THE APPARENTLY MARGINAL ACTIVITIES OF MARCEL DUCHAMP

THE APPARENTLY MARGINAL ACTIVITIES OF MARCEL DUCHAMP

ELENA FILIPOVIC

THE MIT PRESS
CAMBRIDGE, MASSACHUSETTS
LONDON, ENGLAND

The MIT Press
Massachusetts Institute of Technology
77 Massachusetts Avenue, Cambridge, MA 02139
mitpress.mit.edu

First MIT Press paperback edition, 2026

This publication is made possible in part through a grant from the Barr Ferree Foundation Fund for Publications, Department of Art and Archaeology, Princeton University.

Published with support from The Dedalus Foundation.

DEDALUS
FOUNDATION

This book was set in PF Din Pro by the MIT Press. Printed and bound in the United States of America.

Library of Congress Cataloging-in-Publication Data

Names: Filipovic, Elena, author.
Title: The apparently marginal activities of Marcel Duchamp / Elena Filipovic.
Description: Cambridge, MA : The MIT Press, 2016. | Includes bibliographical references and index.
Identifiers: LCCN 2016005202 | ISBN 9780262034821 (hardcover : alk. paper); ISBN 9780262058780 (paperback)
Subjects: LCSH: Duchamp, Marcel, 1887-1968—Criticism and interpretation. | Duchamp, Marcel, 1887–1968--Knowledge and learning. | Artists—Professional relationships—History—20th century. | Art and society—History—20th century.
Classification: LCC N6853.D8 F55 2016 | DDC 709.—dc23 LC record available at http://lccn.loc.gov/2016005202

10 9 8 7 6 5 4 3 2

EU Authorised Representative: Easy Access System Europe, Mustamäe tee 50, 10621 Tallinn, Estonia | Email: gpsr.requests@easproject.com

CONTENTS

ACKNOWLEDGMENTS

More than a book, this has been a life project. The list of people to whom it is indebted, and on whose trust and support it relied, is as lengthy as its development has been. *The Apparently Marginal Activities of Marcel Duchamp* began as a doctoral thesis and was more than fifteen years in the making, far too much time to elegantly explain away except to say that its subject remained both too captivating and too elusive to easily let go of. In all those years this study formed me as much as I was forming it because, more than its subject, Marcel Duchamp offers a model of thinking that shapes me still—as a curator, thinker, writer, historian.

It is from Dorothea Dietrich's darkened lecture hall that I first emerged dumbfounded by images of Marcel Duchamp's exhibitions and *Étant donnés*; it was her intellectual curiosity and rigor that informed this project from its start. Hal Foster generously helped further my inquiry, providing unfailing support along the way. I received grants from the Dedalus Foundation and the French Chateaubriand Foundation, providing early support for my core research in Paris. I remain grateful to these funders, without whom I might never have been able to begin pursuit of such a project at all. And Princeton University's Barr Ferree Foundation Publication Fund generously supported image costs, making the visual richness of this publication possible.

First Virginia Zabriskie and then later Jorge Helft and Adriana Rosenberg entrusted me with the task of curating exhibitions about Duchamp, projects that gave concrete materiality to my research. Adam Boxer offered his bottomless knowledge of avant-garde ephemera. Molly Nesbit and Amelia Jones encouraged my work at an early stage and provided the example of their own diverse ways of thinking about Duchamp. Francis Naumann was a precious source of enthusiasm and guidance; with the assistance of Dana Martin, he was an ever-ready font of images and information. At the Philadelphia Museum of Art, Michael Taylor and then Carlos Basualdo, with the help of Conna Clark, graciously fielded my various questions and image requests. The museum's late director, Anne d'Harnoncourt, kindly agreed to meet me to speak about *Étant donnés* at the beginning of my research and then very elegantly evaded every one of my questions, which was more helpful than she could have known, as it suggested to me that I might indeed be onto something. In Paris, Michel Frizot informally schooled me on all things photographic. The late artists Jean Benoît and Radovan Ivšić and the writers Annie Le Brun and Jean-Michel Goutier shared their memories with me. Gerd Zillner and Monika Pessler of the Austrian Frederick and Lillian Kiesler Foundation in Vienna as well as David and Marcel Fleiss of Galerie 1900–2000 in Paris generously opened up their archives to me, never tiring of my many requests and helping me to represent vital material here. Alexander and Bonin in New York, Jean-Jacques Lebel, Peter C. Jones of the Josef and Yaye Breitenbach Foundation, Eric Le Roy of Les Films de l'Équinoxe—Fonds Photographique Denise Bellon, Stefan Ståhle at the Moderna Museet, Stockholm, Daniel Wildenstein at the Wildenstein Archives, Paris, and Didier Schulmann of the Bibliothèque Kandinsky/Centre Pompidou, Paris, also kindly helped make it possible for me to have crucial images in the book.

In ways more amorphous and all the more vital, Boris Belay, Sophie Berrebi, Eduardo Cadava, Rana Dasgupta, Jonathan Massey, Kevin Moore, Carrie Pilto, Vivian Rehberg, Sambuddha Saha, and Gerardo Sustaeta followed and supported my early writing process through the most precious of friendships. During a later leg of the process, they were joined by Rhea Dall, Barbara Cuglietta, Frances Horn, Gabriel Kuri, Jan Mot, Solveig Øvstebø, Dieter Roelstraete, Lilou Vidal, and the teams at WIELS and Kunsthalle Basel, all of whom offered relentless trust and enthusiasm. Fellow Duchampian and cherished interlocutor Paul Franklin was a boundless source of encouragement and knowledge. Thomas Y. Levin and Danai Anesiadou, at two different stages in the protracted life of this project, tirelessly listened to me speak about it and fortified me with their solidarity, wise advice, and consummate friendship. Andrew Belichesky offered his own form of unconditional belief in me, which mattered more than he could know. With them all I racked up unrepayable debts.

At crucial moments toward the end of the process, Emiliano Battista, Hal Foster, Irene V. Small, and Jan Verwoert kindly read and commented on parts of this manuscript. Antonia Hirsch read all of its parts and was its most devoted and astute commenter, accompanying me through the lonely process of finishing. I readily absorbed many of their suggestions. In a final stage Renate Wagner graciously assisted me in the task of checking captions and securing image rights, and Lindsey Westbrook lent her eagle eyes. And for his part, Roger Conover was the most encouraging and patient of commissioning editors that a writer could hope for. His enthusiasm for this project helped see it to its end. Matthew Abbate edited the manuscript with care, and designer Margarita Encomienda gave it wings. More debts.

Hans Ulrich Obrist gave me my first job and first major distraction from working on this manuscript, in the process fortifying in me the idea that thinking about art and exhibition histories and working with artists to make exhibitions were not at all separable. Adam Szymczyk once told me that he invited me to co-curate the 5th Berlin Biennale in order to "save me from my dissertation." In a way he did, and his trust in me helped make this study infinitely better than it ever would have been. Dirk Snauwaert, because he understood what it meant to me, encouraged my work on this and generously accommodated sabbatical leaves from my job at WIELS in Brussels, allowing my thinking about Duchamp to overlap with exhibition making in ways that irrevocably changed both. The Villa Médicis and its director, Éric de Chassey, provided an idyllic retreat for the writing of the last chapter. I am extremely grateful to them all.

I was at work revising the manuscript as I took up the position of director of Kunsthalle Basel, a model institution if ever there was one for experimenting with how one's research can inspire exhibition making. Many of the artists I worked with along the way inadvertently accompanied this project and nourished it through the examples of their own practices and thinking. This book is dedicated to them.

No study of Duchamp would be the same without the truly exceptional generosity, curiosity, and kindness of Jacqueline Matisse. She became, over the years, not only a source of knowledge and inspiration but also a dear friend and mentor. Her family, Catherine, Robert, Nicolas, and, above all, Antoine, got used to having me around and welcomed me with incredible warmth. And Dona Hochart indefatigably assisted me with all my requests, always with grace. They and the Association Marcel Duchamp supported my research and this publication in every possible way, and with a trust that helped fuel it.

Bojan Šarčević read and accompanied this project's final stages with patience and a love without measure, without which it surely would not have reached its end. Finally, my most profound gratitude goes to my mother, Marlene Belichesky, whose fearlessness has always been my most inspiring model.

IMAGE CREDITS

© 2016 Succession Marcel Duchamp / ADAGP, Paris / Artists Rights Society (ARS), New York: figures 1.1, 1.2, 1.3, 1.4, 1.5, 1.6, 1.7, 1.8, 1.9, 1.13, 1.14, 1.15, 1.16, 1.17, 1.18, 1.19, 1.20, 1.21, 1.22, 1.23, 1.24, 1.25, 1.26, 1.27, 2.1, 2.3, 2.4, 2.7, 2.9, 2.17, 2.20, 2.22, 2.23, 2.24, 2.25, 2.26, 2.27, 2.28, 2.29, 2.30, 2.31, 2.32, 2.33, 2.34, 2.35, 2.36, 2.37, 2.38, 2.39, 2.40, 2.41, 2.42, 3.1, 3.2, 3.7, 3.8, 3.9, 3.10, 3.11, 3.16, 3.17, 3.18, 3.20, 3.21, 3.22, 3.28, 3.31, 3.32, 3.34, 3.35, 3.36, 3.37, 3.38, 3.39, 3.40, 3.41, 3.42, 3.43, 3.45, 3.46, 3.47, 3.48, 3.49, 3.50, 3.51, 3.52, 3.53, 3.54, 3.55, 3.56, 3.57, 3.58, 3.59, 4.1, 4.2, 4.3, 4.4, 4.5, 4.6, 4.7, 4.8; frontispieces to chapters 1, 2, and 3

Courtesy The Philadelphia Museum of Art, Philadelphia: figures 1.1, 1.18, 1.19, 1.20, 2.20, 2.30, 2.37, 3.2, 3.7, 3.8, 3.10, 3.19, 3.20, 3.22, 3.32, 3.33, 3.35, 3.36, 3.37, 3.38, 3.39, 3.40, 3.41, 3.42, 3.43, 3.44, 3.45, 3.46, 3.48, 3.49, 3.50, 3.51, 3.57, 3.59, 4.6, 4.7, 4.8

Courtesy Association Marcel Duchamp: figures 1.2, 1.3, 1.4, 1.8, 1.9, 1.13, 1.16, 1.17, 1.27, 2.3, 2.4, 2.9, 2.23, 2.24, 2.25, 2.26, 2.27, 2.28, 2.29, 2.32, 2.34, 2.36, 2.37, 2.39, 2.40, 2.41, 2.42, 3.21, 3.28, 3.47, 3.52, 3.53, 3.54, 3.58

Courtesy Francis M. Naumann Fine Art, New York: figures 1.5, 1.6, 1.7, 1.21, 1.25, 2.38, 2.43, 4.4, 4.5

Photo: Graydon Wood, 1994 / Philadelphia Museum of Art: figures 1.8, 1.9, 2.4, 2.30, 2.33, 3.1, 3.2, 3.20; frontispiece to chapter 3

© 2016 Estate of Pablo Picasso / Artists Rights Society (ARS), New York: figures 1.10, 1.11, 1.12

Photo: Philippe Migeat © CNAC/MNAM/Dist. RMN-Grand Palais / Art Resource, NY: figures 1.10, 1.22

© RMN-Grand Palais / Art Resource, NY: figure 1.11

Courtesy The Museum of Fine Arts, Houston: figure 1.12

Photo: Jacques Faujour © 2016 Centre Pompidou, MNAM-CC (distribution RMN), Paris: figure 1.14; frontispiece to chapter 1

Courtesy The Philadelphia Museum of Art / Art Resource, NY: figure 1.15

© The Metropolitan Museum of Art, New York / Art Resource, NY: figure 1.23

© 2016 Artists Rights Society (ARS), New York / ADAGP, Paris: figures 1.26, 2.6, 2.17, 2.21, 3.13, 3.23

Courtesy Archives Jean-Jacques Lebel, Paris: figure 2.1; frontispiece to chapter 2

© Estate of Henri-Pierre Roché: figure 2.1; frontispiece to chapter 2

Courtesy Yale Beinecke Rare Book and Manuscript Library / Société Anonyme Archives, New Haven: figures 2.2, 2.5, 2.6

© 2016 Centre Pompidou, MNAM-CCI (distribution RMN), Paris: figures 2.7, 2.8

Courtesy Stadtarchiv Munich: figure 2.10

Courtesy bpk / Zentralarchiv, SMB bpk, Berlin / Art Resource, NY: figure 2.11

© les films de l'équinoxe—fonds photographique Denise Bellon: figures 2.14, 3.16, 3.17, 3.18

© National Gallery of Modern Art, Scotland: figure 2.12

© 2016 Man Ray Trust / Artists Rights Society (ARS), NY / ADAGP, Paris: figures 1.17, 2.13, 2.37

Courtesy Marcel and David Fleiss / Galerie 1900–2000, Paris: figures 2.13, 3.25, 3.26, 3.27, 3.29, 3.30, 3.31

© Collection Schall: 2.15

Courtesy Wildenstein Institute, Paris: figure 2.16

Courtesy Adam Boxer / Ubu Gallery, New York: figure 2.17

Courtesy Author: figure 2.18

© The Josef and Yaye Breitenbach Charitable Trust, New York: figure 2.19

© Arnold Newman / Getty Images: figure 2.22

© 2016 Maurice Jarnoux / Getty Images: figure 2.44

© 2016 The Estate of George Paul Thek. Courtesy Alexander and Bonin, New York: figure 3.3

Courtesy Museum of Modern Art, New York: figure 3.4

© 2016 Vito Acconci / Artists Rights Society (ARS), New York: figures 3.5, 3.6

Photo: Andrea Nuñez / Philadelphia Museum of Art: figures 3.7, 3.22, 3.38, 3.57

Courtesy Moderna Museet, Stockholm: figures 3.11, 3.56

© and Courtesy Austrian Frederick and Lillian Kiesler Private Foundation, Vienna: figures 3.12, 3.13, 3.14, 3.15, 3.17, 3.19, 4.1, 4.2, 4.3; frontispieces to the Introduction and Conclusion; front and back covers

Courtesy Radovan Ivsic: figure 3.24

Courtesy Temple University Libraries, Urban Archives, Philadelphia: figure 3.34

Photo: Will Brown / Philadelphia Museum of Art: figures 3.36, 3.37, 3.39, 3.40, 3.45

Photo: Bertrand Prévost, © CNAC/MNAM/Dist. RMN-Grand Palais / Art Resource, NY: figure 3.55

© 2016 The Estate of Marcel Broodthaers / Artists Rights Society (ARS), New York / SABAM, Brussels: figures 3.60, 3.61

© 2016 Maria Gilissen, Artists Rights Society (ARS), New York / SABAM, Brussels: figures 3.60, 3.61

CAPTIONS FOR THE CHAPTER-OPENING ILLUSTRATIONS

Page xiv:

View of Duchamp's studio, 210 West 14th Street, New York, 1945. Photo by Percy Rainford. Austrian Frederick and Lillian Kiesler Private Foundation, Vienna.

Page 10:

Marcel Duchamp, note with heading "Idée de la Fabrication" from the *Box of 1914*, 1913–14. Photograph of manuscript note, mounted on mat board, 11⅟₁₆ × 9⅜ inches. Centre Pompidou, MNAM-CCI, Paris.

Page 72:

View of Duchamp's studio, with sitter presumed to be Henri-Pierre Roché, 33 West 67th Street, New York, c. 1917. Photographer unknown, perhaps Duchamp or Roché himself. Archives Jean-Jacques Lebel, Paris.

Page 156:

Marcel Duchamp, *Étant donnés: 1° la chute d'eau, 2° le gaz d'éclairage* ... (Given: 1. The Waterfall, 2. The Illuminating Gas ...), 1946–66, detail view of the door as installed at the Philadelphia Museum of Art. Mixed-media assemblage. Exterior: wooden door, iron nails, bricks, and stucco embedded into museum wall. 95½ × 70 × 49 inches. Philadelphia Museum of Art: Gift of the Cassandra Foundation.

Page 268:

Marcel Duchamp (with annotation) in his 210 West 14th Street studio, New York, 1945. Photo by Percy Rainford. Austrian Frederick and Lillian Kiesler Private Foundation, Vienna.

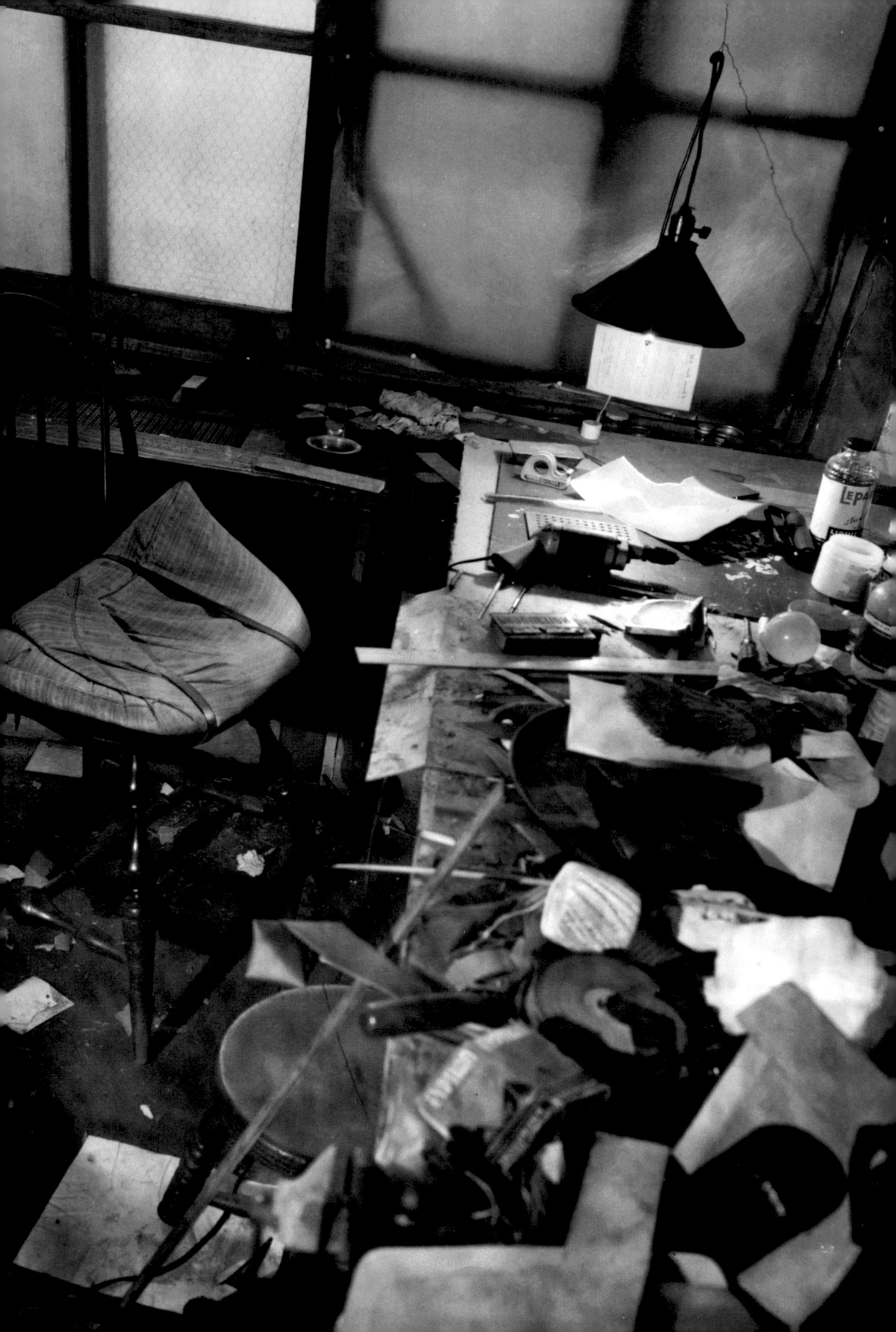

INTRODUCTION

A HISTORY OF
MARCEL
DUCHAMP

AND OTHER
FICTIONS

THE STORIES WE TELL

His story is by now well known. Marcel Duchamp, youngest son of a bourgeois family, began his artistic career as a painter making works in oil on canvas, regularly sized, filled with conventional imagery (portraits of his sister or mother, tree-lined landscapes, chess players ...) and relatively little formal invention. Certainly his paintings followed some of the more avant-garde developments of his time, exploring for instance the formal implications of Cubism and Futurism. He even experienced minor celebrity after one work, *Nude Descending a Staircase* (no. 2, 1912), was rejected for exhibition by his fellow Cubists in 1912—only to be singled out the following year as the most publicized work at the Armory Show in New York. But, as the ever-growing literature on the artist will tell you, had he not "abandoned" painting in favor of nominating store-bought stuff as art or erecting the polysemic enigma that is the 1915–23 *Large Glass* (the works most cited as examples of his new approach), we might not need to speak much about a certain "Marcel Duchamp." Instead, he figures as the twentieth century's most celebrated artistic figure and lodestar to the generations of artists who came after him. Still, the story we tell about him is largely a story of *things*: artworks invented or handmade, original or in copy, influential and in some cases revolutionizing. Some of these objects might not look much like works of art, but all are resolutely material, quantifiable, collectible, historicizable.

The artists of a subsequent generation were perhaps the first to understand that there might be a problem with this Duchamp story. "Marcel Duchamp is all but impossible to write about," Robert Rauschenberg once claimed, adding, "Anything you may say about him is at the same time untrue."[1] The poet David Antin put it slightly differently, but the point is somewhat similar: "any reading for a duchamp work is too stable for it."[2] So it is. To cement in print yet another authoritative interpretation for a "duchamp work" would be to build an edifice of thought more rigid than the uncertainties the artist built into it—not to mention that the lines around what counts as a "duchamp work" could themselves be notoriously slippery when speaking of someone as interested as Duchamp was in ideas trumping "visual products."[3] Indeed, to define the historical relevance of an artist and his oeuvre predominantly through the discrete objects that remain of his practice seems to go against the very specificity of Duchamp as subject. By interrogating originality, aura, authorship, and autonomy, Duchamp put the very notion of what an artwork is and does into question. By regularly involving himself in extra-artistic activities (or so they seemed by the standards of the day) as part of the very "making" of an artwork, he equally put the notion of what an artist is and does into question. Intimately connected, Duchamp's twin destabilizations of artwork and artist call for us to look as carefully at what he orchestrated around the artwork and at what he did in place of conventional art making as at the pieces themselves. Perhaps for this reason, his close friend Henri-Pierre Roché claimed (or was it a warning to the future historian?) that the artist's "finest work" was not this or that element of his material output, but instead "his use of time."[4]

That time was hardly spent conforming to the expected behavior of an artist. Widespread is the perception of Duchamp as someone who, after 1913 (or 1923, depending on whom you ask), "went around for the rest of his life resolutely and masterfully *not* being an artist."[5] Such accounts were replete with mentions of his supposed defection from art making in favor of chess playing, amateur tinkering, or even ironic detachment—all of which suggest alternatives to the traditional image of the "creative" artist. But while such anecdotes satisfy a desire to know about the life of the artist, this study focuses on Duchamp's various activities to a different end: to illuminate not the artist's person, but his *work*. The activities here examined are altogether more mundanely practical and yet inseparable from institutions of art (museum, gallery, archive, art history), and they are entirely related to the recognition, valuation, and understanding of the work of art as such. Motley as these activities are, including as they do Duchamp's role as administrator, archivist, art advisor, note taker, publicist, reproduction maker, and salesman of his own oeuvre, they coalesce around his repeated and engaged role as "curator" from the 1910s to the end of his life.

Although the profession of the curator, as we understand it today, was hardly defined in the early years of Duchamp's career—and he would never explicitly use the term for himself—the role progressively became concretized in the half-century during which he adopted curatorial operations as part of his artistic practice, solidifying into its current sense of an art professional associated with the caretaking of art as well as its public exhibition and mediation. Still, a "curator," no matter how one defined that role specifically, had aims and responsibilities quite distinct from an artist's and vice versa, making it all the more unusual that Duchamp so frequently and insistently engaged in the tasks associated with the "curatorial"—from documenting, administrating, and constructing discursive apparatuses for his artworks to testing whether institutions would feature them in exhibitions; from archiving to collection management; from backdoor negotiating with collectors and museum boards to designing the catalogs and elaborate scenographies of exhibitions.

Through the nineteenth and twentieth centuries, it was not altogether unusual for artists to be involved to some extent in the presentation and dissemination of their work. On a few occasions, some even took an exceptionally active role (think Gustave Courbet's 1855 production of postcards of his paintings and self-financed rogue pavilion staged across the street from the official Paris Salon). More than occasional occupations or ancillary undertakings, however, "curatorial" tasks were in Duchamp's hands a veritable lifework and the pivotal catalyst through which to understand and expose the artwork as such. It was arguably Duchamp's pioneering stance that set the foundations on which subsequent generations developed Conceptual art's "aesthetics of administration," to use Benjamin H. D. Buchloh's formulation, and Institutional Critique, for which curatorial and administrative tasks were a central part of artistic labor.[6]

How, then, to recalibrate the understanding of Duchamp's oeuvre so as to write this and other related activities into its history? Indeed, how to tell the story of a figure whose lifelong preoccupation with these fugitive actions contravenes, precisely, the convention of the oeuvre, understood overwhelmingly in terms of solidified, medium-specific things? If again and again Duchamp held that he had "abandoned painting" and was merely instead a "breather," there might nevertheless be a clue in his curious insistence—suggesting that we attend not only to his production of objects (paintings, for instance) but also to the elusive yet vital actions that "produced" his work in another sense.[7]

Consequently, this study focuses on the production of a still understudied but profoundly influential output, some of it tangible, some of it ephemeral, and all of it rendered through a diversity of apparently marginal activities of an artist who redefined so much of what, henceforth, would be called art. To do so, this study examines and contextualizes a number of undeniably obdurate *things*—whether boxes of replicated notes, suitcases filled with miniature reproductions, documentation of ephemeral exhibitions, or even a wholly permanent and immobile installation. The intention is neither to disavow these objects, or constellations of objects, as quantifiable artifacts nor to refute Duchamp's undeniably material impulse. Instead the premise is that their full significance might only be appreciated by studying the activities that accompanied and even "made" them in a certain sense.

"Marginal" in several senses of the word, these activities have been hitherto largely marginal to an object- and masterpiece-focused scholarship for which the *Large Glass* and the readymades have long been the primary subjects. Likely also they have been considered marginal because ephemeral "activities" remain difficult to classify and amorphous, or, more precisely, because they eschew conventional categorization according to those epistemological systems that long governed art historical scholarship. Duchamp's activities did not declare themselves as art (as did, for instance, Fluxus gestures, performance art, or the activities of artists whose work would later be gathered under the Relational Aesthetics tag), nor were they necessarily "framed" as such (with a public, or at an announced time or place). And finally, they may have been regarded as marginal because instead of seeming to create artworks themselves, they instead produced peripheral supports or framing devices for other, more "proper" artworks. In turn, the marginality of these activities has led to a kind of marginalization of the material objects that relate to or emerge from them. The *Box of 1914* (1913–14) or *Étant donnés* (1946–66), to take two examples, in very different ways each escaped being fully inscribed in the histories of their epochs and, moreover, were not widely recognized as the mordantly critical objects that they are, a fact that this study seeks to address.

A central argument here is that through Duchamp's deep preoccupation with the institutional sites, mechanisms, and conventions that accompany and ostensibly lie outside of the artwork, he radically shifted the artwork's terms (and not solely, as has been so long thought, through an act of "nominalism" that transformed a urinal into *Fountain* in 1917). Of course, to say that Duchamp was interested and engaged in the workings of the institutions of art will seem superfluous, so affirmed may the notion be in readings of the avant-garde. Indeed, the assertions here may at first appear both downright elementary and already long processed by art history. Yet so inured are we to the idea that Duchamp managed to transform the ontology of the artwork that many histories have failed to wonder by what maneuvers this was accomplished. These pages insist on the critical agency of many of the artist's activities that are not, traditionally, considered part of an artistic practice, and all of which refuse conventional conceptions of authorship and objecthood, yet provide the basis for understanding what Walter Benjamin, in an unpublished draft of one of his most influential texts, called Duchamp's advancement of a "theory of the work of art."[8]

This study therefore proposes a methodological path in which the fugitive operations (or what I am calling here "activities") that Duchamp incited in order to test, theorize, contextualize, and position his work might be thought of as constitutive rather than merely procedural, auxiliary, or incidental. I focus on a shift from the stable category of medium-specific objects to the precarious status and ambiguous ontology of acts, which attempted to refigure the making and positioning of the artwork as such. Duchamp's conception of the work of art through curatorial, archival, administrative, and other activities would have worked against Clement Greenberg's understanding of Modernist art as essentially determined by its medium specificity, its ability to constitute itself in relation to the particular and characteristic qualities of its materials ("unique to the nature" of the medium in question).[9] It is no wonder, then, that Duchamp's ordinary-objects-elevated-to-art, chosen as he insisted on the basis of "visual indifference, and, at the same time, on the total absence of good or bad taste,"[10] with all their medium aspecificity, remained in so many of Greenberg's accounts the paragon of the corruption of the pure, autonomous form on which the critic's own understanding of Modernism was built.[11]

The questions this study raises with regard to the treatment of an artist's "activities" were first insinuated through the historicizing of the readymade that began in earnest in the 1960s. Importantly, at the time critics and scholars did not read the readymade (to take the example of *Fountain*) as a porcelain object to be formally compared and discussed alongside the development of other sculptural forms. Instead it was recognized as an artwork whose importance lay elsewhere: in its radical act of selection (or declaration, nominalization, invention) that claimed an ordinary industrial thing as "art," and in that act's revelation of the institutional forces determining what counts as art.[12] Previous to this, and fortified by both the Greenbergian doctrine of Modernism that held so much sway during the critic's reign of influence in the United States (whose heyday was the 1950s and '60s) and the Museum of Modern Art in New York's own acquisition and narrativization of Modernism, the history of modern art was largely told through a progressive, teleological account of objects taken to be formally pure and autonomous. Consequently, the recognition of the paradigmatic shift that was contained in the readymade made the art historical project of reformulating the history and theory of art and the evaluation systems it employed a vital necessity, a reformulation that carried over into readings of new art being made in the 1960s and '70s.

Or was it the other way around? If, as Hal Foster suggests, "'influence' can flow backwards too, at least in interpretation," perhaps Duchamp's readymades only thickened into something legible in the 1960s because of new practices that allowed critics to unthink the presumed autonomy and medium specificity of the artwork.[13] Richard Wollheim's influential 1965 article "Minimal Art," appearing on the heels of Duchamp's 1964 reedition of his readymades, provides an important case in point: it makes a claim for the fundamental importance of Duchamp's reconception of the notion of "work" in the "work of art."[14] Wollheim's reading highlights the shift from making (as in manufacturing) to choosing (as in decision making), a shift that was visible, he argued, in the works of "recent" art that relied on similarly "minimal" gestures and means. Old or new, either might have helped in the reading of the other, no matter which came first chronologically.

Artists in the 1960s and '70s, whether Neo-Dada, Pop, Conceptual, or Minimal, frequently claimed the readymade's influence, but scholars and critics also regularly discussed art production of the time in relation to the readymade, regardless of whether the creators of the artworks acknowledged an affinity.[15] Still, the understanding of the significance of act over object, while it became crucial to the reading of the procedural and immaterial gestures of the generation that followed Duchamp, did not readily (or retroactively) apply itself to other Duchamp works, endowing the readymades with a status that almost holds them apart from his larger oeuvre. Moreover, Duchamp's so-called invention of the readymade must itself be qualified, and the little-discussed, but more labored and layered, set of activities that were crucial in historically positioning the readymade must be highlighted. In this telling, the readymade is not only an object selected and nominated but, perhaps even more importantly, one that is *curated*. And it is precisely the curatorial operations not only of the readymade but also of so many other Duchamp works that turn the discourse, institutions, marketing, and presentational strategies of art into the artist's cardinal if fugitive "medium."[16]

Three chapters, collectively spanning the period between 1913 and 1969, run from Duchamp's first active experiments with reproduction and archiving to the year after his death, when his monumental, semi-posthumous intervention was installed in a museum. Chapter 1 focuses on activities related to his purported invention of the readymade and to the *Large Glass*: Duchamp's note writing, archiving, photographing, and publicizing, resulting in various boxes of photographically replicated notes beginning with his *Box of 1914* and continuing through his *Green Box* in 1934. It examines the peculiar transgressiveness of the methods and media he chose as well as the discursive operation the notes enact in their circulation and posited relationship to other things more readily considered works "of art," shifting and even determining, one could say, those artworks' reception.

Chapter 2 focuses on Duchamp's curatorial activities, dealing, reproducing, and publicizing. These enterprises point to the ways in which art is made visible, valuable, meaningful, or even, at a more primary level, recognizable as such, through acts of exchange, presentation, replication, and dissemination. The chapter addresses Duchamp's participation in, or orchestration of, exhibition contexts, his marketing and sales of artworks, and the conception of the *Boîte-en-valise* in the late 1930s as a series of multiple, miniature monographic retrospectives of his work.

Chapter 3 contextualizes Duchamp's replicating, photographing, administrating, and curating as part of the clandestine construction *Étant donnés*, a curated exhibition of sorts, that the artist meticulously arranged to have installed at the Philadelphia Museum of Art only after his death. Long misread as a return to figuration and an abandonment of the critical impulse that had driven the readymades, and thus ignored or insufficiently contextualized with contemporaneous works, *Étant donnés* is considered here as a complex exploration of some of the most formative ideas advanced by the artist, undergirded by a trenchant criticality and rendered all the more subversive by insinuating itself so carefully into exactly that seat of institutional power and adjudication that it seeks to question.

Inevitably, this is a study of art's institutional apparatuses. The museum—that display space/institution/authority that Duchamp probed when constructing ephemeral exhibition displays for the Surrealists, the *Boîte-en-valise*, and *Étant donnés*—remains a central protagonist in this story. So, too, is the museum's institutional pendant, the archive, at once evoked and mocked in the artist's multiplied boxes of torn and fragmented notes. But other facets of the institution, such as discourse, the market, and presentation strategies, also play a role. Accordingly, the history of Duchamp's oeuvre can also be written as a history of the artist's perennially engaged relationship to the framing sites and discursive or presentational procedures that help construct something as a work "of art" and for which the artist took on the various roles that are the subject here.

This is also a study of photography and reproduction in an age in which the primacy of the original was only beginning to be questioned. "Reproduction," that treacherous word, a threat to the notion of the authentic artwork, plays a signal role in this study, as it did in Duchamp's entire oeuvre. First there were the scribbled notes that he began photographing in 1913–14, then there were more notes and actual artworks that he spent the rest of his life returning to and replicating with painstaking precision, not to mention a final, posthumously released work that would announce the index and reproduction as having been motors for the artist's thinking all along. The pressure of photographic reproduction's response to painting (that "original" and auratic museum-worthy object par excellence), the decontextualization of the reproduced artwork, the refunctionalizing of the object, the shifting of the experience of the artwork: these are what the various boxes actualize. Duchamp's serial reproductions (of notes, of his own artworks), perhaps more than any other project to emerge from the early twentieth century, anticipated and tested the most pressing concerns of Benjamin's essay "The Work of Art in the Age of Its Technological Reproducibility."[17]

Finally, this is also a study of the uneasy reception of a specific segment of Duchamp's practice. It is about the curious ways in which, despite his being claimed as a pivotal figure of the twentieth century with countless publications dissecting his oeuvre, the radical particularity of his practice has not yet been fully examined: his construction of discursive accompaniments to his artworks, his first crucial experiments with photography and reproduction, his lifelong relationship to exhibition making, the ways in which he actively participated in the construction of his own legacy, and finally the complexity of the administrative and curatorial gestures involved in his final work's commentary on the museum. Through them we see that Duchamp understood well that meaning derives just as much from what is *outside* and *around* the artwork as from the subject, technique, and presumed content within the neat contours of the frame or atop the pedestal. Such intangible and transient, context- and situation-specific details (of the presentation) of the artwork are, however, intrinsically difficult to acknowledge and perhaps even more difficult to historicize (they do not sit still as the object itself does). The elision or marginalization of these activities and subsequent misreadings of some of their related, quantifiable output thus points to a blind spot of sorts.

The Apparently Marginal Activities of Marcel Duchamp takes its namesake as its explicit subject, but it might also serve as a case study of the relationship between an artist's agency and the institutional imperatives relative to the construction of an oeuvre, as seen through one of modernity's most pivotal figures. So, too, might it add another layer to the story of Duchamp that we have inherited (and which he himself arguably had some hand in constructing): that of a lapsed painter, obsessive chess player, occasional cross-dresser, and onetime librarian who "abandoned" art making in 1923, spent the rest of the 1920s inventing optical contraptions, and, throughout the 1930s, seemed (according to even his most ardent supporters) to be merely "vacationing" in his past. To tell his story, one must speak of the roles of administrator, archivist, art advisor, curator, publicist, reproduction maker, and salesman that Duchamp repeatedly and obstinately inhabited. Crucially, it was in his apparently marginal activities that Duchamp was at his most profoundly critical, blurring the lines between curatorial and artistic practice in a way that would forever shift notions of artwork and artist alike.

l'Idée de la Fabrication

— Si un fil droit horizontal d'un mètre de longueur tombe d'un mètre de hauteur sur un plan horizontal en se déformant à son gré et donne une figure nouvelle de l'unité de longueur. —

— 3 exemplaires obtenus dans des conditions à peu près semblables ([illegible]): dans leur considération chacun à chacun sont une reconstitution approchée de l'unité de longueur.

les 3 stoppages étalon sont le mètre diminué.

CHAPTER 1

NOTES FOR A THEORY OF THE WORK OF ART

NOT "OF ART"

Scribbled in 1913, apparently carelessly and yet squirreled away preciously, is a torn bit of paper bearing the question: "Can works be made which are not 'of art'?"[1] Perhaps initially meant only for himself, Marcel Duchamp's deceptively simple query conceals radical implications. That year would mark the artist's most famous gesture, the so-called invention of the readymade, as seen in his *Roue de bicyclette* (Bicycle Wheel) and the handful of selected industrial objects that followed in the years after. It was the year as well of his creation of a musical composition dictated by nothing more than chance, *Erratum musical*, and of *3 stoppages étalon* (3 Standard Stoppages), an oddball attempt to create alternate standards for that most standardized form of measurement, the meter. It was, as Duchamp later underscored, his "moment of critical change."[2] And although the various experiments of that year seemed to radiate in many directions, sitting in the background of all of them was the construction of an elaborate discursive operation, at once remarkable and seemingly slapdash, and entirely connected to that most ingenuous but fundamental question about the very nature "of art."

Duchamp had begun, just prior, to make loose notes of hastily written thoughts, and by 1913 he decided that the scrappy jottings should be documented, archived, photographically replicated, and distributed—a highly unusual move for the period. That project, since entitled the *Box of 1914* by historians (but repeatedly dated to 1913–14 by the artist himself), constitutes a mordant commentary on the work of art, authorship, and originality, and it marks the beginning of Duchamp's concerted interest in both the transgressive potentials of reproduction and the discursive parameters of art.[3] It accompanied and informed his thinking about both the readymades and *La Mariée mise à nu par ses célibataires, même* (The Bride Stripped Bare by Her Bachelors, Even, 1915–23), also known as the *Large Glass*, not to mention his experiments with chance and measurement, inaugurating a lifelong interest in those gestures and things that surround or frame an artwork and that might only equivocally appear to be works "of art" in and of themselves. This chapter is about those early replicated notes and their later progeny, here examined through the lenses of various disciplines, including literature, collage, photography, and painting, to which they relate and which they undermine in turn. What emerges is the revelation of their primacy as a project that articulates—and complicates—the conceptual stakes of so much of Duchamp's practice, setting nothing less than the terms of what Walter Benjamin called the artist's "theory of the work of art."[4]

THE *BOX OF 1914*

"Marcel," he told himself in October 1912, "no more painting; go get a job."[5] The scribbling of Duchamp's notes, which first date to 1912, thus coincided with his self-prescribed departure from painting and suggests that an evasion of strict (artistic) productivity in favor of meandering thoughts nevertheless should accompany the business of finding paid work. His good friend Francis Picabia found him some through his uncle Maurice Davanne, who directed Paris's prestigious Bibliothèque Sainte-Geneviève. There Duchamp thought he could get a "grip on an intellectual position, against the manual servitude of the artist."[6] Taking the post was also, he admitted, in defiance of the dogmatism of the Cubists who had refused to exhibit his *Nu descendant un escalier* (Nude Descending a Staircase [no. 2], 1912) in their Salon des Indépendants earlier that year: "as a reaction against such behavior coming from artists who I had believed to be free, I got a job. I became a librarian."[7]

He thus spent the winter of 1912 enrolled in courses on paleography and library studies at the École Nationale des Chartes, a training that introduced him to the exacting logic of the archive.[8] Literary works were plotted along lines of chronology, sequentiality, authorship, and theme; Duchamp learned to follow these so as to put books, manuscripts, and documents in their place. Perspectival manuals, philosophical treatises, and countless books were at his disposal. We know he studied some, even jotted notes about them.[9] Through the end of 1914, his job was to keep and create order in this bastion of the recorded past. In the process, the archive *literally* surrounded him.

Word about his new occupation spread, even to the press. "Having become a librarian at the Sainte-Geneviève library, he arranges books," the *Paris Journal* of May 19, 1914, declared, as if appalled, "and that is why for two years now one hasn't seen any paintings anywhere by Marcel Duchamp."[10] What few knew at the time (they likely would have thought little of it even had they known) was that throughout his training for, and during his work at, the library, Duchamp was very busy writing.

He scribbled on just about anything: torn scraps of paper, the back of a gas bill, hotel letterhead, the underside of a Camembert cheese label. On these he mingled descriptions of futile sexual advances and mechanical frustration; he depicted complex, layered details of machine parts, pulleys, and levers; he advanced hesitant speculations, pseudo-scientific theorems, ridiculous analogies, and random ideas for future productions. He penned them in prose full of misspellings, wordplay, crossed-out phrases, underlined words, and multicolored marginal annotations, and, in a manner no less quirky, he included numerous instructions on how these very "texts" should be written at all. There was nothing precious or composed about his handwriting nor anything refined about the scraps he wrote on.

Unlike those writers whose notes on random scraps of paper suggest a decided sense of economy, also seen in their effort to fit as many lines on a page as possible (think Robert Walser or Walter Benjamin), one has the sense that Duchamp had simply decided to write on what was at hand whenever an idea came to him, and then to preserve this ephemeral output. Hundreds of scribbled, cryptic lines on hundreds of pieces of loose paper "document" his thinking process. As he acknowledged:

> These notes are from just about the time, 1912, when I absolutely changed my life, so to speak, in regard to art and decided to completely forget about the

CHAPTER 1

1.1

Marcel Duchamp, *Box of 1914*, 1913–14. Commercial cardboard photographic supply box containing sixteen photographs of manuscript notes and the drawing *Avoir l'apprenti dans le soleil* (To Have the Apprentice in the Sun) mounted on individual mat boards, and one photographic facsimile of the drawing *Médiocrité* (Mediocrity), unmounted, each 11¹⁄₁₆ × 9⅜ inches. Philadelphia Museum of Art: Gift of Mme Marcel Duchamp, 1991.

> Nude and forget about the Futurisms and so forth. So they are with the intention of doing something else which I did not know at the time what it was going to be, naturally. They were jottings, you see, on a piece of paper. Whatever idea came to me, I would put it on a piece of paper, any piece of paper, so those papers have all kinds of shapes, torn shapes. They are general, without any destination to speak of, just an idea that comes to you when you dream a bit or read and I put them down for eventual use if necessary.[11]

The effort to "forget about the Nude and forget about the Futurisms," which is to say, *to forget about painting*, and the taking up of note writing went hand in hand. Against conventional painting's too-insistent appeal to the eye, the notes were bastions of thought. They held out ideas.

Duchamp's jottings would compose an idiosyncratic score to accompany and prepare the way for an immense work on glass: the enigmatic visual epic of failing machinery and frustrated sexuality that many would consider his most important and inscrutable artwork, the *Large Glass*. Although he only began physical labor on the *Large Glass* in 1915, in a strange act of conjuring an object that was not yet visible, the artist gathered a small sampling of his notes to himself in 1913–14 in order to reproduce and disseminate them.[12] Some of the selected notes bear obscure references to the as-yet-unbuilt glass work, even if countless others not included in this first *Box* are more directly linked to it. Having decided upon his selection, Duchamp made photographic copies of the notes and thus inaugurated an affair with reproduction that would consume him to the end of his life.

For the process, Duchamp laid out his notes and photographed them one by one, making contact prints from large glass plate negatives (13 × 18 cm), rendering a result identical—or almost so in some cases—to the notes' original size. He made gelatin silver prints of fourteen selected notes, as well as of photographic documentation of his 1913 assemblage-experiment *3 Standard Stoppages*, and of a drawing from 1914, *Avoir l'apprenti dans le soleil* (To Have the Apprentice in the Sun), making sixteen elements in all, of which he made five prints each.[13] He then trimmed and mounted the photographic copies (leaving, however, the torn and irregular edges of each note visible) on individual but uniform mat boards and placed each of the respective sets in cardboard boxes that originally held 18 × 24 cm glass photographic plates produced by the companies Eastman Kodak Co. or Lumière Jougla. The result was an edition of five boxes containing five sets of the same scrawled and at times almost illegible writing. He distributed them among friends, cherished patrons, and family, keeping a set for himself. And almost as soon as he had distributed them, they entered a shadow space, not entirely forgotten but definitely not treated as the groundbreaking gesture they were: photographically, conceptually, or otherwise.

The process of writing, selecting, reproducing, and disseminating these notes just about coincided with the choosing of industrial objects, eventually nominated "readymades," many of them inscribed with their own elegant, nonsensical poetics: a 1915 shovel became *In Advance of the Broken Arm*, a 1916 comb became *3 ou 4 gouttes de hauteur n'ont rien à faire avec la sauvagerie* (3 or 4 Drops of Height Have Nothing to Do with Savagery). Language had begun to infect everything Duchamp engaged in. What his notes *say* and how they *mean* is vital, even if it is not the mere conveyance of information in the form of words that is their point. And although language is operative in both the *Box of 1914* and the readymades, one kind of inscription is, nevertheless, omitted from the notes. Duchamp left each of the boxes undated, unsigned, and untitled; it was only later, for simplicity's sake, that they came to be called by scholars the *Box of 1914*. In contrast to those industrially made objects "invented" at roughly the same time—each with no detectable sign of the artist's touch in their manufacture, but which would go on to bear a signature, title, and date as anchors to their work-of-artness—these notes so literally bespoke the artist's hand that Duchamp seems to have dispensed with any additional mark: it was as if the scribbled script itself was its own signature and proof of authority.[14]

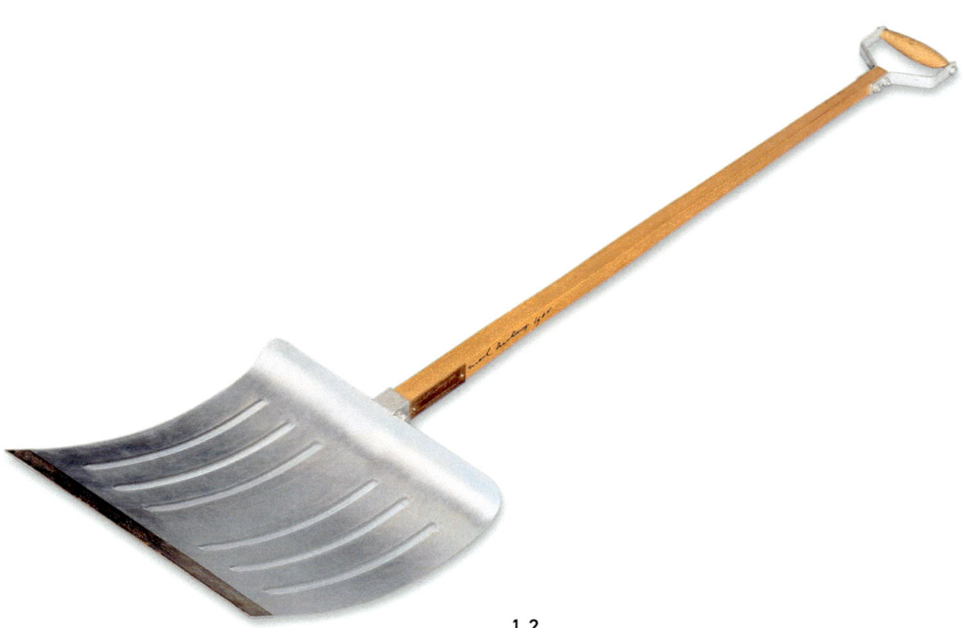

1.2

Marcel Duchamp, *In Advance of the Broken Arm*, 1915/1964 (original version of 1915 lost). Wood and galvanized iron, edition of 8 replicas, 52 inches in height. Indiana University Art Museum, Bloomington: Partial gift of Mrs. William H. Conroy.

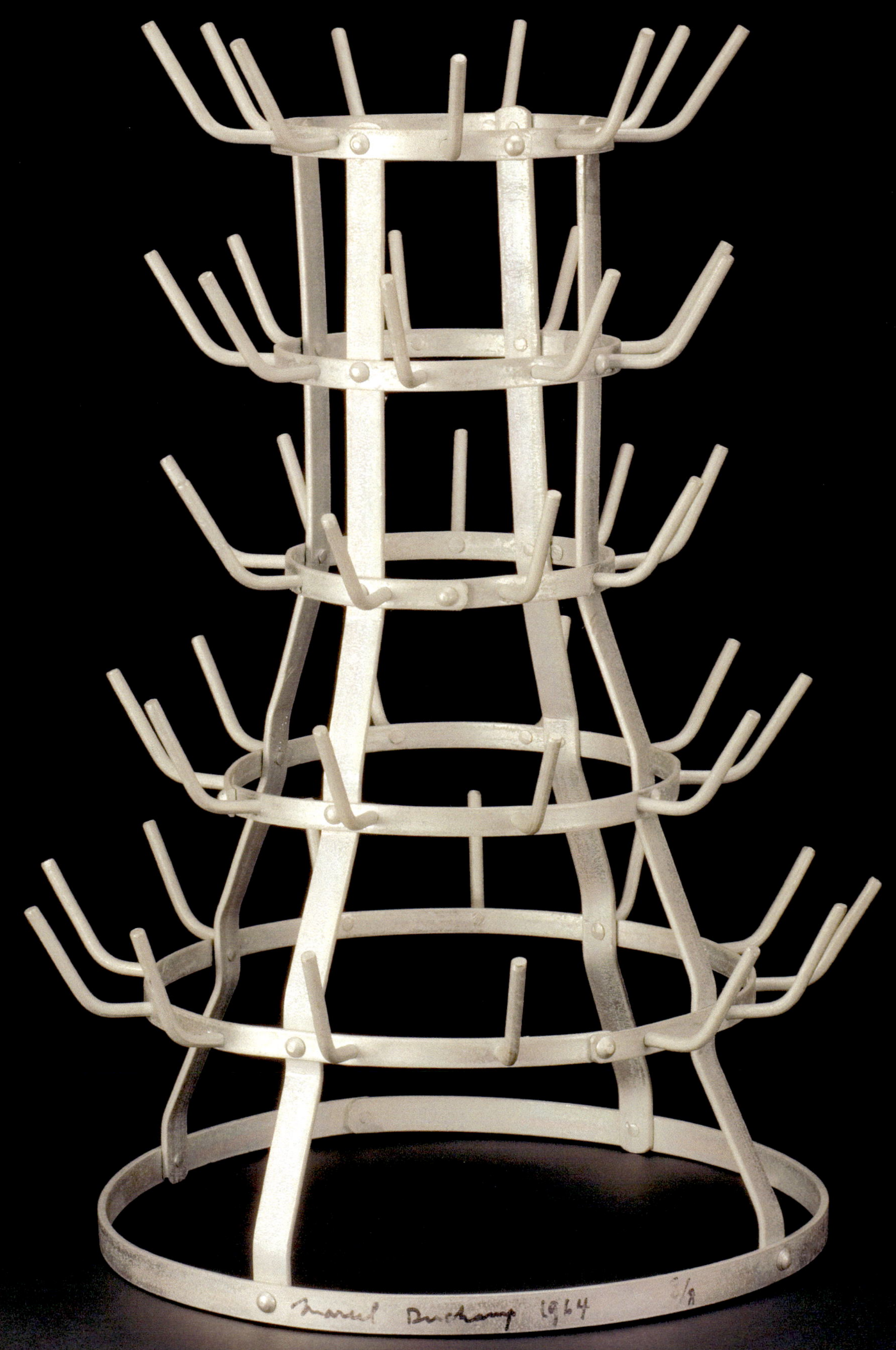
Marcel Duchamp 1964

It might seem an incongruity that at the same moment that the readymades consciously avoided the hand—or *la patte*—of the artist that Duchamp so condemned in painting, his scribbled notes made a show of it.[15] The seeming contradiction did not end there: while the notion of the author was so resolutely questioned with the readymade, Duchamp both reinstated the author in his notes, since they were, after all, made from the artist's hand script, and, in replicating them, put the author in question again. Reproduction—photographic reproduction, more specifically—potentially ad infinitum, would make a mockery of even the most seemingly personal manifestation of an artist's trace. Authorship, in both projects, was a deeply ambiguous notion for the artist, the readymade and the notes simultaneously elevating and disavowing the cult of author or aura.[16] The copied notes became a related gesture, ostensibly at odds with but in fact conceptually allied with the readymades, which were in their time singular examples of potentially limitless industrial objects while the copied notes were multiple examples of that most uniquely singular of traces. The two were the product of a similar probing.

Both strategies queried the foundational premises of what an artwork or an author *is* and *does*, what defines and determines them, but also how that most modern of phenomena, mechanical reproduction, might make or unmake these categories from within. For Duchamp must have known that if each of his notes remained unique, they would likely never be considered more than that: an artist's doodles. They would be doodles that were, moreover, merely signs for something *else*—announcing, encircling, and describing ideas and future artworks, but not artworks in themselves. Ironically, it is precisely in their reproduction that Duchamp heralded them as more than mere scribbles, indeed as something worthy of the effort of his selection, collection, and replication, and thus meriting the attention of others. He doesn't seem to have made any effort at that time to exhibit them as artworks in their own right (as he would, just a few years later, with his readymades), but he did devote a significant effort to multiplying and distributing the five sets. Later he proclaimed, as he would even more vociferously about his second set of replicated notes that followed the *Box of 1914*, that they had been meant to act on the *Large Glass* and shift how it was seen. This first set of replicated notes might thus have been, in its own way, a "test" of sorts, an attempt to see if the notes could effectively change the perception of the artworks they evoked, or whether they could even themselves *be taken for* works "of art." Duchamp, as we will see, enacted many such tests.

1.3

Marcel Duchamp, *Porte-bouteilles* (Bottlerack), 1914/1964 (original version of 1914 lost). Galvanized iron bottle rack, edition of 8 replicas, 25 ¼ inches in height. Private collection.

Calvin Tomkins, perhaps Duchamp's most astute biographer, once asked: "If ideas were what mattered, why wouldn't he have wanted to make those as clear as possible—for example by getting rid of inconsistencies and contradictions?" He went on to speculate: "One reason could have been that the ideas themselves were not as important as the process by which they had come into existence—the *passage* from a thought's conception to its later development."[17] This passage was, clearly, a messy one, revealing the improvised, erratic movements of thought as it made it to the page. If the original notes could be said to be an inventory of ephemeral thought, the data or evidence of conceptualization, then Duchamp's photographic copies are documents of documents of process.

Yet if their form and function in some way evoke an archive of documents, these boxes of replicated notes nevertheless problematize that resemblance. In creating them, Duchamp hardly emulated the docile archivist. The flow of words in his notes does not help relate one scrap to the next, nor do the boxes' undated, unpaginated, unbound pages suggest any logical sequence or order. The fact that the containers hold loose contents underscores all the more a deliberate randomness: there is no system that indicates a predetermined sequence by which the notes are supposed to be put into the box, no logic determining why a particular note makes sense in the whole at all. They look like they just happened to have been included.

Duchamp's ambivalent position regarding the idea of the archive was also reflected in his decision to counteract the exactitude of the photographic reproductions with the way he decided to contain them. He chose readymade boxes and modified their labels, adding his own first name in pencil, underlining words or striking them out with black marker (on at least one occasion he crossed out the word "industrielles" on a box that bore the printed advertisement "photographies industrielles" and underlined "photographies" three times), or affixing additional labels to certain box covers. Duchamp's manufactured labels thus seem to offer more accurate classification (call them photographs, yes, but *not* industrial photographs), even as their scrawled corrections and partial provision of information decidedly refuse to approximate the standards of archival labeling.

Evading narrative, rejecting chronological flow, and held together without the benefit of either thematic or alphabetical order, the project was less a product of ironic detachment than a revision of the rules of the archive. If Duchamp's day job at exactly that moment involved archival classification at the Bibliothèque Sainte-Geneviève, his other vocation involved breaking it down, constructing a kind of counter-archive, one built not on systems, linear time, or progression but instead on haphazard arrangement, repetitive return, and tentative process.

It is evident that something about the bureaucratic archive seduced Duchamp. Indeed, late in his life he admitted that during his youth he had actually considered becoming an official notary, that bureaucrat par excellence, like his father.[18] And when he went to the United States for the first time in 1915, despite the *succès de scandale* of *Nude Descending a Staircase* just a few years before, he vocally declared that he didn't want to make his money from anything like artistic work. ("I would willingly live in New York. ... But only on the condition that I could earn my living as a librarian or something analogous," he told Walter Pach, who was helping to arrange his stay.)[19] Maybe it is no coincidence that when Frederick Kiesler questioned him in the 1940s about the trajectory of his life and work, the architect's schematic notes from the conversation recount: "he retired from exhibiting to a Library St. Genevieve, where Picabia had an uncle-Librarian. (from Oct. 1913–1915) than [*sic*] left for America. Made Filing-cards-exact (no typewriter)."[20] The comment is telling. In any number of interviews from the 1930s onward, Duchamp claimed that he had left the art world for chess or, simply, for "breathing," but in this oral history he was an artist who gave up his creative practice for *administration*—to make filing cards.

The use he would make of the appearance of bureaucracy over the years is striking: he employed a notary public (to certify the "authenticity" of *L.H.O.O.Q.* [1919] years after he made it), printed business cards in 1920 for his alter ego, Rrose Sélavy (announcing her specialty as "Precision Oculism" with offices in "Paris–New York" and a "complete line of whiskers and kicks" on offer), created official-looking rubber stamps (for *Tzanck Check* [1919], the stamp declaring that the handmade simulation of a bank check that the artist actually used to pay his dentist was an "original"), invented fake financial "guarantors" (like the "Teeth's Loan and Trust Company Consolidated" in his abovementioned check, its company name repeatedly stamped across the faux check; later he would invent another backer, the "Bank Mona Lisa," for a 1965 check made out to Philip Bruno), used official gummed-paper French revenue stamps (to "authenticate" his edition of *Obligations pour la roulette de Monte Carlo* [Monte Carlo Bond, 1924], itself a kind of financial document in which Duchamp made himself the "administrator" of a joint stock venture; similar revenue stamps were then used again in many miniature reproductions of his paintings made in the late 1930s), used the aesthetic of the classification binder (for the structure and format of the remarkable publication *Some French Moderns Says McBride* [1922]), and made numerous, even larger archive-like productions (later note boxes but also, most extensively, his *Boîte-en-valise* [Box-in-a-Valise, 1938–42]). In this, as in other instances, the appearance of certified officialdom and, with it, bureaucratic logic, order, and control, are simultaneously evoked and contravened.

In line with what would be a lifetime of flirting with administration, Duchamp's note project sets up layers of administrative ambiguity: How can a seeming testament of artistic process (notes for the "making of" artworks) effectively be such a thing if one cannot gain a sense of how one thought or idea leads to another? Without chronology, taxonomy, narration, cause-effect, or any other (even if highly personal) order to follow between the notes, how can one derive meaning from them? And what, anyway, were the criteria for the inclusion or exclusion of a note?

Informal textual notes by artists were not, of course, unique: artists often included speculations or instructions illustrated with drawings in their sketchbooks. And while the history of art is full of recourse to these "peripheral" artistic materials in order to understand an oeuvre, the difference here lies in the more public nature of Duchamp's

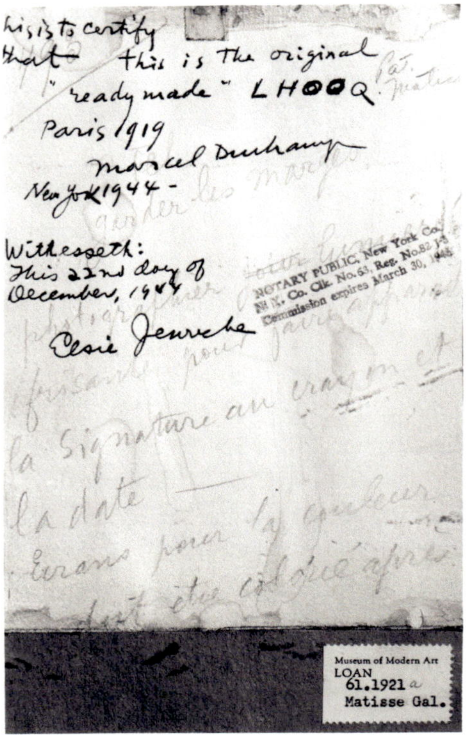

1.4

Marcel Duchamp, *L.H.O.O.Q.*, 1919 (verso). Annotated, notary-certified backside of a reproduction of Leonardo da Vinci's *Mona Lisa* with Duchamp's annotations in pencil, 7 ¾ × 4⅞ inches. Private collection, Geneva.

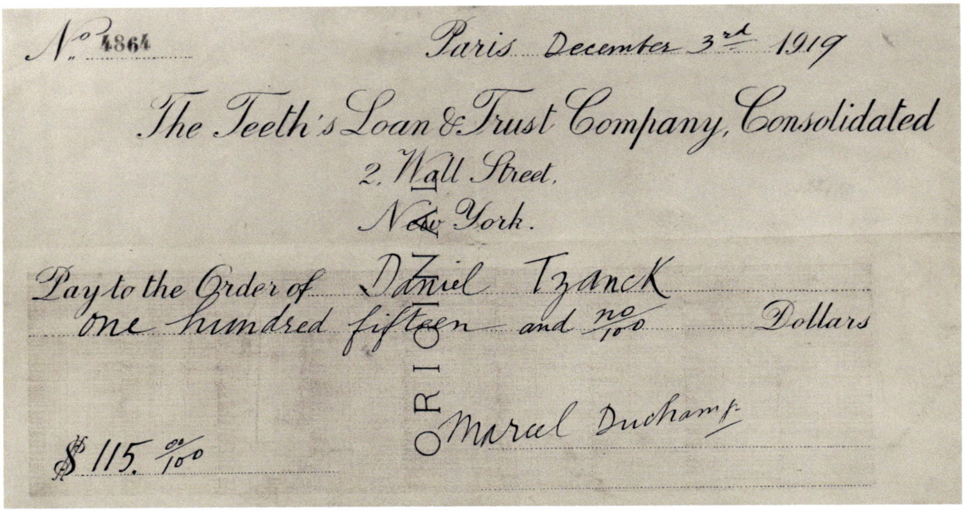

1.5

Marcel Duchamp, *Tzanck Check*, 1919. Ink and rubber stamps on paper, 8 ¼ × 15 ¹⁄₁₆ inches. Israel Museum, Jerusalem: Gift of the Vera and Arturo Schwarz Collection.

1.6 (right)

Marcel Duchamp, *Nu descendant un escalier* (Nude Descending a Staircase), 1937. Reproduction of *Nu descendant un escalier*, 1912, collotype with signed revenue stamp added, sheet: 13 ¼ × 7⅞ inches. Private collection.

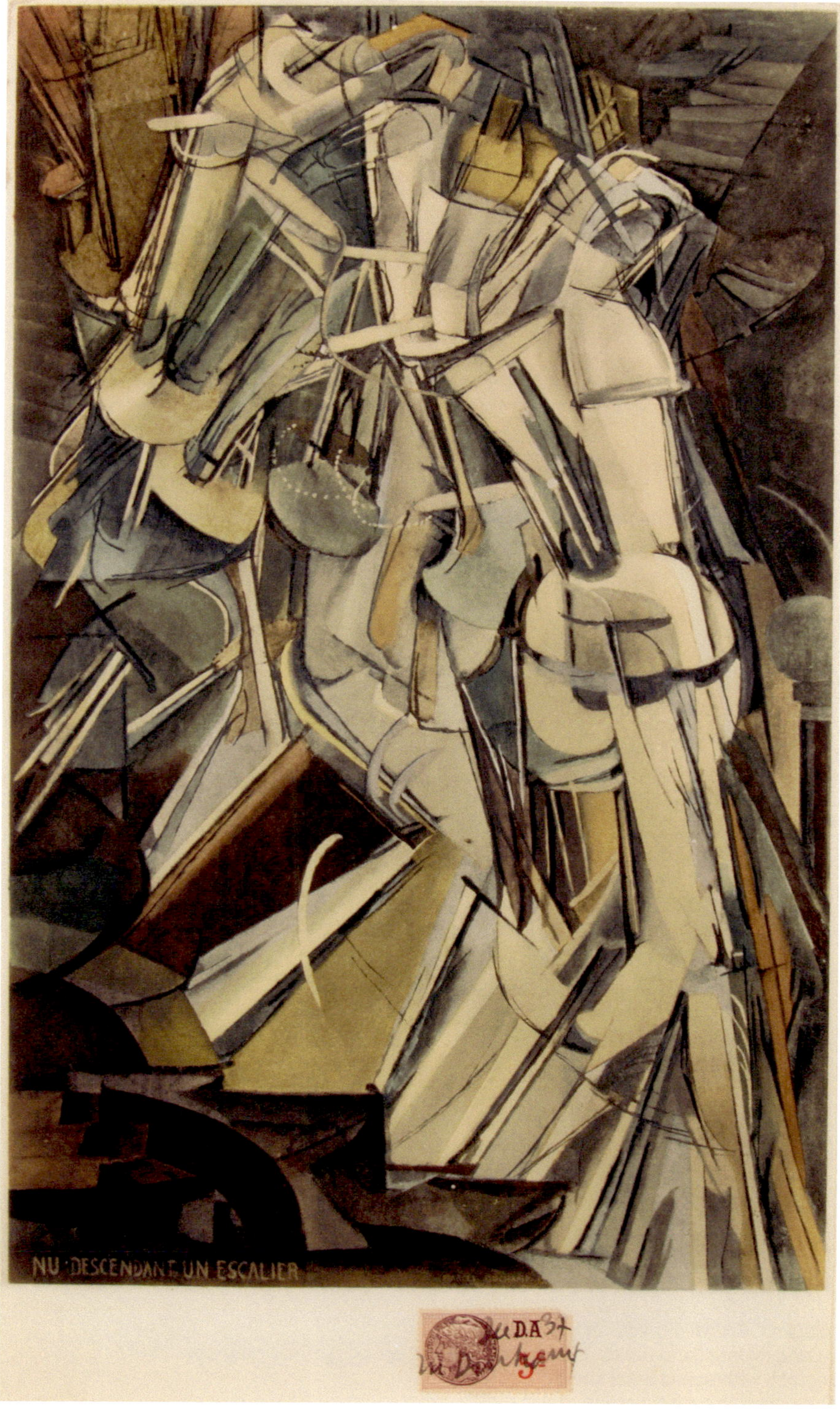
NU·DESCENDANT UN ESCALIER

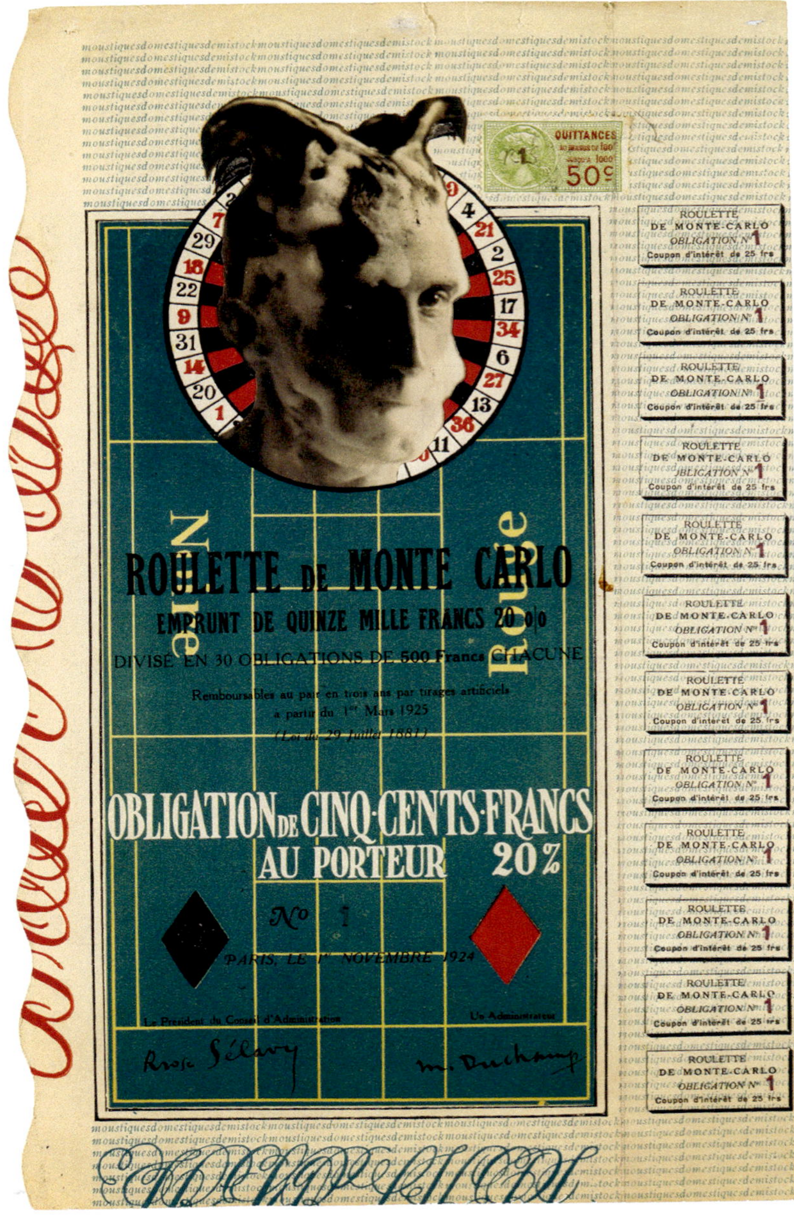

1.7

Marcel Duchamp, *Obligations pour la roulette de Monte Carlo* (Monte Carlo Bond), 1924. Photolithograph with signed fiscal stamp, 12⅜ × 7¹¹⁄₁₆ inches. Private collection.

scribbled scraps. In insisting on their replication and distribution (even if only for a small circle of intimates), and by including them much later in his first monographic and retrospective exhibitions, Duchamp decidedly wanted to bring attention to his notes. This is all the more striking given the artist's notoriously estranged relationship to the preservation of traces: ridding himself of most books once he read them or of any correspondence once he responded to it, and even deliberately destroying vestiges of his romantic liaisons. Thus his meticulously constructed "public" copies of his notes and, later, his carefully preserved administration of the costs, quantities, and locations of his artworks for the production of other archive projects are, as it were, all the more noteworthy.

LITERATURE

"A box containing a dozen or so aphorisms or pseudo thoughts" is how Duchamp described the *Box of 1914* and the nature of the notes it includes.[21] The notes range from reflections on the act of looking, military service, electricity in art, linear perspective, or photographic registration to the equivalence between art and shit. In them much is left to interpretation. After all, what does he mean by his proposed "world in yellow," "painting of frequency," or "electricity edgewise"? Pithy, instructional, or cryptic, these jottings lack pretensions to profundity (implicit in the "pseudo" of Duchamp's description of the "thoughts" traced by the notes) as much as they evade any real connection from one to another. One thing that they do is to transgress literary norms.

From a literary standpoint, the audacity of Duchamp's gesture remains underestimated. The notes have been largely ignored except as a source for citable information, and are rarely examined in light of either the literary or artistic context in which they were first forged. Yet the avant-garde rethinking of the space of the word and of visual attention is a vital context for registering the stakes of Duchamp's unusual project.[22]

Duchamp finished his *Box of 1914* the same year that Stéphane Mallarmé's *Un coup de dés jamais n'abolira le hasard* (A Throw of the Dice Will Never Abolish Chance) was published by the Nouvelle Revue Française in Mallarmé's desired visual form, which was heralded immediately as a poetic and typographic revolution. Mallarmé's poem bestowed a new plasticity upon language through typographic spatialization, and arguably Duchamp's first "box" project achieved a similar effect, but by very different means. It subscribed neither to the Mallarméan *durée du livre*—the particular temporal experience instigated by the sequential unfolding form of the book—nor, say, to the exploded graphics and gestural dynamism of Futurism, with which it was also contemporaneous. Instead, Duchamp's loose, boxed pages insisted on another kind of linguistic and formal unfolding and another engagement on the part of their beholder.

Whether or not Duchamp saw Mallarmé's fresh-off-the-press poem in 1914 is not really the point. Although the artist repeatedly admitted to being deeply interested in Mallarmé's writing and even used a reference to one of his poems in a work from 1915, the groundbreaking version of *Un coup de dés* was published just too late to have influenced the literary form of Duchamp's first notes.[23] The poem might even have come out too late to affect the artist's decision regarding the physical format of the *Box of 1914*, so simultaneous was the "publication" of the two projects. Thus the comparison aims to sketch the landscape into which Duchamp's notes were released rather than to suggest genealogies of thought or form. Mallarmé, for example, worked against the expectation of linguistic order with a radically antigrammatic form, although he paired it with a highly *recherché* language that insisted on itself as nothing if not the modern inheritor of a high tradition of poetry. Alternately, one might evoke concurrent Futurist texts that emerged from 1912 onward, which, with a play of onomatopoeia and dynamic form, freed themselves from the Symbolist tradition and *passéiste* grammatical conventions, but nevertheless held on to such literary staples as simile and poetic aspects of free verse. Duchamp, on the other hand, avoided any literariness at all.

"One can see seeing ..." and "*Arrhe* is to art as *merdre* is to *merde* ... ," Duchamp's photographed notes declare in their meager, calligraphic way. Thus even if one considers the most irreverent of Futurist, Zaum, or Dadaist poetry, little in the associated language strategies of "making strange" or disrupting of sense is operative in Duchamp's textual output. Instead he opted for more pedestrian phrases and words and even dictionary citations, theorems, and formulas. The notes are composed neither of strings of unrelated words nor of playful meaninglessness; their language often does make sense. The words convey information, conjure images, provide instructions for the construction of objects, or propose actions. But for every bit of "information," and every ostensibly stable meaning, there is another note or even a verso side that seems to undo it. There is no plainer way to say it: Duchamp's notes erode their own assertions.

Even the fact that the artist would, throughout his life, so fiercely reject what he called the "retinal" (that superficial appeal only to the eyes prevalent in the history of painting and epitomized, for Duchamp, in the work of Gustave Courbet)[24] is seemingly countered by the fact that he insisted on so exactly replicating the visual appearance of his original notes. Relying on the gestural traces of his handwriting, the artist marked his phrases with hesitancy, incompletion, evasion, and absence, punctuating his phrases with "misspellings," inkblots, and effaced words or letters. His was a language replete with contradictions, ambiguities, and references to other notes (that may or may not have been selected for inclusion). With their orderless scrawls and multiple layers of writing and rewriting, the reader is prevented from mastering or comprehending with certainty anything that is given.

It is hardly surprising, then, that shortly after he had begun his first note project, Duchamp composed a poem, *The* (1915), in which star-shaped forms took the place of what would otherwise have been each instance of the eponymous article. Then, a year later, blank spaces marked strategically missing letters in the words inscribed on the metal surface of the sculpture *À bruit secret* (With Hidden Noise, 1916). Also in 1916 he typed four index cards of discontinuous phrases to make up *Rendez-vous du dimanche 6 février* (Rendezvous of Sunday, February 6). Attacking legibility, continuity, and syntactical systems, these projects (like the notes) operate between the articulation and dissolution of language.

The

If you come into ✱ linen, your time is thirsty
because ✱ ink saw some wood intelligent
enough to get giddiness from a sister.
However, even it should be smilable
to shut ✱ hair whose ✱ water
writes always in ✱ plural, they have avoided
✱ frequency, meaning mother in law; ✱ powder
will take a chance; and ✱ road could
try. But after somebody brought any
multiplication as soon as ✱ stamp
was out, a great many cords refused
to go through. Around ✱ wire's people,
who will be able to sweeten ✱ rug,
that is to say, why must every patents
look for a wife? Pushing four dangers
near ✱ listening-place, ✱ vacation
had not dug absolutely nor this
likeness has eaten.

remplacer chaque ✱ par le mot: the

1.8

Marcel Duchamp, *The*, 1915. Manuscript in ink on paper, 8¾ × 5⅝ inches. Philadelphia Museum of Art: The Louise and Walter Arensberg Collection.

-toir. On manquera,à la fois,de
moins qu'avant cinq élections et
aussi quelque accointance avec q-
-uatre petites bêtes; il faut oc-
-cuper ce délice afin d'en décli-
-ner toute responsabilité. Après
douze photos,notre hésitation de-
-vant vingt fibres était compréh-
-ensible; même le pire accrochage
demande coins porte-bonheur sans
compter interdiction aux lins: C-
-omment ne pas épouser son moind-
-re opticien plutôt que supporter
leurs mèches? Non,décidément,der-
-rière ta canne se cachent marbr-
-ures puis tire-bouchon. "Cepend-
-ant,avouèrent-ils,pourquoi viss-
-er,indisposer? Les autres ont p-
-ris démangeaisons pour construi-
-re,par douzaines,ses lacements.
Dieu sait si nous avons besoin,q-
-uoique nombreux mangeurs,dans un
défalquage." Défense donc au tri-
-ple,quand j'ourlerai ,dis je,pr-

-este pour les profits,devant le-
-squels et,par précaution à prop-
-os,elle défonce desserts,même c-
-eux qu'il est défendu de nouer.
Ensuite,sept ou huit poteaux boi-
-vent quelques conséquences main-
-tenant appointées; ne pas oubli-
-er,entre parenthèses,que sans l'
-économat,puis avec mainte sembl-
-able occasion,reviennent quatre
fois leurs énormes limes; quoi!
alors,si la férocité débouche derrière son propre tapis. Dès dem-
-ain j'aurai enfin mis exactemen-
-t des piles là où plusieurs fen-
-dent,acceptent quoique mandant
le pourtour. D'abord,piquait on
ligues sur bouteilles,malgré le-
-ur importance dans cent séréni-
-tés? Une liquide algarade,après
semaines dénonciatrices,va en y
détester ta valise car un bord
suffit. Nous sommes actuellement
assez essuyés,voyez quel désarro-

-onent,après avoir fini votre ge-
-ne. N'empêche que le fait d'éte-
-indre six boutons l'un ses autr-
-es paraît (sauf si,lui,tourne a-
-utour) faire culbuter les bouto-
-nnières. Reste à choisir: de lo-
-ngues,fortes,extensibles défect-
-ions trouées par trois filets u-
-sés,ou bien,la seule enveloppe
pour étendre. Avez vous accepté
des manches? Pouvais tu prendre
sa file? Peut-être devons nous a-
-ttendre mon pilotis,en même tem-
-ps ma difficulté; avec ces chos-
-es là,impossible ajouter une hu-
-itième laisse. Sur trente misé-
-rables postes deux actuels veul-
-ent errer,remboursés civiquement,
refusent toute compensation hors
leur sphère. Pendant combien,pou-
-rquoi comment,limitera-t-on min-
-ce étiage? autrement dit: clous
refroidissent lorsque beaucoup p-
-lissent enfin derrière,contenant

porte,dès maintenant par grande
quantité,pourront faire valoir l-
-e clan oblong qui,sans ôter auc-
-un traversin ni contourner moin-
-s de grelots,va remettre. Deux
fois seulement,tout élève voudra-
-it traire,quand il facilite la
bascule disséminée; mais,comme q-
-uelqu'un démonte puis avale des
déchirements mains nombreux,soi
compris,on est obligé d'entamer
plusieurs grandes horloges pour
obtenir un tiroir à bas âge. Co-
-nclusion: après maints efforts
en vue du peigne,quel dommage!
tous les fourreurs sont partis e-
-t signifient riz. Aucune deman-
-de ne nettoie l'ignorant ou sc-
-ié teneur; toutefois,étant don-
-nées quelques cages,c'eut une
profonde émotion qu'éxécutent t-
-outes colles alitées. Tenues,v-
-ous auriez manqué si s'était t-
-rouvée là quelque prononciation

Yet the notes are meant to be read. Duchamp's typed transcription of each of the notes contained in the *Box of 1914* for Walter and Louise Arensberg (who sponsored the construction of the *Large Glass* in the later 1910s and planned to own it) underscores that the notes should not be considered merely visual material. Duchamp appended the typewritten transcriptions to the mounted photographs—even though both his patrons were used to reading the artist's characteristic scrawled script, as dozens of letters they exchanged over the years prove. He was, then, emphatically facilitating—and even insisting on—not only the notes' reading but also their role as a referential system (their ability to *mean*). Duchamp was perhaps imagining them laid out, casually available near the *Large Glass* itself and any number of other Duchampian works, fingered by the Arensbergs' bourgeois American guests who should, he thought, be able to understand them, or at the very least read them, even if in French. Thus, however much the notes' scribbled script might seem to put readability at stake, their explicit intent was to accompany and serve as a "guide" for the works they evoke. The notes are, whatever else they might be, a discursive apparatus.

1.9

Marcel Duchamp, *Rendez-vous du dimanche 6 février* (Rendezvous of Sunday, February 6), 1916. Typescript with black ink corrections on four postcards taped together, 11¼ × 511/16 inches. Philadelphia Museum of Art: The Louise and Walter Arensberg Collection.

COLLAGE

One of art history's Duchamp stories, told with varying degrees of sympathy, resolves to the following: unable to rival Cubism despite a number of painterly efforts, Duchamp has virtually no choice but to find an alternative and in the process invents the readymade, thereby gaining a foothold on lasting acclaim.[25] The context of Cubism in relation to Duchamp's earliest painted work and passage to the readymade is thus frequently evoked. His multiple, reproduced notes are, however, never considered in relation to Cubism in general or Cubist collage in particular. The problem is perhaps at least partly an ontological one. The notes most often serve as citable sources from which anecdotes, evidence, or information about Duchamp's oeuvre or thinking are extracted; they are rarely seen as aesthetic objects, or as objects proposing theoretical problems in themselves. According to this understanding, they tell, but they do not *do* anything. On the other hand, as Clement Greenberg announces in no uncertain terms, the advent of collage "was a major turning point of Cubism ... and therefore a major turning point in the whole evolution of modernist art."[26] In this light, what could Duchamp's first publication of a handful of scribbled notes have to do with Cubism's—not to say Modernism's—most triumphant developments?

Duchamp often declared that by the latter part of 1912 he had decided to "avoid all contact with traditional pictorial painting which is found in Cubism and in [his] own *Nude Descending a Staircase*."[27] As it happens, the "Cubism" being made, shown, and sold at the time that Duchamp was writing his notes (1912–13) and photographing and then boxing them (1913–14) corresponds exactly with Pablo Picasso and Georges Braque's "synthetic" phase, in which layered images composed of glued pieces of paper, newsprint, and debris introduced what were called *papiers collés*.[28]

Duchamp's replicated notes and Cubism's *papiers collés* are not only perfectly contemporaneous but could be said to share a medium: both are collages of sorts, collections of cut or torn scraps mounted on a backing. They are both artworks declaring themselves to be such while evading all markers of high art (through their mundane materiality, everyday references, and avoidance of technical skill), rejecting traditional mediums and ambivalently positioning themselves between image and text. Duchamp's copied notes do not attempt to grapple with all of the fundamental issues that Cubist collage does—for instance its meditation on and rejection of the conventional pictorial means of Western representational painting, including perspectival recession, anamorphic distortion, chiaroscuro modeling, or distinction from decoration. But the *Box of 1914* does nevertheless traffic in other reference points crucial to the *papiers collés*. Duchamp's replicated notes might not reference mass production through the use of bits of newspaper or ticket stubs, but their dependence on photographic means of reproduction cannot help evoking that culture. And there is the way in which both examples, *papiers collés* and replicated notes, struggle with that most modernist of concerns, flatness. Moreover, the *Box of 1914* addresses some of the same questions that the *papiers collés* raised regarding the orientation of the picture plane (vertical versus horizontal), the potential objecthood of the pictorial, the relationship between word and image, fragmentation, and the rarefaction of the artwork. Importantly, however, if the two artistic projects applied themselves to certain parallel issues, Duchamp's insinuated altogether different—although just as damning—consequences for the artwork as it was then being conceived.

The importance of the Cubist collage to art history, emerging in part from, and immediately following, Picasso's experimental *Still Life with Chair Caning* (1912), was supposedly not only the introduction of mass-cultural detritus into the artwork, but also a revision of the strict verticality of the two-dimensional painting. In other words, the insistence on reading as opposed to "mere" looking. Yve-Alain Bois points to this:

> Painting's vertical section and completely covered over surface were always opposed to the horizontal and diagrammatic space of writing (with few exceptions man reads seated at a table, especially since the invention of printing), but Picasso annulled that antinomy by a 90-degree pivoting (this is the radical gesture of his *Still Life with Chair Caning* of 1912, a canvas that asks to be read as the horizontal plane of a café table, seen from above): for him the picture had become a system structured by arbitrary signs; henceforth his canvas became a written page.[29]

If *Still Life with Chair Caning* can be called a "written page" of sorts, it is one that nevertheless still deploys the grammar of painting—even a frame, albeit one made of rope—and it was ultimately intended to be viewed on a wall. So too were the *papiers collés*, including *Bouteille de vieux marc* (Bottle of Vieux Marc) made shortly after, in the spring of 1913, and others like it that might seem to approach even more insistently the status of objects to be read: in their remove from the world of oil, turpentine, and gloss finish, in their unapologetic paperness, and in their deployment of newsprint and proliferation of words. Yet many of the paper components of these collages bear holes from the straight pins that Picasso and Braque used to temporarily affix them to a backing while they visualized and repositioned the scraps before finally gluing them down. If the scraps and their backing had been worked upon while lying on a table, the pieces could have been rearranged infinitely without needing to be affixed. But the visual assessment for which the pins were required was that of verticality—of being held up to a wall, that surface upon which painting traditionally hung. There can be no ambiguity about how one is to read them: like a picture.

It is perhaps no coincidence that following on the heels of those works, Picasso began in spring 1914 to make collages comprised of a combination of faux gilded picture frames, museum labels, and wallpaper backgrounds. This series, among them works such as *Pipe et partition* (Pipe and Sheet Music, 1914), reinforced and self-consciously mimicked the resolute verticality of painting and its relationship to the museum collection. Indeed, for all of Picasso's and Braque's efforts with their collages to undo the traditional modes of making and presenting something *as a picture*, many of painting's most stalwart conventions nevertheless remained safely in place.

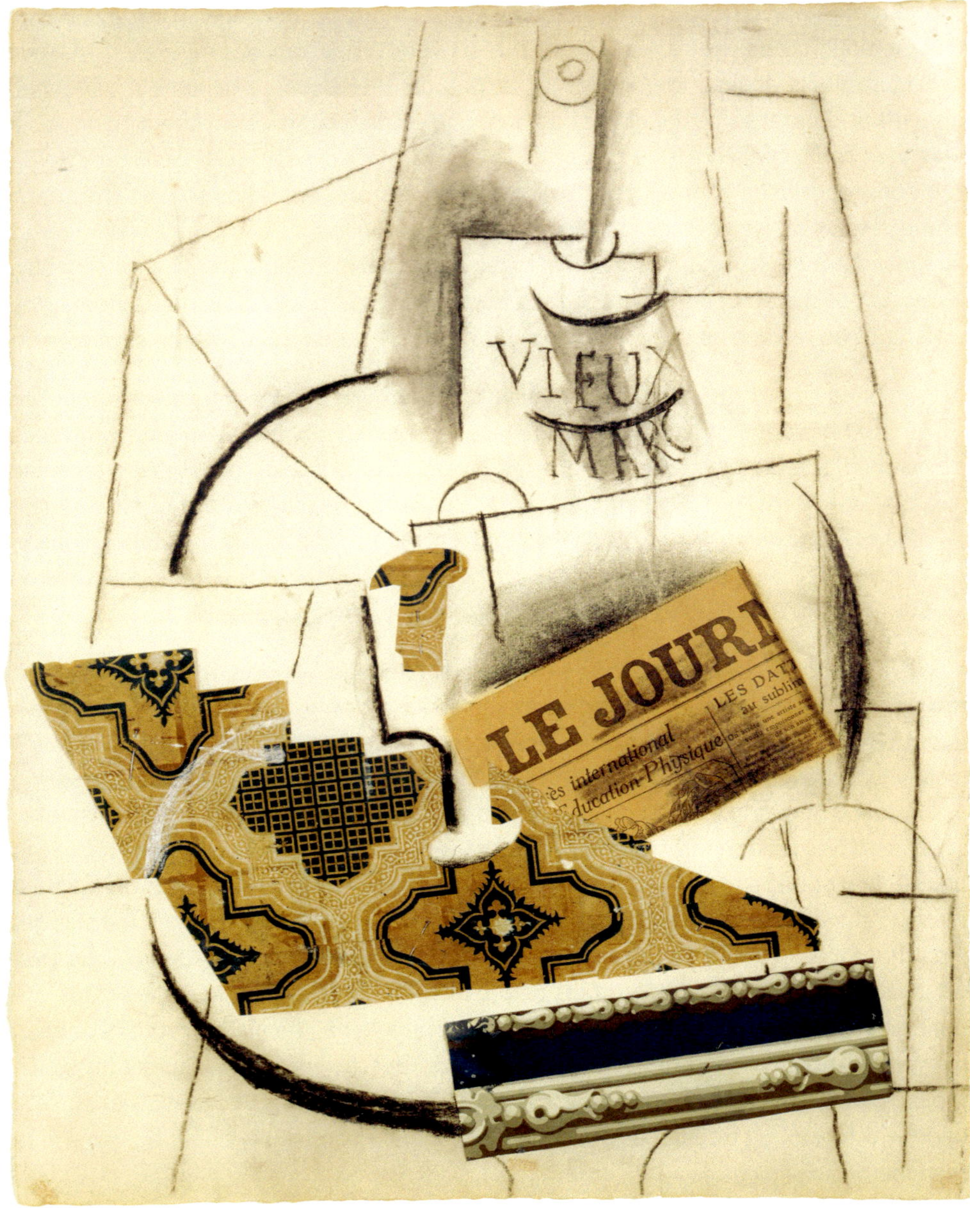

1.10 (top)

Pablo Picasso, *Bouteille de vieux marc* (Bottle of Vieux Marc), 1913. Charcoal, collage, 24¾ × 19¼ inches. Musée National d'Art Moderne, Centre Georges Pompidou, Paris.

1.11 (top right)

Wall of Pablo Picasso's studio at 242 boulevard Raspail, Paris, while he was at work on various *papiers collés*, mid-December 1912 or February 1913. Photographer unknown, possibly Picasso. Musée Picasso, Paris.

1.12 (bottom right)

Pablo Picasso, *Pipe et partition* (Pipe and Sheet Music), 1914. Gouache and graphite on pasted papers, 20 × 26 inches. The Museum of Fine Arts, Houston: Gift of Mr. and Mrs. Maurice McAshan.

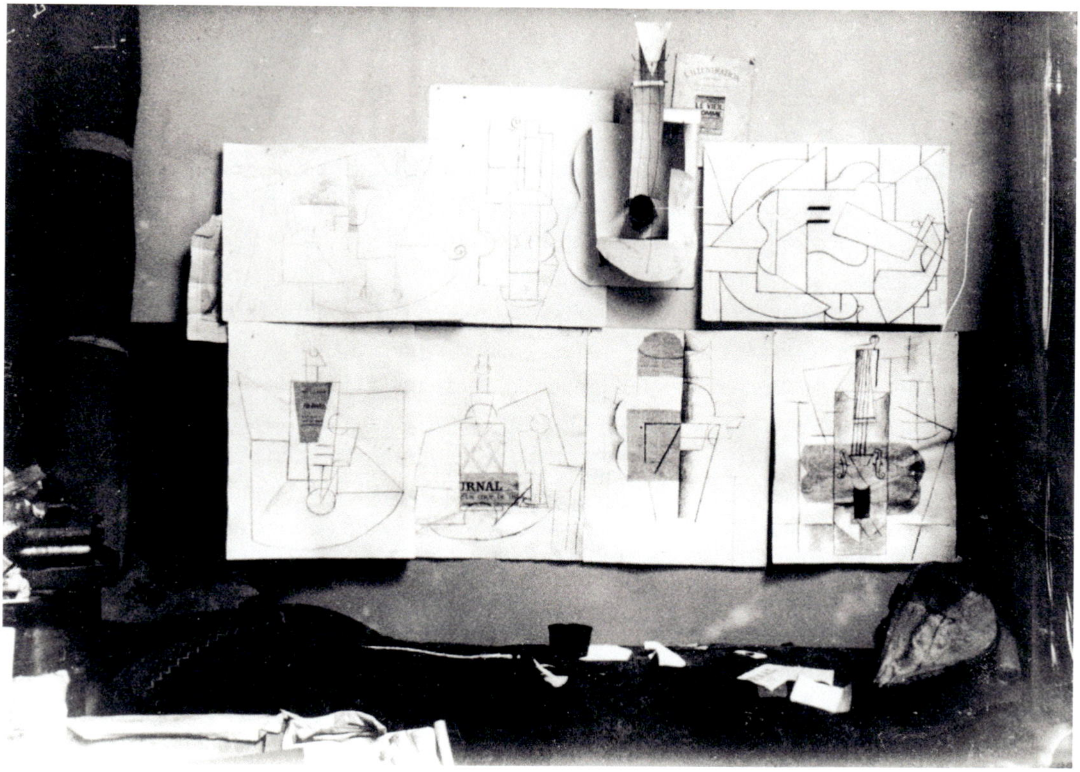

URNAL

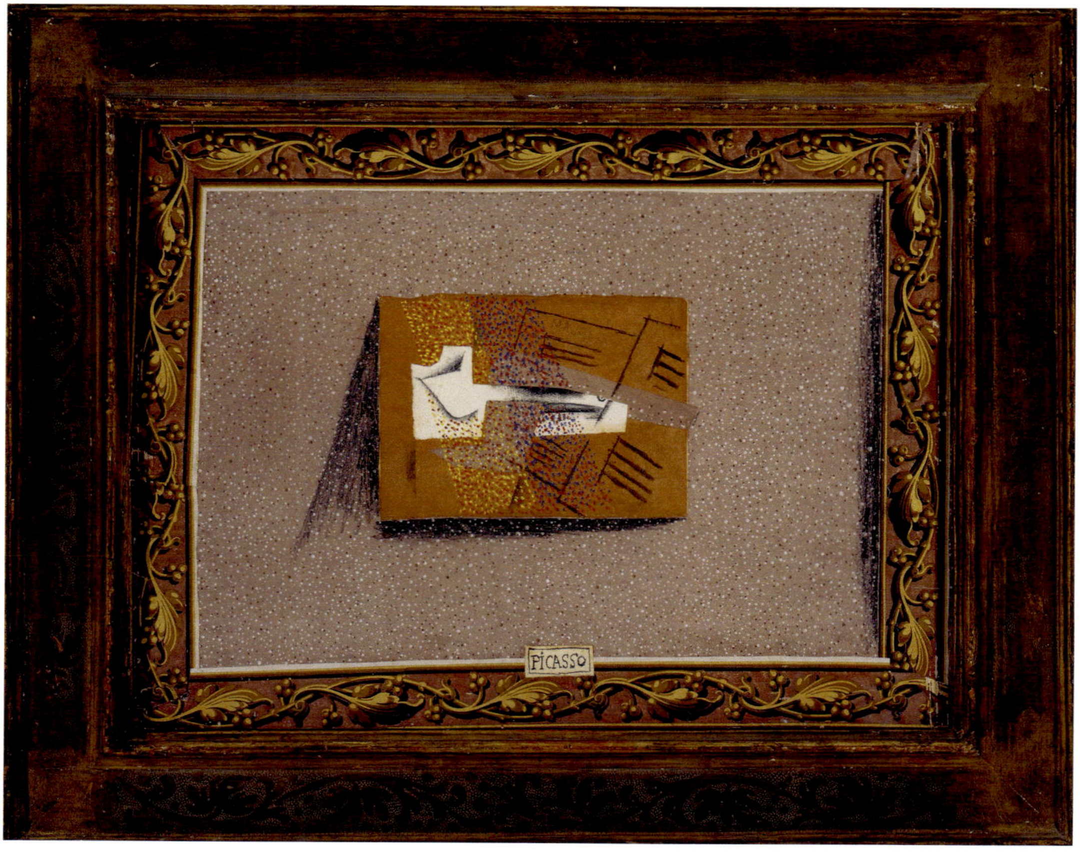

PICASSO

For Duchamp, the notes were not destined for the verticality of display. His boxed fragments of writing incite another form of engagement: looking at them necessitates taking them out of the box and handling them as objects. Still, looking is what one is meant to do because, after all, they are photographs. Duchamp deployed the medium precisely to foreground that his reproduced notes are not to be treated as mere literary specimens.

The apparent conflict between textual reading and aesthetic looking is a particular hallmark of Cubism's *papiers collés*.[30] Lined with bits of newsprint and textual fragments, like so much encrypted innuendo, these collages invite decoding—so much so that scholars literally have begun to read "what the papers say" in search of the "true" meaning of the collages.[31] Nonetheless, the very fragmentation of that language (partial words or phrases such as "Le jou," "urnal," "Un coup de Thé," "Trou ici," et cetera) edges the collages toward the pictorial, because, as Rosalind Krauss argues, "deprived of a linguistic context in which to perform," these partial words or phrases are primarily designed to operate as part of an image.[32]

Duchamp's notes, on the other hand, are too often treated as nothing *but* linguistic articulations, works so much about words that the way in which they are also pictures is overlooked. It is no accident that over the years Duchamp's notes have been *cited* (in order to explain an artwork situated somewhere else and presumably more meaningful) while Cubism's collages have been *deciphered* (the text offering a more complete interpretation of what the collages mean as pictures).[33]

More than a mere combination of the textual and the visual, Duchamp's notes arguably constitute a reconsideration of aesthetic attention and spectatorial experience through a reorientation of the picture plane. One might think of the way Leo Steinberg discusses Robert Rauschenberg's and Jean Dubuffet's work as having radically reconceived the surface of painting, reorienting the position of the viewer through a reconception of the artwork's flatness. Steinberg observes that something "happened in painting around 1950 ... pictures no longer simulate vertical fields, but opaque flatbed horizontals ... a radically new orientation, in which the painted surface is no longer the analogue of a visual experience of nature but of operational processes." And for this, Steinberg argued, Duchamp was perhaps "the most vital source."[34] Although he does not name any specific work of Duchamp, Steinberg's "different order of experience" is, in fact, arguably first performed in the notes.[35] Through them, Duchamp rendered scanning the flat page—*reading*—the operative mode of aesthetic engagement at the same moment at which he transformed the disordered, haphazard, and tentative (documentation of process) into the artwork itself.

While the *Large Glass* would go on to stand erect in space, reflecting the upright spectator in its glass diptych segments, the various notes undermined its verticality as they aimed to keep the piece grounded in the horizontals on which we read and write. More than that, the replicated notes furthered a process begun in 1913–14 and continued in later reproduction projects, which would make of the work of art a thing to be handled, shuffled, laid down—contrary to the way that Cubist collage engaged its spectators. Each note thus offered itself (à la Steinberg) as a "work surface that cannot be construed into anything else," and thus wound up as "a verification of its own opaque surface."[36] It was one way for Duchamp to take the conventional idea of the artwork *down*, literally.

"Sans colle" (without glue), one of Duchamp's notes, written in this period but only published posthumously, announces defiantly, mysteriously.[37] On the heels of Cubism's most fertile investigations and decidedly rejecting its practice of gluing everything in place, Duchamp offered the *papiers* without the *colle*. The individual notes remained materially disconnected fragments. In addition, their language prevented the disparate pieces from ever seeming to connect too readily or to offer linguistic continuity. Compared to the way in which each Cubist collage remains literally unified—with one composition integrating all fragments and assembling them, even sometimes explicitly framing them, on a single planar surface (no matter that what that surface actually pictured contradicted this unity)—Duchamp's readiness simply to present a series of disconnected elements in a box can be understood as an emphatic pursuit of fracture and dissolution, strategies that Cubism claimed as its own.

The discrepancy between the historical treatments of the two parallel efforts is striking. While the two might not immediately look comparable, their commonalities make their juxtaposition not only possible but also an expedient way of understanding the context and contours of each. Perhaps the most significant distinction between them is the following: the *papiers collés*, however unluxurious and however linked to a mass-cultural reality, remained unique and rarefied in their originality even as they advertised their skimpiness, while Duchamp's multiple, photochemically copied scraps, by contrast, refuse both Cubism's originality and its ultimate pictorial, glued-together resolution.[38] In their differences, it also becomes evident that the turn in Duchamp's practice—marked by his reproduction of notes—does not reflect a "failure" to continue down the path of Cubism, as has so long been claimed. Instead, through his note project, Duchamp addressed a number of issues that were the very mainstays of Cubist collage. His photographically reproduced and boxed scraps can be said to have interrogated the limits of the traditional work of art in a way that has been, while different from Cubist collage, even more far-reaching in some respects.

PHOTOGRAPHY

It should be stated, for once, in no uncertain terms: the *Box of 1914* is also a set of photographs. It is odd that this most obvious and technically irrefutable fact, one with vast repercussions, has not much registered in the history of Duchamp, or of photography, for which it could easily provide an important, pioneering object of study. The influence of "the photographic," as scholars such as Jean Clair and Rosalind Krauss have argued, is everywhere felt in Duchamp's oeuvre, even if, as they both note, the artist rarely made photographs himself or directly employed the medium.[39] However, in studying

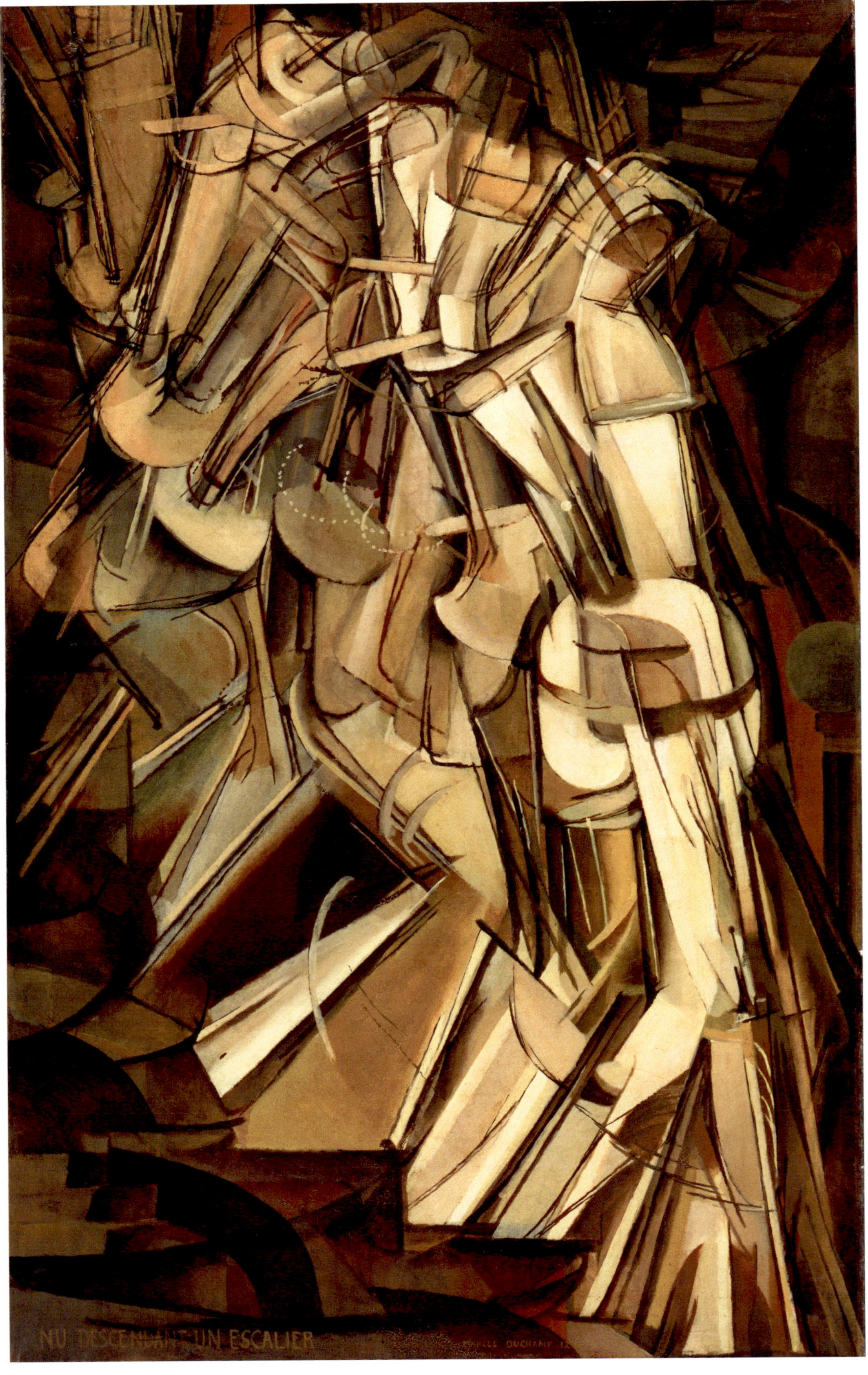
NU DESCENDANT UN ESCALIER
DUCHAMP

the numerous painterly expressions of the *iconography* of early photographic technologies—the chronophotography in *Nude Descending a Staircase*, the emanation painted around the figure's hands in *Portrait of Dr. Dumouchel* (1910), which evoked so-called aura photographs, or even the shadowlike silhouette and stop-motion quality of the early ink drawing of his sister in *Jouer?* (Play?, 1902)—Clair, like most scholars, leaves Duchamp's most complexly developed and richly provocative photographic experiments such as his replication of notes curiously understudied. And this even though Duchamp's publication of all his notes, beginning in 1914, relied so heavily on photography in particular (and on reproduction as a paradigm in general) that the entire project cannot feasibly be considered independent of the photographic medium.

The reasons for the omission are likely technical as much as conceptual. In looking for the ways in which Duchamp was influenced by the conceptual implications of the photographic—its relation to his explorations of delay, shadows, and the index—even as he avoided becoming a "photographer" or making the medium itself a prominent feature in his work, scholars often fail to acknowledge that rare moment when he actually deployed photography. It is as if the directness of Duchamp's photographic gesture with the *Box of 1914* blinded scholars who were looking for "the photographic" and so missed the photograph. In the process, they overlooked not only the repercussions of the artist's first major experimentation with the medium, but also the ways in which it laid the foundations for so much of what historians found important in his later works. In studying the ways in which the "logic of photography" was a central motor of Duchamp's work, they focus almost solely on works that exist as singular originals: note Krauss's interest in *Tu m'* (1918), the *Large Glass*, and *With My Tongue in My Cheek* (1959), or Clair's focus on the paintings *Nude Descending a Staircase* and *Portrait of Dr. Dumouchel*. In failing to take the logic of photography to its final conclusion, they neglect not only to examine Duchamp's very first work to exist in multiple copies, but also to tackle the problem of the photographic head-on.[40]

1.13

Marcel Duchamp, *Nu descendant un escalier* (Nude Descending a Staircase), 1912. Oil on canvas, 57½ × 35⅛ inches. Philadelphia Museum of Art: The Louise and Walter Arensberg Collection.

Duchamp's reproductions of his notes are rarely, if at all, examined in relation to the development of an avant-garde history of photography (never, for instance, has the *Box of 1914* been shown in photography exhibitions about the era). Yet Duchamp's use of the medium arguably reveals more about how the very limits of photography were being pushed than almost any other artwork of the period. The artist's deployment of photography to replicate bits of paper bearing his hand script was neither Dadaist prank nor nihilistic provocation; it was the beginning of a long, and obstinately pursued, theoretical inquiry. In using the medium as no art photographer in his time would, and claiming the result as an artwork in itself and simultaneously as a supplement to, or discursive accompaniment for, another artwork, Duchamp put his finger on photography's troubled relation to contemporary notions of the work of art. In his hands, photography is not a medium entrenched in its own traditions and history, but instead one that evacuates the conditions of the aesthetic medium by becoming a "theoretical object," as Krauss would claim as a potential of photography.[41] This is part of what makes Duchamp's *Box of 1914* so provocative. Against a sense that photography's primary function lies in its technical capacity to arrest and inscribe what is held in front of the camera, he uses it as a conceptual vehicle, challenging accepted ideas of photography's use, utility, and significatory dimensions through a rupturing of the conventions attached to it.

In numerous interviews Duchamp acknowledged his interest in Étienne-Jules Marey, the French pioneer whose chronophotography the artist remembered observing in illustrated magazines around 1911.[42] Marey, the chronophotographer of the successive *instantané*, the physiologist-inventor who devised a means almost simultaneous with Eadweard Muybridge to photographically capture rapid movement, certainly inspired one aspect of Duchamp's photographic impulse. *Nude Descending a Staircase*, for instance, cannot be considered outside the influence of chronophotography (Muybridge himself photographed women descending staircases). But if Duchamp's lifelong and complex relationship to the photographic is to be fully understood, it cannot be entirely encapsulated by the *aesthetics* of chronophotography. Another aspect of Marey's project might have been just as influential: the creation of concrete documents through mechanical (photographic) means. For Marey's utilization of photography was actually little concerned with aesthetics as such. In his pursuit, the photograph was *evidence*. It is this documentary, evidential aspect that seems to have been crucial to Duchamp's complex engagement with the archive, first announced in the *Box of 1914*.

The scholarship regarding Duchamp and photography (or even concerning his brother Raymond Duchamp-Villon's use of photography) consistently focuses on the visual effects of chronophotography.[43] We know that Duchamp had been exposed to the technique through Duchamp-Villon, who as a medical student had worked with Marey's protégé Albert Londe, the staff radiologist and photographer under Dr. Jean-Martin Charcot at the Hôpital de la Salpêtrière. Its banal documentary possibilities, however, may have been a more important shared concern of the two brothers. In the early teens, Duchamp-Villon used photography to document his own sculptural production, and thus Duchamp could have found in his brother a useful instructor or fellow explorer of photography. Whereas Duchamp-Villon would use photography to make a practical record of his artworks, his youngest brother would endeavor to turn the document—even more, the copy of the document—into an artwork.

One should not forget that, at the time, photography had little hope of actually rivaling the place of painting because its indexical quality was inimical to the expectation of transcendence, originality, and autonomy in the modern artwork. If the photograph couldn't hang like the transcendent canvas in the transcendent gallery, the beginning of the twentieth century did nevertheless see an emerging category of "art photography." The 1910s witnessed the apex of the Pictorialist movement (including such names as Edward Steichen, Alfred Stieglitz, Julia Margaret Cameron, and Alvin Langdon Coburn), with its aspirations to firmly root photography in the sensibility and aesthetic of painting. Diametrically opposed to the Pictorialists (with which his work was concurrent), Eugène Atget produced the bulk of what he specifically called his photographic "documents" between 1898 and 1914.[44] His work offers perhaps the best example of a photographic practice that self-consciously strove to eschew a purely aestheticist logic during these crucial years that inaugurated photography's "modern period."[45] One could list Alphonse Bertillon's photos of criminals, Albert Londe's of hysteria patients, and Karl Blossfeldt's of plant specimens in addition to Marey's photos of galloping horses or Atget's of Parisian streets: each has a concrete "documentary" purpose for which its evidential quality offers testimony. Before World War I, as Molly Nesbit attests, the documentary was considered antithetical to the aesthetic: "When Atget started working, documents occupied the lowest scale in the hierarchy: artists *used* documents, but their works were not *like* documents."[46] Yet *that* was precisely what Duchamp was making: photographed copies of notes that approached the appearance of documents, not artworks. At the same time, they quietly worked toward embodying each of the two categories—and undermining both.

Duchamp's black-and-white photographs of notes, housed in five boxes made for photographic glass plates, engaged photography neither to colonize it as high art nor to claim it as an avant-gardist medium with the potential to shock. Instead, the boxes initiated a sustained exploration of the charged intersection of photography and painting, of documentary and aesthetic creation, and of production and reproduction. Before World War I, when the avant-garde as we currently conceive it was but a nascent phenomenon, it was only Futurism that directly used photography in art, capturing blur on film in order to immortalize movement. Dada, with its radical experiments with collage and photomontage, had not yet begun. Thus, during a period when photography was trying to raise its status to that of high art, and before the avant-garde would inaugurate photographic collage and montage as modes to deconstruct photography's pretensions to aesthetic autonomy, Duchamp had already begun an operation that would complicate the status of the photograph.[47]

Entirely rejecting the conventions of art photography of the day—the still-nascent medium was being widely used to make portraits and landscapes, *not* to photograph pieces of paper and even less those with random ideas scribbled on them—Duchamp used the camera as if it were a copying machine, a photocopier *avant la lettre*. Thus with his very first box, Duchamp developed a model of the photograph as a flat and flattened copy and the camera as an emphatically neutral recording instrument. Neither window nor mirror (as the photograph was so often metaphorized), Duchamp's utterly artless and spatially depthless photos of flat scraps of paper seem not to have had the slightest regard for the conventions of the medium.

More akin to the world of archiving and administration than to art photography, these photographs convey information. One can read Duchamp's characteristic hand script, and identify the tears and irregularities of their different pages. Yet the photographs are often overlit, underlit, or black-shadowed, hardly hiding the marks of an amateur approach to the medium. In manifest neglect of specialized skill, Duchamp did not, for instance, photograph his notes under glass, a known technique for eliminating those shadows that almost invariably show beneath the crumpled corners and warped pages of his various notes.[48] Instead, his photographs show the notes' edges. They announce themselves as nothing more than reproductions of notes, which, paradoxically, the artist nevertheless presents as artworks.

Through the medium of photography, Duchamp's fourteen notes and two images, copied five times each, unmoored the unique original paramount to traditional contemporary conceptions of the artwork. Indeed, his very first project using photography was arguably the foundation for his lifelong engagement with reproduction and the questioning of originality. Not only would his photographic paradigm undermine the authenticity and singularity of the work of art; it equally came to question what the photographic could mean.

The replicated notes were thus the perfect ambivalent objects, performing and undoing multiple categories of art and the expectations associated with them. Simultaneously, they also offered fourteen-times-five copies of handwriting, which, like the artwork in a larger sense, is the very graphic trace that is ostensibly inimitable: an original that cannot be copied. What audacity, then, to reproduce hand script by way of the modern medium that was rivaling painting and showing up its mimetic capacities. What perversity to turn the manuscript into a photograph, to turn the scrappy note into a glossy image that pictorializes writing even as it turns that emblematic mark of authenticity—hand script—into a photographic copy.

Photography, so typically an arbiter and conveyer of three-dimensional space, was made to become emphatically about flatness and inscription. For Duchamp's notes neither bear the signs often used to argue for photography as art, such as depth of field, illusion, and accurate rendition of detail, nor convey a sense of the captured instant, with its narrative or symbolic interest. Instead, they willingly exist in a no-man's-land in which their apparent offering of factual testimony is undermined by an unresolved sloppiness, a reticence to actually deliver either pristine, archive-worthy documents or "artlike" photographs.

After photographing his notes, Duchamp trimmed and mounted each on loose cardboard backings, thereby turning these textual artifacts into something more akin to images. In fact, one of the series (a note explaining how he will go about making *3 Standard Stoppages*, bearing the underlined phrase at the top "L'Idée de la Fabrication" [The idea of fabrication]) is composed of two photographs mounted edge to edge on a mat board so as to depict one document which, in turn, is composed of four little scraps of paper aligned to look—although hardly convincingly—like one continuous text. In other words, Duchamp tried to pass off a grouping of little scraps as a single document that would factually qualify as coherent information, yet its constructedness (literally, its visible fabrication) makes this more than questionable. These four little pieces of paper never actually were one page; they are only rendered as one in a picture. Like the other elements in the box, each photograph offers a picture of what a document is supposed to look like, but simultaneously proves not to be what it represents: it is not quite a document, just a fabricated image.

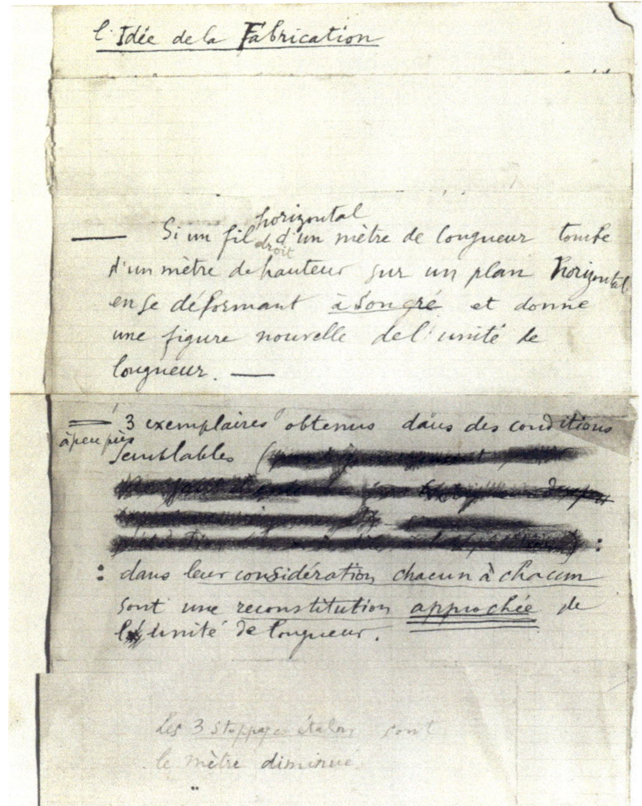
l'Idée de la Fabrication

— Si un fil droit horizontal d'un mètre de longueur tombe d'un mètre de hauteur sur un plan horizontal en se déformant à son gré et donne une figure nouvelle de l'unité de longueur. —

— 3 exemplaires obtenus dans des conditions à peu près semblables (

: dans leur considération chacun à chacun sont une reconstitution approchée de l'unité de longueur.

Les 3 stoppages étalon sont le mètre diminué.

1.14

Marcel Duchamp, detail of note with heading "L'Idée de la Fabrication" from the *Box of 1914*, 1913–14. Photograph of manuscript note, mounted on mat board, 11 1/16 × 9 3/8 inches. Centre Pompidou, MNAM-CCI, Paris.

Several of the boxes into which Duchamp collected his photographed notes in 1914 bore the label "Extra-rapide," a term he would also frequently cite in his notes. In the world of photography at the time, it was a proclamation of how swiftly light-sensitive photographic paper could inscribe an object placed before the lens (useful for photographing objects in motion or persons struggling to sit still). Yet the "extra fast" paper was, in Duchamp's hands, illogically used to reproduce things that were slower than slow, since the note paper and the letters scribbled upon it couldn't have been more immobile or patient. Duchamp thus used photography neither as a sign of his savvy application of an advanced technology nor to make an art object to be hung on the wall, but as a means for recording, documenting, in short blatantly reproducing, all the while insinuating that these photographs, too, could be art.

Cinema theorist André Bazin would publish "The Ontology of the Photographic Image" several decades later, but his theory of photography nevertheless resonates with what Duchamp seems to have been grappling with all along:

> Painting is, after all, an inferior way of making likenesses, an ersatz of the processes of reproduction. Only a photographic lens can give us the kind of image of the object that is capable of satisfying the deep need man has to substitute for it something more than a mere approximation. ... The photographic image is the object itself, the object freed from the conditions of time and space that govern it. No matter how fuzzy, disoriented, or discolored, no matter how lacking in documentary value the image may be, it shares, by virtue of the very process of its becoming, the being of the model of which it is the reproduction; it *is* the model.[49]

Indeed, against either an artistic practice that claimed the photographic as a legitimate rival to painting or a commercial photographic practice that insisted on its dispensable, marketable, mass-cultural role, Duchamp's reproduction of his notes eschews what was in the period considered properly photographic—either a rational, technical precision or an aesthetics of artfulness. Through this, he effectively gets to the heart of what could be called the conditions of the photographic, in essence Bazin's idea of the photograph as "the model of which it is the reproduction."[50]

The exploration of this condition, posited by Rosalind Krauss as one of Duchamp's defining contributions to twentieth-century art, resides in the manifold ways in which the *Large Glass* and other Duchampian works would silently refer to and deploy photographic, indexical means.[51] Her reading is right, although to it I would add other examples and objects of study, the first being the *Box of 1914* and the last being Duchamp's final and most resolutely indexical work, *Étant donnés* (1946–66, discussed in chapter 3).[52] If we fail to consider the significance of the *Box of 1914*, not only for the specific ways it deploys the index (in the process deliberately attempting to position the *Large Glass*) but also for its role as matrix for Duchamp's lifelong exploration of the logic of photography, we might easily overlook those ways in which the artist called for a radical rethinking of the entire definition and valuation of the work of art as a singular, unique, hierarchically stable, and undeniably authentic repository of artistic originality.[53] Before he had given a name to the everyday already-made things he had brought, like stray animals, into his studio, indeed before he had begun the operation that would use those things to test the robustness of the category called "art," Duchamp's replicated notes offered a model of reproduction that sat uneasily between being things in themselves and being references to other artworks, opening an altogether different but related set of questions about where the lines are drawn between and around that thing we call a work "of art."

PAINTING

"Even a few words I don't feel like writing. You know exactly what I think about photography. I would like to see it make people despise painting until something else will make photography unbearable. There we are. Affectionately, Marcel Duchamp. 17 May 1922."[54] Such was the annoyed proclamation of the artist to photographer Alfred Stieglitz's question "Can a photograph have the significance of art?" directed at a select group of artists in 1922. Duchamp had just returned to New York to recommence work on the *Large Glass*, and the conflicted relationship of photography and painting was not far from his mind.

Painting and photography—Duchamp's comment hardly suggests a love for either. But no matter how one construes his words, the artist was deeply engaged in a practice that interrogated both. And the development of both mediums in coexistence was, following Benjamin H. D. Buchloh's logic, central to the avant-garde's various reconceptions of painting.[55] Buchloh's models include not only Duchamp but also Alexander Rodchenko's development of a photomontage aesthetic concomitant with the latter's definition of pure pictoriality around 1921, Robert Rauschenberg's exploration of the photographic in his work at the same moment that he engages with the paradigm of the monochrome in 1949–51, and eventually Gerhard Richter's development of a particularly imbricated practice of painting and archiving photography in the early 1960s. For the art historian, to have continued to paint while ignoring the import of photography was tantamount to missing the boat. Picasso, according to Buchloh, missed it:

> It is the disaster of Picasso after Cubism not to have recognized the historical viability of photography. You cannot work against photography, outside photography, or in denial of photography and pretend that painting remains viable all through the 20s and 30s, when there is an extraordinary photographic culture springing up around and developing in every single country in the most amazing ways. And here is this man who pretends that there is no relevance to be considered and no issue to be addressed.[56]

Duchamp's *Nude Descending a Staircase* and his interpretation of chronophotography, on the other hand, are claimed as exemplary of the imbricated practice Buchloh champions as progressive.[57] It is striking, however, that the critic does not discuss the *Box of 1914*, because it is there that Duchamp was less obviously, but with more

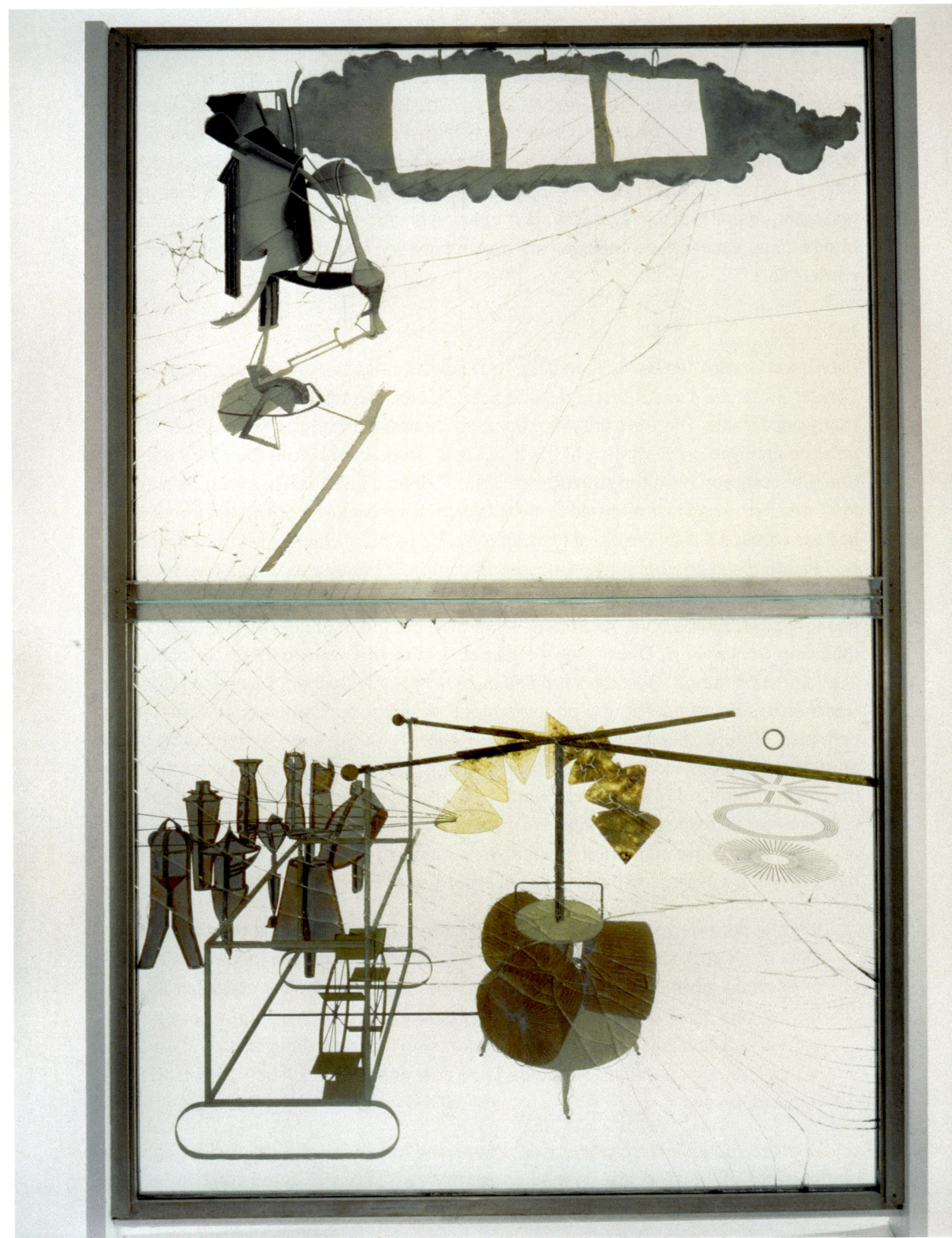

CHAPTER 1

far-reaching consequences, truly reckoning with the conditions of photography, simultaneously with, and explicitly in relation to, the preparation of the "precision painting" that is the *Large Glass*. The *Box of 1914*'s "flat" use of photography as a profane copying technology (in order to replicate the apparently unreplicable: handwriting) provocatively brings the medium to its degree zero—concurrently with the artist's continued engagement with painting. For, whatever one might call the *Large Glass*, it still is a unique, signed, framed, and titled pictorial representation displayed in a vertical manner (a traditional diptych of sorts, no less) and in this sense evokes painting. At that point, in the early teens, both painting and photography played a vital role in Duchamp's practice, and he seems concerned to question the implications of both. In fact, the artist situates himself at the center of the painting-photography dialectic while undermining both and refusing to acknowledge his engagement with either.

It may not be easy to determine Duchamp's strategic objectives within this contested field, but one thing seems clear: he wanted to see photography *affect* painting. For many reasons, the *Large Glass* plays a crucial role in this, making it, as George Baker suggests, an example of "photography by other means."[58] Not only are the notes relating to the *Large Glass* "dominated," as Jean-François Lyotard has written, "by the photographic analogy," with references to snapshots, time-lapse poses, and "extra-rapide" exposures, but the actual use of photography was instrumental in devising several of its motifs.[59] To recount them is to describe a series of oddball photographically inspired methods: Duchamp photographed a sheer curtain in front of an open window, recording the movement of air and its effect on the piece of cloth over the course of three photographs and using these photographic transcriptions of the concrete but miniscule action as the basis for the three irregular forms of the Bride's "love gas," called "Draft Pistons," on the upper panel. Or there were the "Sieves" in the *Large Glass*, "colored" by the dust that Duchamp allowed to accumulate on the surface of the glass over several months so that dust gained an equivalence with light on the photographic plate, leaving what Krauss calls "a kind of physical index for the passage of time."[60] Photography, it seems, is everywhere evoked in what is essentially a massive, standing glass plate, constructed during the period when photographic negatives were typically glass plates upon which an image was inscribed.[61]

1.15

Marcel Duchamp, *La Mariée mise à nu par ses célibataires, même [Grand verre]* (The Bride Stripped Bare by Her Bachelors, Even [The Large Glass]), 1915–23. Oil, varnish, lead foil, lead wire, and dust on two glass panels (cracked), each mounted between two glass panels, with five glass strips, aluminum, foil, and a wood and steel frame, 108 × 1¼ × 69 ¼ inches. Philadelphia Museum of Art: Bequest of Katherine S. Dreier.

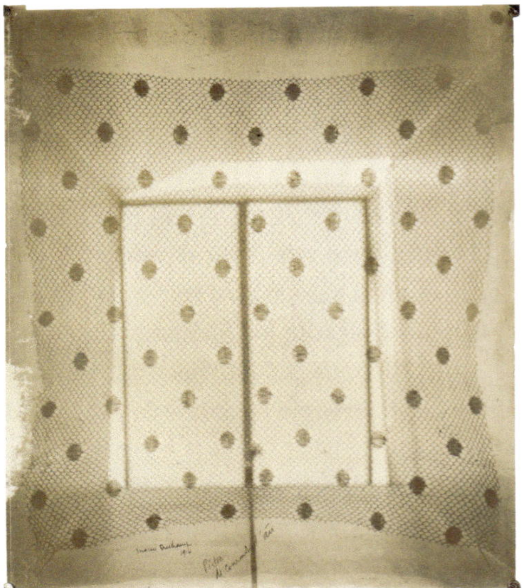

1.16

Marcel Duchamp, *Piston de courant d'air* (Draft Piston), 1914. One of a series of three photographs used by the artist for designing the "Draft Pistons" of the *Large Glass*. Gelatin silver print, 23⅛ × 19¾ inches. The Philadelphia Museum of Art.

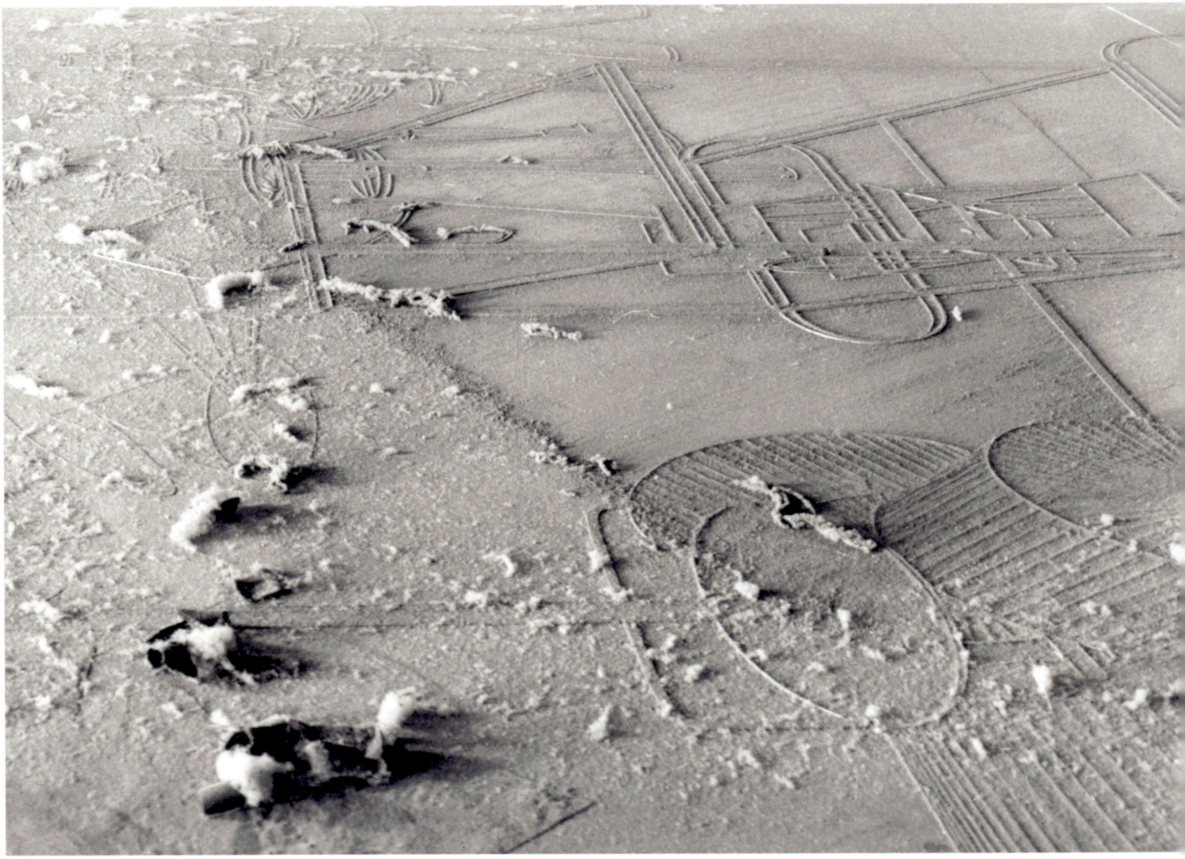

Not only did Duchamp take that index-making process seriously, drafting a sign near the *Large Glass* as it lay resting on a table that read: "Dust breeding. To be respected," but for him to have Man Ray take a photograph of it is to have wanted a veritable index of an index.[62] One can detect the traces of photography in the *Large Glass* in yet another way. For on a fundamental level, photography and, concretely, photography as used in the *Box of 1914*, which is to say, photography as a means of mechanical reproduction, arguably provided the very logic of Duchamp's approach to the *Large Glass* as a painting. About this the artist was unequivocal: he conceived his effort on the *Large Glass* as "mechanical work," labor diametrically opposed to what he again and again described as the *patte* of the painter.[63] Contrary to a certain logic of painterly originality, the artist repeatedly called the *Large Glass* instead a "precision painting," glossing his use of the term "precision" here through references to mechanicity, image transfer, and a negation of the artist's touch. He went so far as to call the labor on the piece a form of "copying," saying further, and explicitly, that he wanted it to resemble an "imitation of photography."[64] In no uncertain terms, then, it is precisely the blatant mechanical reproduction—the act of copying—so central to the *Box of 1914* that serves as the modus operandi for the *Large Glass*, no matter how different the status of the "copying" in each.

This is where things get complicated. At a moment when Duchamp is insisting on turning to the mechanical, imagining a massive glass work that uses photography and attempts to refuse the visible *patte* of the author, he had already surrounded the product of this rejection of the hand with scribbled notes—and had already photographically copied them, and would afterward do so again, using different notes, repeatedly. Perhaps the greatest paradox of the relationship between the two elements—*Large Glass* and notes (those contained in the *Box of 1914* and those that followed)—is, then, that the *Large Glass* is a kind of painting (epitome of the unique, auratic artwork) that attempted and failed to pursue the strategies of the photograph (the epitome of the non-unique, replicable image), yet it is also accompanied by handwritten manuscripts (another epitome of the unique and auratic) that are reproduced (thus non-unique and replicable) and, as such, challenge the idea of a rarefied and unique work through their replication.

1.17

Marcel Duchamp, *Élevage de Poussière* (Dust Breeding), 1920. Photo by Man Ray. Gelatin silver print from original negative, 2 13/16 × 4 3/8 inches. Jedermann Collection, N.A.

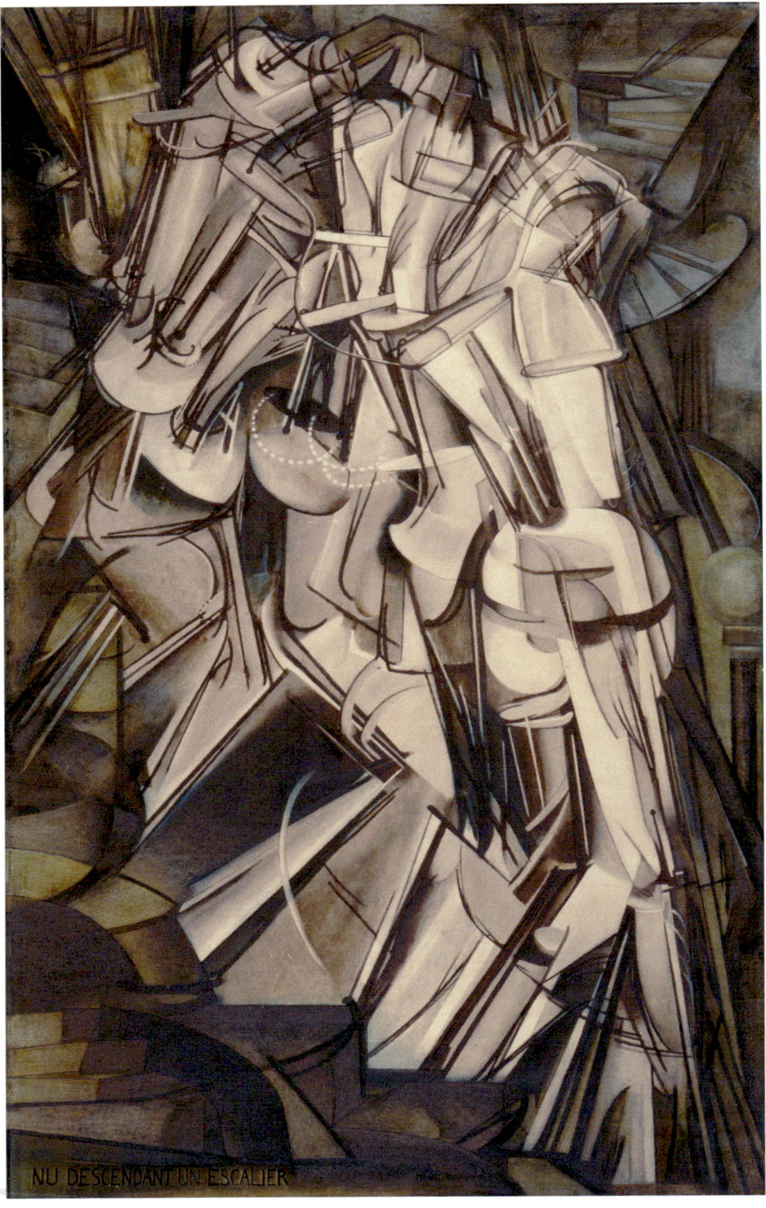

1.18

Marcel Duchamp, *Nude Descending a Staircase* (no. 3), 1916. Graphite, pen and black ink, black paint, colored pencil or crayon, and blue wash on a gelatin silver photograph, $57\frac{5}{16} \times 36\frac{1}{8}$ inches. Philadelphia Museum of Art: The Louise and Walter Arensberg Collection.

If photographed notes served as a model for the *Large Glass* so as to construct a new, albeit conflicted, model for painting, Duchamp used painting in turn to complicate his approach to photography. He did so, notably, with another project made just a year after beginning work on the *Large Glass*. In 1916, in order to satisfy Walter and Louise Arensberg's seemingly unquenchable thirst for Duchampiana and to alleviate their dismay at not being able to possess his *Nude Descending a Staircase*, Duchamp had a life-size photograph taken of the painting, calling it *Nude Descending a Staircase, No. 3*.[65] He then added washes of metallic gray and green gouache to the black-and-white image, highlighting the nude's forms without at all attempting to replicate the original painting's color scheme. According to his signature, even its author was a replica, related but different, a "son" of himself: "Marcel Duchamp (fils) 1912 ... 1916."[66] What he created was a dubious hybrid, neither true painting nor unadulterated mechanical photography. The hand-colored photographic copy of a hand-painted canvas defied both mediums in one blow. The very originality of painting (in this case, Duchamp's single most famous painting on canvas) is unsettled in the act of mechanically producing a photographic copy to take its place. Yet, conversely, the mechanical reproducibility of photography, the medium's single most defining feature, is revoked by turning the photograph into a unique, hand-painted—and thus newly original—artifact.[67]

Reproduction proves to be a complex operation in Duchamp's oeuvre: modus operandi, agent for the questioning of painting, and subject to being undermined in turn. Not as a mode of practical publicity or anything like an easy means of dissemination, and never a mere mechanical process, it would play a decisive, even structural, role for him to the end. In 1930, for instance, in response to Louis Aragon's invitation to contribute to an exhibition entitled "La Peinture au défi" (The Challenge to Painting) organized in March of that year at the Galerie Goemans in Paris, the artist responded with a series of artworks that challenged painting only to deconstruct the very premise on which the challenge was articulated. Duchamp's contributions interpreted the show's title specifically through variations on reproduction and the photographic. To arrive at this response was not as obvious as it might in retrospect seem, especially as Aragon himself saw the key to undermining painting elsewhere. For, as is clear from the exhibition's catalog, Aragon thought the "challenge" could primarily be achieved through what the writer called "collage."[68] Not so much a strict category for works made of actual pasted elements, he understood collage as an artistic strategy that embodied a set of qualities—impoverished, unskilled, ironic, critical, intellectually driven—that were virtually irreconcilable with the bourgeoisie's *bon goût*, and that thus made them quintessentially painting's *other*. Still, the words "reproduction" or "originality," so central to Duchamp's thinking, are absent from the lexicon of Aragon's catalog essay.

Among the works Duchamp contributed to the show was *Pharmacie* (Pharmacy, 1914), one of his edition of three prints of an idyllic landscape, stock images bought from an art supply shop and specifically intended to be copied by students learning to paint, to which Duchamp simply added two small hand-painted dots, transforming a mass

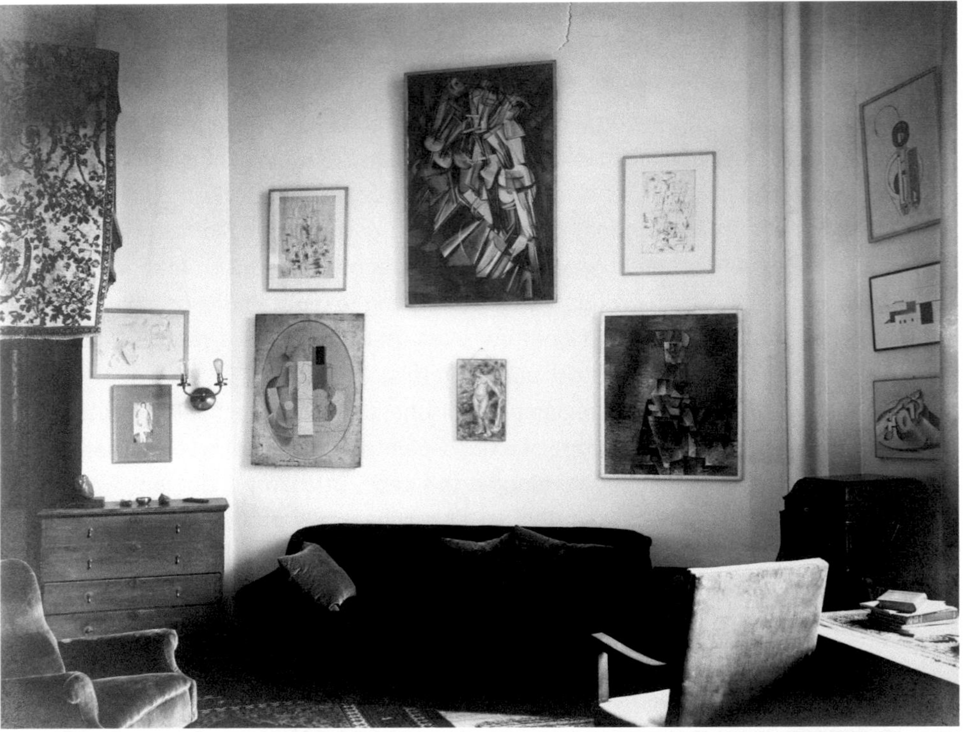

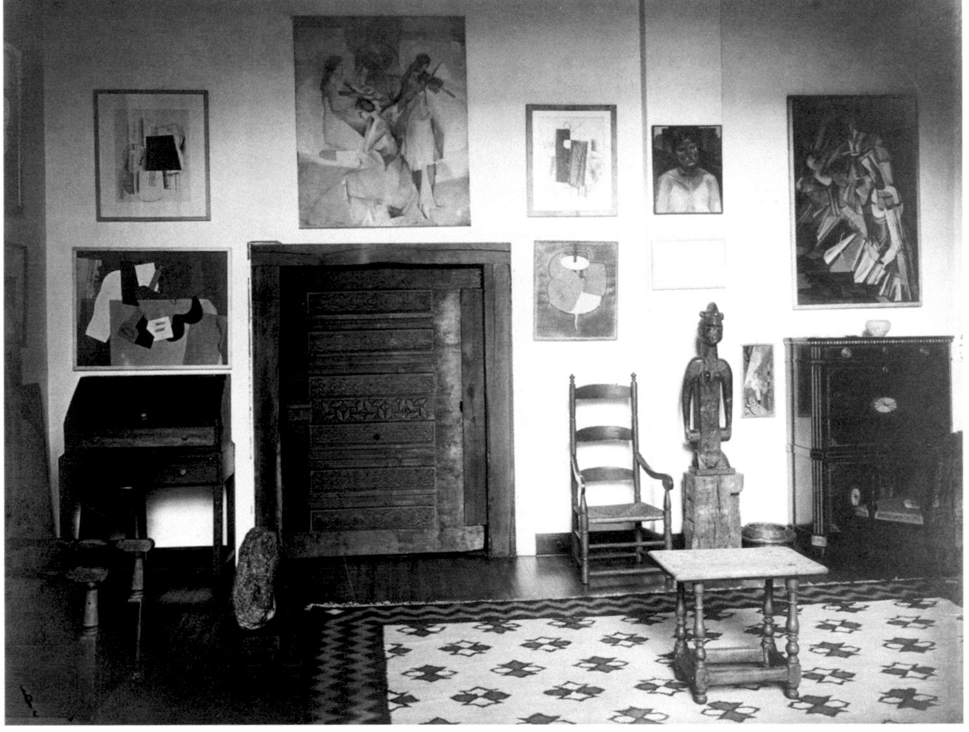

reproduction to be reproduced into an "original" by failing to do what any art student was meant to do with it. The most biting of the artist's submissions, however, were two related works: *L.H.O.O.Q.* (1919), a mass-reproduced postcard bearing a photographic image of the *Mona Lisa* hand-adorned with a moustache, goatee, and signature by Duchamp (itself arguably a commentary on the auratic museum masterpiece and its commodity reproduction), and, presented alongside it, a newly minted *L.H.O.O.Q.*, signed "Marcel Duchamp (réplique 1930)," a copy of the "authentic" manipulated image of 1919 made especially for "La Peinture au défi," although considerably larger than the postcard "original" and, again, hand-signed and hand-altered as *L.H.O.O.Q.* had been. Hanging next to each other (with the second work's eponymous "replica" status unambiguously asserting its ambiguity), they enacted a doubly audacious provocation. The first *L.H.O.O.Q.* inscribes reproduction at the heart of a critique of painting; its copy reinforces this while simultaneously also announcing that even a defiantly graffitied photographic reproduction becomes, de facto, an "original" at the moment it is replicated. In a move that is never as simple as "this will kill that," with mechanical photographic reproduction annihilating or replacing painting, in Duchamp's hands photography and its mechanical reproducibility are undermined in turn.

1.19

Interior of the Arensberg apartment, c. 1920. Photo showing Marcel Duchamp's *Nude Descending a Staircase* (no. 2), 1912, above couch. Photo by Charles Sheeler. Philadelphia Museum of Art: The Louise and Walter Arensberg Collection.

1.20

Interior of the Arensberg apartment, c. 1920. Photo showing (on far right) Marcel Duchamp's *Nude Descending a Staircase* (no. 3), 1916, a photographic replica of the earlier painting featured in another room of the collection. Photo by Charles Sheeler. Philadelphia Museum of Art: The Louise and Walter Arensberg Collection.

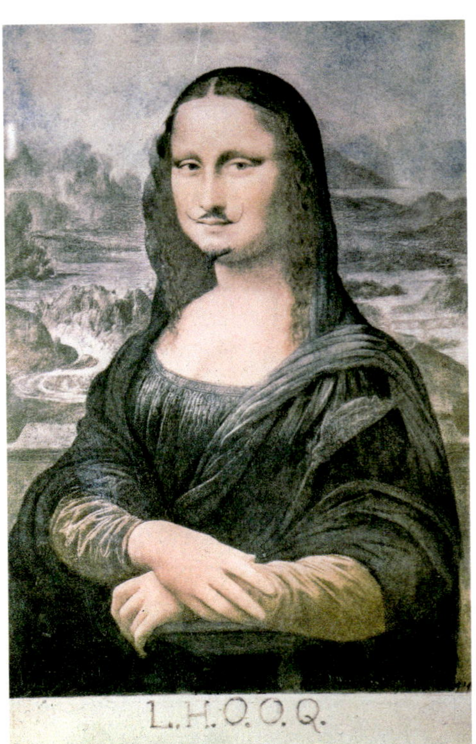

1.21

Marcel Duchamp, *L.H.O.O.Q.*, 1919. Reproduction of Leonardo da Vinci's *Mona Lisa* with annotations in pencil, 7¾ × 4⅞ inches. Private collection, Geneva.

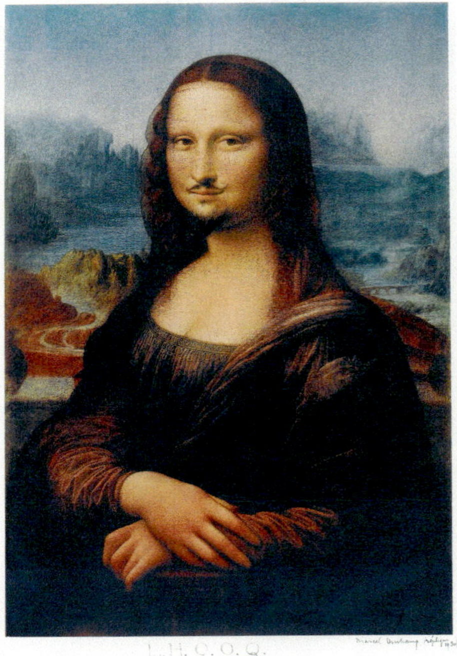

1.22

Marcel Duchamp, *L.H.O.O.Q.*, 1930. Reproduction of Leonardo da Vinci's *Mona Lisa* with annotations in pencil to replicate *L.H.O.O.Q.* from 1919, signed "Marcel Duchamp (réplique 1930)," 25½ × 19 inches. Centre Pompidou, MNAM-CCI, Paris: Deposit of the French National Communist Party, Paris.

Walter Benjamin makes reference to "La Peinture au défi" in his "Second Letter from Paris." Written in November 1936, some years after Aragon's exhibition but at about the same time Benjamin was penning "The Work of Art in the Age of Its Technological Reproducibility," his "letter" discusses the contemporary debate about the relationship between photography and painting.[69] While Aragon consistently speaks about *collage*'s defiant relationship to painting in his exhibition catalog essay, Benjamin insists explicitly on considering the argument in terms of *photography*'s defiance of painting. No mere detail, the difference of position is noteworthy. Although Aragon's understanding of collage was broad, and his choice of artworks and artists reflected this sweeping conception, he never emphasized photography or reproduction as such. Instead, much of what Benjamin attributes to "La Peinture au défi" seems to be found not so much in a reading of Aragon's text as in what may well have been Benjamin's reading of Duchamp's contributions to the show. After all, the only elements in the exhibition that explicitly used photographic reproduction as the mode by which to "challenge" painting were Duchamp's.

As his contributions to the exhibition demonstrate, Duchamp's endeavor to put the originality of the artwork (of painting) at stake by means of reproduction, pioneered with the *Box of 1914*, had become an increasing preoccupation. Concurrently, the threat that the specter of reproduction posed to the auratic work of art—and implicitly to the museum that collects, preserves, and displays it—made itself felt with particular acuity in Europe at this time. By 1929 the German museum establishment, for instance, began to sense the distinct peril that mechanical reproduction posed to the status of the artwork's originality, a peril that Duchamp had so consistently been embracing in his practice.

One example is particularly telling. In May of 1929, Alexander Dorner, the visionary director of Hannover's Provinzialmuseum (now the Landesmuseum) from 1925 to 1937, organized "Original und Reproduktion," an exhibition for Hannover's Kestnergesellschaft gallery composed of thirty-five works on paper, including ink drawings, watercolors, and pastels by artists such as Paul Cézanne, Pierre-Auguste Renoir, Claude Lorrain, and Giovanni Battista Tiepolo.[70] Dorner presented each original artwork next to a high-quality photographic facsimile, both under glass and framed identically. The show challenged spectators to distinguish between originals and copies, a feat that not one visitor (including numerous art professionals) was able to completely and successfully accomplish. News of it quickly reached the circle of artists around Duchamp and his brothers, perhaps because it had aroused widespread controversy over precisely the question of the reproducibility of the aesthetic original.[71] Indeed, the exhibition resulted in more than six months of heated debates among museum authorities, art critics, and university professors in Germany and left a long trail of ink in the Hamburg periodical *Der Kreis*.[72] Typical of the criticism leveled against the show (which resulted in a call to expel Dorner from the International Association of Museum Officials), the art historian and Baden Kunsthalle director Kurt Karl Eberlein argued that what was at stake in patrolling the borders between the original artwork and its reproduction was nothing less than the artwork's sovereignty and, indeed, the very experience proper to art. He lamented:

> But this is just what is so disgraceful and unbearable: that one has to set about explaining why a work of art is a work of art, why it belongs to a different order of production, why it can never be comprehended, represented, or reproduced by the machine and its techniques, why it is not a factory couch, a bicycle, or a toothbrush, and why the experience of art should not ultimately depend upon a well-meaning and commercially clever forgery![73]

For those on Eberlein's side, the mythos of art with its inimitable facture and aura was at stake, so much so that authorities in Berlin even clamored to outlaw facsimile reproductions as "hostile to art."[74] The photographically reproduced original—like the industrial, mass-produced object, "a factory couch, a bicycle, or a toothbrush"—was not only completely incompatible with Eberlein's understanding of the work of art (one cannot help imagining what he would have thought of Duchamp's *Fountain*), but indeed the everyday object was constructed as the exact, and thereby defining, antithesis to the authentic artwork.

Technologies for the reproduction of original works of art were, of course, nothing new (convincing book illustrations and postcards, for instance, had been in circulation for some time). Thus when the complete banning of art's reproduction was demanded by Dorner's angry critics, an important, if so far latent, malaise was exposed: for the first time *a museum* was implicated in staging the proximity between authentic originals and their deceptively mimetic photographic copies. The fact that Dorner brought reproduction into the museum made the inherent threat of that technology manifest. The exhibition confirmed the significance of reproduction as a contemporary cultural phenomenon—a phenomenon, however, that called the museum's very raison d'être into question.

These concerns did not escape Benjamin, whose writing, while not directly participating in the Dorner-inspired debates, was increasingly preoccupied at this same moment with issues of originality, reproduction, the artwork, and photography.[75] Benjamin was attempting to theorize how (photographic) reproductive technologies recast the inherent form, structure, and meaning of the artwork. The very concept of authenticity, autonomy, and ultimately the author was in question: "The presence of the original" was, prior to the advent of these new technologies, "the prerequisite to the concept of authenticity."[76] Since then, as he saw it, "Mechanical reproduction emancipates the work of art from its parasitical dependence on ritual. To an ever greater degree the work of art reproduced becomes the work of art designed for reproducibility. From a photographic negative, for example, one can make any number of prints; to ask for the 'authentic' print makes no sense."[77] It is perhaps precisely this shared concern—questioning the terms of the aesthetic original—that drew Benjamin to Duchamp's production.[78]

"Can works be made which are not 'of art'?" Duchamp had scribbled to himself back in 1913.[79] He must have been wondering whether indeed, as an artist, one could escape conventional definitions of the artwork while still producing or authoring *things*. After all, what exactly makes an artwork "art"? Given his primary activities around the time of writing the query—not only the selection of those infinitely reproducible industrial objects from 1913 to near the end of the 1910s, but also the process of replicating his handmade words in 1913–14 and then again in 1934—*reproduction*, both industrial and photographic, seems to have been a fundamental motor for the shattering of the precious exclusivity "of art" from the "work of art." Thus it is not surprising that Duchamp declared late in life that a longtime goal of his had been "to wipe out the idea of the original."[80] His critical discussion of "the original," a notion "which neither exists in music nor in poetry," made clear that the idea was specifically attached to and propagated by painting, since, as he added, "plenty of manuscripts are sold, but they are unimportant. Even in sculpture, the artist only contributes the final millimeter; the casts and the rest of the work are done by his assistants. *In painting, we still have the cult of the original.*"[81] Duchamp's endeavor was to make an art that might be rid of exactly the precious, ritualistic aura that painting, that symbol of art par excellence, exudes and the museum, its champion, exalts.

Duchamp's thinking about how to make "work" that is not "of art" coincided with preparations for the *Box of 1914* and his so-called invention of the readymade, even if it is only the latter that is regarded as having explosively pushed at the conventional definitions of the artwork (with all that followed for the history of art). Duchamp's question, to which he emphatically returned in the mid-1930s with his next note project, might also be said to define the intersection of his and Benjamin's common interest.

GREEN BOX

Although curiously little has been made of the fact by scholars of either Duchamp or Benjamin, during the same period that Benjamin was drafting his "Work of Art" essay in Paris, he was also studying the second and most elaborate of Duchamp's note replication projects and formulating his own theorization of them.[82] The German writer's most influential essay, begun in 1935, published in German and French in 1936 and revised through 1939, is at once a treatise on the transformation of the conception of the artwork in the face of reproductive advances, a critique of that nebulous phenomenon he called "aura," and an acclamation of the progressive potential of image reproduction technologies. In the notes, variants, and revisions of his essay (unpublished during his life), Benjamin devotes a small section to Duchamp, recording that the "relatively small but influential output" of the artist offered what he considered "one of the most interesting phenomena of the French avant-garde."[83] The comment is revelatory, since what Benjamin had most likely seen of that "small but influential output"—given that Duchamp was still relatively unknown internationally and had little visibility on the exhibition scene in Paris—were, in fact, works deeply engaged with reproduction, such as *Pharmacy*, *L.H.O.O.Q.* (along with its self-conscious later *réplique*), maybe also his *Porte-bouteilles* (Bottlerack, 1914), but, most importantly perhaps, the artist's 1934 follow up to the *Box of 1914*.[84] While none of these use direct photographic means, as the *Box of 1914* did, some of the logic of photography (multiplication, refusal of originality) and its concrete technologies were vital to each of them.

Specifically, the writing of "The Work of Art in the Age of Its Technological Reproducibility" came just in the wake of Duchamp's 1934 edition of note boxes entitled *La Mariée mise à nu par ses célibataires, même* (The Bride Stripped Bare by Her Bachelors, Even), also known in colloquial shorthand as the *Boîte verte* (Green Box). This, the artist's second note project, differs from its predecessor in its edition size and also in the method used for its production, but it was nevertheless conceptually enmeshed in many of the same questions as the *Box of 1914*. Based again on Duchamp's scribblings dating back to the 1910s, it revealed those vagaries of thought and hand that championed the importance of process, speculation, and ideas in relation to other artworks, already realized or not. Importantly, it was a project that explicitly continued the exegesis of the theme of the original and the copy begun with the *Box of 1914*. It should hardly be surprising that Benjamin, at the moment of theorizing reproduction, was captivated by the way Duchamp and his *Green Box* may have literalized many of his own questions.

Made in an edition of 320 (as opposed to the *Box of 1914*'s mere five), the *Green Box* contains ninety-three (as opposed to sixteen) loose copies of Duchamp's jottings and one reproduction of an artwork. Rather than mounted photographs of original notes, these are meticulously made quasi-facsimiles—collotype copies created using photographically based technologies. In some cases they mimic the precise size, form, and aspect of their original so as to make them nearly indistinguishable from it. In other cases, they replicate the script and content of their respective notes and bear the idiosyncratic appearance of being facsimile copies of an original (conforming to the idea of "an original"), but the choice of paper, ink color, or size is manifestly different from the original note.[85] To compare them carefully to their originals is to notice that for all the labor involved in making them, and for all their appearance of idiosyncrasy (reading as authenticity), not all of the boxed notes are precisely identical copies at all.

The *Green Box* notes are thus quite different in appearance from the contents of the *Box of 1914*, which, as mat-board-mounted photographs of notes, were never *actually* meant to be confused with scrappy originals. However distinct in method, both projects used photographic technologies to complicate the status of the handwritten original, the later box pushing further toward offering replicas that could actually pass as originals, all while still putting that relationship in question. Yet as far as Duchamp was concerned, the *Green Box* project was undoubtedly photographic. As he told an American friend in 1934 in whom he was attempting to generate interest in the project, "This book is in fact a box containing photographic reproductions of notes written by hand and photos of pictures."[86] One can imagine, though, that even if the *Green*

Box were not, strictly speaking, a work of photography, it was exactly this grappling with the limits of the auratic original through replication that Benjamin considered exemplary of Duchamp's critical stance. It was a crucial example of aesthetic production that responded to what Benjamin called the then-current "competition between painting and photography."[87]

Benjamin's essay asserts that photography constitutes the "first truly revolutionary means of reproduction," and that the photograph of the work of art invariably separates the artwork from its ritualistic function and singularity, thus ultimately undermining the "authority of the object."[88] Acknowledging the implications of photography in the contemporary transformation of the work of art, Duchamp's various reproductions offered Benjamin's "contemporary man" an essentially new mode for the experience of the artwork, namely that of "objects disengaged from their functional contexts."[89] In the case of the *Green Box*, the "objects" in question are the notes themselves: meticulously reproduced facsimiles (or quasi-facsimiles), replicas, that as artifacts first of all convey a sense of displacement—of being at one distinct remove from authenticity.

The contents of Duchamp's boxes are, quite simply, not what they seem to be. Like the experience of a performance in a film (rather than in the theater), so goes Benjamin's wider reasoning, the experience of the replicated notes is quintessentially a mediated one, an experience *of the mediated*, that is, one offered specifically, and only, by a medium of mechanical reproduction. And it is exactly this experience and aesthetics of the mediated or mechanically reproduced that the writer champions as truly modern and progressive.[90]

That Duchamp had been working toward a paradigm of the mediated or mechanically reproduced, as an aesthetic *sui generis*, becomes evident when one considers the distinctive features and conceptual implications of the *Green Box*.[91] He invested what can only be called maniacal attention to the particular modes and incredibly complicated processes of reproduction. As he recounted to Michel Sanouillet:

> Twelve years after finishing, or rather after putting aside my *Glass*, I fell upon my working notes, scribbled at random on some hundred scraps of paper. I wanted to reproduce them as exactly as possible. So I had all of these thoughts lithographed with the same ink as the originals. To find paper of absolutely the same quality, I had to ransack the most unlikely corners of Paris. Then we had to cut out three hundred copies of each lithograph using zinc patterns that I had trimmed according to the outlines of the original papers. It was tremendous work and I had to hire my concierge to help.[92]

The sheer effort involved in this prolific reiteration project is dizzying as well as deeply significant. So too is Duchamp's insistence on mentioning his efforts to create an exactitude between original and copy that he seems, in fact, to have sometimes deliberately avoided. Still, he *did* scour Paris for different papers and *did* use elaborate and layered technologies of reproduction, all to create the *appearance* of meticulously exact replication. With it, he asserted what would become a central paradigm in his work and an art

1.23

Marcel Duchamp, *La Mariée mise à nu par ses célibataires, même [Boîte verte]* (The Bride Stripped Bare by Her Bachelors, Even [Green Box]), 1934. One color plate and 93 facsimile notes and drawings or photographic reproductions by Marcel Duchamp contained in a green-flocked cardboard box, self-hinged, 13⅛ × 11 × 1 inches. Edition of 320 copies; deluxe edition of 20 and regular edition of 300. The Metropolitan Museum of Art, New York: Anonymous gift, 2002.

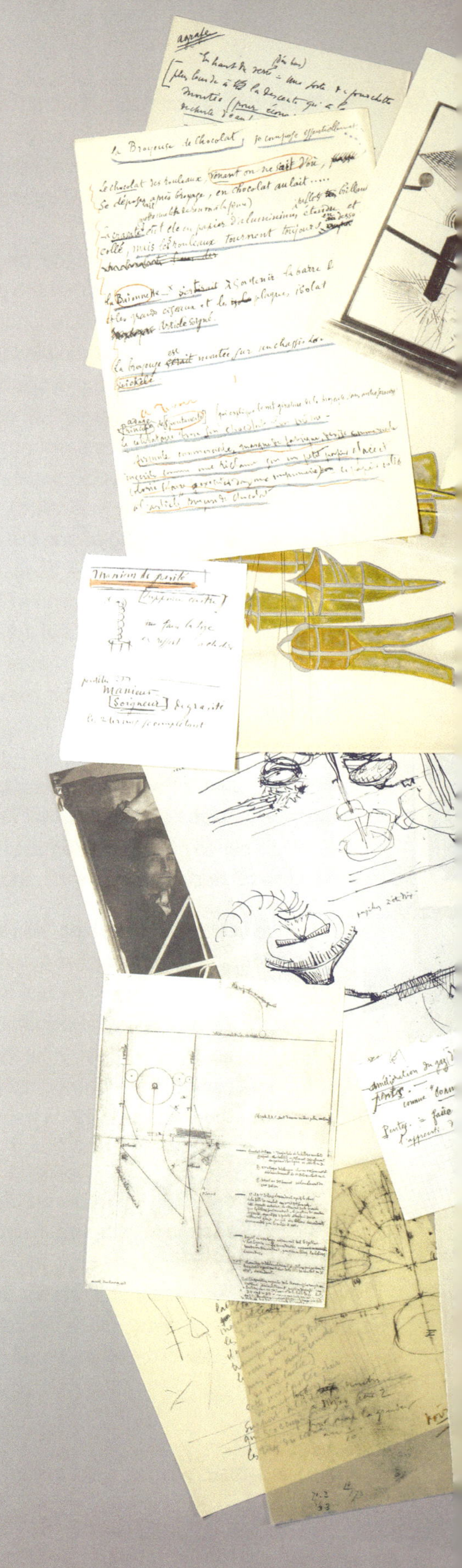

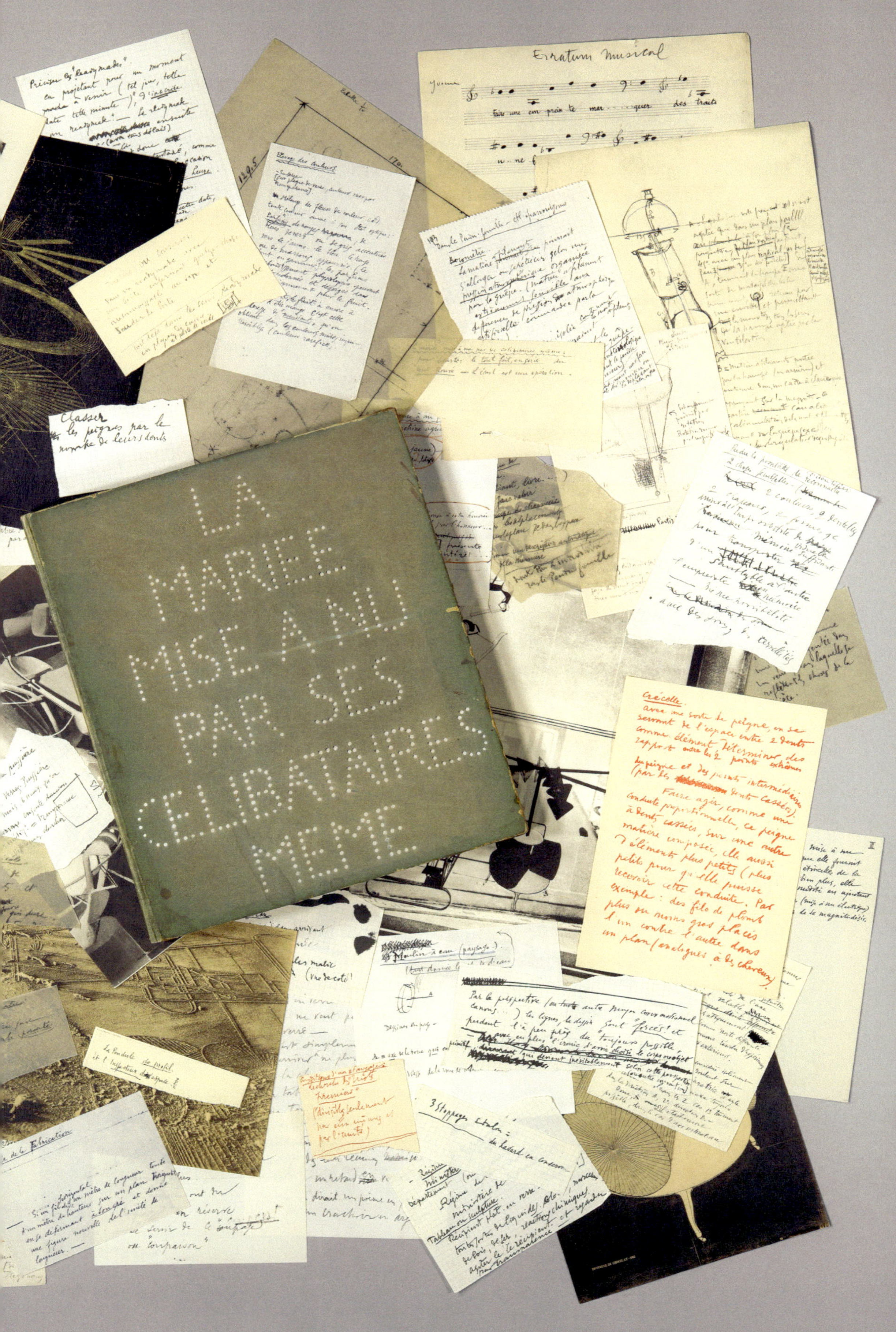
LA MARIEE MISE A NU PAR SES CELIBATAIRES MEME
Erratum Musical
Classer les peignes par le nombre de leurs dents

historically pioneering gesture. With the *Box of 1914*, the *Green Box* is one of the first instances of a multiple or edition that claimed the status of an artwork in its own right, all the while being *about reproduction* and undermining the relationship between the original and copy.

In a letter to the Arensbergs written in early 1934, the artist laid out the main contours of his *Green Box* project, whose details he modified only somewhat along the way.[93] The artist had originally planned to produce a regular edition of five hundred of the "boxes" containing nearly 135 notes and about ten (black-and-white) photographs; he also proposed to make a certain number of more expensive "deluxe" versions of the box and to distinguish them from the regular versions via the addition of a color photograph. The cost of making such an edition is likely a crucial reason for the changes that ensued: the regular edition size dropped by two hundred, at least forty notes were held back, and the approximately ten black-and-white "photographs" were replaced by reproductions using the somewhat less costly (but nevertheless expensive) medium of collotype printing. Perhaps the most important modification, however, was that each of the twenty deluxe versions now included, instead of a color photograph as originally planned, a single handwritten note (a bona fide "original" upon which one of the copies for the ensemble was based). No mere economic compromise, Duchamp's juxtaposition of copy and original, fraudulent and authentic, reproducible and unique, revealed a deliberate ambivalence that would, in fact, accompany all of his replication projects.[94]

By September 1934, iridescent, light-green perforated cards announced the publication of an edition of three hundred standard and twenty deluxe editions of *La Mariée mise à nu par ses célibataires, même*, the full name underscoring its central reference. Duchamp actively promoted his box of notes, and his engagement in its circulation and dissemination was almost part of the work itself. In addition to the special "subscription" form for ordering it by mail, he offered his *Green Box* at a special rate to institutions and made sure that the most avid collectors of his work had their own copy. Each green, flock-covered box contains ninety-three loose slips of paper describing details, preliminary ideas, and projects mostly related to the *Large Glass*, including a doctored photographic reproduction of the piece itself (as seen when it was first exhibited at the Brooklyn Museum in 1926), copies of plans, elevations, and drawings pertaining to sections left incomplete, a copy of Man Ray's photograph *Élevage de poussière* (Dust Breeding, 1920) (picturing the dust accumulating so as to impart "color" to the area of the *Large Glass* known as the "Sieves"), and eight reproductions of artworks related to the *Large Glass*.[95] Each scrappy shard of paper, quickly sketched diagram, and half-finished phrase was torn away from some other context. And, as with its predecessor, the *Box of 1914*, the notes sit in their container without any prescribed order.

While the mere fact of making such an edition would be enough to acknowledge the inherent reproducibility of the artwork, the content of the boxes exponentializes that notion. Duchamp's 320 copies of ninety-three originals amount to almost thirty thousand acts of replication for this one edition of boxes alone. For it should be emphasized that, while being mechanical in some sense, the actual techniques of reproduction that

Duchamp specifically chose involved procedures that required painstaking manual labor and were intensely time-consuming. His original notes were individually photographed in order to be reproduced using a combination of collotype printing (or *phototypie*, as it is known in French) and hand-stenciling or pochoir coloring. For this, the artist enlisted the help of a pochoir studio in Paris to reproduce the chromatic idiosyncrasies of his habitual scribbling. They had an assembly-line-like setup to hand-stencil the colors on the prepared collotypes. An individual zinc stencil was hand-cut for each strikethrough, underlining, or other colored mark, and then a watercolor wash was applied by hand over each stencil in order to simulate the original note. This was the case even when Duchamp introduced a number of small but perceptible and (as his instructions to the collotype studio indicate) seemingly intentional deviations between the original notes and their replicas. Each reproduction delivered to him from the pochoir studio was then hand-cut using a set of zinc tear-templates the artist made in order to mimic the particularities of the irregular tears or frayed edges of its "original." And when the artist tired of doing the work himself (there were, after all, tens of thousands of little bits of paper to cut), he hired his apartment building concierge to complete the task. The whole tedious operation evidently appealed to him. Even if enacted with factory-like repetition, each of his copies was born from application by hand, resulting in inevitable variations. The effect was a perfect *simulation of originality* even as each was, necessarily, slightly distinct—from the others and from its model. Original copies they were, leaving behind a minefield of questions regarding their status as "reproductions."

For still other reasons, it is symptomatic of Duchamp's critical project that he should have chosen the combination of photomechanical reproduction and hand coloring. Several letters written by Albert Gleizes and the French Cubists to Alexander Dorner in 1929 and 1930, likely in response to the "Original und Reproduktion" exhibition, suggest that news of the show made it to Paris and, in particular, to the circle of artists Duchamp knew well through his brother Jacques Villon. The letters show that discussions of the artwork and its copy had been ignited in Paris, where, as Gleizes describes, the new technique of "phototypie finished with pochoir coloring" allowed artists new possibilities for the dissemination of their work. As Gleizes underscores, the method resulted in copies "as real as the painting itself because produced in the same way and from the same material."[96] The letters confirm not only that the French artists around Duchamp were then debating the value of this newly developed method—and of the reproduction of artworks in general—but also that there was a fervent sense that of all the available reproductive methods, the pochoir technique was the most like "painting itself." Whereas Gleizes and the other French Cubists were considering the method as a way of circulating their painterly production precisely because of its apparent fidelity to the original, Duchamp's entire project challenged the very idea of what fidelity to an original might mean. He saw instead the method's equivocal quality and therefore its critical potential. The pochoir technique, more than any other, maintained a highly ambiguous relationship to mass reproduction while retaining the closest (and thus most conflicted) relationship to "the original."

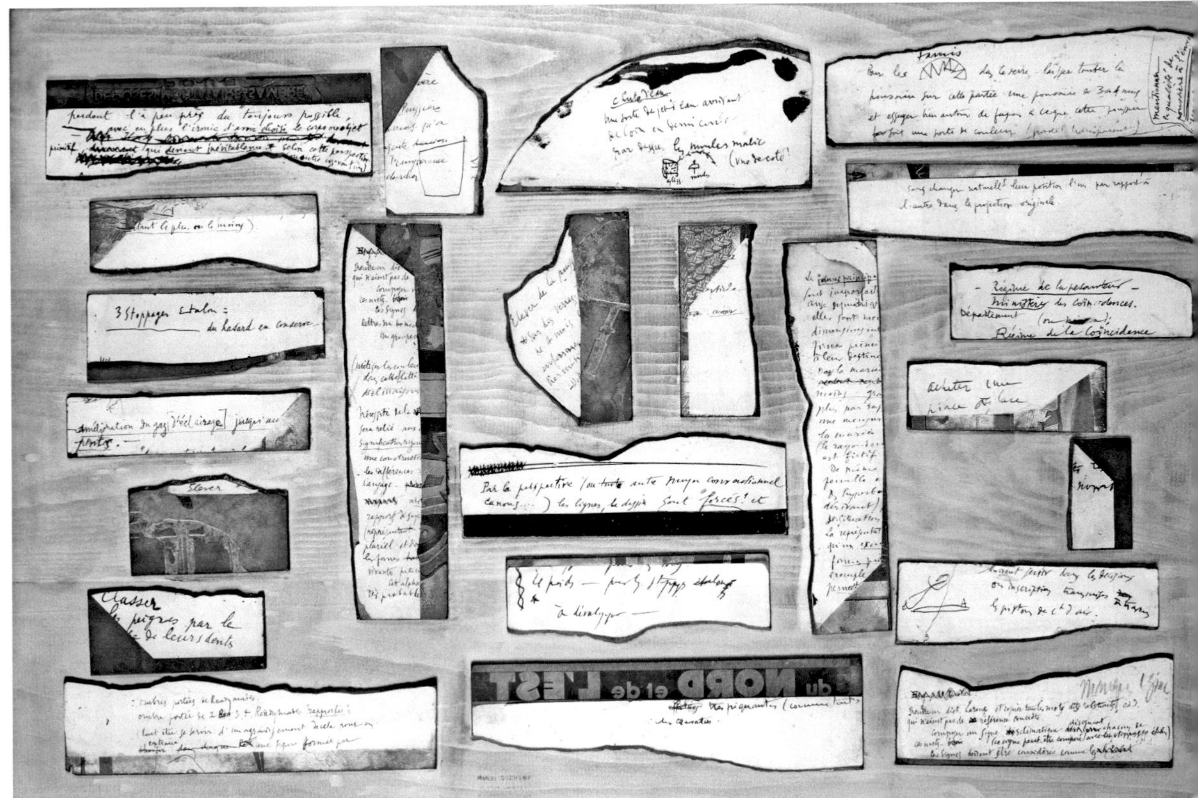

1.24

Marcel Duchamp, elements for making the *Green Box*, 1934. Assemblage, paper on zinc printing blocks mounted on wood, 26 ¾ × 18 ⅛ × 2 15/16 inches. Private collection, Paris.

1.25

Marcel Duchamp, replicated note headed "La Broyeuse de Chocolat" from the *Green Box*, 1934. One of 93 collotype printed facsimile notes. Collection Francis M. Naumann Fine Art, New York.

la Broyeuse de Chocolat se compose essentiellement :

Le chocolat des rouleaux, venant on ne sait d'où, se déposerait après broyage, en chocolat au lait .....

La cravate (mettre une lettre de renvoi à la figure) eût été en papier d'aluminium à reflets brillants étendu et collé, mais les 3 rouleaux tournent toujours en dessous. ×

la Baïonnette × sert à soutenir la barre de compression et les grands ciseaux et les plaques isolatrices.

Article soigné.

La broyeuse est montée sur un chassis Louis XV nickelé.

A revoir

adage de [spontanéité] (qui explique le mt giratoire de la broyeuse sans autre secours)

Le célibataire broie son chocolat lui même —

Formule commerciale, marque de fabrique, devise commerciale inscrite comme une réclame sur un petit papier glacé et colorié (faire exécuter dans une imprimerie) — ce papier collé à l'article "Broyeuse de chocolat"

Edging both toward and away from industrialization, mass culture, and technical reproducibility, pochoir replication held on to something of the handmade against the grain of a mechanically reproduced image. Thus, far from choosing an outmoded or near-obsolete technique, Duchamp used pochoir in order to formulate a complex response to his cultural context: it was *the* method that allowed for copying while retaining a hold on the status of originality. Consequently, not only do the conditions under which he used the method become clearer, but so too does the degree to which his choice meant to underline the necessary ambiguity of the resulting handmade copy.

Duchamp was establishing a paradigm of the mediated or mechanically reproduced: this much is evident based on the sheer quantity of reproductions that he made and the peculiar, complicated, even fetishistic methods he used to go about the business of making them. And yet any such Duchampian paradigm could hardly be without equivocations, because everything about this project—from Duchamp's repeated return to the replication of hand script, in particular, to his creation of intentional differences between some originals and "their" facsimiles or his inclusion of actual original notes in the deluxe boxes—points to the ambiguities of his chosen technologies. Moreover, the degree to which these would go on to infiltrate his practice as a whole attests that Duchamp was articulating the terms of a practice that elevated even as it evacuated the traditional status of the artwork—an artwork here untethered from its ties to originality.

It is perhaps no coincidence that after making the *Box of 1914* and before he went on to reproduce his oeuvre in miniature with the *Boîte-en-valise*, Duchamp chose with the *Green Box* to even more insistently focus on the replication and dispersal of the auratic mark of the artist's hand. Arguably, his paradigm of reproduction was most forcefully (or most perversely) expressed through the "signature," handmade script that is necessarily "a repeatable, iterable, imitable form," as Jacques Derrida put it, while being simultaneously and paradoxically incommensurable with the notion of the copy.[97] The theoretical implications of the artist's gesture run deep, for the signature is, as Duchamp knew very well, entirely bound up in questions of authorship, inscription, and authenticity, often serving as either validation of the artwork or the mark that betrays it as a counterfeit (nothing more than a forged copy).

Paradoxically, Duchamp's scribbled writings were precisely the iconic traces that supported the idea of the author—*this artist*—as a unique thinker. So while he pushed ahead in his explorations of reproduction as a modus operandi for his art practice, he also short-circuited this operation by doggedly constructing aura: the aura of the handwritten, the aura of the delicately handmade and thus in some way always paradoxically unique copy (underscored by the "originals" included in the deluxe editions), and, finally, the aura of hermeticism that he promoted by publicly circulating the relics of an artist's thinking process.

If aura lies at the center of Duchamp's endeavor, it also could not have escaped the attention of Benjamin when looking at the *Green Box*, so preoccupied was the latter at precisely that moment with the ramifications of mechanical reproduction for the unique and auratic work of art. Benjamin's unpublished variant for one of the sections of the "Work of Art" essay reveals an astute understanding of the *Green Box*:

> [Duchamp's] theory of the work of art [*correction by Benjamin, designated with a question mark*: of the value of art] which he demonstrated recently (without explaining it) through a series of large boxes, *La Mariée mise à nu par ses célibataires, même*, is pretty much as follows: once an object is looked at by us as a work of art, it absolutely ceases to function as such. This is why contemporary man would prefer to feel the specific effect of the work of art in the experience of objects disengaged from their functional contexts [*crossed out*: torn from this context or thrown away] ... rather than works nominated to play this role.[98]

The passage is striking for many reasons. The rare commentators of the period who paid attention to Duchamp's notes (most notably André Breton) found in them little more than a story to be disclosed, a citable soap-operatic drama of love, machinery, and frustrated desire. Very likely, Breton's designation of a number for each element or "character" in the *Large Glass* (visible from an annotated photograph of the work found in the writer's archive after his death) was done while he was preparing his essay about the work, which he wrote as a quite conventional romantic plot (complete with a list of characters and descriptions of their intrigue, action, motivation, et cetera) presented as the eloquent legend for the mute map that is the *Large Glass* (an interpretation that helped influence the reading of the notes thereafter).[99] Benjamin, on the other hand, found in Duchamp's notes not the unfolding of a narrative but evidence of nothing less than a "theory of the work of art." He saw in the notes something of the formal, linguistic, and theoretical complexity that others too quickly overlooked in favor of a tale of a Bride and her Bachelors. He does not, in fact, ever refer to the subject matter of the notes—he does not read them as if they were to convey information or elements of a "story." Implicitly understanding that the point is not to put the notes into any such narrative order, Benjamin detects other stakes.

The philosopher's sparse but incisive reflections on Duchamp only begin to suggest the impact that the artist's preoccupation with reproduction might have had on him by way of artistic example, and this even if his reflections on the artist were ultimately not retained in the final, published version of his essay.[100] For it is hard to overlook the fact that one of the most complex theses in the "Work of Art" essay—that the advent of photography has completely transformed art's role, that "to an ever greater degree the work of art reproduced becomes the work of art designed for reproducibility"—was perhaps nowhere more exemplified in the art making of the period than in Duchamp's oeuvre. Even the readymade, "invented" almost simultaneously with the making of the *Box of 1914* and so deeply related to the logic of that note reproduction project, provides an important gloss on Benjamin's thesis, being the first of Duchamp's endeavors to make works that, by dint of their industrially produced nature, are always already *infinitely reproducible*.

THE GUIDE FOR AN ARTWORK

It is perhaps fitting that the artist's most involved exegeses on reproduction up to this point came in implicit relationship to his readymades and in explicit relation to the *Large Glass*, itself constructed as an undeniably auratic masterpiece. When asked, Duchamp recounted in no uncertain terms that he meant for the notes of his *Green Box* to serve as a kind of key or guide, a discursive supplement to the *Large Glass* (as he had once suggested about the *Box of 1914* as well).[101] And indeed many of the notes do identify otherwise entirely cryptic or simply unrealized elements in the *Large Glass*, bestowing meaning on the enigmatic pictured (and unpictured) motifs, communicating otherwise inaccessible ideas, facts, and "explanations" for the work. For instance, according to the *Green Box*, the chocolate grinder in the lower panel operated by the nine individually named headless uniforms (the "Bachelors" in this tale) is a metaphoric masturbatory device, and the insectlike "agricultural machine" in the upper panel is a love-gas-emitting virgin Bride. The *Large Glass*'s materialization of Eros and its discontents is driven by technologies, both obscure and mundanely mechanical, which power the cycle of an endless amorous striptease that never results in consummation—as so many of the scholarly texts written about the *Large Glass* confidently tell us.[102] This description is not based on any visual analysis of the work itself, but instead on the reading of the notes. Indeed, so hermetic is the *Large Glass* itself, so impossible is it to know any of those narrative "facts," that many interpreters contend that the work would be completely impenetrable without the notes.[103] This was supported by Duchamp himself, who repeatedly affirmed that without the notes one could hardly understand the meaning and status of the *Large Glass* as a conceptual—more than visual—endeavor.[104]

1.26

Annotations by André Breton on a photo by John D. Schiff of Marcel Duchamp's *Large Glass*, c. 1934. Centre Pompidou, MNAM-CC, Paris: André Breton Archives, Bibliothèque Kandinsky.

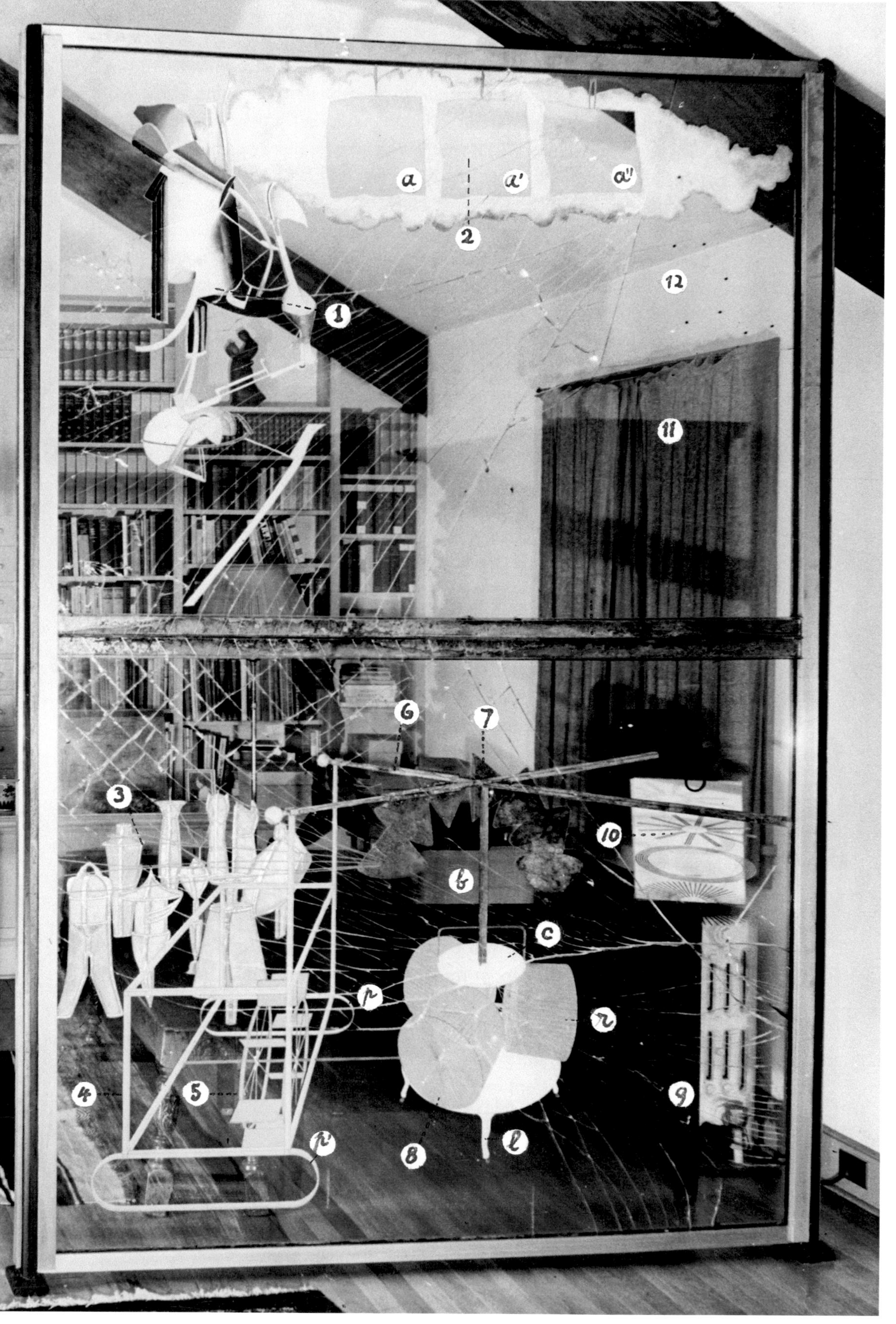
a
a'
a''
2
1
12
11
6
7
3
10
b
c
p
r
4
5
9
p'
8
l

Like the *Box of 1914* before it, the later notes were to be an accompaniment to an object that shouldn't even, according to Duchamp, be looked at. Speaking of the work in 1949, he proclaimed: "The glass was not made to be looked at (with aesthetic eyes); it must be accompanied by a 'literary' text which is as amorphous as possible and never takes form; both elements, the glass for looking at and the text for listening and understanding, had to complement each other and, above all, prevent the other from acquiring a plastic/aesthetic or literary form."[105] As Duchamp would have it, it was through his replicated writings that he aimed to undo the accompanying glass "painting" as a mere observable depiction (a painting for painting's sake), which was tantamount to problematizing painting's raison d'être (and this at a time when visuality was *the* quality that legitimated the very existence of painting). The attempt, with the notes, to prevent the *Large Glass* from taking on the role of an autonomous masterpiece (or necessarily *existing* at all: "whether it is there or not, is not important," as Duchamp said)[106] and, most notably, to keep it from being looked at is all the more interesting when one considers that the notes were reproduced and themselves rendered public at a moment when the *Large Glass* was inaccessible to its owner or any other viewer.[107]

The *Green Box* was being disseminated at a moment when Duchamp could only imagine the *Large Glass*'s future presentation, and the notes would have to serve as something like discursive auxiliaries for the then-unviewable work, while also positioned as things that themselves "never take form" and exist in the absence of their subject. And if Duchamp repeatedly insisted that the *Box of 1914* and *Green Box* were a kind of commercial catalog ("Sears Roebuck-like") for the *Large Glass*, the analogy was no accident: product catalogs accompany, explain, contextualize, even "sell" objects to a potential buyer.[108] They can entirely determine how the viewer sees (or doesn't see) the product on offer. And this, as it happens, has largely proven to be the case in relation to Duchamp's piece, since almost every serious written account of the *Large Glass* makes explicit reference to or acknowledges information that the artist set out in order to "guide" its reading. Some accounts were even written without seeing the work, only the notes.[109]

In their own way, Duchamp's tens of thousands of copies of his notes disseminated in the world to accompany a singular, auratic masterpiece could be seen as another sort of "test." The notes query whether the circulation of an archive of accompanying notes could foil the "aesthetic" aspect of an artwork and, conversely, determine its reading. The magnitude of such a proposition and its significance for the artist's larger thinking are impossible to overstate. One cannot forget how unusual it was at the time for an artist to propose ways to access his or her artworks, something typically only done by gallerists, curators, critics, or auction sales officials. The act was, you could say, quasi-curatorial. Duchamp was attempting to see whether the discourse that surrounds an artwork could complicate, if not entirely influence, its interpretive destiny: positioning it, endorsing a reading, and ultimately steering its reception. And as history has shown us, it could and it did.

CONCLUSION

From about 1913 onward, Duchamp repeatedly offered up copies of notes that existed for the purpose of construing surplus meaning for another artwork. In so doing, the notes' discursive function effectively directed the reception of the *Large Glass*, determining how most Duchamp scholarship to date has understood their elusive pendant. Yet, ironically, the artist's project to undermine autonomy (and the original's aura) did so using handwriting, that most auratic of traces. Duchamp's simultaneously auratic and multiple, autonomous and contingent, photographically replicated handwritten notes present themselves as the perfect "theoretical objects" (to repeat Krauss's term).[110] It is precisely there, in Duchamp's notes as theoretical objects, if you will, that the modernist myth of originality, along with its notion of the author (the source of "authority," the purveyor of the kind of certainty that "settles an argument"), aura, and autonomy, was first established and simultaneously contravened in the artist's oeuvre. This ambiguous maneuver reveals itself as the veritable motor of Duchamp's entire life project. His photographically inflected copies—strange, audacious, inelegant indexes that they are—represent the first instances of a lifelong series of programmatic breaches.[111]

For Duchamp's replication of notes was an engaged and lifelong operation. In the late 1960s, at the very moment when conceptual artists were busy making an art of decidedly unauratic documents (perhaps in no small part as a response to the model that Duchamp himself offered), he went on to "publish" one final box of notes, *À l'infinitif* (In the Infinitive), known as the *Boîte blanche* (White Box), bringing the number of his meticulously copied notes to more than forty thousand variously sized facsimiles in total.[112] The *Box of 1914* is thus the crux not only of the various replication projects that would follow it but also, and even more importantly, of the larger interrogation that Duchamp inaugurated in which the certainty of terms such as "autonomy," "originality," "aura," "author," "artwork," "discursive apparatus," "artist," and even "curator" came undone.

Duchamp's notes forcefully demonstrate several central preoccupations of his entire oeuvre. These include the undermining of painting's singularity by means of photography's infinite multiplicity, a process that grappled with the very definition of the work of art as such, which Benjamin saw as advancing a "theory of the work of art." It was a theory whose foundations were being laid in 1913. Already Duchamp's first box of notes—relating to but not quite in themselves collage, literature, photography, or painting—was at odds with the artistic production of its time. As a result, perhaps, little attempt was made to set the notes into context with the avant-gardist developments among Duchamp's Cubist, Futurist, and other contemporaries, causing them to be generally omitted in histories, which have largely failed to account for their prescient and far-reaching significance.

It was perhaps their means of *operation* as much their indeterminate status as autonomous objects—what they did and how they did it, as much as what they were or weren't—that rendered them so long unaccounted for. Since the notes were almost curatorial in nature (more than traditionally artistic), it was not such a huge leap for Duchamp to move from thinking about the production and circulation of notes that were meant to accompany and shift perceptions of an artwork to thinking about the exhibition spaces that an artwork finds itself in—which would become, increasingly, his concern in the years that followed.

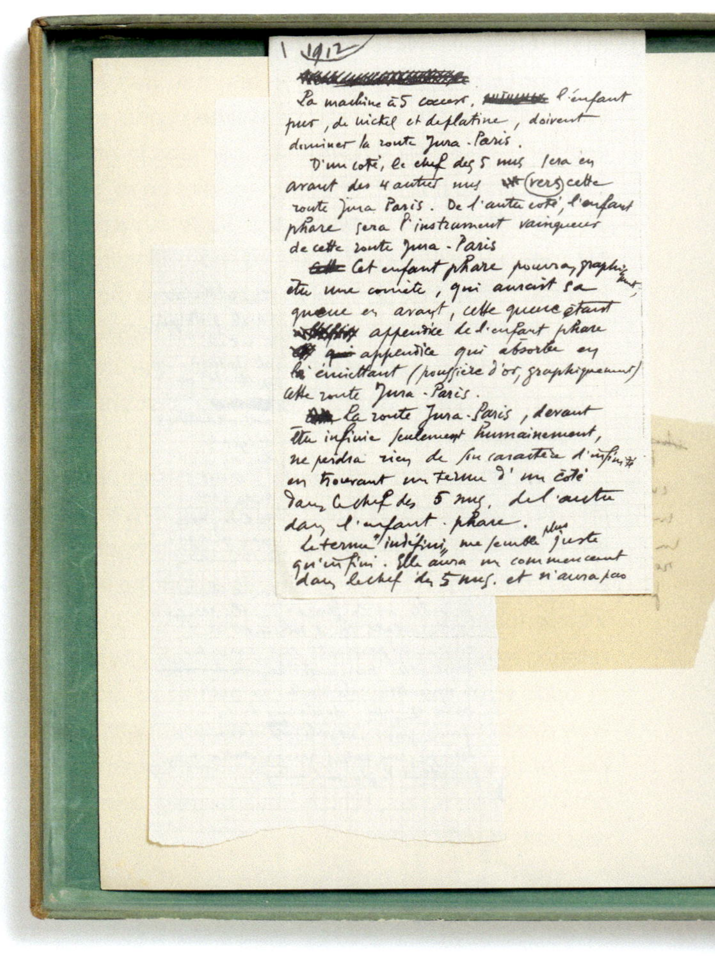
1 1912
La machine à 5 coeurs, l'enfant
pur, de nickel et de platine, doivent
dominer la route Jura-Paris.
D'un côté, le chef des 5 nus sera en
avant des 4 autres nus (vers) cette
route Jura Paris. De l'autre côté, l'enfant
phare sera l'instrument vainqueur
de cette route Jura-Paris
Cet enfant phare pourra, graphiquement,
être une comète, qui aurait sa
queue en avant, cette queue étant
appendice de l'enfant phare
appendice qui absorbe en
l'émiettant (poussière d'or, graphiquement)
cette route Jura-Paris.
La route Jura-Paris, devant
être infinie seulement humainement,
ne perdra rien de son caractère d'infini
en trouvant un terme d'un côté
dans le chef des 5 nus, de l'autre
dans l'enfant-phare.
Le terme "indéfini" me semble plus juste
qu'infini. Elle aura un commencement
dans le chef des 5 nus. et n'aura pas

1.27

Marcel Duchamp, *La Mariée mise à nu par ses célibataires, même* [*Boîte verte*] (The Bride Stripped Bare by Her Bachelors, Even [Green Box]), 1934. One color plate and 93 facsimile notes and drawings or photographic reproductions by Marcel Duchamp contained in a green-flocked cardboard box, self-hinged, 13⅛ × 11 × 1 inches. Edition of 320 copies; deluxe edition of 20 and regular edition of 300. Private collection.

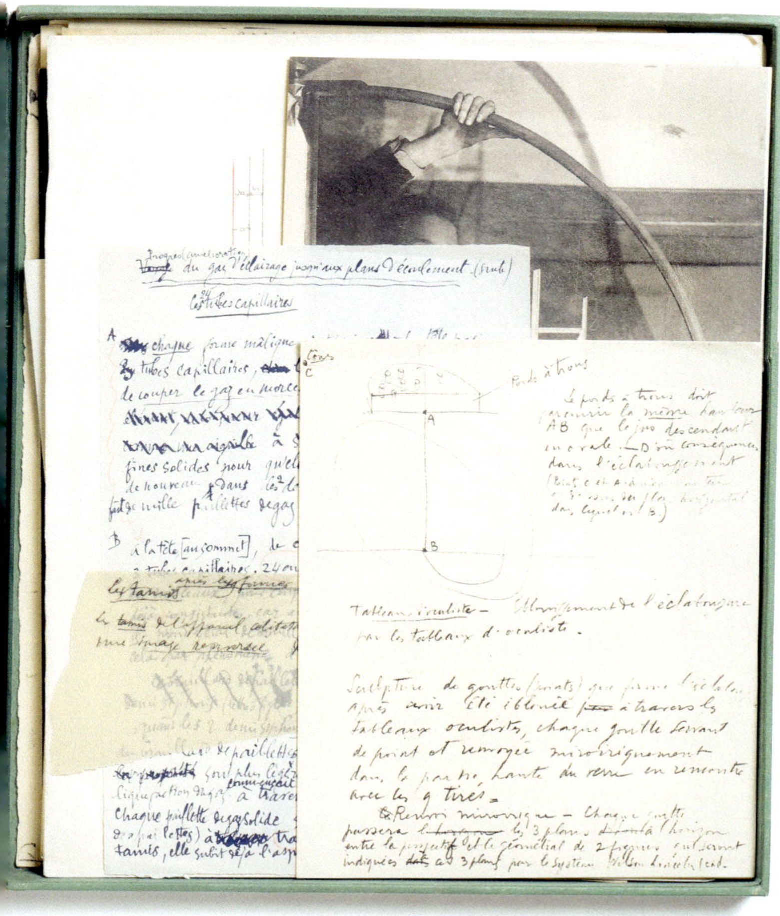

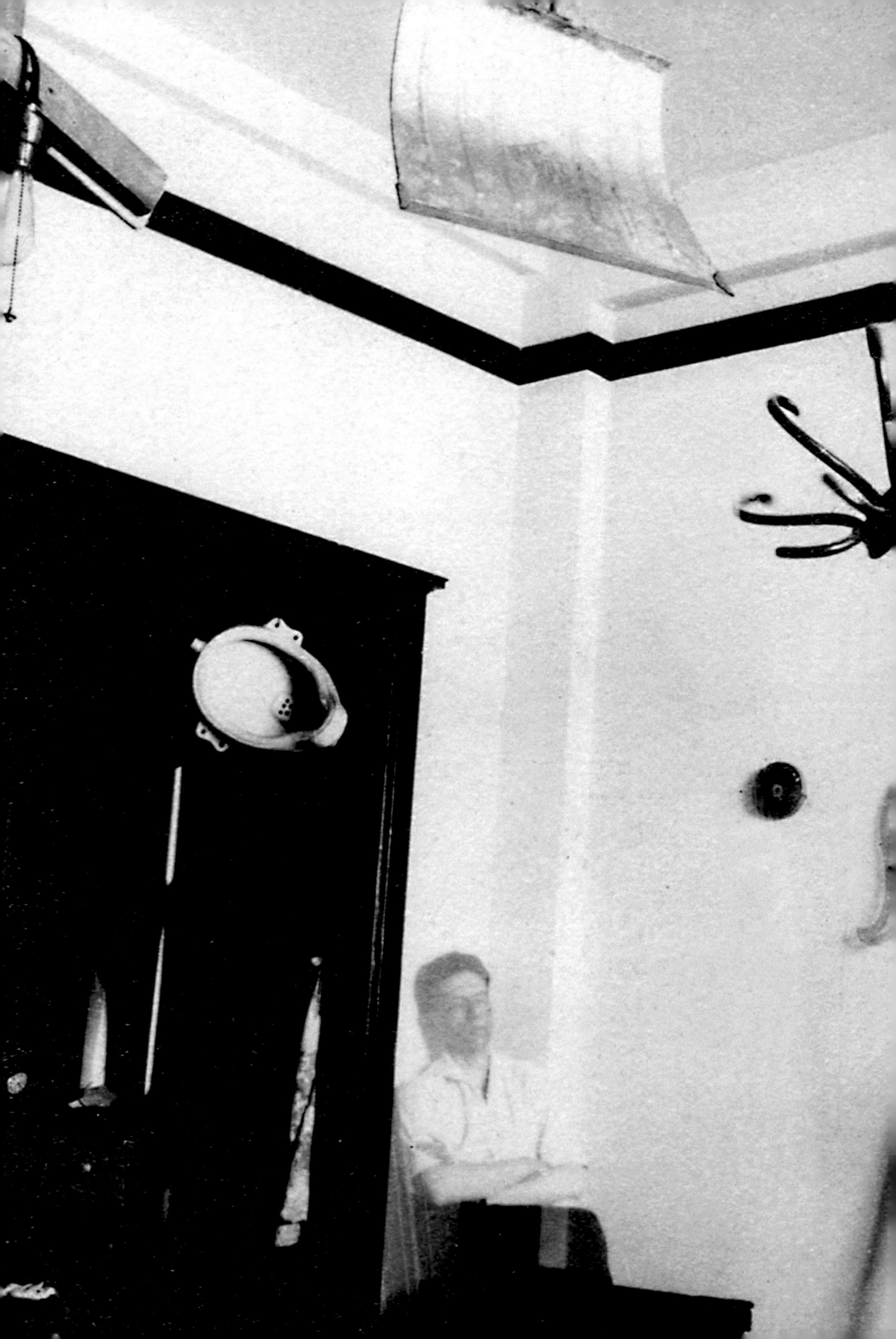

CHAPTER 2

I MYSELF WILL EXHIBIT NOTHING

PRINCIPLES

About few things had Duchamp been so defiant, so seemingly categorical. "I myself will exhibit nothing, in accordance with my principles," he wrote to his friend and most dedicated collector, Walter Arensberg, in 1918.[1] At issue was whether or not the artist would show any of his own work in the Cubist exhibition that he was attempting to organize in Buenos Aires during his short stay there. In the end the exhibition never materialized, but Duchamp's "principles" remained in effect: directing Arensberg from afar, he instructed the collector not to loan any of his work for other exhibitions being planned in New York at the time. A few years later, his answer to his brother-in-law Jean Crotti's solicitation for artworks to be exhibited at the 1921 Salon Dada was perhaps even more explicit. "Balls," he answered, in a telegram with, obviously, no works to follow.[2] Still later, in a 1925 letter to another of his patrons, Jacques Doucet, Duchamp declared, "All exhibitions of painting or sculpture make me ill. And I'd rather not be involved in them."[3] Again he sent orders not to lend one of his pieces—a copper and metal motorized contraption titled *Rotary Demisphere* (1924) then in the hands of Doucet—if requested for exhibition, because, as the artist explained, he didn't want people to see in it "anything other than 'optics.'"[4] Which is to say, he didn't want anyone to get his or her own ideas about what category of object it was. A thing's location and mode of display, its placement in the context "of painting and sculpture," his reticence suggested, has consequences. After all, people might just take anything shown in an exhibition to be a work "of art."

Duchamp's infamous early rejection at the Parisian Salon des Indépendants was the catalyst, so the usual narrative goes, for his critical attitude toward institutions of artistic judgment and presentation.[5] Yet in the years after his fellow Cubists quietly asked him to withdraw the *Nu descendant un escalier* (Nude Descending a Staircase [no. 2], 1912) from their exhibition at the 1912 Indépendants, and despite his seemingly unequivocal declaration of "principles," he was actively involved in many shows, not only as an exhibiting artist but, perhaps more surprisingly, as advisor, organizer, curator, and even quasi-dealer. Indeed, in various ways over the course of more than half a century, Duchamp would make the exhibition a vital component of his thinking about the work of art as such.

One senses when probing Duchamp's active involvement in exhibitions and the function of these within his oeuvre that he obstinately, programmatically refused to reduce the artwork to a discrete, auratic thing unto itself. His perennial involvement in exhibitions in roles other than participating artist in the traditional sense and his repeated adoption of an amateur curatorial role suggest that he comprehended all too well that the display, dissemination, circulation, and sale of an artwork not only construct its value and meaning but also determine the conditions for when, how, and whether at all it enters history, thereby *constituting* the work in a certain sense. Indeed, the centrality of Duchamp's relationship to the exhibition—that is, the ephemeral organization of ideas and objects in (an institutional) space—suggests that it is imperative to write the artist's relationship to exhibitions and his role as curator into the history of his oeuvre. This demands attention not only to his orchestration of opportunities to present his works in particular exhibition configurations and his frequent participation as a curator of exhibitions from the 1910s into the 1960s, but also to his construction of an object literally *as* an exhibition (or an exhibition as an object, depending on one's point of view) with his *De ou par Marcel Duchamp ou Rrose Sélavy* (From or by Marcel Duchamp or Rrose Sélavy, 1938–42), better known as *Boîte-en-valise* (Box-in-a-Valise), a decisive agent in the construction of the legacy of his entire oeuvre.[6]

EXHIBITION AS TEST

That Duchamp understood public exhibitions to be sites with the power to enunciate the work of art as "Art," and in turn to create the conditions for its entrance into history, was perhaps first articulated in relation to the readymades. As we know too well, those everyday industrially made objects *eventually* landed in the annals of art history. But how and when they got there is essential, though still somewhat underdiscussed. To tell this story, one must shift one's attention away from the object itself and instead toward the curious series of Duchampian procedures that made their entrance into history possible.

By 1913–14 Duchamp had a number of as-yet-unnamed readymades in one of his first Parisian studios. They remained there while he temporarily moved to New York until, in his absence, his sister Suzanne threw them all into a dustbin while cleaning up. In a letter sent to her in early 1916 (it arrived too late to save the stuff), Duchamp explained his new category of object and the concept for what he called, then, for the first time, the readymade. He accompanied it with the request that his sister sign his name on the objects, inscribe his chosen titles, date them, and send them to him.[7] (After all his labor to replicate his notes just two years before, it is ironic that the actual hand script of the author was here of little importance to him, although that there should be an author named was clearly crucial.) Much later, in the 1960s, he stated that he had begun fiddling with these objects as a mere "distraction," even claiming that they had begun as "a very personal experiment that [he] had never intended to show to the public."[8] But in actuality, by 1916, he had decided to title, sign, and date them, and even attempt to show them in public exhibitions. He treated them as works of art, even as he repeatedly and vehemently denied their artfulness.[9]

Duchamp's radical act embodied by the readymade was not merely to select a non-art object and treat it as art, because, and as he quickly understood, few might notice, and little about anyone's understanding of art would change: it would be like a tree falling in a forest with no one but himself to witness it. Even his sister, after all, hadn't recognized the status of the objects enough to spare them from the trash bin. Instead, for the profane things that he had selected to "switch function" (as he once described the procedure) and occupy the place of an artwork, a further act was necessary.[10] The conditioning factor that allowed the readymades to enter a wider historical discourse was not so much, or at least not only, their selection or nomination as art, but rather the curation that Duchamp orchestrated for them. As objects that lacked uniqueness, evidence of technical skill, romantic impulse, and clear authorship—precisely because they were store-bought things and thus *not* auratic—they required these curatorial operations. They needed to be put on public exhibition, to be documented and administrated in some way, to successfully appear *as* art in an art context, and to be connected to a larger artistic oeuvre. These efforts are the vital yet little-acknowledged backstory to the readymades and their complex relationship to art history, nowhere more explicitly evident than in the peculiar reception and historicizing of that most iconic of them all, *Fountain* of 1917.

Contrary to the usual discussion of the readymades as an "invention," then, one should more precisely speak of their *curatorial construction*. The shift is more than a question of semantics, and is rather one of implications: instead of their being the result of immediacy or a genial discovery, as "invention" implies, one might instead recognize the labor implied in the administrative, nonartistic aspect of the curatorial. This shift of terms connects the readymade both backward to the artist's replicated note and archiving projects—with their own attempt at a kind of discursive accompaniment to *La Mariée mise à nu par ses célibataires, même* (The Bride Stripped Bare by Her Bachelors, Even, 1915–23), also known as the *Large Glass*—as well as forward to his active involvement in exhibitions, sometimes even in the explicit capacity of curator. All of these roles testify to Duchamp's lifelong preoccupation with the apparatuses that surround the artwork.

The series of curatorial gestures that brought the readymades into being, as it were, has a prologue. In April 1916, just two years before he first made his grand declaration that he would prefer not to exhibit at all, Duchamp tried to get more, rather than fewer, of his works shown. When invited to exhibit one of his paintings in a group show at Bourgeois Gallery in New York, Duchamp bartered with the gallerist, agreeing to participate only if two of his readymades could also be included ("I will give you a painting to show but let me have my readymades also").[11] The readymades were subsequently placed, without fanfare or even indication, in the coat and umbrella stand area near the gallery's entrance. Not surprisingly, they went almost totally unnoticed. ("Nobody knew what was there. There was no description, no denomination, no label.")[12] As Duchamp biographer Bernard Marcadé suggests, "Duchamp, at the time, hardly bent over backwards to get his readymades seen, let alone admired. All that was important to him was that they figure in the show."[13] Why, one must wonder, did he insist so fiercely on showing them?

Duchamp, it seems, was venturing to see whether his readymades might, by dint of being situated in an art space, get noticed, or whether he had effectively determined a kind of artwork that could court invisibility and thus, in a way, both become *and* simultaneously cease to be art. The fact is, he didn't label the two readymades, didn't insist on having them in the exhibition space proper where visitors expected to find "Art," didn't present them in a way that would signal their status as art (by placing them on pedestals, for example), and didn't orchestrate any documentation of the act (as he would, to an extent, a year later with his store-bought urinal). He did not even point out the two pieces to anyone in a way that would have generated discussion about them. In interviews, when recounting the story in passing, decades later, he never mentioned with any consistency which two readymades were shown.[14] And yet, under No. 50 in the exhibition checklist and recorded below the heading "Marcel Duchamp," one could find the mention of "Two Readymades," so a trace of their presence in the exhibition and of the new object/category/genre he devised was deliberately left (no matter that at the time few knew or understood what the term meant).[15] The exercise seems a kind of "test" from which Duchamp might have learned that an object only appears as a work of art under certain conditions, one of which is to be formally and explicitly on exhibit with all the administration (labeling), protocol (pedestal, frame), and contextualization this entails, among other bona fide artworks and decidedly in an exhibition space, not just near an exhibition space.

Less than a year later, an entirely different sort of space served as a testing ground of another sort. While Duchamp never actually called it an exhibition space, and it was in no way properly public, his first New York studio/apartment was as much a place of display as it was a place of labor and living. It is best known from a series of small, grainy photographs, some of them out of focus. A certain Henri-Pierre Roché—a writer, occasional art dealer, and good friend of Duchamp—is thought to have taken them at some point during 1917 (Roché would go on to write *Jules et Jim*, proving him to be arguably a far better novelist than he was a photographer). But the aesthetic quality of the images was not really what mattered. Duchamp kept the pictures and returned to them years later. Manipulated and then left out like his laundry, or as clues, the images would whisper that the configuration of objects in a space holds some secret to their significance.

There isn't a single photograph among them that shows the artist's studio (in this case also his home) cleaned up. Duchamp's drawers are open. His shoes and pillows are strewn across the floor. Dust has collected in the corners. The supposed cold conceptualist, the man who epilated his entire body because he seemed not to like the unkemptness of body hair (and requested that his partner of the moment consider doing the same), the artist of the industrially produced readymades, lived in a pigsty.[16] Yet the photographs reveal that the shiny porcelain urinal on view was not in the bathroom, or even tucked in a corner, but hung over a doorway. Duchamp's snow shovel was not casually leaning against a wall waiting for use, but suspended near the ceiling. His coatrack could be found inconveniently and ridiculously in the middle of the room, nailed to the floor, aptly titled *Trébuchet* (French for "trap" or something one trips over).[17] The disorder of the room might appear careless, except that a urinal, a snow shovel, and a coatrack simply didn't get to where they were by accident. These were selected objects in chosen positions.[18]

In one of the images, Roché positioned himself as if an eerie cousin of Hippolyte Bayard in his famous "portrait of a drowned man," probably also using a long exposure to include himself in the image, his eyes closed and back leaning, a ghostly presence

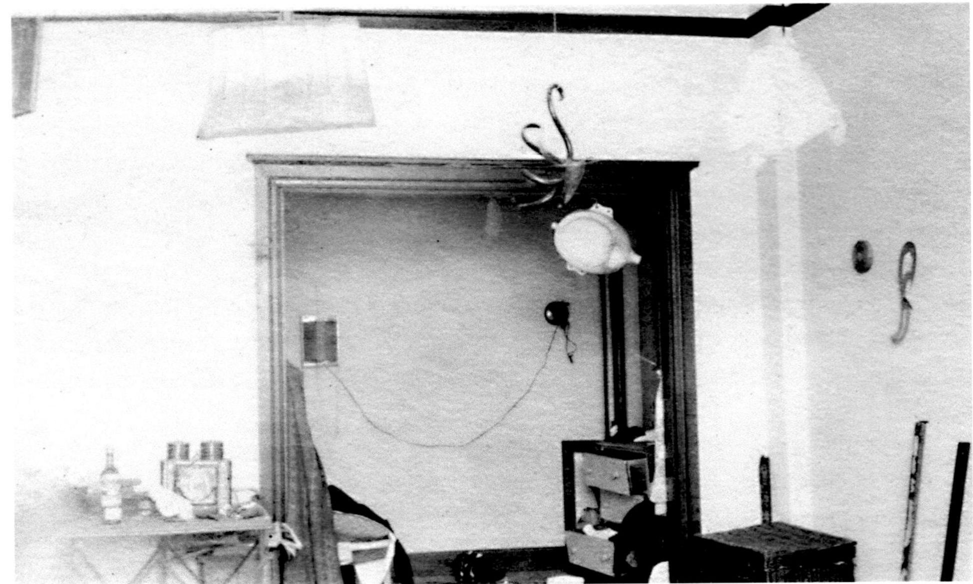

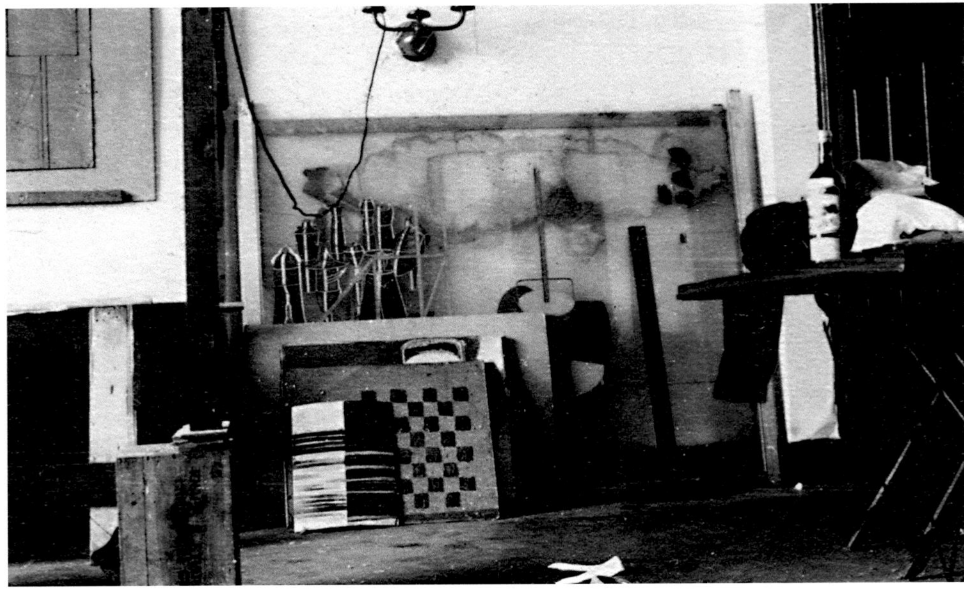

2.1

Views of Duchamp's studio, 33 West 67th Street, New York, c. 1917. Photos presumed to be by Henri-Pierre Roché. Archives Jean-Jacques Lebel, Paris.

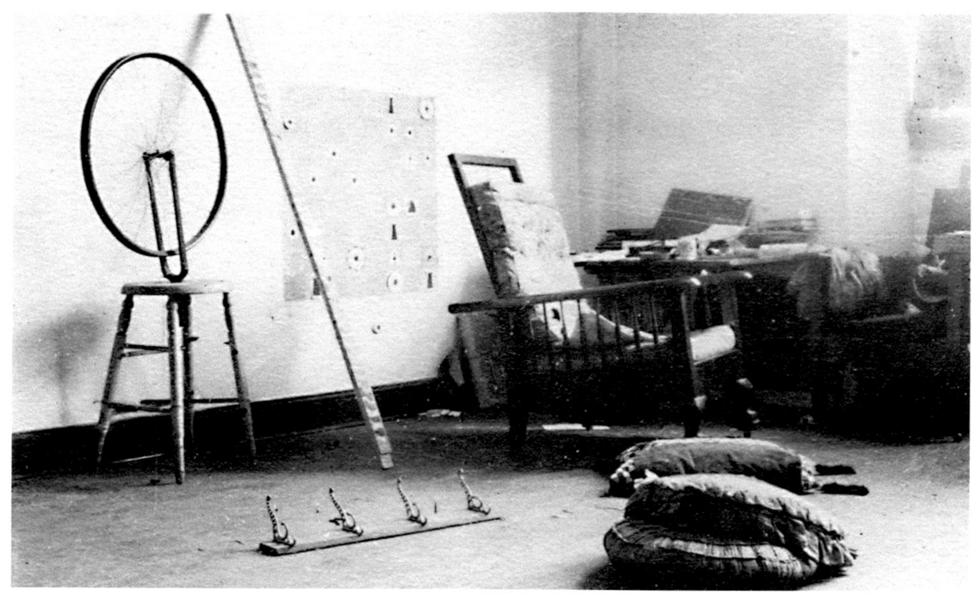

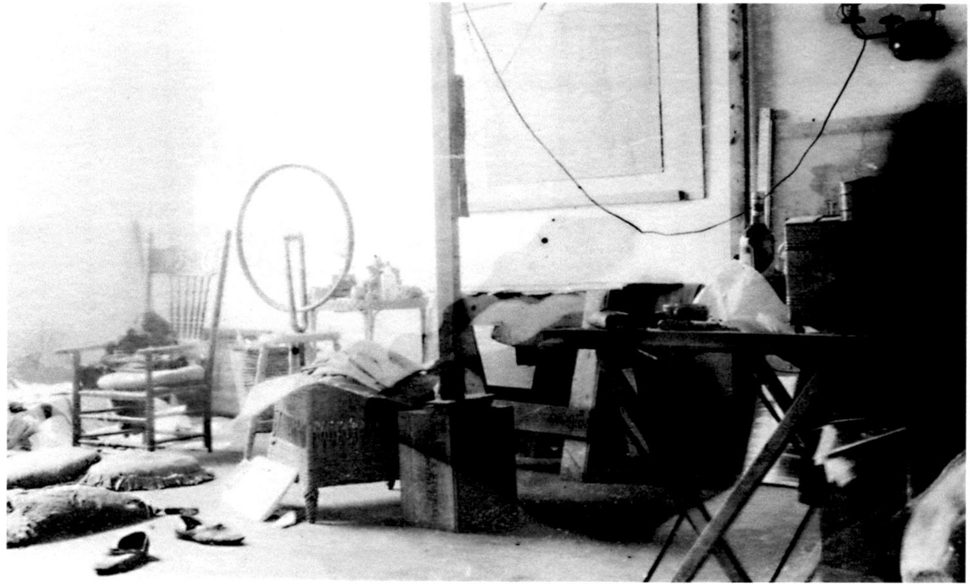

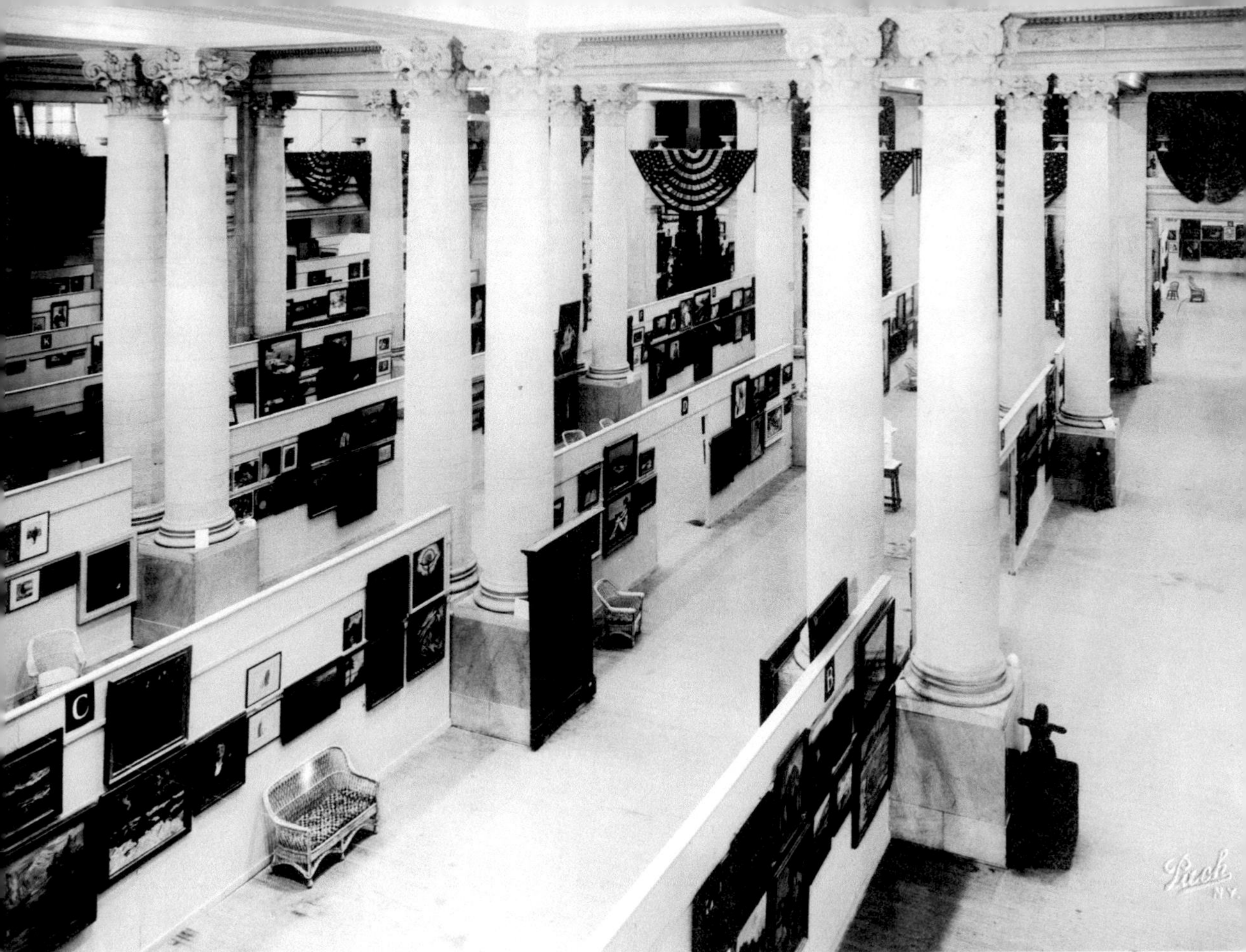

2.2

Installation view, Society of Independent Artists Exhibition, Grand Central Palace, New York, 1917. Yale Beinecke Rare Book and Manuscript Library, New Haven: Katherine S. Dreier Papers.

among Duchamp's strangely suspended objects. This and the other photos give another indication that Duchamp thought of the readymades as more than mere stuff. The pictures show that these everyday objects, because of the way they were arranged or displayed—indeed, exhibited—could not be practical; their utility was undermined so that they became objects of contemplation, or perhaps of laughter, but not of use. The studio, while decidedly not an art institution and not exactly public, was nevertheless frequented by the artist's friends and acquaintances, and it was in a way the readymades' first presentation space, the place that Helen Molesworth rightly calls their "major site of reception."[19] That site of presentation/reception was a place of enunciation. It declared: this is not (only) a urinal (or apparatus to hang coats, or tool to shovel snow).

Around the same time, although the exact chronological relationship of these two events of 1917 remains fuzzy, a time before the word "curator" was in common use, Duchamp was made president of the "hanging committee" for the Society of Independent Artists Exhibition scheduled to take place in New York from April 11 to May 6, 1917. The exhibition was open to all comers, and the president of the hanging committee was responsible for the display strategy and structure of the show, which is to say, was close to being its curator in the contemporary sense. In that capacity Duchamp devised a curious system for the arrangement of the show, proposing to hang the artworks not according to school, style, chronology, or even perceived quality, but alphabetically and according to chance, beginning the exhibition with the first letter selected from a hat. (As it happened, the letter "R" was drawn first.) Images of the resulting show reveal that paintings were hung edge to edge in two rows, with a label near the works indicating the letter of the alphabet to which their author belonged. The *New York Times* would have none of it, condemning the exhibition as "Pictures by the mile, hung in a go-as-you-please manner, in alphabetical order, instead of the order of merit."[20] The comment surely amused Duchamp, as he had already proposed a long-term plan for the recurrent exhibition: in the years after, another letter should be drawn, and then another, thereby ensuring absolutely no favoritism while defying every known system according to which exhibitions are typically organized.

Arguably, it was precisely because Duchamp was president of the hanging committee that he made sure that another gesture he performed would be anonymous: he submitted to the exhibition a store-bought piece of porcelain plumbing to which he gave the name *Fountain*. The urinal, signed "R. Mutt 1917," was, as the famous story goes, rejected. No matter that the exhibition claimed to have "no jury and no prizes" and that anyone who paid the six-dollar member and submission fee, as R. Mutt had, was supposed to be allowed to exhibit. And no matter, indeed, that Duchamp, as president of the hanging committee, himself didn't agree with the rejection and resigned in protest, subsequently pulling out of the exhibition the only (rightfully attributed) work of his own that he had planned to show.[21] A urinal revealed the exhibition's pretense of undogmatic inclusiveness to be, quite simply, a lie.

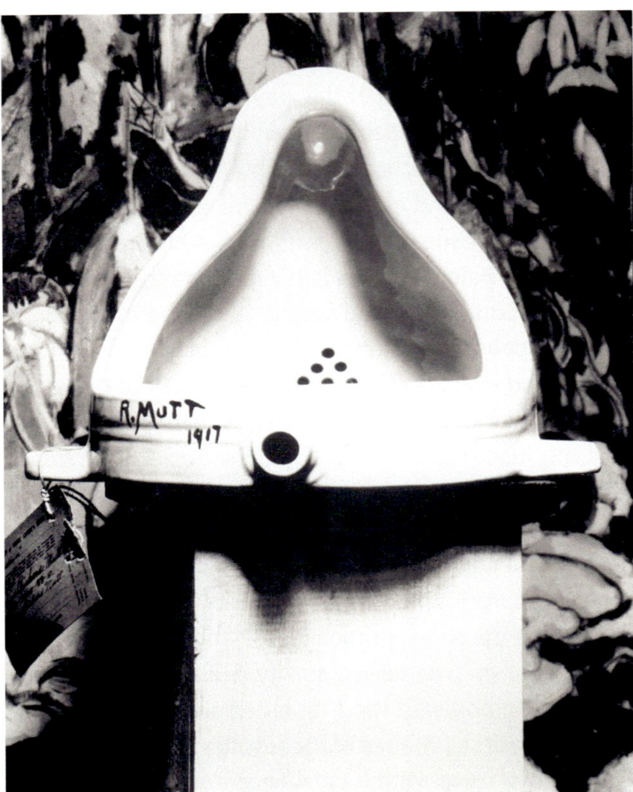

2.3

Marcel Duchamp, *Fountain*, 1917. Gelatin silver print, 9 ¼ × 7 inches. Photo by Alfred Stieglitz. Private collection.

Fountain by R. Mutt

Photograph by Alfred Stieglitz

R.MUTT 1917

THE EXHIBIT REFUSED BY THE INDEPENDENTS

THE BLIND MAN

The Richard Mutt Case

They say any artist paying six dollars may exhibit.

Mr. Richard Mutt sent in a fountain. Without discussion this article disappeared and never was exhibited.

What were the grounds for refusing Mr. Mutt's fountain:—

1. *Some contended it was immoral, vulgar.*
2. *Others, it was plagiarism, a plain piece of plumbing.*

Now Mr. Mutt's fountain is not immoral, that is absurd, no more than a bath tub is immoral. It is a fixture that you see every day in plumbers' show windows.

Whether Mr. Mutt with his own hands made the fountain or not has no importance. He CHOSE it. He took an ordinary article of life, placed it so that its useful significance disappeared under the new title and point of view—created a new thought for that object.

As for plumbing, that is absurd. The only works of art America has given are her plumbing and her bridges.

"Buddha of the Bathroom"

I suppose monkeys hated to lose their tail. Necessary, useful and an ornament, monkey imagination could not stretch to a tailless existence (and frankly, do you see the biological beauty of our loss of them?), yet now that we are used to it, we get on pretty well without them. But evolution is not pleasing to the monkey race; "there is a death in every change" and we monkeys do not love death as we should. We are like those philosophers whom Dante placed in his Inferno with their heads set the wrong way on their shoulders. We walk forward looking backward, each with more of his predecessors' personality than his own. Our eyes are not ours.

The ideas that our ancestors have joined together let no man put asunder! In *La Dissociation des Idees*, Remy de Gourmont, quietly analytic, shows how sacred is the marriage of ideas. At least one charming thing about our human institution is that although a man marry he can never be *only* a husband. Besides being a money-making device and the *one* man that *one* woman can sleep with in legal purity without sin he may even be as well some other woman's very personification of her abstract idea. Sin, while to his employees he is nothing but their "Boss," to his children only their "Father," and to himself certainly something more complex.

But with objects and ideas it is different. Recently we have had a chance to observe their meticulous monogomy.

When the jurors of *The Society of Independent Artists* fairly rushed to remove the bit of sculpture called the *Fountain* sent in by Richard Mutt, because the object was irrevocably associated in their atavistic minds with a certain natural function of a secretive sort. Yet to any "innocent" eye

"[*Fountain*] may be a very useful object in its place," so a rare reporter referring to the event recounted, "but its place is not an art exhibition, and it is, by no definition, a work of art."[22] The verdict was clear: censored from the catalog and the show, *Fountain* was hidden by the nonjury "jurors" behind a wall partition where the public would not see it. It was thereafter lost or accidently broken or deliberately smashed or taken—the stories vary wildly—almost as quickly as it had been chosen from among the lavatory supplies at J. L. Mott's ironwork and appliance showroom, never to be seen again.[23] Or at least almost.

As we know, at some point after that fatal judgment and before the object's ultimate demise, Duchamp had the rejected *pissotière* photographed. That is, he orchestrated the creation of an evidential trace of its existence, while still careful not to reveal that he was the fixture's "author." If anyone wondered at his action, they might have deduced that he was acting in his capacity as president of the hanging committee, in other words, producing documentation in relation to the exhibition in which he was involved. But his commissioning of a photographic document was meant to do something more than prove the existence of *Fountain* to future historians. For in that case, any photographer—even Roché—would have sufficed. Instead Duchamp engaged the services of the most respected art photographer of the day, Alfred Stieglitz, the very man, as Duchamp knew well, responsible for championing the photograph as art.[24] Stieglitz's carefully lit and artful (even reverential) image of Mutt's vulgar salon submission, with the application tag to the exhibition still dangling from the work, was published soon after. It appeared with the captions: "Photograph by Alfred Stieglitz" and "THE EXHIBIT REFUSED BY THE INDEPENDENTS" alongside an unattributed editorial and several texts relating to "The Richard Mutt Case" in the second issue, from May 1917, of the satirical journal *The Blind Man*, founded and anonymously published by Beatrice Wood, Roché, and Duchamp himself. But the circulation of the little journal was extremely limited, and nowhere was Duchamp's name attached to the rejected work. Thus few had any idea that he was behind *Fountain*; no one seems to have probed into the matter at all, and Duchamp didn't publicly mention his connection to the object for decades ("for a period of thirty years nobody talked about them [the readymades], and neither did I").[25] Thus we cannot forget that, back then, the rejection of *Fountain* was no more than a footnote to a small, local story. Not a scandal. Not even noticed. Not yet. The so-called invention of the readymade still needed to be *constructed*.[26]

2.4

Spread from *The Blind Man*, ed. P. B. T. [P: Henri-Pierre Roché, B: Beatrice Wood, and T: Marcel Duchamp], featuring Richard Mutt's *Fountain*, 1917. Philadelphia Museum of Art: Gift of Jacqueline, Peter, and Paul Matisse in memory of their mother, Alexina Duchamp.

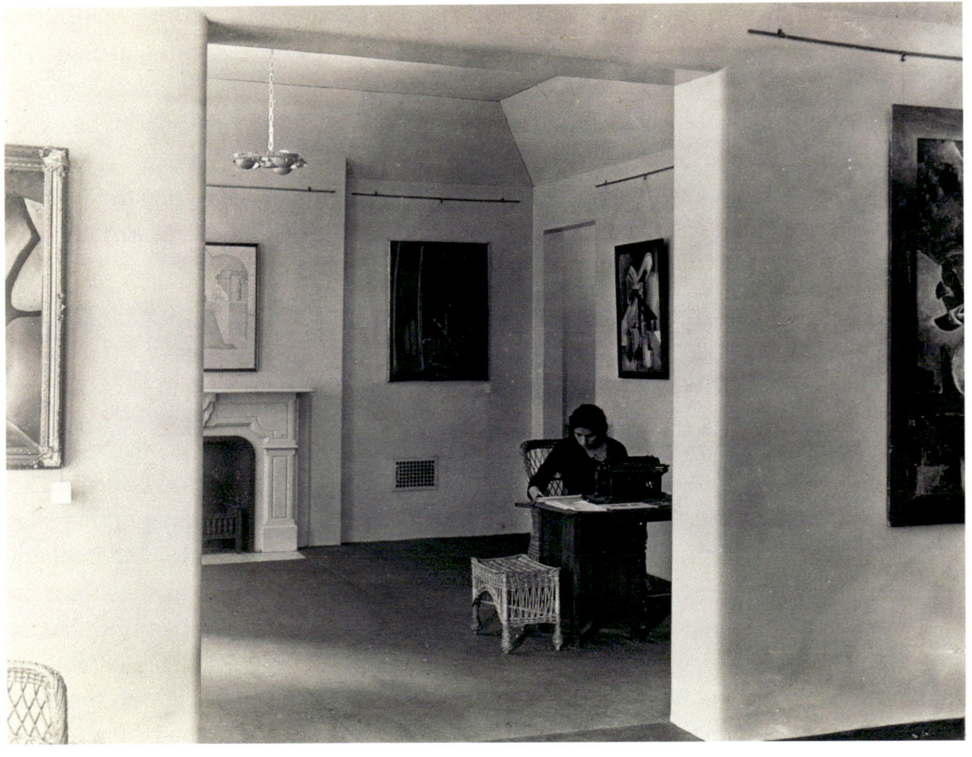

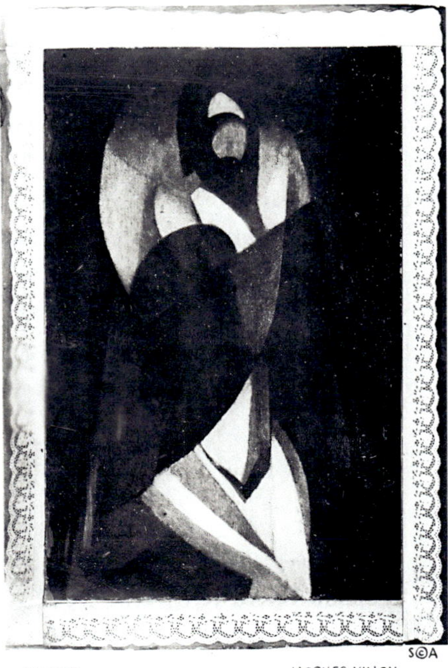

2.5

Installation view, exhibition rooms of the Société Anonyme (with Katherine S. Dreier seated in the background), 19 East 47th Street, New York, 1920. Yale Beinecke Rare Book and Manuscript Library, New Haven: Katherine S. Dreier Papers/Société Anonyme Archives.

2.6

Postcard reproduction of Jacques Villon's *Figure*, 1919, with lace frame, as it was exhibited at the Société Anonyme, c. 1920. Yale Beinecke Rare Book and Manuscript Library, New Haven: Katherine S. Dreier Papers/Société Anonyme Archives.

When Duchamp did finally reveal his connection to *Fountain*, decades later, which is to say, when he began to retroactively acknowledge, contextualize, and create a lineage or genealogy for an object that no longer existed and had made no impact while it did exist, his revelation was entirely bound up with his thinking about exhibitions, art institutions, and their administration of what counts as "art." The readymades, as we know (and *Fountain* more than any other), have since come to be seen as one of the most uncontestably important artistic gestures of the twentieth century. Yet the readymades are arguably the result not only of artistic fiat (invention, declaration, or selection—a logic of "this is art if I say it is"), as has been long understood, but perhaps even more importantly, of another set of actions: the series of "tests" Duchamp enacted between 1916 and 1917 in three very different sorts of spaces (commercial gallery, studio, and supposedly nonjuried exhibition), the documentation and administration of one key readymade (having it photographed, having that image published), and, crucially, decades later, his construction of a public (even if miniature) exhibition in which he finally, successfully, presented it as "art."

Who knows exactly how or why Duchamp returned to the idea of *Fountain* decades after he first selected the piece of porcelain and nominated it as art? What is clear is that the artist had, in the years after 1917, increasingly turned his attention to the frameworks, institutions, and dissemination systems (discursive, exhibitionary, financial) circumscribing the work of art. Starting in 1920 he had a foundational role, together with fellow artists Man Ray and Katherine S. Dreier, in the Société Anonyme, Inc. (dubbed the "Museum of Modern Art" nine years before Alfred Barr Jr. founded the other institution that now operates under that name). Duchamp's official title at the Société was "head of exhibitions." As such, he wrote nearly all the detailed catalog entries on artists for its various publications, made studio visits with artists to select their artworks, and decided on the peculiar display details of its short-lived 47th Street exhibition headquarters, including the choice of bluish oilcloth-covered walls, gray rubber flooring, and paper lace doilies to frame certain paintings. As Kristina Wilson notes, Duchamp's choice of such unusual elements for the exhibition space had the effect of turning "the gallery itself into an artwork: the art no longer was located simply in the canvases hung on the walls but rather comprised the entire atmosphere of the room."[27] More than the idiosyncratic exhibition presentation details, Duchamp was responsible for determining and contextualizing the artworks that would be featured in the exhibitions organized at the Société's headquarters or elsewhere under its banner, a role in which he was deeply involved throughout the 1920s.

Duchamp also carefully surveyed the exchange value of artworks, aware that this, too, had a role to play in the reception and understanding of the object itself.[28] In early 1926 he used money inherited from his father to purchase eighty of his friend Francis Picabia's paintings and organize their public sale at Paris's Hôtel Drouot. Duchamp designed the catalog for the sale and, in his personal copy, carefully noted the price at which he expected each painting to sell as well as the final hammer price. Just a few

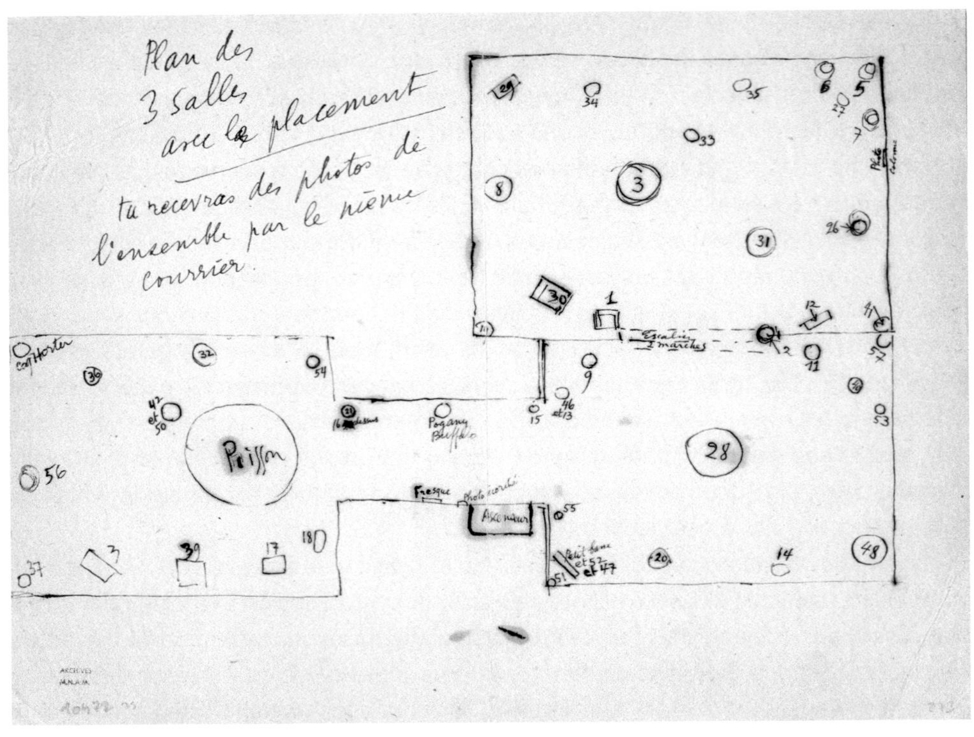

2.7

Marcel Duchamp, floor-plan sketch for the Constantin Brancusi exhibition at Brummer Gallery, New York, 1933. Centre Pompidou, MNAM-CCI, Paris: Brancusi Bequest.

2.8

Installation view, Constantin Brancusi exhibition organized by Marcel Duchamp at Brummer Gallery, New York, 1933. Photo by Soichi Sunami. Centre Pompidou, MNAM-CCI, Paris: Brancusi Bequest.

months later he convinced Roché and a rich heiress to join forces to purchase nearly thirty Constantin Brancusi sculptures during the public sale of the estate of John Quinn, a collector for whom Duchamp had been an informal art advisor. Duchamp, as a result, actively involved himself in the promotion and organization of several Brancusi exhibitions (at Brummer Gallery in New York in 1926 and 1933 and the Arts Club of Chicago in 1933). He became, effectively, Brancusi's American agent, seeking out exhibition and sales opportunities, and even helping to file the initial complaint with the U.S. customs office over the works being levied with import tax when they were taken to be "articles of utility" rather than sculptures. By 1933, with many of the sculptor's works still in his possession, Duchamp seems to have understood that his investment needed to be better exhibited, so he immersed himself wholly in the organization of the Brummer Gallery show that year. He drew rather detailed installation plans for the arrangement of each sculpture (even cutting Brancusi's *Endless Column* down a bit so it would fit upright in the gallery). He wrote to the Romanian sculptor several times over the course of the show's preparation, his last letter accompanied by the calculations of all the sales that the show generated (it mattered to Brancusi what his works sold for, but also to Duchamp, who obviously had a financial interest in the whole affair). These pursuits, like his later sales activities, amounted to nothing more than "small business," as he insisted in his discussion with Calvin Tomkins when probed.[29] But it was business all the same.

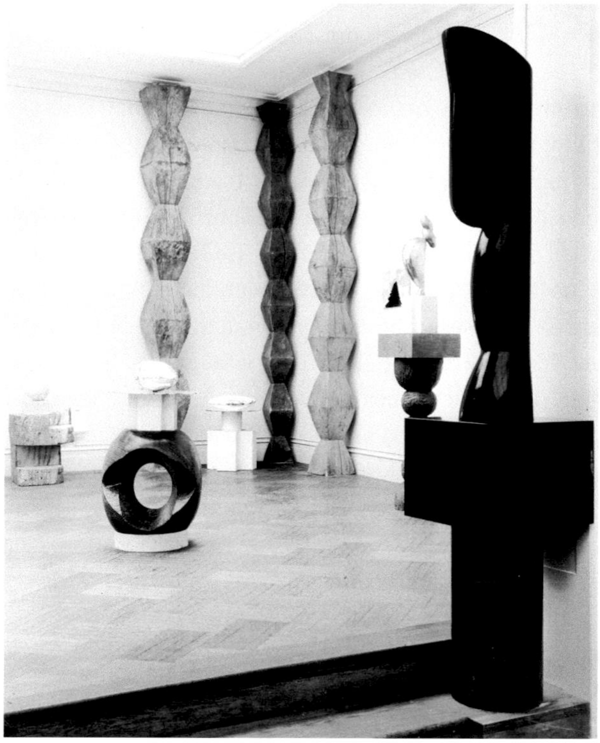

That "business" included Duchamp's lifelong involvement as an art advisor to collectors, organizer of exhibitions for artist friends (among them the first museum exhibition of Florine Stettheimer at the Museum of Modern Art in 1946 and the first solo exhibition of the poet-artist Mina Loy's work in New York at Bodley Gallery in 1959), and even quasi-dealer of his own oeuvre. In the latter case, he ensured that his most dedicated supporters could buy his works once their original owners were willing to part with them, facilitating contact between them or even buying works back himself only to offer them for sale to another. Indeed, Duchamp's art advising was so widespread that critics like Roger Shattuck rightly remind us: "As an advisor to art collectors and galleries and museums, Duchamp had a large influence on the art market in the United States during half a century. John Quinn, Walter Arensberg, Katherine Dreier, Julien Levy, Peggy Guggenheim, Sidney Janis, and Walter Hopps listened to him with confidence."[30] Duchamp's advice to them was, more often than not, rather selfless, generously helping to advance the visibility and value of the art of others he believed in. In a number of cases, however, he successfully managed to capitalize on the fantasies of ownership and desire for possession with regard to his own work. In the process he marshaled private property into public circulation and ensured that the bulk of his oeuvre would remain in the hands of a few patrons, whom he then entreated to donate the works to respectable museum collections. All of these gestures, as well as works that explicitly engage with the artwork's ambiguous commodity status such as *Tzanck Check* (1919) and *Obligations pour la roulette de Monte Carlo* (Monte Carlo Bond, 1924), prove that the artist clearly understood that the value of an artwork was not self-evident. It needed to be helped along, contextualized, perhaps even *created*.

Duchamp's "tests" arguably went in both directions: he not only attempted to see whether everyday objects brought into art exhibitions would get noticed and be taken as valid and valuable, but also brought idiosyncratic creations to nonart contexts to see how they would be understood there. In 1935, as Roché reports, Duchamp "had produced a dozen *Rotoreliefs* [optical discs] in a large edition. ... He rented a tiny stand at the Inventions du Concours Lépine [a Parisian trade fair for inventions and inventors], and waited for the crowd. I went to see him there. The disks were all turning at the same time, some horizontally, others vertically, all around Duchamp, who looked like a smiling salesgirl."[31] Later Roché added: "It was incredibly festive, but one would have said that the little stand was shrouded in invisibility. Not a single one of those visitors, on the lookout for practical inventions, stopped by. A quick glance was all they needed to see that, between the machine to compress and burn garbage, on the left, and the instant vegetable cutter, on the right, this thing wasn't practical. Duchamp smiled and said, 'One hundred percent a mistake. At least it's clear [*net*].'"[32] Neither taken to be art nor of any functional use, Duchamp's obviously impractical spinning disks drew no interest from the visitors to the fair—it being, after all, a site for the dissemination of new, pragmatic solutions to everyday life. As this and other of the artist's quasi-curatorial activities made clear, a thing's (ontological) status and (cultural or financial) value were not inherent in it, but rather ascribed to it: details such as how one spoke about it, how and in what context it was presented, and the financial transactions it incited had a formidable role to play.

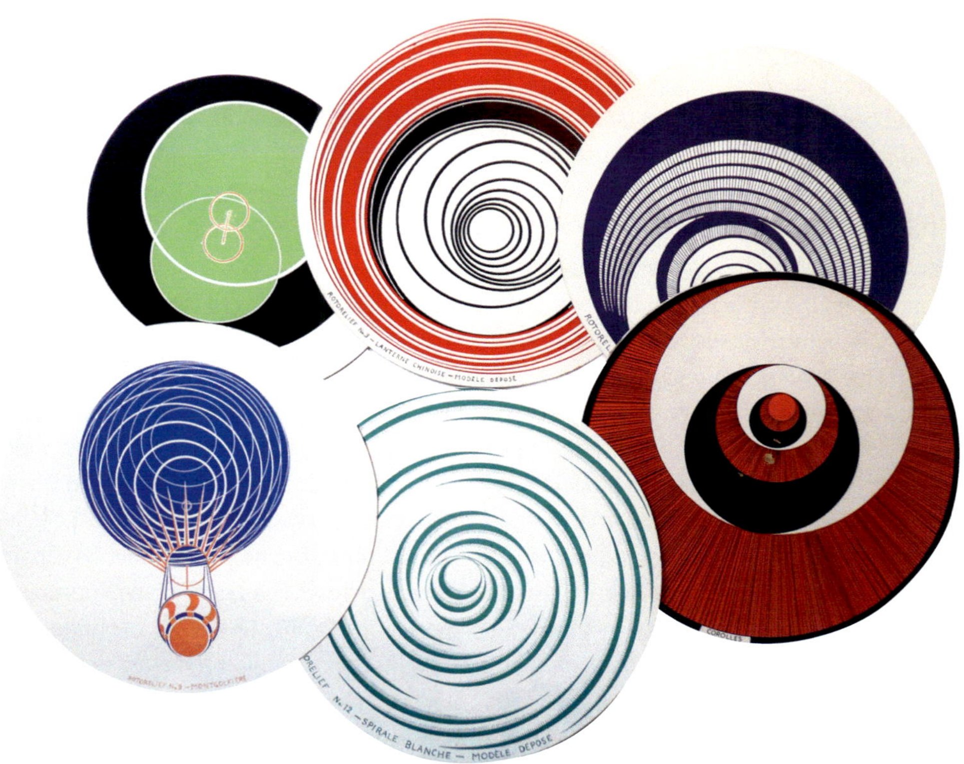

2.9

Marcel Duchamp, *Rotoreliefs*, 1935. Set of six cardboard disks printed on both sides with color offset lithography, each 7⅞ inches in diameter. Original edition of 500 sets, unnumbered and unsigned, in circular holder (c. 300 sets lost during World War II). Private collection.

After his official posts as "president of the hanging committee" or "head of exhibitions" and unofficial role as agent or dealer, by the late 1930s Duchamp would add a new function to his repertoire of apparently marginal activities, that of exhibition "generator-arbitrator." This term, which the Surrealists used for him in 1938, was another way to say, simply, "curator." In that role, in the early months of 1938 he prepared the first of what would be an elaborate and spectacular series of exhibitions for the Surrealists, which took both the conventions of exhibition making and the museum as a countermodel. It is precisely at this moment—with curating, exhibitions, and the museum so much on his mind—that Duchamp was simultaneously at work on the creation of a complex, ambiguous work in multiple copies, which he entitled the *Boîte-en-valise*. Although historians have rarely inquired into the connections between the concurrent activities—Duchamp's curating exhibitions for Surrealists and his creation (and curation) of a personal, miniature retrospective of reproductions, a "portable museum," as he called it—one cannot fully understand the implications of one without examining the other.[33] Nor indeed can one understand their implications without probing the lifelong importance of curating, exhibitions, and the museum for Duchamp.

THIS IS A CURATOR, EXHIBITION, MUSEUM

One might rightfully ask: What exactly was a "curator," an "exhibition," or indeed the "museum" in the early part of the twentieth century? And what sort of curatorial practice or exhibition form or museum paradigm could have been imaginable for Duchamp at the time? However much each of these notions—curator, exhibition, museum—became more formalized in the modern period, the types, purposes, and organization of exhibitions and museums in Europe, and the functionary art guardians who managed their collections, may have seemed as different from one another as the objects within them. Yet whatever their distinctions, many nineteenth- and early twentieth-century art museums shared formal, methodological, and ideological premises built into their very logic as secular temples for the public presentation of artworks.[34] These premises, moreover, came to provide a template from which so many other exhibition sites of modernity would model themselves (and which their curator-keepers would be tasked with maintaining). The adjudication of value (both of exhibition and exchange), preservation of authenticity, celebration of patrimony, defense of visuality, discursive contextualization, and didactic edification were just some of these.

The primacy of the "originality" of the artwork, as Rosalind Krauss argues, was fundamental:

> The theme of originality, encompassing as it does notions of authenticity, originals, and origins, is the shared discursive practice of the museum, the historian, and the maker of art. And throughout the nineteenth century all of these institutions were concerted, together, to find the mark, the warrant, the certification of the original. From this perspective we can see that modernism and the avant-garde are functions of what we could call the discourse of originality.[35]

About the necessary discrediting of the copy that was the flip side of this, she went on to insist that "both the avant-garde and modernism depend on this repression."[36] Indeed, in another essay Krauss put her finger on reproduction's contestatory relationship to "the utopian aspects of the museum's early project"—holder as the museum was of "an original that in its material presence seemed to oppose itself, all the way down the line, to the simulacral drive of photography."[37] And, as the late-1920s controversy around Alexander Dorner's exhibition "Original und Reproduktion" had indicated, the art museum (and those tasked to uphold it) prided itself as being not only a bastion but also a guarantor (provider of Krauss's "warrant" and "certification") for the incontrovertibly original artwork.

Fast-forward for a moment: whereas one might presume that this nineteenth- and early twentieth-century art museum—so focused on the maintenance of order, neutrality, rationality, and originality—was wholly different from its more modern successors, at least as concerns an almost singular interest in the auratic original, "the original" was evidently still an abiding concern of the museum well into the late 1960s. And this regardless of the revolution that we might imagine Duchamp's work had by then instituted or that the 1964 reedition of his readymades should have certainly solidified (and with it Pop art's almost simultaneous multiplications, Conceptual art's dematerializations, and Minimal art's serial repetitions). An anecdote might prove most telling: some time after the 1966 exhibition "Working Drawings and Other Visible Things on Paper Not Necessarily Meant to Be Viewed as Art," which is now widely considered to be both a work of Conceptual art (by its organizer, the artist Mel Bochner) that forms the bedrock of Conceptual art history and the first ever Conceptual art exhibition (featuring photocopies of the submissions of such artists as Sol LeWitt, Donald Judd, Eva Hesse, and Carl Andre, which were collected and displayed in four identical binders), Bochner attempted to donate one of the binders that comprised the exhibition to the collection of the Museum of Modern Art in New York. The museum declined the offer, presumably not seeing the piece as art suitable for its collection, or even as art at all. Instead it proposed to consider the gift for the library, which Bochner refused. In other words, as late as 1966, the Museum of Modern Art was simply not able to conceive of a binder with photocopies of artworks as an artwork in itself. With this in mind, one might not have to strain too much to imagine how troubling Duchamp's various proposals, including his own copies of his artworks, were to museums and to the very idea of the work of art that circulated in earlier decades.

That exhibition walls were not only the ground for display, literally, but also the ground for authority, metaphorically, was certainly another shared tenet of the constellation of institutions tasked with preserving and disseminating art. As Krauss posits:

> Whether public museum, official salon, world's fair, or private showing, the space of exhibition was constituted in part by the continuous surface of wall, a wall increasingly unstructured for any purpose other than the display of art. It was also the ground of ... choice—of either inclusion or exclusion—with everything excluded

from the space of exhibition becoming marginalized with regard to its status as Art. Given its function as the physical vehicle of exhibition, the gallery wall became the signifier of inclusion and, thus, can be seen as constituting in itself a representation of what could be called exhibitionality, or that which was developing as the crucial medium of exchange between patrons and artists within the changing structure of art in the nineteenth century.[38]

The "exhibition," whose appellation reveals its fifteenth-century roots in legal terminology as the displaying of evidence, may well in Duchamp's time still have been depicted as the neutral (evidential) presentation of items to a public within or upon an institution's walls. And this despite the fact that the exhibition—then as now, and whether in a museum, salon, gallery, or inventor's fair—was the context through which art was often first made public, seen, discussed, and circulated. The recognition of the importance of this only seems to have occurred in the modern period, after 1914. As Martha Ward points out, "One way to characterize the period from 1750 to 1914 in relation to our own is that it occurs prior to the articulation of any science or discourse of display." She further notes:

> Despite the appearance during this period of the institutions that are now commonly taken to be synonymous with the creation of autonomous space for art (museums, art societies, salons, galleries), it's nevertheless the case that art installation was not yet a subject of professional discussion, with a language of its own. Nor did the dealers, administrators, entrepreneurs or artists who mounted exhibitions often aim to create startlingly innovative displays of art and so to engineer new modes of visuality.[39]

More than a selection of artworks produced by a list of artists, occupying a given space, and hung more or less high on a wall, the exhibition had come to be considered a vital public and perceptual platform, a veritable medium, comprised of the relationships created between its contents, the dramaturgy around them, the discourse that framed them, and, importantly, the authority of the site or institution in which they found themselves. The avant-gardes of the 1920s, including Duchamp and his contemporaries, seem to have understood this well.

This self-consciousness of the exhibition as a medium begins in the 1920s, as Yve-Alain Bois claims, at the hands of such artists as El Lissitzky, whose pointed interrogation of the conventional visual experience in the exhibition proved influential to later artists and curators alike.[40] It was followed, in the mid-1920s and 1930s, by the efforts of pioneering museum directors, including Dorner in Hannover and Alfred Barr Jr. in New York, through which the development of the modern notion of the curator in Europe and the United States began to take shape. Encompassing *ancien régime* notions of the art historian-cum-museum *conservateur*, principally preoccupied with the cataloguing and preserving of a collection, and the more discursive and conceptual strategist and maker of exhibitions that Dorner and Barr inaugurated, the foundations were laid for the present-day sense of the curator that crystallized in the 1960s. That this figure, the curator, had the role of caring for and making public the artwork meant that he or she was primarily preoccupied not only with policing the borders of art (to ensure the authenticity of what went under its name and to gauge its value for history) but also with creating a discursive context around it, to enact what Benjamin H. D. Buchloh has called the curator's role in the "transformation [of the work] from *practice* to *discourse*."[41] This discourse included lecturing and writing about and contextualizing the artwork but also carefully positioning it within exhibition contexts so that the understanding of the work might accrue differently, or at all.

Duchamp, whatever he might have thought of these definitions, certainly could not ignore the authority of the museum, the exhibition, or the curator for the artist and artwork, nor that each was in the full throes of "modernization" by the 1930s. Some American and European museums had, in the years just prior, taken conscious steps toward changing and "neutralizing" their galleries and modes of display (the inauguration of the Museum of Modern Art in New York in 1929 being an important early example, with its sparse hangings and monk-cloth-covered walls, anathema to the cluttered salon interior that had been the previous norm). Yet the year 1937 marked the beginning of an undeniably scientific approach to the museum and an attempt at the universalization of its display aesthetics and exhibition making in Europe. It was precisely then that the museum, as a crucial tool in the service of history and as a modern enterprise, was officially and publicly *érigé en système*, or turned into a methodology.[42]

From May to November 1937, "Muséologie," an exhibition organized by the French state, set out to define the burgeoning "science" of museum design and installation techniques. Situated between the various national pavilions at the Paris Exposition Universelle, each with its competing claims to technological, cultural, or other advancement, this exhibition insisted that the art museum was not a venture of personal whim ("of either good or bad taste"), not a subjective selection, but rather a complex and precise enterprise of scientific judgment and presentation of museum-worthy, history-making, original artifacts.[43] To demonstrate this, craftsmen created miniaturized dioramas of museum interiors from all over the world—tiny walls lined with tiny paintings, monumental architectures reduced to the scale of dollhouses—all recessed into the walls of the exhibition's carefully organized display spaces. Signs and diagrams mapped out how spatial organization and installation aesthetics enabled viewers to see and experience an exhibition. Next to these didactic elements, graphics charted facts about the history, role, and importance of the museum, highlighting the number and kind of museums maintained by each nation. It was an encyclopedic exhibition on museums and museum technologies.

As a finale, the exhibition offered a full-size "model" retrospective of the work of Vincent van Gogh. Here visitors experienced optimal museological conditions: noiseless rooms, evenly distributed lighting, studied floor and ceiling treatments, appropriately sober surfaces, standardized labels, effusive wall texts about the artist and the works.

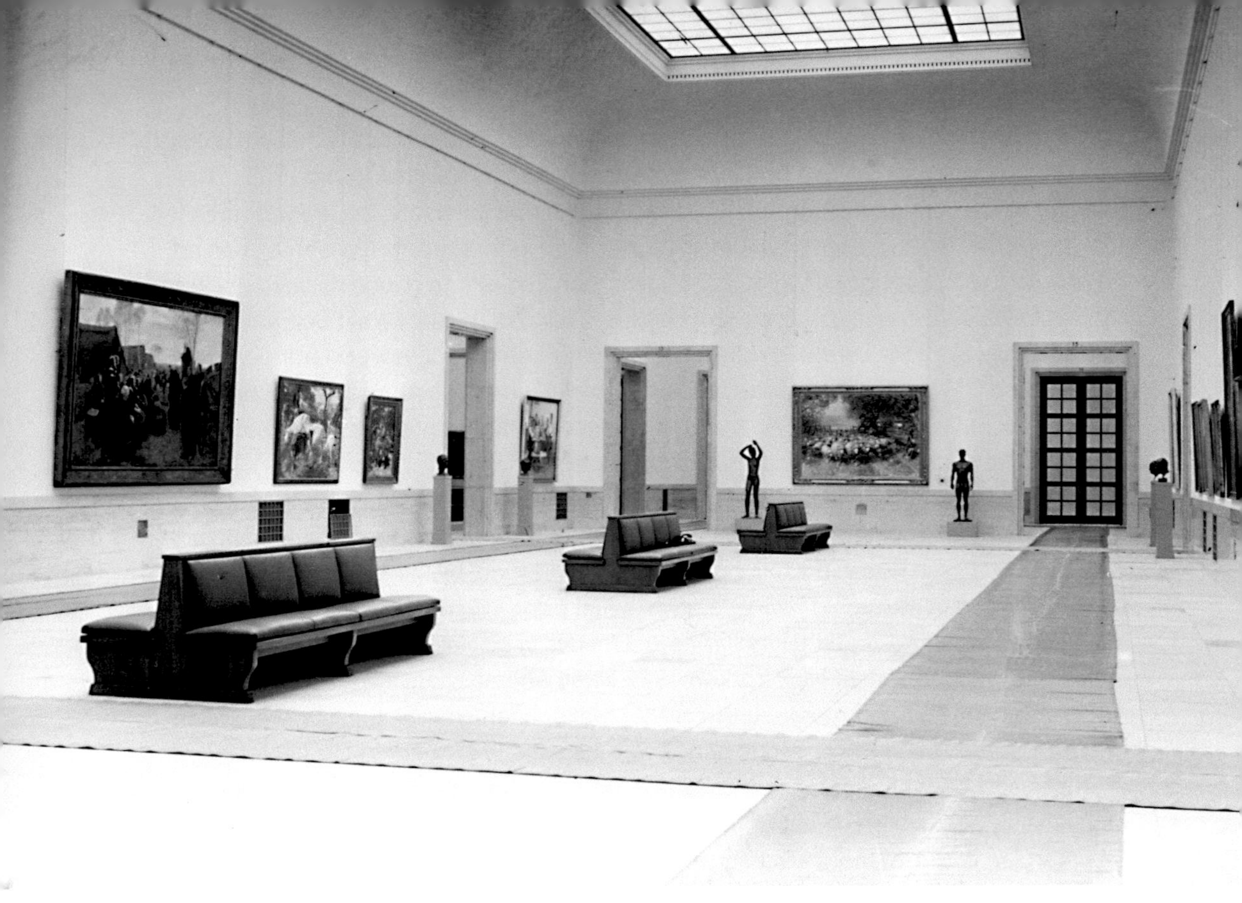

2.10

Installation view, "Grosse Deutsche Kunstausstellung" (Great German Art Exhibition), Haus der Kunst, Munich, 1937. Stadtarchiv, Munich.

2.11

South wall in the third room of the exhibition "Entartete Kunst" (Degenerate Art) in the arcades of the Hofgarten, Munich, 1937. Kunstbibliothek, Staatliche Museen, Berlin.

More than a show to honor the famous painter of sunflowers, it was a didactic *installation-type*, a model demonstrating how one should, if one followed scientific principles, ideally exhibit art. There, as in the museum in general, proper behavior and disciplined observation were the goal.

Amplifying the cult of the visual so important to the very conception of the museum, the exhibition of museology unabashedly touted the primacy of vision.[44] It is thus not surprising that René Descartes, founder of the scientific method in France and considered the quintessential visual philosopher, was omnipresent in this exhibition on exhibition making. Cartesianism was more than simply insinuated; the curators expressly conceived the "Muséologie" exhibition "under the patronage of Descartes."[45] It formed part of France's celebration of the three hundredth anniversary of the *Discours de la méthode*, a text that included *La Dioptrique* and contained the thinker's most extensive examination of optics and vision. Cartesianism, science, reason, truth, order: these were all mobilized to uphold the museum's authority, as exemplified in the whole of this unusual presentation at the Exposition Universelle—very likely the first show ever to explicitly take the museum exhibition as its theme.

Meanwhile, the proclaimed scientificness of the whole museological enterprise neutralized the museum's judgments—the arbitrariness of its artistic choices or the partialness of the narratives it validated. Yet the stakes were just beneath the surface. It was a moment, we should not forget, when Europe was witness to the period's most terrifying collusion between aesthetics and politics—for which both the museum and the art exhibition were fundamental instruments. Munich, for example, witnessed the simultaneous staging of the Nazis' "Grosse Deutsche Kunstausstellung" (Great German Art Exhibition) and "Entartete Kunst" (Degenerate Art) exhibition in 1937. All of this formed the witting or unwitting backdrop to the Paris Exposition Universelle's assertion, central to the newly formed discipline of "museology," that a museum's evaluation of artworks and presentation of history are grounded in empirical, objective truth.

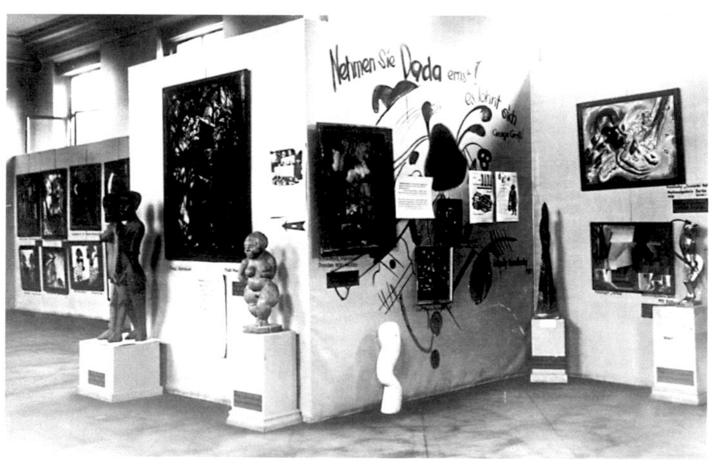

EXHIBITIONISM

On the heels of the 1937 Paris Exposition Universelle's celebration of the rigor and rationalization of the museum, indeed at the precise moment when the modern art museum was becoming an undeniably solidified "scientific" progeny of the Enlightenment, Duchamp was busy interrogating the functions and protocols of exhibitions and museums in a full-scale exhibition. His preoccupation with responding to and defying the conventional form and terms of the art exhibition was deeply connected to his simultaneous work on the *Boîte-en-valise* and, more generally, his conception of the artwork, inextricable as the latter was from his complex relationship to various institutions of art, including the museum.

One can imagine him walking the vast fairgrounds of the 1937 Exposition Universelle, marveling at the displays of scientific technologies, museological gadgetry, and industrial machines. He had made plans to meet friends at the opening, but he disappointed them by missing the festivities.[46] Regardless of whether or not he attended the fair later, he likely took notice of what the popular and art press as well as verbal accounts heralded: 1937 was a formidable moment in the constitution of the modern museum.[47] The dismantling of the Exposition Universelle had not yet begun when Surrealist leader André Breton and poet Paul Éluard convinced Duchamp, at the end of 1937, to begin to conceptualize the installation of what was to be the first Parisian "Exposition internationale du surréalisme." The Surrealists had been invited by Georges Wildenstein to stage a collective show at his Galerie Beaux-Arts and had been given carte blanche for the event that was held (after several date changes) from January 17 to February 24, 1938. It did not go unnoticed by the Surrealists—nor, surely, by Duchamp—that the Galerie Beaux-Arts was among the most respectable galleries of the period, an appendix to the venerated journal *Gazette des Beaux-Arts* (also owned by Wildenstein). More than simply one of Paris's most fashionable galleries, the Galerie Beaux-Arts often organized shows in connection with those offered simultaneously at French institutions. Thus the resulting Surrealist exhibition was not something that the frequenters of the gallery were used to finding at Wildenstein's august establishment. The invitation, as the artists knew well, was a loaded one: if Wildenstein was interested in Surrealism, the movement's self-styled radical position must have been losing its potency. Perhaps for this reason, Breton and Éluard assembled a team with Duchamp at the helm so as to create an exhibition that would position itself against the very bastion of bourgeois good taste that had had the good taste to invite them.[48]

Duchamp's official title was the exhibition's "générateur-arbitre" (generator-arbitrator), a peculiar neologism for the time, announcing his role as motor for and referee of the ideas of the overall display. In his capacity as, essentially, curator, Duchamp's interventions were rather simple, even if spectacular in effect and radical in implication: he imagined Wildenstein's top-lit, cream-colored, elegantly appointed eighteenth-century interior as a dark "grotto." He covered the ornate moldings, ceiling, and banks of lights with suspended coal sacks (1,200 of them, he insistently claimed).[49] Not even justifiable worries about the flammable nature of the coal sacks or an insurance executive's warnings could move Duchamp to significantly alter his project (emptied of their coal and filled instead with equally flammable newspaper, the sacks' residual soot remained). Duchamp installed an electrified iron brazier at the center of the main hall to serve as the show's dim, central source of light. In their inversion of interior and exterior, up and down, the sacks initiated an unsettling of the gallery's architecture, while the faint lighting throughout did everything to refuse an art exhibition's typical clarity. He had department store revolving doors rented for the occasion and brought into the exhibition space to hang paintings and drawings on. In one fell swoop, art and commerce, the art gallery and the department store (the primary site for revolving doors at the time), were incisively conflated. And this while the ceiling above undulated, darkness prevailed, the blackened walls refused the clean, white neutrality of the modern art exhibition, and coal dust fell onto the finery of the exhibition's guests. More than any particular object or detail, Duchamp's determination to comprehensively remodel the entire gallery was a challenge to "those walls accustomed to semi-official exhibits."[50]

As a result, the 1938 installation looked little like the group's previous shows or, for that matter, like any other art exhibition held during the period. The mise-en-scène Duchamp initiated was considerably different from the relatively sober and even conventional displays that characterized the "Exposition surréaliste" of 1925 or the "International Surrealist Exhibition" in London in 1936. Even the 1936 "Exposition surréaliste d'objets"—despite its heterogeneous mix of Surrealist constructions, lava formations, mathematical models, African artifacts, and other found objects that shook the taxonomies of the art gallery and museum—did not radically reconceive the exhibition space as such; indeed, that show could be said to have mimed as closely as possible (with vitrines, pedestals, and an ordered display) some of the most visible codes and systems of art institutions.[51] In 1938, on the other hand, these presentational codes were called into question for the first time when the Surrealists asked Duchamp to conceptualize and, effectively, curate their exhibition. The result introduced a perceptual and performative undermining of the gallery space and exhibition conventions, an endeavor that subsequent Duchamp-curated Surrealist shows took up as their cardinal principle. (Still, the unlikely agreement was among the journalists, all of whom denounced the show on some pretext: on grounds that it had been orchestrated either too well or not well enough, that the art was too academic or not "real" art at all, that the Surrealists were hopelessly occult or the latest darlings of a bourgeois elite. And for some, the exhibition's mise-en-scène seemed to be proof of a lack of artistic aptitude. As François Fosca, writing for *Je Suis Partout*, put it, "If the work of the Surrealists had any real interest, this whole staging wouldn't have been necessary. It is hard to imagine Corot, Delacroix, or Degas running around in this way; it is obvious that those artists had talent.")[52]

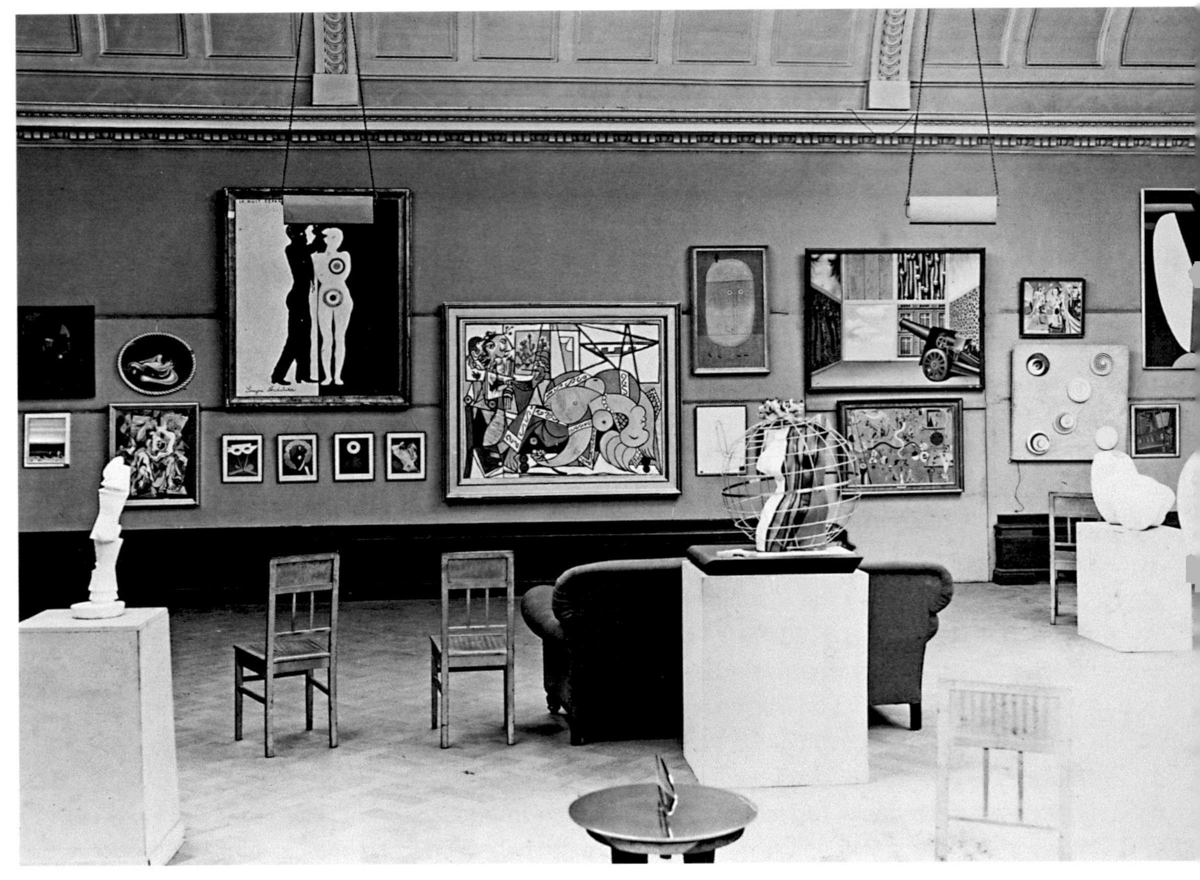

2.12

Installation view (main gallery), "International Surrealist Exhibition," New Burlington Galleries, London, 1936. Photographer unknown, part of a series contained in *Photo Album: International Surrealist Exhibition*. National Gallery of Modern Art, Scotland: Roland Penrose Archive, purchased 1994.

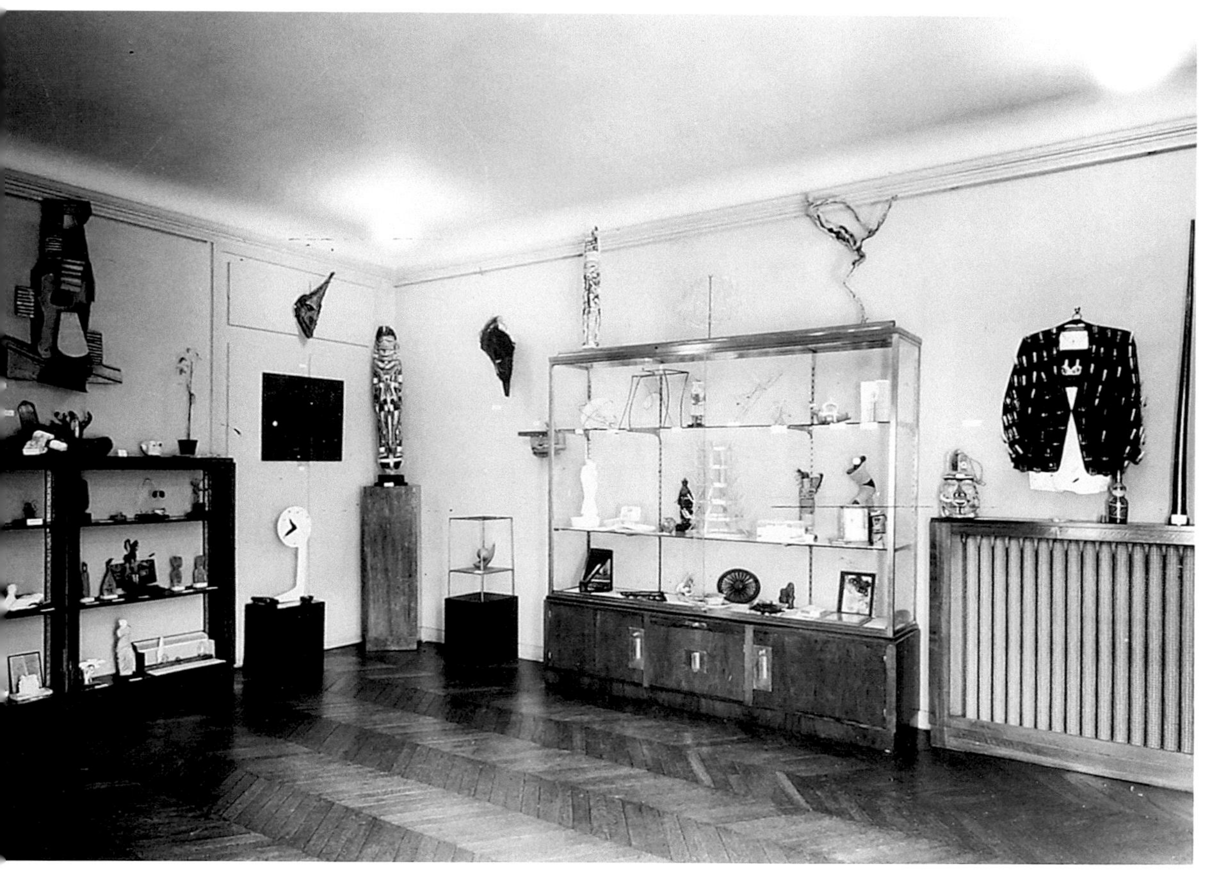

2.13

Installation view, "Exposition surréaliste d'objets," Galerie Charles Ratton, Paris, 1936. Photo by Man Ray.

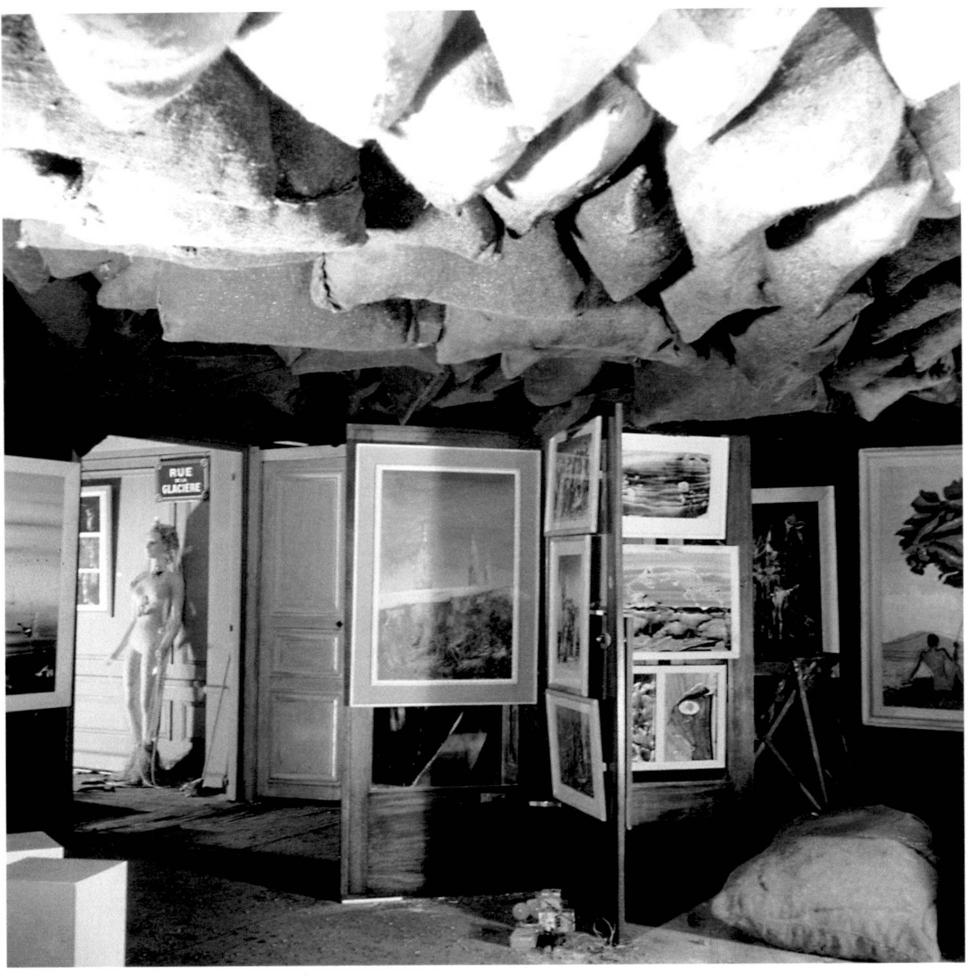

2.14

Installation view of the central grotto with a view toward the "Rue Surréaliste" at the "Exposition internationale du surréalisme," Galerie Beaux-Arts, Paris, 1938. Photo by Denise Bellon.

2.15 (following pages)

Contact sheet of press photos of the "Exposition internationale du surréalisme," Galerie Beaux-Arts, Paris, 1938. Photos by Roger Schall.

In the weeks before the opening, Duchamp's initial ideas for the exhibition design served as an inspiring catalyst for the other participating artists. Salvador Dalí, for example, parked a taxicab—occupied by a begoggled mannequin surrounded by live snails and vegetation—just outside the gallery. Inside, a collectively designed faux urban landscape was the first thing to greet visitors. This streetscape featured fictive Parisian street signs and served as the backdrop for sixteen mannequins, each "dressed" by a different artist. From here one proceeded toward a simulated lake and four elegantly appointed beds in the main hall (that the exhibition interior evoked an oneiric brothel was not lost on journalists attending the vernissage) carpeted, by Wolfgang Paalen, with dead leaves and dirt. A soundtrack consisting of "hysterical laughter recorded at a psychiatric asylum" and "the lockstep of a German army procession," as several artists described it, filled the air.[53] One cannot help imagining that in the twinned evocations of hysteria and the German army, Hitler's Munich shows were not far from anyone's mind.[54] Alongside this aural disruption, the olfactory senses were simultaneously stimulated: behind a screen, roasting coffee beans sent the invitation's promised "odeurs du Brésil" wafting through the air. The lights were turned off, creating near obscurity throughout. For the opening night, a dancer, Hélène Vanel, hired to simulate hysteria, thrashed about from the exhibition's beds to the lake and onto the floor with a live rooster in her hands. Dirty, dark, loud, and lugubrious, the installation of the "Exposition internationale du surréalisme" "destroyed," as Man Ray recalled, "that clinical atmosphere that reigned in the most modern of exhibition spaces."[55]

Even though the wildly fantastic overall scenario might appear more Surrealist in spirit than Duchampian, the various elements not only remained important to Duchamp but also anticipated his own grotto-like final work, *Étant donnés: 1° la chute d'eau, 2° le gaz d'éclairage ...* (Given: 1. The Waterfall, 2. The Illuminating Gas ... , 1946–66), begun years later.[56] More importantly, perhaps, by insisting on the fundamental destabilization of the conventional art space and terms of display, Duchamp deepened his own complex questioning of and engagement with exhibition making.

It was in this space that his *Pharmacie* (Pharmacy, 1914), *9 moules mâlics* (9 Malic Molds, 1914–15), *La Bagarre d'Austerlitz* (The Brawl at Austerlitz, 1921), *Rotary Demisphere*, one readymade, and his alias's contribution to the "Rue Surréaliste" found a temporary showcase. The mannequin "by" Rrose Sélavy was among the sixteen rented storefront mannequins poised behind rope in the corridor of the Galerie Beaux-Arts, each a kind of assisted readymade. Wearing Duchamp's coat, shoes, and hat, with a red illuminated lightbulb in its pocket and the signature "Rrose Sélavy" scribbled across its pubis, the mannequin simultaneously evoked Parisian prostitutes and signed, labeled, roped-off, museified objects. The message was striking: the art object, commerce, the art institution, and desire were entwined, a conflation that appeared elsewhere in the exhibition and appears persistently in Duchamp's larger body of work.[57]

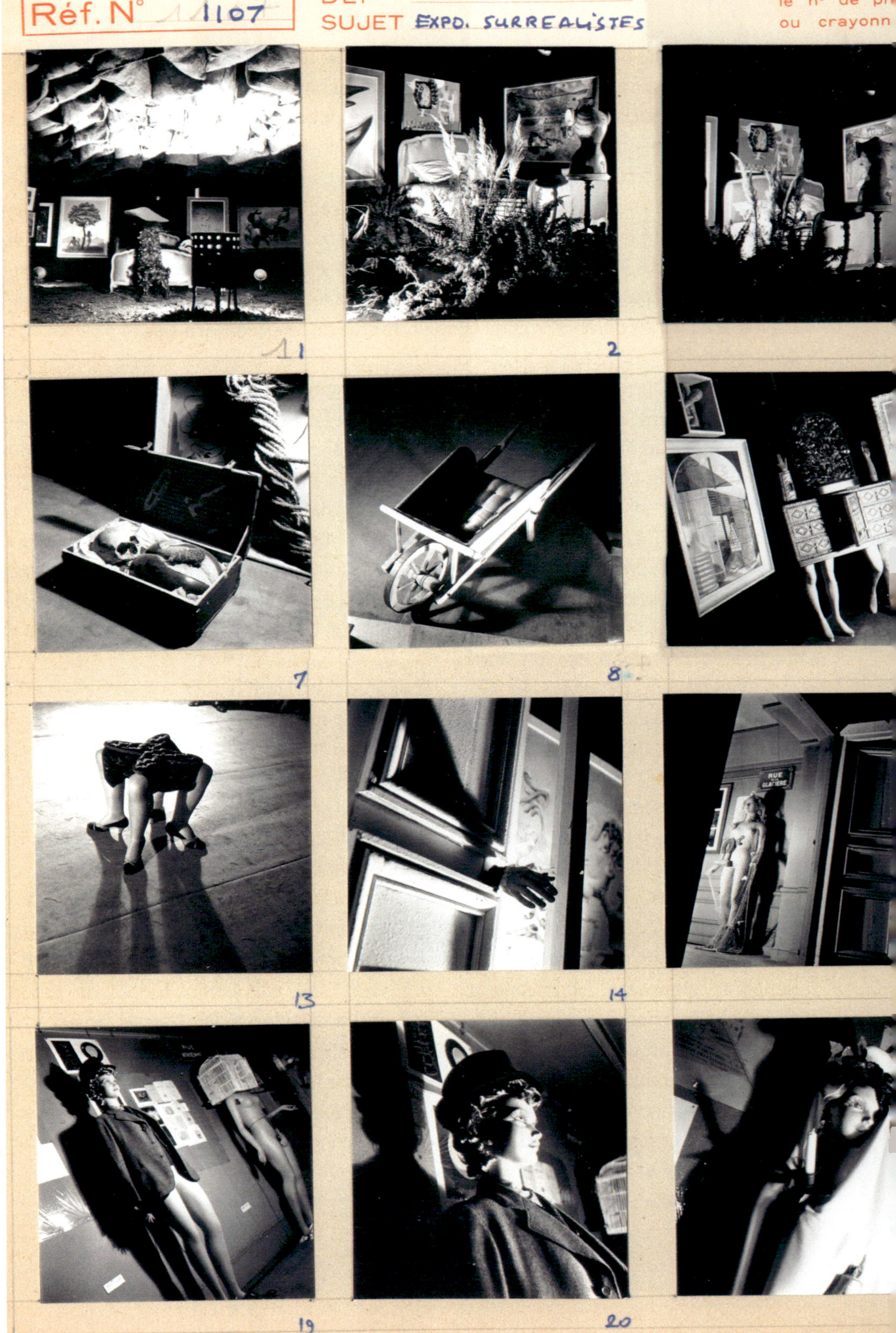
Réf. N° 1107
DÉPT
SUJET EXPO. SURREALISTES
le n° de ph
ou crayonn
1
2
7
8
13
14
19
20

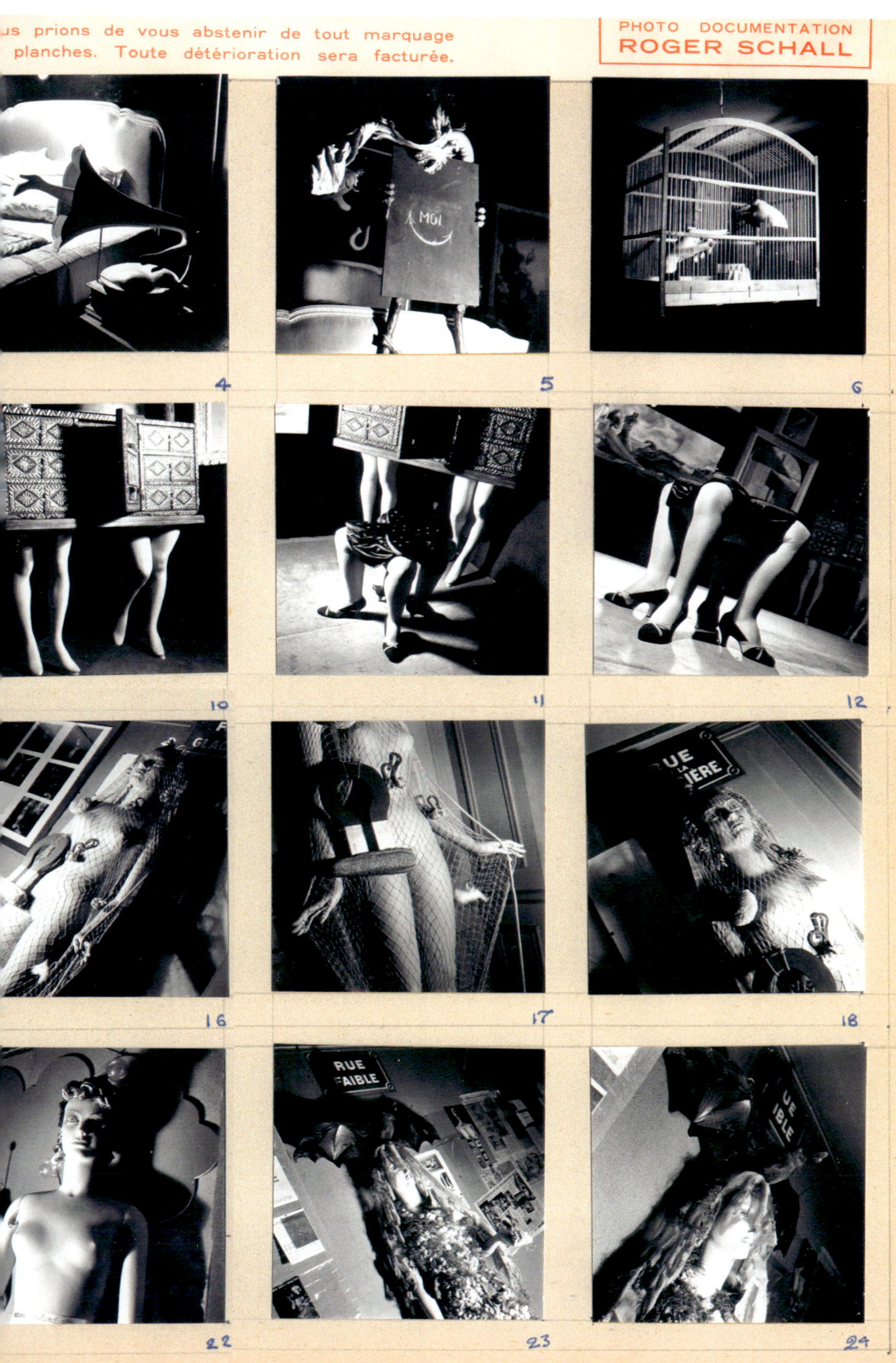
us prions de vous abstenir de tout marquage
planches. Toute détérioration sera facturée.
PHOTO DOCUMENTATION
ROGER SCHALL
MOI
4
5
6
10
11
12
16
17
18
22
23
24
RUE
FAIBLE

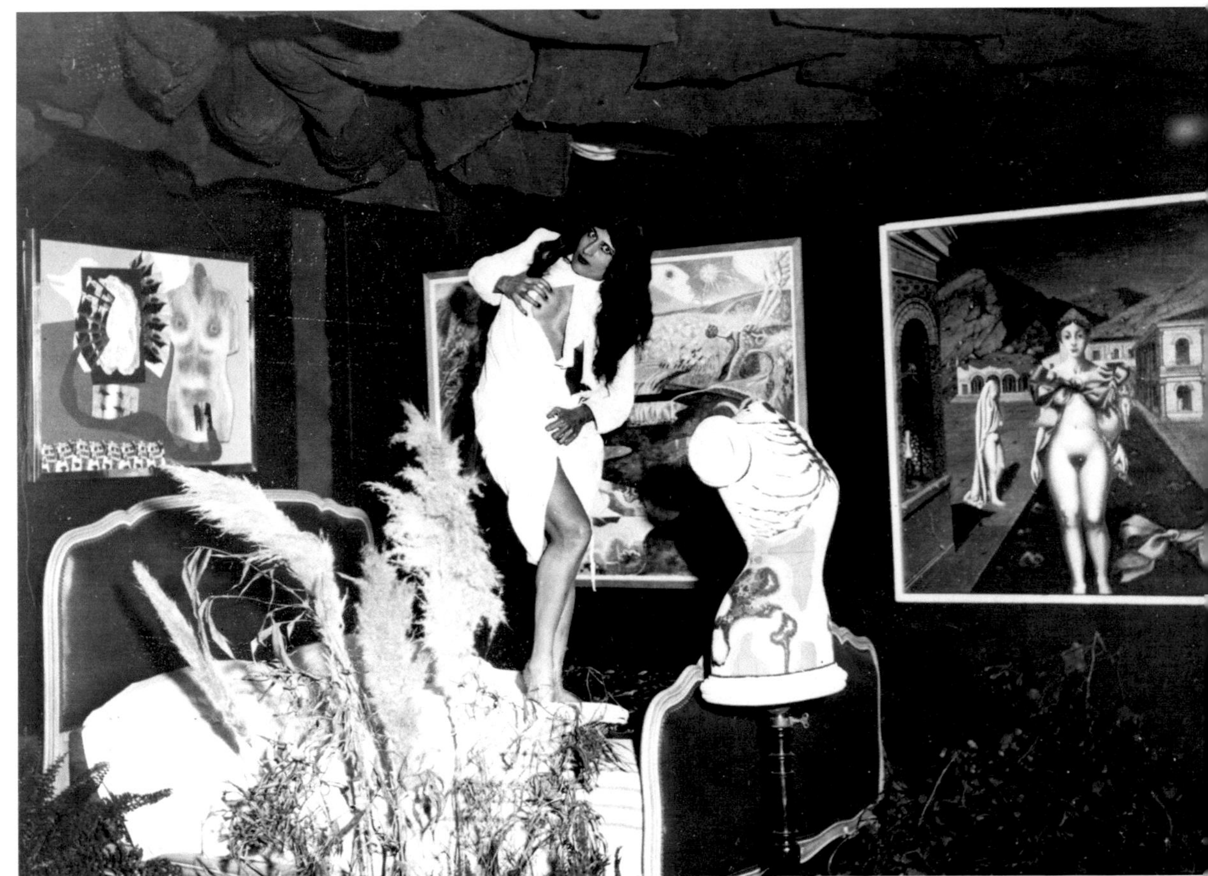

2.16

View of Hélène Vanel rehearsing *L'Acte manqué* (The Unconsummated Act) for the opening-night performance of the "Exposition internationale du surréalisme," Galerie Beaux-Arts, Paris, 1938. Photographer unknown.

Just as significant to an understanding of the exhibition's role in Duchamp's thinking is an element that was not realized. He had originally wanted the entire exhibition to be in the dark with a system of electric lights to illuminate each painting and object in the exhibition individually, but only when triggered by a viewer's approach. When that proved impossible, Man Ray, in his capacity as "master of lighting," proposed a practical alternative: he turned out the gallery's main lights and forced visitors to view the works using pocket flashlights handed out at the entrance.[58] May Ray's solution was largely faithful to Duchamp's original intention: the viewers brought themselves close to the works, hunching forward to focus their handheld electric lights. Thus, even in its adapted form, one notes in this lighting strategy a concern with perception and a continuation of that questioning of visual autonomy found throughout Duchamp's oeuvre, from his efforts to circumvent retinality in painting to his various experiments with what he called "precision optics" to, ultimately, the hunched corporeal looking that would be provoked by his final work.[59] The artist's attempt to create obscurity could not be further from the "enlightening" tenets of the gallery and museum. Engaging the entire body so directly in the act of art viewing, Duchamp's darkness rendered palpable his insistence that seeing and knowing are explicitly corporeal affairs.

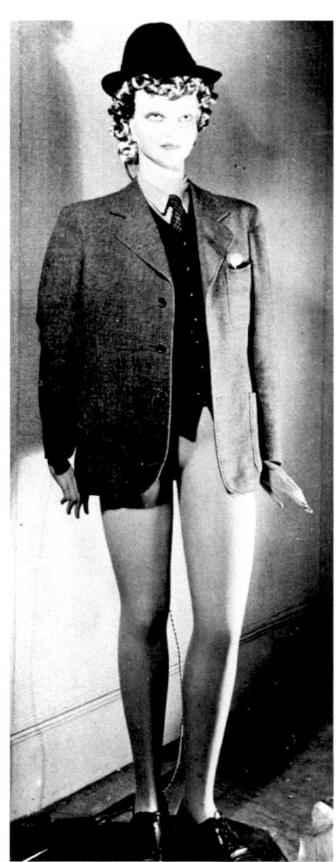

2.17

Marcel Duchamp, *Rrose Sélavy*, 1938. Life-size female mannequin dressed in Duchamp's clothes for the "Exposition internationale du surréalisme," Galerie Beaux-Arts, Paris, 1938. Original lost, dimensions not recorded. Photo by Raoul Ubac.

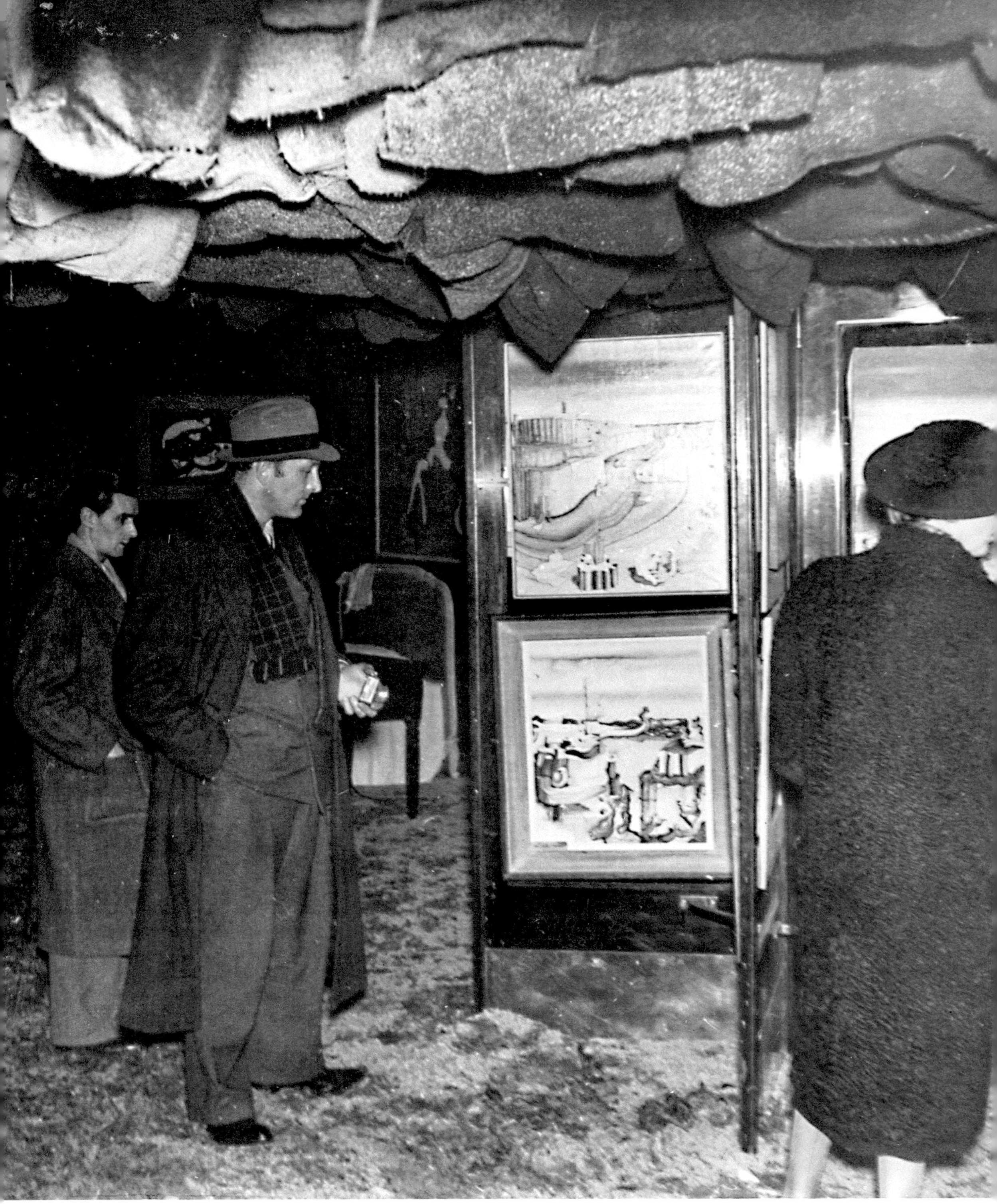

CHAPTER 2

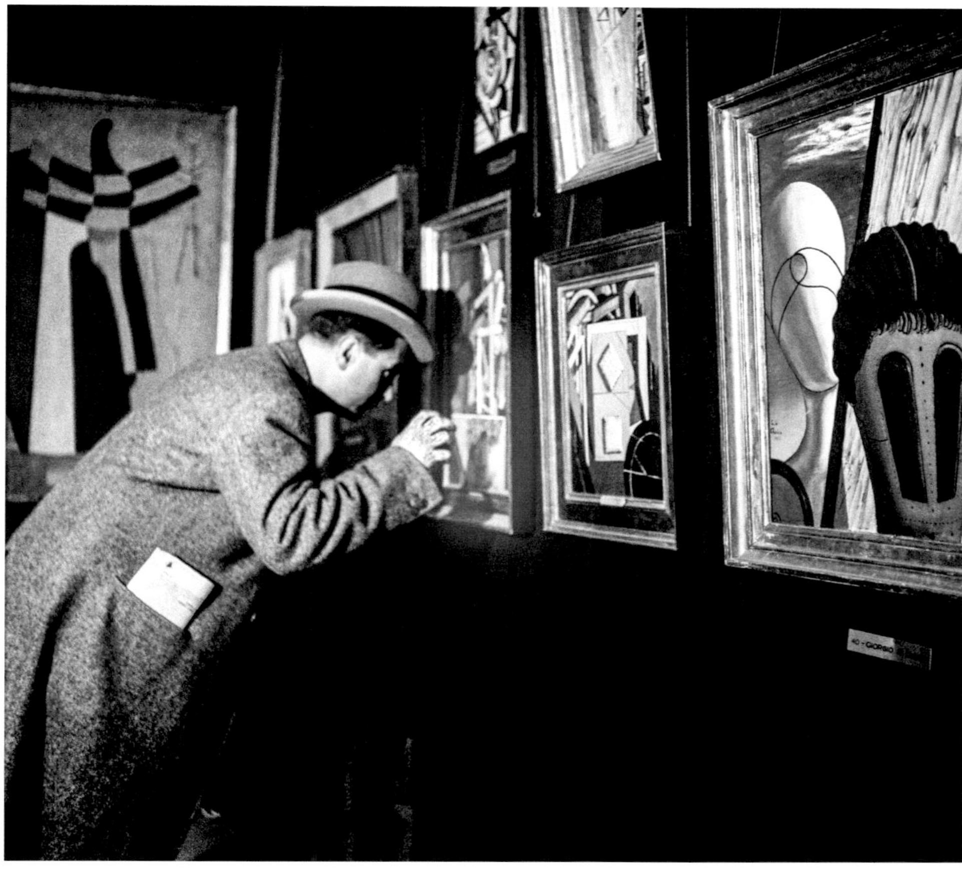

2.18

Installation view of the "Exposition internationale du surréalisme," Galerie Beaux-Arts, Paris, featuring visitors using flashlights, 1938. Photographer unknown. Collection of author.

2.19

Installation view of the "Exposition internationale du surréalisme," Galerie Beaux-Arts, Paris, featuring a visitor using a flashlight to view paintings, 1938. Photograph by Josef Breitenbach. Manipulated silver gelatin print, contemporaneous with negative.

Duchamp's experimentation with exhibition making continued when, after the exodus of many Surrealists from Europe during the Second World War, Breton called on him again to install the first international Surrealist exhibition in the United States. Titled "First Papers of Surrealism" (after the application papers that most of the émigré artists had to submit upon entry into the United States), the show was held from October 14 to November 7, 1942, at the Whitelaw Reid Mansion on Madison Avenue in New York as a benefit event for the Coordinating Council of French Relief Societies. For it, Duchamp devised a simple, economic solution to act against the mansion's faux Florentine interior with its gilded moldings, ornate ceiling paintings, crystal chandeliers, and other opulent architectural details. Having acquired for the installation what he claimed was "sixteen miles" of ordinary white string, he engaged the help of several friends to enmesh the exhibition spaces with it, resulting in a crisscross of white webbing. In the end they used only a fraction of the artist's overzealous purchase (after, that is, the initial installation, which entangled several chandeliers and other furniture, causing the string to be accidentally destroyed by "spontaneous combustion"), but the invocation of colossal numbers already evident in the "1,200 coal sacks" of 1938 remained, and the title for the installation was fixed: *Sixteen Miles of String*.[60] The twine traversed the mansion's former drawing rooms where Duchamp had hung paintings on a series of portable display partitions (paintings being the overwhelming majority of what was on show), thus enacting a far simpler, although no less spectacular, revision of exhibition conventions than he had conceived in 1938.

The tangled mesh did not cut off vision completely—it was the frustration, not elimination, of sight that Duchamp desired. Still, the entwinement between and in front of so many of the things supposedly "on display" constituted a vexing barrier between the spectator and the works of art. As the critic Edward Alden Jewell of the *New York Times* reported:

> The show, installed in what used to be the Whitelaw Reid's drawing room and in adjacent rooms of his Florentine palazzo of the Eighteen Eighties, constitutes a very diverting and flavorsome event. The décor is phrased in just the unexpected sort of labyrinthine wit that we should expect from Marcel Duchamp, who has engagingly entangled this miniature Surrealist "pluriuniverse" in sixteen miles of innocent white string. No use trying in a matter-of-fact way to describe what he has accomplished. The net result, geometrical at least by implication, in its interlacing and festooning, is appropriately weird and devious. It forever gets between you and the assembled art, and in so doing creates the most paradoxically clarifying barrier imaginable. But if this ingenious investiture of Duchamp's clarifies the present occasion by so perversely enmeshing it in a shroud of irrational logic, it also helps make imperative one's effort to determine just what Surrealism really is, how inclusive and to what extent exclusive, is its empire; whether "inner vision" and diabolically serpentine wit are, ipso facto, interchangeable terms.[61]

Several of the artists participating in the exhibition were disappointed that spectators could not properly see their artworks, yet this seemed to be precisely Duchamp's point.

If we are to believe Henry McBride's report in the *New York Sun,* which appeared just after the opening, Duchamp submitted his own painterly contribution to the exhibition to the same visual impediment as the others, obstructing access to his own work even more: "Even Marcel Duchamp ... contributes a hitherto unshown canvas [*Network of Stoppages* (1914)]. It nestles behind a particularly thick wad of cobwebs."[62]

Like the 1938 "Exposition internationale du surréalisme," "First Papers of Surrealism" was a reconsideration not only of the "art" itself but also of how an art exhibition typically regulates viewing: the performative operation of making a viewer aware of what stands, in the words of the *New York Times*, "between you and the assembled art." Duchamp's strategies thereby simultaneously recalled and anticipated his fascination with how the viewer sees, suggested by his persistent interest in optical experiments throughout the late 1910s and the 1920s. Think of such works as *To Be Looked at (from the Other Side of the Glass) with One Eye, Close To, for Almost an Hour* (1918), *Rotary Glass Plates* (1920), and *Rotary Demisphere* (1924), or, most forcefully, the artist's final piece, *Étant donnés*, which is at once an artwork and its own machine for looking.

The exhibition organizers seem to have planned to permeate the air with the invitation's promised "smell of cedar," but ultimately the odor was either omitted or simply went unnoticed by the crowds, since no critic mentions it. For the October 14 opening, however, the eleven-year-old Carroll Janis, son of gallerist Sidney Janis, did show up on schedule with a group of his friends, in full baseball and football regalia (including spiked shoes). Duchamp had sufficiently planned "children playing" as to announce it in the exhibition's catalog and had paid for the children's taxi fare, instructing them to freely run around playing ball, skipping rope, or playing hopscotch. The raucous playing continued into the night, in the midst of the crowded opening, encouraged by Duchamp's request that the children not stop when asked to do so by adults, even though the artist himself didn't attend. The event, as Duchamp could easily have anticipated, caused quite a scene among the tuxedo-clad attendees. But "our instructions were to ignore everybody and just play to our hearts' content," as Janis later recalled. To the visitors' questions or complaints, the children replied, as they had been instructed, "Marcel Duchamp asked us to come and play here."[63] Alongside the reconfigured viewing created by the string webbing, Duchamp's delegated action was an insertion of the body—ludic, running, sweating, squealing—at the center of the exhibition. It was also another test of sorts, an inquiry into whether exhibition visitors (adults and children alike) would respect the authority of an absent artist-curator, even when heeding that authority meant disobeying the tacit rules of the institution they were in.

2.20 (following pages)

Installation view of "First Papers of Surrealism," featuring Marcel Duchamp's *Sixteen Miles of String*, Whitelaw Reid Mansion, New York, 1942. Photo by John D. Schiff. Philadelphia Museum of Art: Gift of Jacqueline, Peter, and Paul Matisse in memory of their mother, Alexina Duchamp.

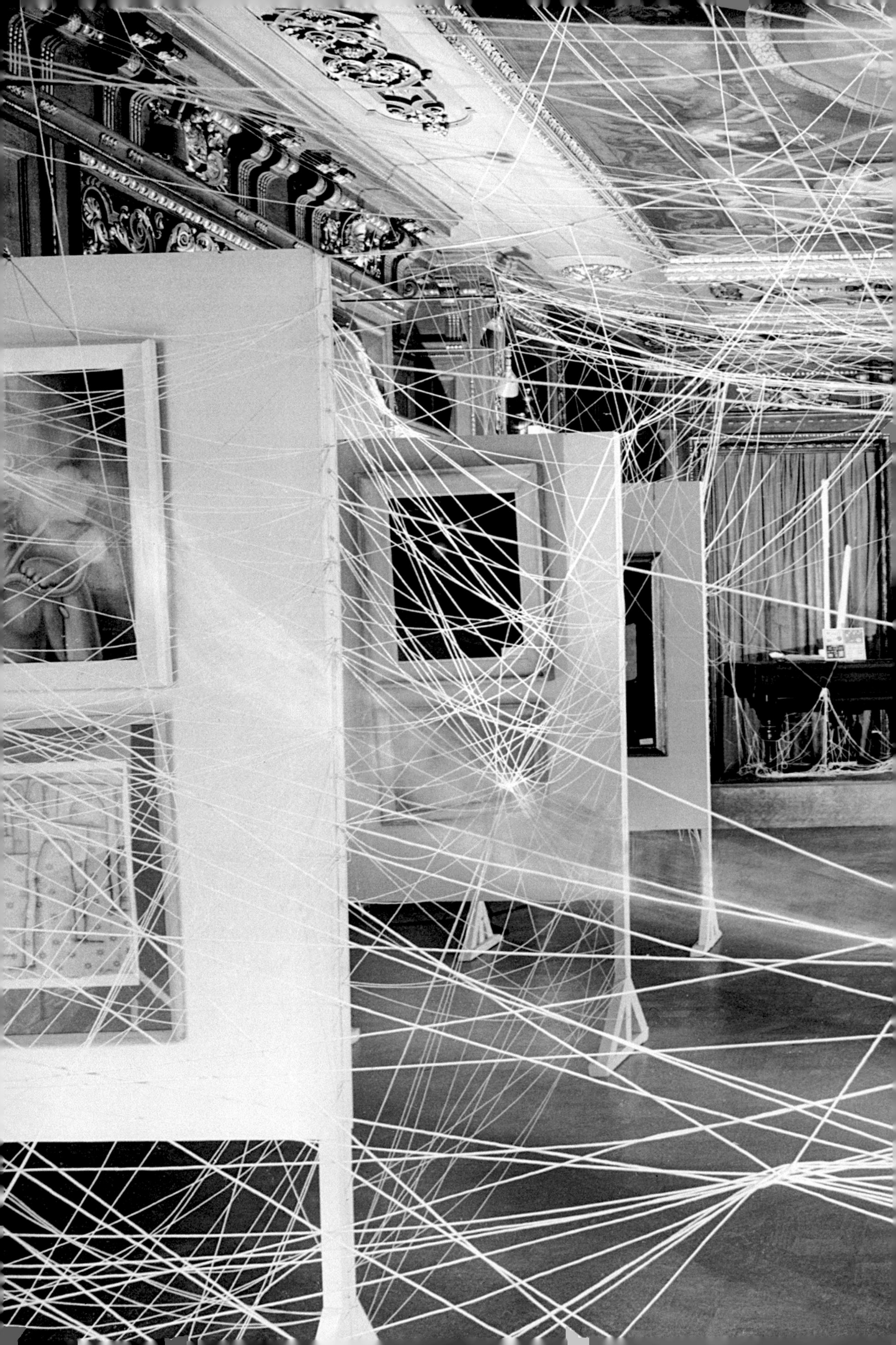

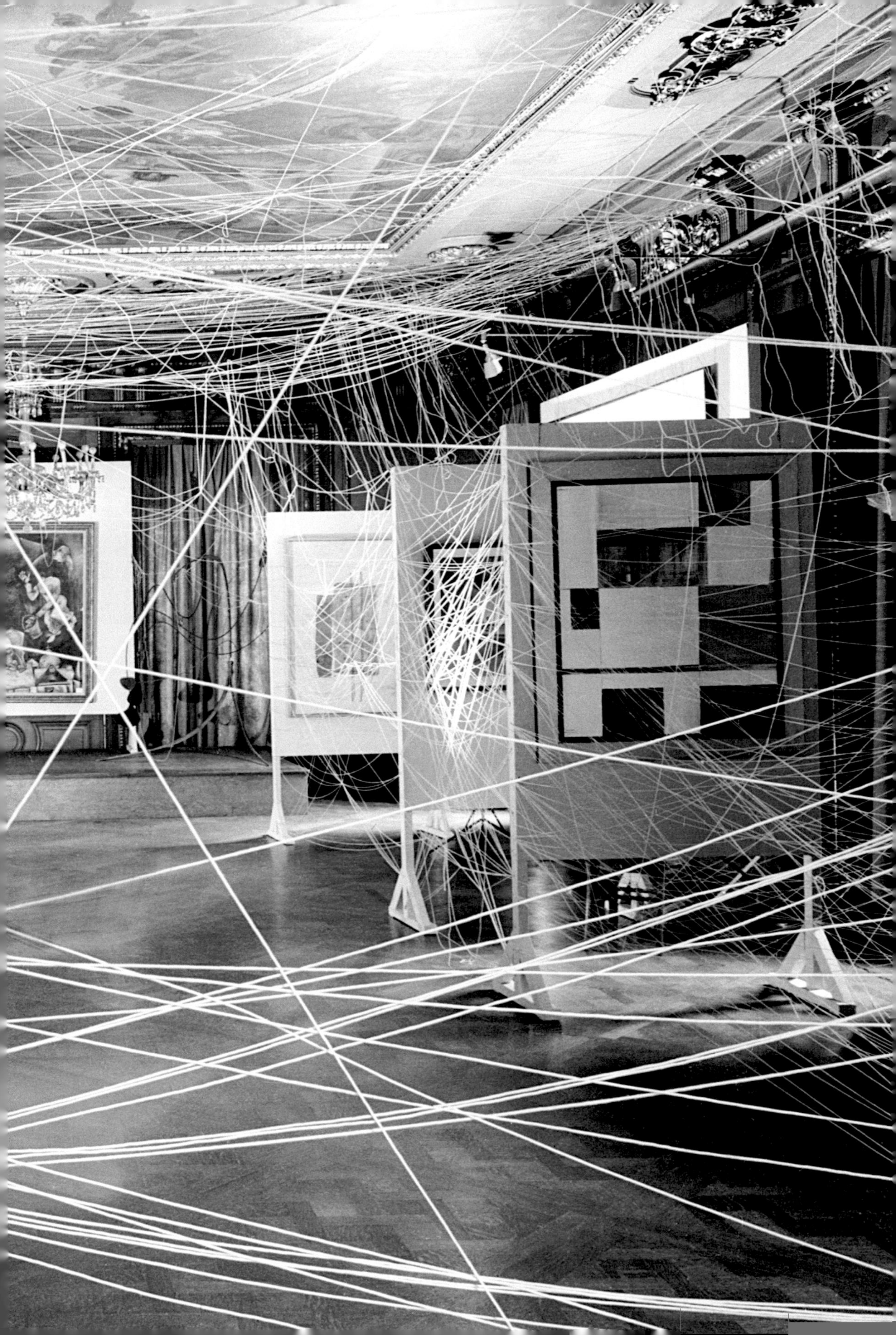

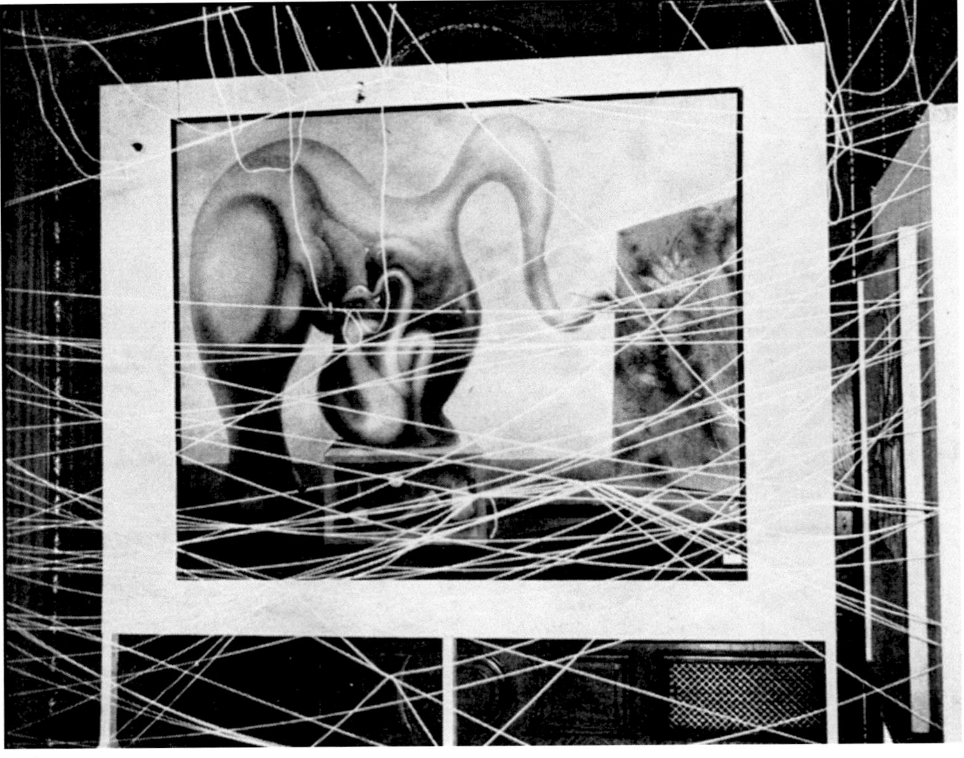

2.21

Installation view of the "First Papers of Surrealism," featuring Max Ernst's *Le Surréalisme et la peinture*, 1942, as installed behind Marcel Duchamp's *Sixteen Miles of String*, Whitelaw Reid Mansion, New York, 1942. As published in *Newsweek*, October 26, 1942.

2.22

Marcel Duchamp with his *Sixteen Miles of String* installation at the "First Papers of Surrealism" exhibition, Whitelaw Reid Mansion, 1942. Photo by Arnold Newman.

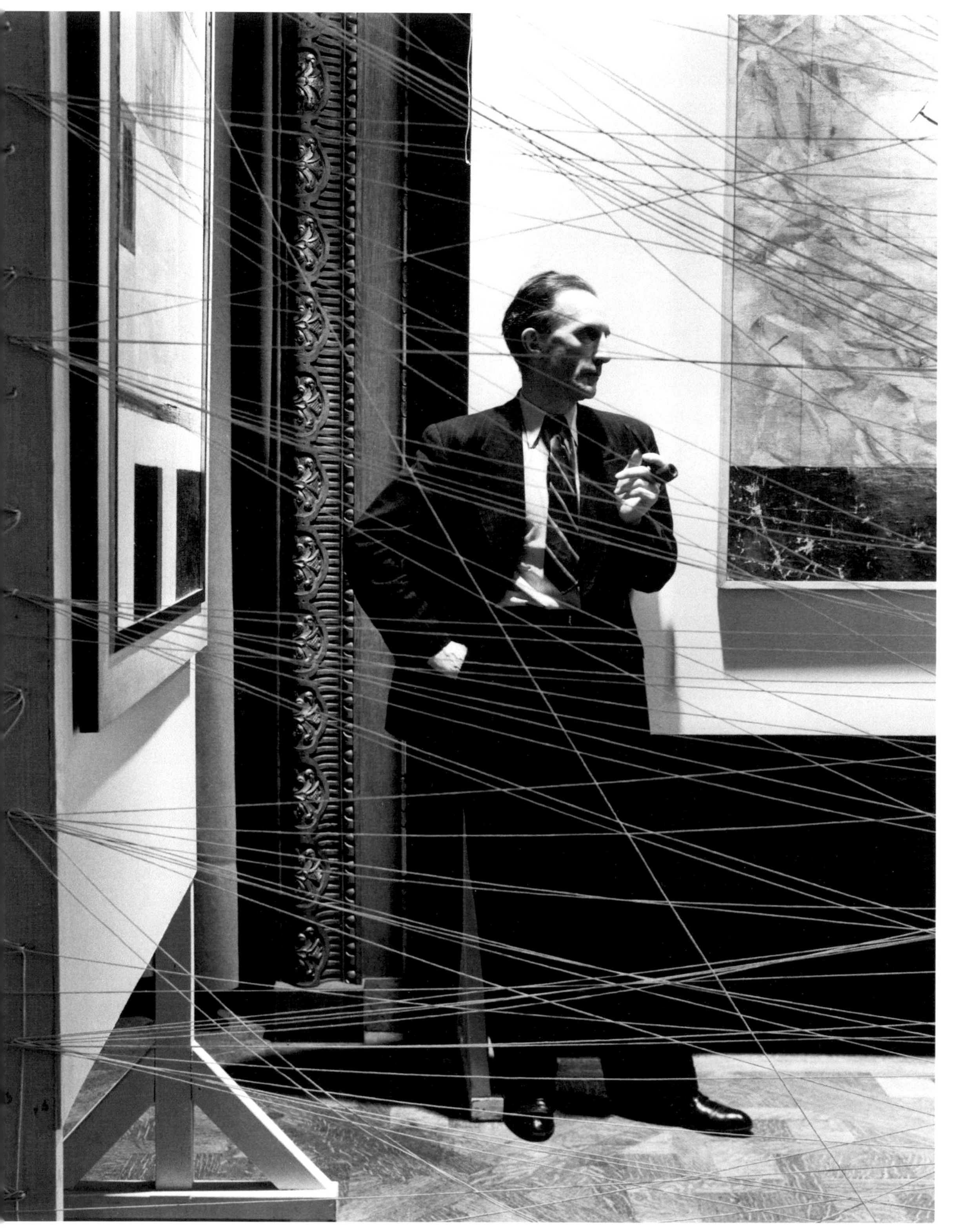

"I MYSELF WILL EXHIBIT NOTHING"

While in many ways "First Papers of Surrealism" in 1942 was less apparently elaborate than the "Exposition internationale du surréalisme" of 1938, both exhibitions contributed a drastic reordering of aesthetic perception and the protocols of institutions for the presentation of art, consequently marking the exhibition itself as a veritable medium of art for Duchamp. To pay attention to the details of both exhibitions is to notice the obvious efforts he took, his consistent commitment to them (he even included two installation views in his 1963 retrospective exhibition and catalog), and the resonance they have with his final, posthumously released work (discussed in the next chapter), regardless of the exhibition's still undermentioned role in critical writing about Duchamp's consideration of the artwork through its display, context, reception, and dissemination.[64] For, however much the spectacular mises-en-scène might appear alien to the supposedly aloof father of the readymade, his involvement in these shows was entirely bound up with his thinking about how artworks—his own and others'—are affected by institutions, frameworks, and distribution, how they find their way into publicness and, eventually, history.

THE BIRTH OF AN AUTHOR

In the background of his curatorial adventures sits Duchamp's creation of an artwork as an exhibition (or an exhibition as an artwork; it is somehow both at once), the *Boîte-en-valise*. He insistently dated it to "1938–42" regardless of the fact that its protracted production actually spanned from 1935 (with his initial conception of the project and preparation for it) through 1936–37 (when the bulk of the actual manufacture took place) to 1941 (when the first deluxe edition of the project was complete).[65] The artist never quite explained the 1938 beginning date or the 1942 end date, and, oddly, no one pressed him to clarify them, even though—despite what he told Pierre Cabanne, Robert Lebel, Calvin Tomkins, and others—there was ample evidence, for example, that the conception and construction of the more than three hundred elaborate boxes containing reproductions in miniature of nearly all of his works began at least three years prior to 1938. This imprecision with regard to fact might have been strategically deliberate, or even decisively conceptual. Duchamp, it seems, wanted to identify the inception of his project (for himself perhaps as much as others) with a series of events that coincided in 1938.

That was the year he took on a role as curator of the Surrealist exhibition in Paris (the inauguration of what would be a three-decade-long commitment to curating for the movement), while 1942, or his claimed completion date, was the year of the "First Papers of Surrealism" show. Formally, the chaotic disorientations that characterized those shows could not be more different from the unassuming and seemingly orderly arrangement of the portable cases filled with facsimiles of Duchamp works that would become the *Boîte-en-valise*.[66] However, if the artist's contribution to the Surrealist exhibitions exposed and shifted the period's normative notion of display and the aesthetic experience proper to it (whether the more dominant bourgeois salon style as manifest in Wildenstein's gallery or the still-nascent white cube that the Museum of Modern Art was advocating at the time), so too did his encased retrospective respond in its own way. Continuing a reflection on the nature of art and the space of display, it rendered explicit the terms and conditions of the art institution's supercharged authority.[67]

More than that, the year 1938 signals a congruence of other, seemingly related events. It marks the moment when Duchamp initiated the miniature reproduction of his 1917 *Fountain*, which was also, necessarily, the moment he returned to questions of the authority of institutions (to decide what counts as art) that his rejected original urinal ineluctably recalled. As we will see, this was also the moment when his initial idea to make a mere flat album of reproductions began instead to take on an exhibition-like configuration.

The boxed form that Duchamp had used previously (on a small scale in 1914 and then in 1934 for the *Boîte verte* [Green Box]) contained photographic reproductions of scraps of notes; they were boxes with loose and disordered contents that ambiguously sat between the two- and the three-dimensional. Had Duchamp continued in this manner, his *Boîte-en-valise* might very well have ended up as another loose-leaf collection of paper and celluloid reproductions in a box. But in the early months of 1938, shortly after taking up the role of exhibition generator-arbitrator for the "Exposition internationale du surréalisme," Duchamp carefully handmade a miniature, three-dimensional replica of the store-bought piece of plumbing he had once called *Fountain*—and this act seems to have changed everything. Practically speaking, Duchamp might well have understood his *Boîte-en-valise* as only having properly *begun* at the moment he realized that it could no longer be the "album" or "book" he had once thought it would be, but would shape itself into a "portable museum" (as he would later describe it). Conceptually speaking, he might well have understood his *Boîte-en-valise* as only having properly *begun* when it could be the kind of place—the kind of exhibition, really—that could (finally) exhibit *Fountain*. Against this background, the (false) dating of the *Boîte-en-valise* takes on particular significance.

The artist returned to the long-lost *Fountain* more than two decades after his defiant 1917 act of "selection." Once he decided to feature it in his retrospective project, he could easily have bought a new urinal from any local plumbing shop and photographed it, as he had done just two years prior for the lost original *Porte-bouteilles* (Bottlerack, 1914). Alternatively, he could have reproduced an extant photograph of the original object, as he would in 1940 with the equally lost snow shovel, *In Advance of the Broken Arm* (1915). After all, he had at least two usable photos of the urinal, having carefully held on to both the Stieglitz image and those little Roché snapshots. And, by 1937, Duchamp had already represented other objects by way of photographic reproduction for use in his envisioned album. Instead he made a sculpture of a urinal (or "remade" the one he had never "made" to begin with, depending on how one looks at things).[68]

Duchamp used the Stieglitz photograph as a reference and turned the *Fountain*'s industrial contours into an odd, miniature, handmade, wire-and-papier-mâché sculpture.

The result was, as Roché described it in his diary, "a little masterpiece of humorous sculpture, the color of a boiled shrimp, with little holes that are so absurd yet done with such care."[69] By the summer of 1938, the artist brought the object, in all its absurdity, to a ceramicist (one of several artisans he would employ for the slow and complicated casting project) to make a mold and porcelain casts for inclusion in the *Boîte-en-valise*. Ironically, Duchamp's modeling of the tiny object introduced a sculptural act never present in the 1917 *Fountain*.

This act of sculpting (based on a photograph, no less) willingly reversed so much of the radical refusal of artfulness embodied by the readymade "original." Literally: the 1917 store-bought urinal had been rotated ninety degrees and signed so as to appear as something like a sculpture for exhibition, but later, Duchamp presented the little white cast *Fountain* in the usual orientation of a urinal when he put it on display in his "portable museum." Showing his first full-size replica of the *Fountain* in a 1950 exhibition organized by Sidney Janis, Duchamp mounted the newly purchased urinal unrotated as well, this one low to the floor and positioned for use, as he put it, by "little boys."[70] The reversal was subtle but noteworthy: if the first version offered a urinal-as-sculpture, these later models seemed to offer a sculpture-as-urinal. In fact, the miniaturized copy was undeniably endowed with the artist's skill and touch ("done with such care"), thus conjuring an auratic object, yet it was reduced to absurdity and based on a mass-produced fixture that was precisely devoid of any aura at its origins.

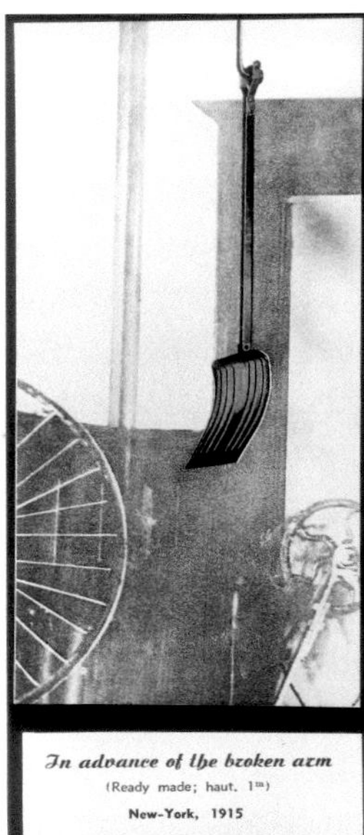

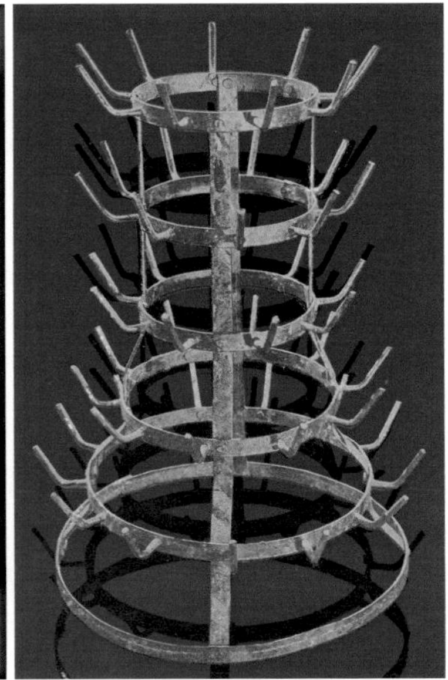

2.23

Marcel Duchamp, reproduction of *In Advance of the Broken Arm* for the *Boîte-en-valise*, c. 1936. Private collection.

2.24

Marcel Duchamp, reproduction of *Porte-Bouteilles* (Bottlerack) for the *Boîte-en-valise*, c. 1936. Private collection.

Whatever else this act might have suggested, it effectively and unequivocally, indeed retroactively, *produced* Duchamp as author—of a pseudonymously signed object that he had not previously directly acknowledged as his own.[71] Since everything in the *Boîte-en-valise*, its viewers understood, was "by or from" Marcel Duchamp (or his alter ego, Rrose Sélavy), to include *Fountain* among his other output was an avowal both surprising and extraordinary. Duchamp thus not only effectively "curated" the first public exhibition of *Fountain*, but he also used it as the first broad public declaration of his authorship of the work.[72] This act is arguably the fundamental precondition for its entrance into the annals of history.

When he remade *Fountain* in 1938, Duchamp dug deep into the past and turned to a memory of the art establishment's authoritative judgment. To replicate the rejected piece of plumbing was to fabricate an object of institutional critique for posterity. The image of *Fountain* stands today as the paragon of Duchamp's assault on the art institution, his most iconic and (perhaps twentieth-century art's) single most influential artwork. But—and we cannot forget this—in 1917, the general public had little way of knowing that R. Mutt was M. Duchamp; the "author" and, correspondingly, the critical potential of the object did not register.[73] *Fountain* simply did not appear on the radar of art history in 1917, nor did it in the few decades that followed.[74]

This fact cannot be overemphasized, since so many of the art historical references to the urinal as the seminal example of Duchampian iconoclasm fail to take note of the work's lack of publicness in its time. They treat *Fountain* as if it were, already in 1917, the art historical icon that it is today and as if one could properly speak of it without considering the fundamental role that its documentation, administration, and re-presentation in an exhibition (all of which could be called, simply, its "curation") have had on its contemporary interpretation. T. J. Demos, for instance, suggests that in the 1930s with the *Boîte-en-valise*, Duchamp was responding to what he calls the "institutionalization of the readymade," adding: "The earlier readymades, such as *Fountain*, had completed their transformation into an artwork in part through an act of institutional recontextualization (from plumbing store to art gallery)," and "by 1938, it was evident that the original strategy of the readymade ... was outmoded."[75] These statements ignore the fact that before Duchamp's completion of the *Boîte-en-valise* in the early 1940s, *Fountain* had never been shown in an art gallery, museum, or institution of any kind, nor had it even circulated as an image apart from its lone appearance in the ephemeral *The Blind Man*, nor, moreover, had it been discussed in any published essay, large or small, as a work by Duchamp. And only two or three of the artist's other readymades had been featured in two or at most three exhibitions (one among them being the umbrella stand area of the Bourgeois Gallery in 1916 and another the 1936 show of Surrealist objects in which the *Bottlerack* sat next to lava rocks, mathematical models, and other nonart trinkets), with virtually no attention accorded them by the press, public, museums, commercial galleries, or in art historical accounts.[76] Not to mention that not a single readymade had been even temporarily shown in a museum, let alone owned by

2.25

Marcel Duchamp, papier-mâché model of *Fountain* and first cast reproduction of *Fountain* for the *Boîte-en-valise*, 1938. Papier mâché covered with paper, metal components; varnished and glazed version with holes marked in black, and signed, each approx. 3.5 × 1.8 inches. Private archives.

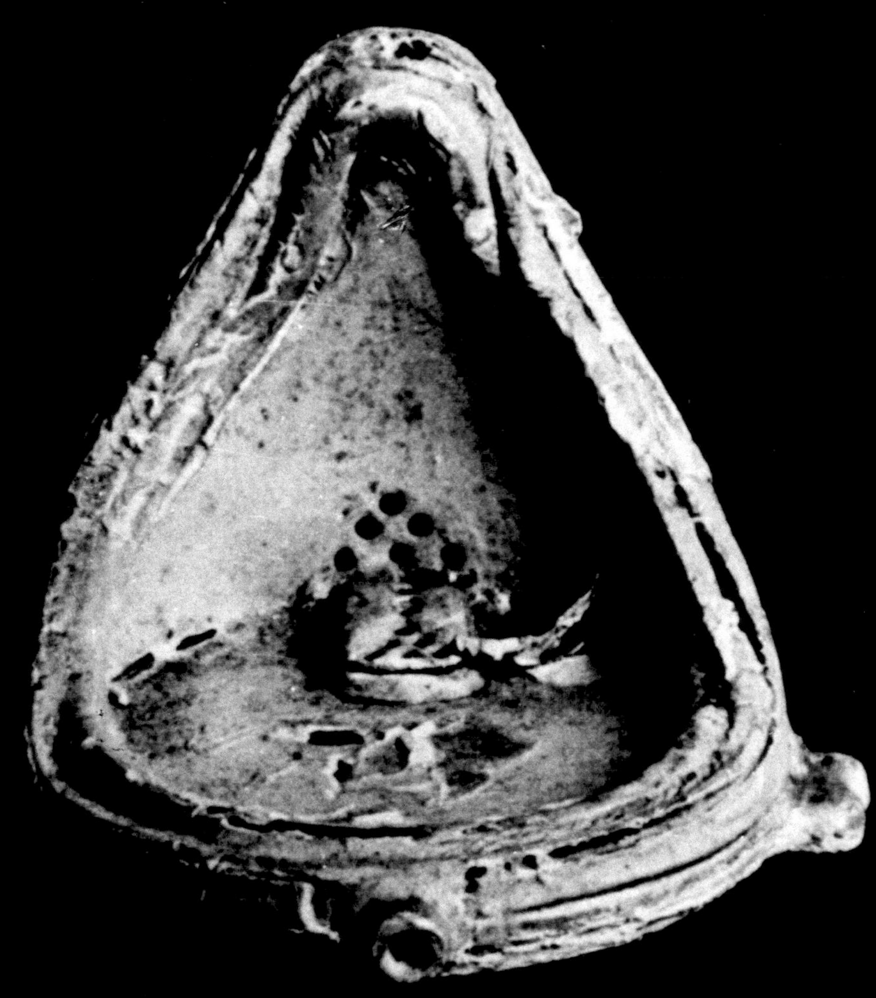

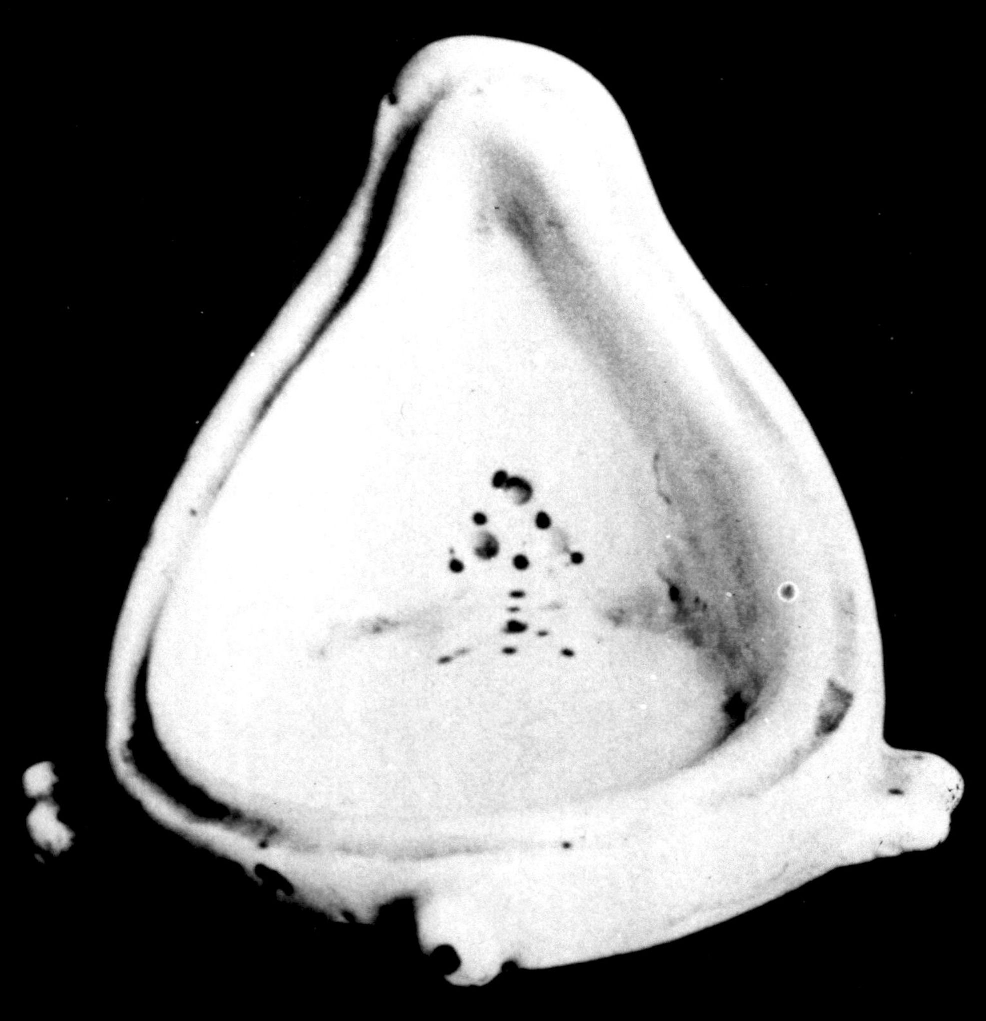

“I MYSELF WILL EXHIBIT NOTHING”

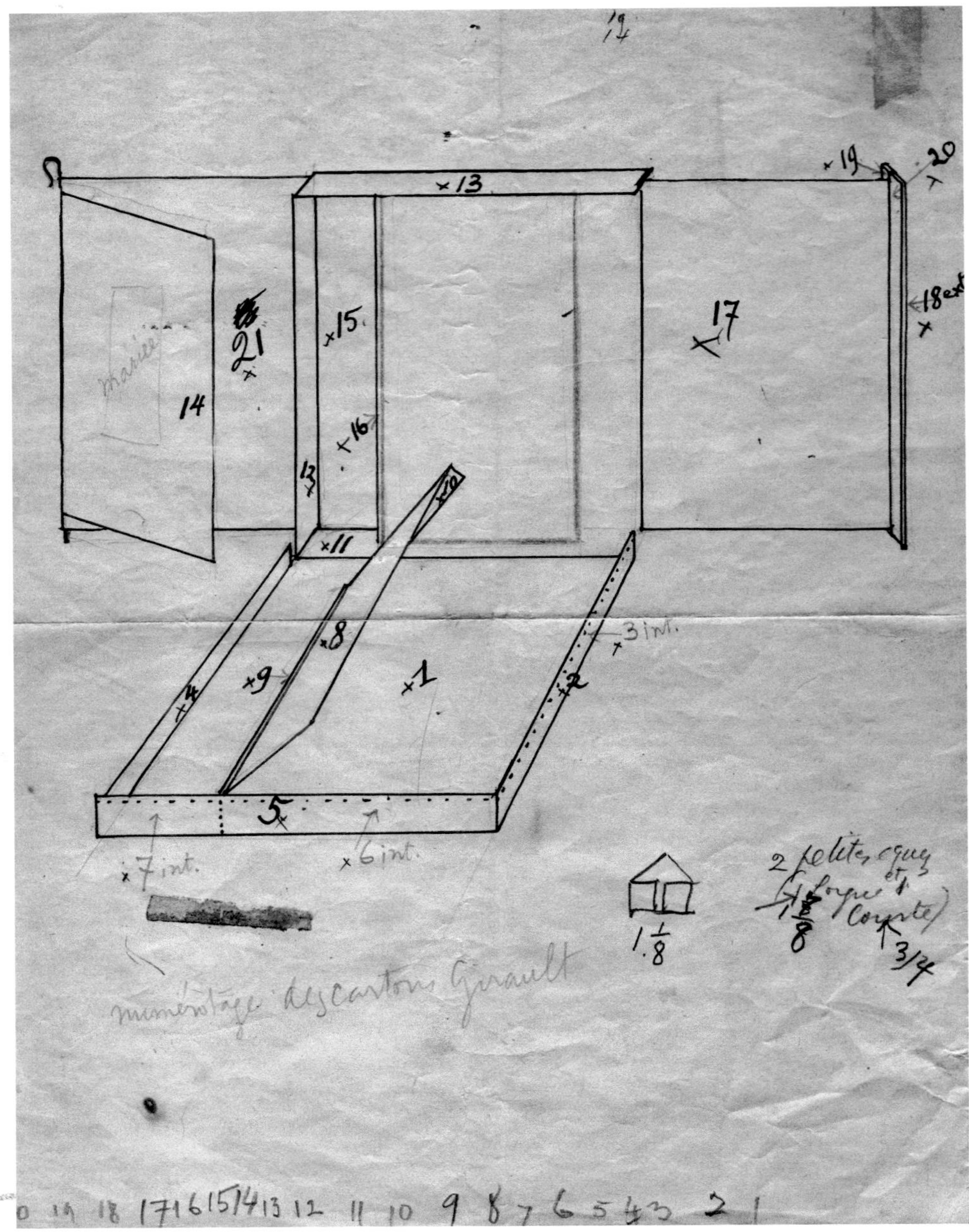

2.26

Marcel Duchamp, plan for assembly of the *Boîte-en-valise*, 1940. India ink and colored pencil on paper, 10 15/16 × 8 7/16 inches. Private archives.

one, until the 1960s. This reality hardly corroborates the vast and early "acculturation" of which Demos speaks. And while he further claims that "the effects of institutionalization on Duchamp's work were more than evident in 1936," historical evidence shows that quite the opposite is the case.[77]

After crafting his miniature *Fountain*, Duchamp went on to make reproductions of two other reduced-size three-dimensional objects (*Air de Paris* [Paris Air, 1919] and *Pliant ... de voyage* [Traveler's Folding Item, 1916]), but the construction of a miniature urinal had already testified to something quite remarkable: Duchamp was no longer thinking of developing his monograph either as anything like an "album," as he had begun describing it in 1935, or even as a simple "boîte" like those he had made previously. While he may not yet have determined the exact nature of the container for the works, in making the tiny sculpted model of the urinal he had already forced himself into a corner—or found a way out, depending on one's perspective. The container for his reproduced corpus, from that point forward, necessarily took on an architecture of a sort, indeed an exhibition-like configuration. The reproduced *Fountain*, along with a whole series of other Duchampian objects, could thus come together in what he would eventually call a "portable museum."

The act was necessarily defiant. An industrially produced urinal had no place in an actual museum (outside of the bathroom, that is). As Duchamp had begun to understand in 1917 (and conditions definitely hadn't changed in the decades that followed), the fate of his *Fountain* would be to remain virtually invisible, *unexhibitable* as such. Given that the original of 1917 had never actually been publicly shown outside his studio, no one had yet seen it in an exhibition until its miniature reconstruction in the *Boîte-en-valise*. In fact, it would reappear in a full-size copy only much later, for the first time in 1950, at the Dada exhibition held at Sidney Janis's gallery in New York, where Duchamp agreed to show a newly store-bought urinal (on which he replicated the faux signature and the 1917 date of the "original"). Two more store-bought versions of *Fountain* appeared in 1953 and 1963, respectively, after which the artist manufactured an edition of eight in 1964 with the Italian gallerist Arturo Schwarz.[78] Thus, as many postwar accounts suggest, Duchamp's most infamous readymade *does* question art's hallowed institutions, but it did so fully only with extraordinary delay, administered through sly curation in Duchamp's retrospective exhibition in a simulated, miniature museum enacted through the *Boîte-en-valise*.

That oft-used Duchampian term *retard*, meaning temporal "delay" or "lateness," is palpably present in the way in which *Fountain* would eventually perform as a work of art (or, simply, become recognized as such).[79] But how far that delay extended and where exactly it manifested are matters of some debate. Thierry de Duve emphasizes the role of Duchamp's photographic documentation of *Fountain*, suggesting: "The urinal's art status was obtained through impeccable, shrewd, and merciless strategy. Once on record, the Richard Mutt case has proven impossible to erase. It has been written into the art history books, which means that it has been registered in the jurisprudence of modern art."[80] So, too, does Dalia Judovitz, who calls Stieglitz's photograph "a strategy of delayed exposure ... [which inscribes] a temporal dimension onto the perception of the urinal," adding that the urinal was "reified through its photographic reproduction, only to come into existence *après-coup,* as a reproduction that replaces the original."[81] Duchamp's creation of photographic documentation and a publication trail is undeniably significant to the operation of its eventual historical inscription, but despite de Duve's suggestion that the photograph *writes* the work "into the art history books," or Judovitz's claim that it is the photographic "reproduction that replaces the original," *Fountain*'s first public appearance in the *Boîte-en-valise* fundamentally contributed to that operation. In the process, it even more radically extended the temporality of what de Duve calls a "delay in porcelain" (playing on Duchamp's reference to his *Large Glass* as a "delay in glass").[82] For the delayed return of the urinal, as a work of "Marcel Duchamp" in a museum, is crucial to the object's belated anti-aesthetic operation. Thus, far from being an intrinsically critical object (performing the questioning of the artwork and institutional context that history now ascribes to it), *Fountain* became so (as Duchamp's various "tests" sufficiently demonstrated) not only because it was selected, rejected, and then photographically recorded, but importantly also because of the *Boîte-en-valise*'s fundamental role in displaying, positioning, contextualizing, and theorizing—in short, *curating*—the readymade for the first time.[83]

MAKING ORIGINAL COPIES, AGAIN

"Approximately all the things I have ever produced" was how Duchamp initially described what he wanted to feature in his retrospective project when the idea first came to him in 1935.[84] It was immediately after his production of the *Green Box*, and he quite quickly began to focus on what he was then calling his "albums," which should represent his artistic output in the way that his boxes of notes represented his ideas. He first mentioned the project in a letter dated March 1935 addressed to Katherine Dreier, ending with a plea for Dreier's discretion regarding his project since, as he warned, "simple ideas" are "stolen easily."[85] No one beat him to the punch, although it is curious to imagine Duchamp nervous that someone else might actually want to embark on such an idiosyncratic project before him. He then commenced preliminary labor on the series of personal "albums" he had in mind.

Although he did not provide Dreier with more details at that point, Duchamp was thinking of making something on the order of the *Green Box*, except, this time around, he had in mind to make loose, paper-backed copies of nearly all of his artworks instead of replicas of his notes. By the end of 1935, the quiet administrative labor that would be the cornerstone of the project had begun: Duchamp drew up lists of all the artworks he had ever made and noted the names of their owners. He wrote to many of them, asking to have professional black-and-white photographs taken of selected paintings, glass works, and objects; he made cross-continental voyages to examine the condition of works and record titles, dates, measurements, and the exact color of the works in

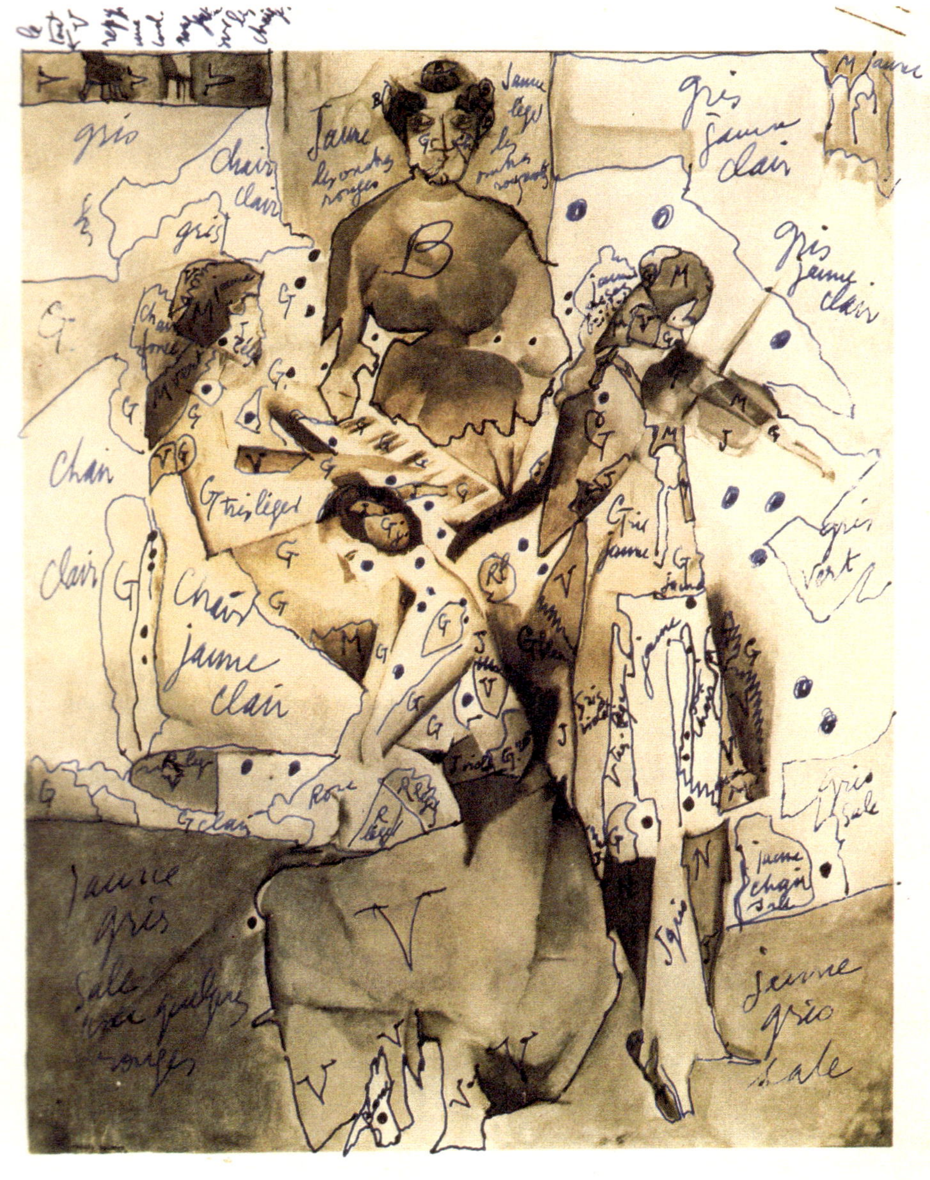

2.27

Marcel Duchamp, annotated reproduction of *Sonata* for inclusion in the *Boîte-en-valise*, c. 1935. Collotype with color notations, 9¼ × 7¹⁄₁₆ inches. Private archives.

public and private collections. He even repurchased or borrowed some pieces to make the required detailed notes about them. The lists were marked with various shorthand codes (e.g., a "Ph" next to the title if the necessary photograph had been taken), and the cost of each step was duly noted.[86] The painstaking labor, like that for his previous note replication job, was deeply invested in the praxis of the archive.

The meticulous listing and recording prepared the way for the period from 1936 to 1940 when Duchamp set in motion the actual reproduction. In a few cases, when he was invited to contribute an illustration to a book or magazine, he took advantage of the request by asking the printer to run off an extra three-hundred-plus copies of the illustration so it could be included in his own album.[87] For the greater part of the reproductions, however, Duchamp opted for complex and labor-intensive methods and avoided burgeoning technologies such as color photography, which could not yet faithfully reflect the colors of the originals. One suspects that he might not have employed such a method even had it proved exact enough. After all, he eschewed other more frequently used and expedient processes, including offset lithography (which he had just previously used for the *Rotoreliefs*), in favor of collotype printing coupled with pochoir coloring (which he had employed most extensively in the reproductions for the *Green Box*).

For many of the chosen pieces, Duchamp made what he called *coloriages originaux* (original colorings)—prototypes containing multitudes of annotations and meticulous lines dividing the image into small colored sections, so as to painstakingly simulate the exact colors and details of the painting or glasswork on which they were based. With these prototypes as color guides for the pochoir production, a group of printers would deploy as many as thirty different, specially designed zinc foil stencils, masks, and templates for any one image, manually applying successive chromatic washes until the print was transformed into a satisfactorily faithful reproduction. In other cases, for instance for his cracked glass pieces, the artist individually numbered and marked each one of the cracks on a photographic version so that these could then be methodically replicated. It would take years to complete all of the copies that Duchamp had in mind, a fact the artist took in stride. Thus, as Ecke Bonk makes clear, to speak of "reproductions" (or even the artist's other generic term for them, "items") hardly conveys the intricacy of the handwork involved.[88] The process was precise and painstaking, often, paradoxically, requiring more labor than the originals had.

Some reproductions were later separated out from the set, individually signed, and even given a "seal" of officialness through the addition of a gummed paper French revenue stamp (a thirty-centime *timbre fiscal*) employed in legal matters to authenticate official documents.[89] There can be little doubt that Duchamp's method, as much as its ambiguous result—somewhere between the handcrafted and the mechanically reproduced—was crucial to the subversive operation of the project. As authorized "original" copies of otherwise original artworks (including some, like the readymades, that were themselves, at their origins, mass-produced industrial *copies*), the *Boîte-en-valise*'s replicas and their manufacture both enacted and evidenced the artist's complex questioning of the aesthetic original.[90]

By 1938 the enterprise of copying his artworks via pochoir reproduction alone had considerably changed. At that time, as we know, Duchamp had taken up the role of curator for the Paris "Exposition internationale du surréalisme" and worked nearly simultaneously on making three-dimensional miniature replicas of a selection of his readymades. It was a watershed moment. Much about the "album" necessarily shifted from that point on; Duchamp would retrospectively date this as the beginning of the project.

He selected a total of sixty-nine of his artworks to be reproduced in one form or another, and, given the magnitude of the edition he envisioned, he often made slightly more than the necessary 320 copies of each. The task was only finished in 1941, a production period, as it happens, overlapping with France's entry into war, surrender to Adolf Hitler, and subsequent occupation.[91] Despite this, Duchamp worked undaunted. As his production jottings so faithfully record, the long list of specialists called upon included more than a few photographers, print shops, typesetters, and pochoir studios as well as several carpenters, glassblowers, china craftsmen, ceramicists, and suitcase makers, among others.[92] The various components for the *Boîte-en-valise*'s "items," as Duchamp explained to Cabanne, had then to be smuggled by the artist (under cover of an official document used by cheese dealers, provided by a friend in the business) through occupied France and across the demarcation line to the "free-zone" in Marseilles, from where he was able to leave for the United States.[93] The artist's "cheese transportation" was spread over several months in the spring of 1941 and enabled the safe passage of the material for some fifty of his boxes.[94] The effort, and all of the various ad hoc records that he used to administrate it, present a picture quite at odds with the frequent treatment of the project as mere idle distraction or negligible endeavor. Indeed, Duchamp's persistence in seeing each step through, despite the attendant hardship, material restraints, and difficulty in transporting supplies through the early months of the occupation, confirm his fierce commitment to the project.

With more than three hundred copies of each of the selected items complete and the assembly of the first few cases under way, a subscription form for preorder announced the imminent availability of a "box of pull-outs" filled with "faithful reproductions ... the ensemble of which (~~69~~ 68 items) represents the almost complete work of Marcel Duchamp between 1910 and 1937."[95] The work's title, by that point, was also set: *De ou par Marcel Duchamp ou Rrose Sélavy* (From or by Marcel Duchamp or Rrose Sélavy) had been imprinted between the four thin wood slats that formed an "M" and graced the lid of the work. The descriptive nomination *Boîte-en-valise* accompanied this official title on advertising literature and became, in the years that followed, the most common shorthand name for the piece.

Quite contrary to the order form's deceptive modesty regarding what was on offer, the so-called "box of pull-outs" opened to reveal an elaborate collapsible interior structure. Hand-colored reproductions of certain works were affixed to loose sheets of black cardboard and sheltered in an inner compartment; reproductions of select glass works on transparent celluloid sheets, also hand-colored, were held erect or pulled along sliding rails; a photographic image of *Why Not Sneeze, Rrose Sélavy?* (1921) was

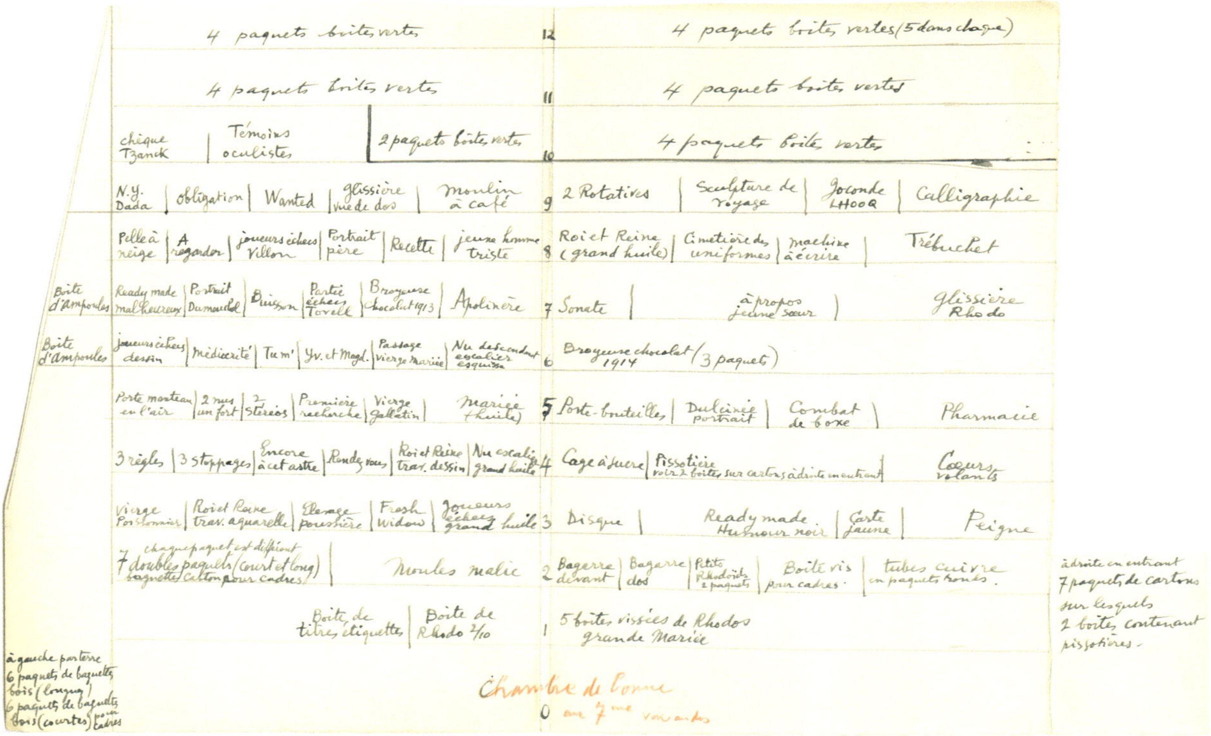

2.28

Marcel Duchamp, accounting of the costs involved in making the *Boîte-en-valise*, from the box labeled "Documents épisodaire (chronologique) Jeux de mots," undated. Philadelphia Museum of Art Archives: Alexina and Marcel Duchamp Papers, series XII, subseries A, box 36.

2.29

Marcel Duchamp, diagram-inventory of the arrangement of various elements for the *Green Box*, *Boîte-en-valise*, and other projects stored in a room on the same floor as his apartment-studio, 11 rue Larrey, Paris, early 1940s. Philadelphia Museum of Art Archives: Alexina and Marcel Duchamp Papers, series XII, subseries A, box 36.

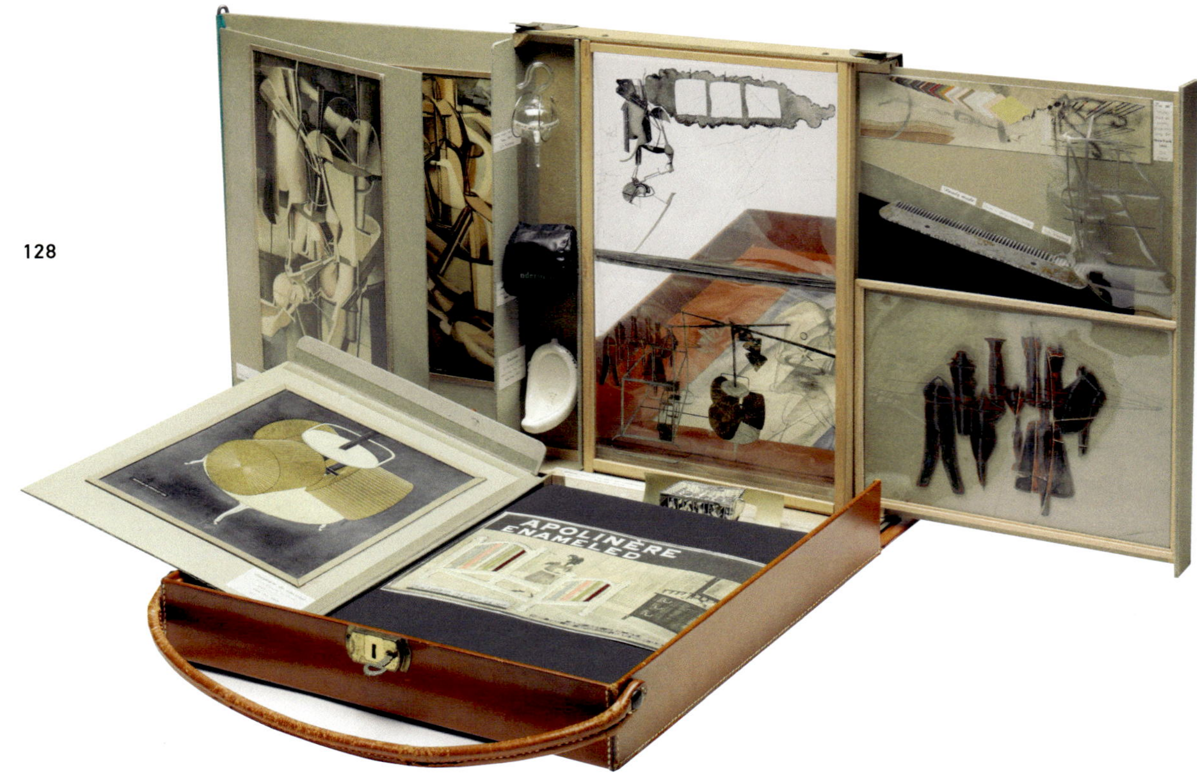

2.30

Marcel Duchamp, deluxe edition n° 0/XX of the *Boîte-en-valise*, made 1943. Brown leather valise with handle containing sixty-nine miniature replicas and printed reproductions and one original, *Virgin (No. 2)*, 1938, hand-colored collotype; valise (closed): 16 × 14¾ × 4¼ inches. Philadelphia Museum of Art: The Louise and Walter Arensberg Collection.

affixed to a little block of plaster, giving the image a three-dimensional quality; there was an accordion-folded image of *3 Stoppages étalon* (3 Standard Stoppages, 1913), and mounted, three-dimensional, palm-size versions of the urinal, glass ampoule of Parisian air, and typewriter cover. In the end, the majority of the miniature museums contained sixty-eight facsimile works (the sixty-ninth piece broke often and was left off later editions), all carefully labeled and neatly organized.

The first few cases were completed at the end of 1941, shortly after the artist arrived in the United States, and the remainder were produced slowly but steadily over the course of subsequent decades. The assembly of the boxes and the arrangement of all the parts took time, and Duchamp, the ultimate precision worker, operated slowly. After the first valises were complete, he employed the help of various friends (including Joseph Cornell, Xenia Cage, and finally his stepdaughter Jacqueline Matisse) to put together the later boxes. They were assembled in seven groupings or "series," each with minute differences. The entire edition of more than three hundred would not, in fact, see its completion until several years after the artist had died. Having devised a project so intricate and time-consuming, with an edition size so large, Duchamp probably knew that his boxed monographs would keep on coming from the makeshift factory he had set up even after his departure from this world.

In addition to three hundred standard copies of the project, Duchamp produced twenty deluxe models. Nearly all of these are distinguished by a reddish-brown leather valise, as opposed to the merely cloth-covered boxes of the standard models, and by the inclusion of a signed "original" work of art. The artist made the deluxe models first, each destined for a specific friend or select patron, and each was numbered and personalized with their name. In many of them a "coloriage original"—one of the prototypes hand-colored by Duchamp used for the creation of the *Boîte-en-valise*'s reproductions—served as the so-called original item. If the *Box of 1914* had inaugurated the then-yet-unnamed concept of the artist edition—an artist-produced object in multiple copies—Duchamp gleefully expanded the notion with the *Green Box* and the *Boîte-en-valise*. The more than three hundred copies of those latter boxes (as compared to the five of the *Box of 1914*) seem practically infinite, as was their potential to reach a wide and unforeseeable audience.

One cannot ignore the irony in the position of Jacques Villon, Duchamp's elder brother, on the question of such a large edition of artworks. In a letter to Jean Fautrier from the 1950s about what Fautrier called his own *originaux multiples* (original multiples)—a series of lithographs produced from 1949 to 1953 in editions of three hundred that were individually hand-colored by Fautrier and others—Villon complained, "To make three hundred copies, it's too much! Every work must retain some originality, something personal. To multiply it excessively devalues it."[96] The comment suggests Villon's likely disapproval of his youngest brother's various projects toward the multiplication of the artwork. But for Duchamp and, later, Fautrier, the devaluing of a certain idea of painting was a deliberate intention of their respective practices. As Fautrier made quite clear:

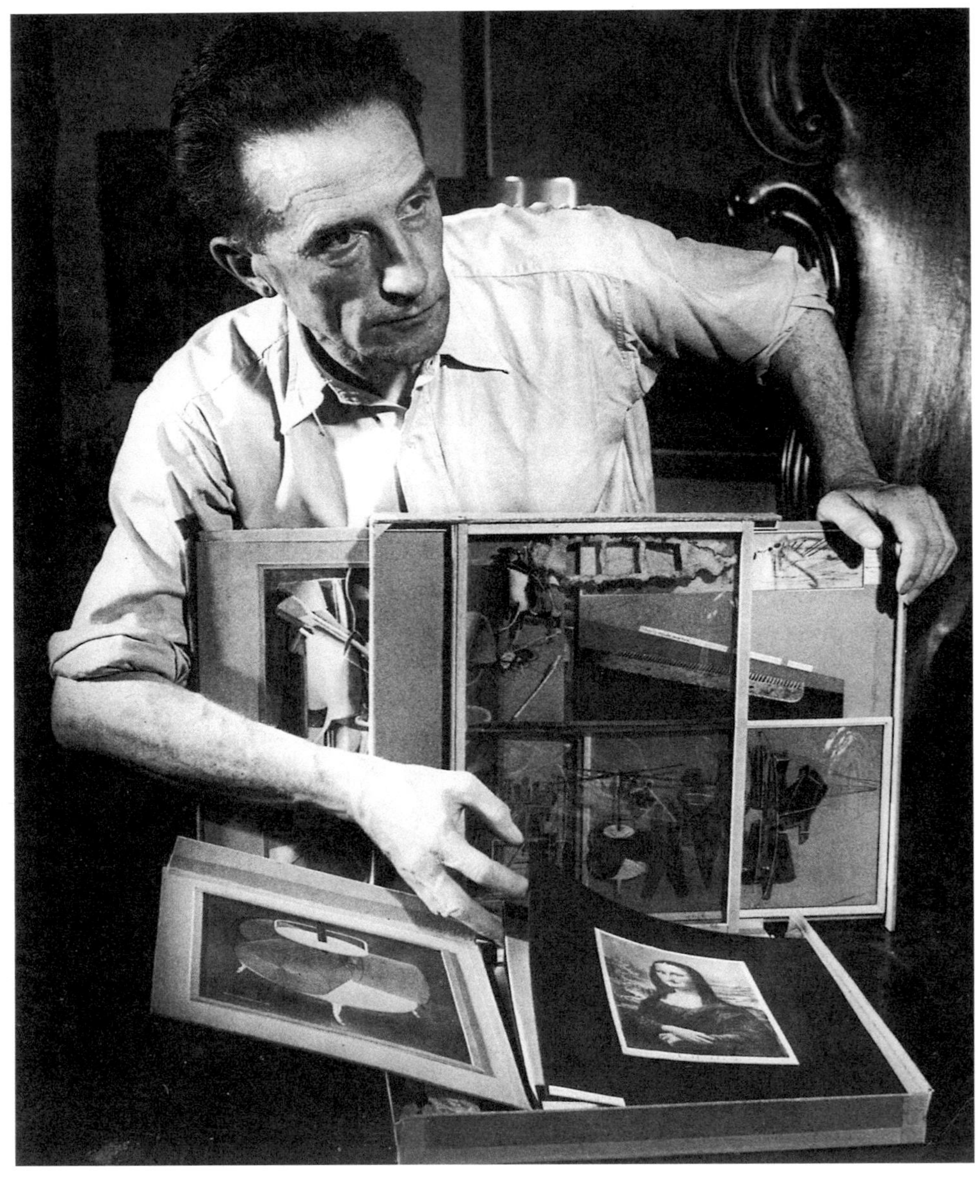

2.31

Marcel Duchamp demonstrating the display possibilities of the *Boîte-en-valise*. Photographer unknown. Published in *Time*, September 7, 1942.

> In any case, as long as the painter limits himself exclusively to a stale technique, exhausted by four centuries—*oil paint*—he will end up with a precious object whose magic has ceased to move us—*the unique work*—with all the disgust it already elicits, for us, at its sacred and ephemeral touch; the work that, through its rarity, pushes against the forward-moving tide of an industrial culture, by its rarity, leads to the sort of historical showplace—*the museum*—where it displays itself in a void.[97]

As the *Boîte-en-valise* exposes the fault lines menacing the ontological stability of the work of art through its sheer numbers (continuing what the previous boxes had begun), one cannot forget that this procedure—as Fautrier vocally acknowledged—also necessarily implicates the museum, at that time still very much a bastion of the artwork as an authentic, authored, auratic, singular original.[98] The idea and functioning of the museum, that "dated showplace," is inseparable from Duchamp's critical project with the *Boîte-en-valise*, as we shall see.

A MUSEUM THAT IS NOT ONE

"Instead of painting something new," Duchamp declared, "my aim was to reproduce the paintings and objects I liked and collect them in as small a space as possible. I did not know how to go about it. I first thought of a book, but I did not like the idea. Then it occurred to me that it could be a box in which all my works would be collected and mounted like in a small museum, a portable museum, so to speak."[99] Benjamin H. D. Buchloh has read the work accordingly:

> All of the functions of the museum, the social institution that transforms the primary language of art into the secondary language of culture, are minutely contained in Duchamp's case: the valorization of the object, the extraction from context and function, the preservation from decay and the dissemination of its abstracted meaning. ... [With it Duchamp] also changes the role of the artist as creator to that of the collector and conservator, who is concerned with the placement and transport, the evaluation and institutionalization, the display and maintenance of a work of art.[100]

This reading is right, though I would add some caveats. A bit like Duchamp's characterization of the readymade as "a work of art that is not one," the *Boîte-en-valise* could be said to be a museum that is not exactly one: not a reproduction of the museum in the traditional sense, even in miniature, it is also not like the museum maquettes that Duchamp might have seen on display in "Muséologie," the exhibition devoted to modern museum techniques at the 1937 Exposition Universelle. Everything about the *Boîte-en-valise* renounces the awe-inspiring scale and physical presence of the museum. The tentative structure, with its Lilliputian dimensions and wobbly frame, seems to always remain in the process of constituting itself through an almost infinite variation

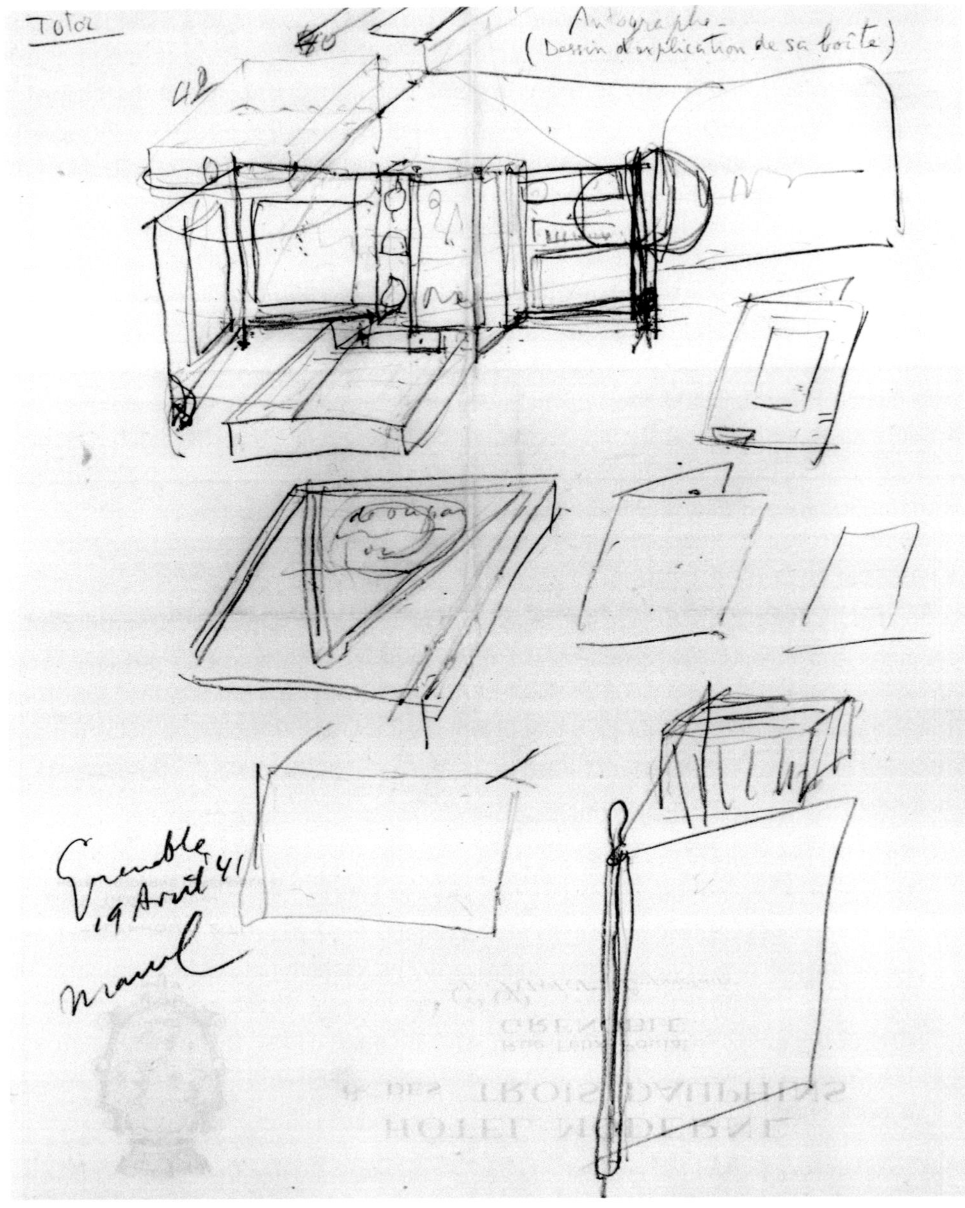

2.32

Marcel Duchamp, explanatory diagram for the *Boîte-en-valise*, 1941. Pencil on notepaper of the Hôtel Moderne & des Trois Dauphins, Grenoble, France, 10½ × 7⅝ inches. Carlton Lake Papers: University of Texas at Austin Archives.

and mutation of presentation—thus hardly akin to the commanding facades and spaces typical of the museum. If a "small museum" does come to mind, it is because the *Boîte-en-valise*, in fact, both invokes *and* contravenes, mimics *and* critiques, the museal.

In this, the *Boîte-en-valise*'s inclusion of "walls"—even if collapsing, movable, and wobbly—was no negligible detail. The functioning of its interior structure is suggested in a sketch Duchamp made for Roché in April 1941. This informal explanatory drawing of his box, laid out on the back of stationery of Grenoble's Hôtel Moderne, conveys with excited lines and axonometric views the various interior components of the complex object that Roché was soon to receive. Little of the specificity of the miniature artworks to be mounted appears; the drawing attends much more to the mobile mechanisms and changeable armatures of display—its exhibition walls, as it were. And yet what is clear in the drawing, as in the presence of the *Boîte-en-valise* itself, is that to expose the art, one needs to unpack the framework; to view the exhibition, one needs to handle the pieces and (re)organize the display. Exhibition walls, in other words, there were, even if unfixed and malleable.

The unfolding of the *Boîte*'s presentation and the sequence of viewing the elements in its "exhibition" are left entirely to the viewer's discretion. And if its boxed structure, complete with handle, suggests that movement and destabilization lay at the core of the project, Duchamp's multiple retrospectives-in-traveling-cases also displaced the museum's function of decontextualizing and sheltering the work of art from the outside world. The *Boîte-en-valise* exposes both the "museum" and its artworks to the impure and ordinary space of the everyday. It was another way of abolishing the distance separating the artwork from the viewer and the world. In its structural aspects alone, then, the exhibition space offered up by the *Boîte-en-valise* reveals a project that is not about constituting an actual museum, even on a small scale; instead it is a "museum" that announces itself as one even as it performs its own negation.

In reality, a museum's defense of visuality is fundamental. As Donald Preziosi has succinctly put it, museums "situate all objects within viewing spaces that evoke and elicit a proper viewing stance and distance. Artworks are spaced, arranged, and composed so as to permit the taking up of proper stances: position for the subject."[101] Duchamp's portable museum must be considered in the context of the performative operation incited in the "visitor" relative to his museum-on-the-move. The miniaturization of the individual works demands that vision be made haptic—in the handling of objects, in the opening and closing of lidded compartments, in the rubbing of fingers across the black creased folders of reproductions, in the sliding and movement of celluloid versions of glass works, in the invitation to touch the palm-size urinal, glass ampoule, and typewriter cover—rejecting the pure ocularcentrism typical of the museum. This is entirely fitting given that elsewhere in his oeuvre Duchamp had repeatedly suggested that there could be no seeing that is not carnal or embodied and therefore unruly, even if he knew too well that, in an institutional context, there is no seeing that is not directed, ruled, and prescribed by the authority of the institution itself.

Duchamp's aim in his early optical experimentation was, as Krauss argues, "to corporealize the visual, restoring to the eye (against the disembodied opticality of modernist painting) that eye's condition as bodily organ, available like any other physical zone to the force of eroticization."[102] One might say, further, that the "disembodied opticality of modernist painting" was, for Duchamp, implicitly tied to the modern gallery and museum. The tactile, mobile looking elicited by the *Boîte-en-valise*, however different from the darkened, disorienting, or twine-ensnarled installations Duchamp had by that point created for the Surrealist exhibitions, nevertheless like them shattered the typical institutional distance between body and vision.

This confrontation of corporeality and museological looking, self and object of display, is emblematized in two "original" works created in 1946 to accompany two of the deluxe versions of the *Boîte-en-valise*. The valise given to Brazilian artist Maria Martins, Duchamp's lover at the time, housed the composition *Paysage fautif*, consisting of an abstract and amorphous "wayward landscape" formed by a spattering of seminal ejaculate on Astralon backed by black satin. Artist Roberto Matta's valise, on the other hand, was augmented with an untitled work composed of four small clumps of head, axillary, and pubic hair affixed to the reverse side of a piece of Plexiglas that displayed a lightly sketched bodily form. One might ask what it means to archive and museify the body in such a way, exhibiting such traces of the mundane (not to say base) fact of corporeality.[103] These works, given to two of Duchamp's close confidants, slyly expose still more of the traditional museum's tenets, at once demystifying the artist (for artistic "mastery" and museal worthiness seem irreconcilable with this most banal functioning and the secretions of the body) while simultaneously evoking the kind of fetishism evident in the display of objects in such eminent French institutions as, for example, the Louvre, where the object's presentation and treatment evoke a cult of the relic. To seriously consider the *Boîte-en-valise*, then, is to ponder the way in which it not only undermines and redirects the purely visual, but also insists on the libidinal and corporeal as both matter of, and point of access to, the museum.

Yet can it be overlooked that there is something decidedly amiss in the *Boîte-en-valise*'s curatorial/archival system? Duchamp understood that a number of seemingly innocuous institutional details play a role in how and what we see in an exhibition: from the information on labels and wall texts to the title of the exhibition and overall organization in a space. His curated grouping of works follows no perceptible logic of chronology, medium, or theme. The selection is arbitrary, the scale of miniaturization variable. Each reproduced item bears a museum-type label with a standardized typeface, and the typical uniform classificatory information accompanies each piece (dimensions, media, collection information). But Duchamp's labels refer to the "original" works (actually still extant or not), no matter that these are distinctly at odds with the reduced dimensions and posterior reproduction of the specimens on offer in the *Boîte-en-valise*. He thus played the museum's game—but he played it his way.

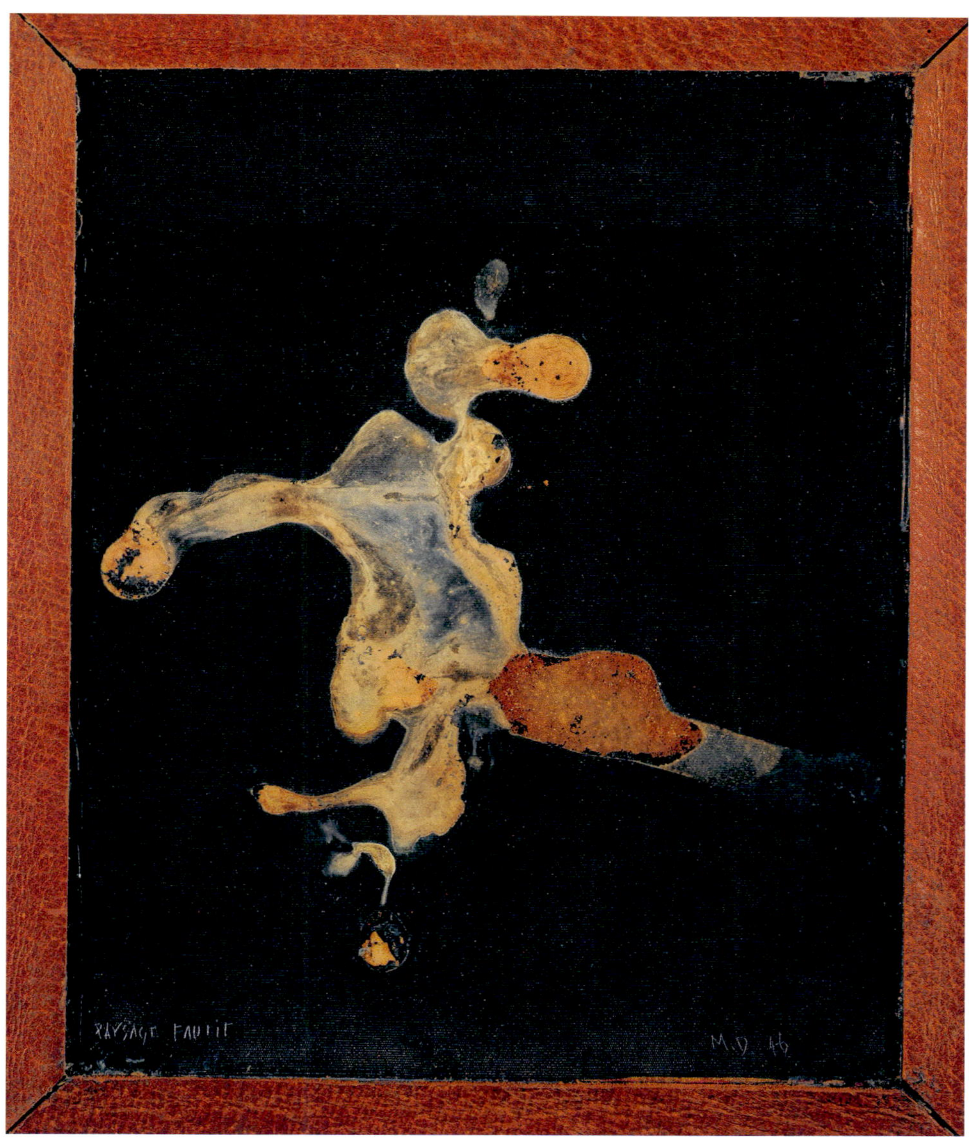

2.33

Marcel Duchamp, *Paysage fautif* (Wayward or Faulty Landscape), 1946. Original artwork from the *Boîte-en-valise*, deluxe edition n° XII/XX. Seminal fluid on Astralon backed with black satin, 8 ¼ × 6 ½ inches. The Museum of Modern Art, Toyama, Japan.

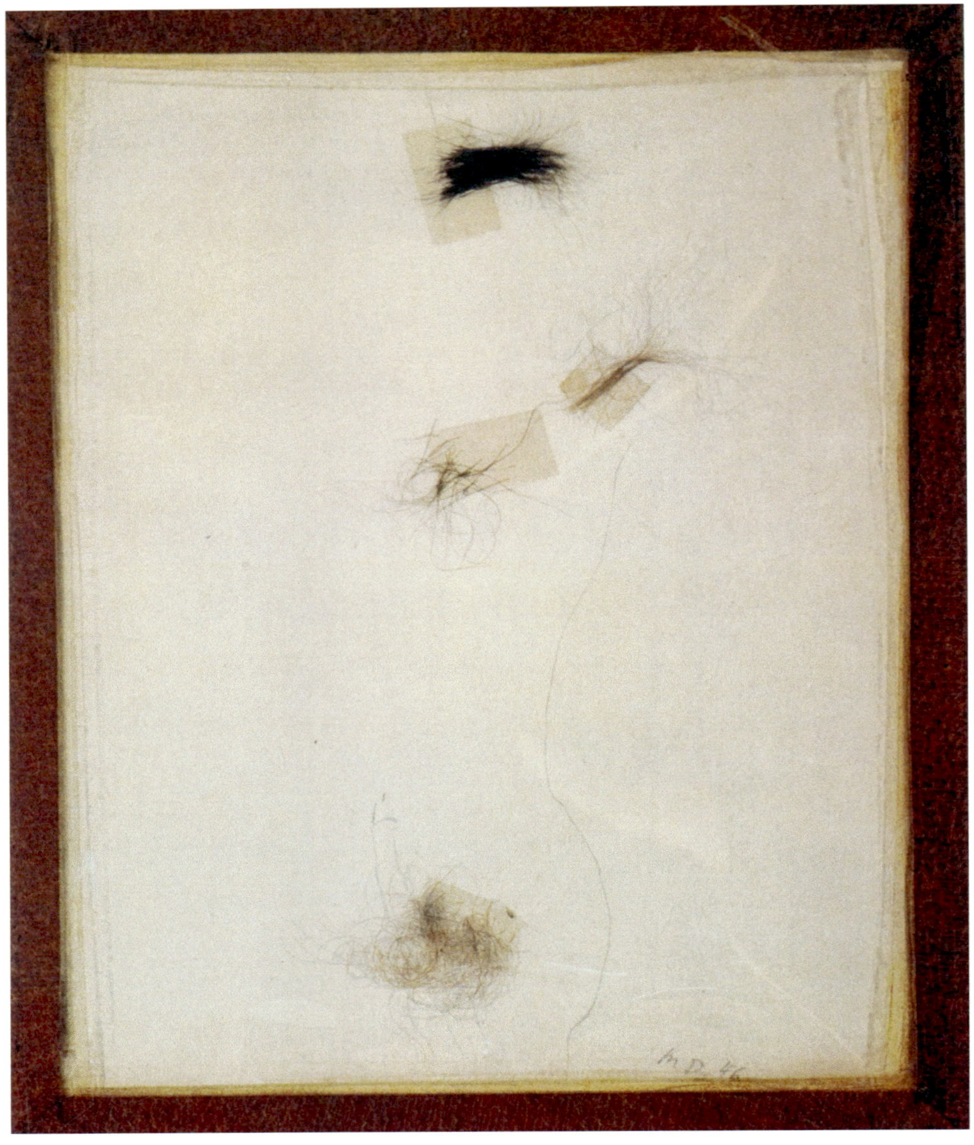

2.34

Marcel Duchamp, *Untitled*, 1946. Original artwork from the *Boîte-en-valise*, deluxe edition n° XIII/XX. Head, axillary, and pubic hair taped to paper, mounted on cardboard, with pencil additions, 7 ½ × 5 ¾ inches. Private collection.

2.35 (following pages)

Marcel Duchamp, annotated labels related to the *Boîte-en-valise*, mounted and included in the box labeled "Documents épisodaire (chronologique) Jeux de mots," undated. Philadelphia Museum of Art Archives: Alexina and Marcel Duchamp Papers, series XII, subseries A, box 36.

Over the years, this artist-as-maker-of-his-own-museum repeatedly revised his collection and its museum labels. To map the movement (or loss/destruction) of the featured originals, he made his own administrative guide: he pasted a copy of each of the work labels from the *Boîte-en-valise* onto a thick mat board backing, revising the information by hand so as to keep his collection information completely up to date. When possible, he corrected and remade labels for the boxes that were still to be assembled. For instance, when in 1954 a great number of Duchamp's works gifted by the Arensbergs finally went on view at the Philadelphia Museum of Art, he noted the change on his mat board and designed new labels for his reproductions to document the transfer. Along the way he also added selected works to his miniature museum (from sixty-eight in the first valises to eighty-three in the last series), including newly made as well as older pieces. Duchamp even tried to keep track of which of his works were *not* represented in the *Boîte-en-valise* and, at one point, thought of including this list in a certain number of the deluxe versions of the box. The idea was abandoned, but nevertheless he did create an administrative list of the "not represented." Duchamp housed it, along with his mat board of annotated labels, in a cloth-covered box that holds no fewer than thirty items—including supply and object inventories, chronologies, methodical accounting statements listing the cost of almost every aspect of the reproductive project, the price and location of each of the deluxe valises, and payment records—each element elaborating the labor (but also the bureaucracy) that accompanied the early preparation for the *Boîte-en-valise*. It was an archive for the portable museum as archive.

It thus becomes clear that Duchamp, a notary's son, had again transformed himself into a kind of (museum) bureaucrat, one whose careful adherence to the institution's protocols and whose standardized, completely up-to-date labels form a part of his effort to underscore the museum's regulative function. Yet an ambivalence pervades Duchamp's operation, for his lists, while strangely and fastidiously complete, are (like his various other notes) also scribbled on the backs of worn receipts and torn pieces of cardboard, so that, like so much else in the entire enterprise, they both marshal and contravene the signs of a museum's authority and administration.

Moreover, just as the inclusion of *Fountain* in the *Boîte-en-valise* announced Duchamp as its author, constructing the conditions for it to be seen as a work of art, so too did his copies of his oeuvre exhibited in a miniature museum act as if they were somehow already museum-worthy—a gesture of incredible hubris, or prescience, depending on how one looks at things. Duchamp first conceived his retrospective project in the mid-1930s, at a moment, it should not be forgotten, when the first large-scale Parisian retrospectives of Pablo Picasso and Henri Matisse hailed them as definitive "masters" of the twentieth century, and when Christian Zervos, founder of France's premier journal of modern art *Les Cahiers d'Art*, published the first lush catalogues raisonnés of these two painters, seeming to confirm their status as art historical icons.[104] The art world, then, had two declared modernist heroes with no place for Duchamp; the truth is, he hardly featured in art histories at that time. Thus the cheekiness of his gesture should

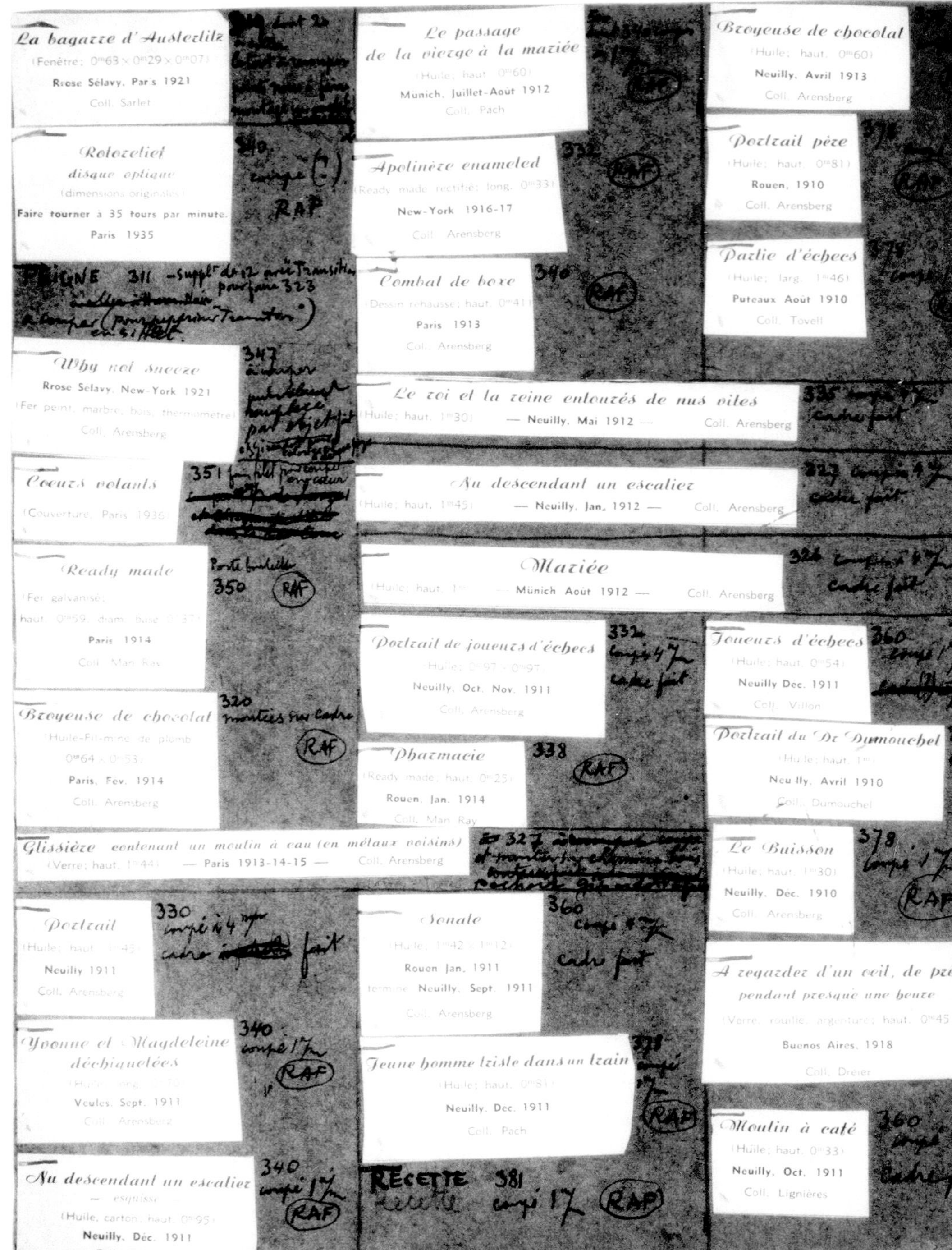
La bagarre d'Austerlitz
(Fenêtre; 0m63 × 0m29 × 0m07)
Rrose Sélavy, Paris 1921
Coll. Sarlet
Rotorelief
disque optique
(dimensions originales)
Faire tourner à 35 tours par minute.
Paris 1935
Why not sneeze
Rrose Sélavy, New-York 1921
(Fer peint, marbre, bois, thermomètre)
Coll. Arensberg
Coeurs volants
(Couverture, Paris 1936)
Ready made
(Fer galvanisé;
haut. 0m59, diam. base 0m37)
Paris 1914
Coll. Man Ray
Broyeuse de chocolat
(Huile-Fil-mine de plomb
0m64 × 0m53)
Paris, Fev. 1914
Coll. Arensberg
Glissière contenant un moulin à eau (en métaux voisins)
(Verre; haut. 1m44) — Paris 1913-14-15 — Coll. Arensberg
Portrait
(Huile; haut. 1m45)
Neuilly 1911
Coll. Arensberg
Yvonne et Magdeleine
déchiquetées
Veules, Sept. 1911
Coll. Arensberg
Nu descendant un escalier
— esquisse
(Huile, carton; haut. 0m95)
Neuilly, Déc. 1911
Coll. Arensberg
Le passage
de la vierge à la mariée
(Huile; haut. 0m60)
Munich, Juillet-Août 1912
Coll. Pach
Apolinère enameled
(Ready made rectifié; long. 0m33)
New-York 1916-17
Coll. Arensberg
Combat de boxe
(Dessin rehaussé; haut. 0m41)
Paris 1913
Coll. Arensberg
Le roi et la reine entourés de nus vites
(Huile; haut. 1m30) — Neuilly, Mai 1912 — Coll. Arensberg
Nu descendant un escalier
(Huile; haut. 1m45) — Neuilly, Jan. 1912 — Coll. Arensberg
Mariée
— Münich Août 1912 — Coll. Arensberg
Portrait de joueurs d'échecs
Neuilly, Oct. Nov. 1911
Coll. Arensberg
Pharmacie
(Ready made; haut. 0m25)
Rouen, Jan. 1914
Coll. Man Ray
Sonate
(Huile; 1m42 × 1m12)
Rouen Jan. 1911
terminé Neuilly, Sept. 1911
Coll. Arensberg
Jeune homme triste dans un train
(Huile; haut. 0m81)
Neuilly, Déc. 1911
Coll. Pach
RECETTE
Broyeuse de chocolat
(Huile; haut. 0m60)
Neuilly, Avril 1913
Coll. Arensberg
Portrait père
(Huile; haut. 0m81)
Rouen, 1910
Coll. Arensberg
Partie d'échecs
(Huile; larg. 1m46)
Puteaux Août 1910
Coll. Tovell
Joueurs d'échecs
(Huile; haut. 0m54)
Neuilly Dec. 1911
Coll. Villon
Portrait du Dr Dumouchel
Neuilly, Avril 1910
Coll. Dumouchel
Le Buisson
(Huile; haut. 1m30)
Neuilly, Dec. 1910
Coll. Arensberg
A regarder d'un oeil, de prè
pendant presque une heure
Buenos Aires, 1918
Coll. Dreier
Moulin à café
(Huile; haut. 0m33)
Neuilly, Oct. 1911
Coll. Lignières

La mariée mise à nu par les célibataires
Munich, 1912
Coll. Candel
Médiocrité
Neuilly, 1912
Coll. Breton
Joueurs d'échecs
Neuilly, 1911
Coll. Arensberg
2 nus : un fort et un vite
Neuilly, 1912
Le roi et la reine traversés par des nus vites
Neuilly, 1912
Coll. Arensberg
50 cc air de Paris
Paris, 1919
Coll. Arensberg
Élevage de poussière
New-York, 1920
Le roi et la reine traversés par des nus vites
Neuilly, 1912
Coll. Arensberg
Fresh Widow
New-York, 1920
Vierge
Munich, 1912
Coll. Arensberg
... pliant, ...de voyage.
New-York, 1917
Stéréoscopie à la main
Buenos Aires, 1918
Rotative plaques verre
New-York, 1920
Encore à cet astre
Neuilly, 1912
Coll. Arensberg
Ready made
New-York, 1917
Glissière
(Vue de dos)
Fountain
New-York, 1917
Paris 1913-14
Coll. Dreier
9 moules malic
Paris, 1914
Coll. Roché
New-York 1915-23
Coll. Dreier
New-York 1918
Coll. Dreier
Paris, 1913
Coll. Arensberg
Munich, 1912
Coll. Gallatin
Cadres bois pour Man Rhodo
Rotative plaques verre
RAF

not be underestimated. At the time, no one was interested in organizing a survey show of Duchamp's oeuvre (one would not come for another few decades), so curating his own—and in miniature reproduction no less—would likely have been seen at the time as both precipitous and preposterous.[105]

Even the artist's most fervent supporters seem to have been uncertain about *Boîte-en-valise*'s function, choosing to see it in terms of the past oeuvre it represented rather than as a new critical work in itself. As early as 1936 Julien Levy wondered: "Are [Duchamp's] present activities indicative of a new advance? Or is he merely 'writing his own memoirs'?"[106] Likewise Walter Arensberg—owner of many of the original artworks upon which the reproductions were based—received a *Boîte-en-valise* in the mail and found it "difficult to know exactly what to say of such an epitome of a life work."[107] And during his seemingly indefatigable discussions with Duchamp, Pierre Cabanne hardly asked about it. One can imagine his reasoning: Why devote much energy to probing Duchamp about a valise filled with reproductions when the "originals" were already being discussed?[108] In short, the three hundred or so retrospectives-in-a-box were seen as a curious enterprise of self-citation, a "vacationing in past time," or were paid no attention at all.[109]

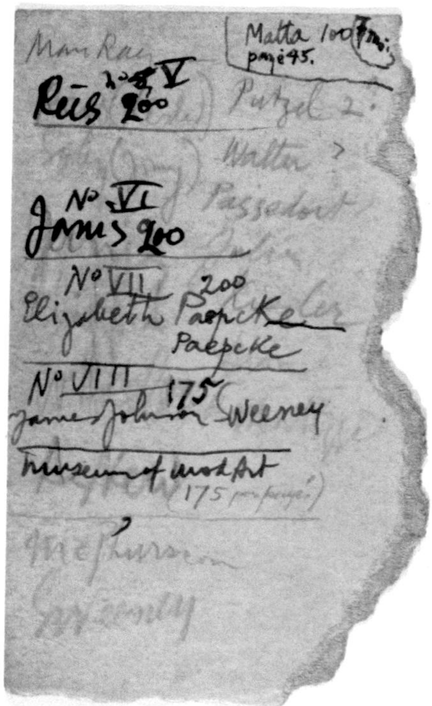
Man Ray
Matta 100 frs.
page 45.
Reis 200
Putzel 2
No VI
James 200
No VII 200
Elizabeth Paepcke
Paepcke
No VIII 175
James Johnson Sweeney
Museum of Mod Art
(175 par page)
McPherson
Sweeney

2.36

Marcel Duchamp, notes recording who purchased various deluxe editions of the *Boîte-en-valise* and accounting of how much they paid, included in the box labeled "Documents épisodaire (chronologique) Jeux de mots," undated. Philadelphia Museum of Art Archives: Alexina and Marcel Duchamp Papers, series XII, subseries A, box 36.

Yet one "museum" retrospective may have helped beget another. Martha Buskirk rightly stresses the relationship of the *Boîte-en-valise* to the artist's efforts to conserve the majority of his works in the hands of a small group of devoted patrons and aid them in the donation of these works to a few major museums. Especially, she adds, "given the degree to which it framed—sometimes quite explicitly—the installation of the Arensberg collection in the Philadelphia Museum, which opened in 1954, and subsequent exhibitions of his work, such as those in 1963 in Stockholm and Pasadena, where aspects of the displays paid direct homage to the arrangement in the box."[110] Ecke Bonk, who so minutely studied and elaborated the details of the monographic project, also sees it in relation to the destination of Duchamp's larger corpus at the Philadelphia Museum of Art. In his account:

> It was not until 1954, when the Arensberg collection was installed in the Philadelphia Museum of Art, with Duchamp's assistance, and opened to the public, that it became possible to accomplish with the originals what had already been achieved in miniature, in the *Boîte*. The permanent installation in the museum, centering on the *Grand Verre* (Large Glass), is a 1:1 equivalent of the folding, miniature ensemble. At a stroke, Philadelphia had become the center around which gravitated all the copies of Duchamp's portable museum, only one-third of which had been issued, in homeopathic doses by 1954.[111]

The mistake would be to perceive the *Boîte-en-valise* as an unequivocal manifestation either of Duchamp's antipathetic position with regard to the museum *or* of his deep longing and strategic efforts to find his way into it, either of which, by itself, would fail to sense the critical tension that lies at the heart of the project as a whole.

Understanding this critical tension might counter the reading of the *Boîte-en-valise* as ultimately compromised, like the readymades before it, as a truly radical project:

> In the work's attempt to dissolve reification within the very medium and the site where they are produced, in the necessity to mimetically anticipate its subjection to ideology by inscribing itself as precisely as possible into those very systems that determine its historical status, it seems to fail to maintain any claim for autonomy and rupture in favor of a complacent, melancholic, and passive contingency upon the conditions of rule it set out to disrupt.[112]

Buchloh's damning appraisal suggests that Duchamp's *Boîte-en-valise* ultimately failed, that any questioning that might be presumed from it could only be rectified by the more potent anti-institutional gestures of the generation that came after, those of Marcel Broodthaers most notably.[113] No matter the remarkable critical force (and aesthetic or intellectual merit) of the projects of Institutional Critique that followed in the *Boîte-en-valise*'s wake, and in some cases even thanks to it, few if any of those later projects can be said to have entirely escaped the "conditions of rule" of the institution, or even necessarily to have meant to do so. As if anticipating this, Duchamp evoked the museum already in an interview in 1915, observing that the "so much misunderstood" Futurist manifesto, which demanded the destruction of the museum, was meant "in symbol only."[114] Maybe he thought that the Futurists could not have been serious about such a proposal while continuing to make easel paintings. Or perhaps Duchamp knew that they did not truly mean it because they must have known, as he did, that to destroy the institution or even simply to insist on remaining outside of it would also mean to remain outside of discourse, reception, and perhaps even eventually art historical accounts. Moreover, it would mean not bringing actual change to an institution that, however lambasted, was nevertheless of interest to the Futurists as much as to Duchamp (and later to Broodthaers and others after him). Perhaps for this reason Duchamp never made any grand claims regarding the museum's destruction, and that fact was not a complacent, passive, or melancholic admission of his own inevitable defeat. Instead he worked to expose the walls that held up its narratives, that disciplined its visitors and contents alike, that confirmed its authority, that displayed its judgments. His was a slow movement toward, around, and within the museum, all the better to reveal its most deeply entrenched premises.

PHOTOGRAPHY AND THE COMMODITY

With the *Boîte-en-valise* Duchamp pushed the implications of reproduction, already raised with the *Box of 1914,* to an extreme. Like his earlier boxes, the *Boîte-en-valise* uses photography for the seemingly most neutral, most inartistic of purposes: for documentary reproduction, in this case of works of art.[115] Yet Duchamp's anonymous "documentation" here is often dubious, at once announcing and evacuating its role of witness to a truth. Given that some of the photographs "represent" artworks that, at the time of making the *Boîte-en-valise*, were no longer extant, photography—and the unreliability that Duchamp built into it—became the perfect emblem for the duplicity of the copy.

Duchamp's involvement in photography in the early 1910s and '20s has long conveyed the impression of a playful lack of seriousness, a kind of goofing around with a photographer friend and his camera. But to look closely is to notice that in almost every instance he used photography (either of his own making or that of his accomplice Man Ray) to literalize the potential duplicity at its heart. From the barren landscape suggested by the layer of dust covering the *Large Glass* in Man Ray's and Duchamp's collaborative photograph *Élevage de poussière* (Dust Breeding, 1920), published with the subtitle *Vu prise en aéroplane* (View Taken from an Airplane), to the numerous portraits of Duchamp in drag as Rrose Sélavy or as the spokesmodel for *Belle haleine—Eau de voilette* (Beautiful Breath—Veil Water) in Man Ray's glossy shots or on labels affixed to perfume bottles, for Duchamp the photograph is the recurrent site of contradiction, deception, visual troubling.

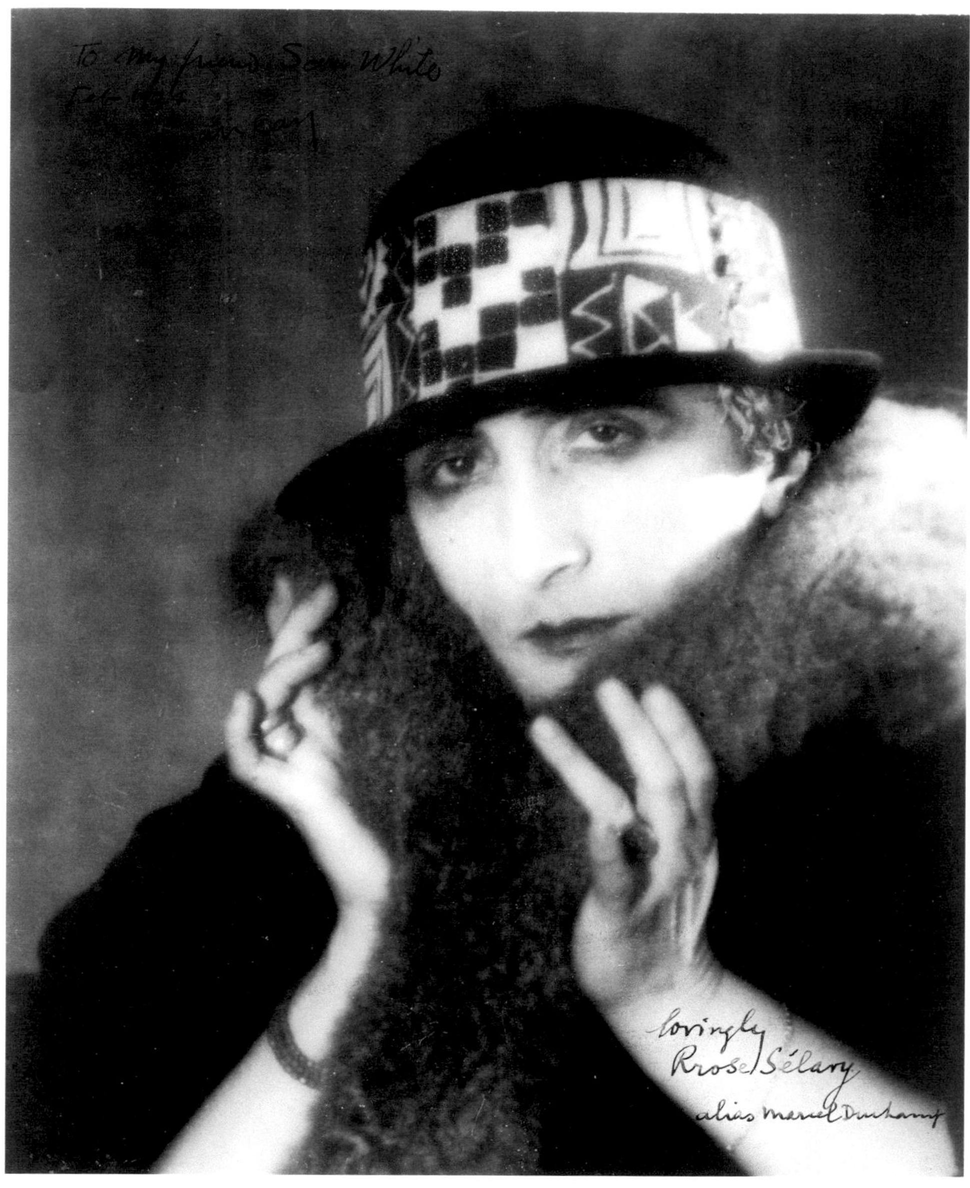

2.37

Marcel Duchamp, *Marcel Duchamp as Rrose Sélavy*, c. 1920–21. Photograph by Man Ray, retouched by Marcel Duchamp. Gelatin silver print, image and sheet 8½ × 6 13/16 inches. Philadelphia Museum of Art: The Samuel S. White 3rd and Vera White Collection, 1957-49-1.

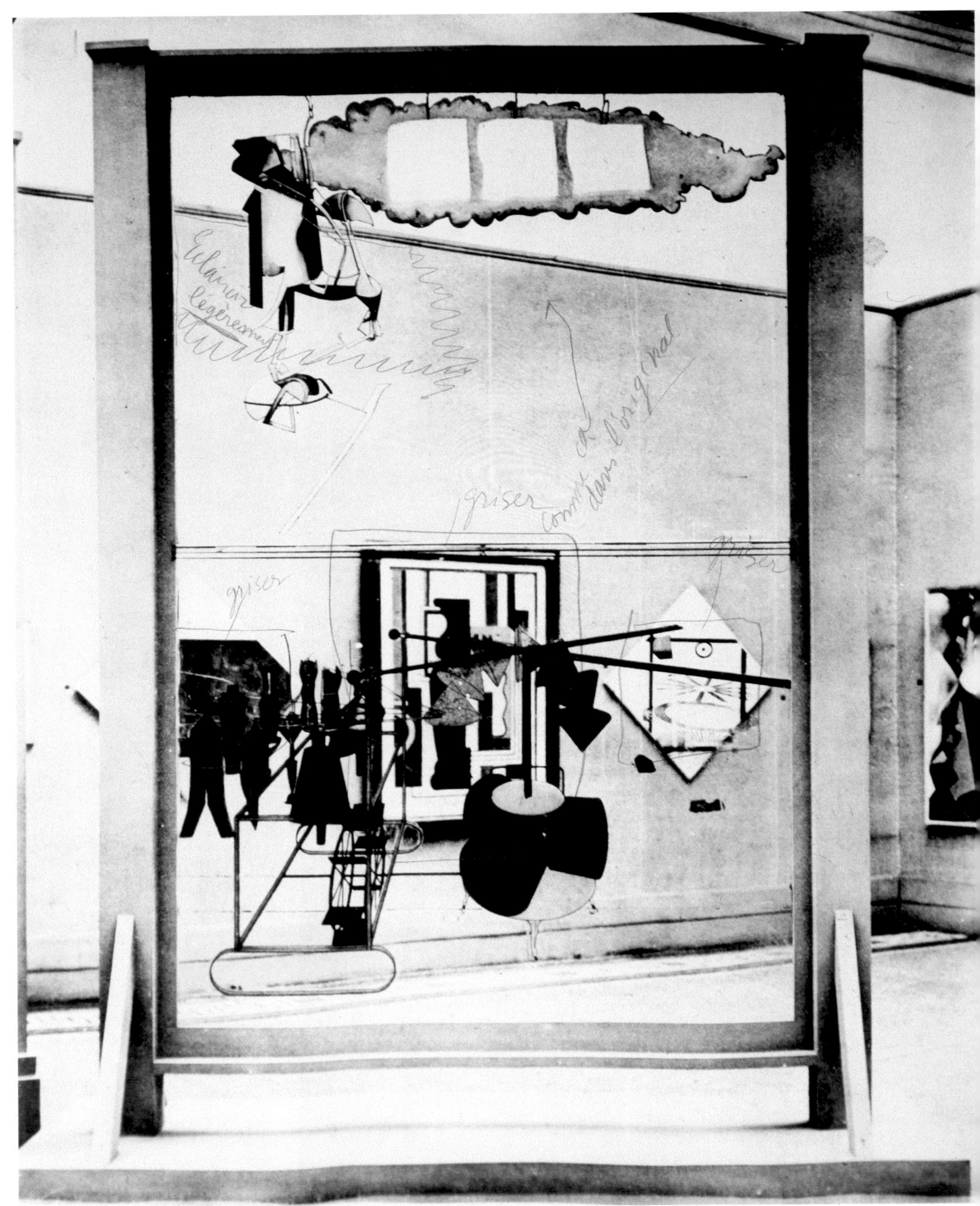

Eclaircir légèrement
griser
comme dans l'original
griser
griser

CHAPTER 2

While preparing the *Green Box*, Duchamp had Man Ray deftly airbrush a soft veil over the reflection of paintings (by Piet Mondrian, Fernand Léger, and Kazimir Malevich) that appeared, a bit too distractingly, in the only existing photograph of the upright, unbroken *Large Glass* as temporarily installed at a Brooklyn Museum exhibition.[116] The corrective airbrushing (which, as Man Ray's multiple attempts at the task reveal, was no easy matter) was amply justified in the interest of rendering the *Large Glass*'s mechanical forms legible; the effect, however, is in keeping with Duchamp's recurrent use of photography against the grain of its oft-claimed truth. In particular, the *Boîte-en-valise*'s reproductions that are based on photographs resist credibility. The image of *Bottlerack* shows false shadows, images of a hatrack, bicycle wheel, and coatrack are visibly retouched, the strange plaster and photographic representation of *Why Not Sneeze, Rrose Sélavy?* stands in a no-man's-land between the second and third dimension, images of *Sculpture de voyage* (Sculpture for Traveling, 1918) or *Readymade malheureux* (Unhappy Readymade, 1919) include blatantly fictive hand-drawn additions, and his rendition of the *Monte Carlo Bond* includes a special gray varnish to create a false "aged" patina.[117] What you see in Duchamp's photographic reproductions is seldom what was actually there.

2.38 (left)

Marcel Duchamp, retouching instructions for the *Large Glass* as installed in 1927 at the Brooklyn Museum of Art and rephotographed for reproduction in the *Green Box*, 1934. Private collection, New York.

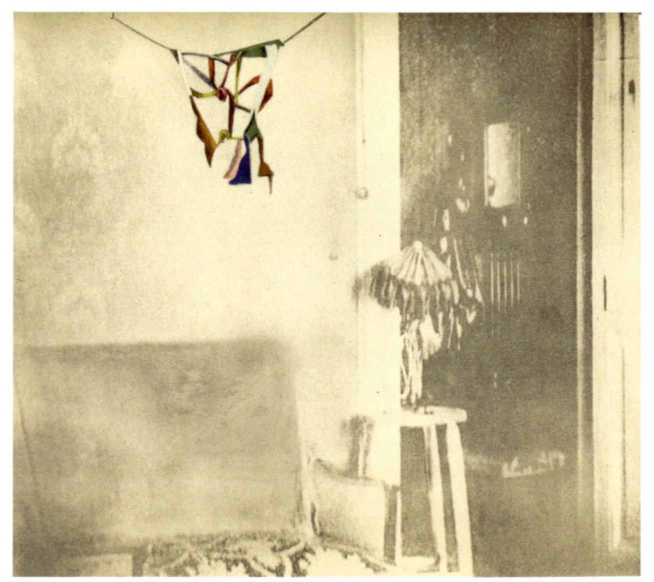

2.39

Marcel Duchamp, reproduction of *Sculpture de voyage* (Sculpture for Traveling) for the *Boîte-en-valise*, c. 1940. Private archives.

In 1940, in order to represent *Trébuchet* (Trap, 1917) in the *Boîte-en-valise*, Duchamp turned to one of the snapshots Roché had taken in his studio (see figure 2.1). He enlarged the image and studied every curve of the by-then-lost coatrack that he had once nailed to the floor of his atelier. After whiting out the object entirely, Duchamp had a tiny but extraordinarily precise line drawing made of the coatrack that exactly replicated the photographic detail he had covered over. Rendered in dry, mechanical lines, the deliberate handwork observed here is exponentially greater than the process of selection that had transformed the store-bought item into an artwork in the first place.[118] Then, through a time-consuming and careful process of hand-coloring, collaging, and repeat printing, he turned the newly drawn *Trébuchet* into something like a photographic "document" (he would later employ variants of this process in images of the suspended snow shovel, hatrack, and bicycle wheel). The result, a new order of image—neither fully photographic nor fully drawn nor fully documentary—introduced a slippage of terms and categories. If photography was so long seen as emulating painting, the father of the readymade effectively reversed this relationship.

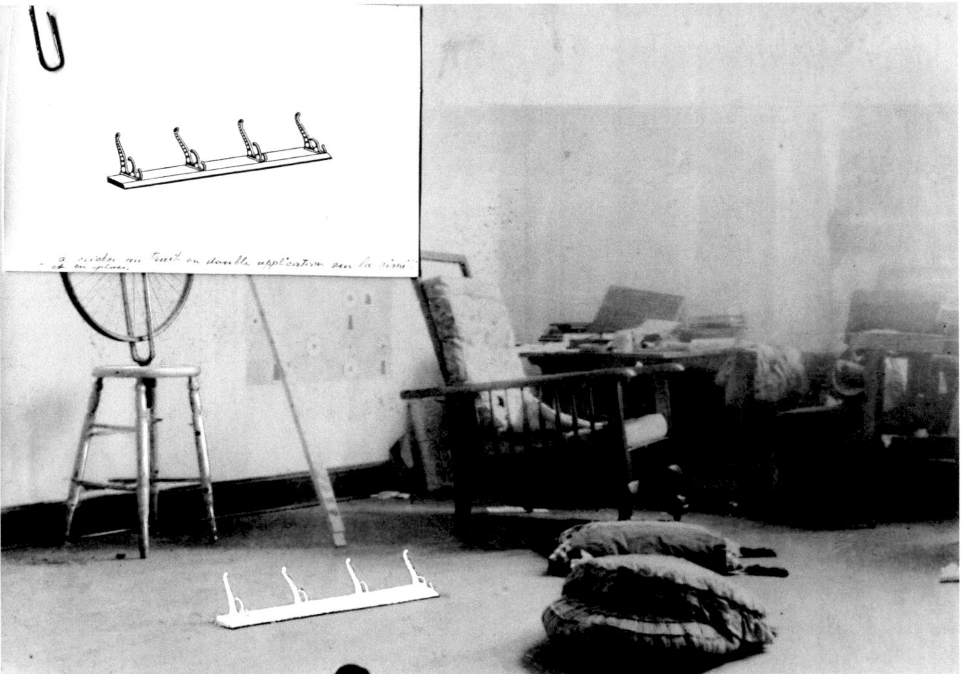

2.40

Marcel Duchamp, enlarged and retouched photo of his studio with *Trébuchet* whited out and, attached, a photographic reduction of a line drawing of *Trébuchet* as used for reproduction in the *Boîte-en-valise*, both c. 1940. 7.5 × 10.2 inches and 3 × 4.4 inches. Private archives.

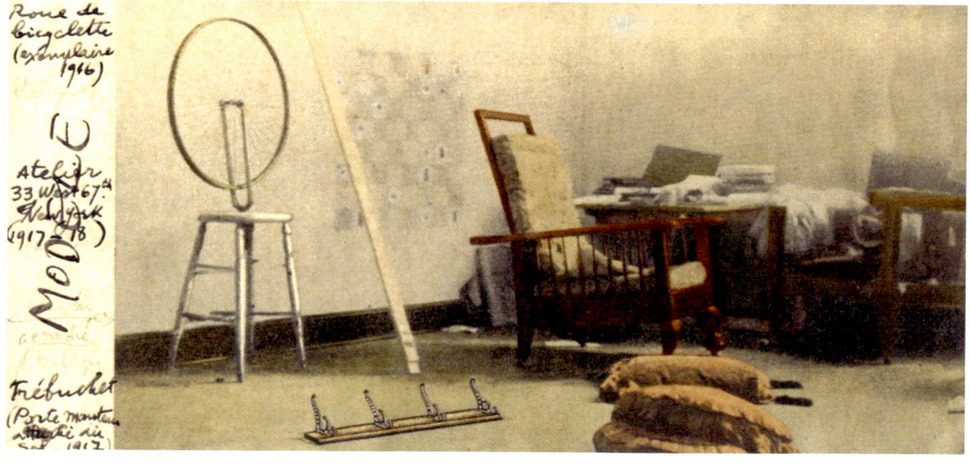

2.41

Marcel Duchamp, model for the reproduction of *Trébuchet* (Trap) in the *Boîte-en-valise*, c. 1940. Private archives.

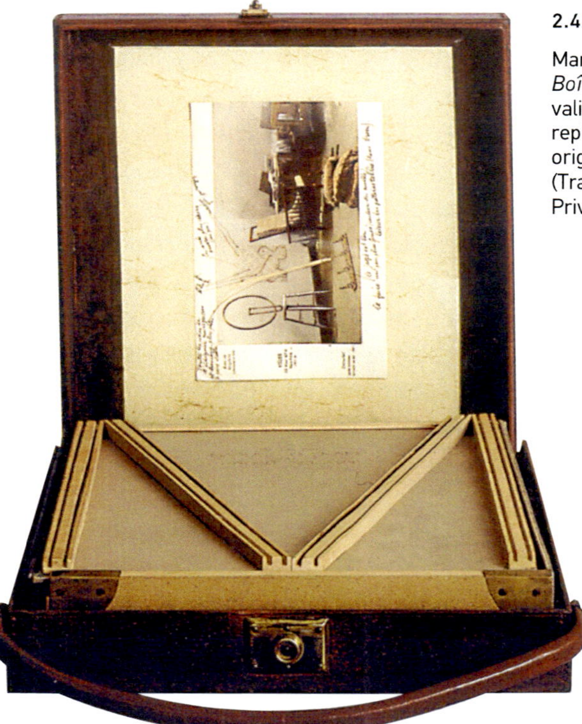

2.42

Marcel Duchamp, deluxe edition n° XIV/XX of the *Boîte-en-valise*, made 1948. Brown leather valise with handle containing sixty-nine miniature replicas and printed reproductions and one original, color notes for reproduction of *Trébuchet* (Trap). Valise (closed): 16 × 14¾ × 4¼ inches. Private collection.

The privileged role of the photograph as evidence for the reality of objects or events (as a direct transcription of the real) had long endowed it with the status of fact. As Roland Barthes would later contend: "Photography never lies; or rather, it can lie as to the meaning of the thing ... never as to its existence."[119] Everything suggests that Duchamp understood the latter point (his orchestration of the Stieglitz photograph of *Fountain* in 1917 suggests as much), even if, in his "museum," he deliberately made photography lie. Again and again, as with the carefully simulated notes of the *Green Box*, the *Boîte-en-valise*'s reproductions reflexively acknowledge the incapacity—indeed, impossibility—of the photographic to deliver its promise of veracity regarding its subjects. Certainly the things that appear in the *Boîte-en-valise*'s reproductions based on photographs actually once had been, but perhaps never quite as Duchamp makes them appear. His photographic/drawn hybrids, so calculated to deceive (and even sometimes to reveal that very deception at the same time), show the *Boîte-en-valise*'s testament to a lifework to be a concerted act of artful construction.

It is perhaps little coincidence that photography sits at the center of Duchamp's questioning not only of how the appearance of the "truth" of the artwork is constructed, but also of how its value is construed. The reproducibility of the work of art, more specifically the *photographability* of the artwork (since, unlike other forms of reproduction, photography retained a perilous proximity to the thing itself), is the subject of Walter Benjamin's "Letter from Paris," where he discusses its relationship to an artwork's value through the example of André Adolphe Eugène Disdéri. An otherwise unremarkable photographer and maker of photographic reproductions of artworks for the Louvre, Disdéri had, in 1854, invented a system of printing inexpensive, multiple photographic portraits on a single page, giving birth to the wildly popular photographic calling card, the *carte de visite*. It was, however, specifically in his work for the Louvre that Benjamin saw an operation that had "put the notion of the work of art in question, because such reproduction of the work accelerates its transformation into merchandise."[120]

The transformation of the artwork into merchandise and vice versa might well have been Duchamp's program, his cunning game, and reproduction was at the center of it. Reproduction, photographic and otherwise, came to challenge the relationship not only between art, art history, and the museum but also between art and the market. If Duchamp's positioning of the readymade in the museum that was the *Boîte-en-valise* had insisted that the commodity could take the place of, and play the role of, an artwork, his production of 320 copies of his own "museum" turned that purportedly noncommercial site into a miniature commodity version of itself.

The museum, however, was the last institution to want to admit such a conflation. As Yve-Alain Bois notes:

> In its desire to substitute itself for the miscellaneousness of the museum as bric-a-brac (which had nothing heterogeneous about it because the interchangeability of extremely varied curiosities directly followed the logic of the commodity and a return to the same), the modern museum did nothing more than engender another

type of homogeneity, one founded not on the infinite extensibility or undifferentiatedness of the collection, but on the structure of exclusion furnished by the history of art and based on decontextualization. In aiming to abstract works from the structure of exchange as a real context for which they were sometimes created, the modern museum, and artists with it, has deluded itself about the possibility of escaping the logic of the commodity [*la loi de la marchandise*].[121]

For Duchamp, the transformation of art into merchandise was a procedure different from that of Art Nouveau or even the Bauhaus, in which the utilitarian and the aesthetic were to be subsumed. His was a gesture without pretense to heroism: there was no claim to bring art to the masses, no effort to make anything that held the least bit of functionality, no beautification of the everyday. If there was something innately disruptive about the commandeering of a real urinal to claim it as a work of art, there was something perhaps even more contentious in reducing its size, in making it toylike and deliberately playful, and casing it up with other items (typewriter cover, comb, bottlerack ...) that in the end serve as nothing so much as placeholders for the "real," once-useful things to which they refer. Thus, insofar as the readymade is seen to expose the tensions between the commodity and the art object, between the serial and the collectable, between the ordinary and the exhibitable, the *Boîte-en-valise* grafts this ambiguity even more emphatically onto the very specific components that make up the museological, including institutional architecture, presentation technologies, archival methodologies, and so on.

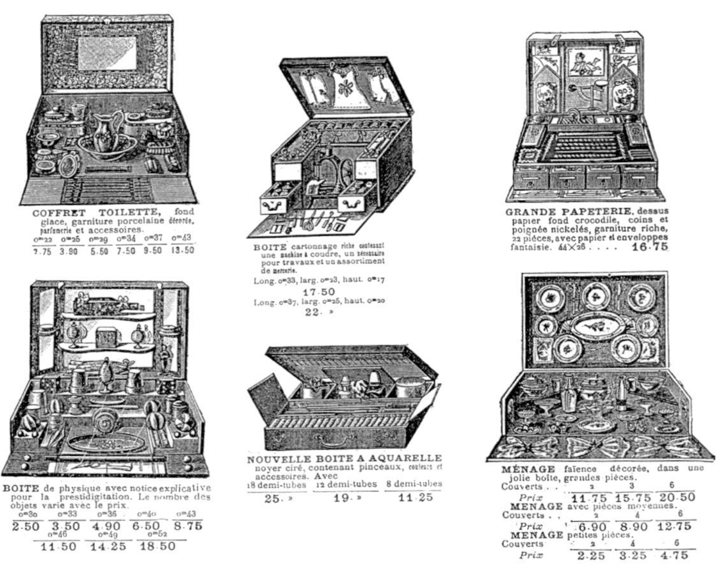

2.43

Page from the *Grands magasins du Louvre*, 1903. Sales catalog (showing boxes to house various items). Ronny van de Velde, Antwerp.

The multiplications of Duchamp's *Boîte-en-valise* asserted that the museum itself had something profoundly in common with both industry and the commodity. And here one cannot help thinking of Duchamp's various efforts over the years as not only curator but quasi-dealer—"cheerfully masquerading as an American-style 'businessman,'" as Robert Lebel put it—as part of his "test" to understand how the implications of presentation and display, as well as circulation and exchange, affect the meaning of the thing called "art."[122] If, in his *Boîte-en-valise*, the "items" (a term itself so resonant of the object's existence as product) within their case resemble, as many observers have pointed out, a traveling salesman's case of wares, they insinuate that art institutions might be closer to the market than the art world cared to admit, or even that the two could be seen as operating in alliance. The artist's miniaturized lifework perfectly packaged in a neat box (the most precious examples resembling suitcases with locks and handles) that could conveniently be purchased by way of subscription and whose descriptive inscription ("This box contains 68 items ...") not only made fuzzy the distinction between art object and commodity product but also claimed for the artist the roles of producer, distributor, curator, salesman, and publicist.

Almost simultaneous with Duchamp's development of his portable museum of reproductions, another provocative conception of the museum was being forged.[123] *Le Musée imaginaire*, André Malraux's book-length study begun in 1936 and first published in 1947, developed the idea that with the invention of the color photolithographic plate, art reproductions could effectively form a new supermuseum-in-a-book, a *musée imaginaire* as he called it (or a "museum without walls," as his American translator radically transformed the phrase). The collection of this "imaginary museum" encompassed any photographically reproducible work of art:

> In our [imaginary museum], picture, fresco, miniature, and stained-glass window seem of one and the same family. For all alike—miniatures, frescoes, stained glass, tapestries, Scythian plaques, pictures, Greek vase paintings, "details" and even statuary have become "color-plates." In the process they have lost their properties as objects; but, by the same token, they have gained something: the utmost significance as to style that they can possibly acquire. Thus it is that, thanks to the rather specious unit imposed by photographic reproduction on a multiplicity of objects, ranging from the statue to the bas-relief, from bas-reliefs to seal-impressions, and from these to the plaques of the nomads, a "Babylonian style" seems to emerge as a real entity, not a mere classification—as something resembling, rather, the life-story of a great creator. Nothing conveys more vividly and compellingly the notion of a destiny shaping human ends than do the great styles, whose evolutions and transformations seem like long scars that Fate has left, in passing, on the face of the earth.[124]

The constellation of museum, photography, reproduction, and reception thus lay at the heart of both Malraux's and Duchamp's projects. They were almost certainly responding to the same historic and museal context, and Benjamin remains a possible conduit

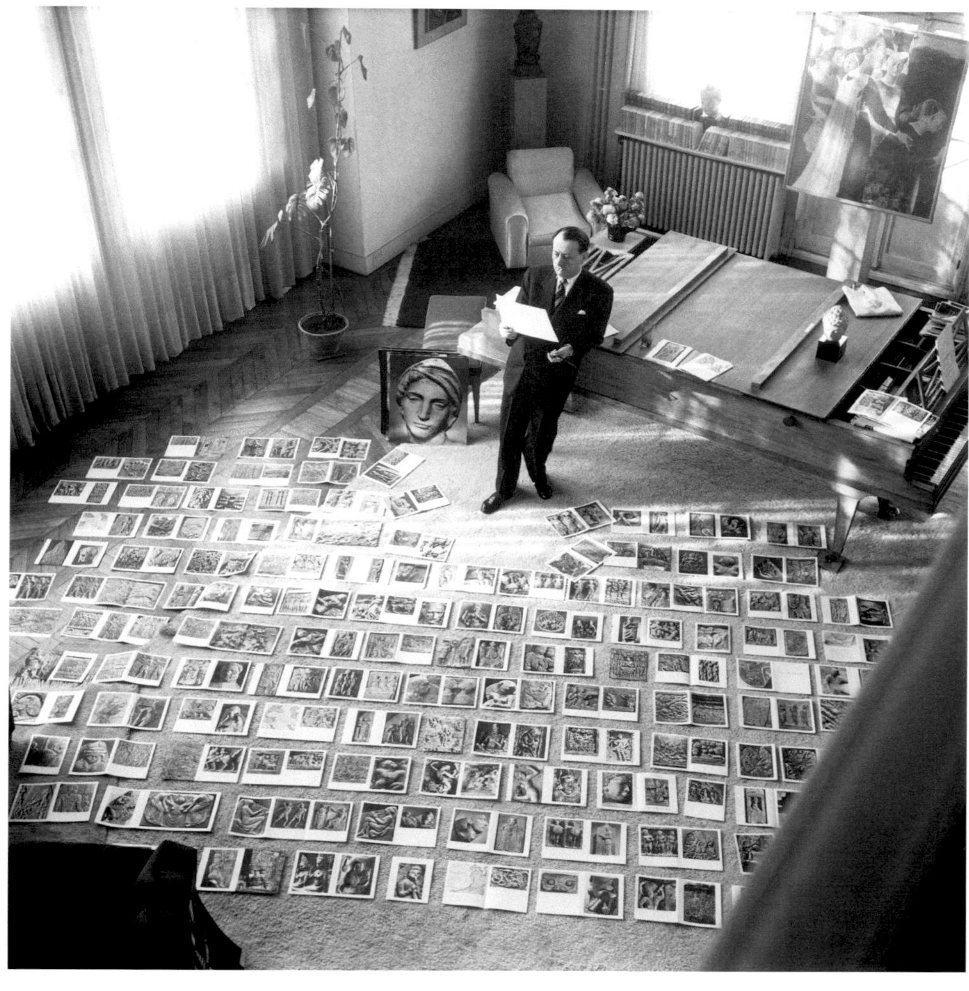

2.44

André Malraux posing with the image plates from his *Musée imaginaire*, 1954. Photo by Maurice Jarnoux. Paris Match Archive.

between them.[125] As Benjamin's letters to Max Horkheimer suggest, in 1936 Malraux had already publicly lectured about Benjamin's "Work of Art" essay and promised "a more detailed consideration of the essay in his next, evidently theoretical, book."[126] Speculative though any real connection between Malraux and Duchamp may be, insofar as Malraux's thinking about the artwork in the age of mechanical reproduction owes something to Benjamin, it might also owe something to Duchamp's advancement of a "theory of the artwork" formulated by Benjamin while working on his essay.

According to Malraux, and it is the foundation on which his entire project is built, art history is the history of *ce qui est photographiable*, the history of that which can be photographed.[127] The future French minister of culture adamantly believed in the direct and ingenuous transmission of information by the photographic medium and by modern photographic reproduction (at least where painting and sculpture are concerned; stained glass escapes accurate reproduction, he admits). With his assemblage of paper reproductions of artworks, Malraux posits the development of *style* (i.e., Classical, Romantic, et cetera), a veritable aesthetic "truth" obtained from decontextualization and formal juxtaposition within a grouping of works. Thus the image of the author seen from above and surrounded by photographic reproductions is the perfect image of the project itself. The contents of the *musée imaginaire* spread across the floor present themselves as anonymous units in an ensemble where their spatial, dimensional, and other distinctions are flattened, homogenized, and decontextualized—each rendered uniformly museum-worthy.

Malraux's project places great faith in the photographic, and more importantly a kind of unquestioned insistence that there *can be* a neutral and objective presentation and representation of the work of art in the art history book—the paper *musée imaginaire*. The logic suggested by his project can be seen to equally inform the ostensibly neutral, objective presentation in the real museum. The English translation's transformation of Malraux's central idea into "museum without walls" covers over yet another important distinction. As scholars have noted, "The original French for this—the *musée imaginaire* (imaginary museum)—brings out the antimateriality of the operation, its drive to reduce the physicality of the object to the virtuality of the image."[128] One could say that Malraux's project—no matter how unthematized—unwittingly advanced a critique of the national museum collection as an ensemble of auratic and original objects housed in a physical edifice: the monolithic position of the museum itself stood uncontested in Malraux's telling, which only suggested that in the future it was to be virtual.

If Duchamp's project shares with Malraux's a critical understanding of the potential of reproduction, Duchamp's is both more emphatically trenchant in its effort to uncover the ideologies upholding artwork and museum alike and, paradoxically, wedded to the idea that an actual, physical, full-size museum should nevertheless one day house the originals on which the *Boîte-en-valise*'s reproductions are based. Like Malraux, Duchamp also perceived the relationship between (art) history and "that which can be photographed," but in Duchamp's case, the use of modern means of mechanical reproduction was to decisively impact the perception and function of the work of art and, in turn and inevitably, the institution's in preserving and celebrating it, in imbuing it with an aura. Indeed, one of several vital places where Malraux and Benjamin differ, and where Benjamin and Duchamp share more than they might have been aware of, is a foregrounding not only of the material and conceptual role of photography but of "exhibition value," by which Benjamin also means "exchange value as it penetrates the institution of art, and transforms both the work of art and its contextual frames."[129]

With the *Boîte-en-valise*, Duchamp may have been at pains to create his own version of a "museum," but his was one without authority, transcendent majesty, secure location, or even "authentic" works of art. That is, he creates a museum as a blatantly commercial enterprise and with only the most tenuous hold on museality. In the process, he neither recuperates nor obliterates the museum; rather, he subjects its idea, rules, and operational givens to a series of questions. Herein lies the core of the artist's project. Through a conflation of seeming order and randomness, the original and its reproduction, the museal and the commercial, the auratic and the ordinary, the *Boîte-en-valise* offers an ambiguous model of the artist as producer and an even more conflicted model of the museum as authoritative guarantor of originality, value, quality, and even, some might contend, a kind of art historical "truth." In doing so, the so-called portable museum exposes what the typical art object and its varied forms of institutional support tended to hide—that the history of art and the museum are both involved in constructing and elevating as expediently "natural" what is little more than an artful construction.

CONCLUSION

Why, in 1916, did Duchamp so deliberately insert his readymades into an exhibition that had not even requested them? Why, in 1938 and then again in 1942, did he curate for the Surrealists when he was not even a member of the group and rarely felt obliged to do things he didn't want to do? Why, indeed, construct his own version of a museum exhibition of reproductions, demanding such painstaking work and long-term commitment? And, lastly, why take part in any of these at all given his declared aversion to exhibitions, based on his own firmly stated principle: "I myself will exhibit nothing"?

The truth is, Duchamp spent much of his lifetime involved in exhibitions of one sort or another, not only presenting his works in them but also using what opportunities there were to curate exhibitions, whether for himself or for other artists, even for artistic groups he didn't belong to. By the late 1930s, at a moment when official spaces for the display of art prided themselves on being rational, objective, and scientific, Duchamp's turn toward idiosyncratic installation and exhibition spaces, including his conception of the *Boîte-en-valise*, highlights the exhibition as fundamental to the artist's practice as a form through which he articulated—to use Benjamin's terms again—a veritable "theory of the artwork."[130] In the end, Duchamp's activities as curator might be understood less as disloyalty to his "principle" not to exhibit and more as the radical consequence of exactly this critical position on the institutions of art that had initially prompted his rejection.

In this regard, his practices of note replication and exhibition making are not as unrelated as they might at first appear. Both were concerned with how one looked at things aesthetically, both aimed to support or frame something else (the ostensibly legitimate aesthetic object), and both ambiguously drew and redrew the lines that delineate an artwork, confounding the established borders that dictated what was and wasn't "art." Indeed, in Duchamp's body of work, it is through, and because of, the apparently marginal matter *around* the work of art—whether the notes about an artwork, the administration that records it, the display codes that present it, or the institutional forces that affirm it—that the very definition of the art object was put in crisis, which is to say, brought to a turning point.

Duchamp's selection of everyday things inaugurated, according to Dorothea von Hantelmann, what she calls a "curatorial paradigm": "In the field of art it was Marcel Duchamp who anticipated, paradigmatically performed, and articulated this transition. For in this context the readymade occupies the position of a junction."[131] In her reading, and in accordance with much Duchamp scholarship, it was his *choice* of the ordinary store-bought items that was radical, with his vindication of the act of selection allowing the readymade to mark "the transition of a production-oriented society to a selection-oriented society."[132] She adds: "Duchamp turned the act of choosing into a new paradigm of creativity. Or, rather, he sharpened a practice that has always existed into something like a paradigm."[133] She is, in one major respect, quite right. Duchamp arguably *is* the catalyst of a new "curatorial paradigm." But if the readymade is, as Duchamp described it, a "work of art without an artist to make it," it might more properly be thought of as the creation of the artist *as curator*.[134] And this redefinition of the artist as curator must consequently be considered particularly significant to avant-garde practices (and the scholarship) that followed in its wake.

Contrary to von Hantelmann's assertion, this chapter proposes that it is Duchamp's staging of the documentation, deadpan presentation, publication of texts illustrated by precisely that documentation (even the curious dematerialization of the object itself), and (importantly here) the object's miniaturization, replication, display, and dissemination, rather than an act of selection, that define the "curatorial" paradigm of his practice. And it is this far more labored and complex enterprise that was of fundamental importance to the reception of the readymades as well as their profound impact on artists and art history thereafter. Such a reconsideration of Duchamp's "effect" acknowledges that, for the artist, the orchestration of the elements *around* the artwork was a means of orchestrating the conditions for the work of art to "appear" as such, and this might well constitute his major and still underdiscussed contribution to the twentieth century.[135]

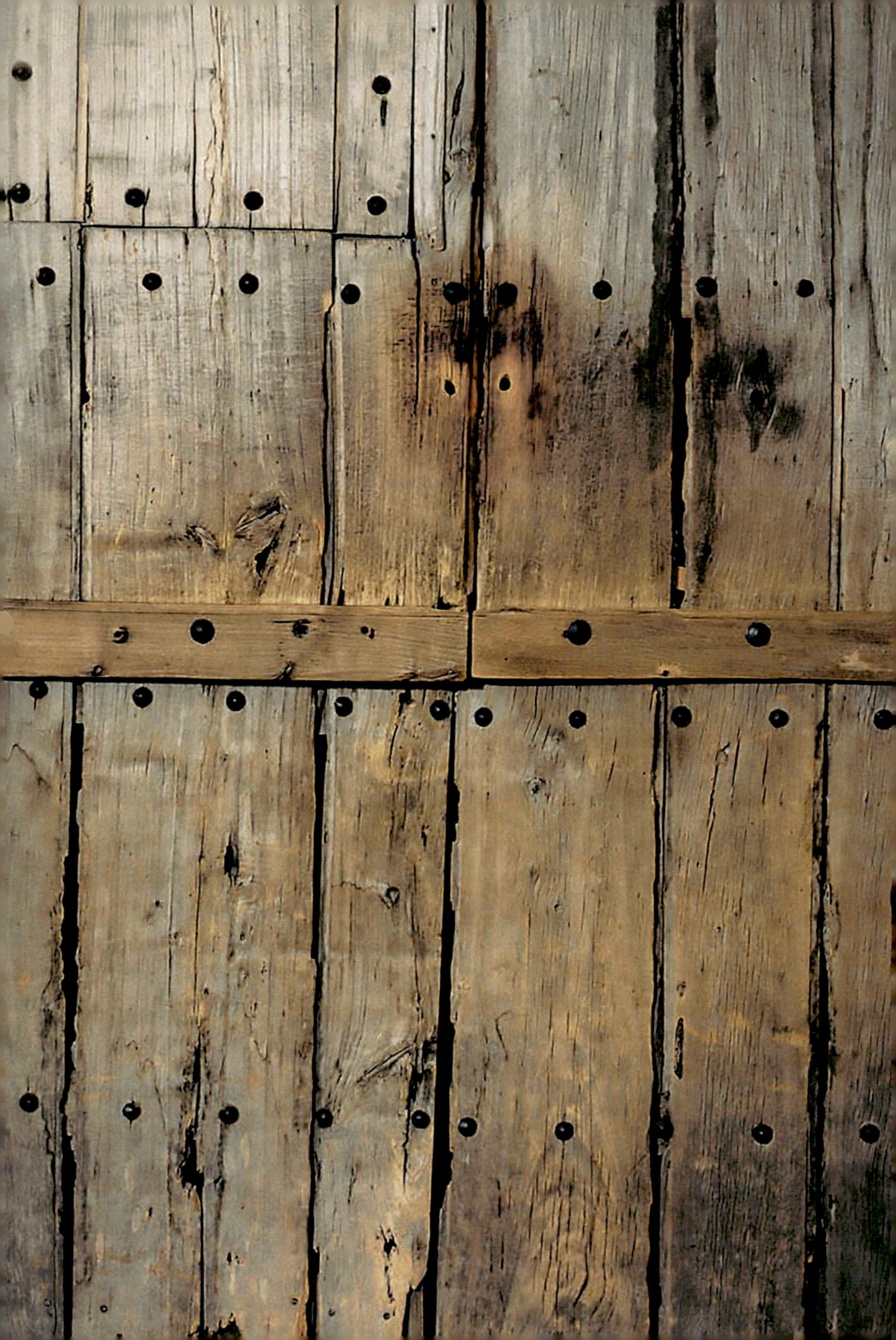

CHAPTER 3

THE DEAD END OF THE MUSEUM

MAUSOLEUMS

Duchamp had doubts—this is how he put it—about the judgments that determined whether a particular artwork entered a museum or not. He claimed, even well into the 1960s, that he thus didn't see the point of going to visit museums, and he peppered his interviews with asides critical of the "mausoleums of art history."[1] His understanding was that art history and the museum were linked, inevitably and irrevocably, like twin machines in the dubious but authoritative arbitration of the artwork's value:

> The history of art is something very different from aesthetics. For me, the history of art is what remains of an epoch in a museum. ... [I] almost never go [to museums]. I haven't been to the Louvre for twenty years. It doesn't interest me, because I have these doubts about the value of the judgments which decided that these pictures should be presented at the Louvre, instead of others which weren't even considered, and which might have been there.[2]

However, everyone knows that Duchamp's own work ended up in exactly that institutional context, and over his lifetime he spent considerable energy to ensure its placement in precisely that citadel of taste and rule. The seeming paradox, however, was neither inconsistent nor a betrayal, but instead wholly in keeping with his critical position, and his final, posthumous installation, *Étant donnés: 1° la chute d'eau, 2° le gaz d'éclairage ...* (Given: 1. The Waterfall, 2. The Illuminating Gas ... , 1946–66), would take that position to its obstinate end.

It might, then, be stating the obvious to declare that no project more firmly reveals Duchamp's vested interest in the museum than *Étant donnés*. After all, it is known not only that the artist constructed the work with the museum in mind, but also that he specifically devised the elaborate instructions for its entry into the Philadelphia Museum of Art, where it now permanently resides. Considering the trajectory initiated with the *Box of 1914* (1913–14) and the readymades, passing through his exhibition making and creation of his own miniature museums, and finding its end point in *Étant donnés*, it might seem utterly redundant to state that Duchamp's final work was concerned, perhaps above all, with the institution of art. For *Étant donnés* is a decidedly site-specific work *avant la lettre*, and the museum is its deliberate and permanent site. It is therefore curious that the manifold implications of the work's museal context and the extraordinary administrative apparatus mobilized by the artist in order to ensure its final destination remain among the least discussed aspects of this profoundly elusive work.[3]

This chapter is about *Étant donnés*, both the complexity of its twenty-year production as seen in the context of Duchamp's larger oeuvre and its relatively meager reflection in an art history that seems to have been long unable or unwilling to adequately account for it, despite the remarkable impact the artist has had on the generations that followed him. I am not here lamenting the general lack of writing about Duchamp's final work, even if it is surprising that it has taken so long for more to follow Jean-François Lyotard's nearly lone *Les TRANSformateurs Duchamp*, published in French in the 1970s.[4]

However, it is both astonishing and revealing that *Étant donnés* has, with few exceptions, not been more widely inscribed in broader art histories of the epoch—which would have reckoned with it in relation to contemporary practices.[5]

Production and reception are intimately related in the work, for production here encompasses not only the labor on the installation in the classical sense, but also the elaborate and equally significant activities that Duchamp conceived in order to direct its reception by situating the piece in its final, institutional resting place. These activities and the resultant display conditions are arguably as much a part of the work's "making" as anything else, even if the critical reception of Duchamp has been slow to acknowledge these activities, which didn't necessarily—or literally—produce the artwork so much as situate, contextualize, and frame it.[6]

MAKING ART HISTORY

Duchamp himself repeatedly commented on the determinant nature of art history: "In the last analysis, the artist may shout from all the rooftops that he is a genius; he will have to wait for the verdict of the spectator in order that his declaration take a social value and that, finally, posterity includes him in the primers of Art history."[7] The reasons for the awkward relationship of *Étant donnés* to "the primers of Art history," or those narratives that attempt to provide broad overviews of art historical eras and movements, although surprising, are perhaps nevertheless not so hard to understand. Strange, overtly shocking, and rapturously visual, Duchamp's elaborate *tableau mort* has often been read through the lens of what one can see of it, through its iconography—a tangle of visual details suggesting possible connections to the vast and cryptic world of *La Mariée mise à nu par ses célibataires, même* (The Bride Stripped Bare by Her Bachelors, Even, 1915–23). Perhaps, say the Duchamp scholars and critics, the unattainable bride of the *Large Glass* has finally, literally, been stripped bare by her thwarted bachelors, with the frustrated desire and electromagnetic erotics of the earlier work now embodied in the waterfall and gas lighting. While those readings attempt to pin down the work through recourse to an explicitly visual narrative, *Étant donnés* has long eluded adequate description (and representation).

Numerous authors have struggled, to varying degrees, to provide a "straight accounting" of (visible) facts that reduce largely to the following: a white and empty half-lit room with a massive, aged wooden door at one end, perforated by two eyeholes, through which one can see (if one ventures to look) the scene of a broken aperture of bricks behind which lies a glowingly illuminated, recumbent, awkwardly spread-legged nude female figure holding a gas lamp in her left hand. This nude and her bared sex are situated in an eerie but bucolic setting of dead twigs and leaves, and all of this is seen against a photo-collage backdrop with a seemingly moving waterfall. These visual facts, however, hardly manage to adequately account for the actual experience of the piece. Accordingly, almost every discussion of *Étant donnés* bears some variant of "No photograph can ever render justice to the beauty and complexity of this work. ... The shock of discovering the piece cannot be captured by a photo or description. Viewing the item is a unique and untranslatable experience."[8] Right, perhaps, this is, but "ultimately," as Helen Molesworth has recently noted, "this contemporary iconoclasm has meant that the work hovered like air: crucial but unremarked."[9] And this in spite of a veritable cottage industry of writing on Duchamp and his seemingly unshakable place as doyen of radical art of the twentieth century.

Certainly *Étant donnés* divided critics when it was first revealed, many seeing it as the senile lapse of an old man and something better not compared with his earlier "great" work. Art historian Joseph Masheck's comment, published in 1974, speaks to the negativity of the work's initial reception: "If earlier works by Duchamp are in the most dubious ways still lovely, this one seems startlingly gross and amateurish. It dissolves into a senile hobby, altogether private in its psychological function, out of place and embarrassingly unengaging—it is not a masterwork of any kind."[10] But this kind of disparagement, however prevalent at the time, hardly explains the work's uneasy place in the art history written in the several decades since. No matter how confrontational, obscene, or morbid its critics may have found it, there is little to justify its almost complete invisibility in the most basic narratives of the development of the art of its time. To best gauge this, peruse just a few representative examples of publications that purport to define and discuss the production of postwar art: *Modernism in Dispute: Art since the Forties*; *A Companion to Contemporary Art since 1945*; *New Art in the 60s and 70s: Redefining Reality*; or *The Rise of the Sixties: American and European Art in the Era of Dissent 1955–1969*.[11] *Étant donnés* is not discussed in any of these despite its perfect coincidence with the publications' stated temporal scope, which spans in most cases from the 1940s to the end of the 1970s. Browse alongside them essays meant to specifically address Duchamp's influence, such as John Tancock's "The Influence of Marcel Duchamp," commissioned for and printed in the catalog accompanying the first large-scale retrospective of the artist after his death, in 1973, and taking as its explicit subject Duchamp's importance to and shared interests with younger artists of the 1960s and '70s, or, similarly, Robert Pincus-Witten's "'Quality Material ...': Duchamp Disseminated in the Sixties and Seventies," where one will not find *Étant donnés* mentioned at all.[12] Even more revealing than the critical condemnations, then, is the long-standing art historical silence.

The problem perhaps already begins with defining its "time." Despite its secure place in the museum, *Étant donnés* has long been without a firm place in art history: an irony, given Duchamp's understanding of the inseparability of the museum and art history. Made over a twenty-year period from 1946 to 1966 and unveiled to the public in 1969, the assemblage seems to fall out of sync with the strict periodizations that are (still) the cornerstone of art history: proper neither to the heroic years of the avant-garde, like the readymades or *Large Glass*, nor to the "new" art and artists of the postwar period, it sits in a no-man's-land. There is a belatedness (or an anticipation, it is difficult to tell which) that has seemingly prevented the work from belonging fully to its present—that

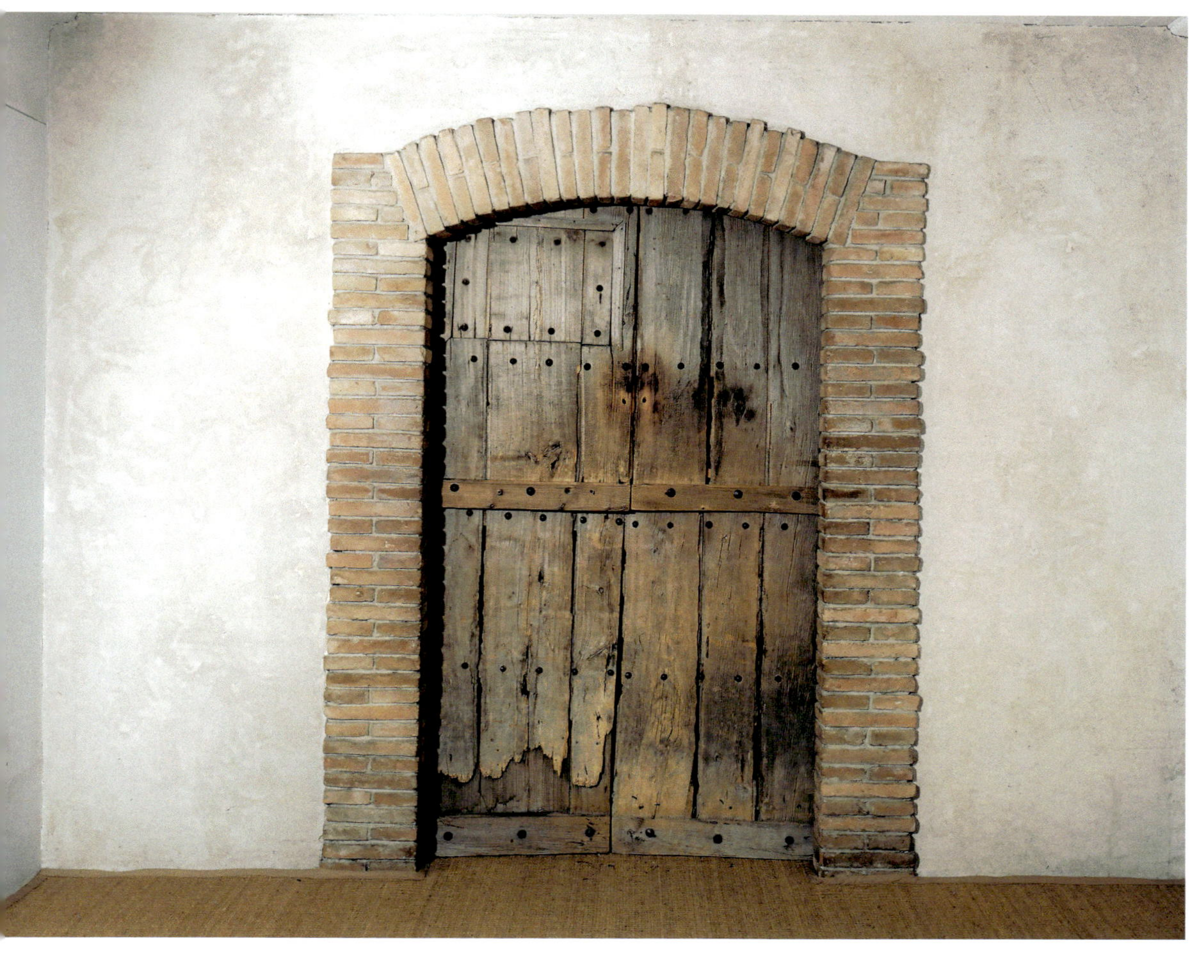

3.1

Marcel Duchamp, *Étant donnés: 1° la chute d'eau, 2° le gaz d'éclairage ...* (Given: 1. The Waterfall, 2. The Illuminating Gas ...), 1946–66, exterior as installed at the Philadelphia Museum of Art. Mixed-media assemblage. Exterior: wooden door, iron nails, bricks, and stucco embedded into museum wall. 95 ½ × 70 × 49 inches. Philadelphia Museum of Art: Gift of the Cassandra Foundation.

3.2

Marcel Duchamp, *Étant donnés: 1° la chute d'eau, 2° le gaz d'éclairage ...* (Given: 1. The Waterfall, 2. The Illuminating Gas ...), 1946–66, interior as installed at the Philadelphia Museum of Art. Mixed-media assemblage. Interior: bricks, velvet, wood, parchment over an armature of lead, steel, brass, synthetic putties and adhesives, aluminum sheet, welded steel-wire screen, Peg-Board, hair, oil paint, plastic, steel binder clips, plastic clothespins, twigs, leaves, glass, plywood, brass piano hinge, nails, screws, cotton, collotype prints, acrylic varnish, chalk, graphite, paper, cardboard, tape, pen ink, electric light fixtures, gas lamp (Bec Auer type), foam rubber, cork, electric motor, and cookie tin, 95½ × 70 × 49 inches. Philadelphia Museum of Art: Gift of the Cassandra Foundation.

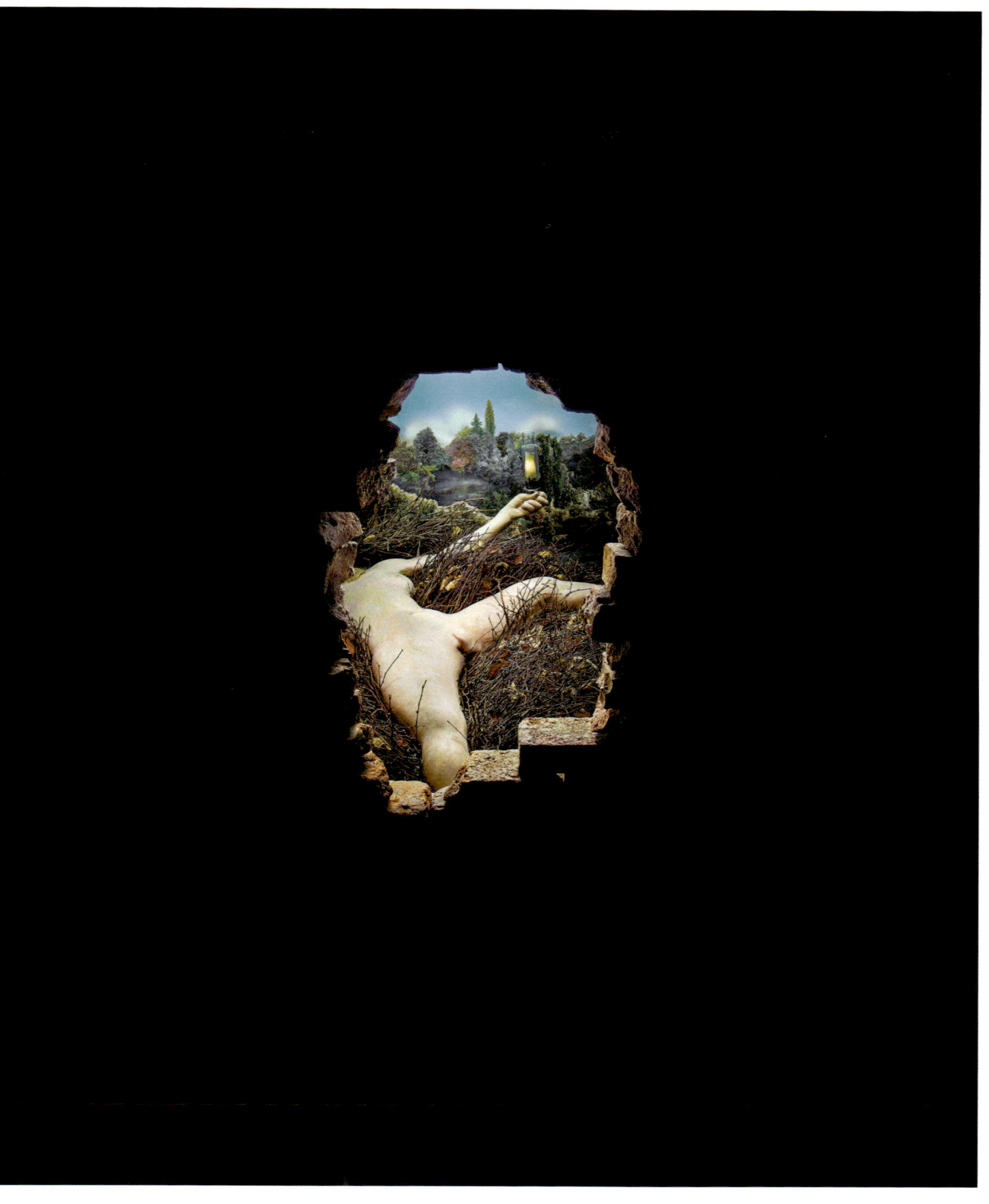

THE DEAD END OF THE MUSEUM

"present" being the twenty years of its becoming. It would be tempting to think that this is one more example of the "delay" that was part of Duchamp's practice, but it is hard to believe that he could have so fully orchestrated, or even anticipated, the historical afterlife of this work. Its absence from postwar art histories is all the more surprising when one remembers that *Étant donnés*'s unveiling was both contemporaneous with, and profoundly relevant to, the diverse expansion of art forms witnessed in the postwar period.[13]

If one wants to speak to the "decade"—that temporal category wholly artificial when employed as a discursive tool in art and cultural histories—one might well ask in relation to which decade we should speak of Duchamp's final work. Although its central, nude figure began to take shape materially in the late 1940s, to compare *Étant donnés* with the production of that epoch would lead to little more than vague formal associations. For, however seemingly connected Duchamp's suggestive assemblage was, for instance, to the sexual provocations of the Surrealists, their fascination with dolls and mannequins and other uncanny female surrogates, Duchamp's suggestively poised nude is but one small part of a larger construction, both literally and conceptually. The 1950s are, technically, the decade in which the background and structure of *Étant donnés* were beginning to be built up. Yet it would also make little sense to fully situate the work in this period or to imagine *Étant donnés* as any kind of influence on its artistic production, since it was unfinished and totally unknown at that point (and, anyway, Duchamp himself was then still little known). The final form of the work was concretized in the 1960s, and the institutional maneuverings that ensured its permanent museal home were mostly orchestrated by Duchamp in these years, even if the work itself was not made visible until the very end of that tumultuous decade. Still, it resonates perhaps more closely with the concerns of that period than with those of any other before it.

With his final work, Duchamp delivers on what can be considered promissory notes left in earlier works, building on and extending his own previous ideas. But *Étant donnés* also in some way reflects—as do most artworks, consciously or not—the development of the culture that saw its appearance. As it happens, in the 1960s the inheritors of the avant-garde were also beginning to grapple with and translate many of those very ideas that Duchamp had begun to lay out since the first decade of the twentieth century. Why, then, has so little attention been paid to the work's relationship with the contemporary art historical context from which, and into which, it emerged? The attempt to situate Duchamp's final work in terms of its broader aesthetic milieu is not to argue for its direct influence on any one art historically defined period per se, nor is it even to suggest the inverse, that any particular stage of the work so defined the whole that one could think of it entirely as a product of notions "in the air" at the time. Instead, it is vital to understand in what ways *Étant donnés* can be historically located, examined—as are all other art historical objects—in relation to the context of its ultimate production and reception.

On the surface, the developments in art of the 1960s might seem the least likely place to "locate" *Étant donnés*. Its idiosyncrasy and visceral thingness, its flimsy awkwardness and blatant constructedness—being obviously something made *by hand*—could hardly seem further from Minimalism's embrace of industrial facture, for instance, or from Greenbergian formalism or language- and systems-based Conceptualism, all of which were being championed at the time. Yet the embodied viewing that Duchamp's work presupposes, a veritable phenomenological inquiry into the conditions of (museum) perception, and the rhetorical theatricality of his diorama-like installation suggest productive ways to read it against, for example, Michael Fried's polemical understanding of Minimalism or the ideas driving Conceptual art.[14] For there is some irony to the fact that in those famous "six years" from 1966 to 1972, when art was apparently "dematerializing," Duchamp completed and presented his arguably most materialist work—a work that, paradoxically, echoes many of the precise ideas and systems that Conceptual art was also questioning.[15] Not least among those concerns were the autonomy of the artwork, the value of the copy, the logic of photography, and the insistence on administration as a part of the artwork itself. And whereas the historian might argue that many of those ideas were already suggested in the readymades or duplicated notes from the first decade of the twentieth century (no matter the historical delay that effectively kept both the readymades and the notes in a holding pattern until the 1960s), *Étant donnés* not only critically rearticulates some of Duchamp's most radical ideas, but also introduces a complex site-specific format directly aimed at the exhibition as a form and the museum as its privileged institutional site. The work's requirement of bodily presence and its questioning of museum conventions leveled new challenges at the conceptions of the artwork and conditions of presentation/reception alike.

Étant donnés's unveiling also coincided with Happenings, installation art, the strategy of "site specificity," the perception-oriented and participatory post-Cagean paradigms of the 1960s, and the beginnings of what was later called Institutional Critique, each of which could usefully be read against the backdrop of Duchamp's final work.[16] When *Étant donnés* finally opened to the public, it did so at about the same moment as such projects as Christo and Jeanne-Claude's *Wrapped Art Institute of Chicago* (1968–69), Marcel Broodthaers's fictitious *Musée d'Art Moderne* (1968–72), and Lawrence Weiner's removal of an exhibition space's wall lathing for Seth Siegelaub's exhibition "January 5–31, 1969" (1969), each differently targeting the art institution. Duchamp's final work, in retrospect, resonates deeply with these, its contemporaries. *Étant donnés* also became public just before such exhibitions as "Spaces" at the Museum of Modern Art, New York (December 30, 1969–March 1, 1970), and "Using Walls" at the Jewish Museum, New York (May 13–June 21, 1970), both specifically inviting artists to make the very space and walls of the museum part of their work. Indeed Duchamp's final work, one should not forget, was on view not long after Paul Thek's *The Tomb* (1967), a ziggurat structure to be entered and containing a life-size cast of the artist in the guise of a "dead hippie," and was almost simultaneous with projects such as Bruce Nauman's *Live Taped Video*

Corner (1969–70), which literally made the spectator's viewing in the exhibition space the subject and object of the piece, or John Baldessari's proposal for an unrealized project for the "Information" exhibition of 1970 at the Museum of Modern Art in New York, mentioned and sketched in its catalog, in which a real corpse was to be exposed in a "special room ... with a glass peephole."[17] *Étant donnés* also preceded Vito Acconci's *Seedbed* (1972), in which the artist's prone masturbating body performed for an audience of aural "voyeurs" in an installation built into the architecture of the gallery (in this case the floor).[18] In their own way, these latter projects performed their own troubling of the terms of institutional display, specifically through the introduction of a corporeality usually not admitted into the dignified space for the showing of art. If the former examples (Christo and Jeanne-Claude, Broodthaers, Weiner, but also the cited exhibitions) suggest conceptual or ideological links between certain artists' critical exposure of the institution and Duchamp's *Étant donnés*, the latter examples (Thek, Baldessari, Acconci, and Nauman) formally and almost directly feature aspects of the prone nude or the explicit voyeurism of *Étant donnés*. The near-simultaneity of the projects, and their commonalities, seem so flagrant that one cannot help wondering why critics at the time almost never evoked comparisons between them and *Étant donnés*.[19]

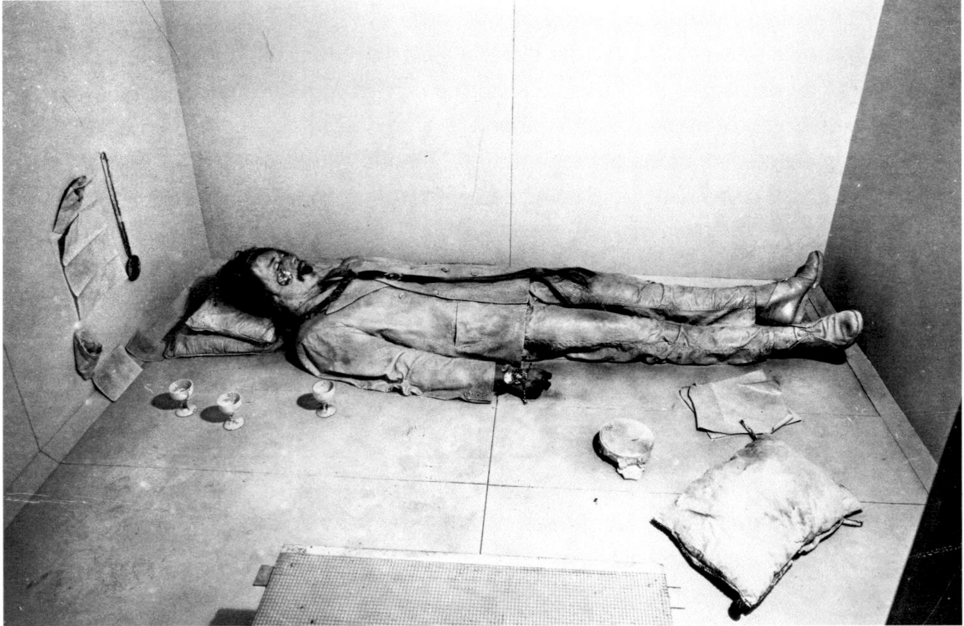

3.3

Paul Thek, *The Tomb*, 1967, interior view, Stable Gallery, New York. Photo by John D. Schiff.

John BALDESSARI
Born 1931, National City, California
Lives in National City

PROPOSAL: Possibly an impossible project. The idea is to exhibit a cadaver, rather than a facsimile person. What is intended is a double play of sorts. One would possibly be appalled at seeing the corpse, i.e., the factor of aesthetic distance would be broken down; but by controlling the lighting, staging, etc., so that it approximates Andrea Mantegna's Dead Christ (making it look like art, refer to what is established as art), the shock would be cancelled and one might be able to look at the tableau with little or no discomfort. The subject is not the cadaver. The subject is rather the issue of breaking and mending aesthetic distance.

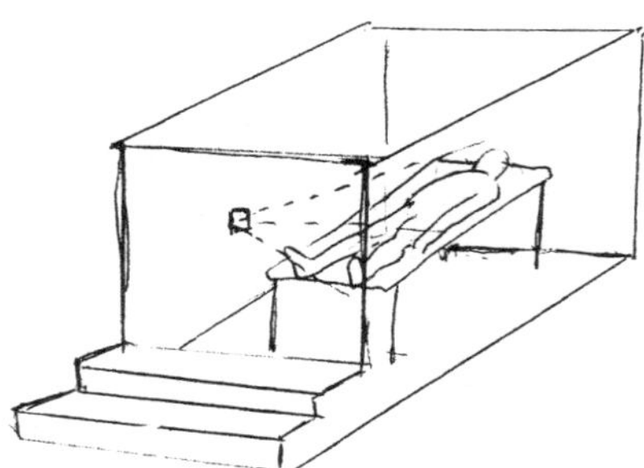

Special room would be built with a glass peephole. Rheostat lighting, refrigeration unit would be concealed.

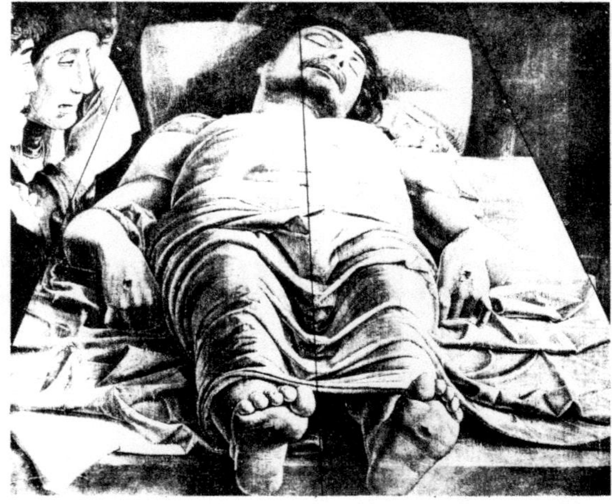

16

3.4

Page from the exhibition catalog *Information* (New York: Museum of Modern Art, 1970), picturing John Baldessari's unrealized proposal for the exhibition.

3.5

Vito Acconci, *Seedbed*, 1972, visitor on top of ramp. Installation/performance, 9 days, 8 hours per day, Sonnabend Gallery, New York, 1972. Photo by Bernadette Mayer.

3.6

Vito Acconci, *Seedbed*, 1972, view of the artist under the ramp. Installation/performance, 9 days, 8 hours per day, Sonnabend Gallery, New York, 1972. Photo by Bernadette Mayer.

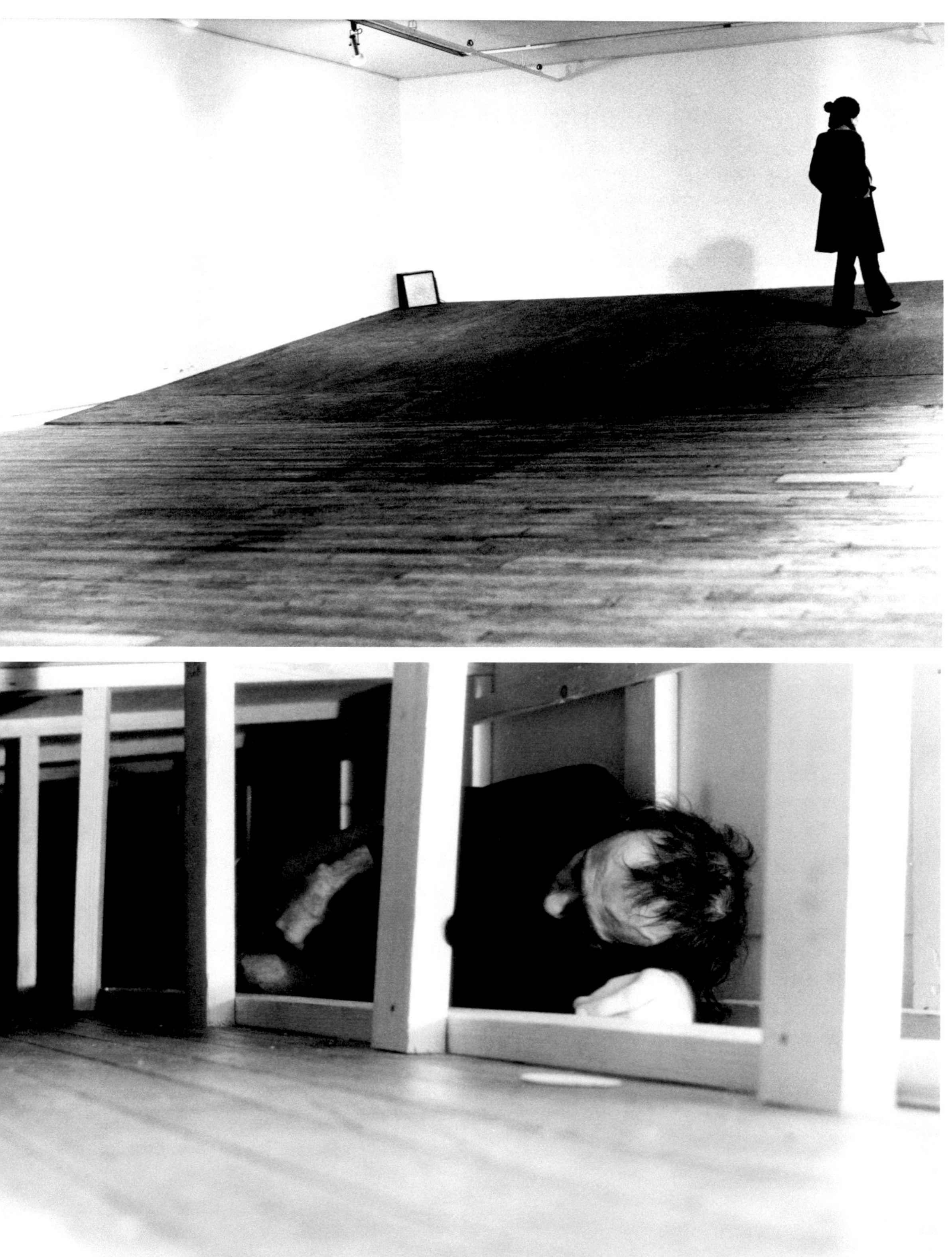

Yes, Duchamp is often mentioned in relation to this period and, in fact, to many of these specific practices. John Cage's interest in Duchamp in the late 1950s and his introduction of the French artist's work to a whole generation of younger practitioners are frequently cited as the catalyst for Duchamp's rediscovery in the United States. But it is the Duchamp of the readymades that is mentioned, the Duchamp of chance and language games, even the Duchamp of the *Large Glass*, with its deployment of the photographic index. It is not the Duchamp of *Étant donnés*.[20]

If some sort of temporal or contextual confusion is to blame (historians not knowing whether to consider it a 1940s or '50s or '60s work, or even whether to consider it fully European or American), this still does not fully explain why *Étant donnés* remains undetectable even in those rather recent genre- and medium-specific histories of installation art, participatory art, Institutional Critique, or contemporary photography that are less strictly bound to temporal schemas, and to which *Étant donnés* would so interestingly contribute. The list of studies to be cited here is long.[21] Why the silence? Why for instance did Brian O'Doherty's brilliant and prescient trilogy of essays about the ideology of exhibition spaces, which appeared in *Artforum* starting in 1976 and which repeatedly mention Duchamp's readymades and his exhibition practice as pioneering, not devote a word to the artist's final work?[22] After all, *Étant donnés* took even more direct aim at exactly the ideological framework that was O'Doherty's subject, and the work had already been sitting in a museum for several years by that point. O'Doherty is more than just an isolated example. Why did there not appear a single article on *Étant donnés* in the pages of *Artforum* in 1969 when it was first made public (or even, just as strangely, in the several years after)?[23] That most engaged and critical hotbed of contemporary criticism at the time not only regularly featured writings by artists (such as Robert Morris, Sol LeWitt, Robert Smithson, and Donald Judd) who themselves certainly knew of Duchamp's last work and who referred to his readymades in their other writings for the magazine; it was also precisely the place where contemporaneous developments in art were being vigorously debated.[24]

And in the rare instances when someone in more recent times does question the larger art historical context in which the work was produced and received, there has often been a blanket refusal to acknowledge the ways in which the work might relate to the progressive art production of its time. T. J. Demos's reading is exemplary of this. *Étant donnés*, he says, "disconnects from the historical paradigm that his wartime work elaborated. But it also severs ties to its own historical field, in terms of any connection to contemporary avant-garde production (corresponding from 1946–66 to the development of abstract expressionism, pop art, minimalism, Happenings, and conceptual art, with which it shares next to nothing)."[25] Such a view of history not only ignores *Étant donnés*'s deep connection and relevance to Duchamp's previous productions, including most specifically his "wartime" exhibition designs and *Boîte-en-valise* (Box-in-a-Valise, 1938–42), but it also takes a myopic view of "contemporary avant-garde production."

The irony of the work's occlusion is all the more remarkable considering that it was around the time of its unveiling that Duchamp came to be internationally acclaimed and the focus of attention for a whole generation of younger artists—what has been called "the Duchamp effect." This was roughly the decade and a half—bracketed by the publication of the first monograph on Duchamp, in 1959, the first English publication of his translated *Boîte verte* (Green Box, 1934) notes in 1960, the reedition of thirteen of his original readymades in 1964, and his first retrospectives in America and Europe (in 1963 in Pasadena, in 1966 in London, and in 1977 in Paris, that last being his first major solo show in his native France)—that marks the establishment of the artist's extraordinary reign of influence, not only as a retroactive "master" of the first half of the twentieth century, but also as the lodestar to so many younger artists. Yet in the 1994 introduction to a special issue of *October*, Benjamin H. D. Buchloh asks "whether the reception of Duchamp's work, manifold and labyrinthine as it is, has not fallen short of the work's actual historical potential—and the near total silence surrounding the hidden enigma in Philadelphia would attest to that."[26] Still, and surprisingly, that very journal devoted but a meager few lines to "the hidden enigma in Philadelphia" in an entire issue devoted to Duchamp's influence on artists after him. And aside from a few recent publications (even if a notable one is massive), little in the way it has been received in the nearly two decades since Buchloh's observation has rectified this situation.[27]

To question the relative silence around Duchamp's most recalcitrant work is to point to the disjuncture between *Étant donnés*'s reception and the imbrication and inner workings of Art History (with a capital A and H) and the Museum (with a capital M) that were the quiet subjects of so much of his oeuvre all along. How strange that precisely this work—Duchamp's coda of sorts—has ended up insufficiently contextualized and thus uneasily located in the very history that it addresses.

THE GIVENS

To tell *Étant donnés*'s story, it is necessary to start from the beginning. Already one of the scraps of paper in Duchamp's *Green Box* of 1934 bearing the heading "Préface" declares: "Étant donnés: 1. la chute d'eau, 2. le gaz d'éclairage ... ." However, as we know, among the jumble of the *Green Box*'s ninety-three pages, there is neither an essay per se nor a linear narrative that develops in any traditional sense, and thus no recognizable way in which this particular torn scrap could "preface" any of the others.

In fact, in recording the title for Duchamp's posthumous work, the note suggested that—for decades—it had been lying in wait, delayed in appearance yet already in the works. Retrospectively, the note takes on the character of a purloined letter, under our noses but unrecognizable as a clue. This trickery was fitting for an artist who had spent the last two decades of his life building *Étant donnés* in utmost secrecy while releasing into the world an array of works that quietly alluded to or referenced the larger installation. Because no one detected what those clues, references, and anatomical quotations were pointing to, their connections to something larger only became known to the

Préface

Etant donnés 1°. la chute d'eau
2°. le gaz d'éclairage,

on déterminera
nous déterminerons les conditions, du Repos instantané (ou apparence allégorique) d'une succession [d'un ensemble] de faits divers semblant se nécessiter l'un l'autre par des lois, pour isoler le signe de la concordance entre, d'une part, ce Repos (capable de toutes les excentricités innombrables (?)) et, d'autre part, un choix de Possibilités légitimées par ces lois et aussi les occasionnant.

Pour repos instantané = faire entrer l'expression extra-rapide

// On déterminera les conditions de [la] meilleure exposition du Repos extra-rapide [de la pose extra-rapide (= apparence allégorique) d'un ensemble ..... etc public, and even to many of the artist's closest friends and family, after his death, when *Étant donnés* entered the collection of the Philadelphia Museum of Art. Significantly, here the artist's notes again establish themselves as an odd administrative structure for the work of art that they covertly announce and circumscribe.

Constructed over two decades, *Étant donnés* was begun in Duchamp's top-floor apartment-atelier at 210 West 14th Street in an aging brownstone walk-up, which he started renting in October 1943.[28] At some point in the summer or autumn of 1949 he rented an additional room that adjoined his apartment. Even after he married Alexina (Teeny) Sattler in 1954 and went to live with his new wife in a somewhat more fashionable midtown location, he held on to the two spaces on West 14th Street. The part that had served as both a living and working space for years would thus, from 1954 forward, remain his "official" studio. It was kept as all his previous spaces had been, spartan and dusty. His additional atelier, secured by a locked door, was accessible—aptly—from the official studio's bathroom (who can forget that so many of the artist's pieces pivoted on that Duchampian confluence of the bodily intimacy found in the lavatory and the messy stuff of the studio?). This second space remained unknown to visitors, who would have found that, in the "public" studio into which they were invited, Duchamp had eliminated most signs of art making (as he stated, he had since about 1923 supposedly "given up" art for other primary occupations, such as playing chess and breathing). The secret studio was where his clandestine figure and her flimsy house could, in all freedom, take form. When his lease for both spaces ran out in the winter of 1965–66, the artist was forced to move. Before dismantling and transporting the nearly complete installation to a fourth-floor space in a banal office building at 80 East 11th Street, Duchamp took some photographs of it and wrote out a few notes to help him remember how to put his construction back together again. Then, in that tiny new room, a mere eighteen by twenty feet, neighbor to Local 662 of the AFL-CIO Poultry Workers' Union and secreted from all friends and colleagues (he went unlisted in the building's directory), his installation was finalized.[29] In the early months of 1966, the artist signed and dated the piece and set to work making an exhaustive manual that would indicate how it could be disassembled and reassembled without his direct involvement. One senses in this action that he knew he might live neither to see the piece taken apart nor to see it enter the final resting place he was so carefully plotting for it.

3.7

Marcel Duchamp, *Préface Étant donnés: 1° la chute d'eau, 2° le gaz d'éclairage* (Preface Given: 1. Waterfall, 2. The Illuminating Gas). Facsimile of manuscript note in the *Green Box*, 1934. Collotype on paper, 8¼ × 5 inches. Philadelphia Museum of Art: The Louise and Walter Arensberg Collection.

Without him, in the months after his death, *Étant donnés* was transported to the Philadelphia Museum of Art, and finally on July 7, 1969, it quietly opened to the public in a gallery adjoining others already displaying the largest collection of the artist's work. If the work's arrival at the museum was destined to signal a kind of conclusion for the piece, its date of inception remains the subject of much speculation. The "preface" in the *Green Box* suggests that ideas for it were already brewing by the early 1910s, when Duchamp had scripted the idiosyncratic title that was eventually published in 1934. Another claim sees its beginnings in a remark made to art dealer Julien Levy in the 1920s about wanting to make a "life-sized articulated dummy, a mechanical woman whose vagina, contrived of mesh springs and ball bearings, would be contractile, possibly self-lubricating."[30] And then of course there are those who locate the work's genesis and most important reference point in the *Large Glass* of 1915–23, rendering the nude of *Étant donnés* little more than a physical manifestation of the fallen bride.[31] That last, oft-repeated reference has largely obscured the importance of another probable trajectory of *Étant donnés*'s development, found in the late 1930s, the moment when the artist was avidly investigating the implications of the museum and exhibition through the work on his *Boîte-en-valise* and various exhibition and display endeavors—projects to which *Étant donnés* has, until recently, only rarely been compared.[32]

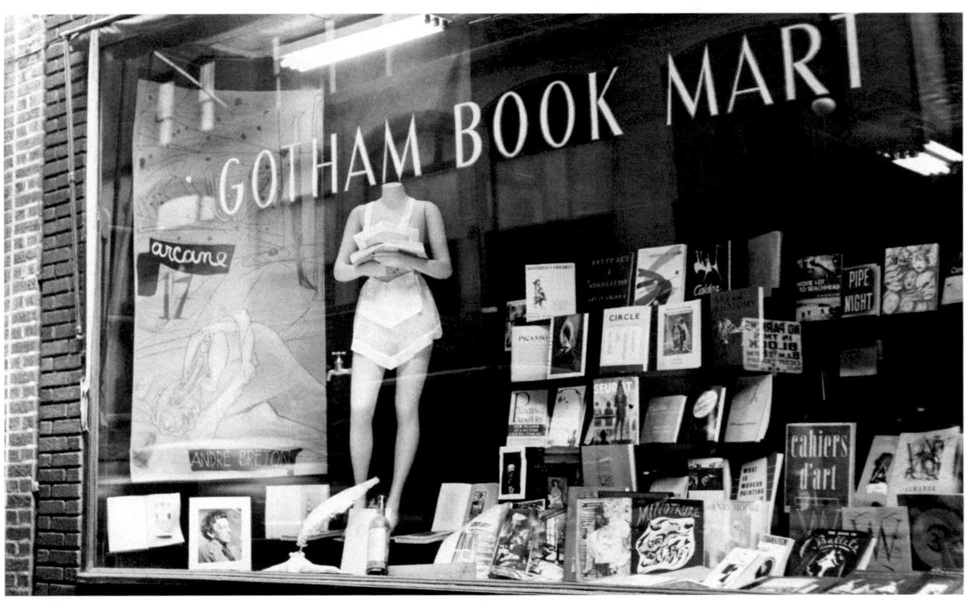

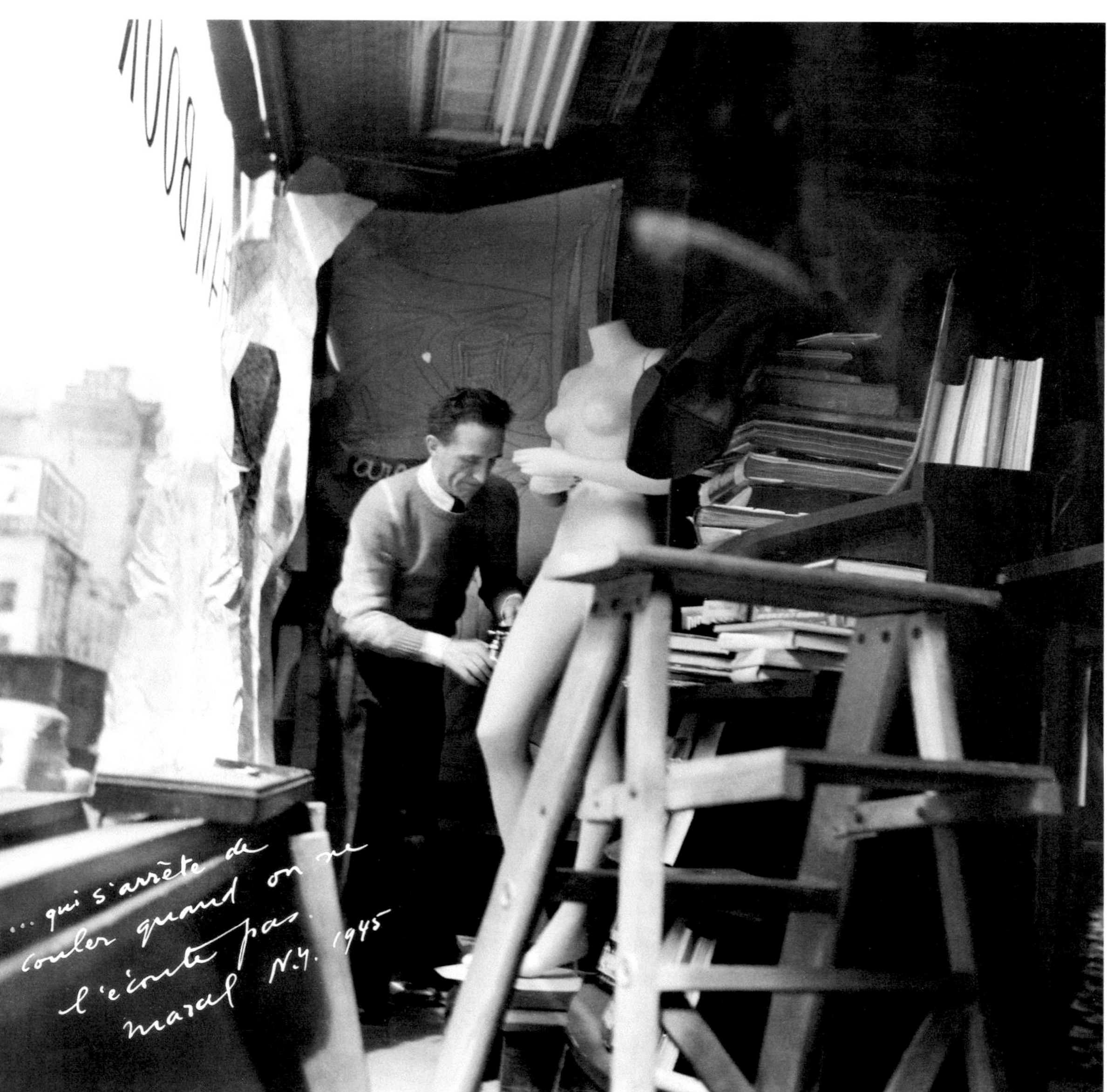

3.8

Marcel Duchamp, *Lazy Hardware*, window display at the Gotham Book Mart, New York, 1945. Photo by Maya Deren. Philadelphia Museum of Art: Gift of Jacqueline, Peter, and Paul Matisse in memory of their mother, Alexina Duchamp.

3.9

Marcel Duchamp installing *Lazy Hardware*, window display at the Gotham Book Mart, New York, 1945. Photo by Maya Deren, signed and annotated by Marcel Duchamp. Centre Pompidou, MNAM-CC, Paris: André Breton Archives, Bibliothèque Kandinsky.

EXHIBITION MAKER

The slow but determined labor on *Étant donnés* followed the production of Duchamp's museum in a box, the *Boîte-en-valise*, whose conception and replications had kept him busy from 1935 to the early 1940s, when the first of the boxes were released. It is worth remembering as well that, predating his conscientious work on *Étant donnés*, Duchamp had already conceived the hyperbolic spectacles that were the 1938 "Exposition internationale du surréalisme" and the 1942 "First Papers of Surrealism." In the two decades that followed those exhibitions, his interest in display and exhibition making continued unabated, resulting in elaborate mises-en-scène for Surrealist exhibitions in 1947, 1959, and 1960, which entirely overlapped work on *Étant donnés*. In this activity—where again he essentially took on the role of a curator—he confronted anew questions regarding the rituals of display, organization of vision, and the role of discursive and other frameworks in the reception of an artwork; in short, the function of the exhibition-as-institution. Together, these investigations could not have been more apt foundations for the major project Duchamp had in mind.

Also significant in this context were the artist's shop window designs, made at the behest of André Breton to help promote and sell the latter's publications.[33] At the Gotham Book Mart in New York in 1945, Duchamp put together a display that he entitled *Lazy Hardware*, featuring a scantily clad headless mannequin with a faucet attached to her thigh—a lifeless half-nude behind glass purveying (the promise of) running water that already manifested various elements of *Étant donnés* as a three-dimensional tableau. That same year, his design for Brentano's bookstore, also in New York, included a partial female figure constructed of chicken wire, a waterfall-like cascade of paper strips, and the sculpture of a female torso by Isabelle Walberg, arranged by Duchamp so that "the head and one arm [were] hidden, the other outstretched, legs spread far apart, one straight and the other sharply bent at the knee, the triangle of genitalia exposed."[34] Iconographically, both of these window designs have been said to anticipate different elements and even the central figure of Duchamp's final work. However, one cannot help thinking of how they perhaps more importantly exemplified the artist's various approaches to presentation, display, and—not negligibly—sales over the years (whether through his Brancusi exhibition, his Concours Lépine stand of *Rotoreliefs*, or even his *Boîte-en-valise*) as much as they looked forward to similar issues in *Étant donnés*. Through these store window designs, he seems to have understood that the shop window, like the exhibition, *produces* value just as much as, if not more than, it puts it on display.

Whenever its actual beginnings, Duchamp dated *Étant donnés* to 1946–66, and the first known studies indeed originated in 1946 when the artist set to work on the concrete plans for, and actual construction of, the piece. The first drawn study for it is also thought to date from 1946, and on a visit to Switzerland in the summer of that same year, Duchamp took photographs of the waterfall that would serve as the backdrop of the installation. In the first known letter mentioning the piece, dating from July 1947,

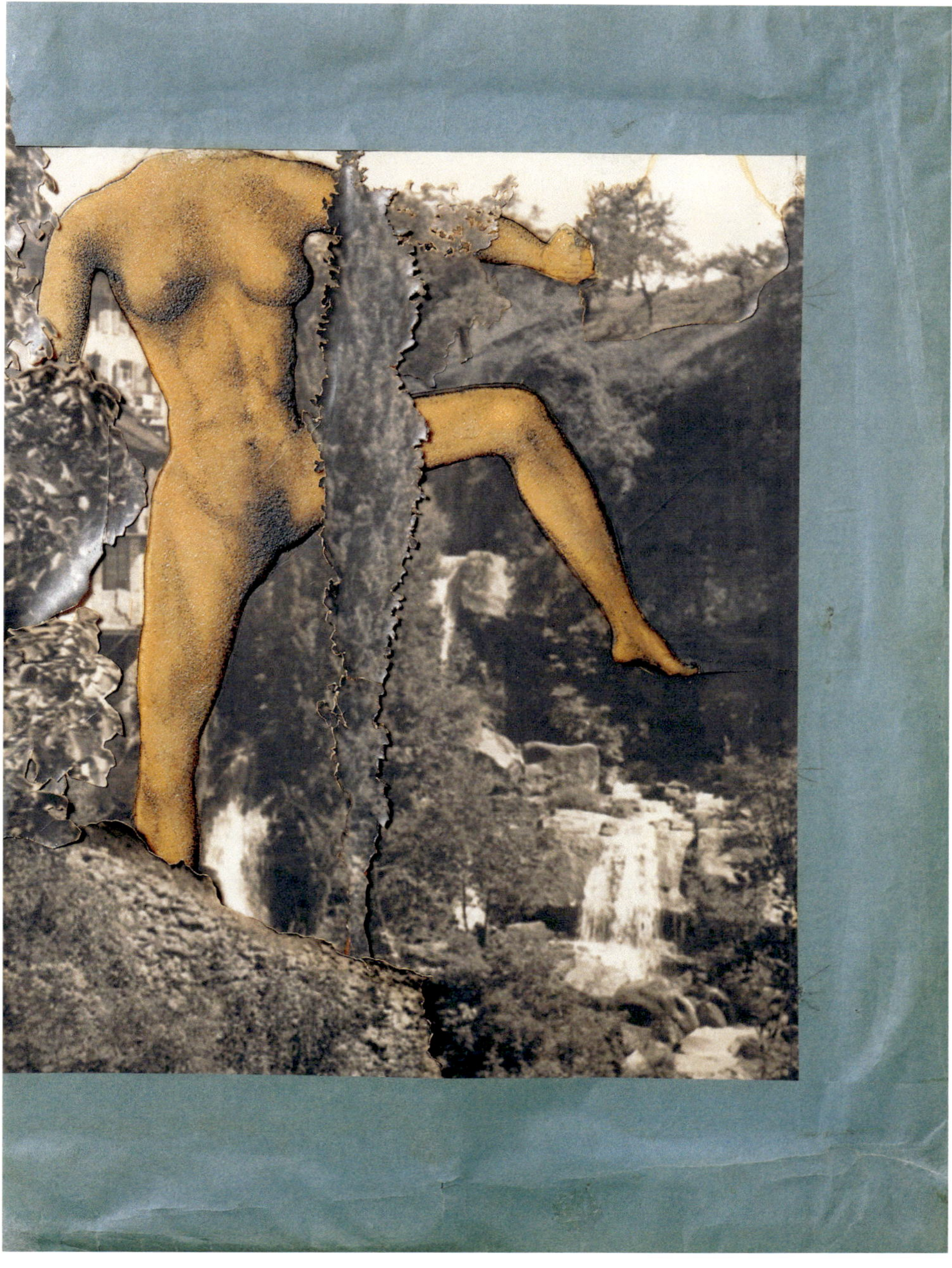

3.10

Marcel Duchamp, photocollage landscape for *Étant donnés,* c. 1946. Textured wax, pencil, ink on paper, and cut gelatin silver photographs, mounted on board, 17 × 12¼ inches. Private collection.

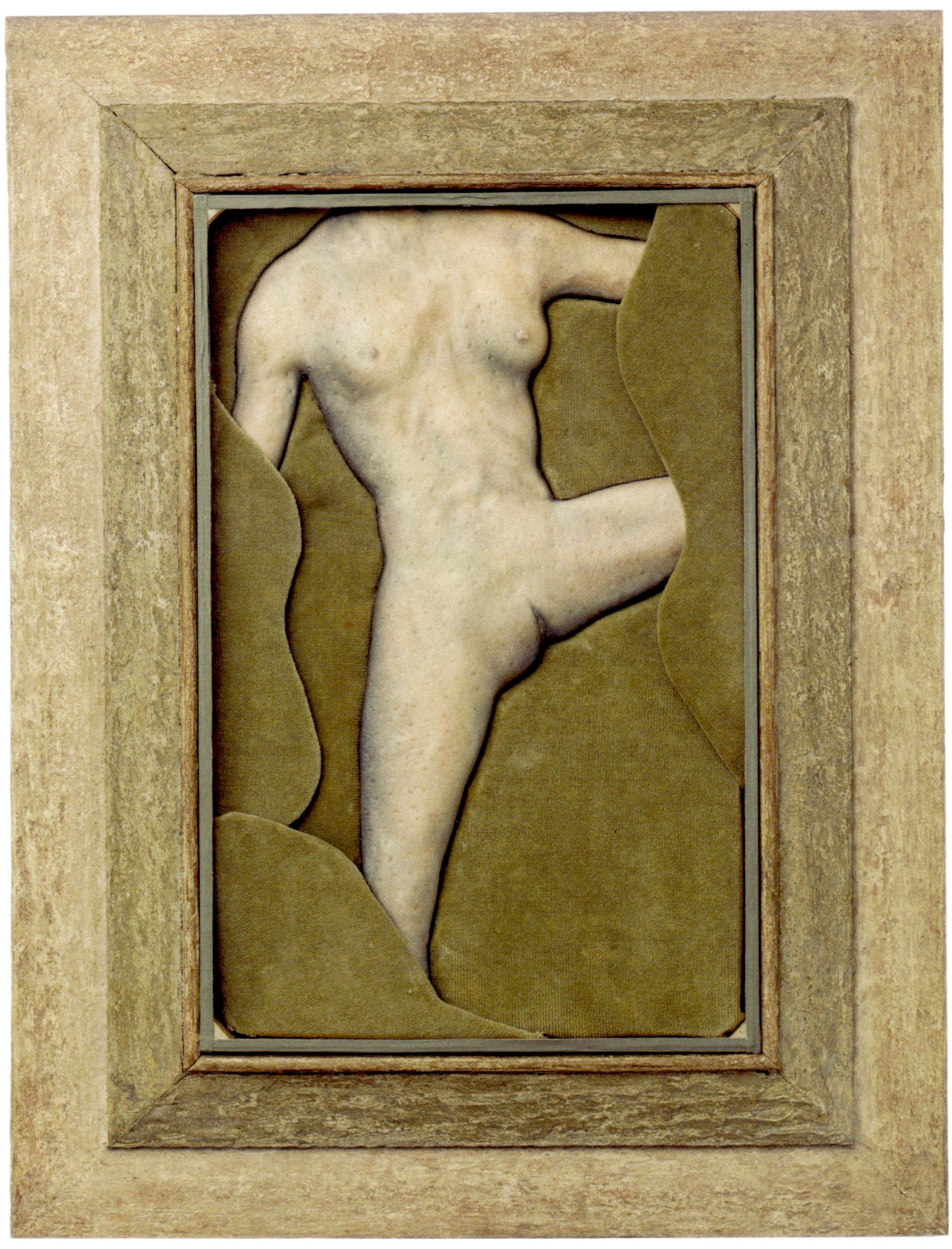

3.11

Marcel Duchamp, study for *Étant donnés*, c. 1946–48. Pigment and graphite on leather over plaster with velvet, 19¾ × 12¼ inches. Moderna Museet, Stockholm: Gift, 1985, dedicated to Ulf Linde from Tomas Fischer.

the artist writes to his then-lover, the Brazilian artist Maria Martins, whose body served as the model for the nude of *Étant donnés*, about his worries concerning the "skin" of the figure he was then making.[35] In the same letter Duchamp reveals that he was awaiting news of a Paris exhibition, since at that very moment, in the tony spaces owned by Aimé Maeght as his new Galerie Maeght in Paris, the 1947 "Exposition internationale du surréalisme" had been erected based on Duchamp's initial conception for the space. The invested nature of Duchamp's involvement in those postwar Surrealist exhibitions suggests not only the degree to which he continually sought to probe the space of presentation and display, but also how much these projects became the site for conceptually articulating ideas important to his simultaneous thinking about *Étant donnés*. I therefore examine these exhibitions in some detail here and specifically in relation to Duchamp's contributions in order to bring focus to the particular parallels and reverberations with his final work.

For this first collective Surrealist exhibition to be held in Paris after the war, André Breton had again asked Duchamp to help design the spatial organization of the show, which ran from July 7 to September 30, 1947. Breton hoped the exhibition would mark the postwar return of Surrealism to French intellectual life, offering "initiation," "superstition," and "a new myth" as the show's implicit themes. Unlike with previous exhibitions for the movement, for which Duchamp was present on site and directly involved in the execution of his design ideas, in this case he was unwilling to go back and forth between Paris and New York to oversee the installation. He thus proposed to work out the scheme and general plans with Breton in Paris before returning to New York, where he appointed architect Frederick Kiesler, himself a pioneer in avant-garde exhibition design, to erect the elaborate interior layout and several smaller installations in his stead.[36] Kiesler, who was based in New York at the time, spent several months in Paris overseeing the construction of the complex exhibition installation. Duchamp's desire to design the exhibition from a distance may have owed something to the fact that he was then engrossed in the labor on the nude of *Étant donnés* at his New York studio.

Following Duchamp's conceptual guidelines, and not only inventing technical solutions for the realization of the artist's ideas but also incorporating much of his own vision of architecture into the whole, Kiesler designed and constructed a decidedly nonlinear, labyrinthine structure that spanned the two floors of Galerie Maeght's decorous spaces.[37] The passageway through the exhibition literalized Breton's esoteric mandate, being laid out, as Eva Kraus notes, "in the manner of a ceremonial path, a 'parade spirituelle' ... intended to trace the stages of an initiation rite—meeting, cleansing and purification."[38] The "initiation" of visitors to the exhibition began with Breton's flight of twenty-one stairs (each representing a book spine bearing the names of Surrealism's most cherished authors), which led to a Duchamp-styled grotto, the main part of the exhibition. For this space, entitled the "Hall of Superstitions," Kiesler stretched thick, dark-green fabric on a curvilinear metal framework roughly following the walls of the various rooms and suspended by rope between the floor and ceiling. Enveloping artworks and visitors alike between these undulating "walls," the exhibition acted as a "single organism," in Kiesler's words; Jean Arp compared it to a large egg that held the spectator "like in the bosom of his mother."[39] Artworks by the show's more than one hundred artists were bathed in a dim, greenish light (like the haze of old gas lamps) and occasionally hung, as was Max Ernst's *Euclide* (1945), behind the stretched fabric that had peepholes cut into it to allow for their viewing.

3.12

Frederick Kiesler, architectural drawing for the "Hall of Superstitions" at the 1947 "Exposition internationale du surréalisme," published in his "Manifeste du Corréalisme," *L'Architecture d'Aujourd'hui* 2 (June 1949).

3.13

Installation view of the "Hall of Superstitions" at the "Exposition internationale du surréalisme," conceived by Marcel Duchamp and designed by Frederick Kiesler, with Max Ernst's *Euclide* (1945) behind a peephole, Galerie Maeght, Paris, 1947. Photo by Rémy Duval.

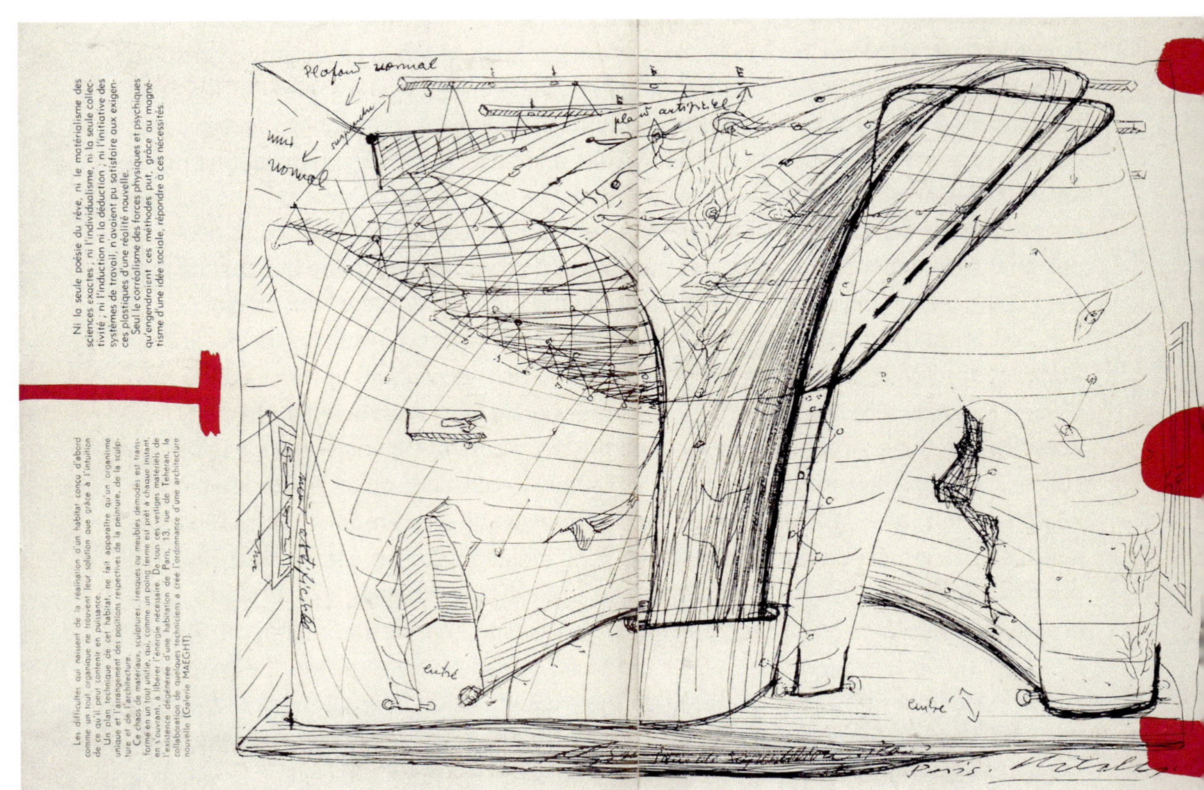

Les difficultés qui naissent de la réalisation d'un habitat conçu d'abord comme un tout organique ne trouvent leur solution que grâce à l'intuition de ce qu'il peut contenir en puissance.

Un plan technique de cet habitat, ne fait apparaître qu'un organisme unique et l'arrangement des positions respectives de la peinture, de la sculpture et de l'architecture.

Ce chaos de matériaux, sculptures, fresques ou meubles démodés est transformé en un tout unifié, qui, comme un poing fermé est prêt à chaque instant, en s'ouvrant, à libérer l'énergie nécessaire. De tous ces vestiges matériels de l'existence dégénérée d'une habitation de Paris, 13, rue de Téhéran, la collaboration de quelques techniciens a créé l'ordonnance d'une architecture nouvelle (Galerie MAEGHT).

Ni la seule poésie du rêve, ni le matérialisme des sciences exactes ; ni l'individualisme, ni la seule collectivité ; ni l'induction ni la déduction ; ni l'initiative des systèmes de travail, n'avaient pu satisfaire aux exigences plastiques d'une réalité nouvelle.

Seul le corréalisme des forces physiques et psychiques qu'engendraient ces méthodes put, grâce au magnétisme d'une idée sociale, répondre à ces nécessités.

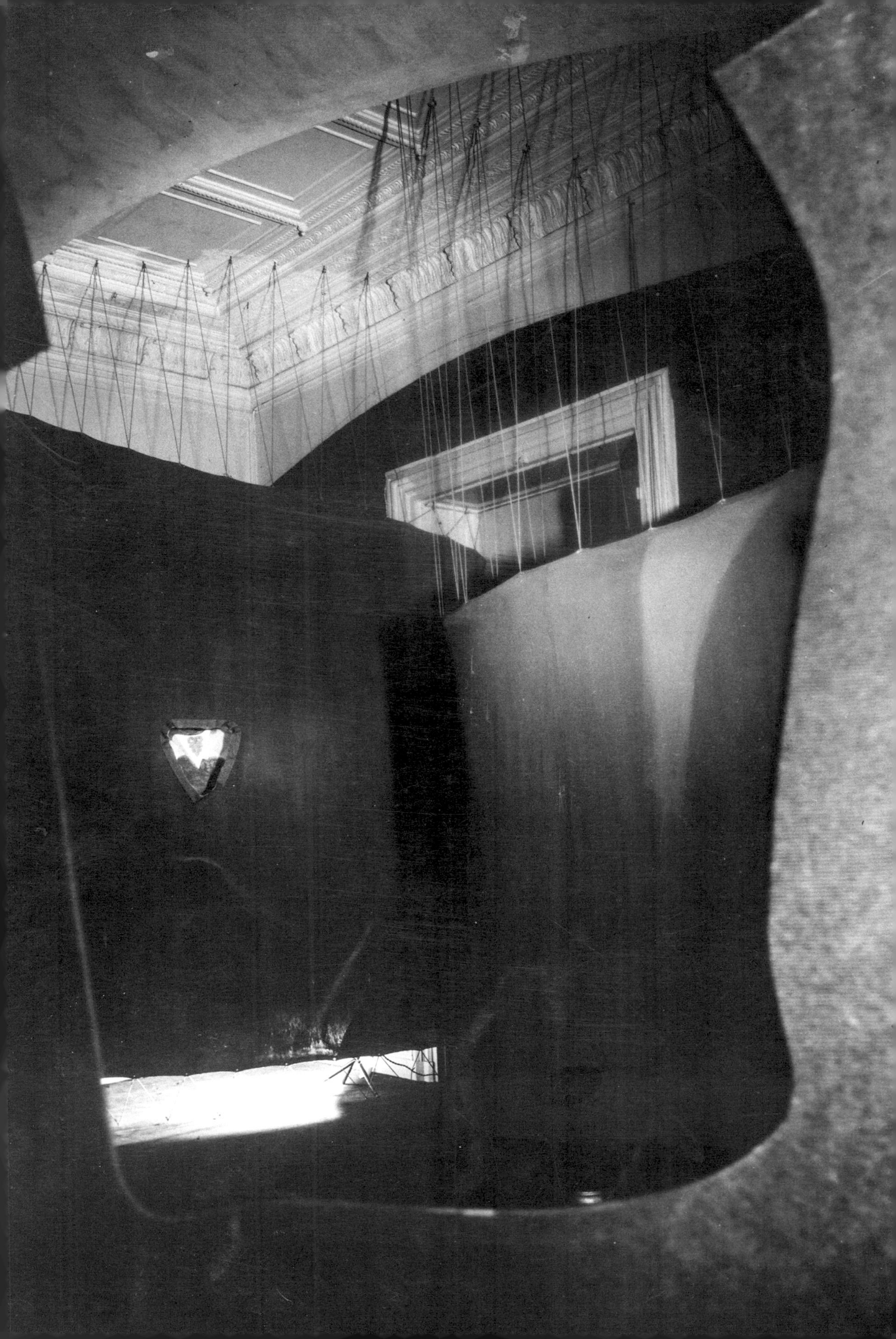

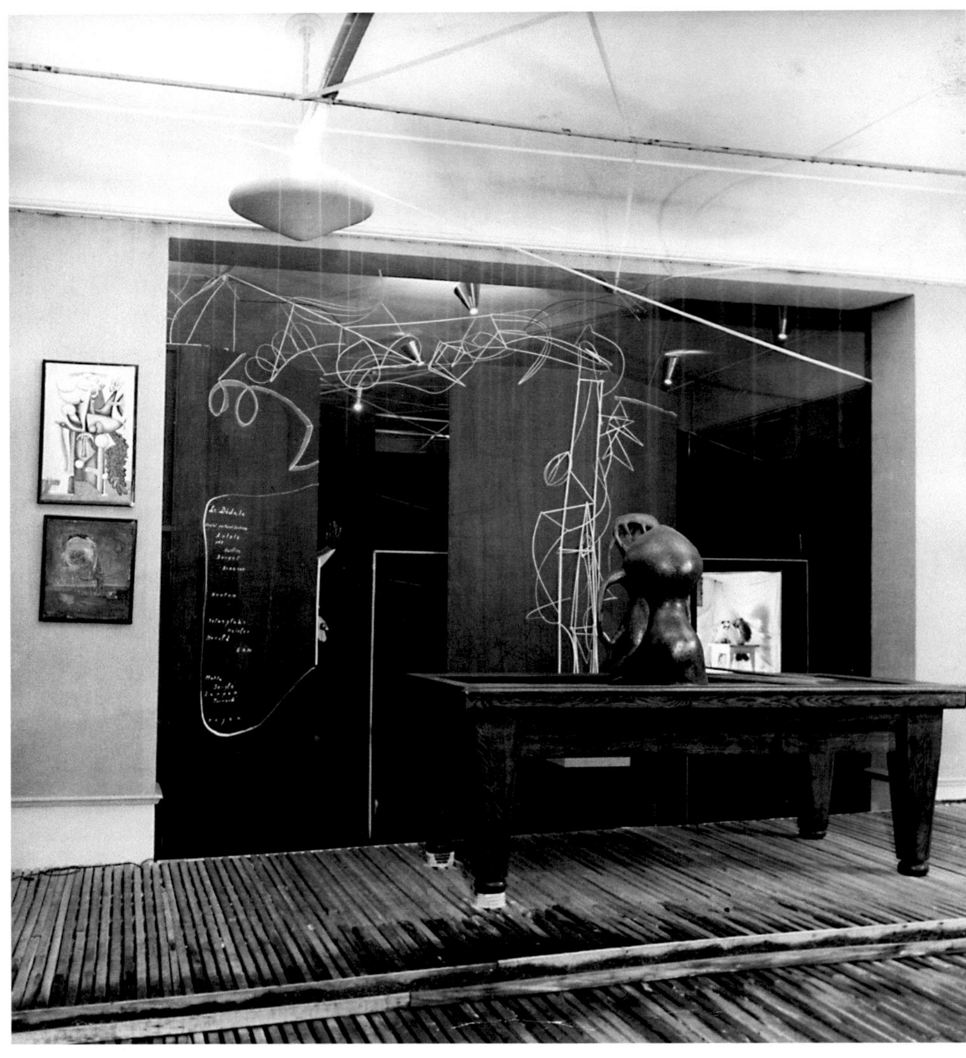

3.14

Installation view of the "Rain Room" at the "Exposition internationale du surréalisme," conceived by Marcel Duchamp and designed by Frederick Kiesler, with Maria Martins's sculpture *Impossible* (1946) on a billiard table, Galerie Maeght, Paris, 1947. Photo by Willy Maywald.

3.15

Installation view of the "Rain Room" at the "Exposition internationale du surréalisme," conceived by Marcel Duchamp and designed by Frederick Kiesler, showing various artworks, including (at center) Maria Martins's sculpture *Le Chemin, l'ombre, trop long, trop étroit* (The Path, the Shadow, Too Long, Too Narrow), 1946–47, Galerie Maeght, Paris, 1947. Photo by Rémy Duval.

To enact the exhibition's requisite "cleansing," the Hall of Superstitions gave way to the "Rain Room," also modeled on ideas by Duchamp. There, water fell from pipes running along the ceiling and directly onto the two figures in Maria Martins's massive bronze sculpture *Le chemin, l'ombre, trop long, trop étroit* (The Path, the Shadow, Too Long, Too Narrow, 1946–47). Shallow vessels of planted earth ran alongside the piece (so that the "rain" would make its grass seeds grow over the course of the exhibition), while the installation of a special latticed wood floor across the whole of the space allowed the water to drain. Adjacent to this simulated waterfall, Duchamp had asked that a functioning billiard table be installed, the latter serving as an oversize and eccentric pedestal for another of Martins's bronze sculptures, *Impossible* (1946).[40] This area of the exhibition opened onto a mazelike structure made of twelve octagonal compartments, Breton's "Labyrinth of Initiations," which served as niches for fantastic pagan votive "altars," each designed by a different artist. Among them was Duchamp's altar to *Le Soigneur de gravité* (Juggler of Gravity, an invisible but apparently crucial figure from the *Large Glass*), built by Roberto Matta according to Duchamp's instructions.[41]

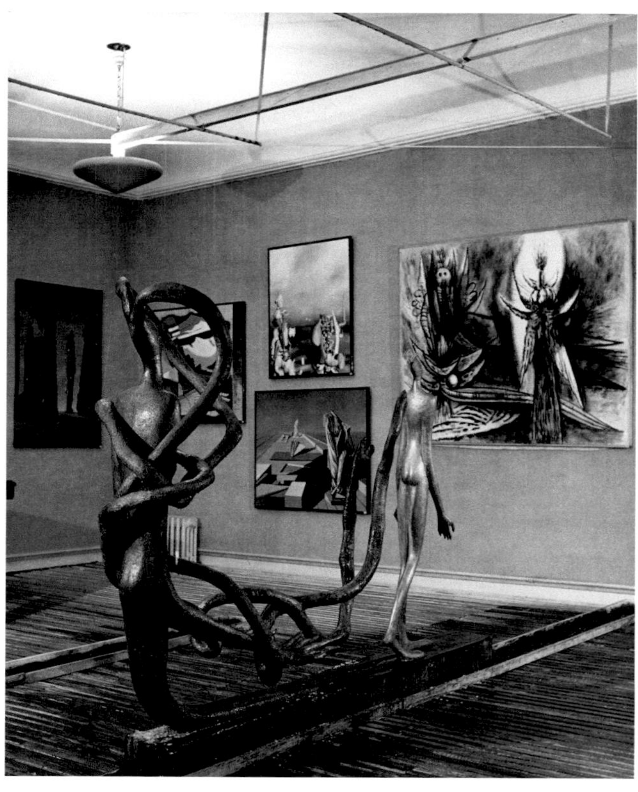

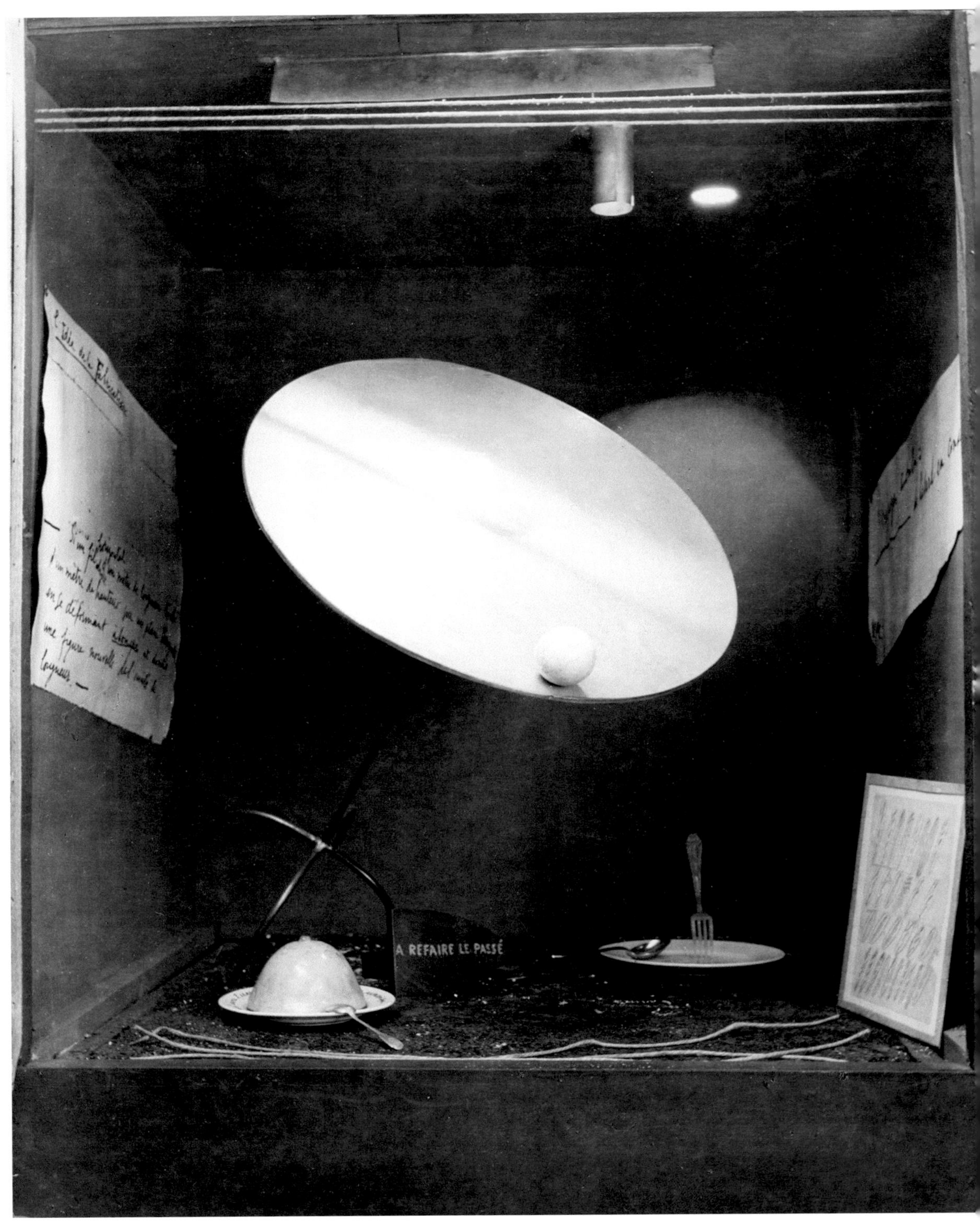

CHAPTER 3

No less spectacular than the 1938 "Exposition internationale du surréalisme," this first postwar manifestation of Surrealism was a peculiar mix of Breton's mythical-initiatory concerns, Kiesler's interest in what he called "correlation" or "continuity-architecture-painting-sculpture," and details prompted by Duchamp (among them, a darkened grotto interior with peepholes built into exhibition walls, "gaseous" light, the steady stream of falling water, the evocation of nature, and a participatory game—all idiosyncratic means of tampering with exhibition conventions, but also means of testing crucial elements of what would become *Etant donnés*).[42]

Duchamp requested that Kiesler specifically make a new work, entitled *Rayon vert* (Green Ray), on his behalf. The work was to be visible through a roughly thirty-centimeter-wide, perfectly cut hole in a part of the fabric "wall" that made up the Hall of Superstitions. It referred, as did the eponymous Jules Verne novel that it took as its inspiration, to an optical illusion, a green luminescence that can be observed at sea under particular climatic conditions at dusk. Although the exact physical details of Duchamp's piece remain appropriately elusive (based as it was on a rare optical phenomenon), Kiesler's sketches and photographer Denise Bellon's images suggest that it was composed of a tilted box frame, a photograph of the sea, a neon light, and two transparent gelatin filters, one in yellow and the other in blue—resulting in green, when layered between two panes of glass. A slit was cut into the photographic paper so that the light placed behind it seemed to emerge from the image's horizon. This illuminated photographic seascape reminds us of the strange foothold that water and gas have in all of Duchamp's work, as well as of the role that photography and voyeurism specifically play in *Étant donnés*. The seascape was likely only illuminated at intervals. This fleeting luminescence and the work's reclusive placement behind a hole no doubt obscured it from most visitors. Few seem to have noticed it at all, and none of the reports of the exhibition mention it, despite the fact that the exhibition catalog buoyantly announced: "Through a porthole shines the green ray by Marcel Duchamp."[43] *Rayon vert* contended, for those who noticed it, and much like the later *Étant donnés*, that the viewing of what is on the gallery's walls is an illusion on all fronts.[44] As far as visual tests go, it might also have been—like Duchamp's totally overlooked introduction of readymades into the Bourgeois Gallery exhibition in New York in 1916—an attempt to investigate under what conditions the work of art, placed behind a hole in the "wall" of an exhibition, would become recognizable as such.

3.16

Installation view of the altar to *Le Soigneur de gravité* (Juggler of Gravity) at the "Exposition internationale du surréalisme," conceived by Marcel Duchamp and installed by Roberto Matta, Galerie Maeght, Paris, 1947. Photo by Denise Bellon.

3.17

Frederick Kiesler in front of his *Anti-Taboo* with Marcel Duchamp's *Rayon vert* (Green Ray) in the background, as installed in the "Exposition internationale du surréalisme," Galerie Maeght, Paris, 1947. Photo by Denise Bellon.

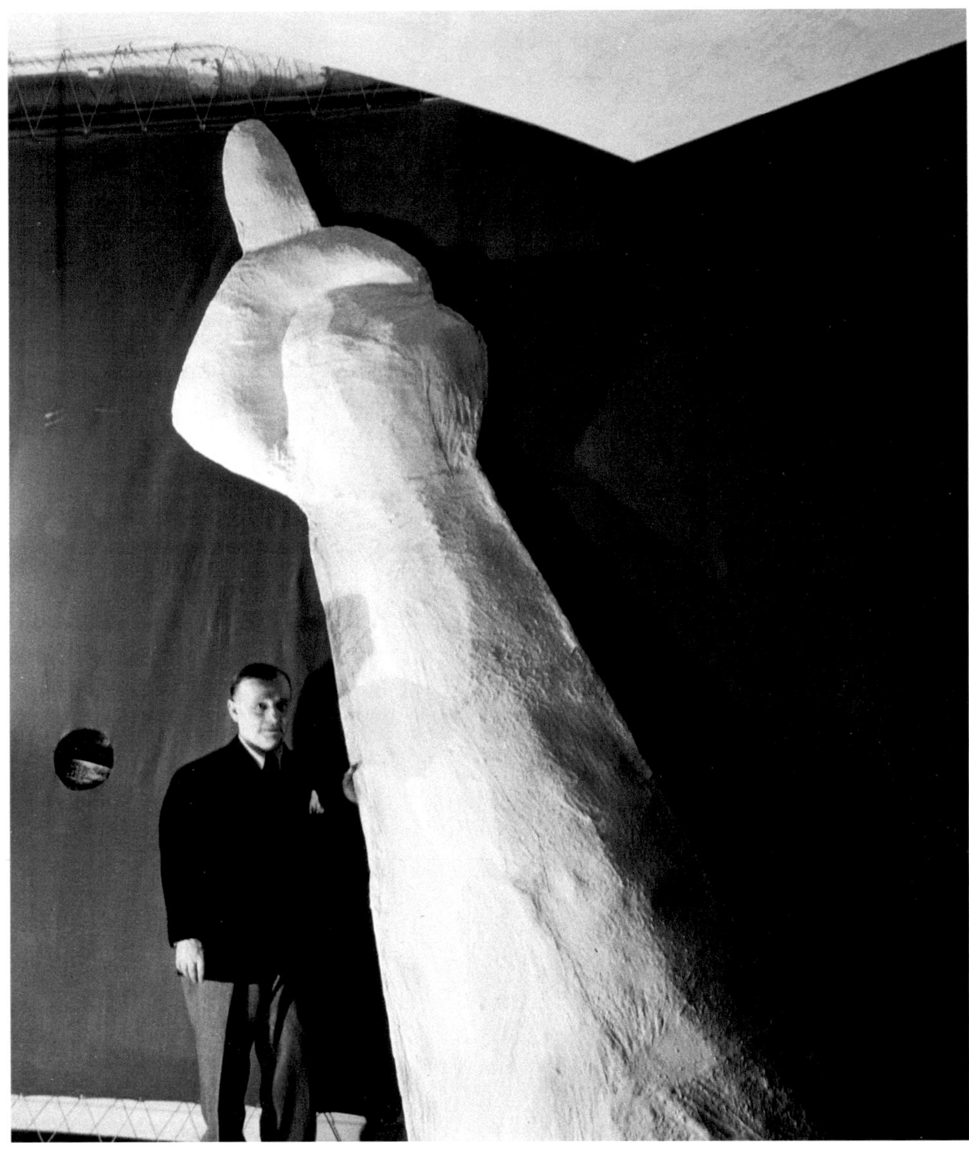

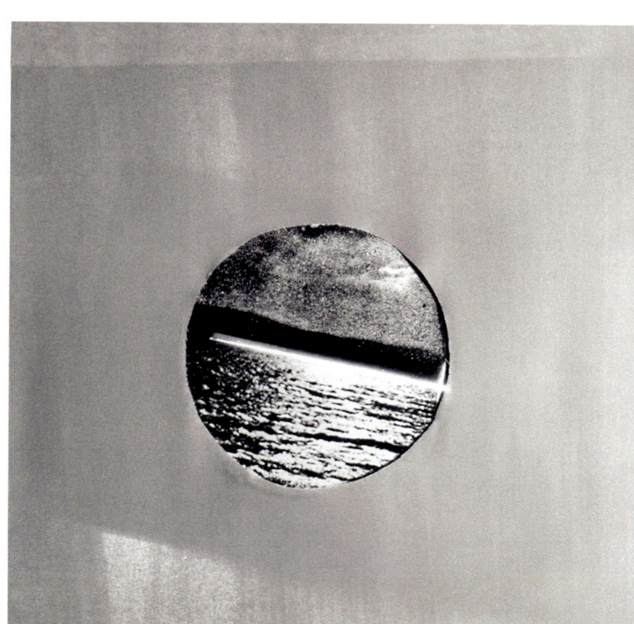

3.18

Marcel Duchamp, *Rayon vert* (Green Ray), 1947, now lost, as installed in the "Exposition internationale du surréalisme," Galerie Maeght, Paris, 1947. Photo by Denise Bellon.

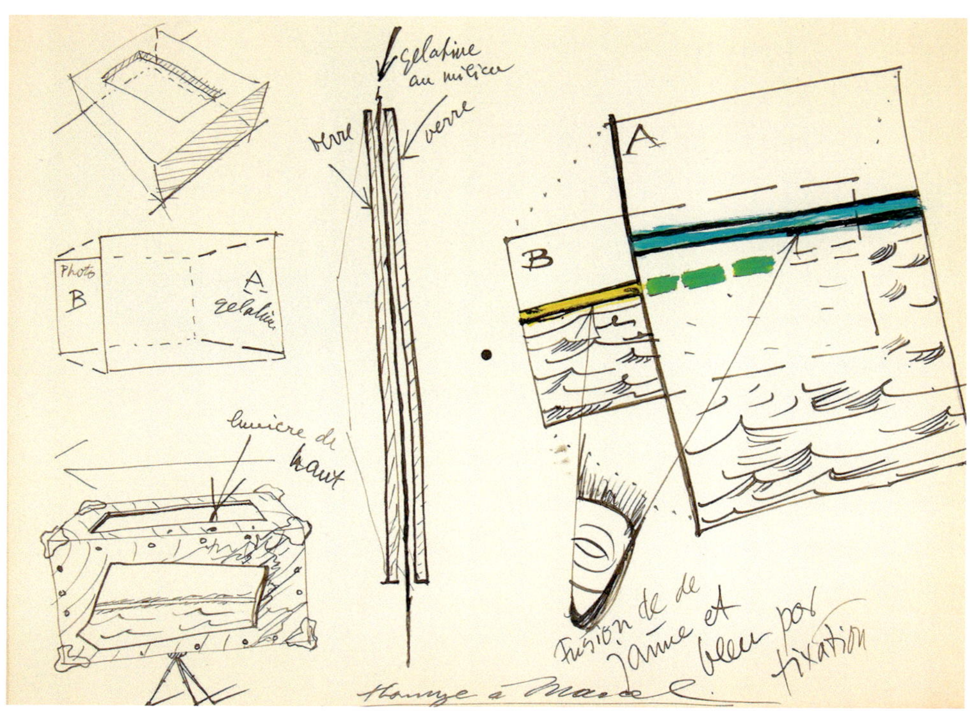

3.19

Frederick Kiesler, study for Marcel Duchamp's *Rayon vert* (Green Ray) for the "Exposition internationale du surréalisme," Galerie Maeght, Paris, 1947. Ink and opaque watercolor on paper, 9 15/16 × 13 15/16 inches. Philadelphia Museum of Art: Purchased with the Katharine Levin Farrell Fund.

3.20

Marcel Duchamp, study for *Prière de toucher* (Please Touch), 1947. Plaster, 8 5⁄8 × 7 1⁄8 inches. Philadelphia Museum of Art: Gift of Enrico Donati.

3.21

Marcel Duchamp with Enrico Donati, *Prière de toucher* (Please Touch), 1947. Numbered edition of exhibition catalog for *Le Surréalisme en 1947* (Paris: Pierre à Feu/Maeght). Bound book with collage of foam rubber, pigment, velvet, and cardboard, adhered to removable cover, 9 1⁄4 × 8 1⁄16 inches. Philadelphia Museum of Art: Purchased with the Gertrud A. White Memorial Fund.

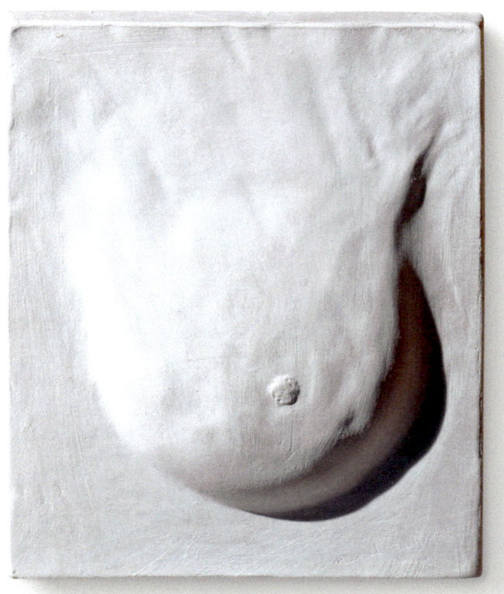

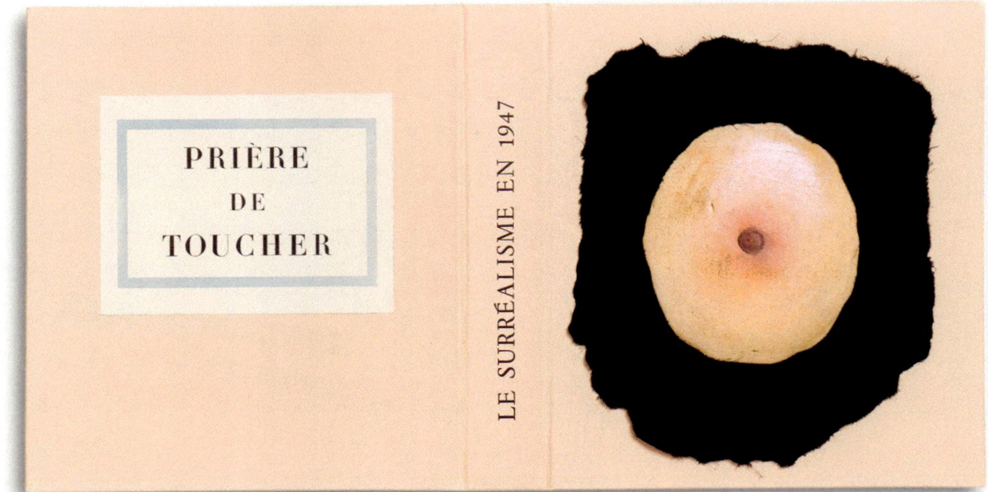

Although *Étant donnés* would remain a guarded secret throughout the entirety of Duchamp's arrangements for the 1947 exhibition in Paris, he wanted to have a cast of Martins's left breast (made as a result of the preparations for his covert work) replicated as a shallow plaster relief to serve as a cover for the deluxe edition of the catalog to accompany the show. The process would have been onerous, involving casting and then fitting nearly one thousand relatively bulky reliefs to the covers of books, and since the deluxe edition had to be produced in a short time, another solution had to be found (but it is telling that Duchamp was so attached to the idea). Fellow artist Enrico Donati suggested using what was colloquially called a "falsie"—a store-bought foam rubber breast employed by women to pad their bras—and he apparently also helped convince a Brooklyn-based manufacturer to make a batch based on Duchamp's plaster cast model.[45] The two artists then hand-painted the nipples of each of the spongy breasts and attached them to a backing of black velvet; both elements were then adhered to the front cover of the catalog slipcase. Hence, the body of Duchamp's lover became the model for industrially made replicas that were, in turn, individually hand-painted to eventually become a series of artistic originals. Rather than simply leaving a clue to his covert work in the form of an anatomical quotation, as is often suggested, Duchamp more importantly left behind this and countless other conceptual allusions to his deep and persistent concerns regarding embodiment, the copy, and the original.

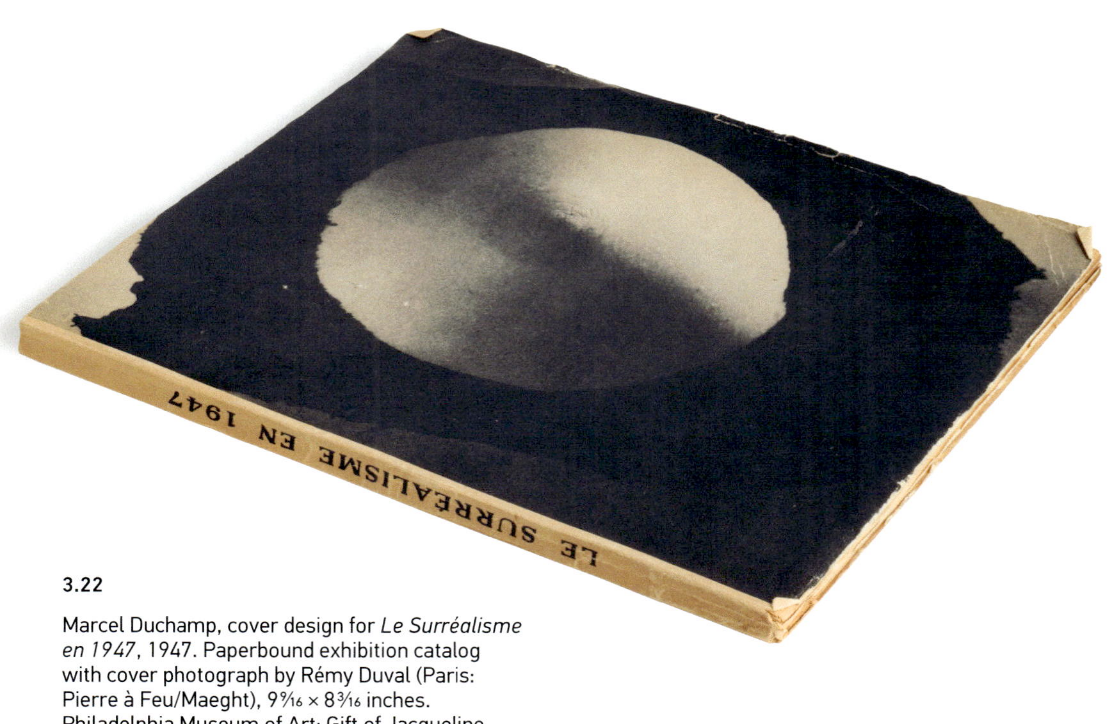

3.22

Marcel Duchamp, cover design for *Le Surréalisme en 1947*, 1947. Paperbound exhibition catalog with cover photograph by Rémy Duval (Paris: Pierre à Feu/Maeght), $9\frac{9}{16} \times 8\frac{3}{16}$ inches. Philadelphia Museum of Art: Gift of Jacqueline, Peter, and Paul Matisse in memory of their mother, Alexina Duchamp.

Slyly extending these queries even further while also continuing an investigation into the photographic medium, the cover of the standard paperback edition of the 1947 Surrealist exhibition catalog featured a photographic reproduction of an actual breast emerging from a swath of black cloth (the seemingly "real" referent of the foam rubber falsie), captioned as follows: "This cover is the photographic reproduction of the original cover by Marcel Duchamp."[46] Yet the photograph was in reality neither of Martins's breast—on which the specially made "falsies" were based—nor of the actual cover with its industrial foam breast. The photograph was of yet another breast, a real one, in this case belonging to a model apparently engaged for the task. At Duchamp's request, French photographer Rémy Duval made this image for the standard-edition covers and to include as a loose print in deluxe editions of the catalog, but it was in no way an actual "photographic reproduction of the original cover by Marcel Duchamp" as announced. Instead, it further complicated the deluxe cover's positing of an "original" or authentic referent while attesting to photography's crucial role in this maneuver.[47]

To the backside of the deluxe-edition cover, Duchamp had attached a sober label bearing the instruction "*Prière de toucher*" (Please touch). The association was irreverent, defiantly mixing erotics and tactility in a publication, rendering reading a corporeal venture. More than that, the catalog arguably served as a kind of manifesto for the rethinking of display conventions surrounding art. For the come-on "please touch" had a specific target: Duchamp explicitly requested of the printer that the lettering mimic the exact typeface used for the famous warning sign accompanying works everywhere in French museums—"*Prière de ne pas toucher*" (Please do not touch).[48] The catalog cover thus quietly points to one of the particular operations of the *Boîte-en-valise*; in a cunning reversal of the museum's regulatory function, Duchamp encourages the transgression of the institution's rules by offering a suggestive summons to touch.

Some years later, for the next major Surrealist group show, this one held from December 15, 1959, to February 15, 1960, at the Galerie Daniel Cordier in Paris, Duchamp was again invited to generate the exhibition's design. The exhibition announced "Eros" as its explicit theme, typographically expressed in the title, "Exposition inteRnatiOnale du Surréalisme." While it is not known whether the theme had already been decided before Duchamp was brought in or whether he suggested it himself, it suited him well in those years in which he was deeply involved in the erotic implications of his secret work.

Again Duchamp designed the space from a distance, and Breton's notes of his conversations with the artist reveal that Duchamp had an initial plan to convert the entire ceiling into a large-scale, spinning apparatus based on his *Rotoreliefs*. Given the theme of Eros, it is telling that Duchamp proposed making use of one of his optical devices; the erotic implications of the otherwise innocuous-seeming disks (first presented by the artist next to vegetable slicers and other practical utilities at a Paris inventors' fair), with their evocations of carnal viewing and pulsating penetration, were now clear.[49] Likely for technical reasons, the idea of a massive ceiling-mounted *Rotorelief* had to be abandoned, but based on French graphic designer Pierre Faucheux's drawing for the

1) Aménagement (I

d) PLAFOND PULSANT (idée de Marcel Duchamp

Tout ce que nous avons pu envisager, à ce propos, au cours de nos conversations de St Cirq me paraît, en définitive, d'une réalisation technique difficile et coûteuse

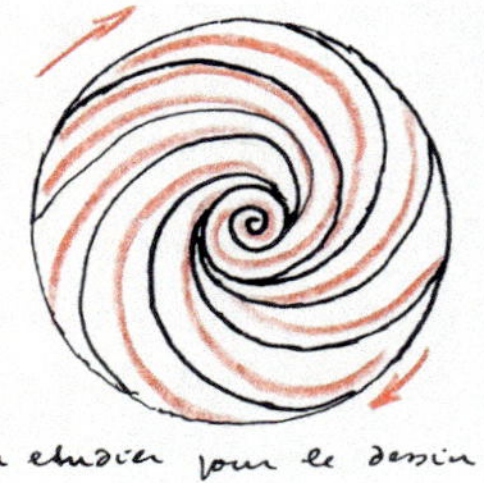

(à étudier pour le dessin)

Je crois que la meilleure solution pourrait être trouvée en utilisant un grand Roto-Relief orné d'un dessin spirale, capable de produire – par rotation du disque – l'effet optique recherché

(Voir les disques déjà réalisés par Duchamp aussi leur utilisation au cinéma)

Peut être ce roto-relief de plafond gagnerait-il à être légèrement incurvé en coupole très plate.

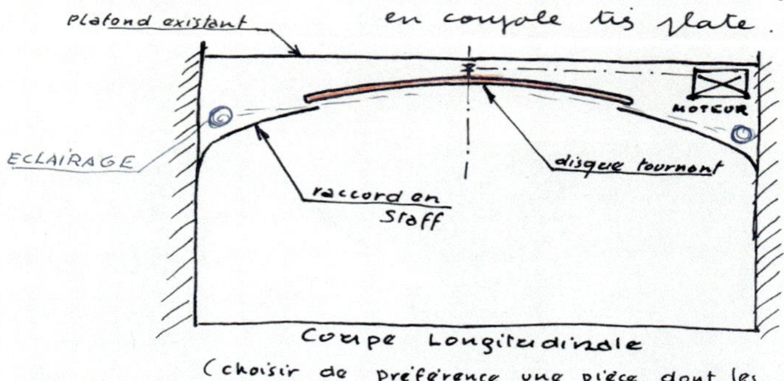

Coupe Longitudinale

(choisir de préférence une pièce dont les proportions sont voisines du carré.)

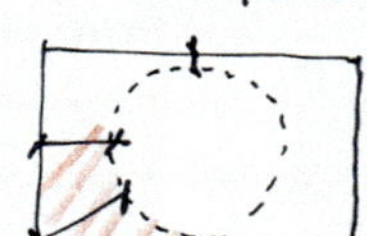

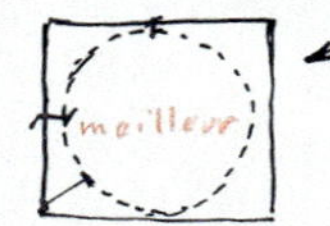

Le raccordement avec les murs peut être facilement réalisé en staff

Cet habillage doit permettre le camouflage des bords du disque

Il peut aussi dissimuler l'éclairage et le mécanisme moteur

L'entraînement du Roto-relief (réalisé en matériaux légers, sur armature) peut être facilement assuré par un moteur à vitesses variables. (accélération et ralentissement des vitesses à régler suivant le rythme de pulsations recherché..) Peut être à synchroniser avec un fond sonore – bruit rythmique imposant l'idée d'une respiration.. (le bruit de la mer, par exemple.)

3.23

André Breton, manuscript of letter to artists concerning the "Exposition inteRnatiOnale du Surréalisme (EROS)," Galerie Daniel Cordier, Paris, 1959. Centre Pompidou, MNAM-CC, Paris: André Breton Archives, Bibliothèque Kandinsky.

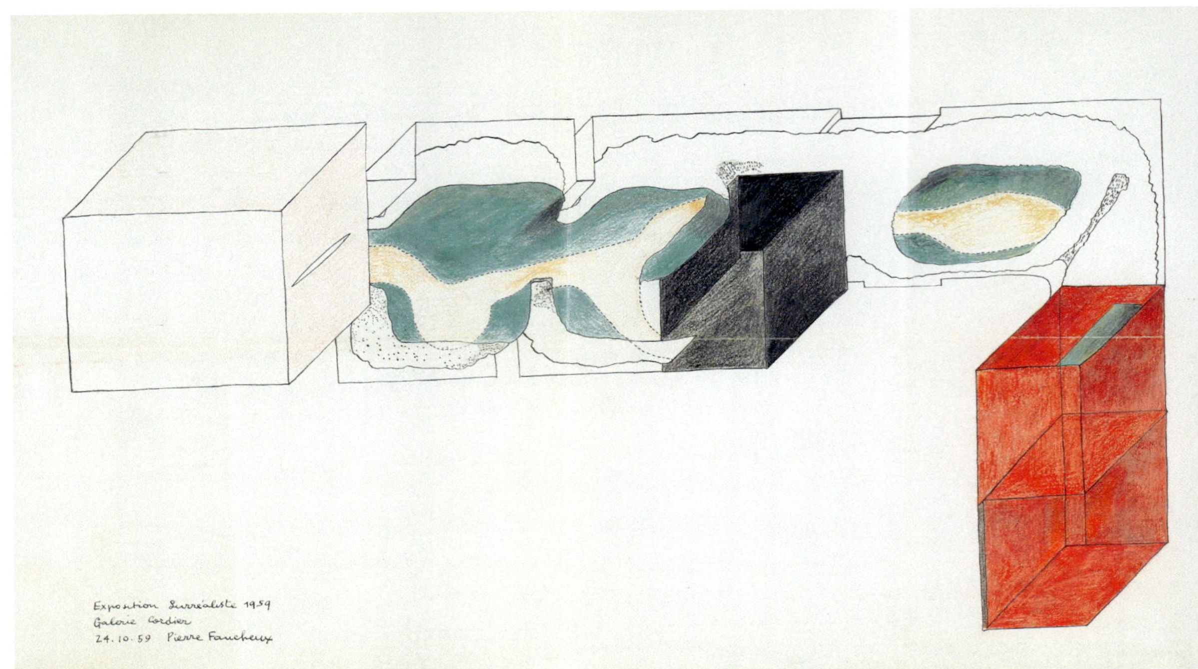
Exposition Surréaliste 1959
Galerie Cordier
24.10.59 Pierre Faucheux

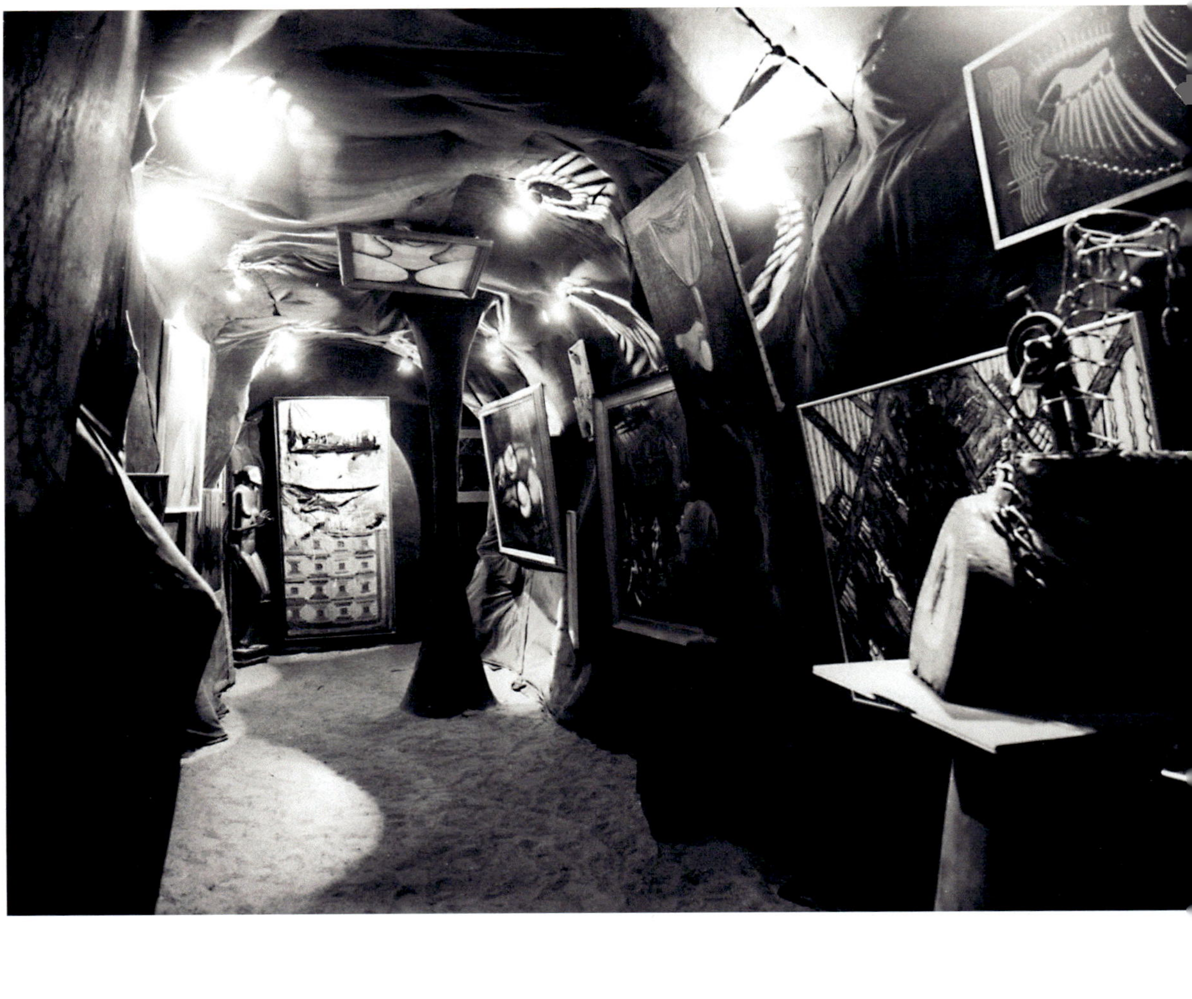

3.24

Pierre Faucheux, floor plans for the "Exposition inteRnatiOnale du Surréalisme (EROS)," Galerie Daniel Cordier, Paris, 1959. Private collection, Paris.

3.25

Installation view of "Exposition inteRnatiOnale du Surréalisme (EROS)," Galerie Daniel Cordier, Paris, 1959. Photo by Henri Glaeser.

3.26

Installation view of "Exposition inteRnatiOnale du Surréalisme (EROS)," Galerie Daniel Cordier, Paris, 1959. Photo by Roger van Hecke.

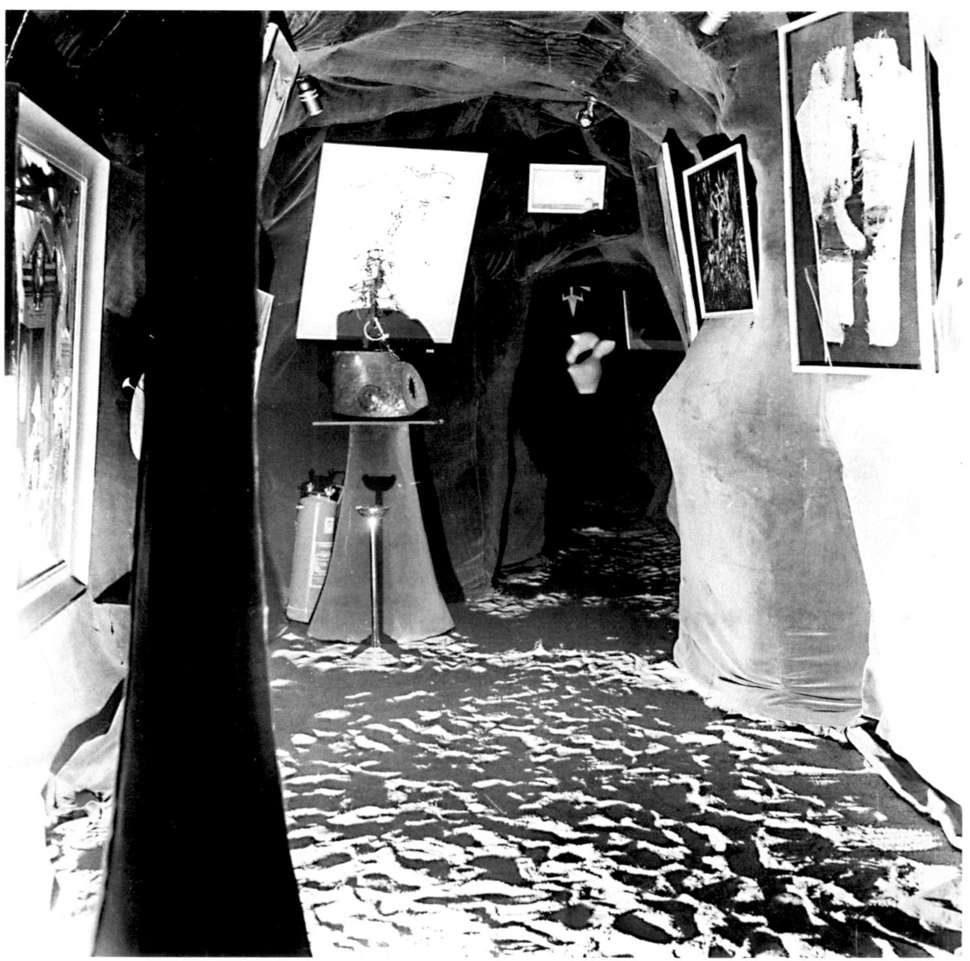

final interior and a handful of surviving photographs, we can make out the nature of the project that resulted in its place. Even before fully entering the exhibition, one might have spied holes at eye level cut into a curtain covering the front window of the gallery, beckoning visitors to peep at the spectacle within. Given how involved Duchamp was in envisioning the details of the exhibition, his early conversations with Breton likely gave rise to the specific notion of the spectator as "voyeur," a definition the poet-leader of Surrealism put forward in a letter to invited artists. The "voyeur," after all, was also how Duchamp would refer to the viewer of his then-still-under-construction *Étant donnés*.[50]

The suitably dramatic pink-satin-covered entrance space of the exhibition featured a ceiling with air pumps hidden behind its fabric so as to create a rhythmic, undulating movement, suggesting that the space itself was a living, corporeal being. At the end of the entrance portal, visitors passed through a pearl curtain set into an ogival doorway that Surrealist artist and historian Robert Benayoun called, in no uncertain terms, "'vaginal' ... with beads of dew."[51] It replaced Duchamp's unrealized hope for an entrance portal in the shape of a "vagina in rubber, badly made but evocative."[52] Can one imagine that the artist who had by that point completed the nude figure of his *Étant donnés*, with her own badly made but evocative orifice—the artist who was in the process of constructing that work's backdrop and architectural surround—did not have his ultimate work in mind when making suggestions for this 1959 exhibition?

More than seventy-five works of art conveyed the "erotics" of the exhibition's title through the mostly explicit iconography of (male) desire.[53] Artworks were immersed in dim lighting, almost as if one with the various organic, womblike spaces and passageways that Duchamp had envisioned. The rooms also included a lugubrious interior lined with moss-green velvet walls (the architect's solution to Duchamp's specific request for moss in the exhibition), and the floor featured a thick layer of sand instead of carpeting, from which protruded provocative stalagmite-like forms. The whole seemed to pulsate to the sound of the poet Radovan Ivšić's recorded acoustics of heavy breathing and erotic sighs, and the smell of cheap perfume, strategically released, permeated the air. Ceilings, walls, and floors, the structural elements so rationally designed and invariably stable in the traditional exhibition, were here rendered volatile and undulant.

The last room of the exhibition, lined in red velvet, featured Meret Oppenheim's *Festin*, a deliciously spectacular contribution to the exhibition's mingling of the carnal and the visual: the artist staged an opening-night feast of lobsters, exotic fruit, and other delicacies spread out on the naked, painted body of a live model hired for the occasion. Selected visitors at the opening were invited into the installation-performance to sit and eat from the erotic "buffet." After the opening night, a gold-patinated wax mannequin with two tuxedoed male mannequins who joined her as simulated "guests" replaced Oppenheim's live model.[54] Duchamp also had his hand in directing the display terms of this, the exhibition's last chamber, specifically requesting that the scene include "stagnant water" and that a barrier of iron grating not only interrupt lines of vision but

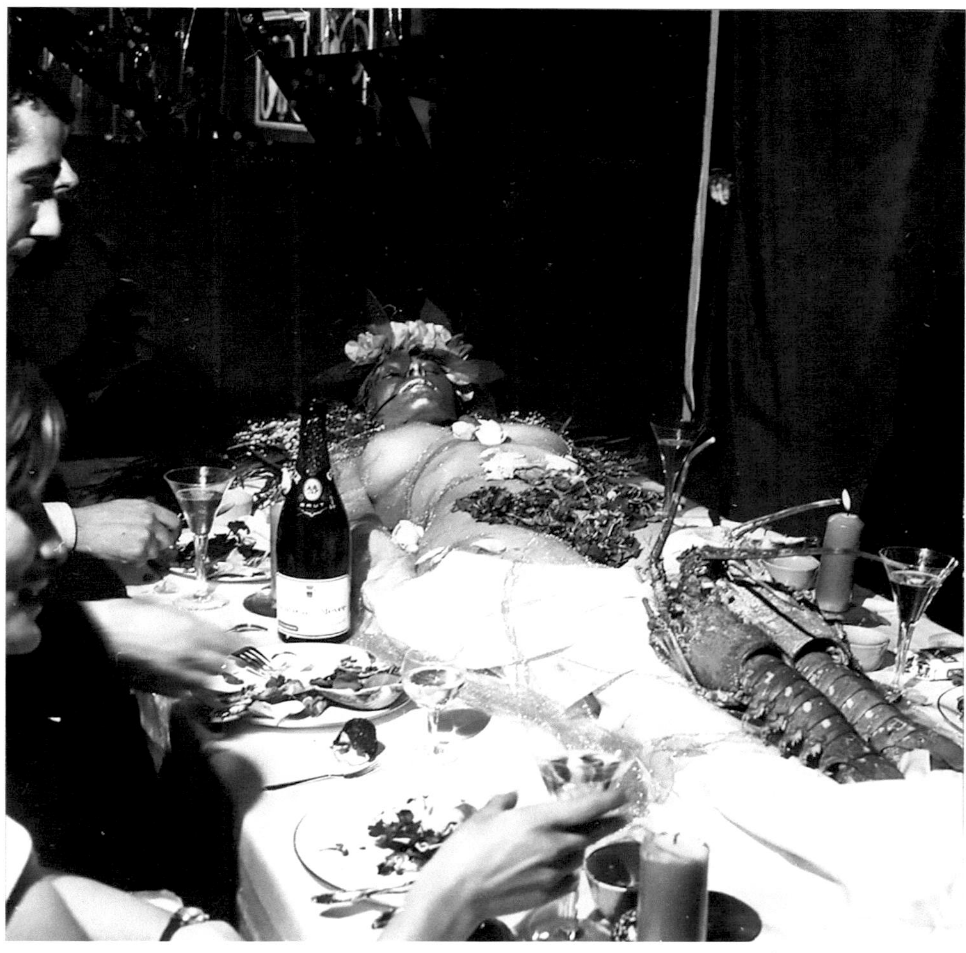

3.27

Visitors eating at Meret Oppenheim's *Festin* during the "Exposition inteRnatiOnale du Surréalisme (EROS)," Galerie Daniel Cordier, Paris, 1959. Photo by Roger van Hecke.

effectively serve to physically separate the spectator from Oppenheim's sprawled nude in her hedonistic landscape.[55] If the whole of the exhibition underscored the connections between the exhibition space and the female body and between looking and carnal pleasure, one cannot but recognize a direct antecedent to Duchamp's last project.

His conception of the catalog also underscored the central role he had occupied in the show's organization. The deluxe edition of the catalog consisted of fifty green mailbox-shaped cases entitled *Boîte alerte!* (Emergency Box!)—a play on a letter box and the artist's own previous *boîte* projects. Among what the cover announced as "lascivious missives," the box contained various erotic letters and paraphernalia, including the facsimile of a suggestive telegram Duchamp had sent Breton before the opening of the exhibition, as well as what Duchamp called his *Couple of Laundress's Aprons*: two playful potholders with "male" and "female" genitalia made of fabric and fur concealed behind tiny tartan fabric flaps—objects that he had the artist Mimi Parent fabricate for him in Paris based on a readymade set purchased in New York. If the *Boîte alerte!*, like the 1947 exhibition catalog, suggestively constructed a relationship between (carnal) desire and (aesthetic) looking as a central concern, it was in the exhibition space itself that one might have found the most telling signs of Duchamp's attempt to underscore the inherent corporeal implications of exhibitions.

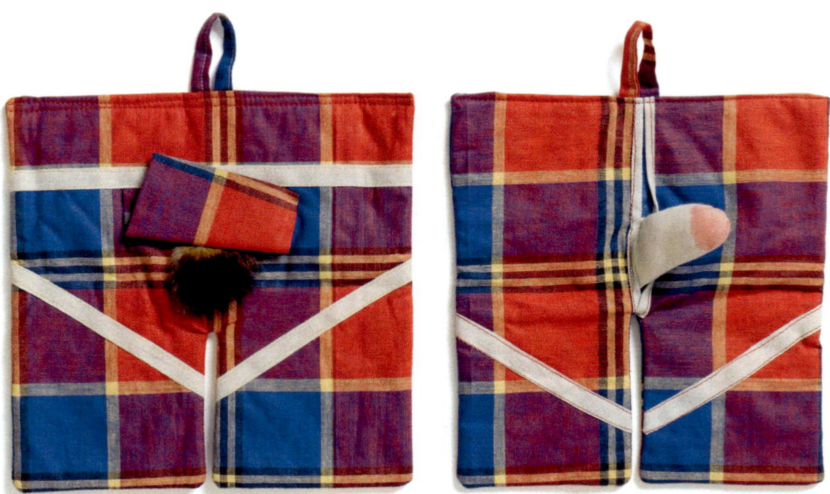

3.28

Marcel Duchamp, *Couple of Laundress's Aprons*, 1959. Two potholders (male and female) made of cloth and fur in an edition of 20 as part of the deluxe edition of *Boîte alerte!* (Emergency Box!), the catalog of the "Exposition inteRnatiOnale du Surréalisme (EROS)," 1959. Male: 8 × 6 15/16 inches; female: 8 1/16 × 7 13/16 inches. Private collection.

"The Surrealist Intrusion in the Enchanters' Domain" was held just a year later, from November 28, 1960, to January 14, 1961, at the D'Arcy Gallery in New York. It would be the last of the Surrealist exhibitions that Duchamp would curate, and for it he devised a hanging that might have seemed rather conventional apart from some small, but suitably odd, interventions. As he was in New York at the time, he conceived and directly oversaw the implementation of the various elements—of which he seemed particularly proud, as his letters to Breton suggest.[56] At the entrance, visitors could punch their invitation at a time-card machine, and could have their future predicted by a fortune-teller who was hired for the occasion and kept busy the entire opening night. Inside, the excruciating sound of a child's blundered piano practice filled the air, clocks bearing different times hung from the ceilings of the gallery's rooms, a ray of light (suggesting either the setting or rising sun) traversed the gallery, and snaking through each of the different exhibition spaces was a garden hose (invoking once again the *eau et gaz* that Duchamp so persistently brought into exhibitions he curated).[57] There were roughly 150 artworks, each with a little flag nearby denoting the nationality of the artist who had created it. Not far away, an electric train circled in a bay window, its string of cars bearing the names of the exhibition's artists. Both gestures served as Duchamp's parodic response to the standard exhibition label.

As his own contribution to the show, the artist created an installation in a corner cupboard comprised of three live hens and their freshly laid eggs under a green light; the poultry was behind a wire fence against which one had to position oneself for viewing. The corner, it goes without saying, became progressively foul-smelling and disturbing as the exhibition wore on. The area bore a handmade sign composed of a piece of ordinary cardboard onto which nickels were glued, spelling out the words "coin sale" (which literally means "dirty corner" in French, a colloquial term for vagina). The elements in the exhibition quietly pointed to ideas developing in *Étant donnés*, each striving to reconfigure the conventional exhibition space and the means by which visitors experience the looking central to an exhibition's functioning.

A shared iconography undoubtedly connects the Surrealist exhibitions and *Étant donnés*, and Duchamp might have been probing how lugubrious interiors, darkened rooms, and corporeal allusions functioned as exhibition space.[58] Yet, arguably, the more vital connection between the Surrealist exhibitions and Duchamp's overall oeuvre lies in their consideration of what an exhibition *is* and *could be*: the artist-curated exhibitions point to the need to rethink the typical space of display, to reconfigure conventions of spectatorial looking, and to allow desire to enter into that place where only a disincarnate viewer was otherwise permitted to be present. In retrospect, each of Duchamp's various curatorial projects—and I consider *Boîte-en-valise* one of them—seems to have served as an important testing ground for the questions he secretly pursued with *Étant donnés*.

That, however, is only half the story. Although the scholarship on Duchamp has long tended to privilege object production over the ephemeral (in this case, short-lived

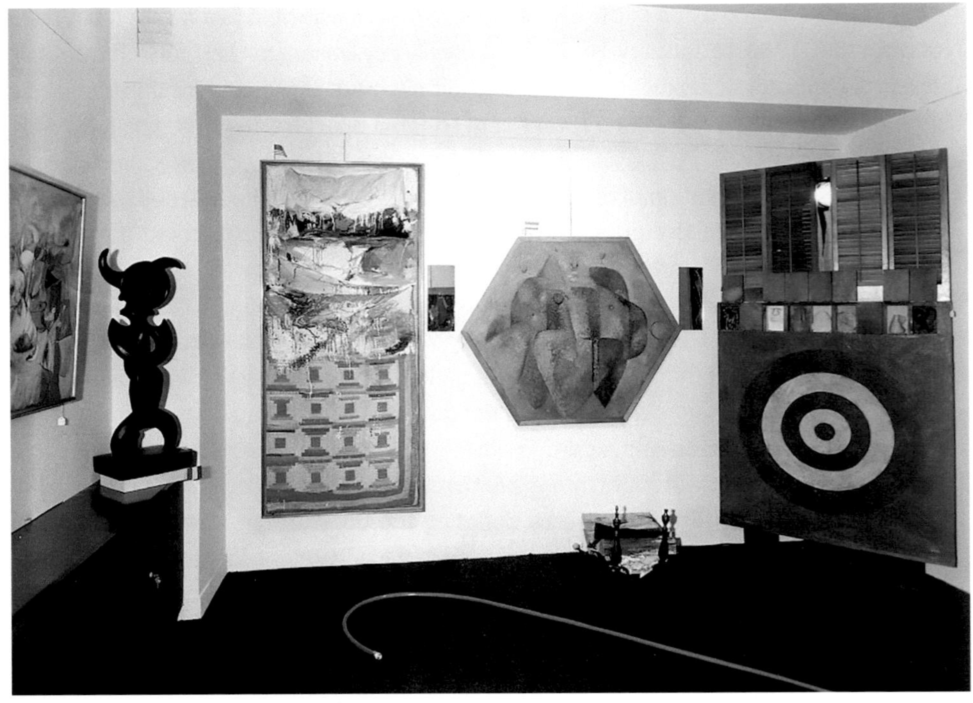

3.29

Installation view of Marcel Duchamp's water hose snaking through the exhibition "The Surrealist Intrusion in the Enchanters' Domain," D'Arcy Gallery, New York, 1960. Photographer unknown.

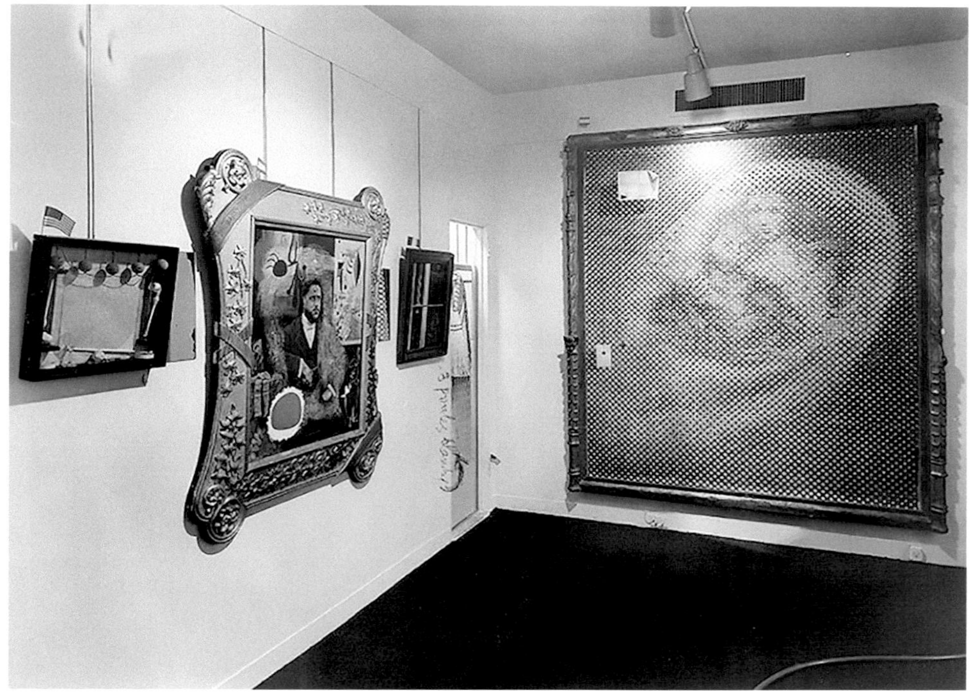

3.30

Installation view of Marcel Duchamp's water hose snaking through the exhibition and *Coin Sale* (left corner, identified on the photo by a handwritten annotation "3 poules blanches" [three white hens]), at the exhibition "The Surrealist Intrusion in the Enchanters' Domain," D'Arcy Gallery, New York, 1960. Photographer unknown.

3.31

Detail view of Marcel Duchamp's *Coin Sale* at the exhibition "The Surrealist Intrusion in the Enchanters' Domain," D'Arcy Gallery, New York, 1960. Photographer unknown.

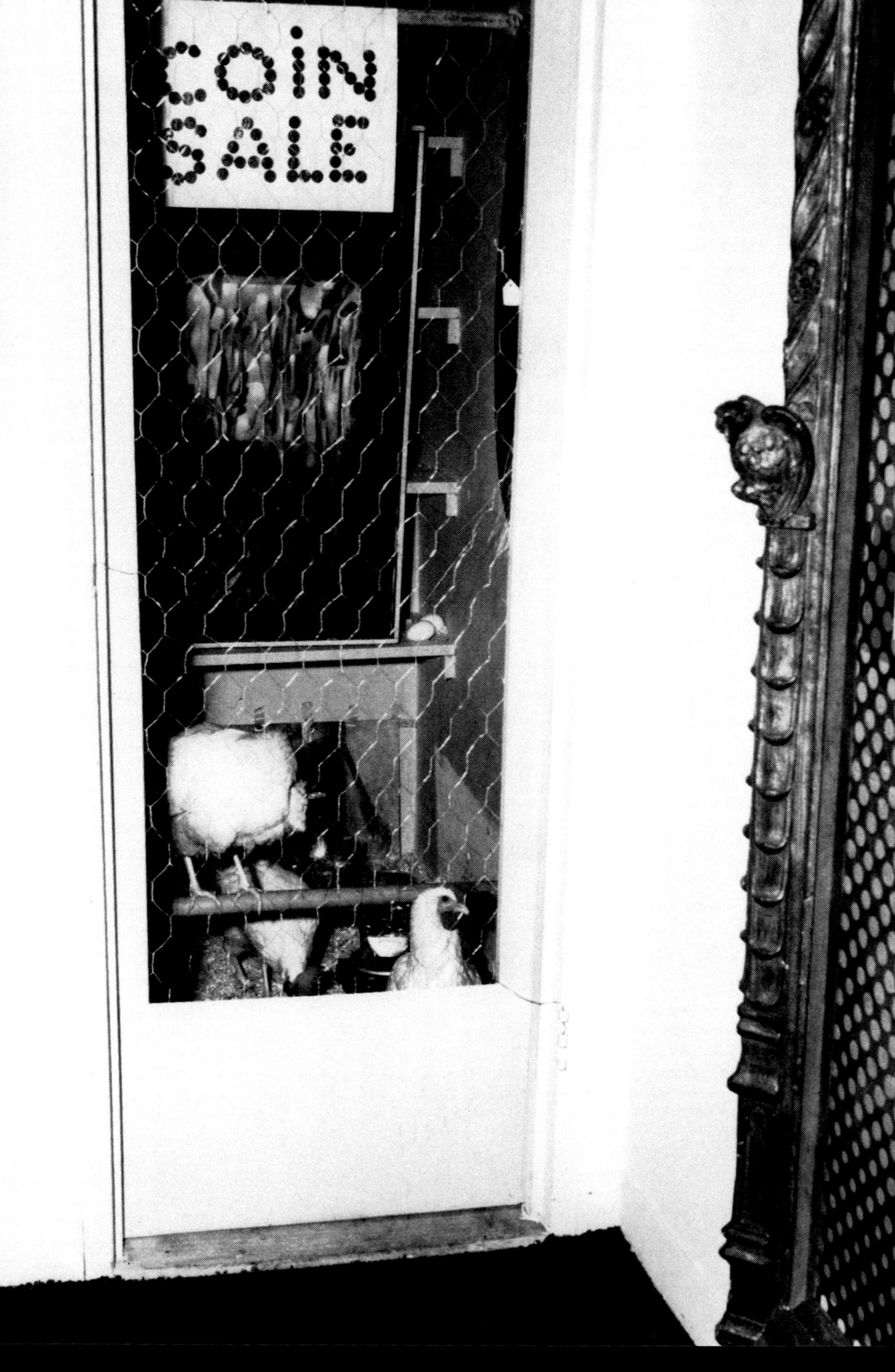
COIN
SALE

exhibition and store window displays), the output of tangible objects was explicitly not the conclusive endpoint of the artist's practice. Instead of conceiving of the flow of ideas in only one direction (the exhibitions as preparation for the production of more permanent things), one might see Duchamp's exhibition making as an artistic strategy in itself, which catalyzed shifts in his thinking about the potential form and meaning of objects. For it seems just as likely that what Duchamp was working through in *Étant donnés* figured in the exhibitions as vice versa, both projects actively materializing and simultaneously transforming his notions of how artworks come to be what they are: how they perform in and are constituted by the spaces and objects around them.

THE ART OF A COLLECTION

Duchamp's development of *Étant donnés* also coincided with a less spectacular but no doubt equally influential task: in the late 1940s, Walter and Louise Arensberg enlisted him to carry out the negotiations with museums to which the couple might potentially entrust their art collection. It was to be no small museum gift: more than forty major Duchamp pieces (nearly every major painting, quite a few readymades, as well as a number of important sketches: by far the most substantial ensemble of his artworks in a single place) and roughly eight hundred ancient artifacts and artworks by other notable artists (many of which had been collected on Duchamp's advice). For this task, the artist met with a number of officials from different American museums to negotiate the donation and terms of its display.[59] Among them, the Philadelphia Museum of Art offered the most long-term perspective for the expansive collection, committing to show it as a unit for a minimum of twenty-five years.[60] Letters sent to the Arensbergs in California so as to help them with their decision making attest to Duchamp's committed involvement with the entire process.[61] Over the course of the deal making, the artist came to know the galleries and interior architecture of the stately Philadelphia Museum building extremely well. He sketched out plans of its galleries, carefully noting such details as entryways, room dimensions, light sources, and other architectural particularities, and is known to have assuaged his nervous patrons by emphasizing the "good air of permanency of the building."[62] In 1949 and then again in 1950, Duchamp sent them various hand-drawn plans to convey the proportions and layout of several galleries in the museum where their collection could potentially be presented. Duchamp's repeated visits to the museum spanned more than a year, and the study of its architectural particularities quietly entered into his preparatory work for *Étant donnés*.

3.32

Marcel Duchamp's proposed floor plan for the modern art wing at the Philadelphia Museum of Art, September 7, 1950. Philadelphia Museum of Art: The Louise and Walter Arensberg Archives.

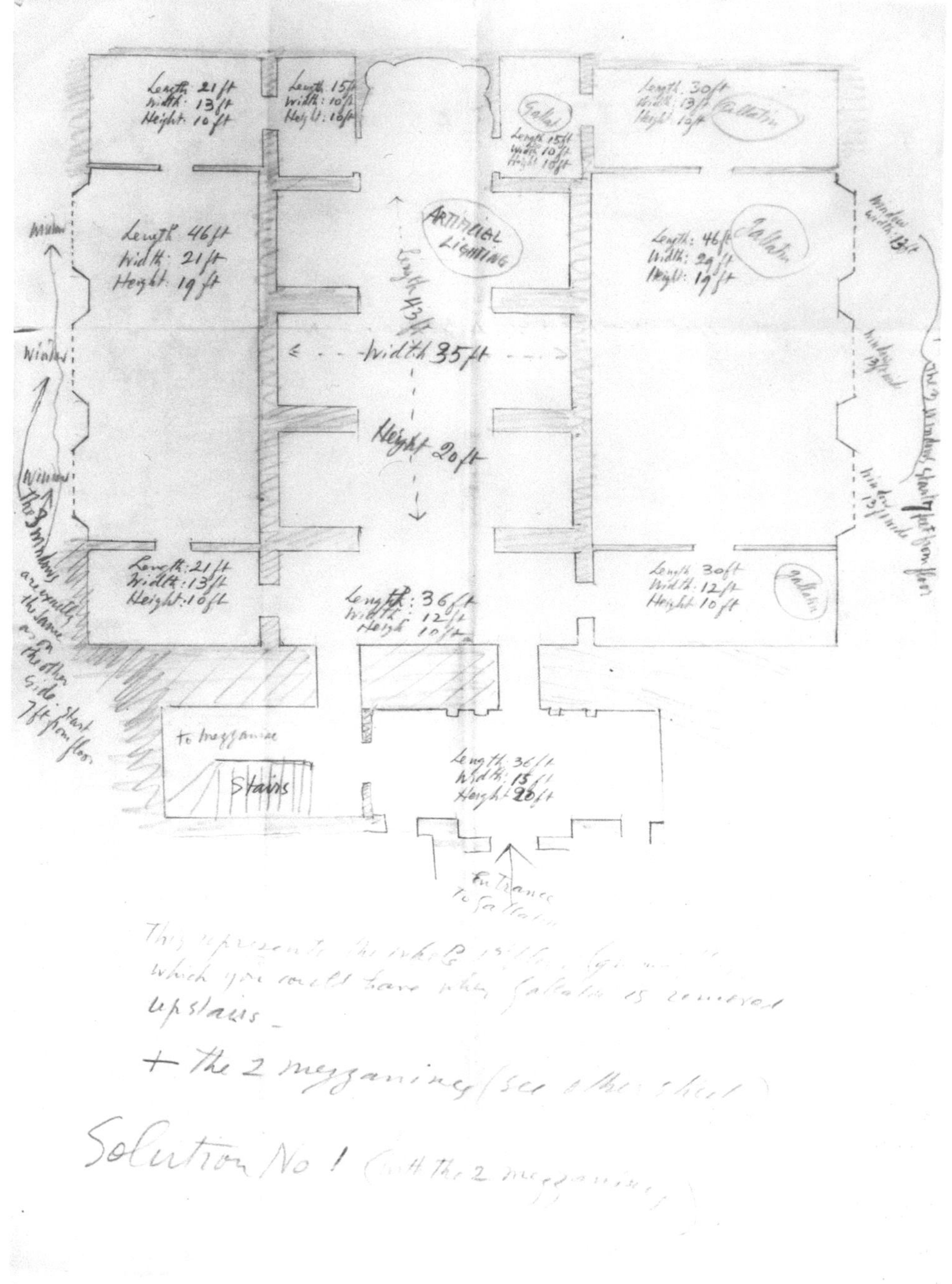
Length 21 ft
Width 13 ft
Height 10 ft
Length 15 ft
Width 10 ft
Height 10 ft
Gallatin
Length 15 ft
Width 10 ft
Height 10 ft
Length 30 ft
Width 13 ft
Height 10 ft
Gallatin
Artificial Lighting
Length 46 ft
Width 21 ft
Height 19 ft
Length 43 ft
Width 35 ft
Height 20 ft
Gallatin
Length 46 ft
Width 29 ft
Height 19 ft
Length 21 ft
Width 13 ft
Height 10 ft
Length 36 ft
Width 12 ft
Height 10 ft
Length 30 ft
Width 12 ft
Height 10 ft
Gallatin
to mezzanine
Stairs
Length 36 ft
Width 15 ft
Height 20 ft
Entrance to Gallatin
upstairs –
+ the 2 mezzanines (see other sheet)
Solution No 1

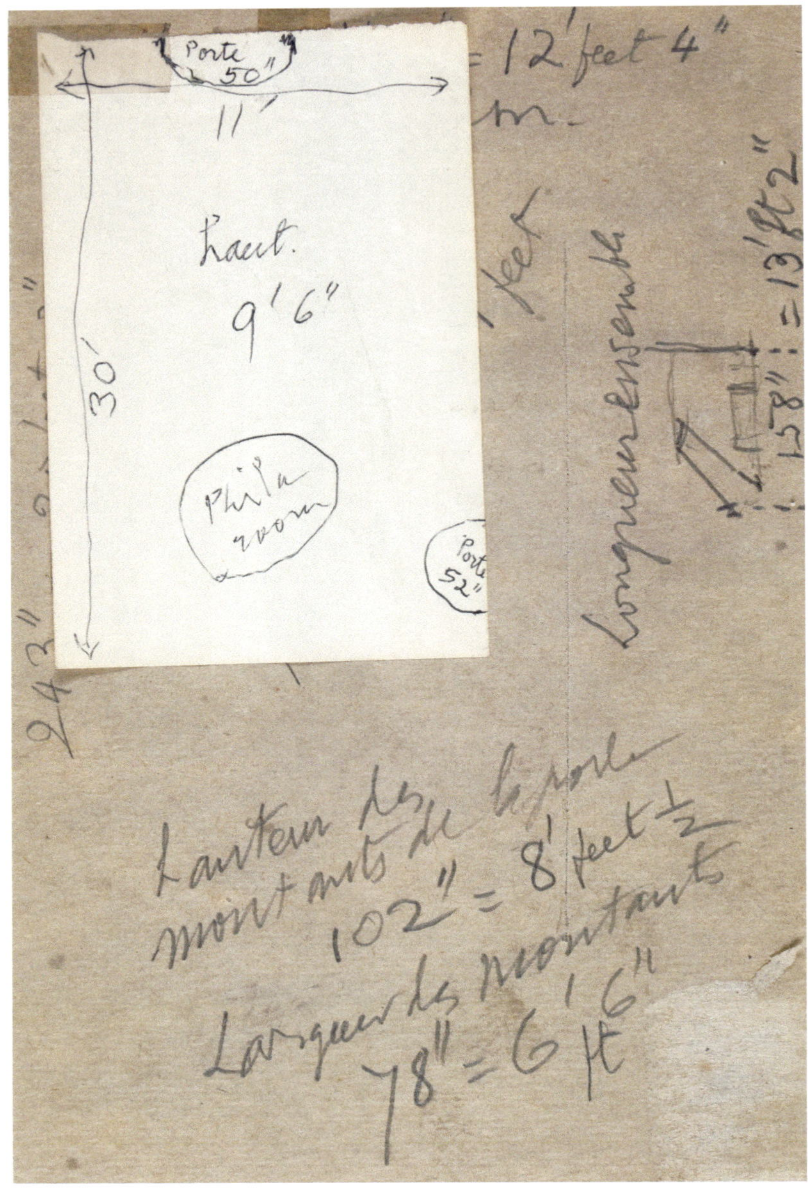

3.33

Marcel Duchamp's floor plan for Gallery 1759 at the Philadelphia Museum of Art, c. 1954. Philadelphia Museum of Art: Archives, Anne d'Harnoncourt Records.

Those hand-drawn plans, to scale and measured with precision, include the famous galleries where the Duchamp works are displayed to this day. Measured and marked as well is a small room—gallery 1759 in the museum's original numbering system—where *Étant donnés* would be housed nearly two decades later. Indeed, among the items found in Duchamp's secret studio after his death was a drawing on a scrap of carton, used as a cutting surface and marked "Phila room," with the measurements of gallery 1759, relative to which the artist evidently developed the proportions of his installation. In selecting the galleries for the Arensbergs' collection, Duchamp specifically chose those for his own works with said adjacent room at one end. There was only one entry to that final, small gallery space and no other way out—it was one of those dead ends of the museum.[63]

In the last days of 1950, the Arensbergs confirmed the donation to the Philadelphia Museum of Art that Duchamp had helped orchestrate. The multiyear preparation of the transfer and installation immediately followed. However, with Louise's death in 1953 and Walter's in early 1954, both missed being able to see their vast collection installed in those spaces the artist had chosen and whose considerable renovations he had overseen. Duchamp directed the placement as well as the lighting of each of the works, setting up the entirety of his pieces previously owned by the Arensbergs around and in relation to the *Large Glass* (which the artist, as executor of Katherine Dreier's will, had also steered toward the Philadelphia Museum).[64] It is not a minor detail that the artist was so involved in stewarding the final resting place for his works; one notes his repeated letters to Dreier to dissuade her from permanently committing works by Duchamp to the distant countryside location of her planned "house museum," and his eventual decision, as trustee of her estate, to donate the *Large Glass* to the Philadelphia Museum. Equally significant is the method the artist used to—literally—secure the piece there for posterity: institutional officials agreed to have its metal frame cemented deep into the floor, ostensibly a safety precaution, but one whose consequence was that displacing or removing the *Large Glass* would entail significant damage to either the work or the museum.[65] In addition, Duchamp requested a quite unusual thing of the institution: he had a doorway cut into the gallery's exterior wall in front of which his *Large Glass* was installed so that there would be a connection between his *Glass* and Maria Martins's bronze fountain *Yara* (c. 1920–42), depicting a naked mythological figure, which had been in the collection of the museum since 1942 and was presented on the eastern terrace just outside.[66] Beyond merely installing his works, then, Duchamp effectively reconfigured the architecture of the museum to suit his works and vision, and it is astounding that the museum abided by his wishes. The curious hold he had over those spaces extended beyond the initial display of the Arensberg collection; it is known that he spent considerable time rethinking and reinstalling the collection even years later, in 1961, when the bulk of it returned from a temporary exhibition at the Guggenheim Museum in New York. In all of these efforts, he acted almost as if a regular museum curator.

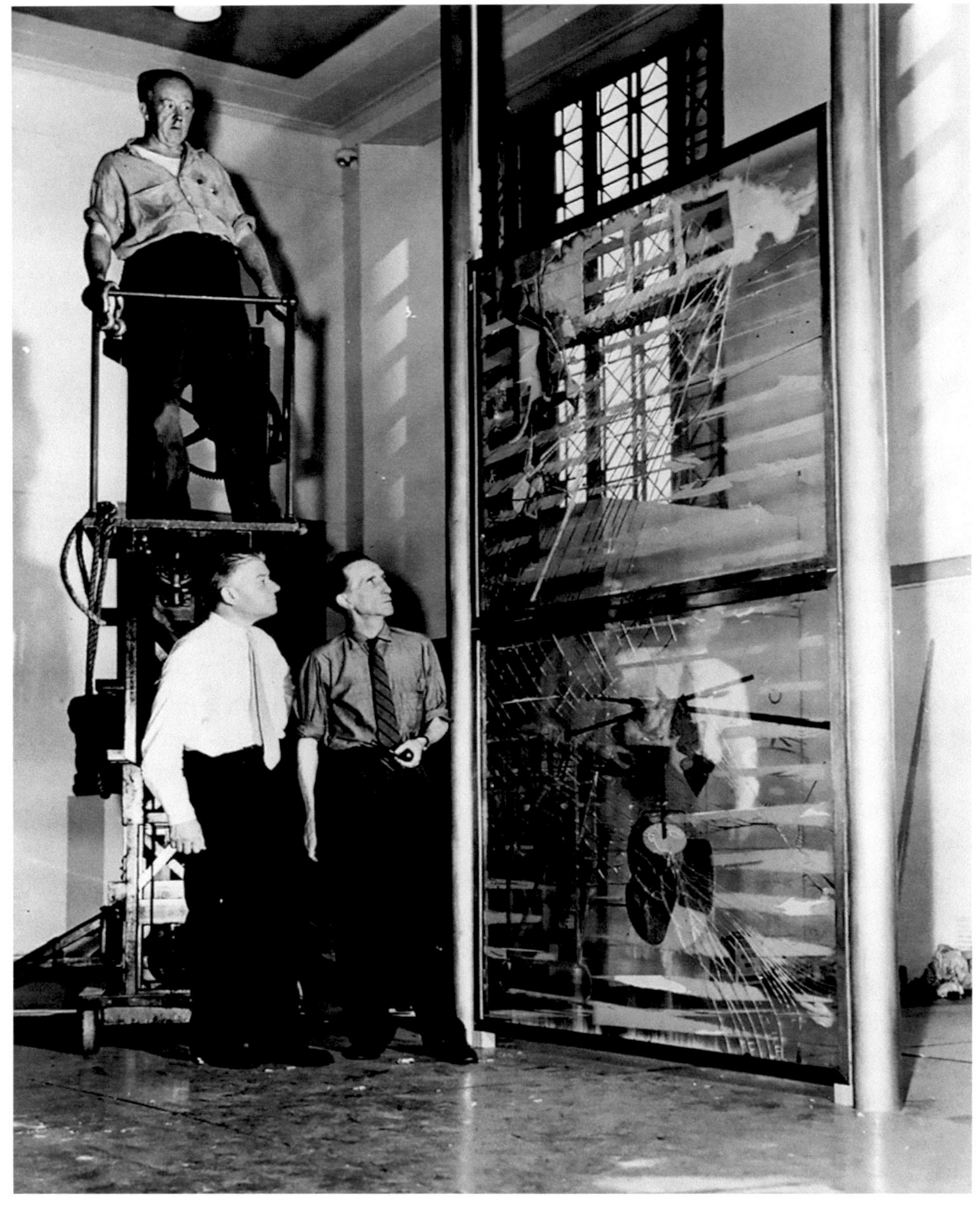

3.34

Marcel Duchamp with workers installing the *Large Glass* in Gallery 1729 at the Philadelphia Museum of Art, 1954.

It was Duchamp's friend Henri-Pierre Roché who commented that the artist "had the same concern to reunite reproductions of all of his works in a suitcase as he had to reunite all of his actual artworks in a single museum."[67] In fact, Duchamp's administration of the Arensberg collection (and, differently, also the Dreier collection), making it into the single most important reservoir of his work, had been a lifelong process.[68] This had been possible not only because the collectors were deeply interested in accumulating pieces by the artist, but because Duchamp himself took an active role in funneling his work to them: specifically reserving items for them, gifting them works, facilitating the purchase of his pieces on the secondary market, and even spending his own inheritance money to buy back works to resell to them.

To do so, he went to significant lengths to inform himself of the exact whereabouts of each of his works. It was a process that began with the construction of his *Boîte-en-valise*, for which he visited many collectors in order to take notes about the exact colors of his artworks to facilitate accurate reproduction. But it didn't end there. When in 1950 Walter Arensberg needed for tax purposes a list of the works he had purchased from Duchamp, the artist produced an up-to-date, itemized list, including all titles and prices.[69] As a result of these efforts, he managed to concentrate a remarkable part of his production in only two places, a fact that the collections at the Philadelphia Museum of Art and, to a slightly lesser extent, the Yale University Art Gallery now make apparent. The significance of this labor seems to have been, in Duchamp's mind, not merely a benevolent gesture or impartial advising, but instead part of his understanding of an artistic practice per se: in a comment made in an interview, he declared that a collection itself might be considered a work "of art."[70] Consequently, one could regard his efforts to install the Arensberg collection in the Philadelphia Museum of Art not only as a prolegomenon to *Étant donnés*, but as part of the very conception of that work.

Based on his experience with museum directors and their board members, Duchamp understood that, even as late as 1951, the *Large Glass* would be "hard to swallow for a 'museum'" (as he admitted in a letter to the Arensbergs). He must therefore have been able to imagine all too well what a challenge *Étant donnés* would represent for the museum, even after his death (and, in fact, perhaps he understood that the work would become ultimately admissible only after his death). Despite this, and unlike so many artists (Constantin Brancusi, Auguste Rodin, and Gustave Moreau, to name just a few) who bequeathed art to the state on the condition that their studios or work spaces be made into quasi-institutions or sites of pilgrimage, Duchamp never seems to have intended to turn his studio into the site for his final work's viewing, even though that might have been a considerably easier task. The artist wanted *Étant donnés* in a museum, and its display there is pivotal to the work's very functioning. Significantly, our viewing experience begins outside the work, in the approach through the succession of rooms and objects that precede the small white antechamber adjoining the main gallery filled with Duchamp's works. Thus it is surprising that so few studies see *Étant donnés* and indeed the entire Duchamp presentation spread across several rooms as a result of his willful

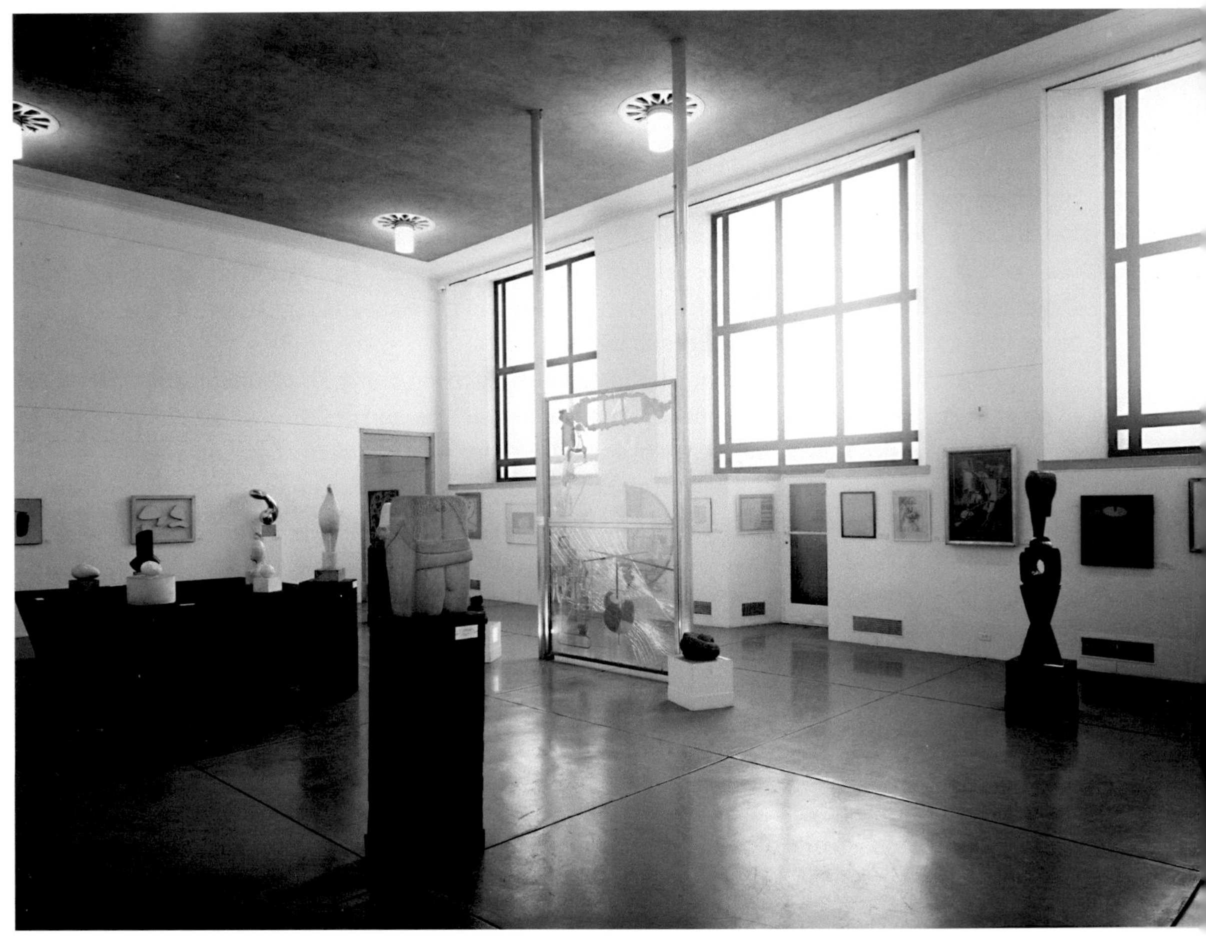

3.35

View of various sculptures, including the *Large Glass*, installed in Gallery 1729 at the Philadelphia Museum of Art, 1965; visible at the back left is the door leading to gallery 1759, where *Etant donnés* would eventually be installed.

management of and commentary on the museum itself.[71] Together these are the culmination of his self-curated exhibition, and perhaps his most significant work of art.

Rather than a negligible detail, the location of *Étant donnés* in an art museum entirely circumscribes one's experience of it. And yet the question of how exactly to read the effort that went into securing the work's placement there is rarely posed by scholars. One might say that an impressive and extraordinary aspect of the "artwork" that is called *Étant donnés* is not so much (or at least certainly not only) the elaborate vision before the eyes of the viewer, but instead the invisible legal and administrative tasks Duchamp performed to put it there—all of which mimic the museum's own rituals and functioning.

In the spring of 1966, once he had completed the piece, he arranged to show the work to his trusted friend William Copley and quietly offered it for sale (for $60,000, it is rumored), so that the foundation shared by Copley and his wife would officially "own" it. As an informal addendum to the sale, Duchamp even requested that the name of their foundation be changed to a new name of his choosing. In keeping with his wishes, the William and Noma Copley Foundation was rebranded the Cassandra Foundation.[72] A lawyer was consulted and legal documents drawn up, making Duchamp among the "officers and directors" of the foundation and stipulating the eventual donation of the work from the Cassandra Foundation to the Philadelphia Museum of Art. This charitable transfer was presumably intended to aid the acceptance of the provocative installation into the museum, and one cannot but imagine Duchamp pondering the museum's particular logic and protocol in order to facilitate that scenario. Moreover, the name he chose for the foundation that would thereafter be listed as donor effectively scripted the work's future museum label: *Étant donnés* ... Gift of the Cassandra Foundation.

It is now known that once the piece was finished, the artist arranged meetings with the Philadelphia Museum of Art's director, Evan Turner, and several of its high-ranking trustees. Lunches were followed by private trips to show them the installation of *Étant donnés* in the artist's secret studio as part of his mission to ensure that, when a museum board meeting would be called—as Duchamp knew one surely would be—there would be supporters who would defend the work's final resting place in the museum.[73] Acting as his own dealer or agent, he must have understood that this kind of art of persuasion among the elite in power at an institution was common procedure, determining so many of the decisions by the museum. Spanning from 1966 through his death in 1968, Duchamp's intricate institutional maneuvers reveal that he had carefully observed the museum's operating procedure in order to construct his elaborate response to the institution's fiction of "objectivity."

Constituent to this, he devised an incredible object—part bureaucratic binder, part technical instruction manual, part photographic cipher, part discursive accompaniment, part authentication tool (connecting the artist to his construction, even in death)—called by historians the *Manual of Instructions*, which anticipated and wrote the script for the reassembly of the installation in its final institutional site. Nearly everything had been set up for the work's final uncovering so that, by 1969, Duchamp "curated" one last show—from the grave. Yet another set of legal documents was drafted, this time between the Philadelphia Museum of Art and the Cassandra Foundation, stipulating the responsibility of the museum for the installation and future maintenance of the work, demanding "at least the same high degree of care" as it exercised with its "other collections," and the condition that the work "will not, under any circumstances, be permitted to leave the premises of the museum."[74] Resulting from this, and just over nine months after his death, with the close involvement of the museum's then young curator, Anne d'Harnoncourt, and Teeny's son, Paul Matisse, both of whom discovered the work upon his passing, Duchamp's installation appeared one day in the back of that small dark room in the museum. Similar to his role as perfect museum bureaucrat when constructing the *Boîte-en-valise*, Duchamp's manifold efforts to organize the precise conditions for the display of his final work—so long taken as merely functional or negligible—must be seen in fact as more properly *rhetorical*: perfectly mimicking the vectors of interest and power of the institution, they rendered the normally nearly invisible rituals and administrative functions of the museum and its curator into a critical element of *Étant donnés*. The curatorial is here nothing less than a medium of *Étant donnés*, even.

THE FRAME

It has long been an accepted truth that the nude female figure—legs spread to reveal her scandalously bared sex and arm aloft—is the central subject of *Étant donnés*. And if not her, then the two eponymous "givens"—the falling water and illuminating gas—are looked to as the work's focus, so literally are they named as the work's center. But what if one understood, instead, the work's context as more than merely auxiliary, more than merely extraneous, as one of its central subjects, even?

It would not be incorrect to call the piece site-specific, even if it was first conceived before that term was in use, and even though when the term did come into widespread use, in the late 1960s (just as *Étant donnés* was completed), it largely denoted industrial wastelands or deserted nature to which artists were turning in order, precisely, to escape from the ideologically compromised white cube of the gallery and museum.[75] But *Étant donnés* was tailor-built not only for the specific proportions of an actual museum space but also, more significantly, in response to the institutional and conceptual underpinnings of what that space stands for. It is, in that way, similar to the genre of site-specific works made in the 1960s and '70s that are often described in the following terms: each "took the 'site' as an actual location, a tangible reality, its identity composed of a unique combination of constitutive physical elements: length, depth, height, texture, and shape of walls and rooms ... existing conditions of lighting, ventilation ... [and] gave itself up to its environmental context, being formally determined or directed by it."[76] With *Étant donnés* there is, in short (and conforming to the very definition of a practice that once would have been called site-specific), "an inextricable and indivisible relationship between the work and its site."[77]

Duchamp chose the museum—that institutional apparatus intimately connected to the validation of the work of art—not only as *Étant donnés*'s "site" but as its frame (of reference) and arguably also its very subject. The museum thus functions as figure and ground, target and weapon, all at once. As this chapter argues, it is through means both covert and explicit, behind the scenes and glaringly on view (perhaps so much so that it blinded), that Duchamp used *Étant donnés* to frame the institutional frame—and in framing the museum, to reveal how it functions, what it upholds, and what it requires to continue to exist.

To begin with, one must speak of the supposed autonomy of the artwork and the museum's relationship to it. Painting, sculpture, and the very idea of an artwork as a totally autonomous material object (à la Clement Greenberg)—defined by contained surface and delimiting edge—depended for their privileged status on the apparently neutral conditions of the museum or gallery space (O'Doherty's famous "white cube").[78] The opposite is also true: the museum and gallery seem to need the "autonomous" art object in order to prevail; it is their raison d'être. The space of the white cube is fundamental to the Modernist precept, its foundational myth: the conviction of the artwork's self-grounding, its existence as something "in and of itself ... [with] a fixed and transhistorical meaning."[79] The readymade was preoccupied with the fallacy of this characterization. With the readymade, the artist arguably spent a lifetime probing these conditions in various art and nonart spaces. *Étant donnés* is the last of his "tests," and the museum is its testing ground. Not only does *Étant donnés* declare, already in its external presentation (brick-lined, inset into the museum's architecture), that it is literally not autonomous—requiring the museum's walls, its institutional authority and specialized viewing conditions—but it also concentrates what were the hallmarks of the museum at that time into its very substance.

As we know, the artist's elaborate institutional maneuvers guaranteed that his final work could occupy the museum as if a tenant with a long-term lease. Still, it is peculiar that discussions of the work fail to mention how exceedingly strange it is—even if we were to accept as commonplace that an artist might manage to insert any work of his own into a museum—that the thing Duchamp insinuated into the museum's collection is not a painting to be displayed on a wall or a sculpture to be shown in the round, but an artwork that makes the very walls of the museum its own. His critics, more than his champions, were the first to detect the threat this posed. John Canaday's caustic article in the *New York Times*, written upon the opening of the piece to the public, condemned it as "a parasitic appendage."[80] However dismissive Canaday's reading, there is something to his critique: from the moment *Étant donnés* opened, it had, in a way, appropriated the museum and would use it, like a parasite, for its own ends.

Insofar as the work makes the walls of the museum its own, it implicates the succession of rooms before it as part of the experience of *Étant donnés*: the museum is revealed as a spatialized articulation of a system of values (reflecting not only bourgeois conventions but also masculine heterosexual fantasies) that end in an oddly lit ersatz crotch, a hole that is the endpoint of a whole series of other holes that Duchamp, one could say, burrowed into the museum. It is not by chance that the work makes so much of the museum's thresholds. In perception as in architecture, a threshold marks the point of transition, the passage toward or away from the perceptible, into or out of a place. Considered in these terms, *Étant donnés* follows a decidedly confounding architectural logic, offering an elaborate behind-the-scenes structure whose visible "front" is a weathered, exterior door found inside the museum that should logically lead vision outside the door, which is to say, outside the museum, but instead brings vision past a broken brick aperture to an illusionistic idyll, purportedly outside (in nature, in the world) but rendered so unconvincingly that it is, in fact, very clearly inside.[81] But inside what exactly? A structure of thresholds, *Étant donnés* explores this limit of architecture, uncovering the place in which it stands, and in the process lifting the whole of the (usually normalized and therefore inconspicuous) museum into view as the site at which the work's perceptual unfolding begins.

A VIEWING APPARATUS

If demonstration is the very purpose of museal display, Duchamp's installation is a kind of monstrous viewing machine: fixing viewers in place, turning them into peeping voyeurs, disrupting demarcations between inside and outside, the artist-curator-impresario posthumously escorting us to an indeterminate place that is veritably inside and yet projecting an outside of the museum. There the viewer is an actor in Duchamp's final work, not a mere observer. As Octavio Paz once put it: "The person peeping through the holes in the Spanish door is not outside the Assemblage: he is part of the spectacle. *Given* is realized by means of his look: it is a spectacle in which someone sees himself seeing something."[82]

Someone sees himself seeing something: in a note written in the teens, Duchamp anticipated this idea by articulating his interest in an ocular reversal, "On peut regarder voir" (One can look at seeing).[83] While this "seeing" has been the subject of considerable Duchamp scholarship, it is the seeing in this specific place that I want to question here. For it had to be in the museum, the very place built on the primacy of visuality, that Duchamp inserted his strange vision-machine-as-crypt.[84] *Étant donnés* might thus be the perfect example of the artwork that, as phenomenologist Maurice Merleau-Ponty posited in 1961, one doesn't actually see, but rather *according to which one sees*; in other words, it is a work that simultaneously actuates and reveals parameters of seeing.[85]

In *Étant donnés* Duchamp carefully determined the perspectival focus of the viewer's gaze; he organized, even plotted it. And though it might not look like the product of anything wholly scientific, the artist undoubtedly found his models in science. Duchamp's perspectival and other semiscientific research, manifest in works from the *Large Glass* through to *Étant donnés*, is legendary.[86] His boxes of notes are testament to this research.

While none of the notes in his vast collections seems to speak directly to the details or construction of *Étant donnés*, it is clear that Duchamp's interest in, and application of, the laws of perspective and stereoscopy were decisive in that work.[87] After all, the following description of stereoscopic space could be said equally to describe *Étant donnés*:

> perspectival space raised to a higher power. Organized as a kind of tunnel vision, the experience of deep recession is insistent and inescapable. ... [As the spectator] views the image in an ideal isolation, his surrounds, with their walls and floors, are banished from sight. The apparatus of the stereoscope mechanically focuses all attention on the matter at hand and precludes the visual meandering experienced in the gallery as one's eyes wander from picture to picture and to surrounding space.[88]

To create such an experience, the artist abided by the customary structuring of stereoscopic views "around a vertical marker in fore- or middle-ground that works to *center* space, forming a representation within the visual field of the eyes' convergence at a vanishing point."[89] Following these parameters to the letter, Duchamp constructed *Étant donnés* so that the vanishing point (in the "perspectivist sense," as Jean-François Lyotard would say), viewed through the eyeholes and past the gaping hole in the brick wall, would coincide with yet another hole: the supine figure's exposed vulva.[90] Just so one would not miss it, the *Manual of Instructions* specified that a spotlight of 150 watts "has to fall vertically, exactly, on the cunt."[91]

Duchamp determined not only where the viewer should look, but also *how*. He went to considerable lengths, using large swaths of black velvet to line the back of the Spanish door and to cover the sides of the structure from the backside of the front door to the broken brick wall, to ensure that the viewer would not be able to see in by any other way than the two eyeholes provided. When looking through these, the point of view and the vanishing point coincide, and, as Lyotard points out, a cunning reversal ensues:

> The device would be specular. ... The plane of the breach would be that of a picture that would cut the visive pyramids that have as their summits the voyeur's holes. In an organization of this type, the viewing point and the vanishing point are symmetrical: If it is true that the latter is the vulva, then the vulva is the specular image of the voyeur-eyes; or: When these eyes think they see the vulva, they are seeing themselves.[92]

In the process, roles switch, relationships are inverted, the gaze turns back on itself: we are seen looking. "Con celui qui voit" is how Lyotard put it, simply and directly, like a finger pointing at a fault line: he who sees is a cunt.[93]

This cunt you see (this cunt that you are, in Lyotard's scenario) is awkward, gaping, failed, and unnatural. Even more than the rest of the body, it is a mix of aborted realism and ambiguity, familiarity and strangeness, seemingly threatening to deliquesce at any moment into undifferentiated matter, and suggesting that Duchamp did not want to present a nude either as an ideal or as a libidinal object (could there be any arousal found in this distorted thing?). Rather, it is a *simulacrum*, a placeholder for the thing that the artist really wants to compel you to see: the museum. Following Lyotard's logic, then: the museum is the cunt.

The work's private, one-to-one mode of address and its imperative of bodily contact violate many museum protocols and fundamental precepts—it is almost impossible not to lean too closely, touching the door, your nose pressed against it while your eyes peer into this display that has the formal structure of the peep show and the diorama at once. This very combination and their respective bodily implications were anathema to the art museum. As we know, in place of embodied viewing, the museum champions a pure, universal, and disinterested gaze (the 1937 "museology" exhibition in Paris, with all its Cartesian fanfare, made this explicit). Indeed, the story of the museum is the story of control over the carnal body of a visitor who does not eat or drink or run or speak too loudly or touch anything in its pristine space. In the museum, surveillance of the body and, as scholars such as Tony Bennett argue, the formation of civic subjecthood go hand in hand.[94] Yet with *Étant donnés*, as Mason Klein has pointed out, Duchamp "dramatically questions the greatest conceit of the modernist epoch: the unexamined idea that vision emerges autonomously from within the opaque, psychophysiological source of the observer's body."[95] It should hardly surprise us, though, as this might well have been the lesson of so many of Duchamp's curated exhibitions. Each of them, in their own way, assaulted the Cartesian premises of a disembodied museum-like viewing, thus thwarting and complicating one of the central and expected givens of the exhibition as such.

It is Rosalind Krauss, following Lyotard's lead, who has best theorized the way vision operates in so many Duchampian works, having understood that the throb of his pulsating optical games and devices is erotic to the core. Her reading is unequivocal: "The optic chiasma that Duchamp suggests is unthinkable apart from vision that is carnal through and through."[96] *Étant donnés* is arguably the culmination of Duchamp's understanding of vision as carnal, cutting through "the idea that a museum is a public space within which one is disincarnated, one where carnal conditions don't count, an ideal space—the one of Kant's conditions of the shareable, communicable 'universal voice'—which is not one where you have to go to the bathroom or where you leave your galoshes."[97] Instead, the particular contemplation that *Étant donnés* devises is one in which you are always potentially "caught in the act" like Jean-Paul Sartre's protagonist at the keyhole in *Being and Nothingness* (1943), which Krauss persuasively evokes relative to Duchamp's final project.[98]

Étant donnés similarly unsettles by way of constructing a potential site of shame: with its antechamber, it places its viewers in the position of being seen by other museum visitors, surprised while hunched and peering in rapt attention at the lewd scene. If, as Krauss further observes, "the scenario of the voyeur caught by another in the very midst of taking his pleasure is never far from consciousness as one plies the peepholes of Duchamp's construction, doubly become a body aware that its rear-guard is down," it is so because Duchamp has deliberately sited this process in the unavoidably public space of the museum.[99]

No longer a contemplative museum spectator, you are, according to Duchamp's explicit wording in the *Manual of Instructions*, a "voyeur."[100] And, as a voyeur, the undeniably embodied position you must take thus becomes not only a commentary on the museum's conscientious construction of "proper" viewing and behavior relative to the auratic artwork (as a step toward forming model subjects/citizens, museum historians would tell you). It becomes a public answer to it. You cannot but be a body in front of Duchamp's piece.

Yet vision deceives us in *Étant donnés*. It manipulates. We might press our noses to the door, position our eyes over the holes, focus our perception, attempt to distinguish figure from ground, illusion from "reality," inside from outside, but in the process what we cannot see exceeds what we can (so much has clearly been constructed behind the scene). And even what we can see leaves us riddled with doubt. The whole piece staunchly upsets the presumed equivalence between seeing and knowing: one looks directly upon the nude figure's sex, that vanishing point of the image where every perspectival line converges, the point where—as a result of the invisible relay of Duchamp's nearly thirty electrical cords and precariously attached wires to illuminate exactly that point—the light shines at its brightest. Yet it is also exactly there—despite light being a symbol of truth, reason, and knowledge, despite the fact that it shines most emphatically *sur le con*—that we know very little and can be sure of nothing: Is she dead or alive? Is she whole behind the dead angles of what we see, or decapitated, footless? What is that oddly shaped gash placed where a vagina should be? Sitting at the threshold of life and death, interiority and exteriority, singularity and repetition, and even among photography, painting, and sculpture, the work irreverently unhinges knowability.

It isn't a secret that Duchamp had the camera obscura—that product of seventeenth-century epistemology and Cartesian reason—in mind as he worked.[101] In the *Manual of Instructions*, he himself compared the effect of the black velvet curtain to "a kind of completely dark camera obscura when looking through the voyeur's peepholes."[102] As its name implies, that "dark room," illuminated by only a single beam of light let in through a peephole, projects whatever is outside onto the interior wall opposite that aperture. The camera obscura was, as Jonathan Crary's important treatise on vision in modernity suggests, "a complex technique of power ... a means of legislating for an observer what constitutes perceptual 'truth.'"[103] And, as Mason Klein points out, it is precisely the logic of this apparatus—"historically thought to clarify and stabilize the visual"—that is thoroughly reversed and made "decidedly confounding" in *Étant donnés*.[104]

Lyotard characterized *Étant donnés* as based on a system of classical perspective; and the classical perspective (like the camera obscura) that Duchamp was at pains to both use and undermine could be said to be representative also of Cartesian thinking, rationalist ideology, and authoritative organization—those things that the museum at the time still very much stood for.[105] Thus it is no coincidence that *Étant donnés* takes on the appearance of a striptease: the museum's codes are exposed, from the conventional representation of the nude in a pastoral landscape as seen in a perspectival space, and the autonomy of the object, to the means through which artworks are validated and "enter" the institution, and the ways that that institution disciplines the bodies that "gaze" within its walls. The tender sensibilities of critics and onlookers were shaken because they thought they were looking at pornography when in fact, all along, they were being forced to confront an institutional site that Duchamp had revealed as obscene.

Étant donnés thus might have begun with a question: how to open up a hole in the museum, a hole that is also a frame for viewing, that is also architectural, also corporeal, that also becomes part of the work itself. The hole that the work burrows into the museum serves to demystify and upset everything around it. As Krauss has noted, "By lodging itself at the heart of the museum—public protector of the values of disincarnated disinterest—the *Étant donnés* was able to pour its logic along the very fault lines of the aesthetic system, making its framing conditions appear in startling clarity only to make them 'strange.'"[106]

THE MANUAL

> The Boxes refer to a work in progress,
> unfinished, perhaps unfinishable, delayed;
> the Instructions [of the Manual] are those of a
> last will and testament: it is finished, I have made it,
> you can only remake it, here's how.
>
> **Jean-François Lyotard**[107]

In order to accompany and constitute *Étant donnés* in its intended resting place, Duchamp devised what scholars have called for lack of a better name his *Manual of Instructions*, comprised of page after page of handwritten texts, penciled diagrams, and photographs held together in plastic sleeves in a black ring binder. Bearing the heading "approximation démontable" (an approximation that can be taken apart, or disassembled), its mode of address contrasts with the artist's various loose and self-consciously replicated notes, written from the first decade of the twentieth century onward, whose tone was speculative, abstract, imagistic, and full of word games. The unique original that is the *Manual of Instructions* is by contrast excessively concrete, detailing in a direct and bare-bones way the precise steps necessary to dismantle and reinstall the elements that make up the installation. Everything about it seems to say that it offers instructions, information. And yet it would be a mistake not to see it in relation to the discursive operation of Duchamp's previous notes. Although the *Manual* is singular (as opposed to replicated) and its visibility initially limited (as opposed to widely disseminated), although indeed it is in other ways different from all his previous note projects, it nevertheless, like them, crucially directs our reading.

The contents of the binder are, according to nearly all Duchamp scholarship, extraordinary but ultimately merely practical. And, to be fair, for the first fifteen years of the public life of the work it accompanied, the manual itself was only semivisible, consultable by request. Yet anyone writing seriously on the work, avid scholars, amateurs of Duchamp, not to mention friends and a curious band of artists inspired by Duchamp, did in fact consult the manual. Still, and surprisingly, even in serious studies devoted to *Étant donnés*, little is said of the *Manual of Instructions* as an object in and of itself.[108] Although many have "used" it, gleaning from it a valuable understanding of the behind-the-scenes machinery of the piece (Lyotard, perhaps its most astute reader, deduces innumerable conclusions from it), few have taken it—much like Duchamp's notes—as more than a mere purveyor of technical facts. Few have noticed the particular ways in which the manual actually functions (as opposed to what it instructs), the role of photography at the heart of it, or the behavior (of the museum and its staff) it so skillfully imposes. As opposed to the installation's construction of a singular, highly regulated view (the voyeur can only see one way and one thing through the peepholes), the manual deliberately opens up a multiplicity of vantage points, effectively an excess of views. The curious nature of the artifact seems to announce—to want us to see—that it is more than a workman's tool, more than procedural residue, that it is instead something more profoundly meaningful and deliberately ambiguous.

Duchamp actually made two manuals. A first version, dating from late 1965, which the artist seems to have made for himself, is full of quickly jotted notes and shorthand reminders for his own deinstallation and reinstallation of the piece when he moved to 80 East 11th Street. It resembles but is much expanded upon in the later version, which probably was only possible because Duchamp himself had practiced how to fully "instruct" the deinstalling and reinstalling of the work. The later album, more publicly known through the facsimile version the Philadelphia Museum of Art published in 1987 (and then reeditioned in 2009), is composed of thirty-five pages of lengthy, handwritten, numbered instructions (called "operations" by Duchamp) and 116 pasted, cut, and collaged photographs as well as a tiny, foldout architectural scale model, the whole providing considerable evidence not only for reading *Étant donnés* but also for Duchamp's relationship to such things as administration, photography, and the museum in the larger sense.

Looking at the final manual, we see what is behind the scenes. The artist had cobbled together a bizarrely functioning object from materials at hand and held together with Scotch tape, with clouds made of cotton, dangling electrical wires attached with twist ties, and a waterfall light machine encased in a Peek Frean's biscuit tin—nothing like the gleam of readymade commodity objects with their perfected, assembly-line efficiency. The inner elements and crudely composed mechanisms of Duchamp's final work, so seemingly far from the impeccable surfaces of an industrial object, were like the handiwork of a promiscuous amateur, using whatever seems to have been available, not abiding by the rules of electricians or carpenters or any other professionalism.

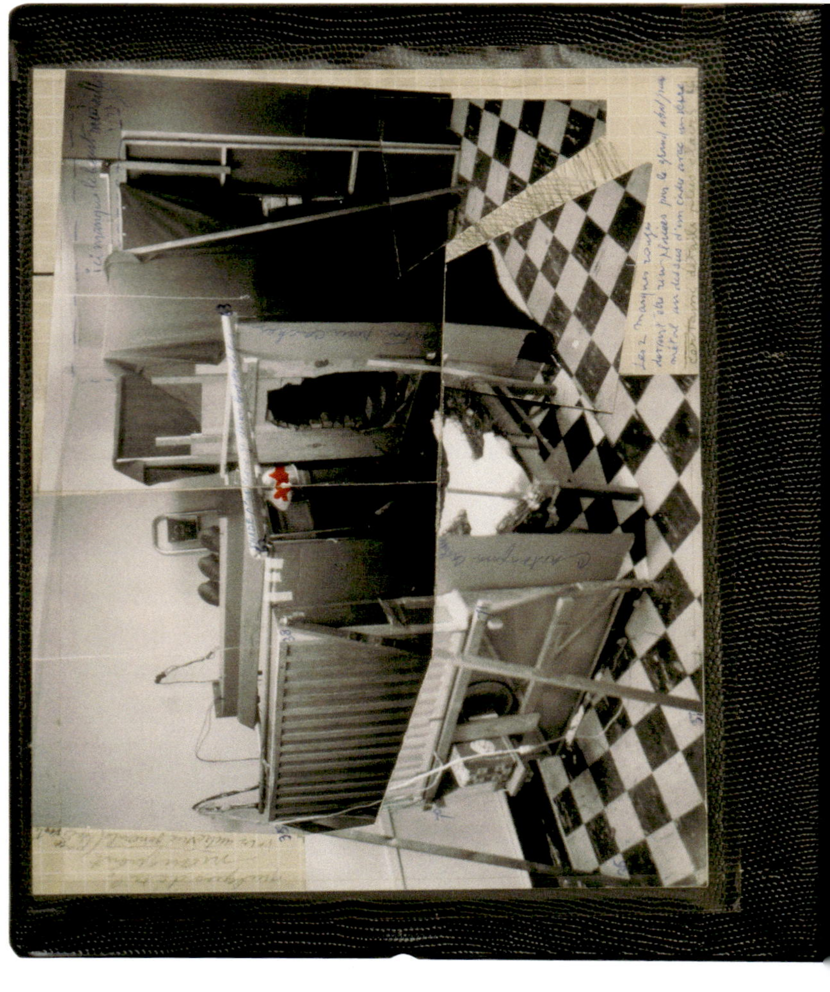

3.36

Marcel Duchamp, *Manual of Instructions* for the assembly of *Étant donnés*, view of the collaged interior of the front cover, 1966. Black vinyl binder with gelatin silver photographs with graphite, colored inks, and paint in clear vinyl sheet protectors, 11⅝ × 9¹³⁄₁₆ × 1¾ inches. Philadelphia Museum of Art: Gift of the Cassandra Foundation.

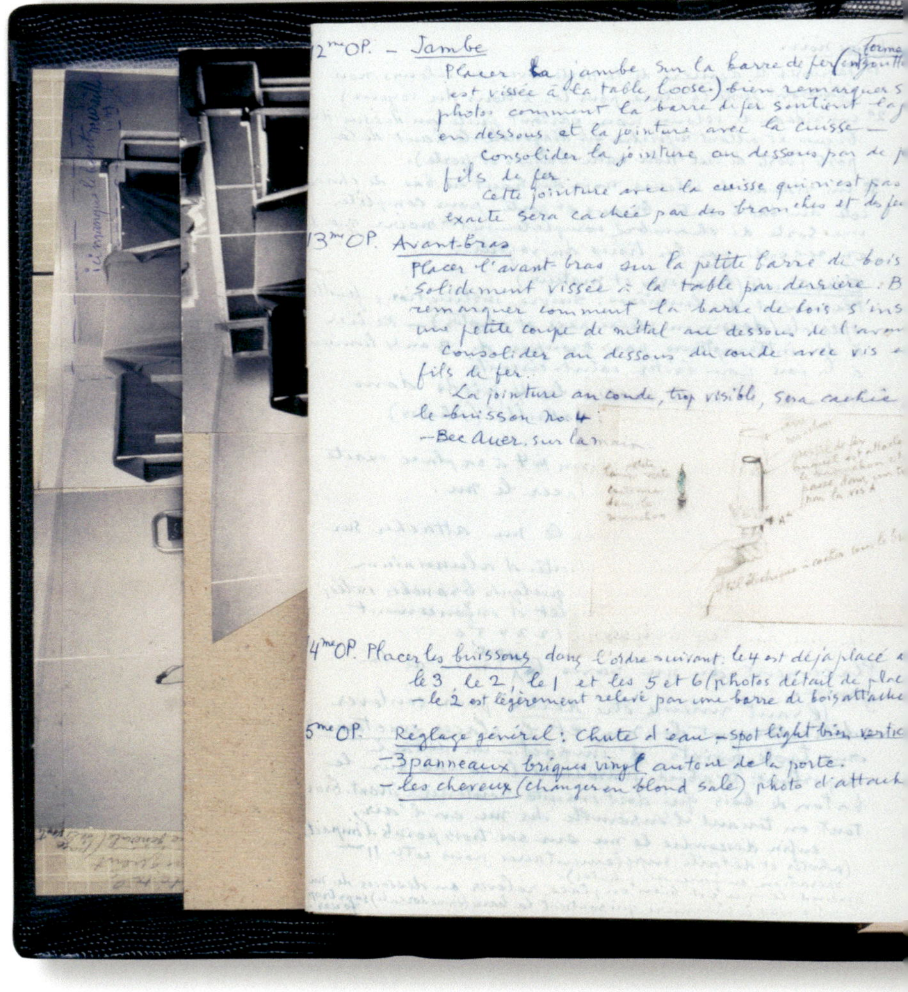

3.37

Marcel Duchamp, *Manual of Instructions* for the assembly of *Étant donnés*, 1966. Black vinyl binder with gelatin silver photographs with graphite, colored inks, and paint in clear vinyl sheet protectors, 11⅝ × 9¹³⁄₁₆ × 1¾ inches. Philadelphia Museum of Art: Gift of the Cassandra Foundation.

3.38

Marcel Duchamp, folding model of *Étant donnés*, c. 1966. Graphite and ballpoint pen on cut cardboard assembled with adhesive and clear pressure-sensitive tape, inserted into page 1 of the *Manual of Instructions* for the assembly of *Étant donnés*, 1966. Maximum dimensions 12 × 4⅜ × 2 inches. Philadelphia Museum of Art: Gift of the Cassandra Foundation.

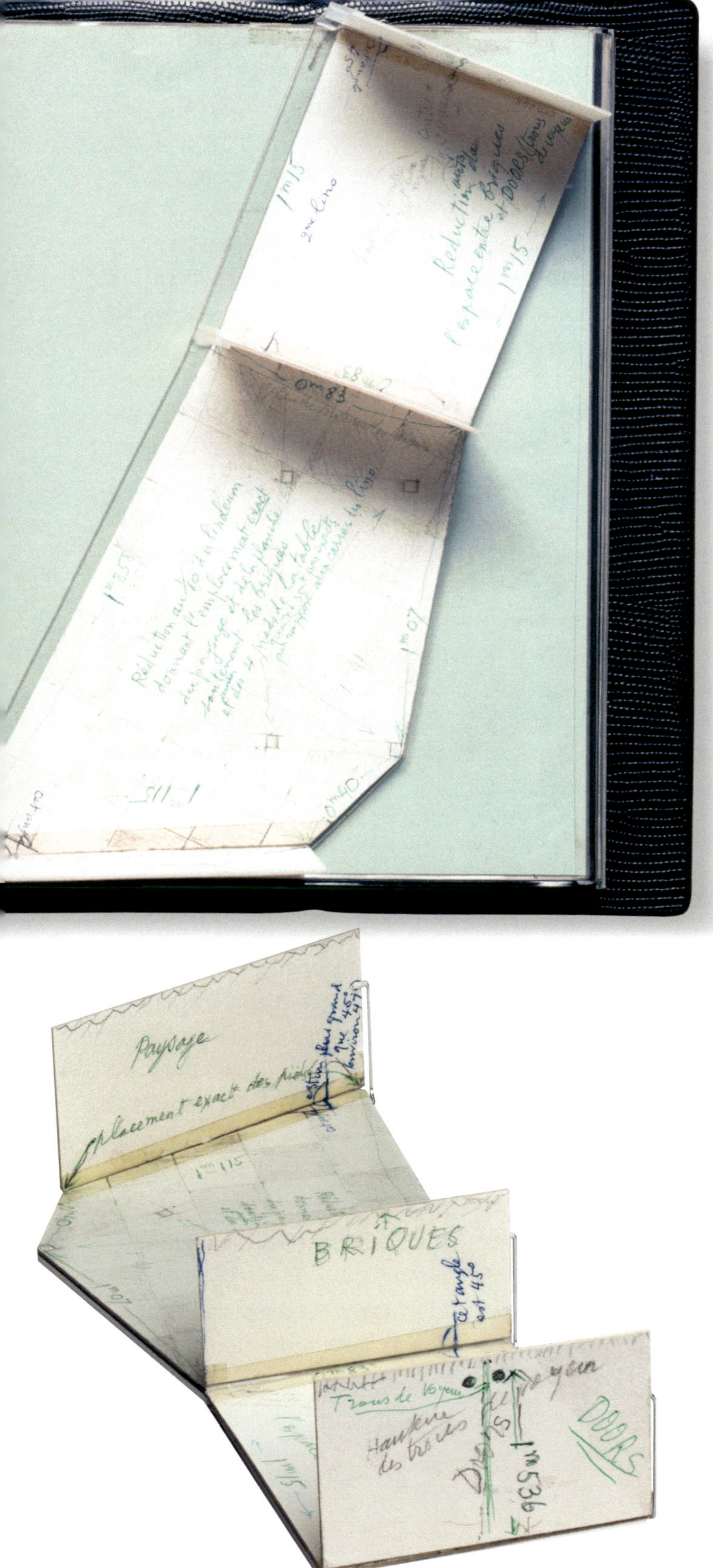
Paysage
BRIQUES
DOORS

He must have taken some pleasure in its functional chaos, a ricketiness that could not be less like the pristine environment and stability of the museum and would also go against every one of its impulses for order, security, and standardization within its walls (not to mention the demands of its insurance handlers and other associated bureaucrats). In short, the manual reveals both what the museum in its caretaking would be required to maintain and what museum visitors would not be able to see or even perhaps divine behind the apertures of the tightly regulated image they are allowed to view.

Duchamp drew the whole installation piecemeal for the museum. Nearly every operation is accompanied by small, hand-drawn illustrations, indicating where the checkerboard linoleum floor should be placed, how each of the sixty-nine numbered bricks should be arranged, not to mention the measurements and degree of angle for positioning various elements. He used a combination of photography and drawing, together with the accompanying written instructions, to meticulously control the ensemble, from the best way to place the blonde wig's curl of hair (so that it lay between the breasts of the figure) to the brand of lightbulb to use ("very white [General Electric] or pinkish"), the degree the landscape should tilt ("at an obtuse angle of 91° or 92°"), and how the figure should be moved ("better to have *two* people to delicately lift the nude and place it *exactly* on the 3 points of impact").[109] Nothing, or almost nothing, was left to chance. The "*ad libidum*" announced in the manual's opening lines concerns the cotton fluff that makes up the scene's "clouds," whose unregulated placement is the only liberty the artist explicitly permitted the institution. What perversity to make the museum tiptoe around the hanging wires and crumbling bricks, to fret that a piece of Duchamp's tape or a twist tie might come unstuck. Where, after all, does this artwork begin and end? Duchamp left that for the museum to mull over.

THE PHOTOGRAPHIC

The manual reveals the astonishing array of materials and methods that make up *Étant donnés*, but it also speaks volumes regarding the particular and vital role of the photographic for the project as a whole. For if Duchamp used a panoply of different media for the making of his final work, he turned in particular to photography, not only literally, as a medium to construct the backdrop for the work and the documentation in the manual, but also procedurally, internalizing the photographic principle of the copy and the trace as the very matrix for the work. Photography's impact on Duchamp's *Étant donnés* is, in fact, inseparable from the foundational, even "structural" role photography arguably had for his entire practice.[110]

Duchamp's use of and interest in photography was, as we already know, curious. Unlike his friend Brancusi, who was so fastidious about the photographs of his sculptures that at a certain point he refused all documentation except his own, or even Rodin's use of commissioned photographs of his studio and sculptures as part of the dissemination of his oeuvre, Duchamp's relationship to photography was both more detached and more complex. There was, of course, his peculiar recourse to the medium inaugurated with the *Box of 1914* and his use of photography over the years in so many of his previously discussed replication projects; in each of these, he employed photography primarily in what appeared to be an almost backhanded, indirect way, even as the medium's logic of inscription, repetition, and reproduction was, again and again, fundamental to his larger thinking about the work of art. Thus despite the fact that Duchamp is rarely thought of as an artist involved with photography, an abundance of evidence points to the medium being an abiding concern.

Not unlike the photographs of the *Box of 1914*, those within the *Manual of Instructions* have all the hallmarks of amateur photography, eschewing deliberate artfulness and aesthetic pretense. Both partake in that particular look and form of address that Benjamin H. D. Buchloh characterized, in relation to certain strands of Conceptualism, as the "aesthetics of administration."[111] Around the time Duchamp was producing the bulk of the photographic images for his manual, he solicited some photographic advice from his friend, the photographer Denise Browne Hare, who only understood why he had been asking when the piece was revealed after the artist's death.[112] In the 116 Polaroid photographs included in the *Manual*, photography explicitly functions to aid the museum in dismantling and reassembling *Étant donnés*. The images look, for all practical purposes, like little more than crude but deadpan documentation or even, as one scholar has pointed out, like crime scene photos, that deadest of deadpan documentation.[113] As a *New York Times* critic put it in 2009, "The Polaroids are documents, not of a fabled retirement, not of cerebral dandyism, but of effort, effort, effort, and the strain and anxiety Duchamp was under as he began to form, through photographs, the rudiments of an instruction manual for dismantling and reassembling the flimsy product of nearly twenty years' work."[114] But, more than evidence of fanatical management by someone anxious for a museum to technically reconstruct his piece as he intended, there are many signs to indicate that the manual was intended to shape the work's reception.

Cropped, blown up, doctored, marked and drawn on, collaged together, sometimes annotated: the sheer materiality of the agglomerated fragments of photographic images somewhat mirrors the installation's. Like the artwork they depict, the photographs in the manual are resolutely homemade, seemingly rudimentary, but astonishingly efficient. To look at them is to confront not only photography's capacity to capture the intractable muteness of things—any one of those photographs that include the figure's lumpish simulation of flesh underscores this—but also its ability to speak of what we might not see in the picture. The nude is the unquestionable protagonist of many of these photographs (so are, in different images, a biscuit box or precarious grouping of wires), but the invisible process that took place for the shutter is inscribed here, too. And here I don't mean the construction of the ensemble, those twenty years of "effort, effort, effort," but rather the construction *of the images* as compositions of long-secreted information.

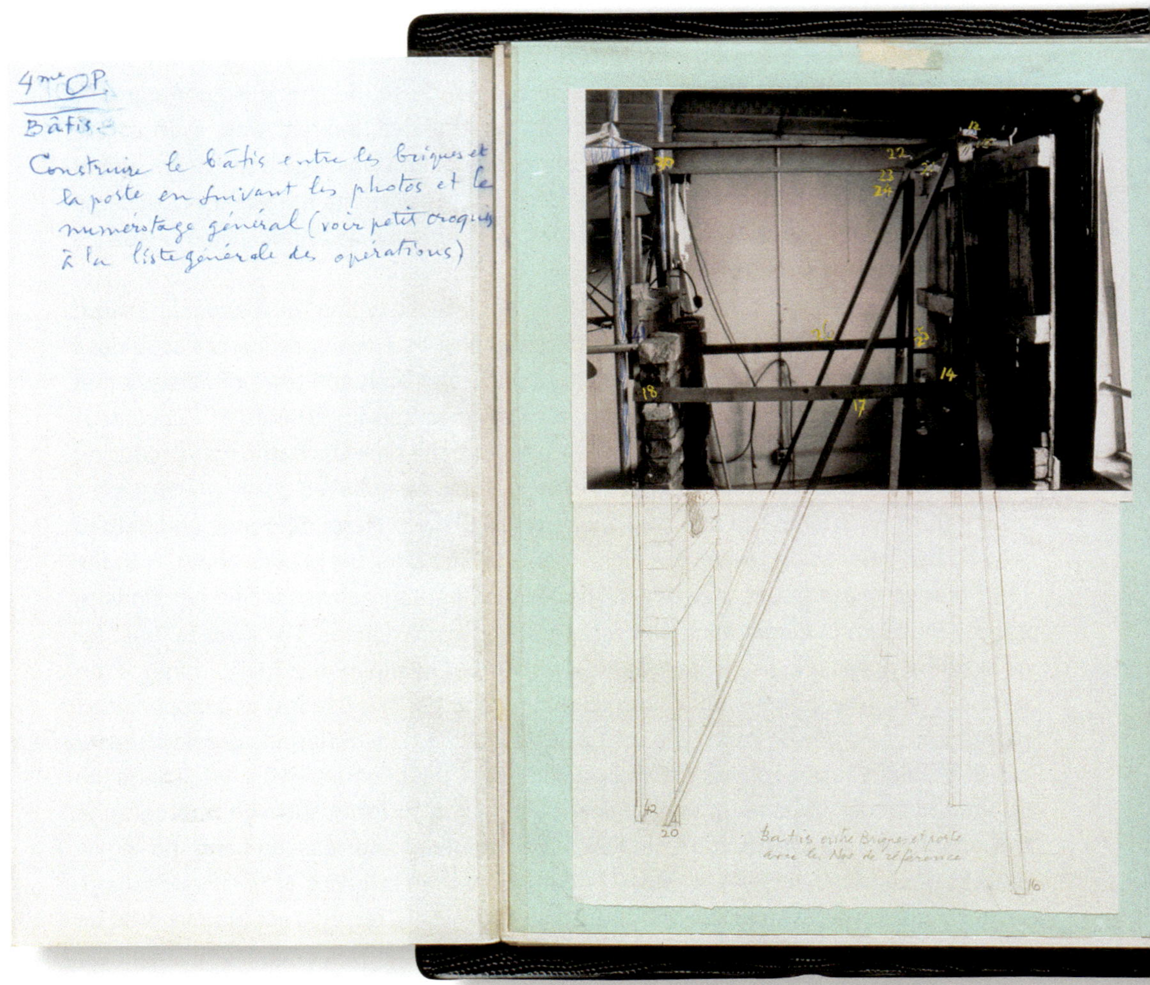

3.39

Marcel Duchamp, *Manual of Instructions* for the assembly of *Étant donnés*, 1966. Black vinyl binder with gelatin silver photographs with graphite, colored inks, and paint in clear vinyl sheet protectors, 11 5/8 × 9 13/16 × 1 3/4 inches. Philadelphia Museum of Art: Gift of the Cassandra Foundation.

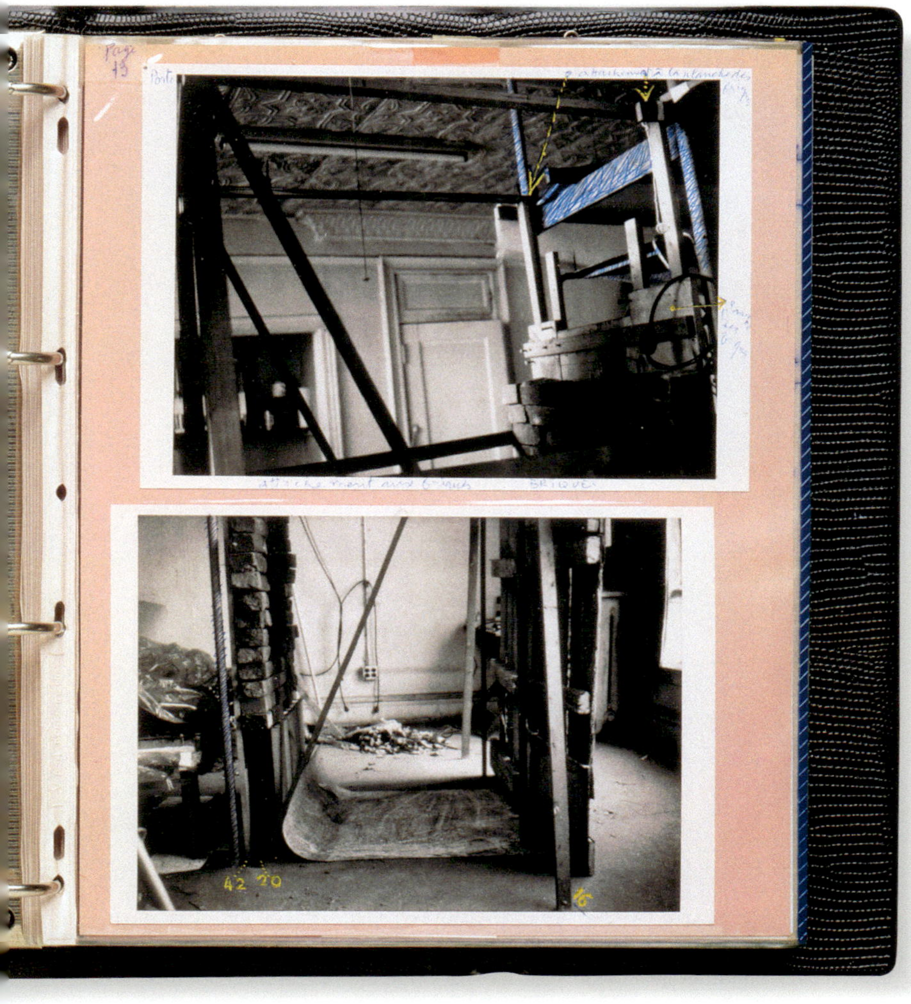

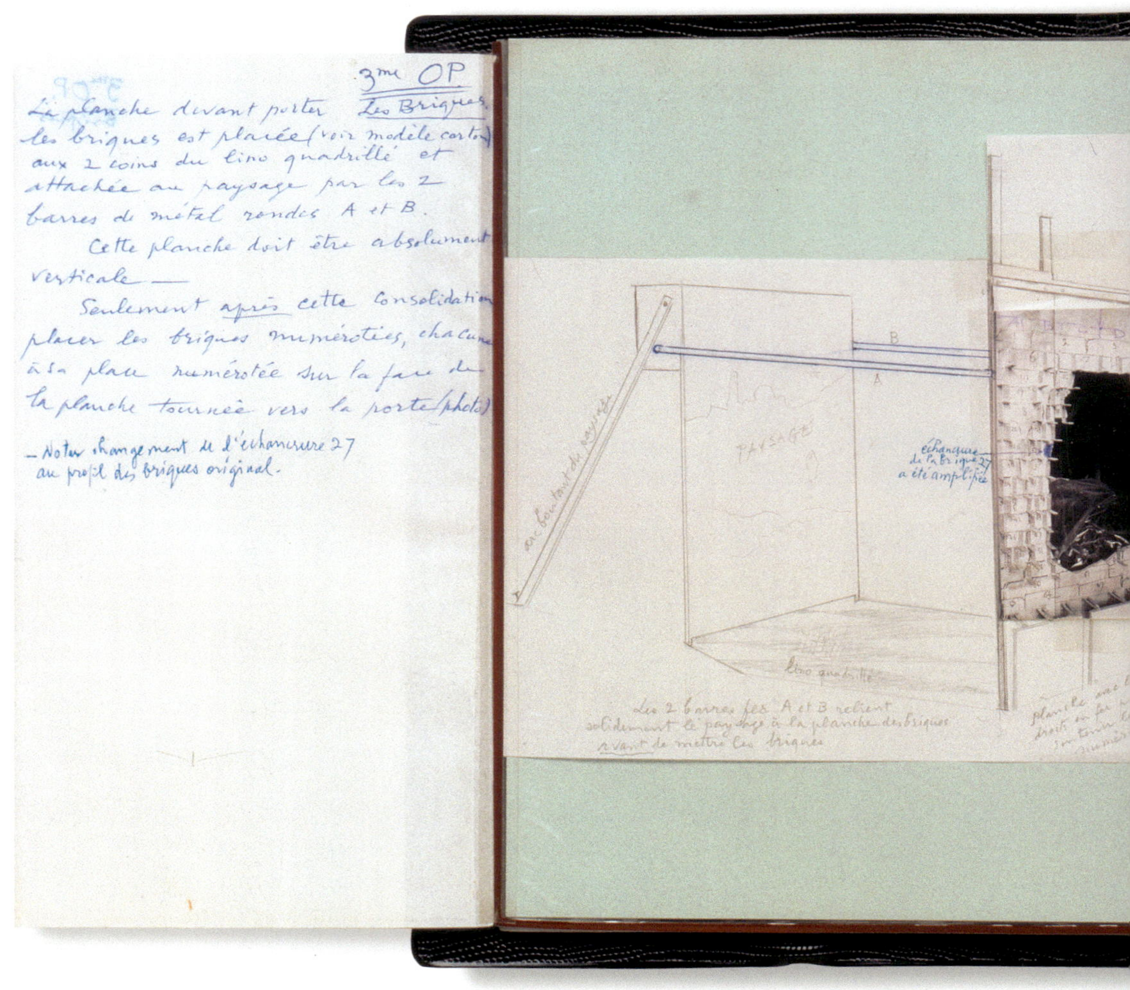

3.40

Marcel Duchamp, *Manual of Instructions* for the assembly of *Étant donnés*, 1966. Black vinyl binder with gelatin silver photographs with graphite, colored inks, and paint in clear vinyl sheet protectors, 11⅝ × 9 13/16 × 1¾ inches. Philadelphia Museum of Art: Gift of the Cassandra Foundation.

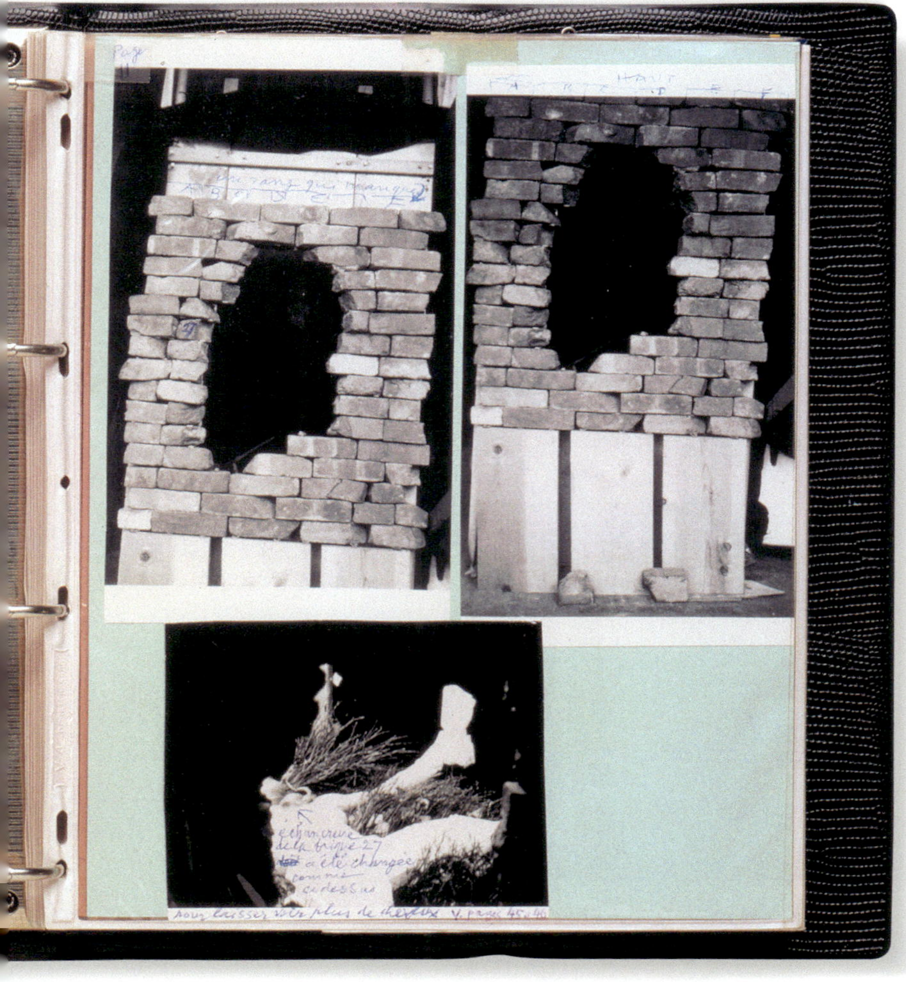

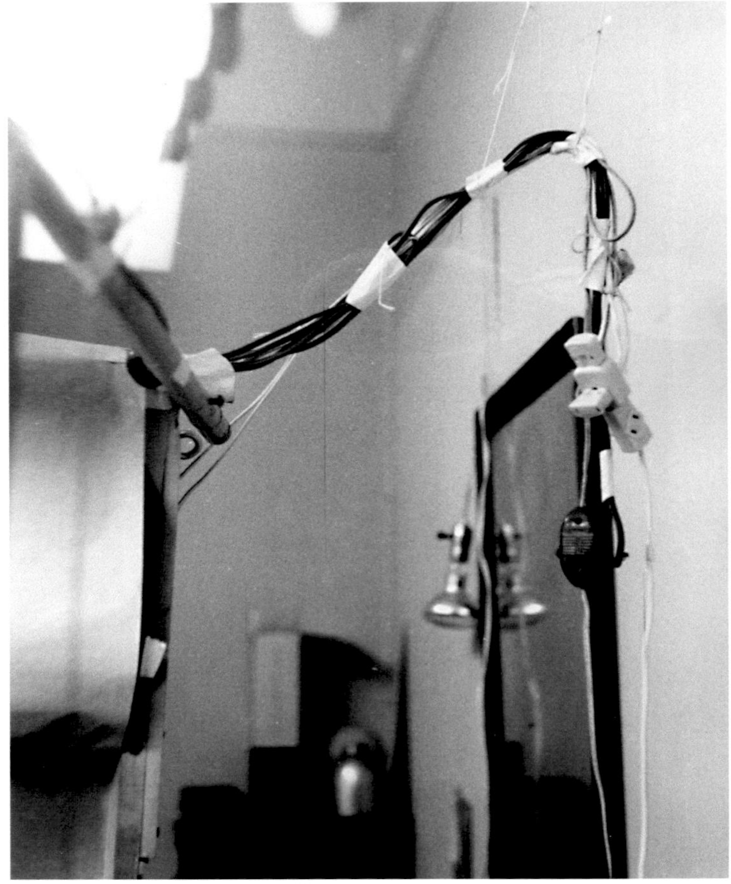

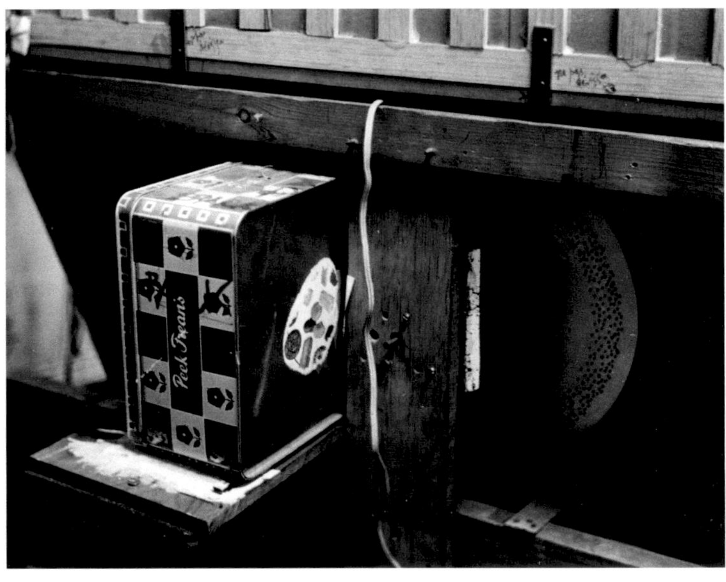
Peek Freans

The photographs consigned to the plastic sleeves of the ring-bound manual are culled from a far bigger mass of photographs that the artist took. He selected. And in preferring one exposure over another, Duchamp—like any photographer, amateur or professional—imposed an idea, a standard, on his subject. Unusually, Duchamp did not involve Man Ray, his close friend and regular accomplice in most matters of photography. In accordance with Duchamp's vow of secrecy, the photographs in the *Manual of Instructions* needed to be taken by the artist himself. There is one exception to this in the whole manual: a single photograph was clearly taken by one of the very few people who accompanied him in the development of the project, his wife, Teeny. It was shot most probably according to the artist's specific instructions and shows Duchamp from the back, leaning forward and holding the figure of the nude to position it. It is included in the manual immediately next to the image of Teeny performing the same task.[115] They are the only two images that picture humans in this collection of documentation that is, in the end, a panoply of stuff. Neither imparts much information except a vague sense of how to best handle the figure: with both hands, one behind the figure's shoulder and the other bracing the torso and leg. But if assuring correct handling were the purpose of such an image, one alone would surely suffice. Instead Duchamp included them both, and next to each other, not only uniting him and his wife in the strange portrait that the manual offers of the artist, but also confirming (to us, future readers of this discursive and pictorial apparatus for the work) that she helped, and that his was a labor that was secreted from nearly everyone but her.

3.41 and 3.42

Detail photos of Marcel Duchamp's *Étant donnés* as secretly installed in the artist's 80 East 11th Street studio, 1968. Photos by Denise Browne Hare.

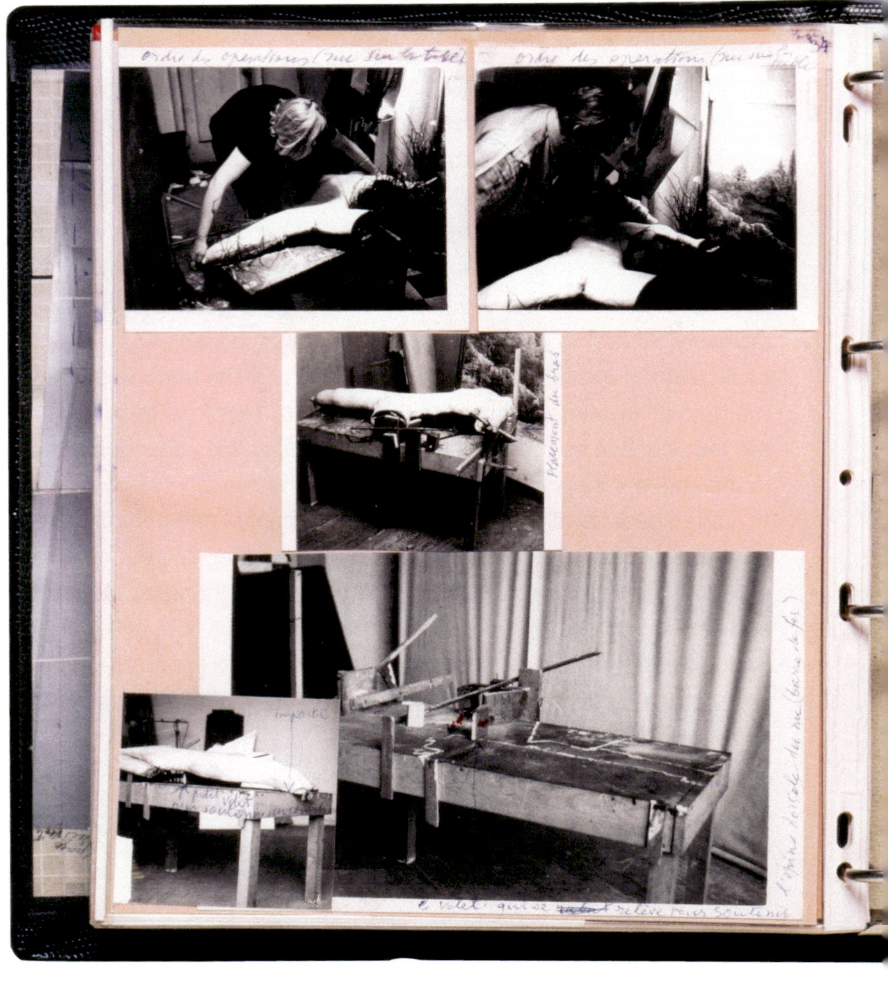

3.43

Marcel Duchamp, photographs picturing Teeny and Marcel Duchamp from the *Manual of Instructions* for the assembly of *Étant donnés*, 1966. Black vinyl binder with gelatin silver photographs with graphite, colored inks, and paint in clear vinyl sheet protectors, 11⅝ × 9$^{13}/_{16}$ × 1¾ inches. Philadelphia Museum of Art: Gift of the Cassandra Foundation.

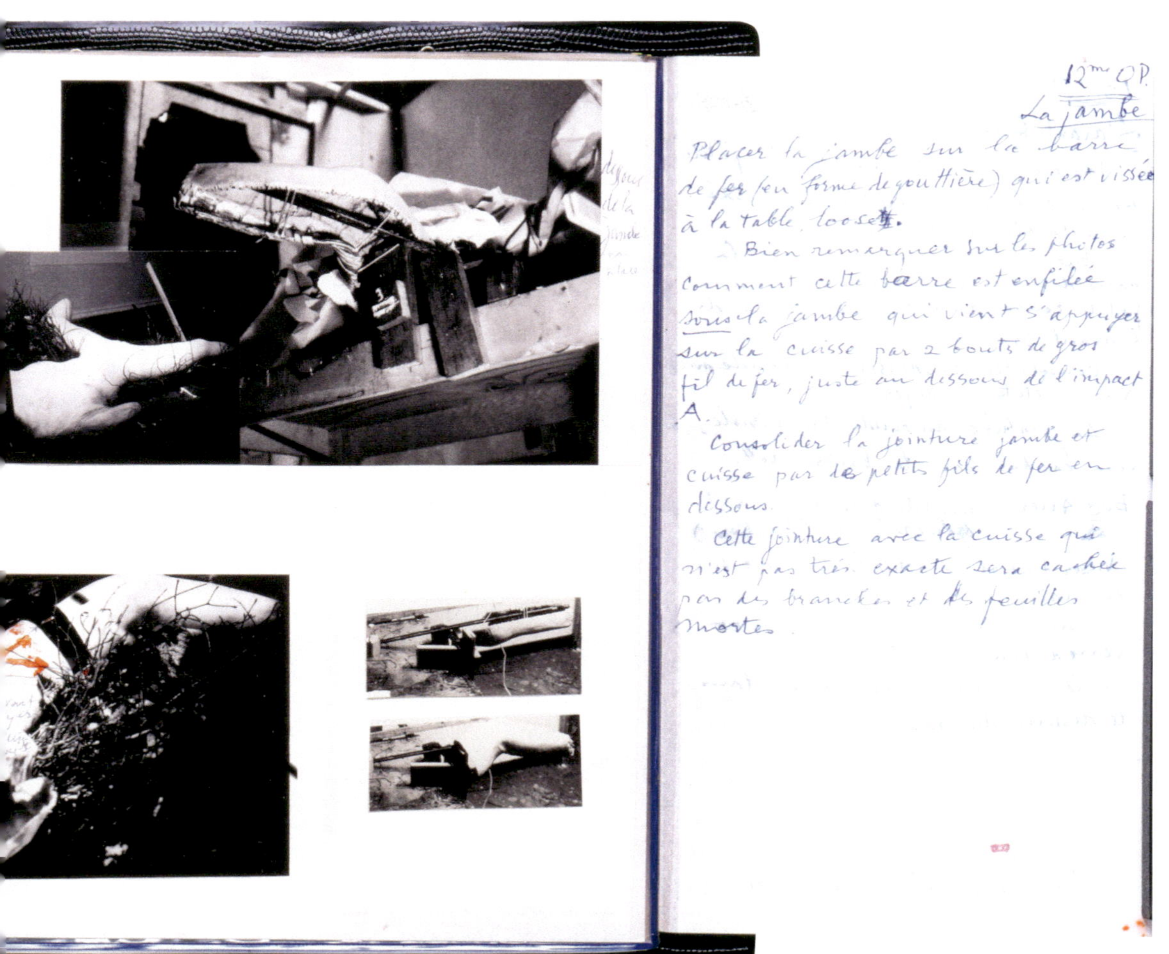
12me QP.

La jambe

Placer la jambe sur la barre de fer (en forme de gouttière) qui est vissée à la table tooset.

Bien remarquer sur les photos comment cette barre est enfilée sous la jambe qui vient s'appuyer sur la cuisse par 2 bouts de gros fil de fer, juste au dessous de l'impact A.

Consolider la jointure jambe et cuisse par des petits fils de fer en dessous.

Cette jointure avec la cuisse qui n'est pas très exacte sera cachée par des branches et des feuilles mortes.

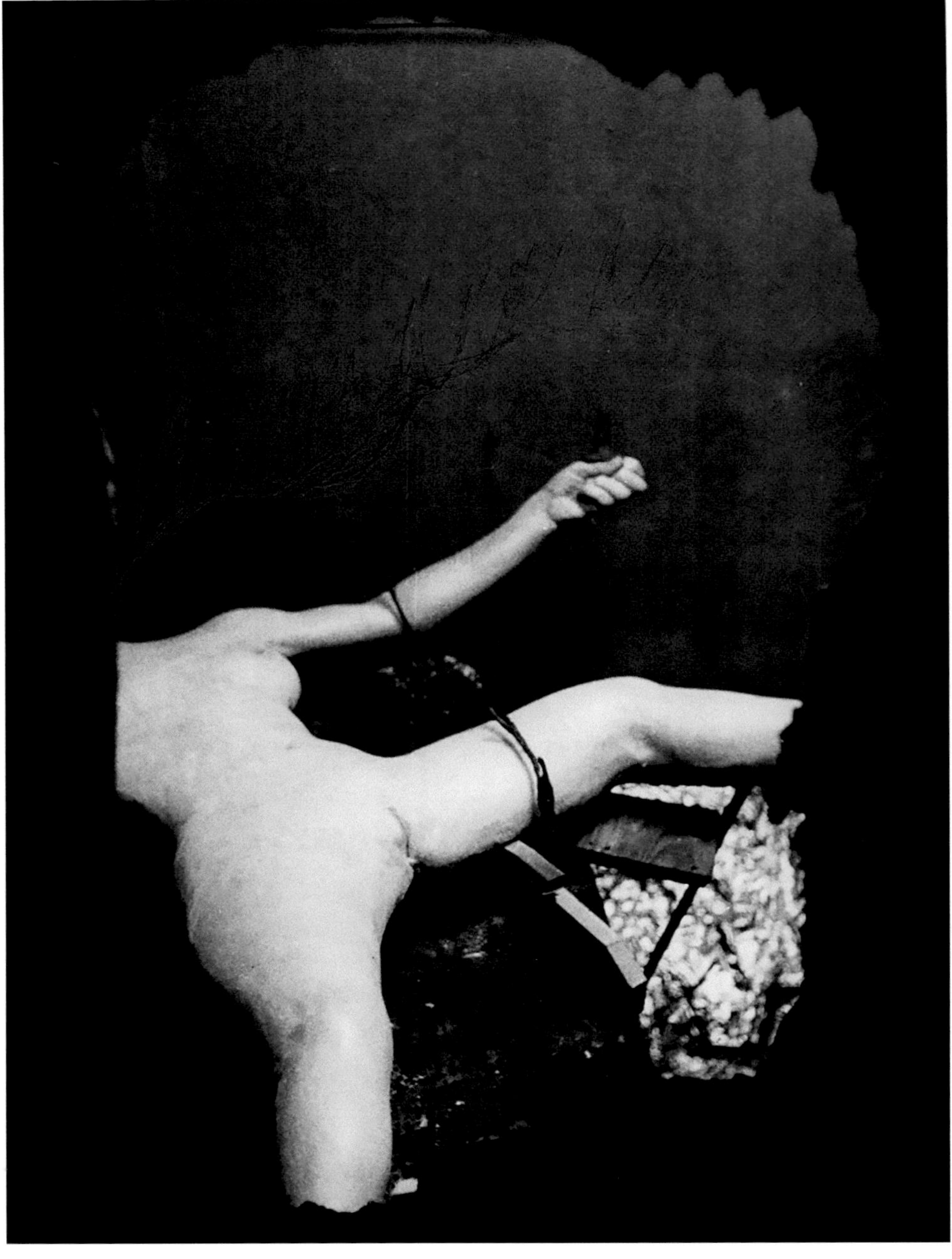

3.44

Marcel Duchamp, photograph of a plaster study for the figure in *Étant donnés*, 1959. Gelatin silver print with red crayon annotations, 11¼ × 10 inches. Philadelphia Museum of Art Archives: Alexina and Marcel Duchamp Papers. Gift of Jacqueline, Paul, and Peter Matisse in memory of their mother, Alexina Duchamp.

In the housekeeping of death, much was found in the small, secret studio that saw the making of *Étant donnés*. In addition to photographs included in the *Manual of Instructions*, Duchamp evidently took more than seventy additional Polaroids that didn't make it into the binder, including a handful of color images. There was also a Dom Pérignon champagne box filled with various attempts at constructing stereoscopic color images of the scene. In all, more than two hundred photographs exist of the single work, from nearly every angle. Two of the loose photographs of the nude figure found in the studio are known to precede those that fill the manuals; the images are identical except for a red crayon mark added to one (as if contemplating the possibility of a smaller opening and tighter view on the nude). Both were seemingly taken in 1959, not long after the artist had completed the painstaking labor on the final nude figure, but before he had constructed the broken brick aperture or any of the architecture around it. Instead he used a piece of dark fabric with a large hole gouged in it to simulate what would later become the broken brick wall. With photography as a tool, he seems to have been testing the position of the nude, the architectural aperture, and the position of the viewer.

The 1959 photographs were evidently enacted for the camera's eye (a stand-in for the viewer's own). Like some of the photographs in the manual, and still other loose images that were not finally included in it, they confirm that Duchamp used photography avidly and repeatedly, yet none of the resulting images could be called documents of process per se. They don't show Duchamp building up the work in any technical or literal sense throughout its various stages of development over twenty years. Nor do they record anything about the elaborate process of manufacturing the nude figure. Nor even does a single photographic trace picture Maria Martins submitting to the repeated and involved casting sessions. Instead, one important use of the medium seems to have been to help simulate the view of the spectator and thus define the work for the artist himself. One can imagine this being the case even if he understood well that the monocular, static view of a camera and its resulting photograph could not actually compare to the roving, binocular, and carnal gaze of the viewer's body looking through the two holes in the door. Still, the doggedness with which the artist took photographs from the "voyeur's" position is telling. What Duchamp's photographs reveal is that the whole of *Étant donnés*, a work that so many historical accounts have described as impossible to adequately capture in a picture, was constructed (at least in its final stages) with the artist frequently looking through the lens of a camera. Duchamp seems to have been using photography to try to anticipate *Étant donnés*'s reception—attempting, however inadequately, to simulate how future viewers might see the work, all while staging the utter discrepancy between the experience of the work and its photographic representation.[116]

Importantly, *Étant donnés* did not exist *as an image* for nearly fifteen years after it opened to the public. One couldn't simply "see" it without experiencing it in person and in its specific museal context—conditions of viewing that are lost in a photograph. An official museum decree prevented any photographs from being published or being taken by the public, and, for more than a decade, the Philadelphia Museum of Art did not itself release any photographs of the behind-the-scenes view offered by the manual (only an image of the door was reproduced).[117] Regardless of whether Duchamp would have stipulated an interdiction of any sort (let alone this one), he was well aware that the work would sooner or later be photographed.[118] Consequently, he left very specific instructions in his manual and even built a system into the structure to allow for the ideal photographic position in the event of the work's photographic reproduction:

> To take good color photos: 1st remove the black velvet that covers the rear of the door/ 2nd/ unscrew the 4 battens 4, 5, 6, 7, which fix the 4 panels of the door together and slide the 2 upper panels to the left and right along the big round steel rail.[119]

We thus know that Duchamp wanted the work, were it to be reproduced, to be represented in such a way as to replicate as accurately as possible what the museum spectator sees. Any image that might circulate of the work should not show any other angle, nor any possible additional view, and definitely not the rickety interior construction, but instead the scene exactly as the artist composed it for the "voyeur." The place of the (potential future) photographer and that of the visitor/voyeur are necessarily—and painstakingly—aligned in the artist's conception of the piece. Duchamp had already, then, taken into account the dissemination of the artwork, leaving careful instructions not only for how its image should circulate popularly, but also for the perspective (quite literally) that its scholarship would be afforded.

In a few of the photographs included in the manual, Duchamp experimented with brick placement, angle of vision, and other elements that affect what a view would ultimately reveal. On the very last page of images in the album, he included two photographs that were taken earlier than the others, and for the production of which the camera literally stands in the place of the imagined spectator.[120] The artist framed and reframed the scene, with the figure ever so slightly more, or less, visible behind the bricks. Minutely changing angle and viewing distance, he made about twenty photographs of almost exactly the same view, although he didn't include all these images in the manual. In some that he did include he added bricks here and there, first penning them in, then emphasizing them on the photograph with red marker, and finally adding them to the actual construction. The question is, if the manual was to aid the museum in its job of reconstruction, why include these shots—the alignments he later discarded along with the final views—at all? Why include details not necessarily useful for the reassembly of the installation? What seems at stake in these final images is not so much to convey information about the scene itself, but to convey to the museum (and to eventual readers of the *Manual*) Duchamp's imperative to minutely control what the viewer would see.

There is more. Among those particular photographs, the two that predate the others were taken before Duchamp had changed the wig of his figure—from the earlier brunette version to the figure's final, blonde tresses. This hair color change, known to those who have studied the manual, has long and probably correctly been read as

Duchamp's desire to change an important reference in the work: from the raven-haired Martins to the blonde Teeny, who had become his wife just about midway through the construction of the piece. Over time, the form and materiality of the nude figure itself have been understood by scholars as a composite of allusions to his most important lovers: the "skin" of Mary Reynolds, his on-again, off-again companion from the 1920s to the '40s who, as a bookbinder, was trained in using leather and probably inspired Duchamp's use of it and might also have helped him procure the parchment skin for his project; the body of Martins, his voluptuous lover for most of the 1940s, who sexually transfixed him but finally left him; and the hair, raised arm, and clenched fist of Teeny, the last of the women in Duchamp's life. If this supposition has animated scholarly discussions for years, it was partly fueled—at least regarding the detail of the change of hair—by the artist himself. For, excepting those two last images in the manual, all other photographs picture the central figure with blonde tresses, and thus there would have been no question about the figure's hair color in the final installation. Indeed, given the secrecy surrounding the work, no one would have known that it started out with brown hair at all. Those two images—utterly unnecessary to the technical task of reassembling the work—annotated in Duchamp's hand to tell us that the wig had been "changed" to blonde, reveal that the change has significance. Here again, photography and note writing were the means through which Duchamp conveyed details that he wanted posterity to know.

Photography figures prominently not only in the manual but also in the pictorial elements visible in the larger work. In 1946 Duchamp took seven photographs of the picturesque Le Forestay waterfall near Chexbres, Switzerland, during his weeklong visit there with Reynolds. These images were evidently the starting point for the construction of *Étant donnés*'s backdrop, and in later years Duchamp substantially manipulated them. After enlarging one of them several times, he cut out parts and duplicated others, reassembling the different elements as a photographic collage on a piece of plywood. He then used a combination of paint, graphite, crayon, and ballpoint pen to hand-color the whole. The result was reproduced as a black-and-white collotype, which he hand-colored in turn, enhancing details in black and colored pencil as well as adding elements, as he had with the collage on plywood, according to the careful notes he had taken in 1946 about the color of the foliage and waterfall. This extenuated process of replicating color was much the same as the one he had employed while working on his *Boîte-en-valise* some decades earlier.

For his *Boîte-en-valise*, he had visited collections holding his original artworks in order to make detailed color notations so that he could create accurate reproductions. But whereas arguably in that case an exactness in representing a particular extant painting or sculpture made sense, here the act is both odd and extremely telling. Duchamp did not have to exactly reproduce the particular waterfall that he had seen and didn't name; he could have rendered it more or less as he remembered it or more or less akin to a general conception of a waterfall and foliage. Yet he took great pains to accurately

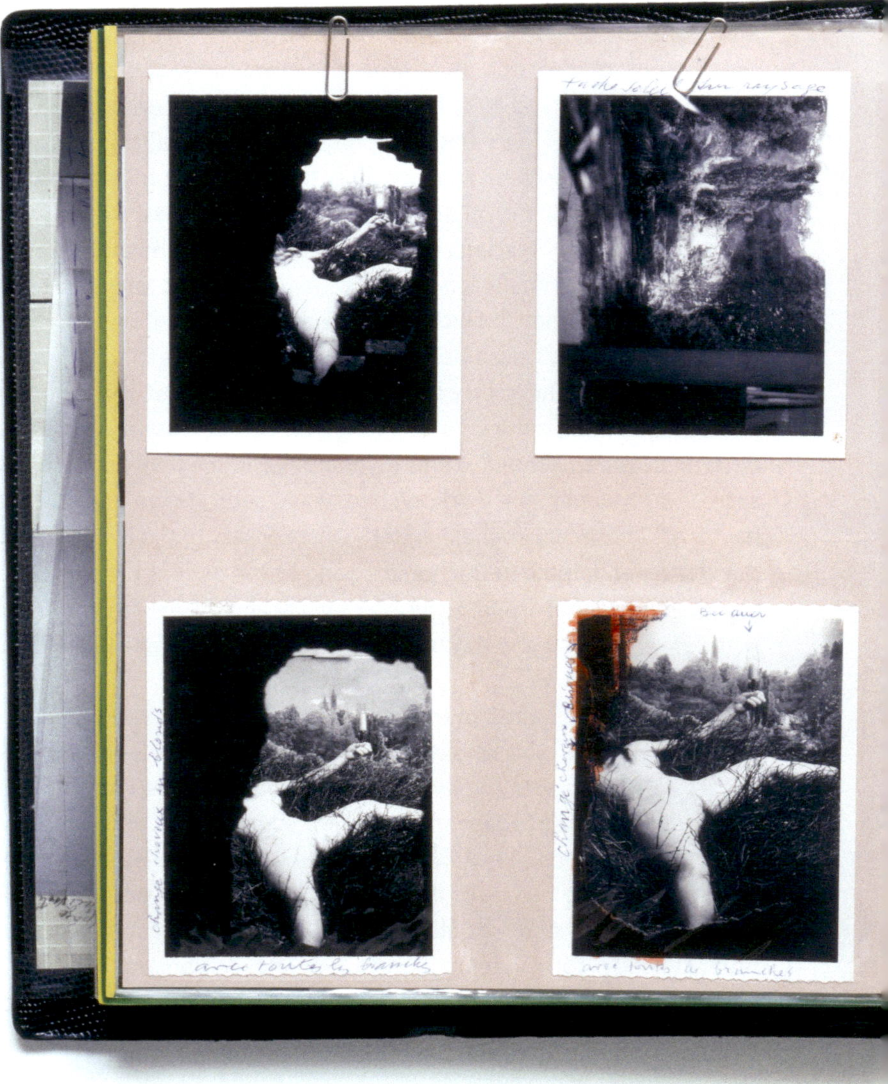
change cheveux en blonds
avec toutes les branches
avec toutes les branches

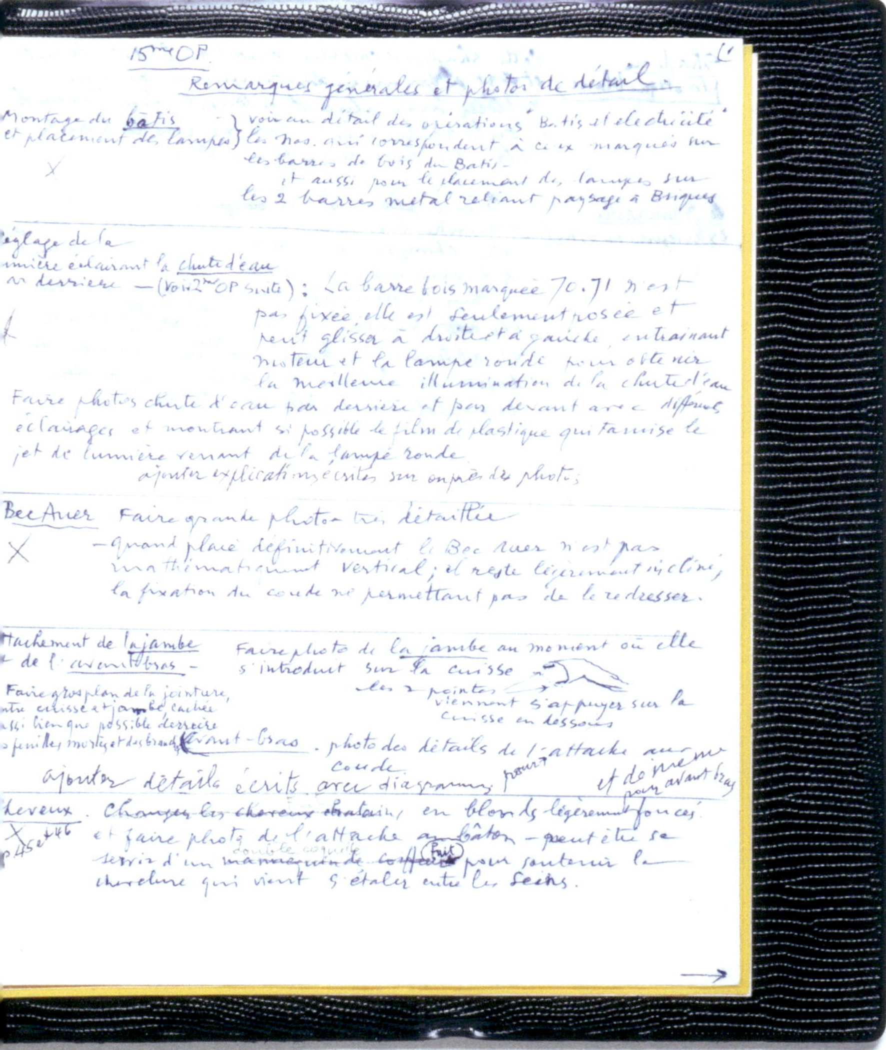

15me OP

Remarques générales et photos de détail

Montage du bâtis et placement des lampes } voir au détail des opérations "Bâtis et électricité" les nos. qui correspondent à ceux marqués sur les barres de bois du Bâtis – et aussi pour le placement des lampes sur les 2 barres métal reliant paysage à Briques

églage de la mière éclairant la chute d'eau r derrière — (voir 2me OP suite) ; La barre bois marquée 70.71 n'est pas fixée, elle est seulement vissée et peut glisser à droite et à gauche, entraînant moteur et la lampe ronde pour obtenir la meilleure illumination de la chute d'eau

Faire photos chute d'eau par derrière et par devant avec différents éclairages et montrant si possible le film de plastique qui tamise le jet de lumière venant de la lampe ronde

ajouter explications écrites sur ou près des photos

Bec Auer Faire grande photo très détaillée — quand placé définitivement le Bec Auer n'est pas mathématiquement vertical ; il reste légèrement incliné, la fixation du coude ne permettant pas de le redresser.

ttachement de la jambe de l'avant-bras – Faire photo de la jambe au moment où elle s'introduit sur la cuisse – les 2 pointes viennent s'appuyer sur la cuisse en dessous

Faire gros plan de la jointure, entre cuisse et jambe cachée aussi bien que possible derrière les feuilles mortes et des branches

avant-bras . photo des détails de l'attache au coude

ajouter détails écrits avec diagrammes

heveux . Changer les cheveux châtain, en blonds légèrement foncés. et faire photo de l'attache au bâton – peut-être se servir d'un mannequin de coiffeur pour soutenir la chevelure qui vient s'étaler entre les seins.

3.45

Marcel Duchamp, final image spread of *Manual of Instructions* for the assembly of *Étant donnés*, 1966. Black vinyl binder with gelatin silver photographs with graphite, colored inks, and paint in clear vinyl sheet protectors, 11⅝ × 9 13/16 × 1¾ inches. Philadelphia Museum of Art: Gift of the Cassandra Foundation.

3.46 (following pages)

Marcel Duchamp, study for landscape backdrop of *Étant donnés*, 1959. Collage of cut gelatin silver photographs over paper, with paint, graphite, crayon, ballpoint pen, and adhesive on plywood panel, with pressure-sensitive tape, 26⅜ × 39⅛ inches. Philadelphia Museum of Art: Gift of Mme Marcel Duchamp, 1969.

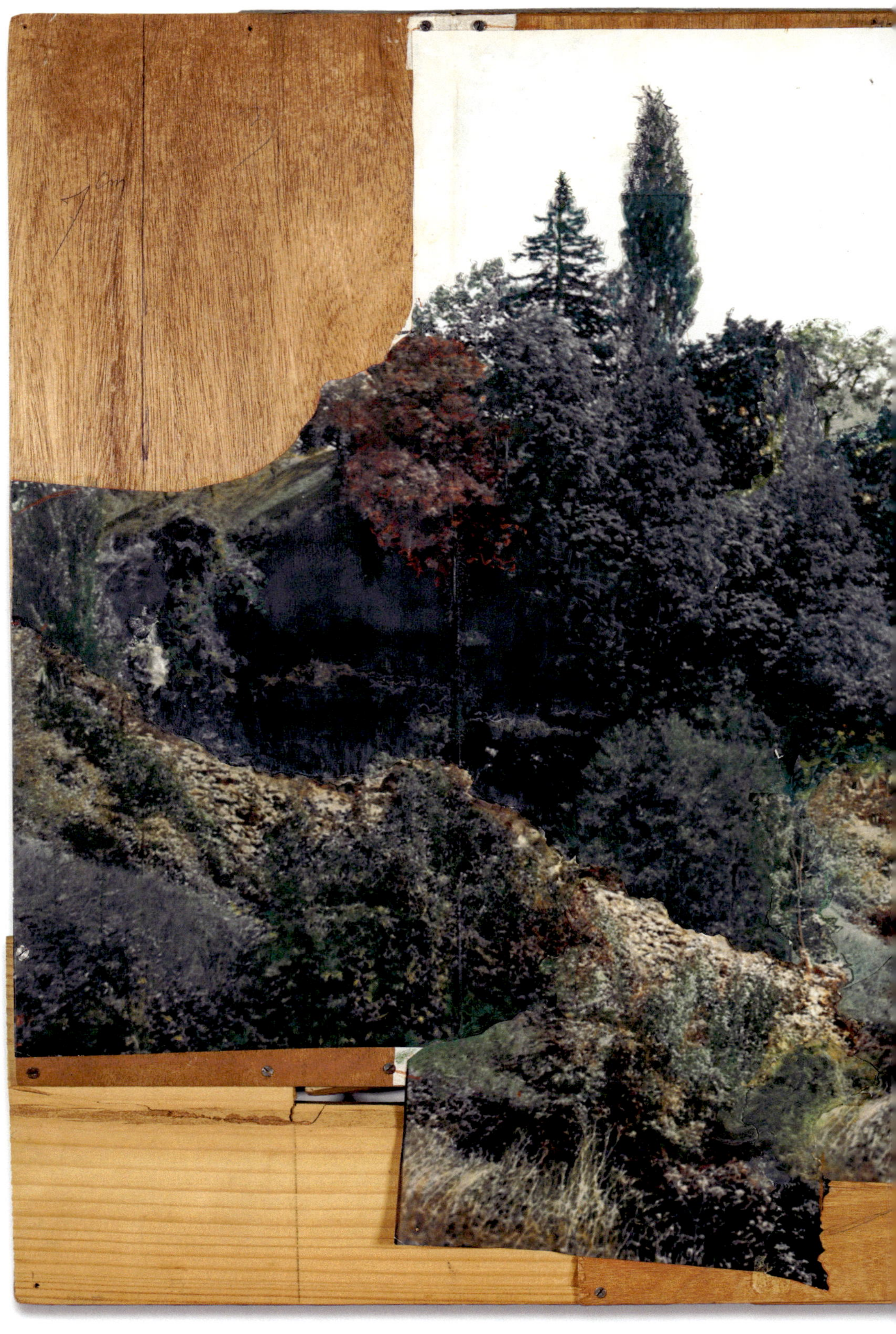

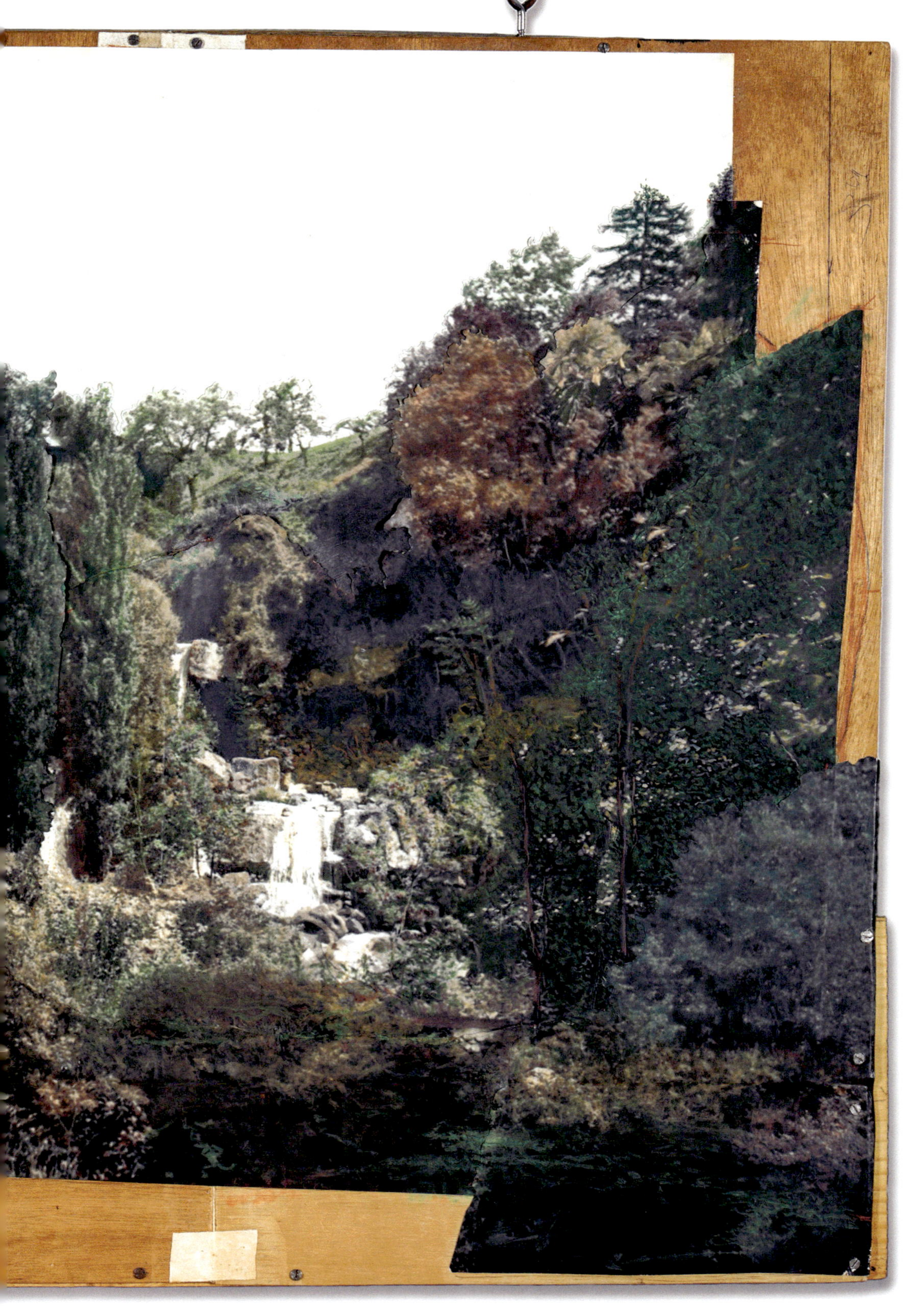

record *that* waterfall, cutting out imagination or idealization in favor of something far more mundane. This elaborate and multiple-step procedure makes clear that, in the whole of *Étant donnés*, he was at pains to replicate, as faithfully as possible, a specific referent, *an original*, if you will.

It should hardly be surprising that "the photographic" provides the guiding logic for *Étant donnés*. It was a continuation of Duchamp's lifelong critical project, exemplified in the *Box of 1914*, *Green Box*, and *Boîte-en-valise*, in which photography is the medium through which the artist sounds the depths of the fraught relationship between originality and reproduction. Photography and its logic form the *chantier*, the work site, at which *Étant donnés* is built, not just literally, as visual instructions, but conceptually, too. Inevitably, for the artist, photography also stands for the manipulation of perception, and the manual operates hand in hand with the installation in order to argue for the demise of certainty, be it photographic or other. This is one of the stories that the manual tells.

THE AURATIC

It is in the manual that Duchamp calls *Étant donnés* an "*approximation démontable*," avoiding such descriptors as "painting" or "sculpture" or even a neologism that would anticipate a new category, something like "installation." This latter classification, so often used today to refer to the artist's final work and describing the "discipline" in which Modernism's quest for medium specificity collapsed, did not yet then exist. His own gloss on the "*approximation démontable*" ("By approximation I mean the margin of *ad libitum* in the dismantling and remounting")[121] suggests that he intended to refer not to some category to which it fit, but instead to the agency he offers the people installing the work: the result of their *approximating* his ideal of the piece. But the choice of words is revealing and perhaps more meaningful than hitherto recognized. From Latin *ad-* and *proximare* "to come near," the dictionary tells us that an approximation is something that approaches something else by way of similarity, for instance "a mathematical quantity that is close in value to but not the same as a desired quantity."[122] To have used it for his project suggests that this dismountable thing, *Étant donnés*, is defined by the fact that it can approximate something else: a replica of the real that is "close to" but "not the same as" the real thing. It is, in other words, a kind of *copy*.

One might here look to the artist's 1937 formulation of the concept of the *inframince* (infrathin), the Duchampian neologism that refers to the minutely thin interval between two nearly identical things and which bears considerable relevance to the artist's thinking about the aesthetic original and its reproduction, with particular reference to the cast and mold.[123] No two things, in the artist's estimation, can ever be the same: repetition inevitably generates difference, even if only infinitesimal. It was this infinitely "thin" distinction that interested him. The *inframince* is the "practical approximation of similarity," as he declared in a note that was published posthumously.[124] Duchamp used the term to describe the difference between otherwise undifferentiated objects produced mechanically in a series: "the difference / (dimensional) between /

2 mass-produced objects / from the same mold / is an infrathin / when the maximum precision is obtained."[125] Or, in another note, written on both sides of a piece of paper:

> [recto] 2 forms cast in / the same mold (?) / differ / from each other / by infrathin separative / amount—All 'identicals' as / identical as they may be, (and / the more identical they are) / move toward this / infrathin separative / difference. Two men are not / an example of identicality / and to the contrary move away / from a determinable / infrathin difference—but
>
> [verso] there exists the crude conception / of the déjà vu which leads from / generic grouping / (2 trees, 2 boats) / to the most identical 'castings' / It would be better / to try / to go / into the / infrathin / interval which separates / 2 'identicals' than / to conveniently accept / the verbal generalization / which makes / 2 twins look like 2 / drops of water. Copenhagen / July 29, [19]37.[126]

With these speculations, Duchamp reveals that any so-called "precision technique" of copying, whether casting and molding or another replication method to make serial things, only produces approximations that are similar but decidedly not the same. The infinitely small but nevertheless nonnegligible distinction between them is, in a word, *inframince*.[127]

The deep and willfully complicated relationship of *Étant donnés* to the idea of the copy—a copy still somehow inextricably tied to aura, but also, as we have seen, to the workings of photography—sits at the very heart of the work's functioning. Thus if photography might, even more directly or literally than any bachelor machine in the *Large Glass*, be *Étant donnés*'s motor of operation and signification, aura would be its consistent yet elusive fuel, its love gas. Duchamp's entire final work persistently strives to maintain a connection to, and simultaneous distance from, its auratic original (the lover's body), and the whole of the artist's reproductive quest in *Étant donnés* serves to construct a situation by which "she" is infinitesimally present even if in actuality lost, which is, as it happens, the perfect analogy for any work of art once it enters the museum—at once preserved (on offer) and inevitably constrained (set at a distance from viewers, regulated, controlled).

ANOTHER ORIGINAL

If ever the photographic was structural, indeed procedural, for Duchamp, it was in *Étant donnés*. Photography's logic takes hold perhaps most saliently in the work's central figure. "She" is a series of art historical quotations, her body a mere "pattern book of nudes": that is what some scholars say.[128] To read their lists is to revisit the whole history of art to which Duchamp apparently refers: "*Origin of the World*, *Woman with a Parrot* and *Studio of the Painter* by Courbet, *Virgin of the Rocks* and the *Mona Lisa* by Da Vinci, *Luncheon on the Grass* and *Olympia* by Manet, the *Statue of Liberty* by Bartholdi, *Saint Theresa* by Bernini, *Woman Bit by a Serpent* by Clésinger, *Ideal City* and many others by Dürer, Titian, Ingres, Chassériau, Cabanel, etc., ad infinitum."[129] But is it so? Much like a viewer who sees the "original"—say, a particular Douglas Sirk film, a certain B-movie starlet—in Cindy Sherman's *Untitled Film Stills* from the 1970s, historians who claim they see the art historical references in Duchamp's *Étant donnés* likewise miss the forest for the trees.[130] They overlook the fact that there is no exact or singular art historical reference, no clear citation, in other words, no actual "original" in Duchamp's monstrously complex copy, at least not one to be found in any history books. That the work is a tangible material remnant—an attempted copy—of its corporeal origins is another story. Yet in its assemblage of these traced origins and in a way similar to Sherman's *Untitled Film Stills*, modeled on various mass-cultural archetypes, figures that stand as "woman" in patriarchal culture, so too is *Étant donnés* a "concatenation of stereotypes" lying in the splendor of an equally concatenated ensemble of staid pictorial conventions (the nude, the pastoral landscape, perspectival space).[131]

This nude, however, is not only an ambiguous pastiche of archetypes (presented in that very pantheon of the art history that Duchamp is meant to have referenced); she is also, emphatically, based on a real woman (or, strictly speaking, three women, if one is counting the details that "belong" to the loves in Duchamp's life). It is obvious that he could have used a readymade figure—a mannequin, a life-size doll; alternatively, he could have sculpted one. But the point, it seems, was not simply to offer a nude for viewing and definitely not to find one ready-made, but to enact something far more convoluted and unsettling. To make his figure, Duchamp turned to live body casting—a denigrated artistic method in which the body itself is the primary generator of the sculptural form. The resultant nude was from its very beginnings, then, meant to be an approximation of a real body, a one-to-one rendering of the object of the artist's forlorn love at the time—not just a lump of parchment, and not either an arty idealization or an abstraction, but a form of direct *copy*.[132]

As letters by Duchamp reveal, not only was Martins's body the starting point for the piece, but its replication might well have been a way to capture that body's very real and dogged evasiveness.[133] He and Martins had met in 1943 and began an impassioned affair that carried them through the beginning of the following decade. The tenor of Duchamp's desire, grasped mostly through his letters to her (her replies are presumed lost), defies much of what we thought we knew about the man repeatedly described in terms similar to Ettie Stettheimer's 1923 assessment: "a cold-blooded fish, who can lose his head over no one, and doesn't pretend to."[134] Indeed, as Helen Molesworth notes, "One of the most persistent pieces of received wisdom about Duchamp is that he was a paragon of indifference in matters both personal and aesthetic."[135] *Étant donnés* belies both counts. He was anything but indifferent to Martins, and in the suite of letters that were written contemporaneously with his first frustrating years of constructing the figure he told her much about the early process of making the work that would only later be titled *Étant donnés*.[136] Martins was not only its muse, model (the original "original"), and the woman to whom he sent so many missives between 1946 and 1951 mixing the technical and the amorous, but, in matters of sculpture, she was also his consultant.

In early 1950 she permanently moved to Brazil with her husband, effectively putting an end to her affair with Duchamp. One senses, though, that it was perhaps as much Martins's consistent unattainability as her presence in the artist's life—refusing to leave her husband and child to sequester herself in Duchamp's studio as he so repeatedly implored of her—that left its permanent trace in his final work. The mix of love, frustrated desire, and loss that is apparent in Duchamp's letters seems to drive the peculiar obsession that is *Étant donnés*, a work that he somehow couldn't finish, or part with, for two decades—two decades that, as it happened, made up just about the rest of his life.

The process of making the nude figure began in the mid-1940s with lessons in body casting that Duchamp took, together with Martins, under the instruction of Italian sculptor Ettore Salvatore, a specialist in the technique.[137] These were followed by sessions with Martins, duplicating individual body parts such as legs, arms, breasts, and her torso through several stages of mold making and casting. The first full-scale figure, based on the life casts and made of modeling clay, was in turn cast in plaster (for that he commissioned Salvatore), and was completed in May 1949. "My plaster cast is back home," Duchamp wrote to Martins later that summer, "and I am working on the sterile surface of the intractable plaster, with the inevitable mishaps. What is ugly about plaster is the impression it gives of having been molded, that very top layer has to be removed by reworking the contours and then you have another original."[138]

One might speculate about why Duchamp opted to cast Martins's body in the first place. In terms of the artistic fashions of the day, life casting would hardly have been an evident choice. Reproduction by casting not only ostensibly evaded the need for the inventiveness or skill required to make a form from scratch, but a single matrix or mold also often allowed multiple identical casts to be made: both factors discredited the method as a legitimate artistic tool. Take, for example, the scandal that had erupted at the 1877 Salon de Paris over Rodin's *Age of Bronze*, where the allegation that the artist had cast the figure from life, later proven untrue, was tantamount to an accusation of fraud. And even though more than a half-century had passed between the Rodin incident and Duchamp's forays into casting, the art world had not yet rehabilitated the technique. As Molesworth explains, "Under the aesthetic regime of modernism, casting came to be denigrated because it was presumed to offer the repetition of an existing form, or to enable the production of identical forms—both of which were seen to be antithetical to the privileging of the sculptural object as unique."[139] In defiance of precisely that hierarchy (that Duchamp had defied, differently but no less adamantly, with his use of pochoir printing and his general fascination with reproduction), the artist made the technique, and with it the whole procedural logic that it shares with photography, central to the development of *Étant donnés*.[140]

The result of the casting procedure Duchamp employed is in fact less naturalistic (and in places, strictly speaking, less anatomically correct) than it might have been had he sculpted the figure to scale based on the body of Martins. But naturalism seems not to have been the point. What is more, we now know from his letters to her that the process was anything but straightforward and easy; he struggled and failed on repeated occasions to arrive at the desired result.[141] The methods he used were complex, time-consuming (by his own accounts he often worked eight hours a day on his project), and frustratingly characterized by trial and error. He was forced to construct and then abandon several versions, searching throughout for better methods and materials to render the form. To see any number of partially broken plaster cast body elements, discarded parchment studies, or even the large Plexiglas element drilled with countless holes filling in the contours of an outline of the figure (the precise use of which, to this day, no one seems to fully understand), all found in the secret studio after Duchamp's death, is to palpably recognize the extent of his struggle. Yet he continued undaunted. As a result, there is something to be said of the incredible *physicality* of the work—not only in relation to Martins's physicality as sitter, whose skin is literally remade, and correspondingly our physicality as viewers, crouching slightly, held in place, controlled as bodies engaged in the act of looking, but also to Duchamp's as its maker, who so tirelessly labored to hand-shape countless elements of the installation.

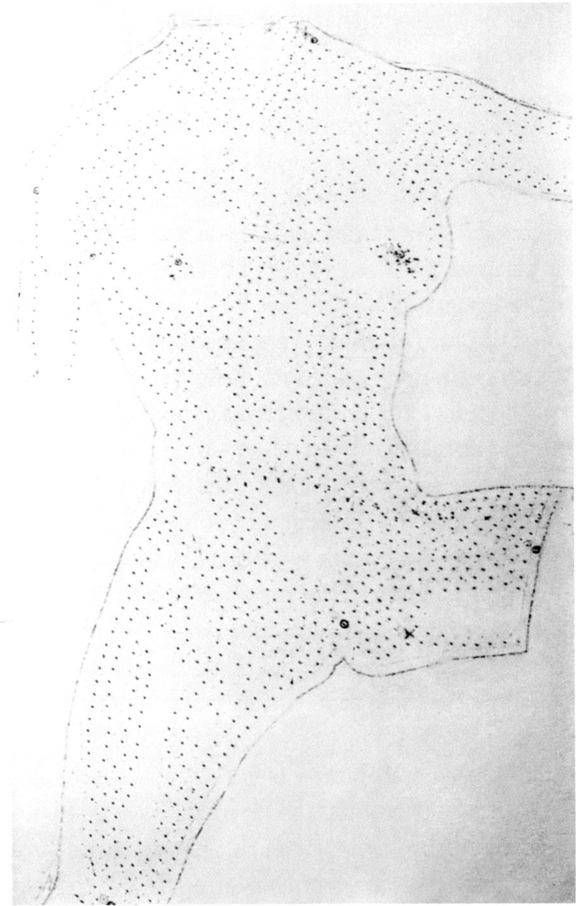

3.47

Marcel Duchamp, preparatory study for the figure in *Étant donnés*, c. 1950. Gouache on transparent perforated Plexiglas, 36 × 22 inches. Private collection.

A clue to his reasons for devising such complex methods seems contained in the letter where he admits that he is producing, as he claims, "another original." For no method other than casting could have garnered the same results: not only did it reproduce the (desired, elusive) body, but also, in being an imprint, the figure in *Étant donnés* forever retained a physical trace of that body. In other words, it was representation's opposite: not a *mere* mimetic likeness, it was a bit of the thing itself. And perhaps it is precisely this hold on a real referent that is responsible for the work's unsettlingly existential corporeality. For Duchamp, the point, it seems, was to turn the figure in his installation *into an index*. The defining quality of the cast, like the particular and irreducible condition of the photograph, is its indexicality. It was the American semiotician Charles Sanders Peirce who, in the late nineteenth century, first gave that quality its name, distinguishing it from the iconic or the symbolic sign whose relationship to things is a question either of resemblance or merely of custom. The index is an altogether different order of sign, bearing a causal, factual, and physical connection to its referent, like the relation between a fingerprint and the digit that made it or a weathervane and the wind that pushed it.[142] The photograph, scholars have told us, is the index's modern embodiment, rendered by the passage of light from a subject to a light-sensitive surface and thus endowed with an intimate, material, physical, not just conceptual, relation to its referent. The cast, similarly made by physical imprint, in this case of mold meeting matter, is a direct registration of the real, and as such is evidence of it.[143] Duchamp himself saw parallels between the mold and photography: a mold is "the (photographic) negative ... from the perspective of form and color," he announced in his notes collected in 1966 in his last box, *À l'infinitif* (In the Infinitive).[144] Both are certifications of a sort, testifying undeniably to a quality of the thing depicted—what Barthes, years later and referring to the photograph, called the "having-been-there."[145] Here the lover's ersatz is a product of fastidious casting and molding, with those casts cast and molded again, always maintaining a chain of indexicality connecting Martins's physical topography to *Étant donnés* as a material witness that the lover undeniably once had been there. Like the elements in the *Box of 1914*, Duchamp's nude figure is, no matter whatever else, a document, a record—evidence, even.

The cast of Martins's body repeats, as Barthes wrote of the photograph, "that which can no longer be existentially repeated."[146] What a strange mnemotechny, then, repeating and as such reminding Duchamp of his lover, holding her vestigial copy in place (locked up) at the very moment that her real body was threatening to evade him. "It is *your* leg and of such beauty!" the artist wrote to his model of her cast.[147] Just as the photograph serves as indexical evidence, so too does the cast. Both are equally relevant to what André Bazin (coincidentally, at the very moment Duchamp was finishing his figure) theorized about the specificity of photography, which can be effectively extended to casting: "it *is* the model it reproduces."[148]

Yet another cast, which Duchamp mentioned in a July 1949 letter to Martins, appears in the only photograph of the figure from the early period of preparatory work. Speculated to have been taken by Duchamp himself, the stark but elegant photographic composition and clean black backdrop suggest that he used the single image as a kind of "portrait" of his cast to share with Martins. Using this and other partial plaster casts produced by this same method (one must imagine him slathering plaster, building molds in individual bodily sections, putting that body together and taking it apart again), Duchamp assembled the final model. He stretched a thin layer of taut wet parchment over the plaster (after trying and discarding various vellums) to make the figure's "skin." It was, from the start, clearly the skin—that vast surface of contact of the body—rather than the body's actual form that Duchamp was concerned with ("the surface produced by the Plastilene gives me more or less what I am looking for, namely the epidermis and not the sculpture of the bones or the volumes," he wrote to Martins, adding, "in any case this plaster cast was only made with a view to the skin that will go on it").[149] He painted the surfaces and the undersides of various studies, testing them to find what he considered the most natural skinlike result (not "too candy-pink," he hoped). In the end, the final eerie, hand-colored, parchment-clad nude took in itself more than a decade for Duchamp to complete, the labor spanning the period between the mid-1940s until the late 1950s and introducing, indeed, "another original" to the complex meditation on the copy that is this final work.

The result of his efforts is, no matter how you look at it, resolutely artificial. What Lyotard aptly called the "last nude" is a life-size yet foreshortened figure with a thin skin of painted parchment. Screwed to a support of crisscrossed wire, tin sheeting, Peg-Board, and gray putty propped on angled joists, she features a raised arm and clenched fist that are out of proportion with the rest of the body and a "vulva" that is, by all accounts, a strangely shaped crevice.[150] Endless is the scholarly conjecture about that orifice, about why Duchamp bestowed the "woman with the open pussy," as he called it in letters to Martins, with a vulva that is so anatomically incorrect, so insolently awkward (violation, castration, *mere* mutilation?).[151] One possible answer would be not to speculate but to acknowledge, again, that however much the impression of an actual, specific body remained fundamental to the entire project, exactitude of translation was evidently not the ambition. In fact, the oddness of her sex could at least partly have been the result of the casting process itself, which required different body parts to be cast individually and then put together, sometimes with awkward joins.[152] Still, whatever may have been the initial technical or other causes, the fact that Duchamp didn't correct or modify the form to make the obviously strange cleft appear more correct is revealing. After all, this was not a man afraid of the labor or time it would take to get his figure *exactly* as he wanted it.

And, as with the vulva, the same might be said of the nude's out-of-scale left arm and hand. During the hot summer of 1959 the original Plastilene arms melted and cracked while Duchamp was away. Both parchment arms of the then recently finished figure fractured so severely that Duchamp was forced to revise the viewing angle of the nude slightly (to conceal the part of her truncated right limb that had fallen off). He also decided to cast Teeny's raised arm and hand to take the place of the extant upright left arm, originally modeled by Martins, which had been damaged beyond repair.[153] While practical, this new partial casting session with another model seems unlikely to have been the only possible solution, not to mention that, since Teeny's arm was somewhat larger than Martins's, the literal incorporation of this new body part caused an odd disruption of scale to the whole. Duchamp doesn't seem to have minded. By that point, with his relationship with Martins long over, it appears that she didn't need to be the only indexical reference of the piece, even if it should—without question—still be *an index*. In other words, the expanse of the figure's cast form—so hard-won by Duchamp—seemingly had to be the indelible imprint of real bodies (actual lovers), but in the very process of production the artist also determined the figure's uncanny regress from the real. He effectively created a result that evinces its own willfully uneasy reciprocity between the actual body and the cast body, between original and replication.

One cannot help thinking here of George Baker's compelling claim in relation to one of Duchamp's close friends that "reproduction, for [Francis] Picabia, never remained simply a mechanical process; it was conceived, instead, as both machinic *and* bodily, both technical and corporeal, with reproduction understood in its full sexual sense, marching indeed to the drum beat of desire and the bodily drives."[154] It is so obvious, and yet one wonders if it had ever been stated so directly. How could we have forgotten that double sense of "reproduction" which, all along, for Duchamp as much as for Picabia, was understood as a question of *the body*? After all, it seems no coincidence that Duchamp's perhaps most famous commentary on reproduction in the very period to which Baker is referring was *L.H.O.O.Q.* (1919). So many scholars have dutifully told us that this literally translates to "she has a hot ass" (indeed, never have I read another translation of the title). But in failing to note the flagrant colloquial meaning of that phrase—which is, in fact, "she's so horny"—they turn the title into a mere comment on its subject's physiognomy, rather than on her own base, corporeal desire. *Étant donnés* makes this libidinous understanding of reproduction explicit and magnified, one last and final time.

Whether one recognizes reproduction as libidinal or not, one cannot deny that the ontological promise of photography is precisely its capacity to beget, again and again, virtually without end, duplicates of itself. The cast, like the photograph or even the signature, is not merely the product *of* a repeatable, iterable form, but also inevitably holds within it the potential *for* further reproduction. Baker's description of the photograph is applicable to the cast as well, since it "also bears its own relation to the condition of the multiple spun through a logic of serialization in which each individual instance of a photograph presents itself as only one of a potentially infinite number of copies."[155] What perversity, then, for Duchamp to have used the logic of both throughout his oeuvre in just that way and to then alter his strategy, right at the end, by suddenly using those methods to make something paradoxically original, undeniably singular, inevitably *unreplicable*. After a lifetime of playing fast and loose with originality and reproduction, Duchamp's final work is a willfully unique, auratic object—singular to an extreme and, as it is unmovable, demanding the experiential presence of the viewer—even as it is (and this is its incredible paradox) also a kind of copy.

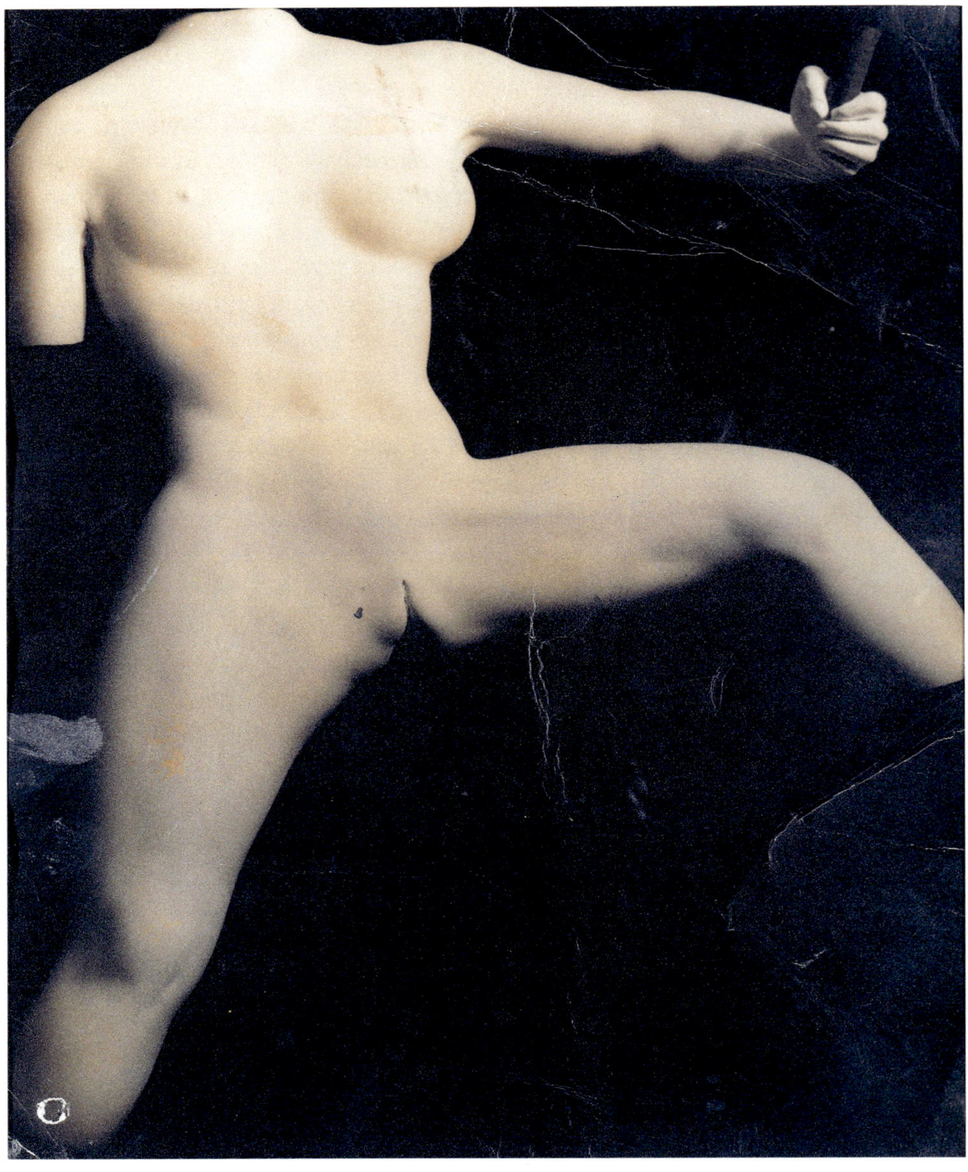

3.48

Marcel Duchamp, photograph sent to Maria Martins of a plaster study for the figure in *Étant donnés*, 1949. Gelatin silver print, 9¼ × 7½ inches. Collection of Norman and Norah Stone, San Francisco.

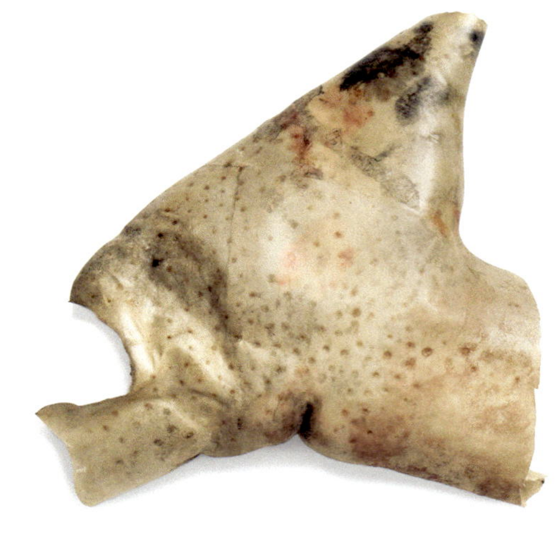

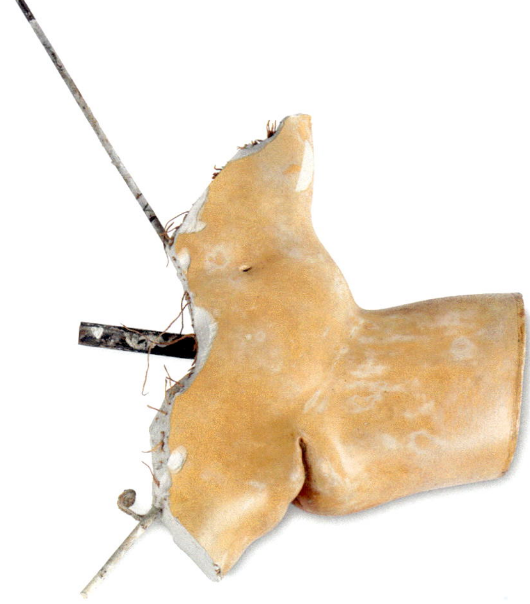

3.49

Marcel Duchamp, untitled (skin for lower torso of *Étant donnés* figure), c. 1948–49. Parchment with paint, graphite, wax, and resin, 11¾ × 11¾ inches. Philadelphia Museum of Art: Gift of Mme Marcel Duchamp.

3.50

Marcel Duchamp, untitled (torso fragment), c. 1949. Plaster with iron and cloth armature, 21¾ × 7½ inches. Philadelphia Museum of Art: Gift of Mme Marcel Duchamp.

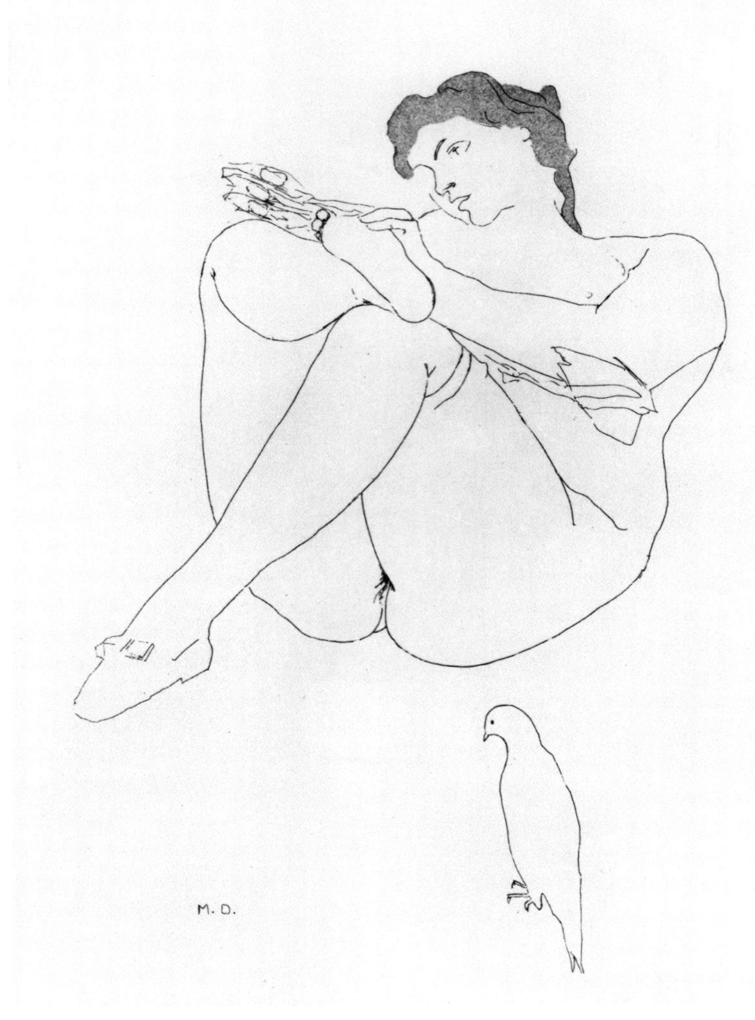

3.51

Marcel Duchamp, *Morceaux choisis d'après Courbet* (Selected Details after Courbet), 1968. From *The Large Glass and Related Works, with Nine Etchings by Marcel Duchamp on the Theme of The Lovers*, vol. 2 (Milan: Galleria Schwarz, 1968). Etching and aquatint on paper, plate: 13⁹⁄₁₆ × 9⅛ inches, sheet: 16⁹⁄₁₆ × 10¹⁄₁₆ inches. Philadelphia Museum of Art: Gift of Mme Marcel Duchamp.

COPIES OF A COPY

If the copy emerges as a central transgressive force of the deliberately auratic work that is *Étant donnés*, one can retroactively detect the concern in several works that Duchamp released well before his secret work went public—from straightforward-looking etchings to curious bodily metonymies. Think of the series of works on paper that he produced in 1968 under the title *Morceaux choisis*. Those "selected details" were essentially nine etchings of line drawings made in the "style of" Ingres, Rodin, and Courbet; they were modified imitations of iconic, erotic works by each artist. The poses of the figures or themes of the images cannot help recalling *Étant donnés*, but of course this is only apparent in hindsight. The *Morceaux choisis*, some even signed MARCELLUS D, didn't hide their debt to copying. On the contrary, these literal imitations of the well-known images of "famed" artists made a show of it.

These were not the only meditations on the copy released in the years before *Étant donnés* was unveiled. Duchamp employed casting for the production of a series of objects that were made public in the 1950s, long before people could connect them to *Étant donnés* and without divulging from what they were themselves cast. A trilogy of what have been called his "erotic objects," *Feuille de vigne femelle* (Female Fig Leaf) from 1950, *Objet-dard* (Dart-Object) from 1951, and *Coin de chasteté* (Wedge of Chastity) from 1954, emerged into the world, one by one, as art objects in their own right. The *New York Times*, at the time of their first showing, deemed them "bizarre artifacts," an attribute that they likely provoked not only because of their eerie corporeality but also, and even if the reporter couldn't know it at the time, because of their double role as both things in themselves and preambles to something yet impenetrable beyond them.[156]

Almost defiantly unlike the first readymades, the erotic objects were carefully molded and cast elements, the product of something that, at its origins, is handmade, as Helen Molesworth reminds us.[157] And although we now know their curious provenance, few at the time of their first public exhibition in the 1950s and '60s could imagine the larger project's production from which they were the residue: *Feuille de vigne femelle* seems to have been used originally as a countermold, helping to press and hold moistened parchment in the crevices and contours of the vaginal opening of a positive plaster mold as it dried.[158] The palm-size object is thus a positive of the figure's lower regions, a vulva turned inside out, literally making the secret nude's sex visible in those years before *Étant donnés* exposed it to the public. The *Objet-dard*, at once phallic and scatological with a title that plays on "art object" and French slang for "penis," had been fabricated from a reinforced plaster armature used as a brace to help press down the parchment slightly below the breast of the nude figure. The two-part *Coin de chasteté*'s original function seems less clear, although it is now known that one of the two elements that make up the piece, its galvanized plaster wedge, fits snugly into the sex of one of Duchamp's abandoned parchment elements related to the production of the nude. Replicating this same sense of bodily union, Duchamp made the second part of *Coin de chasteté* from pink dental plastic and inserted the galvanized plaster part into it.

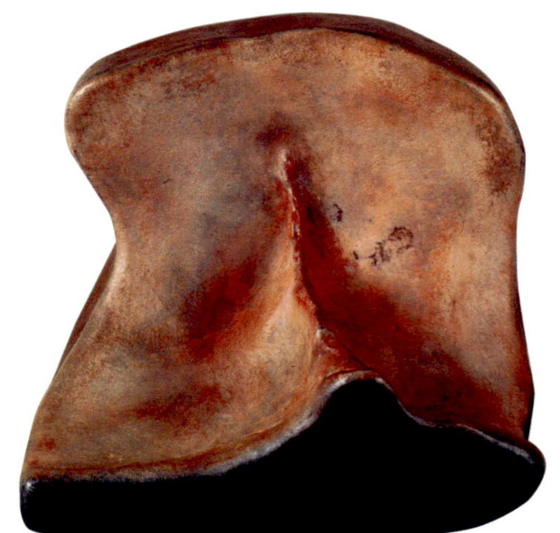

3.52

Marcel Duchamp, *Feuille de vigne femelle* (Female Fig Leaf), 1950. Painted plaster cast, $3\frac{1}{2} \times 5\frac{1}{2} \times 4\frac{15}{16}$ inches. Private collection.

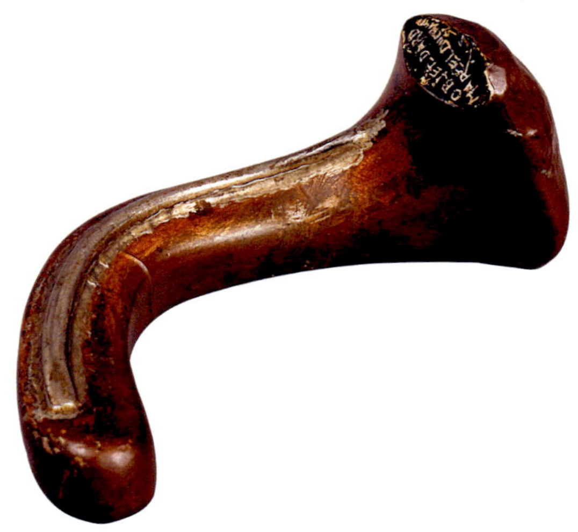

3.53

Marcel Duchamp, *Objet-dard* (Dart-Object), 1951. Copper-electroplated plaster cast with inlaid lead rib, $2\frac{15}{16} \times 7\frac{15}{16} \times 2\frac{3}{8}$ inches. Private collection.

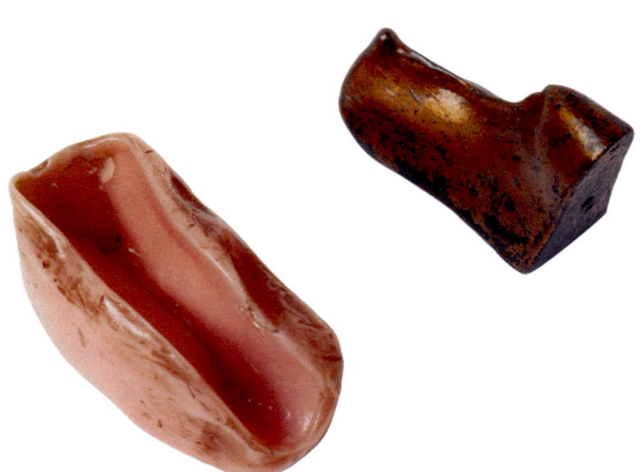

3.54

Marcel Duchamp, *Coin de chasteté* (Wedge of Chastity), 1954. Sculpture in two sections, copper-electroplated plaster and dental plastic, $2\frac{3}{16} \times 3\frac{3}{8} \times 1\frac{5}{8}$ inches. Private collection.

3.55 (right)

[Marcel Duchamp], mold for making copies of *Feuille de vigne femelle* (Female Fig Leaf), c. 1950. Centre Pompidou, MNAM-CCI, Paris.

To separate the two parts is to be confronted with an uncannily evocative vaginal crevice formed as the perfect imprint of the wedge that so delicately sits in it. As multiple countermolds to the secret installation, the little erotic objects were eagerly made public by Duchamp: exhibited whenever there was an opportunity, gifted to friends, and even quite immediately included in reproduction in updated versions of the *Boîte-en-valise*.[159]

Duchamp gave one of his two casts of *Feuille de vigne femelle* to Man Ray as a gift, offering as well that his friend could make another ten copies of that "original" cast to sell off to make himself some money, which Man Ray did.[160] (Testament to this is found in the multipart plaster mold dating from around 1950 that was used for making copies of *Feuille de vigne femelle* and long in Man Ray's possession.) In time, each of the erotic objects would be replicated, in small bronze editions, molded and cast from those "first-generation" already-replicated objects. If the first-generation objects were themselves at a remove from the original—Martins's body—being themselves molds of a cast (the figure in *Étant donnés*), their further replication continued Duchamp's convoluted replication project, all while maintaining an inexorable grip on the index.

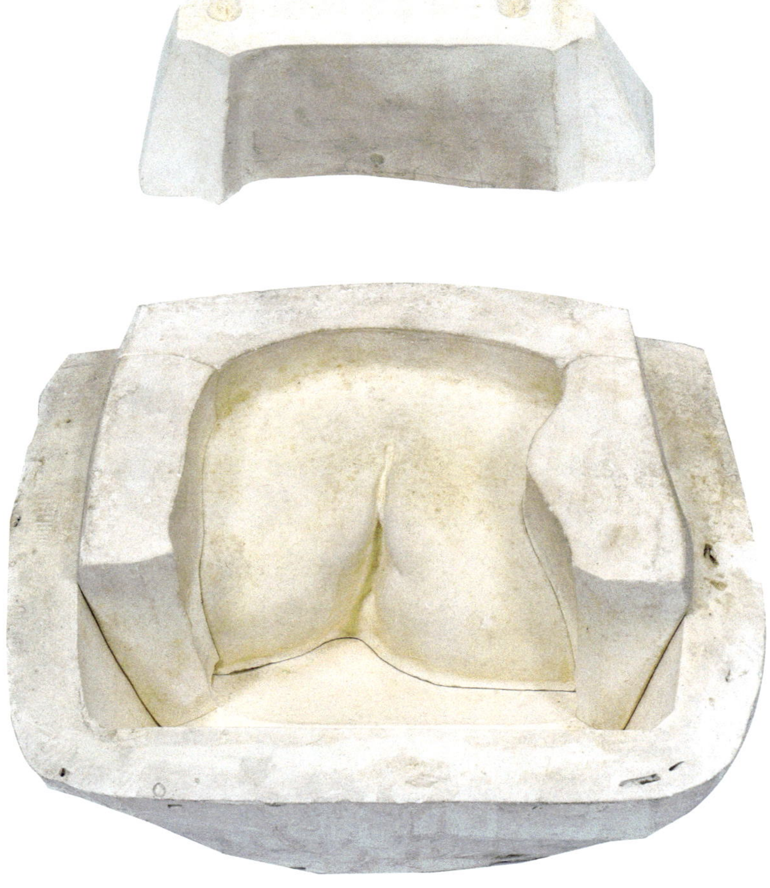

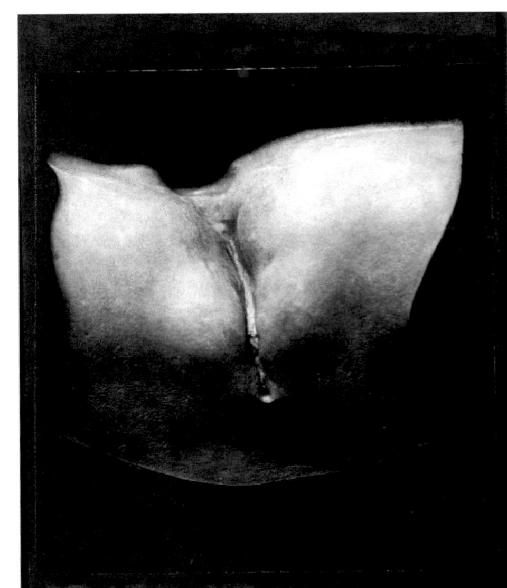

3.56

Marcel Duchamp, *Feuille de vigne femelle* (Female Fig Leaf), c. 1956. Photograph for cover of *Le Surréalisme, même*, no. 1. Hand-retouched photograph, $12 \times 8\frac{1}{8}$ inches. Photographer unknown. Moderna Museet, Stockholm: Museum purchase.

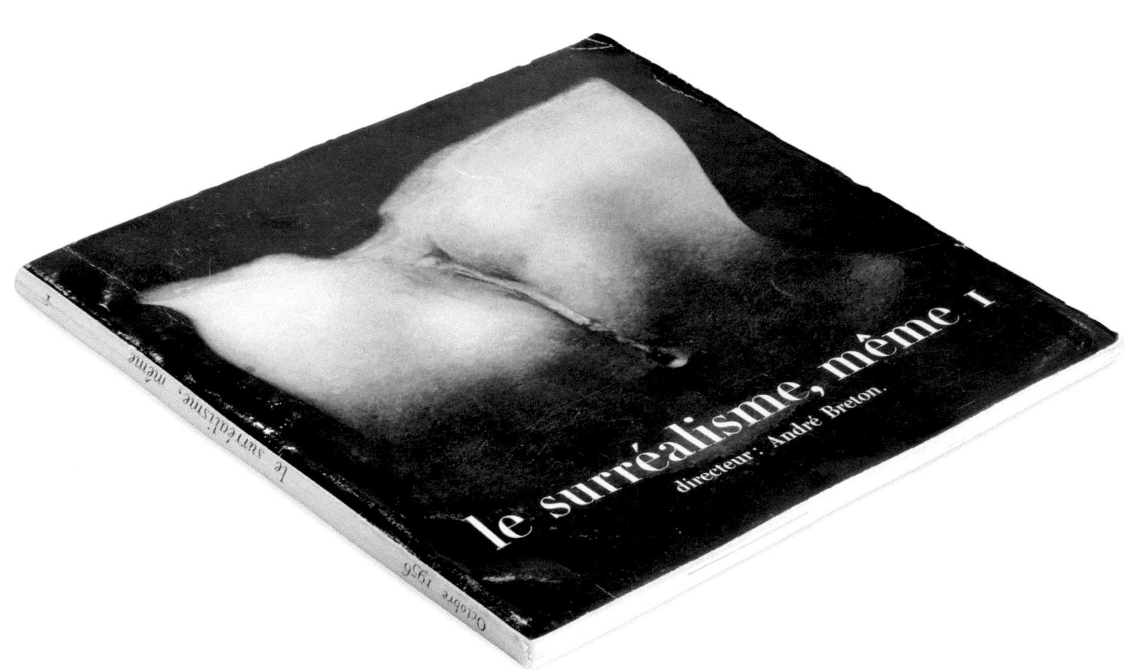

3.57

Marcel Duchamp, cover design for *Le Surréalisme, même*, no. 1 (Winter 1956). Paperbound serial journal, $7\frac{11}{16} \times 7\frac{11}{16}$ inches. Philadelphia Museum of Art: Gift of Jacqueline, Peter, and Paul Matisse in memory of their mother, Alexina Duchamp.

Photography's implication in this, not only structurally but also literally, should not be forgotten. One example perhaps suffices: a hand-retouched photograph of *Feuille de vigne femelle*, most probably made in 1956, to be used for the cover of the first issue of *Le Surréalisme, même*, published in October of that same year. Having been asked by Breton to make the inaugural cover of the new magazine, Duchamp engaged a photographer in New York to reproduce his *Feuille de vigne femelle*, specifically requesting that it be made to look convex rather than concave, in other words, like a negative image of itself, which would be, in fact, a positive reproduction of its source. Duchamp then hand-colored the photo, adding details to emphasize its contours and to enhance the illusion. Through the photographic process, *Feuille de vigne femelle* becomes an inversion of itself; its representation shows it as if it were an image of the "original" model/body, not something at several removes. Like the playful inversions of original and copy for the cover of the 1947 Surrealist exhibition catalog, Duchamp here deploys photography as if to remind us of its central place in the work that it covertly announces.

There were still other indexical works that emerged in the same period, this time not of the lover's body but of the artist's own, no longer feminine but masculine. In 1959, when Duchamp had to make new casts (from Teeny's body) of the arm and hand for *Étant donnés*'s nude figure, he conceived two new works, *With My Tongue in My Cheek* and *Torture morte* (both 1959), that were cast from his cheek and the sole of his foot, respectively. Originally made to be included in Robert Lebel's first monograph on Duchamp when Trianon Press, the publisher, requested new works from the artist, they were rejected in the end. They were not at all, it seems, what admirers of Duchamp had come to expect from him. The artist doesn't seem to have been daunted; he showed them instead at the Surrealist exhibition that he was curating that same year. Even before *Étant donnés* itself was visible, to anyone who paid close enough attention, Duchamp's curatorial practice throughout this period revealed his unrelenting interrogation of presentation and dissemination sites for the work of art. So too did the various blatant copies and bodily metonymies that he circulated suggest that reproduction, eroticism, and the body (as a model but also as a means of handmade production) remained an ardent preoccupation for him right up until the end of his life.

And if all of these essentially handmade objects employing the technique of casting may have seemed odd at the time, thoroughly un-Duchampian, it is telling that they gave way to the actual reproduction of his readymades on the larger scale that we now know today. Duchamp made an official bronze edition of two of the trilogy of his lumpen "erotic" objects in 1962 and '63, just before beginning the project of replicating thirteen of his most important readymades from the 1910s and '20s with the Italian gallerist Arturo Schwarz in 1964. A few reduxes of his readymades had circulated in the 1950s, but they were sporadic and haphazard one-off responses to exhibitions, like Sidney Janis's gallery shows "Challenge and Defy" (1950) and "Dada 1916–1923" (1953), for which Janis picked up a store-bought urinal on Duchamp's behalf. Before 1964, when with Schwarz he authorized an official, signed, numbered, limited edition of eight of each of the thirteen

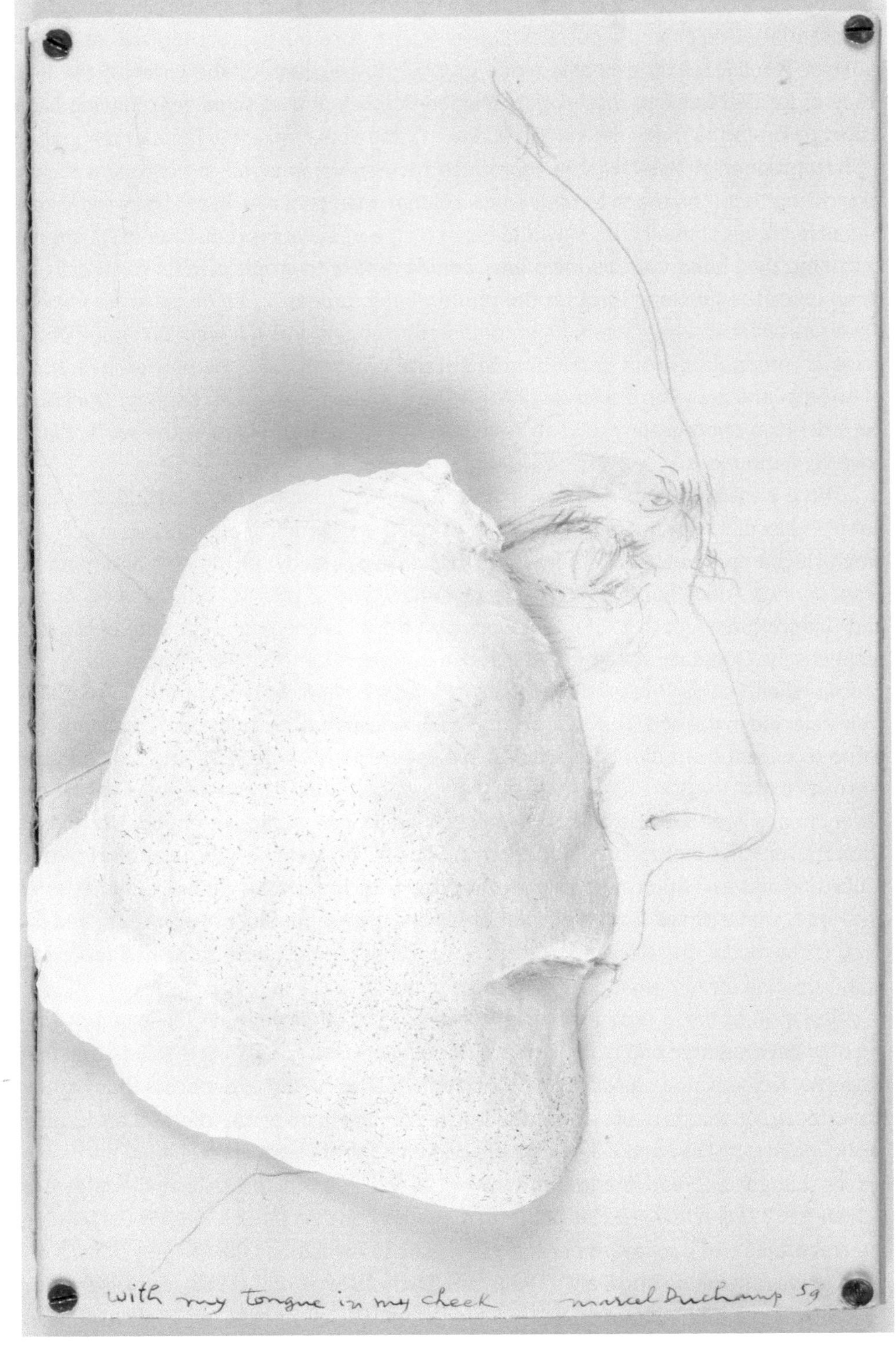
with my tongue in my cheek
marcel Duchamp 59

objects, he had never produced anything of that scale, nor with such implications, with respect to the readymades. In a curious twist, then, it was arguably those little cast handmade objects, by-products of a larger cast figure of a then still clandestine project, that helped set in motion Duchamp's most iconic reproductions of originally mass-produced things. As Helen Molesworth has observed, "The temporal proximity of the intimate, handmade erotic sculptures and the replicas of the readymades suggests that the erotics of the body and the allure of the commodity are connected in Duchamp's practice."[161] The conjunction goes further: through the process of finalizing *Étant donnés*, Duchamp was thinking anew about the messy imbrication of bodily erotics with precisely the questions of originality and reproducibility that had preoccupied him throughout his life.

CONCLUSION

At once a copy and an original, an approximation and an auratic, psychic, phenomenological thing, in a museum and also part of that museum, specular and cuntish, Duchamp's *Étant donnés* is the untenable combination of all of these things at once. If the *Boîte-en-valise*, with its three-hundred-plus copies of artworks and its abstraction of display space (it is an *any* space) seems to celebrate art's power to undermine the original even as it holds on to it, *Étant donnés* does the opposite: it insists on the resurgence of an original object—rare, undeniably unique, authentic in every way—that traffics in, and was made through, outmoded sculptural techniques based on copying. As the culmination of a lifetime of reproduction and thwarting the aesthetic original, *Étant donnés* might seem surprising for being, ostensibly, a unique work. And yet Duchamp positions us in front of an auratic object that is distinctly bound up with the question of the copy, and in a museum no less.

Photography is the operative model in much of this. For Duchamp, the photographic logic (to which casting subscribes) was not only a motor for the destruction of the idea of the unique original and offerer of the ontological promise of the multiple (of more of the same); it was also the bearer of material traces and thus, ambiguously, a perpetuator of originality, producing reliquaries of sorts, containing within it a grain of the thing itself. It was all of these contradictory things at once. This is another story that the *Manual of Instructions* tells, for there Duchamp speaks not only about the task at hand—the reassembly of *Étant donnés*—but importantly also of the centrality of the photographic to the entire work. It informs the viewer that all along Duchamp had used a photographic logic structurally, as a destabilizing agent, a tool that, in its mobilization, renders ambivalent the conditions of its own constitution as an original that is, simultaneously, a copy.

3.58

Marcel Duchamp, *With My Tongue in My Cheek*, 1959. Plaster and pencil on paper mounted on wood, 9.8 × 5.9 × 2 inches. Centre Pompidou, MNAM-CCI, Paris.

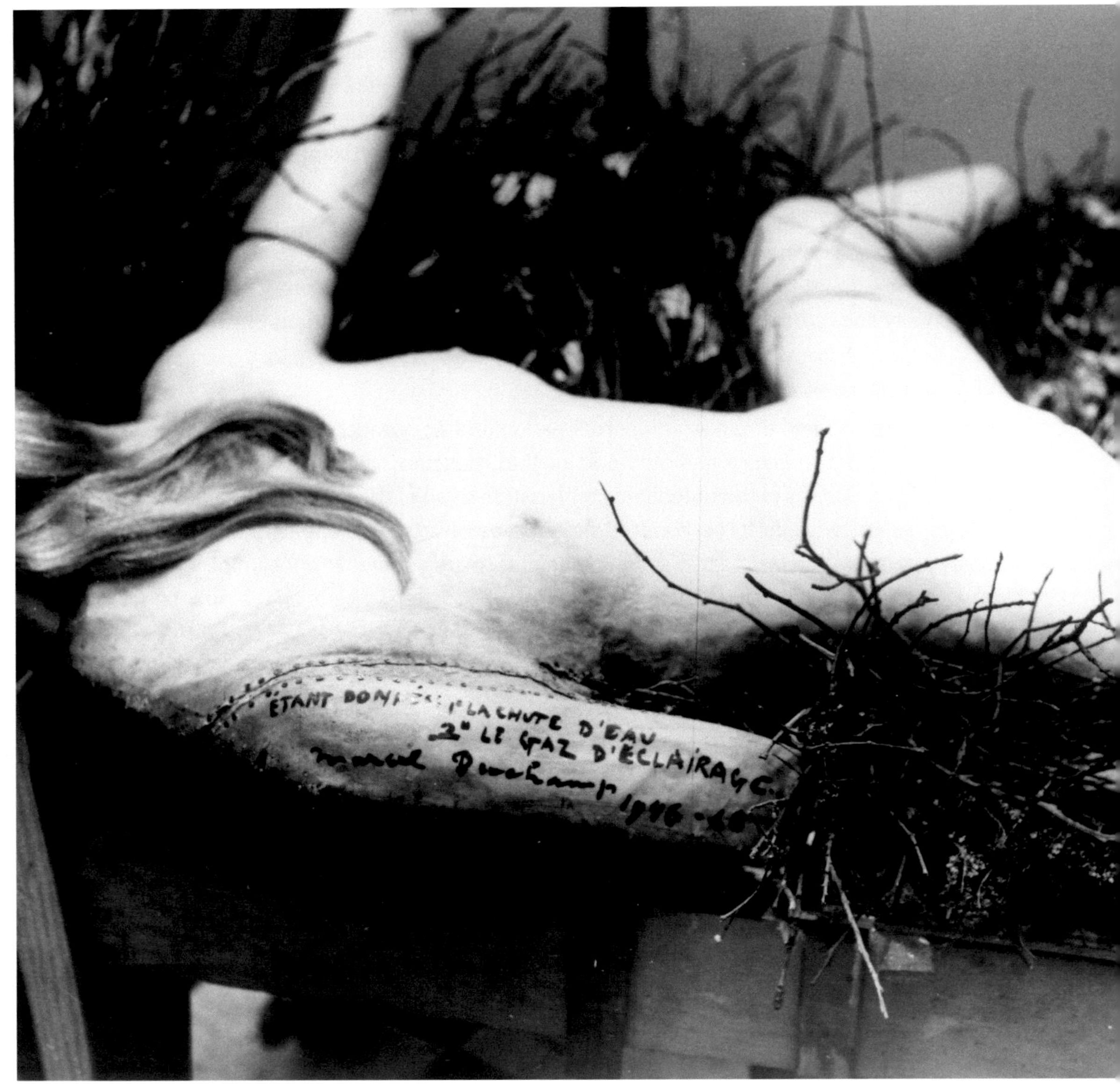

3.59

Detail view of the signed figure in Marcel Duchamp's *Étant donnés* as secretly installed in the artist's 80 East 11th Street studio, 1968. Photo by Denise Browne Hare. Philadelphia Museum of Art: Archives, Anne d'Harnoncourt Records.

The artist took ordinary stuff (tape, cotton, plaster, parchment) and transmogrified it into one of the most radical and transgressive artworks of the twentieth century, and, as Jasper Johns famously observed, "the strangest work of art any museum has ever had in it."[162] But, as this chapter has set out, the work's radicalism and transgressivity is based less on the apparently shocking scene it displays, or what it dares to represent (the subject of so much of the existing writing about it), than on *how* it does so, which is to say, how it managed to insert itself into the museum, how it continues to insist on exposing that context from within, and how, in the process, Duchamp lays bare the properties of that very institutional site so it could never be seen in quite the same way again. For the museum—with its subjective role in the production of value and taste, its unchecked ability to constitute the work of art as much as frame it, its supposed neutrality, its implication in power and self-interest, and importantly also its investment in originality—is the veritable subject in *Étant donnés*. And in positioning its future viewers in place, making their voyeurism part of his work, Duchamp hardly hid that he was exposing the museum to them, one by one, as nothing less than obscene.

Duchamp's steadfast interest in thinking about the meaning of the artwork through, with, and even against its institutional context, and in particular through his investigations of the curatorial and administrative aspects of this context in the physical space of exhibitions through all of the postwar period, is deeply pertinent here. The museum, for which *Étant donnés* was imagined and into which the artist curated it, could be said to determine the piece, even as that work acts like a Trojan horse once inside. Duchamp's final work thus extends so much of what the artist was grappling with from the first decade of the twentieth century onward, but if his earlier projects have long been seen as epistemologically focused investigations of the object, *Étant donnés* exposed the institution as both figure and ground of the artist's oeuvre all along. It was his final artist-curated exhibition.

It is a gauntlet thrown at the feet of the museum, effective precisely because it doesn't let go of its grip on the institution: it sits defiantly within it.[163] Those visible and invisible (or at least oft-ignored because supposedly neutral) support structures are physically integrated into *Étant donnés*. Rosalind Krauss perhaps said it best when she noted that *Étant donnés* "would settle into its permanent institutional context to form the most total and devastating critique of how the aesthetic itself operates and is legitimized."[164] The force of Duchamp's particular practice of criticality lies in precisely this. After more than half a century of shaking up the terms of aesthetic legitimation with his readymades, *Étant donnés* importantly extends but also differently articulates an attack on the institution that amounts to this "most total and devastating critique."

Yet for all of its distinctly transgressive implications, pushing in entirely new ways at issues first introduced in the 1910s with the readymades, it is remarkable that the reception of Duchamp's final work was characterized by a critical silence that, in fact, performed what the artist worked his whole life to reveal: the ultimate power of the forces outside the artwork, including the discourses that historicize it.

In one of his rare public lectures, "The Creative Act," given when Duchamp was almost exactly halfway through his construction of *Étant donnés*, he stated: "Let us consider two poles of the creation of art: the artist on the one hand, and on the other the spectator who later becomes posterity."[165] Elsewhere he continued the thought: "After all, the public represents half of the matter; art is also made through the admiration one has for it; the masterpiece is declared in the final analysis by the spectator."[166] The viewer "*makes* the work."[167] And if this is the case, did the viewers of *Étant donnés*, once it was unveiled and in the several decades that followed, simply decide it didn't deserve to be thus *made*?

Why, one might rightly ask, did it take so long for *Étant donnés* to be inscribed in those very histories and in relation to the very ideas that it so audaciously set out to question? And why, to return to the set of questions evoked early in this chapter, is *Étant donnés* largely still absent from so many studies on simultaneous developments in "advanced art" that are themselves declared to be paradigmatic? To be clear: these questions do not mean to suggest that Duchamp's final work need be claimed as responsible for, or directly influential on, those artists and practices. This is not an effort to establish cause and effect, or heroic origin and disingenuous repetition (and, in some cases, the very simultaneity of some projects I have mentioned suggests that the authors couldn't have known about *Étant donnés* at the point at which they started their own projects). Instead my questions mean to provoke debate about how such a highly spectacular final work by an artist who himself is claimed to be so important for the generation of artists and their practices that came after him (a work that exactly those artists and critics could not pretend *not* to have heard about at the time) could so systematically be excised from critical discussion contextualizing exactly these practices. The inverse is also the case: Given the understanding that those practices incited, why haven't more historians returned to *Étant donnés* to parse it more carefully and read its situated critique in light of the subversive operations attributed to a younger generation?

Even Krauss, who had in the 1970s so presciently seen the indexical functioning of Duchamp's other works, left *Étant donnés* curiously out of her consideration. There, and once again, Duchamp was claimed the progenitor of a generation, but it was not the Duchamp of *Étant donnés*, and this regardless of the fact that the work offered, even more directly and programmatically, a key instance of the very "indexicality" that Krauss was discussing.[168] Several decades later, Krauss would come to see that *Étant donnés* had, in fact, grappled with the photographic in fundamental ways, saying: "And if his art had used photography as a structural, procedural element through which to reveal the operations of the index, here [in *Étant donnés*] 'the photographic' seemed to manifest itself in its crassest incarnation, merely as a drive toward the brutally simulacral: the substitution of the mimetic copy for reality itself."[169] I would inflect her arguments differently, suggesting that there is not only no "reality itself" to see in *Étant donnés* (except if one speaks of the museum itself, although I am not convinced that is what Krauss meant) but instead *only* a bizarrely auratic but nevertheless mimetic copy; and that the "crassest incarnation" of the photographic is the cast itself, responsible for *Étant donnés*'s hyperrealism and its eerie artifice but also, and importantly, for the work's equally paradoxical and simultaneous evocation and refusal of the cult of auratic, authentic originality so cherished by the museum. It is Duchamp's siting of precisely this tension in the museum, I have sought to argue, that lies at the heart of how the work operates but also perhaps explains how it managed to fall so decisively into disfavor among critics who failed to recognize the full implications of that gesture. Comfortably sited within a structure of power, it looked, quite simply, like complicity, a sellout, something better ignored as an artistic dead end.

For twenty years Duchamp had labored on the construction of something seemingly anathema to the uncompromisingly critical oeuvre that had come before it. "Retardataire," in a word, was how the *New York Times* dismissed it when it opened to the public, suggesting that it had "arrived a bit late to make a sensation," and comparing its "spent and sterile slickness" to William-Adolphe Bouguereau, that most ridiculed of nineteenth-century Salon painters.[170] The highly figurative and stridently material (rather than conceptual) aspects of *Étant donnés* were seen as deeply disappointing to many of Duchamp's close friends and nearly every journalist reporting on the installation when it was first made public. For them, it simply made no sense that the dry and cerebral chess-playing father of both the readymade and the allusive *Large Glass* had for so long and with such effort clandestinely crafted something so apparently naturalistic and crassly literal, so tied up with the labor of the hand, so ridiculously like a poor man's Technicolor peep show. Either as an incongruity in his oeuvre or as a *retour à l'ordre* were the explicit terms by which they saw it, failing to understand it as the most elaborate and consistent declaration of the most central of Duchamp's concerns: the questioning of the apparatuses for the legitimation, valuation, and circulation of the artwork.[171]

What if Duchamp's final work, so long repressed from histories of the practices and movements of art developed in the epoch in which it was unveiled, might all along have revealed that era's most tenacious and perhaps still repressed concerns? Although the beginning of this chapter sketches a diverse body of resonant works with which *Étant donnés* could have been, but wasn't, compared—from the practices of John Baldessari and Bruce Nauman to those of Paul Thek and Vito Acconci—it might be productive to focus on one pregnant example to better understand the stakes and consequences of its reception.

It was around the moment of *Étant donnés*'s unveiling, in the late 1960s and early 1970s, that the questioning of the role and power of institutions of art thrived among the most progressive of artists. In his 1970 essay "Critical Limits," Daniel Buren laments the attention "fixed only on the object shown, its meaning, without looking at or discussing even once the place where it is shown."[172] In 1972 Robert Smithson declared in an interview that "the great issue" of contemporary practice, which he predicted would continue to be the "growing issue" throughout the rest of the 1970s, would be "the investigation of the apparatus the artist is threaded through."[173] Critics, for their part, agreed, finding just such an investigation manifested "in the practices of Marcel Broodthaers, Daniel Buren, Michael Asher, Hans Haacke, and Louise Lawler."[174] Numerous were those who, speaking of the filiation of the artists dealing with a critique of the institution, began to connect many practices that actually resonated deeply with *Étant donnés* somewhere else.[175] Craig Owens, for example, admitted:

> It is customary to attribute the recognition of the importance of the frame in constituting the work of art to Duchamp (the readymade requires its institutional setting in order to be perceived as a work of art), and to regard the investigation of the apparatus that the artist is threaded through which took place in the 1970s as a revival of the productivist line elaborated in the 1920s and 1930s, specifically, of the demand (to paraphrase Walter Benjamin) that artists refuse to supply the existing productive apparatus without attempting to change it. I am arguing, however, that the "death of the author" constitutes a historical watershed between the avant-gardes of the '10s and '20s and the institutional critiques of the '70s, and that to regard the latter as a revival or renewal of the former can only lead to misapprehensions about contemporary practice.[176]

It is striking how much *Étant donnés* shares with so many neo-avant-garde projects of the late 1960s and 1970s in their observations about, and complex understanding of, the functioning of art institutions; each could be described as artwork that is, in fact, about the frame of art, including display systems, labels, scenography, administration, et cetera, which organize meaning, interest, and power in the museum.[177]

No artist seems to better exemplify the postwar era's paradigmatic concern with the institution than Marcel Broodthaers, whose *Musée d'Art Moderne* (1968–72) provides an interesting parallel case to *Étant donnés*. It is all the more revealing that the Belgian artist's fictional museum project is repeatedly described as having absorbed the lesson of Duchamp's readymade in order to herald a related but presumably more expanded and emphatic form of critical inquiry, an inquiry that would be hailed as "Institutional Critique." Benjamin H. D. Buchloh, one of Broodthaers's most important advocates and most sensitive readers, in particular makes the claim that Broodthaers succeeded where Duchamp's readymades and *Boîte-en-valise* failed (*Étant donnés* is never mentioned), although sometimes the successes with which Buchloh credits Broodthaers (or other artists involved in Institutional Critique, such as Michael Asher, Daniel Buren, Hans Haacke, or Louise Lawler) are difficult to distinguish from the failures he ascribes to Duchamp.[178] Krauss, for her part, announced that nothing less than "the whole practice of what came to be called 'institutional critique' derived from" Broodthaers, whose practice was one of "calling attention to the supposedly neutral containers of culture and questioning this putative neutrality."[179] And much of the scholarship that followed echoed this genealogy.

I hardly wish to displace Broodthaers from his place as reigning father of Institutional Critique, nor do I wish to claim one more feather in the cap of Duchamp. Still, I cannot but be surprised that for the generation of scholars who celebrated Broodthaers's packing crates, postcard reproductions of paintings, signs for directing visitors (coat check this way, information desk over there), opening and closing "ceremonies," hired art transport vans parked outside his events, and ironic adaptation of the role of museum "conservateur," Duchamp's enactment of institutional rituals for *Étant donnés* went unremarked.[180] Indeed even when, in an open letter written in 1969, Broodthaers argued that one should see his *Musée d'Art Moderne, Département des Aigles* as "a situation, a system defined by objects, by inscriptions, by various activities such as, in this instance, my writing of this letter to you," a conception that critics of his work wholly embraced, none of them seemed to notice the radical critique of the systems of value and meaning constructed by the museum that Duchamp had also orchestrated, that very same year, with the release of his own version of "a situation, a system defined by objects, by inscriptions, by various activities"—including, in this instance, behind-the-scenes museum trustee meetings, elaboration of museum contracts, writing and construction of a *Manual of Instructions*, reorganization of a whole section of the museum's contents and display, and even insertion of the work into the museum itself.[181]

While the readymades had, by the mid-1960s, unquestionably begun to leave their mark on the collective unconscious of contemporary artists and art history—claimed as the primal scene of so much advanced artistic practice—*Étant donnés* provoked an almost opposite response. In the writings of artists and critics speaking about Institutional Critique, it is treated (to this day) as if it simply does not exist, although the concurrence of the inception of Institutional Critique and the public unveiling of the final, remarkable, and eminently public work of an artist who was so influential on the artists forging that critique is too striking not to provoke some questions.[182] Didn't *Étant donnés* involve, precisely, a "critically reflexive site specificity" that has been understood as the founding methodology of Institutional Critique?[183] Didn't it "problematize" the museum, refusing to "affirm, expand, or reinforce" the historically and ideologically loaded site? And didn't Duchamp exact a "reflection on the discursive and systematic mechanisms of reification and instrumentalization" within the institution, revealing how it defines, validates, frames, isolates, excludes, and naturalizes? Did he not, indeed, depart from his own more epistemologically focused investigation of the work of art to treat its frame as, quite explicitly, both "target and weapon"?[184] I cite here the terms used to define Institutional Critique and its methods because applying them to Duchamp's final work makes apparent how selective history has been about who and what it discusses, and how. And this, in the end, is one of the very critiques *Étant donnés* aimed to wage against art history and the museum.

The questions that remain are these: Could the most passionately committed critics of the 1970s and beyond simply not have seen what *Étant donnés* so fiercely aims to show us—holes burrowed in a seat of power that reveal that there is much behind

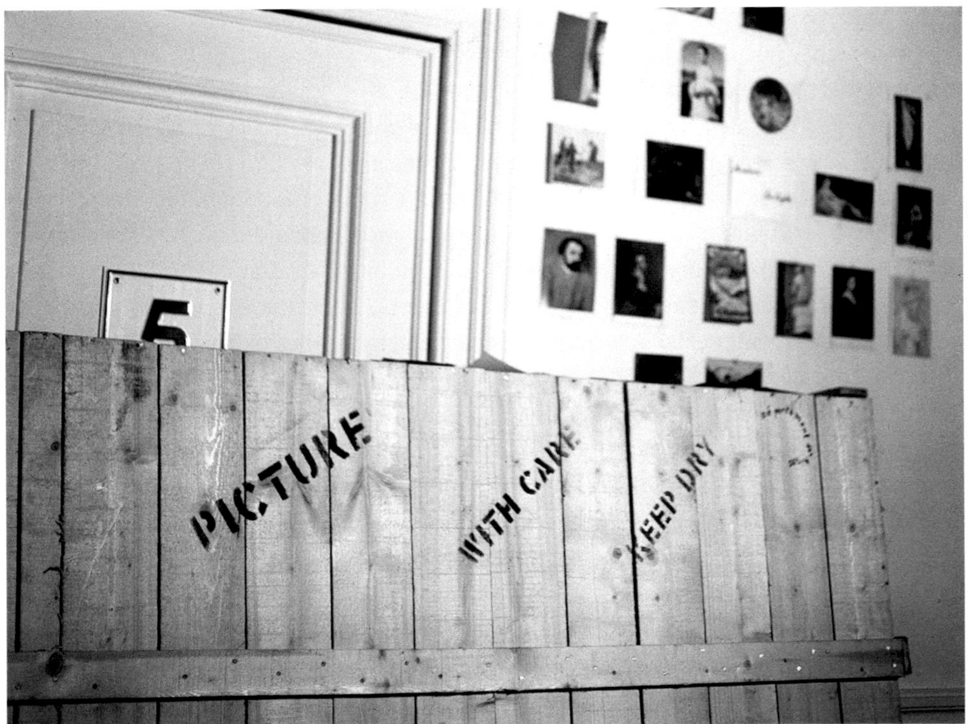
5
PICTURE
WITH CARE
KEEP DRY

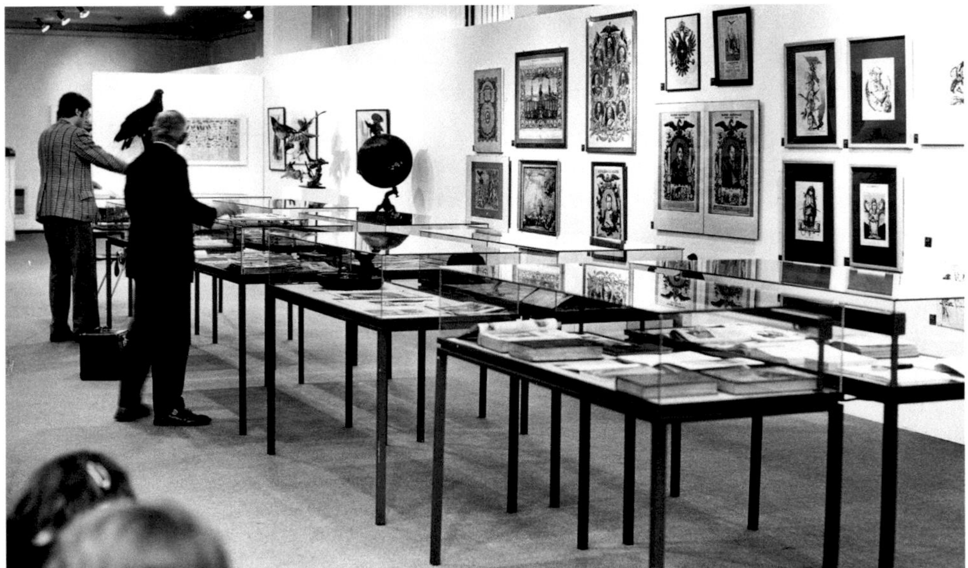

3.60

Marcel Broodthaers, postcard reproductions of artworks and artwork packing crates as part of the *Musée d'Art Moderne, Département des Aigles, Section XIXème Siècle*, Brussels, 1968. Photo by Maria Gilissen.

3.61

Marcel Broodthaers, *Musée d'Art Moderne, Département des Aigles, Section des Figures,* Düsseldorf Kunsthalle, 1972. Photo by Maria Gilissen.

the scenes of the museum that demands interrogation, including how works enter an institution (the wheeling and dealing that is typically not seen), how the discourse that surrounds a work determines reception, how museums dictate perception and behavior, and how value is constructed, culture naturalized, the author affirmed, aura produced? Or, conversely, were artists and scholars at the time so embarrassed for Duchamp (as some accounts imply) that they avoided mention of his final work because they wanted to preserve a pristine image of the "truly" radical gestures for which they held him responsible?[185] In only seeing the inexplicably crass and incongruous hyperrealism of the work, had they so thoroughly missed the critical force of *Étant donnés* in relation to the "apparatus through which the artist is threaded" and the ways—distinct from the readymades' gestures—in which it enacted the period's very questioning of the various institutional forces and relations impacting artistic production?

In the 1980s and '90s, a number of scholars hailed the generation of artists who had come of age after the embers of the avant-garde's fire had apparently cooled. They acclaimed the paradigmatic value of this generation's work, and defended them against reactionary accusations that they were merely compromised and impotent "neo" repetitions of the past. One of the most virulent of the accusations had been waged in Peter Bürger's *Theory of the Avant-Garde*, first published in German in 1974 and translated into English in 1984, prompting immediate and heated debate upon its English release.[186] Responding to it, Hal Foster proposed a reversal of the fatalist teleology of Bürger's thesis, making way for a more complex "temporal exchange" between the historical and neo-avant-gardes: "Rather than cancel the project of the historical avant-garde, might the neo-avant-garde have *comprehended it* for the first time?"[187] The argument, however, might turn on a necessary disavowal, one that was echoed in numerous readings of the operations and strategies of the neo-avant-garde that followed.[188] To argue for the innovation of the new generation, critics might have wittingly or unwittingly constructed a horizon for an avant-garde that did not always, in fact, neatly fit into the categories to which it was being assigned, at least not as far as Duchamp's final work was concerned: Duchamp, who was understood as belonging to the first-generation avant-garde, was almost wholly associated with the readymade (which itself was seen by the 1970s as at least partially compromised as a radical project).[189] In that scenario, by the 1960s and '70s he could only serve through "legacy." The conclusion drawn was that the generation that followed Duchamp, the neo-avant-garde, "grasps" (in Foster's terms) what Duchamp and the avant-garde could not, and while not canceling the importance of their historic predecessors, the neo-avant-garde "enacts its [the avant-garde's] project for the first time."[190]

But what if history were more complex and convoluted than either Bürger or his detractors could admit? What if—instead of either a utopian notion of linear progress (and ultimate failure) followed by meaningless repetition, or, contrarily, an avant-gardism only fully realized in an interpretation and enactment by its successors—there might have been yet other paths for history? For what to do with a figure who grasps the implications of his own radical previous projects and enacts them himself, critically taking on the museum and acting as a curator at the same time that a new generation was doing so as well? What to do with a figure who defies the temporal categories of "avant" and "neo" by creating a coda at the very end of his life that returns to ideas he had put forth in the 1910s but intuits their consequences a half-century later (and perhaps even absorbs the *reception* of his ideas by others) and, further, opens them up for future new directions?[191]

The suggestion here is not to reestablish the original celebration of the historic avant-garde, as Bürger was at pains to do, nor to declare, as Clement Greenberg did (speaking of Duchamp generally), that the artist "locked advanced-advanced art into what has amounted to hardly more than elaborations, variations on, and recapitulations of his original ideas."[192] Instead we might recognize how much Duchamp's final work was not the "retardataire" lapse of an old man who "arrived a bit too late" but instead the neo-avant-garde gesture of an artist who never stopped articulating the terms of a criticality that operates in, through, as well as against the institution of art, and who had found one last way to do so.

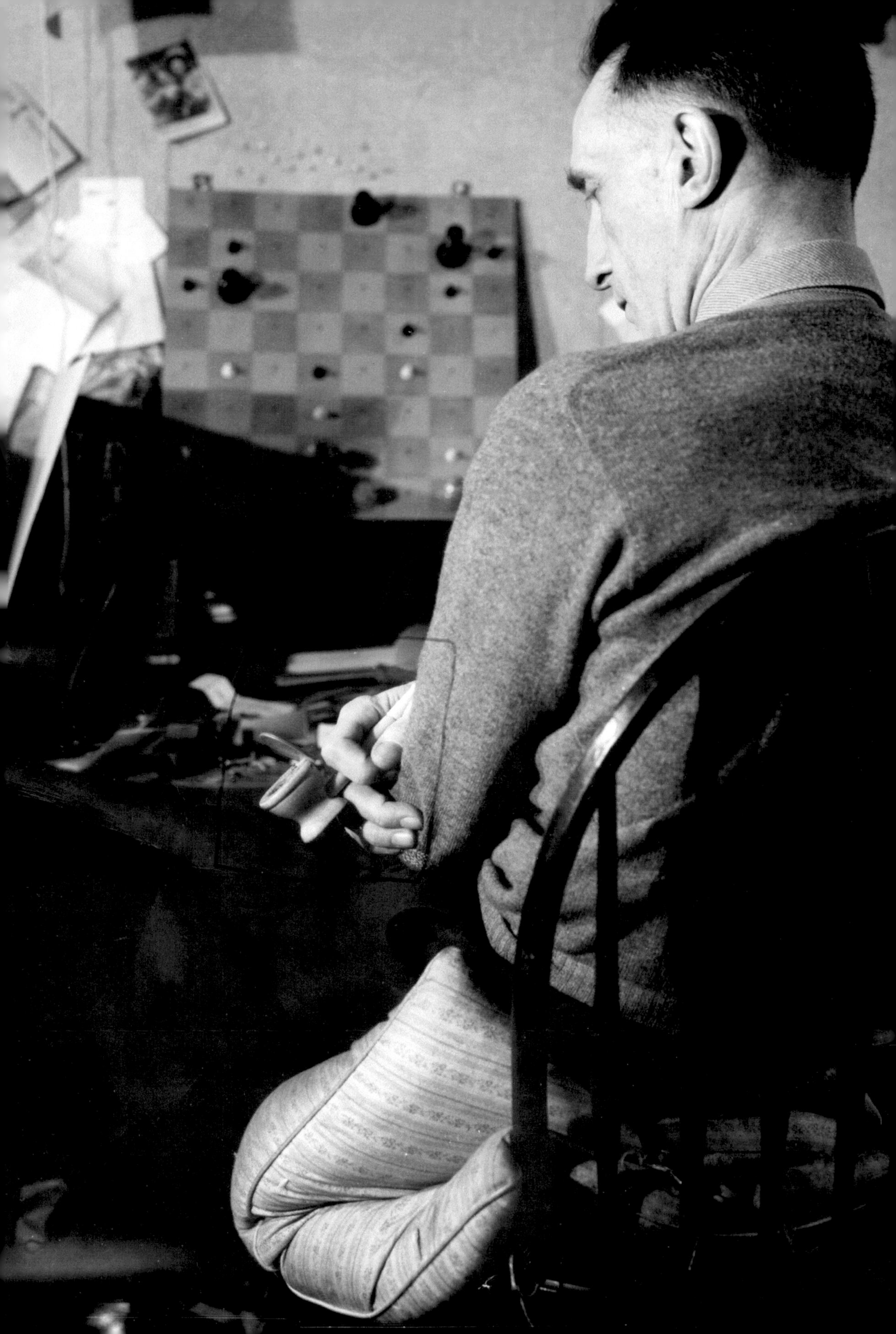

CONCLUSION

THE INVENTION OF AN EMPTY STUDIO

WHERE THERE'S SMOKE ...

Marcel Duchamp sits, his back to a photographer, almost in three-quarter profile with a pipe in the form of a miniature toilet delicately poised between his fingers. He is surrounded by the unkemptness of his studio, a belt holding a folded pillow to the chair on which he rests, a chessboard tacked to the wall alongside scraps of paper, and a photograph (of Maria Martins, as it happens) hanging askew near a dangling electrical wire. But the way he holds the curious pipe is almost too demonstrative not to be posed. He will begin his preliminary studies for *Étant donnés* (1946–66) about a year later, although nothing in his studio gives that information away. Duchamp does, however, want you to see that little pipe. The picture, one of several taken in his 210 West 14th Street studio in January 1945, was part of a photo shoot by photographer Percy Rainford taken at the behest of architect Frederick Kiesler. The architect wanted images of Duchamp and his workspace for a visual essay he was planning for a special issue of *View* devoted to Duchamp.[1] A hand-drawn square surrounds the pipe in one of the photographs, asking that attention be paid to the object. Whether the marking is by Duchamp's hand or Kiesler's (in whose archive the image ended up), it is revealing, even if that particular photograph didn't ultimately get published. Kiesler used an almost identical image, combined with yet another taken from a different angle, along with various other photomontaged elements and visual allusions to make his folding triptych centerfold in the magazine, *POÈME ESPACE dédié à H(ieronymous) Duch'amp* (POEM SPACE Dedicated to H[ieronymous] Duch'amp, 1945). To compose the complex and composite result—as strange as it was inspired—Kiesler (perhaps with Duchamp) cut, overlaid, pinned up on a peg board, and rephotographed various found images, reproductions of artworks by Duchamp, and several of Rainford's commissioned photographs. Duchamp likely contributed a number of elements, among them a subtle but central detail not yet visible in the pegboard study but decidedly present in the published photomontage: smoke wafting up from the toilet pipe he was holding. From his contribution to the magazine one senses that Kiesler was most interested in the artist's approach to perspective, enigmatic mechanics, and the *Large Glass* (1915–23), whose ghostly presence (as if projected onto the walls of Duchamp's New York studio) haunts the triptych. Duchamp, on the other hand, may have had other priorities: amid the abundance of visual signs on the page, his sly reference to a lavatory appliance is like a smoking gun.

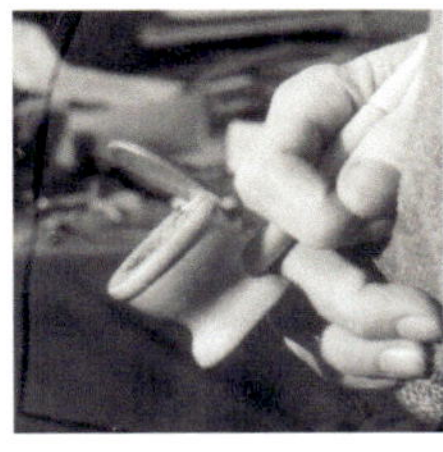
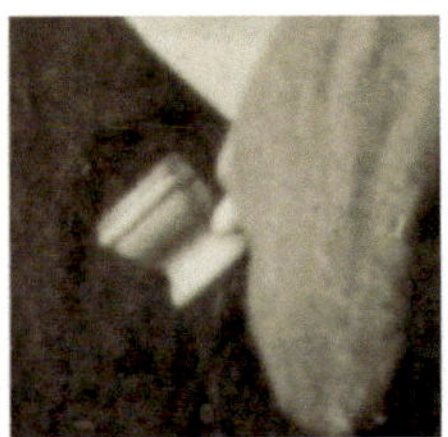
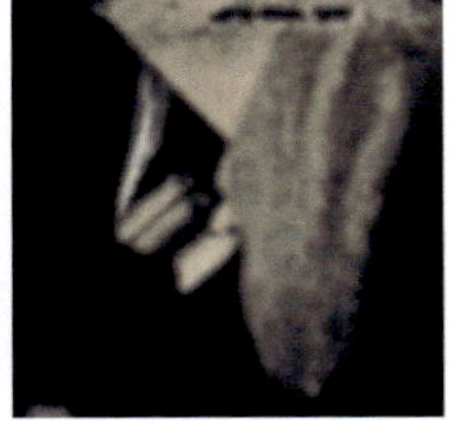

4.1

Details of the chapter frontispiece and figures 4.2 and 4.3.

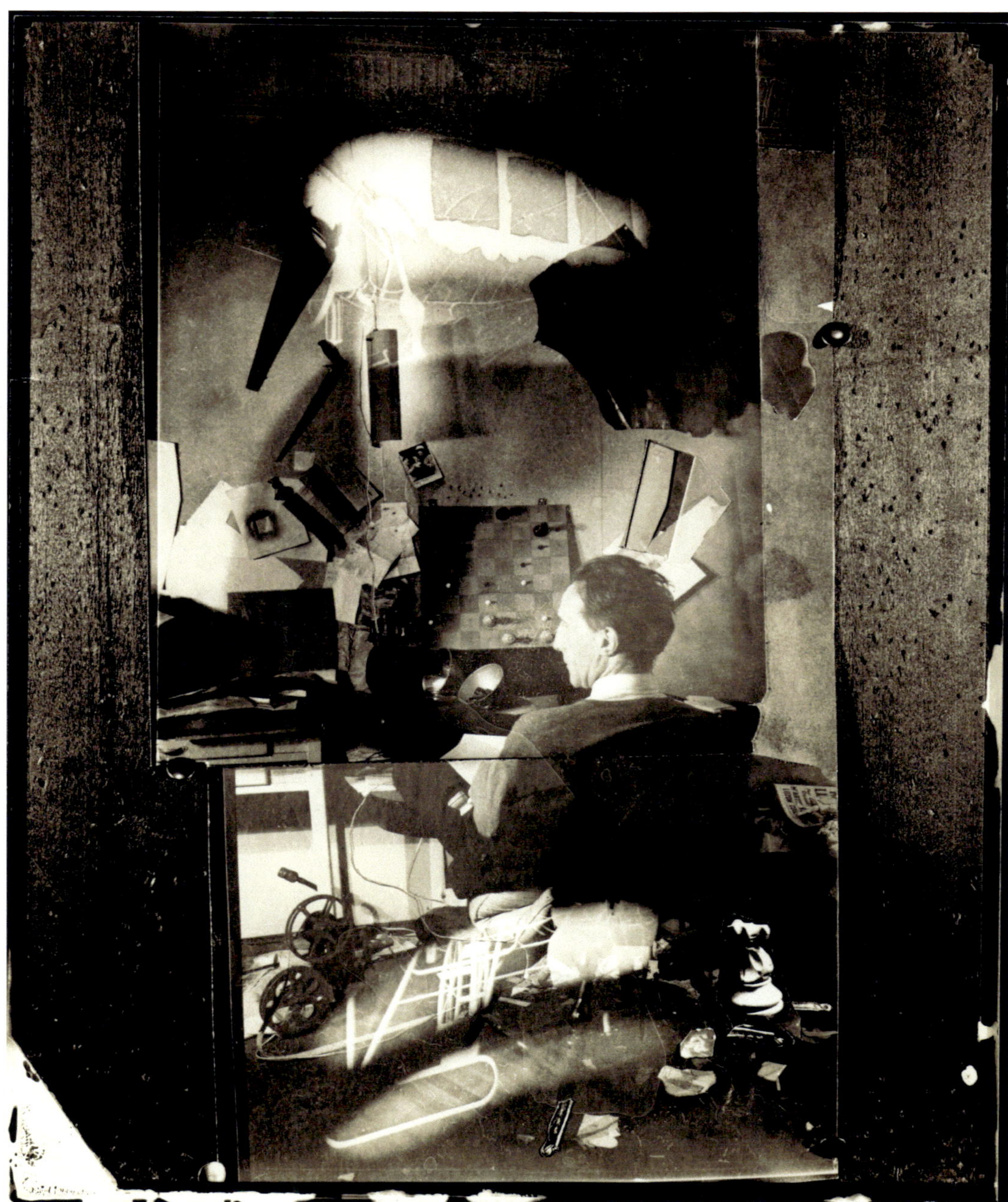

4.2

Frederick Kiesler, preparatory photograph for *POÈME ESPACE dédié à H(ieronymous) Duch'amp* (POEM SPACE Dedicated to H[ieronymous] Duch'amp), 1945. Austrian Frederick and Lillian Kiesler Private Foundation, Vienna.

4.3 (following pages)

Frederick Kiesler, center spread, open view of *POÈME ESPACE dédié à H(ieronymous) Duch'amp* (POEM SPACE Dedicated to H[ieronymous] Duch'amp), 1945. Photomontage with pullouts published in *View: The Modern Magazine* 5, no. 1 (March 1945). Austrian Frederick and Lillian Kiesler Private Foundation, Vienna.

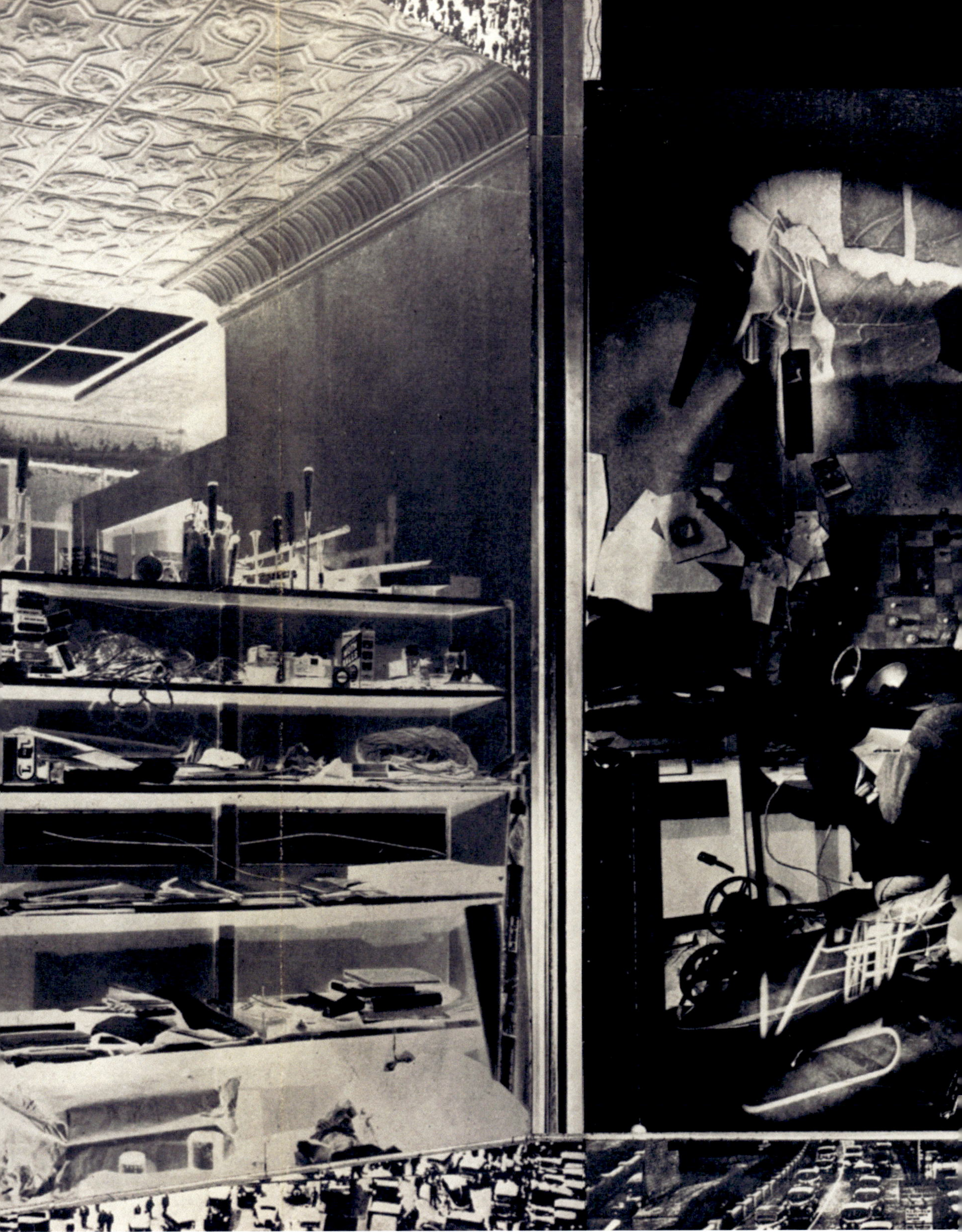

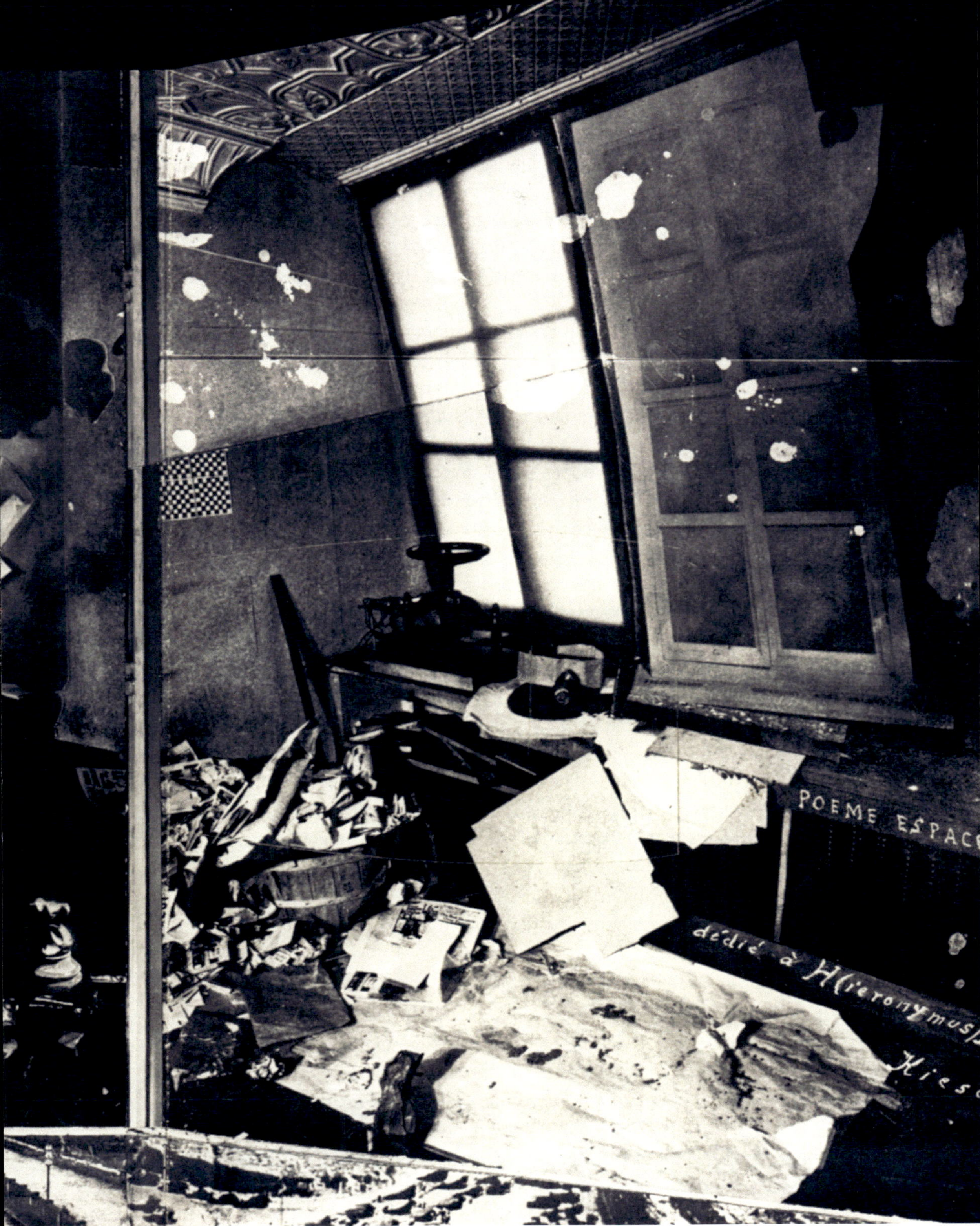
POEME ESPAC
dédié à H(ieronymus)

Duchamp holds out his toilet, (still) smoking, for anyone to see. In fact, the smoke was an illusion, carefully crafted through the magic of photography like so many of the other photographic illusions that line his oeuvre. It seems perfectly at home in the midst of Kiesler's highly manipulated whole.[2] Opening the central flap of the elaborate *View* foldout, one will find that when all other references are masked, a peephole of sorts (apt for an artist preoccupied with peepholes) focuses our gaze on the center of the image, with its curious allusion to Duchamp's history with one particular toilet. At the time the shot was staged, the first batch of the artist's *Boîte-en-valise* (1938–42) had begun to circulate among friends, patrons, and interested institutions.[3] The announcement it contained about Duchamp's authorship of *Fountain* (1917) had thus also begun to make the rounds. The news didn't hit like a bombshell; it was slow and trickling. *Fountain*'s appointment to the place in art history that it holds today was the result of innumerable small maneuvers that connected Duchamp to the industrial piece of plumbing that made him the "father" of the readymade forever after. These included testing to see whether anyone would even notice something like it in an exhibition space, or at least in the vicinity of one (at the Bourgeois Gallery in 1916), or would have it in their supposedly "free to all who apply" exhibition (at the Society of Independent Artists in 1917). Long after having it photographed (by a famous photographer, no less) and publishing the urinal's image (in the equivalent of a self-published fanzine in 1917), he finally signed for it (as R. Mutt had once signed for Duchamp) at the moment that he miniaturized and reproduced it for his portable retrospective in 1938. After admitting (or, more accurately, *publicizing*) that he was *Fountain*'s author, another round of acts followed, including helping the young Harriet and Sidney Janis theorize the readymade in the first article to discuss it seriously (published in the same 1945 issue of *View* in which Duchamp appeared with his smoking toilet pipe). He then signed and exhibited an altogether new replacement urinal (bought for him at a Parisian flea market by Sidney Janis) in Janis's New York gallery in 1950 and then showed the same replacement urinal again in 1953. In 1963, he accepted that Swedish artist Ulf Linde would make a replica for an exhibition in Stockholm, and finally, in 1964, the original Stieglitz photograph served as the basis for the replication of the urinal in an official edition of eight copies. Its entrance into history, as you see, was hardly swift or readymade.

MARGINAL ACTIVITIES

Although the process of its myth building was slow, once *Fountain* had been firmly associated with its author, it became the most emblematic ambassador of the ideas for which the other members of the same category also stood. By the mid-1960s and early '70s, no single artist or artwork was more celebrated, debated, or influential than Duchamp and his urinal. But if no readymade is more iconic than *Fountain* today, it is in no small part due to Duchamp's elaborate efforts to assert its place for posterity. For no readymade was more *curated* than this one. And the 1945 studio photograph in which Duchamp presents himself with a toilet pipe in hand is one element of that larger endeavor.

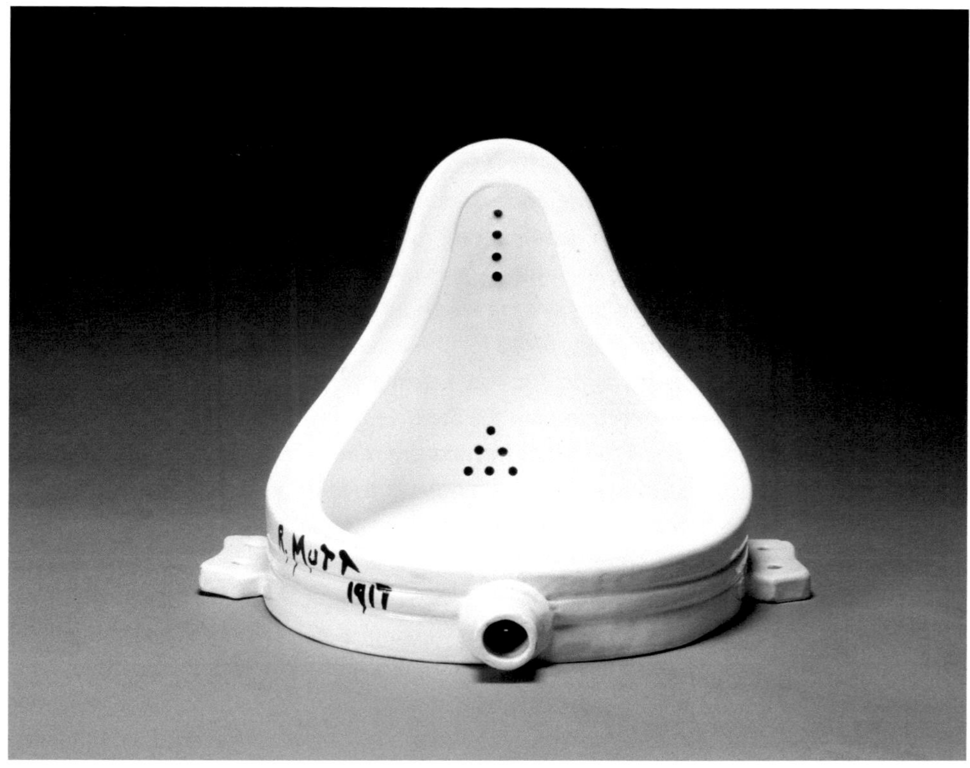

4.4

Marcel Duchamp, *Fountain*, 1917/1964 (original version of 1917 lost). Porcelain urinal turned on its back and signed "R. Mutt 1917." Edition of eight replicas, each 14⅛ × 18⅞ × 24 inches. Private collection.

In its refusal to claim the artist as vessel of technical skill, craft, romantic vision, and authentic experience channeled into the making of unique and auratic objects, the readymade is generally claimed to have promulgated a demystification of artisthood. Yet this was not the result of the fact that Duchamp simply "chose" something and used the rest of his time, as he enjoyed asserting, merely for "breathing." He replaced the creative and generative processes traditionally associated with the artist with a multitude of seemingly practical activities—administrating, archiving, curating, dealing, historicizing, publicizing, reproducing, et cetera—that became themselves veritable artistic procedures.[4] Largely unnoticed or perhaps taken as excessively mundane in their day, these would gain phenomenal importance for the artistic generation that followed him, a generation that, for its part, is said to have similarly "assumed the function of the dealer, curator, the critic—everything but the creative artist."[5]

This counterconception of the artist formed the matrix for Duchamp's unorthodox approach to art, focused on revealing the aesthetic and ideological fault lines of the institutions that governed it and leaving behind a legacy of radical questioning. Yet accounts of Duchamp, and indeed art history in general, have proved slow to know what exactly to do with *activities* that eschew acting as *things*. Without the material sturdiness of an object, or even the spectacularity or bodilyness of a performance, indeed without attempting to be recognized as art at all, Duchamp's fugitive operations disavowed anything like medium specificity. These activities, some of them resulting in what could be considered "artworks" under arrived conventions, were as a consequence either long ignored or inadequately analyzed, perhaps because of their ontologically liminal status. They included the creation of various discursive "manuals" for artworks, curated exhibitions, administration, organization of publicity, reproduction of miniature versions of his art and assembly of them into a traveling case, constitution of several art collections of his work, involvement in the display and renovation of a whole section of a museum, and, finally, the painstaking semi-posthumous insertion of his work into a museum.

Throughout this study, photography and the exhibition represent two axes along which Duchamp ordered his thinking. He used photography and its logic of copying to displace the singular material existence of an artwork as the primary repository of meaning and worth. But his was not exactly a pitting of original *against* reproduction. Rather it was an inquiry into the economy of their relationship and how the elevation or denigration of each might shift meaning, reception, exhibition value, and so on. His *Box of 1914* (1913–14) was, in many ways, the matrix. In 1913–14, after he had brought objects into his studio but before he had endeavored to have them "switch function" (by means of decision, speech act, or even curation), which is to say, before he began to use the readymade to unravel and disclose the institutional conditions for the work of art, he replicated and disseminated his notes, setting the foundations for later work in which questions of repetition, indexicality, and the testing of the apparatus around the work itself would be crucial. Consideration of reproduction in Duchamp's work is thus here set against lengthy discussions of his involvement in exhibitions, aiming to take seriously what he used exhibitions for, how he saw them participating in the construction of (the meaning of) the items they presented, or indeed how he deployed them to articulate his own understanding of what an artwork, oeuvre, artist, or artistic autonomy could be. Consequently, it has been the aim of this study to demonstrate the deep connections that bind the *Box of 1914* (and the related "note" boxes that it spawned), the readymades, the curated exhibitions, the *Boîte-en-valise*, and finally *Étant donnés* to an imbricated logic, one that values what surrounds the artwork as much as the artwork itself.[6] And whereas *Étant donnés* has long been understood as the readymade's *other*, the former's highly worked manufacture, hyperrealism, and museum aspirations seeming utterly anathema to the authorless, conceptual elegance of Duchamp's selected industrial objects, the two projects are here interwoven in a reading that makes them pendants, bookending the career of an artist who was deeply aware of the discursive, historic, administrative, institutional, and presentational mechanisms that condition art.

HIS DEAD END

The temporal distance that separates us from *Étant donnés* today both allows and obliges us to take it seriously, as Duchamp clearly did. An anatomy of the work's critical operations has been attempted here; but also, and precisely because it is a work so much about how artworks are constructed in and through mechanisms that are outside of them, this study has queried the ways in which it has been received. If I have wondered here why Duchamp's last work was not contextualized among similarly critical interventions in the late 1960s or even the decades after, the question aims neither to establish influence nor to propose a revised genealogy. Instead one must ask what was at stake with regard to the neutralization of the critical agency of *Étant donnés*, and how its particular methods and discomfiting result might modify the ways in which we understand what a critique of the institution in the postwar period was—and what it can perhaps still be. Following a lure, so many saw (or wanted to see) a bared sex at the center of Duchamp's last work, and not the obscene spectacle of the museum infiltrated, its conventions of power and rule, ideological and economic investment, exposed. *Étant donnés* is, quite simply, the reflexive culmination of a lifetime of institutional questioning, deliberately set within and working against the very structure of power that it seeks to question. And yet, its critics will counter, the institution *still stands* after its acceptance of the readymade and after one of the most singular and stubbornly unsettling works of all time quietly burrowed itself into its walls. But we, the viewers, are arguably not quite the same after seeing it. The work's allusive but insistent effect continues to inhere in its experience even to this day. And if there is one lesson to be learned from both the scathing dismissals and the awkward historical omissions surrounding *Étant donnés*, it is that Duchamp's final work, decades after its unveiling, indeed managed to resist being fully acculturated, by art history or by the museum.

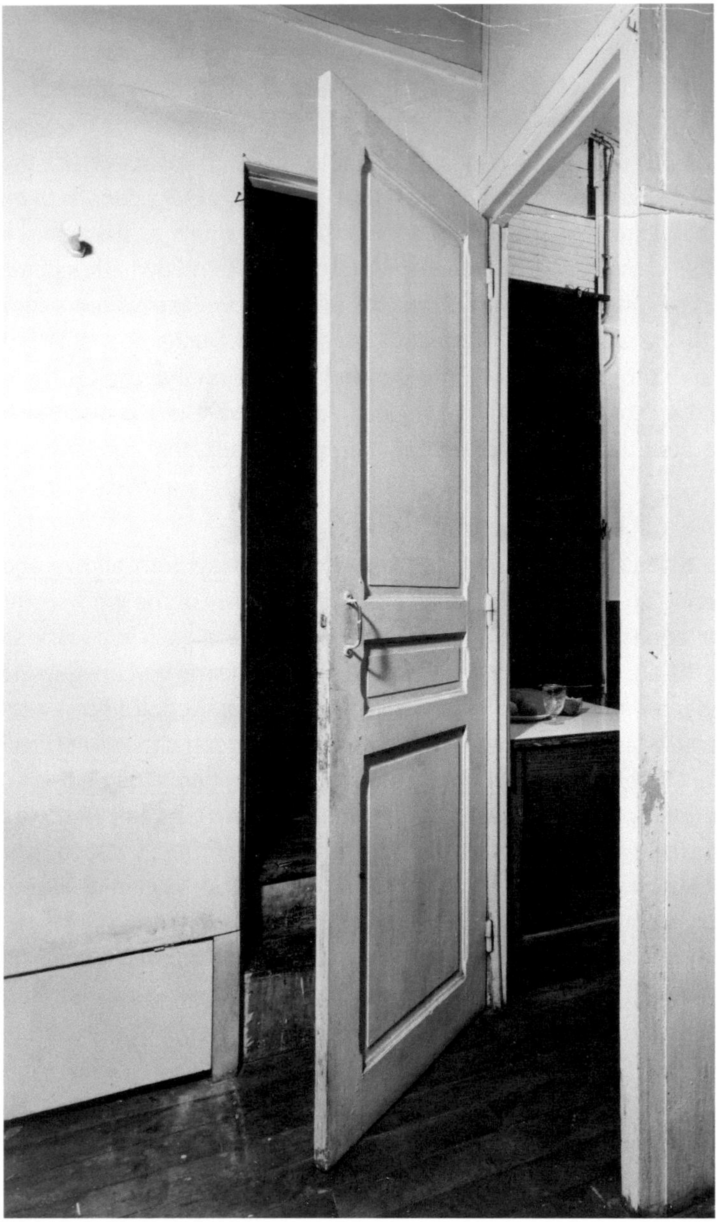

4.5

Marcel Duchamp, *Door, 11 rue Larrey*, 1927/1963. Custom-made wooden door and double door frame, $86\frac{5}{8} \times 24\frac{11}{16}$ inches. Private collection, Italy.

POSTSCRIPT

Étant donnés was an end, in many senses of the word. Duchamp constructed his elaborate, final work over twenty years. How did he manage to conceal the installation and his years of labor from the world? Hiding such a massive project from nearly all of his friends and family, avoiding mention of it in conversations and interviews, and evading any suspicions about what he was actually doing can have been no small undertaking. As we now know, he managed this feat by keeping two studios. The first studio was a decoy—another *exhibition* of sorts—so that the second could be secreted, hiding his labor. Let us return to them for a moment: in one studio he was building his awkward nude and her broken brick house, while in the other he sat around, receiving friends, guests, groupies, chess mates. He gave interviews there. He told anyone who came around that he was doing nothing, simply breathing, that he had given up making art. Of course this was evidently not true. Even if one didn't know about the secret project, Duchamp "released" all sorts of objects during those years—all those books, store windows, and exhibition designs—many of them in fact pointing to ideas developed in *Étant donnés.* There were also the series of erotic objects derived directly from parts or casts of the secret installation, each enigmatic item a key sent out into the world to an as-yet-invisible door. He even, in 1963, quite literally claimed the door from a previous studio as an artwork, *Door, 11 rue Larrey* (1927/1963), at a moment when the question of a door that can both reveal and hide was ever present in his mind.[7]

Still, anyone who came to the "public" studio saw few signs of production or artistic activity (in John Cage's words, there was "nothing going on" there).[8] Duchamp could simply have gotten rid of the first studio and received visitors at home. But he wanted to have a public studio, just next door to the secret studio, so that he could show—literally exhibit—that he was doing nothing. Brian O'Doherty says it best when he notes: "The empty studio, site of production, is displayed as evidence of nonproduction, a mask for an activity in process elsewhere. A creative gesture—the invention of an empty studio—is presented as evidence of sterility, the paralysis of the creative act."[9] Duchamp fooled them all. When he died, nearly no one knew that the sterility and "nonactivity" of the official studio had long hidden the libidinous fecundity of a secret one—not his closest friends, not the interviewers, not even Arturo Schwarz, who was just then going to press with *The Complete Works of Marcel Duchamp.*[10]

"I myself will exhibit nothing," Duchamp had once said, resolutely, defiantly, while a lifetime of curatorial involvement and participation in exhibitions seemingly betrayed that declaration. And yet there, in the "invention of an empty studio" as a quasi-public space, was his pendant statement to that of the spectacularly visual *Étant donnés* in the museum: that the exhibition of "nothing," like those apparently marginal activities which in their own way also looked like nothing at all, might in fact be the key to everything.

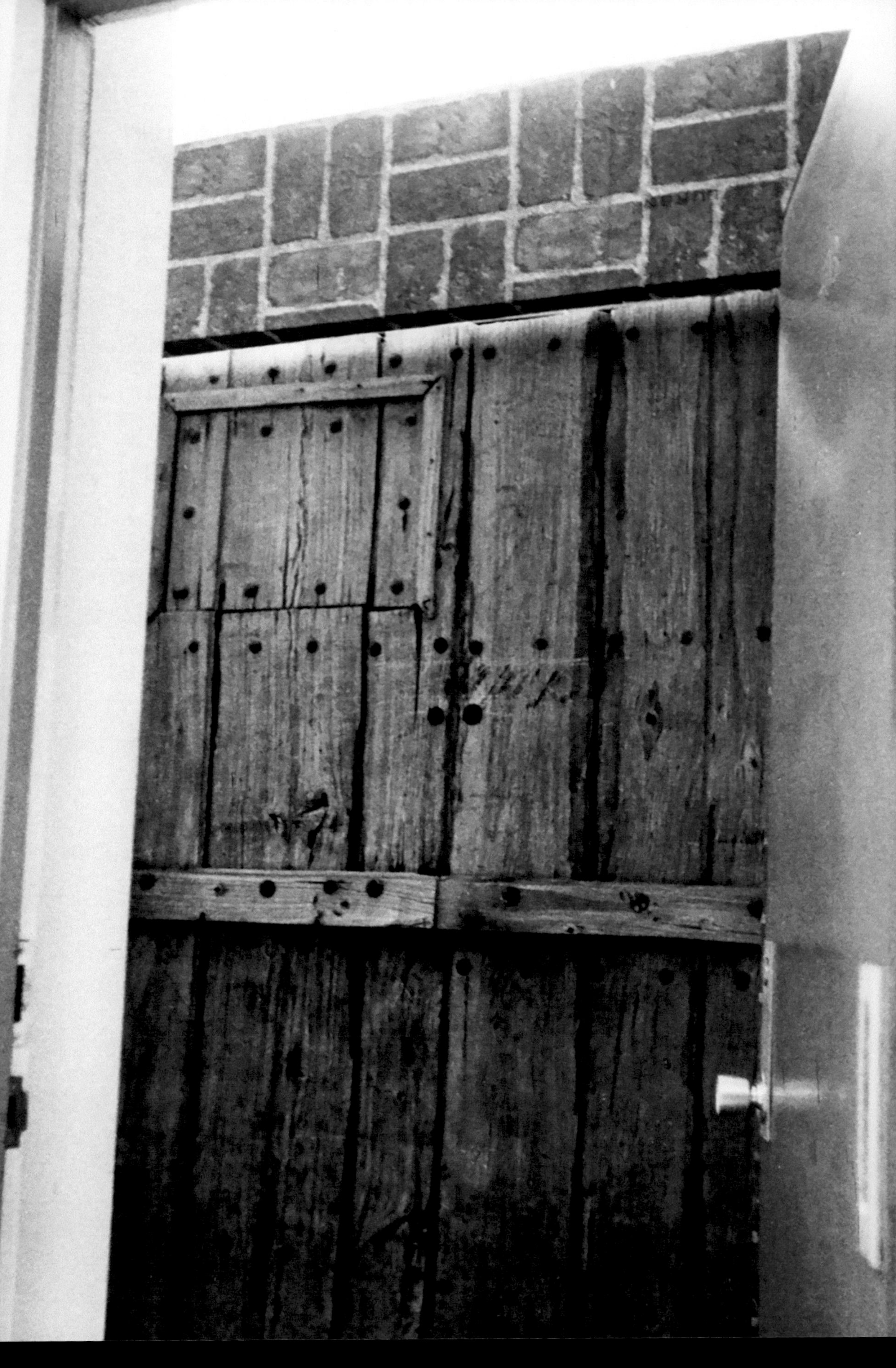

4.6

View of the door into Marcel Duchamp's 80 East 11th Street studio, where *Étant donnés* was secretly installed, 1968. Photo by Denise Browne Hare. Philadelphia Museum of Art: Archives, Anne d'Harnoncourt Records.

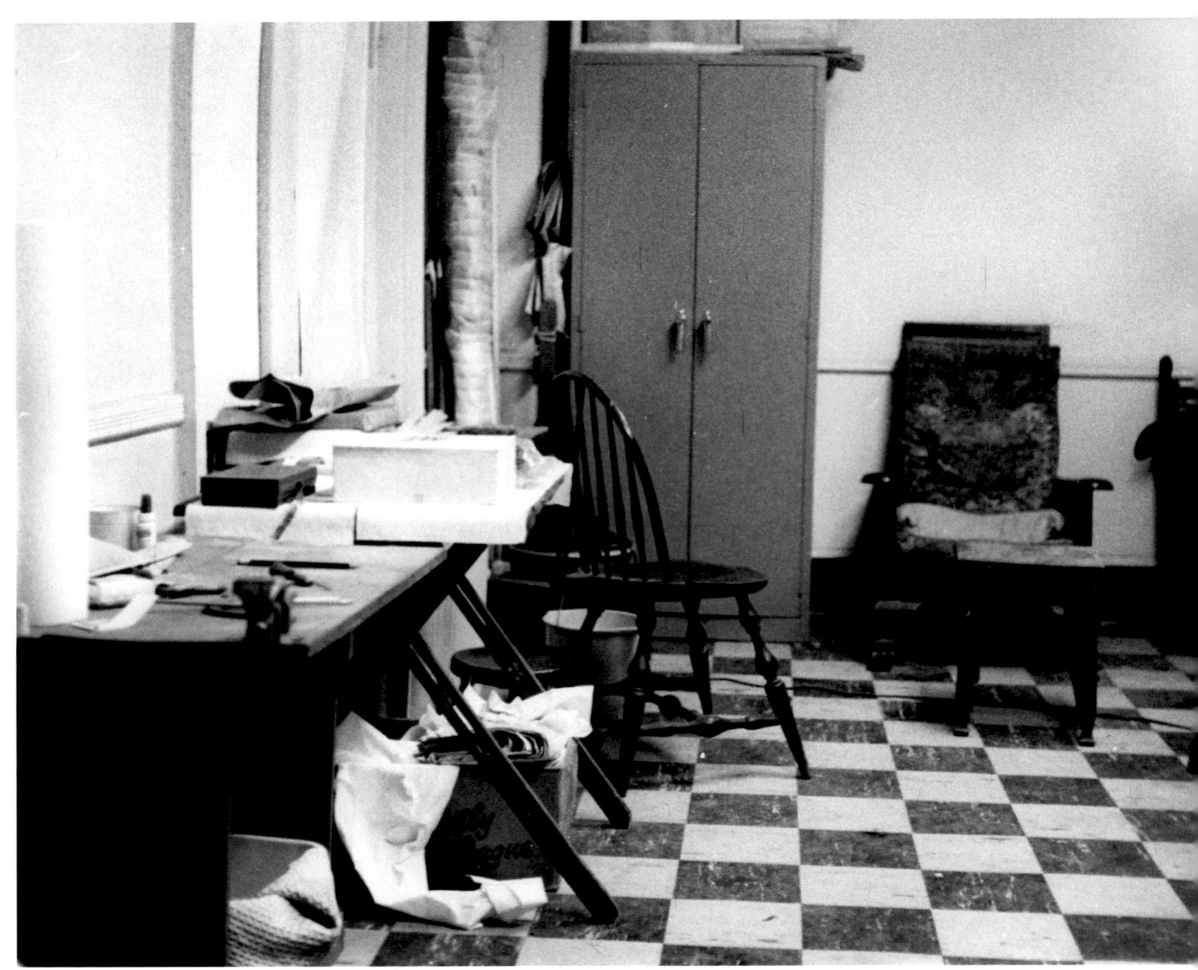

4.7 and 4.8

Views of Marcel Duchamp's 80 East 11th Street studio, where *Étant donnés* was secretly installed, 1968. Photos by Denise Browne Hare. Philadelphia Museum of Art: Archives, Anne d'Harnoncourt Records.

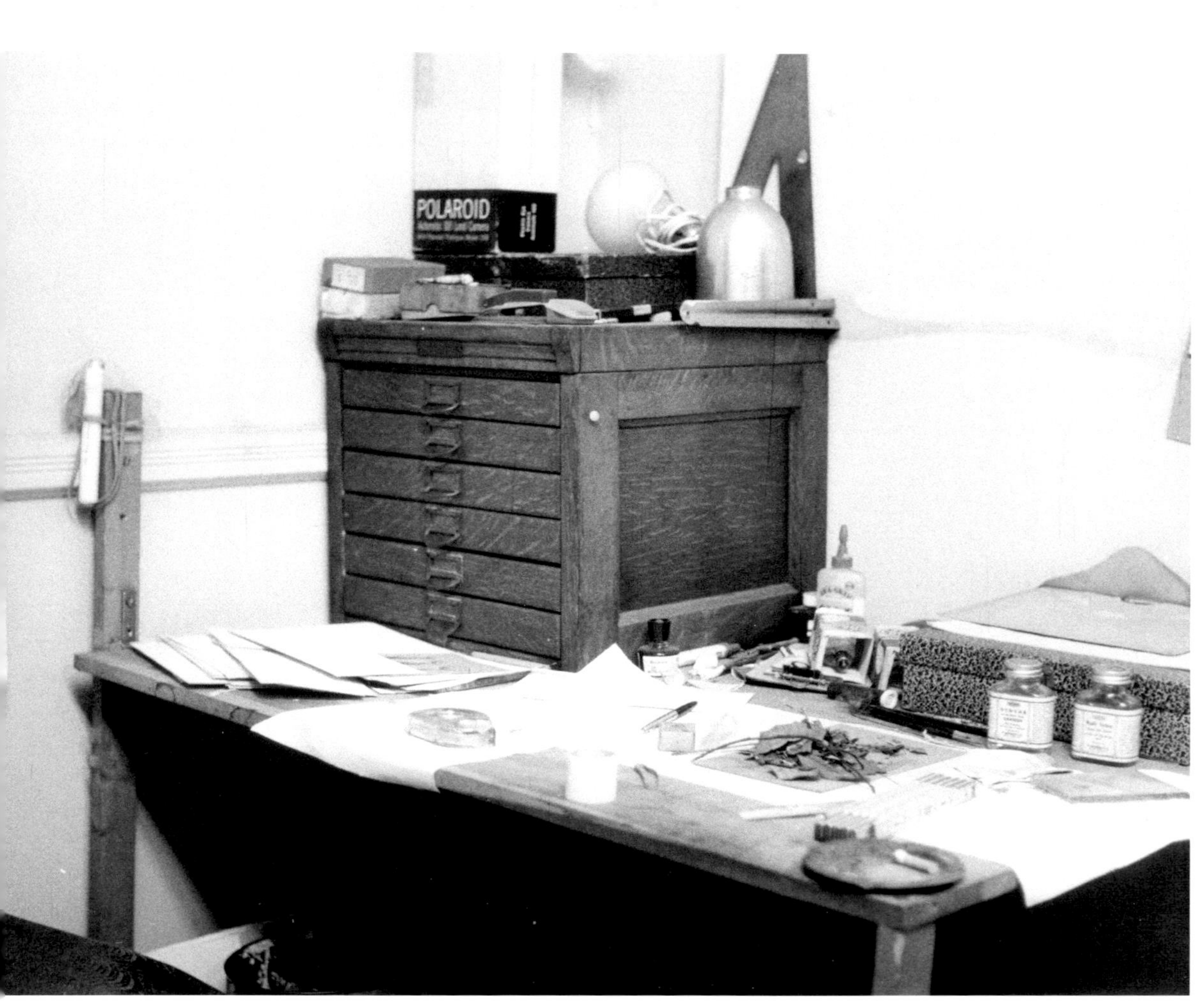

THE INVENTION OF AN EMPTY STUDIO

NOTES

INTRODUCTION

1. Robert Rauschenberg, statement in Anne d'Harnoncourt and Kynaston McShine, eds., *Marcel Duchamp: A Retrospective Exhibition* (Philadelphia: Philadelphia Museum of Art, 1973), 217.
2. David Antin, "duchamp and language," in d'Harnoncourt and McShine, *Marcel Duchamp*, 114. Itself a piece of conceptual poetics, Antin's center-justified, stream-of-conscious reflection in typewriter-style font, lacking both punctuation and capital letters, remains one of the most insightful texts to date on Duchampian language, proclaiming such things as: "by building defectiveness into any reading duchamp ensured the instability of it ... the defects drive his machine."
3. "I was interested in ideas—not merely in visual products," he insisted. Duchamp, quoted in James Johnson Sweeney, "Eleven Europeans in America," *Bulletin of the Museum of Modern Art* 13, nos. 4–5 (1946), 20.
4. Henri-Pierre Roché, "Souvenirs of Marcel Duchamp," trans. William Copley, in Robert Lebel, ed., *Marcel Duchamp* (New York: Paragraphic Books, 1959), 87.
5. Roger Shattuck, *The Innocent Eye: On Modern Literature and the Arts* (New York: Farrar Straus Giroux, 1984), 56. See also Harriet and Sidney Janis, "Marcel Duchamp: Anti-Artist," *View: The Modern Magazine* 5, no. 1 (March 1945), reprinted in Robert Motherwell, ed., *The Dada Painters and Poets* (Cambridge, MA: Belknap Press of Harvard University Press, 1981), 306.
6. Benjamin H. D. Buchloh, "Conceptual Art 1962–1969: From the Aesthetic of Administration to the Critique of Institutions," *October* 55 (Winter 1990), 105–143.
7. Duchamp regularly described himself as a "breather" in lectures, panels, and interviews. See in particular Serge Stauffer, *Marcel Duchamp, Interviews and Statements* (Stuttgart: Editions Cantz, 1992), 85; and Pierre Cabanne, *Dialogues with Marcel Duchamp*, trans. Ron Padgett (New York: Da Capo Press, 1987), 69, 78.
8. Walter Benjamin, *Gesammelte Schriften*, ed. Rolf Tiedemann and Hermann Schweppenhäuser (Frankfurt: Suhrkamp, 1980), I, vol. 3, 1045f; included in "Paralipomènes et variants de la version definitive" (Variants and Notes for the "Work of Art" essay), *Ecrits français* (Paris: Gallimard, 1991), 179–180 (from manuscript page 394).
9. See "Modernist Painting," written in 1960, one of the most influential of his essays, where medium specificity is most programmatically laid out; in Clement Greenberg, *The Collected Essays and Criticism*, ed. John O'Brian, vol. 4 (Chicago: University of Chicago Press, 1993).
10. Duchamp in Cabanne, *Dialogues with Marcel Duchamp*, 48.
11. See Clement Greenberg, "Counter Avant-garde," *Art International* 15, no. 5 (May 20, 1971), 16–19, reprinted in Joseph Masheck, ed., *Marcel Duchamp in Perspective* (New York: Da Capo, 2002), 122–133. See also his Bennington College seminars from 1971, reprinted in Clement Greenberg, *Homemade Esthetics: Observations on Art and Taste* (Oxford: Oxford University Press, 1999), especially "Night Five," 133–134; "Night Seven," 157–159; and "Night Eight," 172–180. I borrow the notion of "medium aspecificity" from Irene V. Small, "Medium Aspecificity/Autopoietic Form," in Alexander Dumbadze and Suzanne Hudson, eds., *Contemporary Art: 1989 to the Present* (London: Wiley-Blackwell, 2013), 117–125.
12. André Breton invokes the readymade in his 1922 essay "Marcel Duchamp," reprinted in Motherwell, *The Dada Painters and Poets*, though without naming any of the artist's "manufactured objects." The first sustained essay on the readymades appeared in the 1945 special issue of *View* magazine devoted to Duchamp, shortly after the artist's *Boîte-en-valise*

brought them into circulation, as it were (some for the first time). Following that, it was Robert Lebel's 1959 monograph on the artist that helped spur scholarship and interest among artists in the 1960s, helping to give the readymade the foothold that it has had subsequently in the history of twentieth-century art.

13. Hal Foster, "A Missing Part," in Foster, *Prosthetic Gods* (Cambridge, MA: MIT Press, 2006), 328.
14. Richard Wollheim, "Minimal Art," *Arts Magazine* (January 1965), reprinted in Gregory Battcock, ed., *Minimal Art: A Critical Anthology* (New York: Dutton, 1968), 387–399.

15. See for example Donald Judd, "Specific Objects," *Arts Yearbook* 8 (1965), reprinted in Judd, *Complete Writings 1959–1975* (Halifax: Press of the Nova Scotia College of Art and Design, 2005), 181–189; Barbara Rose, "ABC Art," *Art in America* (October–November 1965), reprinted in Battcock, *Minimal Art: A Critical Anthology*, 274–297; Robert Morris, "Notes on Sculpture 4: Beyond Objects," *Artforum* (April 1969), reprinted in Charles Harrison and Paul Wood, eds., *Art in Theory 1900–1990* (Oxford: Blackwell, 1992), 868–873; Joseph Kosuth, "Art after Philosophy" (1969), reprinted in Harrison and Wood, *Art in Theory 1900–1990*, 840–857; Leo Steinberg, "Reflections on the State of Criticism," *Artforum* (March 1972), which appeared in its definitive form in *Other Criteria* (New York: Oxford University Press, 1972), see esp. "The Flatbed Picture Plane," 82–91; and Jack Burnham, *Great Western Salt Works: Essays on the Meaning of Post-Formalist Art* (New York: George Braziller, 1974).
16. One might think of this in the way that the "institution," as Irene V. Small has argued, could be said to be the medium of Institutional Critique. As Small notes, "The practice of institutional critique *produces* institutionality as a medium just as the medium of the institution allows for a configuration of elements to form into institutional critique." Small, "Medium Aspecificity/Autopoietic Form," 119–120.
17. See Walther Benjamin, *The Work of Art in the Age of Its Technological Reproducibility and Other Writings on Media*, ed. Michael Jennings, Thomas Y. Levin, and Brigid Doherty (Cambridge, MA: Belknap Press of Harvard University Press, 2008).

CHAPTER 1

1. First written in 1913, the note would not appear in print until more than half a century later, in the notes reproduced and assembled in *À l'infinitif*, also known as the *Boîte blanche*, published in 1967; translated and reprinted in *In the Infinitive: A Typotranslation by Richard Hamilton and Ecke Bonk of Marcel Duchamp's White Box*, trans. Jackie Matisse, Richard Hamilton, and Ecke Bonk (Northend: Typosophic Society, 1999), 1.
2. See *By or of Marcel Duchamp or Rrose Sélavy*, catalog for Duchamp's 1963 Pasadena Art Museum exhibition, unpaginated.
3. Duchamp would repeatedly locate the notes' production to 1913–14, calling them *Box of 1913–14* in his conversation with Pierre Cabanne, in Cabanne, *Dialogues with Marcel Duchamp*, trans. Ron Padgett (New York: Da Capo Press, 1987), 42; or using the title *Box of 1914* but dating them to 1913–14 in Robert Lebel's first monograph on the artist, *Sur Marcel Duchamp* (Paris: Trianon Press, 1959), and his first retrospective catalog, *De ou par Marcel Duchamp ou Rrose Sélavy* (Pasadena: Pasadena Art Museum, 1963).
4. Walter Benjamin, *Gesammelte Schriften*, ed. Rolf Tiedemann and Hermann Schweppenhäuser (Frankfurt: Suhrkamp, 1980), I, vol. 3, 1045f; included in "Paralipomènes et variants de la version définitive" (Variants and Notes for the "Work of Art" essay), in Walter Benjamin, *Ecrits français* (Paris: Gallimard, 1991), 179–180 (from manuscript page 394).

5. Duchamp, interview with James Johnson Sweeney, reprinted in *Salt Seller: The Writings of Marcel Duchamp*, ed. Michel Sanouillet and Elmer Peterson (New York: Oxford University Press, 1973), 133.
6. Duchamp in Cabanne, *Dialogues with Marcel Duchamp*, 41.
7. Ibid., 17. Hereafter I will omit the "no. 2" from mentions of *Nude Descending a Staircase*; this version from 1912 is the one almost universally meant when the title is mentioned.
8. Details of Duchamp's library training, including a course on "bibliography and the organization/classification of libraries and archives," are given in François Le Penven, *L'Art d'écrire de Marcel Duchamp: À propos des ses notes manuscrites* (Nîmes, France: Editions Jacqueline Chambon, 2003).
9. Notes written in this period but only published much later in *À l'infinitif* (1967) make explicit reference to scientific studies such as Henri Poincaré, *Thaumaturgus opticus*; Jean-François Nicéron, *La Perspective curieuse ou magie artificielle des effets merveilleux*; and Esprit Pascal Jouffret, *Traité élémentaire de géométrie à quatre dimensions*, among others.
10. Cited in Guillaume Apollinaire, *Marcel Duchamp, 1910–1918* (Paris: Editions L'Echoppe, 1994), 19–20.
11. Duchamp in "Some Late Thoughts of Marcel Duchamp, from an Interview with Jeanne Siegel," *Arts Magazine* 43 (December–January 1969), 21.
12. Why these sixteen notes and not others? In each of his note projects, from the *Box of 1914* until the last, *À l'Infinitif*, published shortly before his death, Duchamp would deliberately include some and exclude other notes, even leaving a folder of numerous unpublished notes behind when he died. He never fully explained his reasoning. To Serge Stauffer in 1961 he said of the *Box of 1914* that they were "simply a reunion of notes written at random." Duchamp to Serge Stauffer, May 28, 1961, cited in Ecke Bonk, "delay included," in *Joseph Cornell/Marcel Duchamp ... in Resonance* (Houston: Menil Foundation, 1998), 98.
13. Duchamp's memory of the total number of sets he made was either decidedly faulty or willingly evasive. He only recalled two or three sets, when asked, although at least five are known to have existed and four are currently in public collections, with one thought to be lost.
14. It is noteworthy that although Duchamp had brought the profane objects that would become his "readymades" into his studio as early as 1913 (for the stool mounted with a bicycle wheel; the unmodified bottlerack came a year later), it wouldn't be until 1915, *after* the reproduction of his notes, that he would both find the term that would give his objects a category or genre and begin to conceive of them as things deserving of a signature, title, dating, et cetera.
15. Literally an animal's "paw," the *patte* was the artist's characteristic, unique, and thus "signature" touch, a term Duchamp used often with reference to painting. See Jane Blackwell interview with Marcel Duchamp for the BBC, June 5, 1968, reprinted in Francis Naumann, *Marcel Duchamp: The Art of Making Art in the Age of Mechanical Reproduction* (Ghent: Ludion Press, 1999), 302.
16. The notes arguably inaugurated a number of other authenticating devices in Duchamp's work: legal certificates, the use of notary publics, and, last but not least, fingerprints to signify and parody "evidence" of authorship (either his or that of his alter ego Rrose Sélavy).
17. Calvin Tomkins, *Duchamp: A Biography* (New York: Henry Holt, 1996), 297.
18. See interview with Francis Steegmuller, "Duchamp: Fifty Years After," *Show* (February 1963), 28; cited in Francis Naumann, "Money Is No Object," *Art in America* 91, no. 3 (March 2003), 67.

19. Duchamp, letter to Walter Pach, April 2, [1915], reprinted in *Affectionately, Marcel: The Selected Correspondence of Marcel Duchamp*, ed. Francis Naumann and Hector Obalk (Ghent: Ludion, 2000), 34.

20. Duchamp, interview with Frederick Kiesler, presumed to date from 1945; a photocopy of Kiesler's handwritten notes is preserved in the Frederick and Lillian Kiesler Foundation Archive, Vienna.

21. Duchamp, explanatory comment to Robert Lebel (June 20, 1953), serving to aid in the preparation of the art historian's monograph *Sur Marcel Duchamp*; original manuscript in the Robert Lebel Archives, now housed at the Getty Research Institute, Los Angeles.

22. Marjorie Perloff's insightful discussion of Duchampian linguistic works, an exceedingly rare consideration of Duchamp's work in the context of avant-garde poetry, spends curiously little time on the actual construction of language and frustration of legibility in the notes. See Perloff, "The Conceptual Poetics of Marcel Duchamp," in her *21st-Century Modernism: The "New" Poetics* (London: Blackwell, 2002), 92–105.

23. Still, the work clearly impressed Duchamp once he did discover it. By 1918 he would declare to his friend Henri-Pierre Roché that nothing new had been written since *Un coup de dés*. See Jennifer Gough-Cooper and Jacques Caumont, *Ephemerides on and about Marcel Duchamp and Rrose Sélavy* (Milan: Bompiani, 1993), unpaginated, March 26, 1918.

24. Duchamp expressed his disdain for the retinal impulse in painting in numerous interviews and conversations, particularly in the postwar period, when he defined his own approach as antithetical to Courbet's, in which "the emphasis has been on the eye, the retina. Colors and forms only, always on the surface." Duchamp, quoted in the article "Art Was a Dream ..." (unsigned), *Newsweek*, November 9, 1959, 118.

25. Most striking in this regard is Thomas B. Hess's "J'accuse Marcel Duchamp," *Art News* 63, no. 10 (February 1965), 44–45, 52–54, and Clement Greenberg's "Counter Avant-garde," *Art International* 15, no. 5 (May 20, 1971), 16–19. It was subsequently left to Michael Fried to carry the torch; his reading of American painting through the lens of Duchamp's and Dada's "failure" is telling: "It is important to bear in mind that, at bottom, Dada in any of its manifestations and modernist painting are antithetical to one another. Where the former aspires to obliterate all distinctions between work of art and other kinds of objects or occurrences in the world, the latter has sought to isolate, assert and work with what is essential to the art of painting at a given moment. It would, however, be mistaken to think of Dada—the most precocious of the movements—as opposed to art. Rather Dada stands opposed to the notion of *value* or *quality* in art, and in that sense represents a reaction against the unprecedented demands modernist painting makes of its practitioners. (It is, I think, significant that Duchamp was a failed modernist—more exactly a failed cubist—before he turned his hand to the amusing inventions by which he is best known.)" Michael Fried, *Three American Painters* (Cambridge, MA: Fogg Art Museum, 1965), 47. Cubism figures differently in some exceptional publications, such as Thierry de Duve's discussion of Duchamp's shift from pictorial practice to "naming" in *Pictorial Nominalism: Duchamp's Passage from Painting to the Readymade*, trans. Dana Polan (Minneapolis: University of Minnesota Press, 1991). See also David Joselit's discussion of the ways in which Duchamp recodes Cubism's suppression of the body in exchange for a conception of vision as an entanglement of carnality, seeing, language, and painting, in Joselit, *Infinite Regress* (Cambridge, MA: MIT Press, 2001), 9–70.

26. Clement Greenberg, "Collage" (1959), in *Art and Culture* (Boston: Beacon Press, 1961), 70–83. Greenberg's writings have, since the early 1970s, come increasingly under attack by the generation of art historians that followed him, and his essay "Collage" has been particularly blighted in art historical scholarship. Yet if his particular methods and investments have been questioned, his estimation of Cubist collage's primacy has nevertheless stood.

See Lisa Florman, "The Flattening of 'Collage,'" *October* 102 (Fall 2002), 59–86, and Rosalind E. Krauss, "In the Name of Picasso," in *The Originality of the Avant-Garde and Other Modernist Myths* (Cambridge, MA: MIT Press, 1985), 23–41.

27. Duchamp in Cabanne, *Dialogues with Marcel Duchamp*, 37.

28. Duchamp likely knew of these through Guillaume Apollinaire, a crucial conduit for information about the developments of Cubism both among artists and to the public. Through the encouragement of Francis Picabia, Apollinaire became increasingly interested in, and close to, Duchamp by late 1912 (though he had virtually ignored the artist in his reviews of 1909–11). Apollinaire was particularly interested in Duchamp's place within his reading of Cubism. Given this and Duchamp's repeated visits to both Daniel-Henry Kahnweiler's gallery on the rue Vignon and Gertrude and Leo Stein's 42 rue Fleuris apartment, it is difficult to imagine (however one construes Duchamp's developing indifference to the art world) that the artist did not know of Cubism's *papiers collés* in the immediate aftermath of their invention. Although his discussion with Cabanne addressed the early Cubist paintings more than the later collages per se, Duchamp nevertheless mentioned that he "sometimes went to Kahnweiler's gallery on the rue Vignon" and that "it was there that Cubism got me." See Cabanne, *Dialogues with Marcel Duchamp*, 25.

29. Yve-Alain Bois, "Introduction," in *Formless: A User's Guide* (Cambridge, MA: MIT Press, 1997), 27–28.

30. "It is, of course, in Cubism," as Buchloh pronounces, "that elements of language—the legacy of Mallarmé—surface programmatically within the visual for the first time in the history of Modern Painting and that a parallel between the emerging structural analysis of language and the formalist analysis of representation is established." Benjamin H. D. Buchloh, "The Aesthetics of Administration," in *L'Art conceptuel, une perspective* (Paris: ARC, 1991), 41. This accepted understanding of Cubism as the only valid or "programmatic" contemporaneous aesthetic response to the literary invention of Mallarmé symptomatically overlooks Duchamp's *Box of 1914*.

31. The title of David Cottington's article says it all: "What the Papers Say: Politics and Ideology in Picasso's Collages of 1912," *Art Journal* 47, no. 4, "Revising Cubism" (Winter 1988), 350–359.

32. Rosalind E. Krauss, *Passages in Modern Sculpture* (Cambridge, MA: MIT Press, 1977), 51.

33. Key readings of the semiology of Cubism's language include Rosalind E. Krauss, "In the Name of Picasso" and "Motivation of the Sign," in Lynn Zelevansky, ed., *Picasso and Braque: A Symposium* (New York: Museum of Modern Art, 1992); as well as Yve-Alain Bois, "Kahnweiler's Lesson," in *Painting as Model* (Cambridge MA: MIT Press, 1990) and "Semiology of Cubism," in *Picasso and Braque: A Symposium*. Finally, see Krauss, "Circulation of the Sign," in *The Picasso Papers* (Cambridge, MA: MIT Press 1999), 25–88.

34. Leo Steinberg, *Other Criteria: Confrontations with Twentieth Century Art* (New York: Oxford University Press, 1972), 85.

35. Ibid., 84–85.

36. Such is Steinberg's formulation of Rauschenberg's flatbed picture plane operation. See *Other Criteria*, 85.

37. *Marcel Duchamp: Notes*, ed. Paul Matisse (Paris: Musée National d'Art Moderne, Centre Georges Pompidou, 1980), 167.

38. This essential difference might indeed have sealed the notes' fate, for, as Alexander Alberro notes, "there are few things more problematic in the history of modern art than the

concept of the copy." Perhaps as a result, scholars have hardly considered how these two concurrent projects might be usefully compared. Alexander Alberro, "Meaning at the Margins: The Semiological Inversions of John Knight," in John C. Welchman, ed., *Institutional Critique and After* (Zurich: JRP Ringier, 2006), 60.

39. Clair argues, "One could say that if it is rarely *by* the photograph/photography that Duchamp found a new mode of expressing himself, it is in fact always *in relation to* it that he defined the new means of his expression." Jean Clair, *Duchamp et la photographie: Essai d'analyse d'un primat technique sur le développement d'une oeuvre* (Paris: Le Chêne, 1977), 6–7 (translation mine). See also Rosalind E. Krauss, "Notes on the Index: Seventies Art in America," *October* 3 (Spring 1977), 68–81, reprinted as "Notes on the Index: Part 1" in Krauss, *The Originality of the Avant-Garde and Other Modernist Myths*; and Krauss, "Duchamp ou le champ imaginaire," *Degrés* 26–27 (Spring 1981), reprinted in Krauss, *Le Photographique: Pour une théorie des écarts* (Paris: Macula, 1990).

40. So, too, the exhibition and catalog essay by Georges Didi-Huberman, *L'Empreint* (Paris: Flammarion, 1997), argues for Duchamp's crucial role in the reconception of the singular original through his deployment of the *empreint*—a nearly untranslatable term that approaches "impression" and implies reproduction or replication through touch—while barely addressing the *Box of 1914*.

41. Although Krauss locates this in "1960s photography," she suggests that "photography's emergence as a theoretical object had already occurred at the hands of Benjamin in the years that elapsed between his 'A Small History of Photography' in 1931 and his more famous text of 1936 ... in which photography is not just claiming the specificity of its own (technologically inflected) medium, but, in denying the values of the aesthetic itself, will cashier the very idea of the independent medium, including that of photography." Rosalind E. Krauss, "Reinventing the Medium," *Critical Inquiry* 25, no. 2 (Winter 1999), 289–305. Much of this chapter argues for ways in which the *Box of 1914* anticipates and tests out concerns that would become Duchamp's and Benjamin's shared preoccupation in the mid-1930s and would be further realized in the practices of the generation of artists starting in the 1960s who were influenced by Duchamp; in this sense, the use of Krauss's notion is not meant to be anachronistic but instead to suggest the critical potential already inscribed in this prescient work.

42. See Douglas Gorsline's 1962 discussion with Duchamp in which the latter recalls seeing Marey's chronophotography in a magazine sometime toward the end of 1911; the impact, he says, was "immediate," and he "felt that this visual strategy might be [his]." Manuscript of interview and notes housed in the Douglas Gorsline Collection (#901), East Carolina Manuscript Collection, J. Y. Joyner Library, East Carolina University, Greenville, North Carolina.

43. See *Duchamp-Villon, sculpteur* (Paris: Centre Georges Pompidou, 1999) and *Duchamp-Villon, dessinateur et photographe* (Rouen: Musée des Beaux-Arts, 1999), 10–11.

44. Between 1898 and 1914 Atget received commissions from and sold photographs to various archives, city bureaus, and even the newly created Musée Carnavalet dedicated to preserving a record of the history of Paris. Into the 1920s and before Berenice Abbott and the Surrealists would discover him, he also produced records for a clientele of stage designers, architects, publishers, and artists, always insisting that his work was mere *documentation*. But his example is rare; few other photographers were determined to present their work as something wholly outside the category of art. See Molly Nesbit's landmark study *Atget's Seven Albums* (New Haven: Yale University Press, 1992).

45. It was Walter Benjamin who, in 1936, understood their evidential dimension, noting "the incomparable significance of Atget, who, around 1900, took photographs of deserted Paris streets. It has quite justly been said of him that he photographed them like scenes of crime. The scene of the crime, too, is deserted: it is photographed for the purpose of establishing evidence." Benjamin, "The Work of Art in the Age of Mechanical Reproduction," in *Illuminations*, ed. Hannah Arendt, trans. Harry Zohn (New York: Schocken, 1969), 226.

46. Molly Nesbit, "La Photographie et l'histoire, Eugène Atget," in Michel Frizot, ed., *Nouvelle histoire de la photographie* (Paris: Larousse, 2001), 399–409 (translation mine).

47. To give some further perspective, one should not forget that even if Picasso had photographically recorded his work off and on since he first bought a camera in 1906, and Brancusi would begin taking photographs of his sculpture in the 1920s, neither treated the photographs of works as artworks in themselves, neither included them in their retrospectives (as Duchamp would go on to do), and neither was photographing anything as atypical (for the photographic conventions of the day) as notes in order to make two-dimensional facsimiles in multiple copies.

48. See A. Courrèges, *Reproduction des gravures, dessins, plans, manuscrits* (Paris: Gauthier-Villars, 1900).

49. André Bazin's 1958 French original was translated as "The Ontology of the Photographic Image," in *What Is Cinema?*, trans. Hugh Grey (Berkeley: University of California Press, 1967), 14; cited in Krauss, "Notes on the Index: Part 1," in *The Originality of the Avant-Garde and Other Modernist Myths*, 203.

50. If one accepts Hubert Damisch's claim that photography is "nothing other than a process of recording, a technique of *inscribing*, in an emulsion of silver salts, a stable image generated by a ray of light," the contents of the *Box of 1914* are records recorded, inscriptions inscribed. Doubly inscriptive, or, rather, records also about recording, they reveal themselves to be about photography and its relationship, above all, to a logic of reproduction.

51. See Krauss, "Duchamp ou le champ imaginaire," in *Le Photographique*, 71–88.

52. As Krauss attests, Duchamp was "less preoccupied by realization of the photographic than by a reflection of the nature of it" (translation mine). This might seem to explain Krauss's and others' silence about the *Box of 1914*; this silence, however, marginalized a veritable matrix for much of what would come after in terms of Duchamp's interest in the photographic. See Krauss, "Duchamp ou le champ imaginaire," 75.

53. See Krauss's seminal discussion of the original and copy in "The Originality of the Avant-Garde" and "Sincerely Yours," in *The Originality of the Avant-Garde and Other Modernist Myths*, 151–170, 175–194.

54. The replies of artists questioned by Stieglitz were published in *MSS* [Manuscripts], no. 4, New York (December 1922), 2. Duchamp's response is reprinted in *Affectionately, Marcel*, 109.

55. Benjamin H. D. Buchloh, "Gerhard Richter: Painting after the Subject of History" (PhD diss., City University of New York, 1994), xviii.

56. Benjamin H. D. Buchloh, "The Politics of Representation," in *The Photographic Paradigm* (Amsterdam: Editions Rodolpi, 1997), 26.

57. Buchloh says: "Duchamp's particular fusion of the indexical traces of chronophotography with the painterly category of the female nude seemed to enact that very contradiction integral to the dialectic of enlightenment operative in the project of cubist painting." Buchloh, "Gerhard Richter," 68–69.

58. George Baker, *The Artwork Caught by the Tail* (Cambridge, MA: MIT Press, 2007), 202.

59. Jean-François Lyotard speaks of the *Large Glass* in no uncertain terms as related to photography throughout his *Les TRANS/formateurs Duchamp* (Paris: Éditions Galilée, 1977).

60. As Krauss further suggests, "If Duchamp was indeed thinking of the *Large Glass* as a kind of photograph, its processes become absolutely logical, not only the marking of the surface with instances of the index and the suspension of the images as physical substances within the field of the picture; but also, the opacity of the image in relation to its meaning." Krauss, "Notes on the Index: Part 1," 203.

61. See Krauss, "Duchamp ou le champ imaginaire."

62. Henri-Pierre Roché describes Duchamp's dust-making studio in his *Victor* (Paris: Centre Georges Pompidou, 1977), 65.

63. Jane Blackwell, interview with Marcel Duchamp for the BBC, June 5, 1968, reprinted in Naumann, *Marcel Duchamp: The Art of Making Art*, 302.

64. "It was more recopying, copying some sketches that I'd done on glass already, so there was no creativeness there, no invention anymore, it was just a translation of a thing already done, to my mind at least, onto glass." Outtake of Richard Hamilton's interview with Duchamp for BBC's *The Monitor* program, cited in Gough-Cooper and Caumont, *Ephemerides on and about Marcel Duchamp and Rrose Sélavy*, unpaginated, September 27, 1961. See also *Marcel Duchamp: Notes*, n. 147. Of the *Large Glass* Duchamp also said: "I wanted to go to a completely dry drawing, a dry conception of art. ... And the mechanical drawing for me was the best form of this dry form of art." Unpublished manuscript from James Johnson Sweeney interview, Philadelphia, 1955, cited in Ecke Bonk, *The Box in a Valise: de ou par Marcel Duchamp ou Rrose Sélavy: Inventory of an Edition* (New York: Rizzoli, 1989), 9, n. 1.

65. In fact, the painting the Arensbergs actually coveted was *Nude Descending a Staircase* (no. 2, 1912), itself already a kind of redux that Duchamp had made of a first similar version of the painting based on the same subject. The second version is the more famous of the two; it is the one that caused such a scandal in New York when it was shown, and the one most people think of when the title is mentioned. The photographic replica (no. 3) was, as Francis Naumann reports, "prominently displayed in the main studio of the Arensberg apartment in New York, and even after the original painting was acquired in 1919, the photographic replica remained on display, as it would in the Arensbergs' Hollywood home in the 1930s and '40s." Naumann, *Marcel Duchamp: The Art of Making Art*, 20. Fittingly, and not unlike the artist's placement of his 1919 *L.H.O.O.Q.* next to its 1930 *réplique* at the exhibition "La Peinture au défi" (see below), Duchamp also showed the Arensbergs' two *Nudes* side by side at his first retrospective in Pasadena in 1963.

66. In a mocking gesture that can be read as a delayed "conversation" with both Duchamp's 1913–14 note project and this copy of *Nude Descending a Staircase* as well as a questioning of authenticity and originality embodied in two Duchampian works from 1919, *L.H.O.O.Q.* and *Tzanck Check*, Picabia offered his own reflection on replication, authenticity, and authorship on the cover of the November 1920 issue of his journal *391*. There he reproduced what the cover announced as a "copie d'un autographe d'Ingres," that is, a copy of a hand-scripted document as well as its original's fake but official-looking notary stamp, beginning, "I, the undersigned Jean-Auguste-Dominique Ingres ... " To the note's final, validating signature Picabia added his own: "Francis Ingres." *Picabia*, a drawing done that same year of the artist's own signature and countersigned by the artist, might similarly be understood in terms of a creative dialogue between Duchamp and Picabia spanning many years and particularly centered, as George Baker compellingly argues, on the question of the copy.

Baker advances that "Picabia's lifelong dedication to the copy" was a preoccupation he shared with Duchamp, uniting them in an intense series of artistic volleys about authority, reproduction, and originality. See Baker, *The Artwork Caught by the Tail*, 75.

67. The workings of this operation to turn the (photographic) copy into an original (painting) are, in some ways, the mirror opposite of *Tzanck Check*, an original that sought to look like a copy. In 1919, Duchamp constructed a carefully handmade, larger-than-life drawing of a check made to look every bit as if it were little more than a banal, commercially printed, bank-issued document of legal tender (complete with the ink-stamped words "ORIGINAL" in red diagonally across the front). The artist specifically concocted the elaborate facsimile to pay his dentist, Daniel Tzanck, to whom the check was made out.

68. Louis Aragon, *La Peinture au défi* (Paris: Goemans Gallery, 1930), unpaginated, catalog for the exhibition at the gallery located at 49 rue de Seine in Paris's chic art gallery district.

69. Walter Benjamin, "Malerei und Photographie," in *Gesammelte Schriften*, III (Frankfurt: Suhrkamp, 1972), 495–507; translated as "Second Letter from Paris: Painting and Photography," in Walter Benjamin, *Selected Writings*, ed. Howard Eiland and Michael W. Jennings, trans. Edmund Jephcott, Howard Eiland, et al., vol. 3, *1935–1938* (Cambridge, MA: Harvard University Press, 2002), 236–248. Though this is lost in the translation of the title as "The Work of Art in the Age of Mechanical Reproduction" (familiar to readers in English through Harry Zohn's translation of the essay for the collection *Illuminations*), the sense of *possibility* suggested in "reproducibility" is inscribed in Benjamin's original "technischen Reproduzierbarkeit" in the German title, which means something akin to "the possibility of technical reproduction." I have used here and throughout the more recent translation of the title, "The Work of Art in the Age of Its Technological Reproducibility," which comes closest to expressing Benjamin's desired sense of latency and possibility, ideas no less crucial to understanding the connection between Benjamin and Duchamp's relationship to replication. For a contemporary review of Aragon's exhibition, see Carl Einstein, "Exposition de collages," *Documents*, 2ème année, v. 4 (1930), 245.

70. Alexander Dorner is best known for commissioning El Lissitzky to construct his *Abstraktes Kabinett* (Abstract Cabinet) in 1927–28 in the provincial Landesmuseum (an installation that would be destroyed by the Nazis in 1937) and for commissioning László Moholy-Nagy's installation *Room of Our Time*, which could never be completed. See Samuel Cauman, *The Living Museum: Experiences of an Art Historian and Museum Director—Alexander Dorner* (New York: New York University Press, 1958).

71. See the letters from Albert Gleizes to Dorner, discussed further below, and cited in Cauman, *The Living Museum*, 116.

72. See Joan Ockman, "The Road Not Taken: Alexander Dorner's Way beyond Art," in R. E. Somol, ed., *Autonomy and Ideology* (New York: Monocelli, 1997), 82–120.

73. Kurt Karl Eberlein, "Zur Frage: 'Original oder Faksimilereproduktion?,'" *Der Kreis* 6, no. 11 (November 1929), 650–653, reprinted in translation in Christopher Phillips, ed., *Photography in the Modern Era: European Documents, 1913–1940* (New York: Metropolitan Museum of Art, 1989), 145–150. See also Dorner's essay "Original and Facsimile," in the same volume, 151–154, and the texts in Olivier Lugon, *La Photographie en Allemagne: Anthologie des texts (1919–1939)* (Nîmes, France: Editions Jacqueline Cambon, 1997), 385–396.

74. It was the director of the Hamburg Museum of Arts and Crafts, Max Sauerlandt, who opened the discussions on the facsimile "problem" in the September 1929 issue of *Der Kreis* and also instigated the push to outlaw facsimile reproductions of art. A discussion of the debate in *Der Kreis* can be found in Ockman, "The Road Not Taken," 94–96, and esp. fn. 35.

75. Benjamin's first discussion of the photographic reproduction of works of art appeared in print just months after the opening of Dorner's exhibition. In an entry in his Paris journal dated February 4, 1930, Benjamin critically reflects on his friend Adrienne Monnier's defense of photographs of artworks, a topic that he classifies as his own "old *bête noir*." Benjamin's position would shift between the writing of the Paris journal and his first "little" exposé on photography in 1931, and then again between the latter and his more famous "Work of Art" essay of 1936.

76. Benjamin, *Illuminations*, 220.

77. Ibid., 224.

78. For a perceptive reading of Duchamp's interest in mechanical reproduction with reference to Benjamin, see Sarat Maharaj, "'A Monster of Veracity, a Crystalline Transubstantiation': Typotranslating the Green Box," in Mignon Nixon and Martha Buskirk, eds., *The Duchamp Effect* (Cambridge, MA: MIT Press, 1996), 60–91.

79. *À l'infinitif*, translated and reprinted in *In the Infinitive*, 1.

80. Otto Hahn, "Interview with Marcel Duchamp," first published in *L'Express*, no. 684 (July 1964), 22–23, reprinted in Anthony Hill, ed., *Duchamp: Passim, A Marcel Duchamp Anthology* (Langhorne, PA: G&B Arts International, 1994), 69.

81. Ibid. (italics mine).

82. The notes and variants to the "Work of Art" essay cited here and relating to Duchamp date from early 1936. Georges Didi-Huberman, in *L'Empreint*, and Rosalind E. Krauss, in "Reinventing the Medium," are among the few to comment on this draft to Benjamin's most famous treatise in light of its discussion of Duchamp. See Didi-Huberman, *L'Empreint*, reprinted as *La Ressemblance par contact: archéologie, anachronisme, et modernité de l'empreint* (Paris: Editions du Minuit, 2008), 300; and Krauss, "Reinventing the Medium," 293, parts of which reappear in "Reinventing the Medium: Introduction to *Photograph*," in George Baker, ed., *James Coleman* (Cambridge, MA: MIT Press, 2003), 195–196.

83. Benjamin, *Gesammelte Schriften*, I, vol. 3, pp. 1045f; Walter Benjamin, "Paralipomènes et variants de la version définitive," in *Ecrits français* (Paris: Gallimard, 1991), 179–180. As Michael W. Jennings and Tobias Wilke note in their editors' introduction to the first English translation of the first version of the "Work of Art" essay, "Benjamin's repeated rewriting of his essay suggests its importance to him: the successive versions are not so much corrections of his first one but shifts of emphasis." Jennings and Wilke, "Editors' Introduction. Walter Benjamin's Media Tactics: Optics, Perception, and the Work of Art," *Grey Room* 39 (Spring 2010), 6–9. A related conclusion could be drawn from his ample notes and variants, unpublished in his lifetime and to date untranslated into English, which trace not only their author's careful deliberation of the thoughts in this evidently important treatise, but also the degree to which contemporary developments in culture—including Duchamp's note project—inflected his thinking on the project, whether they made it into the final draft or not.

84. Benjamin would have seen these pieces in the exhibition "La Peinture au défi," either in person or through its catalog, which he clearly knew, as well as in the "Exposition surréaliste d'objets," held May 22–31, 1936, at the Galerie Charles Ratton, which he evidently also saw while in Paris.

85. See Rhonda Roland Shearer and Stephen Jay Gould, "The *Green Box* Stripped Bare: Marcel Duchamp's 1934 'Facsimiles' Yield Surprises," *Tout fait* 1, no. 1 (December 1999); accessible at: http://www.toutfait.com/issues/issue_1/News/GreenBoxNote.html.

86. Duchamp, letter to Alice Roullier, cited in Gough-Cooper and Caumont, *Ephemerides on and about Marcel Duchamp and Rrose Sélavy*, unpaginated, October 16, 1934.

87. Benjamin, "Paralipomènes et variants de la version définitive," 179–180.

88. Walter Benjamin, *Selected Writings*, vol. 2, *1927–1934* (Cambridge, MA: Harvard University Press, 1999), 348.

89. Benjamin, "Paralipomènes et variants de la version définitive," 179–180.

90. See Walter Benjamin, *The Work of Art in the Age of Its Technological Reproducibility and Other Writings on Media*, ed. Michael Jennings, Thomas Y. Levin, and Brigid Doherty (Cambridge, MA: Belknap Press of Harvard University Press, 2008).

91. Unlike the very long tradition of artist's etchings or lithographs, for instance, which maintained a status inferior or secondary to the original (painting) as *mere* reproductions, Duchamp's involvement in complex reproductive projects not only attempted to render ambiguous the borderline between original and reproduction, but also insisted on the value of his reproductions and editions as bona fide artworks, often, in fact, exhibited alongside the models on which they were based. His display of the photographic copy of the *Nude Descending a Staircase* next to the original in the Arensbergs' home and in his own first retrospective in 1963, as well as his efforts to insert his *Boîte-en-valise* into and exhibit it in museums and institutions of art, are just two examples. On Duchamp's other projects involving reproduction, see Francis Naumann's *Marcel Duchamp: The Art of Making Art.* Naumann's copiously illustrated book is by far the most thorough and well-documented treatment of the multiple and replication in Duchamp's oeuvre.

92. Interview with Michel Sanouillet, "Dans l'atelier de Marcel Duchamp," *Les Nouvelles Littéraires*, no. 1424 (December 16, 1954), 5; Arturo Schwarz's translation in *Notes and Projects for the Large Glass* (p. 6) is slightly modified here (see note 104 below).

93. Duchamp, letter to Walter and Louise Arensberg, February 20, 1934, reprinted in *Affectionately, Marcel*, 187.

94. The fact that Duchamp included a different "original" note in each of the deluxe editions of the *Box* could be said to further complicate the tension between original and copy, since he effectively negated the possibility of a "master" original box. With his originals divided up and some of them dispersed over the deluxe editions, no single box could contain *all* the auratic notes from which the copies were made.

95. Those works include *Coffee Mill* (1911); *Passage from Virgin to Bride* (1912); *Chocolate Grinder* (1913); *Bride* (1912); *Oculist Witnesses* (1920); *Glider Containing a Water Mill in Neighboring Metals* (1913–15); *9 Malic Molds*; and *To Be Looked at (from the Other Side of the Glass) with One Eye, Close To, for Almost an Hour* (1918). Duchamp used the complicated pochoir method for only one of them, the *9 Malic Molds*, and ordered mere black-and-white collotypes for all the others, curiously reserving the much more elaborate and pictorial form of pochoir color reproduction for his notes and not the bulk of his actual paintings.

96. Letters cited in Cauman, *The Living Museum*, 116.

97. As Derrida argues: "In order to function, that is, in order to be legible, a signature must have a repeatable, iterable, imitable form; it must detach itself from the present and singular intention of its production. It is its sameness which, in altering its identity and singularity, divides the seal." Jacques Derrida, "Signature Event Context," in *Margins of Philosophy*, trans. Alan Bass (Chicago: University of Chicago Press, 1982), 328–329. The signature thus *must* be able to be repeated (otherwise, without the possibility of another with which to compare, how would we recognize it as the reliable mark of this or that person?) but should not, *for it to be authentic*, be able to be copied by someone other than the author.

98. Benjamin, "Paralipomènes et variants de la version définitive," 179–180 (translation mine).

99. In 1932 and 1933, thus before Duchamp had embarked on the process of replicating the notes in the *Green Box*, he shared his notes with André Breton, who published a text transcription of several of the notes pertaining to the *Large Glass*. Prefacing them with a short introduction, he stressed the "considerable value" of the documents and captioned the transcriptions with a careful description of the particularities of each of the original notes—including underlinings, cross-outs, and the color of the ink employed. See André Breton, "Marcel Duchamp: The Bride Stripped Bare by Her Own Bachelors," *This Quarter* 5, no. 1, Surrealist special issue (September 1932), 189–191, as well as "La Mariée mis à nu par ses célibataires mêmes," *Le Surréalisme au Service de la Révolution*, no. 5 (May 1933), 1–2. Later, following the publication of the *Green Box*, Breton would write a more extensive interpretive essay, notable in this context for a number of reasons: first, he had not seen the actual *Large Glass*, so his article is based entirely on a viewing of it via *reproduction* and the details gleaned from the notes; secondly, he organized the chaos and fragmentation of the notes into a neat, continuous, romantic story; thirdly, his was the only published essay on the notes to have appeared before the end of the 1950s, when Duchamp's work and legacy were starting to be reassessed. See André Breton, "La Phare de la mariée," *Minotaure* 2, no. 6 (Winter 1934–35), 45–49; translated as André Breton, "Lighthouse for the Bride," in Robert Lebel, *Marcel Duchamp* (New York: Paragraph Books, 1959), 88–94. Dorothy Dudley's unpublished review of the box suggests that the American writer also found symbolic value in the notes, a "mechanical-physical set of symbols for the modern artist; just as the Gothic artist had a religious set from which to construct windows and frescoes." Dudley, alias Clos Vert, "Paris Letter," dated November 3, 1934, unpublished manuscript, cited in Naumann, *Marcel Duchamp: The Art of Making Art*, 116–117.

100. Inevitably, one must wonder why Benjamin didn't include these reflections in the final essay. Although this can only be speculation, perhaps it was because, when he was writing, he was on one side of a world war and looking into the face of another. His reflections, which he wrote and rewrote until nearly the end of his life, on the transformations of the work of art were not the rantings of a nostalgist clinging to an idea of the auratic artwork, but instead a way of grappling with the vast social transformations that he was experiencing and wondering what role mechanical reproduction had in all of it. The work of art had a role to play in social cohesion, which was a fundamental concern of Benjamin's, but one that—and perhaps he sensed this—Duchamp was apparently not much interested in, no matter that his replicated notes advanced a theory of the artwork.

101. See Cabanne, *Dialogues with Marcel Duchamp*, 42.

102. Just a few notable examples across the last four decades would include: Lawrence D. Steefel Jr., "The Position of *La Mariée mise à nu par ses célibataires, même* (1915–1923) in the Stylistic and Iconographic Development of Marcel Duchamp" (PhD diss., Princeton University, 1961); Jack Burnham, "Duchamp's Bride Stripped Bare: The Meaning of the 'Large Glass,' Part I," *Arts Magazine* (March 1972), 28–32, Part II (April 1972), 41–45, and Part III (May 1972), 58–61; Arturo Schwarz, "The Alchemist Stripped Bare, in the Bachelor, Even," in Anne d'Harnoncourt and Kynaston McShine, eds., *Marcel Duchamp* (Philadelphia: Philadelphia Museum of Art; New York: Museum of Modern Art, 1973), 81–98; Jean Clair, "Duchamp and the Classical Perspectivists," *Artforum* 16, no. 7 (March 1978), 40–49; Craig Adcock, *Marcel Duchamp's Notes from the Large Glass: An N-Dimensional Analysis* (Ann Arbor, MI: UMI Research Press, 1983); and Linda Dalrymple Henderson, *Duchamp in Context: Science and Technology in* The Large Glass *and Related Works* (Princeton, NJ: Princeton University Press, 1998).

103. Craig Adcock suggests, "Looking at the *Large Glass* alone, the viewer would have almost no inkling of what it was supposed to represent." Adcock, *Marcel Duchamp's Notes*, text published to accompany the exhibition of the same name (Tallahassee: Florida State University Fine Arts Gallery, 1985), unpaginated. The indeterminate status of the notes, however, is suggested by Susi Bloch, who observes that Breton's important early essay on the *Large Glass* and the notes, "La Phare de la mariée," first published in *Minotaure* in 1934–35 and later included in Robert Lebel's monograph on the artist, is largely responsible for the persistent understanding of the notes as a key rather than a work in themselves. "If anything," she notes, "it is the *Large Glass* which could be seen as a supplement to the *Green Box*, the incomplete realization of a ruminating idea that could never satisfactorily articulate itself in purely visual terms." See Susi Bloch, "The Green Box," *Art Journal* 34, no. 1 (Fall 1974), 27.

104. Speaking about the *Large Glass* late in life, Duchamp observed: "I still have pleasure seeing it again, even though it is not finished or even intended to be looked at. It certainly isn't *L'Embarquement pour Cythère* [by Antoine Watteau]. *It isn't even a picture; it is a mass of ideas*." His interviewer Michel Sanouillet probed: "If one accepts your definition of the *Large Glass*, why did you feel the need to write all the notes which are found in the *Green Box*?" To which Duchamp retorted: "Certain ideas, to prevent betrayal, call for a graphic language: that's my glass. But as a commentary, the notes can be useful, like captions, which accompany photos in a catalogue of the Galeries Lafayette. That's the *raison d'être* for my Box." Michel Sanouillet, "Dans l'atelier de Marcel Duchamp," reprinted in Arturo Schwarz, ed., *Notes and Projects for the Large Glass,* trans. George H. Hamilton, Cleve Gray, and Arturo Schwarz (London: Thames and Hudson, 1969).

105. Duchamp, letter to Jean Suquet, December 25, 1949, in Suquet, *Miroir de la mariée* (Paris: Flammarion, 1974), 247.

106. George Heard Hamilton, "A Radio Interview," conducted on January 19, 1959, for BBC Radio; transcription printed in Hill, *Duchamp: Passim*, 77 (italics mine).

107. The fragile glass piece had been shattered while being returned to its owner, Katherine Dreier, after it was first publicly exhibited at the Brooklyn Museum in 1926. The damage, however, was only discovered when the work was finally uncrated five years later. When Duchamp released the facsimile edition of notes in 1934 and announced them as specifically relating to the *Large Glass*, it was two years before repair on it had even begun (and consequently before the *Large Glass* could be viewed again).

108. "When I made my *Glass*, it was not my intention *to make a painting to be looked at*, but a painting in which I had used a tube of paint as an accessory and not as an end in itself. ... I wanted, then, to add a book, or rather a catalogue like the *Armes et Cycles de Saint Etienne* [a contemporary French mail order company], in which every detail would be explained, catalogued. And this idea to bring these two things together does not at all, in my opinion, have a literary character. ... My mix had the advantage of getting rid of the idea of painting for painting's sake, which, in 1913, had been my point of departure." Alain Jouffroy, "Conversations avec Marcel Duchamp" (1954 and 1961), in *Une révolution du regard: A props de quelques peintres et sculpteurs contemporains* (Paris: Gallimard, 1964), 107–124 (translation mine).

109. Breton notoriously wrote his "Lighthouse for the Bride" without having seen the *Large Glass* and on the basis of only Duchamp's notes and photographs: see note 99 above.

110. Krauss, "Reinventing the Medium," 290–291.

111. It is exactly there, for example, in the 1913–14 act of reproducing his notes (of making *documents*), that the seeds may have been sown for Duchamp's 1917 *Fountain*, whose existence as a copy without an original was first announced and made visible because of Duchamp's careful photographic documentation (and the subsequent publication of the documentation) and, later, by the replication of the piece (on the basis of the documentation). The act of engaging Alfred Stieglitz to photograph the rejected urinal has recently been acknowledged by scholars as the precursor to conceptual photography. However, I would argue that Duchamp prepared for and rehearsed the implications of the gesture through his *Box of 1914* (as he later developed them through his *Boîte-en-valise*, discussed in chapter 2). See Mark Godfrey and Jessica Morgan, eds., *The Unruly History of the Readymade* (Mexico City: Jumex Collection, 2008); and Erik Verhagen, "La Photographie conceptuelle: Paradoxes, contradictions, et impossibilités," *Études Photographiques* 22 (September 2008), 118–139.

112. Even before the 1967 publication of *À l'infinitif*, a small sampling of Duchamp's notes from the forthcoming box were published under the title "Speculations" in *Art in America* (March–April 1966). One can only imagine that the information in the notes must have spoken volumes to artists working in this period, but even more consequential than what the notes said—in their musings on optical illusion, the photographic, plastic duration, et cetera—were the form these speculative documents took and their role in the discursive administration of the artwork they supposedly related to. The four-page spread in *Art in America* was covered with a scatter of notes—notes that formed the faint background upon which Duchamp's words from a selection of notes appeared in translation in black boldface letters. There were images, too: photographs of Marcel at a desk, Marcel sifting through his notes, Marcel writing. It is striking how much these photos looked like an emerging Conceptualism's own cherished bureaucratic aesthetic—with their penchant for representing their projects through photographs of desks and chairs, books, and notes. And though, when asked in interviews, Duchamp denied that there were any further unpublished notes, after his death a package of nearly a hundred more was found, carefully lying in wait like some message in a bottle meant to be posthumously sent to sea. They were published more than a decade later under the straightforward title *Marcel Duchamp: Notes* (Paris: Centre Georges Pompidou, 1980).

CHAPTER 2

1. Duchamp, letter to Walter Arensberg, November 8, 1918, reprinted in *Affectionately, Marcel: The Selected Correspondence of Marcel Duchamp*, ed. Francis Naumann and Hector Obalk (Ghent: Ludion, 2000), 64.
2. "Pode bal," literally, the "skin of the ball" means "nothing" or "not at all" or, in more vernacular French, "balls (to you)." *Salt Seller: The Writings of Marcel Duchamp*, ed. Michel Sanouillet and Elmer Peterson (New York: Oxford University Press, 1973), 180.
3. Duchamp, letter to Jacques Doucet, October 19, [1925], reprinted in *Affectionately, Marcel*, 152.
4. Ibid. Duchamp would later relent, allowing this and other optical works to be displayed in exhibitions of painting and sculpture.
5. Duchamp had exhibited his early paintings at the two main French salons of the period, the Salon d'Automne, from 1908 to 1912, and the Salon des Indépendants, from 1909 to 1912. At the Salon des Indépendants of 1912 Duchamp experienced perhaps his first real brush with artistic rejection when the hanging committee of the Cubist room (which included his artist brothers) asked him to withdraw his *Nude Descending a Staircase* (no. 2, 1912).

The wound of that rejection stung, and as a result, according to Duchamp, "he retired from exhibiting." See Frederick Kiesler's notes from a conversation with the artist, presumed to date from 1945, a photocopy of which is preserved in the Frederick and Lillian Kiesler Foundation Archive, Vienna.

6. The connections made in this chapter between Duchamp's curating, interest in display techniques, and the museum were first explored in my exhibition and accompanying booklet *Duchamp on Display: Optics, Exhibition Installations, Portable Museums* (New York: Zabriskie Gallery, 2001).

7. Duchamp's first mention of the category/title/genre name "readymade" can be found in a letter to his sister of January 15, [1916]: "You saw the bicycle wheel and a bottlerack in my studio. I bought that as an already finished sculpture. And I have an idea about the bottlerack: listen. Here in New York I have bought some objects of a similar style and called them 'readymade.' You know enough English to understand the meaning of 'already finished' that I have assigned to these objects—I sign them and put an inscription on them in English. I'll give you a few examples: I bought a big snow shovel upon which I wrote 'In advance of the broken arm ...' Don't try too hard to understand this in a romantic or impressionistic or cubistic way—it doesn't have anything to do with that; another 'ready-made' is called 'Emergency in favor of twice.' ... This whole preamble is for one reason: Go get the bottlerack. I am making it into a readymade from afar. On the inside of the bottom ring you will write the inscription I will give you at the end here, using small letters and painting them on with a brush and silver-white paint, and in the same lettering you are to sign it as follows: Marcel Duchamp." Reprinted in *Affectionately, Marcel*, 43.

8. Duchamp cited in "Artist Marcel Duchamp Visits U-classes, Exhibits at Walker," *Minnesota Daily*, October 22, 1965, cited in Thomas Girst, "(Ab)Using Marcel Duchamp: The Concept of the Readymade in Post-War and Contemporary American Art," *Tout-Fait*, http://www.toutfait.com/issues/volume2/issue_5/articles/girst2/girst1.html (accessed May 13, 2016).

9. The paradoxes of this assertion are inescapable. While Duchamp endowed his readymades with many of the signs of being artworks, he fervently and repeatedly claimed that they were not in fact aesthetic objects. As he declared in a public lecture: "A point which I want very much to establish is that the choice of these 'readymades' was never dictated by aesthetic delectation. The choice was based on a reaction of *visual* indifference with at the same time a total absence of good or bad taste ... in fact a complete anaesthesia." Lecture published as "Apropos of 'Readymades'" (1961) in *Salt Seller*, 141. As a further example of his numerous assertions on this topic, he told interviewer Philippe Collin: "The fundamental truth is that it [the readymade] should not be looked at. It just *is* there. One's eyes merely convey the fact of its existence. But it is not to be contemplated as if it were a painting. The very idea of contemplation is evacuated. There is just a taking note that it is a bottlerack, or that it is a bottlerack that has *switched function*." Collin, *Marcel Duchamp parle des Ready-mades* (1967) (Paris: L'Echoppe, 1998), 14 (translation and italics mine). Complicating these assertions, in another interview Duchamp claims: "A readymade [laughs] is first of all the invented word I used to designate *a work of art that is not one*. In other words, that is not handmade. Handmade by the artist. It's a work of art that becomes so by the fact of my or the artist's declaration of it as a work of art, without there being any participation of the hand of the artist in question to make it." Guy Viau, interview with Marcel Duchamp, "Changer de nom, simplement," on Canadian Radio Television, July 17, 1960, transcribed and printed in *Fin*, no. 5 (Galerie Pierre Brullé, June 2000), 12 (translation and italics mine).

10. Collin, *Marcel Duchamp parle des Ready-mades*, 14.

11. Duchamp, interview with R. B. Kitaj, Richard Hamilton, Robert Melville, and David Sylvester, London, June 19, 1966, unpublished transcript, Marcel Duchamp Archives, France, cited in Bernard Marcadé, "Concept of Nothing," in *Voids* (Zurich/Paris: JRP Ringier/Centre Pompidou, 2009), 236. The show in question was "Exhibition of Modern Art" at the Bourgeois Gallery, April 3–29, 1916.

12. Ibid. An unidentified critic did mention Duchamp's presentation of "Two readymades," without identifying or saying anything further about them. "Exhibitions On Now," *American Art News* (New York) 14, no. 27 (April 8, 1916), 3, cited in William Camfield, *Marcel Duchamp/Fountain* (Houston: Menil Collection, Houston Fine Arts Press, 1989), 17n6.

13. Ibid.

14. See the discussion of this exhibition and Duchamp's inconsistency about which readymades were included in Thierry de Duve, *Kant after Duchamp* (Cambridge, MA: MIT Press, 1996), 102.

15. Listed in *Exhibition of Modern Art*, the booklet accompanying the show (New York: Bourgeois Gallery, 1916), unpaginated. See Marcadé, "Concept of Nothing," 236.

16. See Lydie Fischer Sarazin-Levassor, *A Marriage in Check: The Heart of the Bride Stripped Bare by Her Bachelor, Even* (Lyon: Les presses du réel, 2007). On Duchamp's studio in relation to his readymades, see Helen Molesworth, "Work Avoidance: The Everyday Life of Marcel Duchamp's Readymades," *Art Journal* 57 (1998), 50–61.

17. *Trébucher*, "to trip," is the verb used to describe stumbling over something one does not properly see or notice. The related noun is also a French technical term in chess, where it means a "trap": the *trébuchet* is a chess piece one sacrifices, a piece willingly set out as a trap to win a piece from one's opponent. Between the two French meanings of the word, *Trébuchet* names the idiosyncratically displayed readymade coatrack as a thing which, nailed to the floor, one might literally stumble over, but whose agency might also go unnoticed.

18. It is noteworthy that Duchamp would use several of these display strategies also in more public exhibitions: the snow shovel was repeatedly suspended from the ceiling in various exhibitions throughout his life, and he famously placed a replica of the "original" *Fountain* over the doorway of Sidney Janis's gallery for the "Dada 1916–1923" exhibition, held from April 25 to May 9, 1953.

19. Molesworth, "Work Avoidance," 50.

20. Anonymous, "Society of Independent Artists Exhibition at the Grand Central Palace," *New York Times*, April 11, 1917, cited in Camfield, *Marcel Duchamp/Fountain*.

21. It is not known which work Duchamp had planned to show, only that he decided not to show any when he resigned to protest an exhibition that wouldn't accept R. Mutt's signed urinal.

22. "His Art Is Too Crude for Independents," *New York Herald*, April 11, 1917, 6. I thank Francis Naumann for this reference.

23. For the most extensive research on the different accounts of *Fountain*, see Camfield, *Marcel Duchamp/Fountain*.

24. Duchamp uses exactly this description of Stieglitz in his 1963 lecture on the occasion of the fiftieth anniversary of the Armory Show of 1913. See Duchamp, "Armory Show Lecture, 1963," reproduced in *Fin*, no. 18 (Galerie Pierre Brullé, June 2003), 21–32. For more on Duchamp's strategic choice of Stieglitz, see de Duve, *Kant after Duchamp*, 120–123.

25. Duchamp, "Marcel Duchamp Talking about Readymades," interview with Philippe Collin, June 21, 1967, reprinted in Museum Jean Tinguely, Basel, *Marcel Duchamp* (Ostfildern: Hatje Cantz, 2002), 40.

26. I borrow the idea of the artwork "appearing" and being subjected to a "test" from both Thierry de Duve's brilliant reading of the readymade in *Kant after Duchamp* and Michael Newman, the latter of whom notes: "The 'original' *Fountain* did not appear in the exhibition to which it was submitted, and through its nonappearance showed up the conditions for appearance—or exclusion—of a work of art as both institutional and historical: in that time, in that place, under such circumstances, a urinal could not appear as a work of art, even if it could be conceived as such by an artist." Michael Newman, "After Conceptual Art: Joe Scanlan's Nesting Bookcases, Duchamp, Design and the Impossibility of Disappearing," in Michael Newman and Jon Bird, eds., *Rewriting Conceptual Art* (London: Reaktion, 1999), 217.

27. As she further notes, "These decorating choices also instigated a quintessential Dada challenge to art-viewing precedent: the oilcloth walls created an almost industrial backdrop for the art, and the lace transformed the picture frames from props conferring (masculine) importance and establishment into ephemeral (feminine) accessories." Kristina Wilson, "'One Big Painting': A New View of Modern Art at the Brooklyn Museum," in Jennifer R. Gross, ed., *The Société Anonyme: Modernism for America* (New Haven: Yale University Press, 2006), 77.
28. The commercial implications of many of his activities remain an important yet still relatively unexplored topic in Duchamp studies. As Dalia Judovitz put it: "There is one detail in Marcel Duchamp's lengthy artistic career that troubles both his sympathizers and critics alike: the fact that he bought and sold paintings, those of others, as well as his own." Judovitz, "Art and Economics: From the Urinal to the Bank," in *Unpacking Duchamp: Art in Transit* (Berkeley: University of California Press, 1995), 169–194; Francis Naumann, "Money Is No Object," *Art in America*, no. 3 (March 2003), 67–73; and David Joselit, "The Artist Readymade: Marcel Duchamp and the Société Anonyme," in Gross, *The Société Anonyme*, 33–43.
29. Marcel Duchamp quoted in Calvin Tomkins, *The Bride and the Bachelors* (New York: Viking Press, 1965), 60.
30. Roger Shattuck, "Confidence Man," *New York Times Review of Books*, May 27, 1997, http://www.nybooks.com/articles/archives/1997/mar/27/confidence-man/?pagination=false (accessed January 1, 2013).
31. Henri-Pierre Roché, "MARCELDUCHAMPSOPTICALDISKS," *Phases*, no. 1 (January 1954), reprinted in *Salt Seller*, 191.
32. Henri-Pierre Roché, "Souvenirs de Marcel Duchamp," in Robert Lebel, ed., *Sur Marcel Duchamp* (Paris: Editions Trianon, 1959), 79.
33. Duchamp specifically refers to his project as a "portable museum" in "A Conversation with Marcel Duchamp," filmed interview with James Johnson Sweeney, conducted in the Arensberg rooms at the Philadelphia Museum of Art in 1955. Transcribed and printed in *Salt Seller*, 136.
34. On the history and ideological "birth" of the art museum, see Tony Bennett, *The Birth of the Museum: History, Theory, Politics* (London: Routledge, 1995), and Donald Preziosi, *The Brain of the Earth's Body: Art, Museums, and the Phantasms of Modernity* (Minneapolis: University of Minnesota Press, 2003).
35. Rosalind E. Krauss, "The Originality of the Avant-Garde," in *The Originality of the Avant-Garde and Other Modernist Myths* (Cambridge, MA: MIT Press, 1985), 162.
36. Ibid., 168.
37. Rosalind E. Krauss, "Louise Lawler: Souvenir Memories," in Helen Molesworth with Taylor Walsh, eds., *Louise Lawler*, October Files 14 (Cambridge, MA: MIT Press, 2013), 31.

38. Rosalind E. Krauss, "Photography's Discursive Spaces," *Art Journal* (Winter 1982), 312.

39. Martha Ward, "What's Important about the History of Modern Art Exhibitions?," in Reesa Greenberg, Bruce W. Ferguson, and Sandy Naire, eds., *Thinking about Exhibitions* (London: Routledge, 1996), 452–453.

40. Yve-Alain Bois, "Exposition: Esthétique de la distraction, espace de démonstration," *Cahiers du Musée National d'Art Moderne* 29 (Autumn 1989), 57–79.

41. "The curator observes his/her operation within the institutional apparatus of art: most prominently the procedure of abstraction and centralization that seems to be an inescapable consequence of the work's entry into the superstructure apparatus, its transformation from *practice* to discourse." Benjamin H. D. Buchloh, "Since Realism There Was ... (On the Current Conditions of Factographic Art)," in *L'Exposition imaginaire: The Art of Exhibiting in the Eighties* (The Hague: Rijksdienst Beeldende Kunst, 1989), 96–117.

42. *L'Amour de l'Art*, in its special issue devoted to the exhibition, mentioned 1926—when the journal *Mouseion* was created—as the official beginning of museology, "with its rules and its laws." One might argue, however, that museology had only truly started to become a formalized field, and the modern museum a legitimate object of study, by 1937, marked in part by the exhibition "Muséologie." See *Exposition internationale de 1937. Groupe I. Classe III. Musées et expositions. Section I. Muséographie*, published as a special issue of *L'Amour de l'Art*, no. 18 (June 1937). The effect of this exhibition can be seen in the subsequent transformation of European museum interiors such as that of the Stedelijk Museum in Amsterdam, which in 1938 covered its moldings, plinths, and bricks in a uniform white. All this in time to welcome an exhibition of abstract art (with works by Wassily Kandinsky, Constantin Brancusi, Theo van Doesburg, Piet Mondrian, and Sophie Taeuber-Arp, among others).

43. Albert S. Henraux, "Preface," *Exposition internationale de 1937*, 1.

44. See the various pages of photographs and diagrams in the official guide to the museology exhibition, which reproduced the interior of the exhibition along with sketches of visitors' "vision lines": *Exposition internationale de 1937*, esp. 2–23 and 28. For an elaboration of the primacy of the visual in the museum from the nineteenth century to the present, see Tony Bennett, "Pedagogic Objects, Clean Eyes, and Popular Instruction: On Sensory Regimes and Museum Didactics," *Configurations* 6, no. 3 (1998), 345–371.

45. Henraux, "Preface," in *Exposition internationale de 1937*, 1. Commenting on the breadth of the publicity surrounding the Exposition Universelle's celebration of Descartes's *Discours de la méthode*, Geneviève Rodis-Lewis notes, "The tricentenary which assembled an international congress of philosophers in Paris was marked by the publication of numerous newspaper articles as well as special issues dedicated to Descartes in prestigious French and international journals from Milan to Buenos Aires, and from the Hague to Berlin and Bucharest" (translation mine). Rodis-Lewis, "Préface," in *Discours de la méthode* (Paris: Flammarion, 1992), 8. Descartes's relationship to French ocularcentrism is discussed in Martin Jay, *Downcast Eyes: The Denigration of Vision in Twentieth Century French Thought* (Berkeley: University of California Press, 1993).

46. In *A Complaint for Mary and Marcel*, Kay Boyle playfully teases Duchamp and Mary Reynolds for not having come to the opening festivities. Cited in Jennifer Gough-Cooper and Jacques Caumont, "Ephemerides on and around Marcel Duchamp or Rrose Sélavy," in Pontus Hulten, ed., *Marcel Duchamp* (Venice: Bompiani, 1993), unpaginated, May 24, 1937.

47. The publicity around the 1937 Exposition Universelle was widespread, and Duchamp would certainly have learned about its various components, if not firsthand then either from the

general and specialized art press or from friends who attended. The museology exhibition did not go unnoticed by those who frequented the same circles. Notably, Georges Salles, a curator, collector, and friend of Robert Lebel, later included his thoughts on the show in a 1939 collection of writings. Georges Bataille, too, spent time there, as evidenced in his essay on the "Muséologie" exhibition's model Van Gogh show. Georges Salles, "Le Musée," in *Le Regard* (Paris: Plon, 1939; reprint, Paris: Réunion des Musées Nationaux, 1992), 51; and Georges Bataille, "Van Gogh Prométhée," *Verve* 1, no. 1 (December 1937), 20.

48. Even if Duchamp positioned himself explicitly as uninterested in politics, and even if the Surrealists knew better than to approach him to sign their various manifestos and declarations (he never was an official member of the group), his sustained critique of art was vital to the Surrealist effort in 1938. And, given his repeated collaborations on exhibitions for and with the Surrealists over the years, Duchamp's position cannot be easily dismissed as either cynical or critically derisive of Surrealism. The political stakes of the exhibition space in the period are discussed in my "Surrealism in 1938: The Exhibition at War," in Raymond Spiteri and Donald LaCoss, eds., *Surrealism, Politics and Culture* (London: Ashgate, 2003), 179–203.

49. The Surrealist exhibition has been discussed in lively detail by Bruce Altshuler, *The Avant-Garde in Exhibition: New Art in the Twentieth Century* (New York: Harry Abrams, 1994); Martica Sawin, *Surrealism in Exile and the Beginning of the New York School* (Cambridge, MA: MIT Press, 1994); James D. Herbert, *Paris 1937: Worlds on Exhibition* (Ithaca, NY: Cornell University Press, 1998); and, most extensively among these, Lewis Kachur, *Displaying the Marvelous: Marcel Duchamp, Salvador Dalí and the Surrealist Exhibition* (Cambridge, MA: MIT Press, 2001).

50. Georges Hugnet, "L'Exposition internationale du surréalisme," *Preuves* 91 (September 1958), 38–47. Hugnet's account is one of the most vivid and detailed narrations of the exhibition preparations. See also other descriptions of the event by its participants: Marcel Jean with Arpad Mezei, *Histoire de la peinture surréaliste* (Paris: Seuil, 1959), 280–289, and Man Ray, *Self-Portrait* (Paris: Éditions Robert Laffort, 1964), 205–206, 243–244.

51. See Janine Mileaf, "Body to Politics: Surrealist Exhibition of the Tribal and the Modern at the Anti-Imperialist Exhibition and the Galerie Charles Ratton," *Res*, no. 40 (Fall 2001), 239–255.

52. See François Fosca, "Les Arts: La Duperie du surréalisme," *Je Suis Partout*, January 28, 1938, archived on microfilm at the Bibliothèque Nationale, Paris.

53. See Jean with Mezei, *Histoire de la peinture surréaliste*, and Man Ray, *Self-Portrait*.

54. See my "Surrealism in 1938."

55. Man Ray, *Self-Portrait*, 243.

56. For the Surrealist movement, so committed to disturbing rational and aesthetic categories and blurring the borders between dream and reality, the exhibition as a whole reflected these desires. And even if the Surrealists differently expressed the nature of their ideological commitments, the collective recasting of the gallery space seems to have been as important to their project as it was to Duchamp. The latter explained his participation to Pierre Cabanne as follows: "I had been borrowed from the ordinary world by the Surrealists. They liked me a lot; Breton liked me a lot; we were very good together. They had a lot of confidence in the ideas I could bring them, ideas which weren't anti-surrealist, but which weren't always surrealist, either." Duchamp in Pierre Cabanne, *Dialogues with Marcel Duchamp* (London: Thames and Hudson, 1971), 81. Benjamin H. D. Buchloh asserts—and T. J. Demos reiterates—that Duchamp's exhibition installations for the Surrealists were covertly and critically aimed against Surrealist aesthetics and practices, a reading that

hardly holds up against the evidence to the contrary. I see Duchamp's position as being more ambivalent, with a point of attack at once more general and more specific: his recurrent practice of curating exhibitions with the Surrealists allowed him the opportunity to systematically pressure exhibition conventions as well as the notions they turned around, from traditional modes of viewing to the uniqueness of the work of art. See Benjamin H. D. Buchloh, "The Museum Fictions of Marcel Broodthaers," in A. A. Bronson and Peggy Gale, eds., *Museums by Artists* (Toronto: Art Metropole, 1983), 46; Benjamin H. D. Buchloh, "The Dialectic of Design and Destruction: The *Degenerate Art* Exhibition (1937) and the *Exhibition international du Surréalisme* (1938)," *October* 150 (Fall 2014), 49–62; and T. J. Demos, *The Exiles of Marcel Duchamp* (Cambridge, MA: MIT Press, 2007), 127–188.

57. Like so many of Duchamp's gestures, the mannequin stood *between*: between Marcel and Rrose, self and other, object of contemplation and object of desire, autographed auratic work and banal mass-produced thing. Several of these issues are discussed in depth in Amelia Jones, *Postmodernism and the Engendering of Marcel Duchamp* (Cambridge: Cambridge University Press, 1994), 78–79, and Michael R. Taylor, "Rrose Sélavy, prostituée de la Rue aux Lèvres: Levant le voile sur l'alter ego érotique de Marcel Duchamp," in Marie-Laure Bernadac and Bernard Marcadé, eds., *Féminimasculin: Le Sexe de l'art*, exh. cat. (Paris: Musée Nationale d'Art Moderne, Centre Georges Pompidou, 1995), 272–290. The status of the ensemble of dressed mannequins at the 1938 Surrealist exhibition in relation to art, photography, and commerce is the subject of my "Abwesende Kunstobjekte: Mannequins und die *Exposition Internationale du Surréalisme* von 1938," in Pia Müller-Tamm and Katharina Sykora, eds., *Puppen, Körper, Automaten: Phantasmen der Moderne* (Cologne: Oktagon, 1999), 200–218.

58. As Marcel Jean recollected, "Duchamp had thought of installing 'magic eyes' so that the lights would have gone on automatically as soon as the spectator had broken an invisible ray when passing in front of a painting." Marcel Jean, *History of Surrealist Painting* (New York: Grove Press, 1967), 281–282.

59. In her sustained work on Duchamp's optical games, Rosalind Krauss, extending the analysis of Jean-François Lyotard, has underlined the ways in which the artist's vision experiments and optical illusions work to "corporealize the visual," offering counterpositions to those very notions of good form and pure opticality central to aesthetic modernism. See in particular Krauss, "The Im/pulse to See," in Hal Foster, ed., *Vision and Visuality* (Seattle: Bay Press, 1988), 51–75, and Krauss, "The Blink of an Eye," in David Carroll, ed., *The States of "Theory": History, Art, and Critical Discourse* (New York: Columbia University Press, 1990), 175–199. Also see Lyotard, *Les TRANSformateurs DUchamp* (Paris: Galilée, 1977). Among the examples of Duchampian optics in this Surrealist show, reproductions of a *Rotorelief* and the 1935 *Minotaure* cover (picturing a montage of *Dust Breeding* and a *Corolla* disk) were visible along the gallery corridor behind Rrose Sélavy's mannequin, while his *Rotary Demisphere* (the optical machine that Duchamp had not wanted Jacques Doucet to show in art exhibitions just a decade earlier) swirled and pulsated in another room.

60. Duchamp speaks about the exhibition preparation, the string purchase, and the spontaneous combustion of the first webbing of string in his interview with Harriet, Sidney, and Carroll Janis, 1953. Typescript, Philadelphia Museum of Art, Duchamp Archives; and see also Cabanne, *Dialogues with Marcel Duchamp*, 86.

61. Edward Alden Jewell, "Inner Visions and Out of Bounds: Sidelights and Afterthoughts on the Rise of the Surrealist School and Its Limitations—Other New Exhibitions," *New York Times*, October 18, 1942.

62. Henry McBride, "Surrealism Gets Nearer: The Old Whitelaw Reid Mansion Is Invaded by Modernists," *New York Sun*, October 16, 1942, newspaper clipping collected in the Kurt Seligmann archives, New York.

63. Carroll Janis, conversation with the author, 2001.

64. Surprisingly, although several studies of the Surrealist exhibitions have been published, few have ventured to read in Duchamp's curatorial role evidence of his larger thinking about the artwork. T. J. Demos attempts this, rather unconvincingly, in relation to Duchamp's supposed "post-nationalist" impulse, in *The Exiles of Marcel Duchamp.* Michael Taylor, on the other hand, does not much discuss the Surrealist exhibitions in relation to Duchamp's larger output, not least of which should be the *Boîte-en-valise*, but he does advance a compelling trajectory that connects the Surrealist exhibitions to *Étant donnés* in the exhibition catalog *Marcel Duchamp: Étant donnés* (Philadelphia: Philadelphia Museum of Art, 2009).

65. In the first monograph on the artist, Duchamp and Robert Lebel provide the following dates for the *Boîte-en-valise*: 1938 (Paris) and 1941–42 (New York); see Lebel, *Sur Marcel Duchamp*, item no. 173. Likewise, in his interview with Pierre Cabanne, Duchamp dates the *Boîte-en-valise* "from 1938 to '42." Cabanne, *Dialogues with Marcel Duchamp*, 79. This dating is repeated in the catalog for Duchamp's first American retrospective in Pasadena in 1963 (entitled "De ou par Marcel Duchamp ou Rrose Sélavy," like the Duchampian work on which the exhibition was in part modeled), and has become the standard (unquestioned) dating in many Duchamp studies since.

66. It is perhaps not surprising that the artist included photographs of precisely these two exhibitions from 1938 and 1942 not far from the display of his *Boîte-en-valise* in his first retrospective at the Pasadena Art Museum in 1963. Nor perhaps is it surprising that if he had somehow used these actual exhibitions to influence his conception of the *Boîte-en-valise*, at that Pasadena show he in turn used the *Boîte-en-valise* to influence his hanging of certain works in the exhibition space, mimicking the positions of display in his miniature retrospective. The flow of influence between actual exhibitions and the simulation of a miniature exhibition was, it seems, a two-way street.

67. Even if the white-cube aesthetic that would soon become the norm in many galleries and museums of modern art was not yet prevalent, Wildenstein's gallery (with its baroquely elegant fittings and velvet-lined walls) was every bit as much an assertion of a certain institutional authority, in this case modeled on the luxe bourgeois interior still very much in use by most museums.

68. For reproduction in the *Boîte-en-valise*, Duchamp included Man Ray's photograph of the *second* store-bought bottlerack (1936), which was, as the first had been (and as was the case with so many of the quotidian readymade objects), subsequently lost.

69. Henri-Pierre Roché, from the letters and unpublished documents housed in the Roché archive of the Carlton Lake Collection in the Harry Ransom Research Center at the University of Texas, Austin. Cited in Ecke Bonk, *The Box in a Valise: de ou par Marcel Duchamp ou Rrose Sélavy: Inventory of an Edition* (New York: Rizzoli, 1989), 204.

70. Janis interview cited in Francis Naumann, *Marcel Duchamp: The Art of Making Art in the Age of Mechanical Reproduction* (Ghent: Ludion Press, 1999), 168.

71. The act almost literalizes Gordon Fyfe's assertion: "Art reproduction is exegesis about an original which changes the relationship between the artist and the public meaning of the work of art. It cannot be judged as posterior to the authorship of the original. Reproduction does not translate or encode a pre-established authorship, it is a medium through which authorship is produced. … If we are to talk about the social construction of the artist then we must also talk about the social construction of impersonal process work. The individuality

of the artist has been produced through a struggle to determine the meaning of reproductions." Fyfe, "Art and Its Objects: William Ivins and the Reproduction of Art," in Gordon Fyfe and John Law, eds., *Picturing Power: Visual Depiction and Social Relations* (London: Routledge, 1988), 83–84.

72. In addition to the publication in *The Blind Man*, an oblique reference to *Fountain* surfaced in the chronology section of the catalog for the 1936 "Fantastic Art, Dada, Surrealism" show at the Museum of Modern Art in New York. However, for the vast public—professional and amateur alike—that didn't know that Duchamp was involved in the affair, Alfred Barr's brief and somewhat enigmatic reference to the artist's "rejected submission of a ready-made piece of plumbing" under the events of "1917" was easily overlooked. Perhaps the only readers who paid any attention to it were the administrators of the Society for Independent Artists, who noticed the mention and felt that their good name was slighted by Barr's allusion to the event. Writing to Barr on behalf of the group, John Sloan insisted that it could not "be permitted to place in the exhibition an object which by its nature would have aroused such disgust and resentment among the members and visitors of the society as to endanger the continuance of the work which had been undertaken and carried out steadily since [the inception of the organization]." And so, according to his own admission, the act of rejection was not one of "judgment" but rather some sort of public morality policing. Sloan thus objects to Barr putting the Society in the position "of rejecting an exhibit offered as a work of art when, as you know, we were dealing with a matter totally unrelated with art," a comment that underscores how little had changed about the perception of the work in question in the years between 1917 and 1936. See exchange of letters between Alfred Barr Jr. and the Society of Independent Artists in 1937 regarding the *Fountain* affair in Clark Marlor, *The Society of Independent Artists: The Exhibition Record, 1917–1944* (Park Ridge, NJ: Noyes Press, 1984), 37–39.

73. William Camfield's investigation of *Fountain* confirms its virtual invisibility in public history throughout the 1920s and 1930s. See Camfield, *Marcel Duchamp/Fountain*. Indeed Apollinaire's June 16, 1918, *Mercure de France* article "Le cas de Richard Mutt," reporting on art events in New York (likely suggested by Duchamp or one of his entourage without letting Apollinaire in on the details), never once mentions Duchamp in connection with the scandalous "case." However, if Duchamp solicited little public attention connecting himself and *Fountain* before the object's remake in 1938, his authorship was nevertheless spoken about over the years among a small circle of his friends, some of whom mention it in their own writings (Anaïs Nin and André Breton, for instance). Additionally, Paul Franklin points to several works by Duchamp and his friends Francis Picabia and Pierre de Massot that invoke or make reference to his 1917 affair with the men's public toilet. See Franklin, "Object Choice: Marcel Duchamp's *Fountain* and the Art of Queer Art History," *Oxford Art Journal* 23, no. 1 (2000), 27–49. The first text to discuss the readymades in a sustained way appears in 1945, Sidney and Harriet Janis's "Marcel Duchamp: Anti-Artist," in which they state (evidently having been guided by Duchamp himself): "The ready-mades may be unique as a concept but they are not necessarily intended to be unique as examples. For instance, the bottle rack was lost and replaced by another. Although the original inscription was forgotten and no other substituted, the act of replacing the object itself grants to the product of mass production the same validity as nature grants to any star in the skies or grain of sand upon the earth." Harriet and Sidney Janis, "Marcel Duchamp: Anti-Artist," *View: The Modern Magazine* 5, no. 1 (March 1945), 23, reprinted in Robert Motherwell's 1951 anthology *The Dada Painters and Poets* (Cambridge, MA: Belknap Press of Harvard University, 1981), 3–11.

74. Demos, *The Exiles of Marcel Duchamp*, 144, 146.

75. Ibid.

76. Although just about any history book of the period would yield similar information, one example may speak to the critical silence that surrounded the readymades until after the *Boîte-en-valise* effectively staged their exhibition: Clement Greenberg did not mention Duchamp in his seminal 1939 essay "Avant-Garde and Kitsch" (where the avant-garde art of "Picasso, Braque, Mondrian, Miro, Kandinsky, Brancusi, even Klee, Matisse and Cézanne" is discussed). Greenberg, "Avant-Garde and Kitsch," *Partisan Review* 6, no. 5 (1939), 34–49, reprinted in Charles Harrison and Paul Wood, eds., *Art in Theory 1900–1990* (Oxford: Blackwell, 1992), 529–541.

77. Demos, *The Exiles of Marcel Duchamp*, 26.

78. On the history of the various incarnations of *Fountain*, see Camfield, *Marcel Duchamp/ Fountain*.

79. Duchamp's notes are peppered with references to *retard*. See Thierry de Duve's discussion of these in *Kant after Duchamp*, 85, 97, 101, 134, 139.

80. De Duve, *Kant after Duchamp*, 135; see also his section "Given the Richard Mutt Case."

81. Judovitz, *Unpacking Duchamp*, 127–129. See also Martha Buskirk, "Thoroughly Modern Marcel," in Martha Buskirk and Mignon Nixon, eds., *The Duchamp Effect* (Cambridge, MA: MIT Press, 1996), 197. The example of *Fountain* and its museum thus points to a larger problematic in teleological narrations of the history of art, highlighting, for instance, the blind spot of Peter Bürger's reading of the way the avant-garde work and its reception operates, discussed further in chapter 3. See Peter Bürger, *Theory of the Avant-Garde*, trans. Michael Shaw (Minneapolis: University of Minnesota Press, 1984). For a compelling reading of the discrepancies in Bürger's argument as they relate to the relationship between avant-garde and neo-avant-garde practices, a reading to which my own here is indebted, see Hal Foster, "Who's Afraid of the Neo-Avant-Garde?," in *The Return of the Real* (Cambridge, MA: MIT Press, 1996), 1–32.

82. De Duve, *Kant after Duchamp*, 134.

83. Indicative of this was the kind of exhibition that Duchamp was offered before the *Boîte-en-valise* inscribed *Fountain* (and with it, other readymades) into the artist's oeuvre: his first solo show opened in Chicago in 1937 and included twelve oil paintings from Duchamp's early period (without a single readymade). A proper retrospective did not follow until more than twenty-five years later, in Pasadena, California. Histories of the avant-garde too often only see the readymades from the vantage point of their current place within art institutions (in art historical narratives and in the art museum), a place that testifies, in some accounts, to their being *compromised* as truly radical objects. Benjamin H. D. Buchloh and T. J. Demos after him see the *Boîte-en-valise* as responding to the "failure" of the readymade. See Buchloh, "The Museum Fictions of Marcel Broodthaers," and Demos, *The Exiles of Marcel Duchamp*.

84. Duchamp, letter to Dreier, March 5, 1935, cited in Bonk, *The Box in a Valise*, 147.

85. Ibid., 148.

86. All these appeared in true Duchampian form—on odd scraps of paper, torn fragments of cardboard, and the backsides of unrelated documents—and were housed in a brown cloth-covered box scribbled with the words "Documents épisodaire (chronologique) Jeux de mots." This box contains an ensemble of chronologies, lists of works, valuations, locations, and several photographs of reproductions, about thirty pieces in all, most of which relate directly to the work and planning for the *Boîte-en-valise*.

87. This was the case, for instance, for his *Coeurs volants* (Fluttering Hearts, 1936), which featured on the cover of a 1936 issue of *Cahiers d'Art* and for which Duchamp had asked the printer run off roughly 320 extra copies of the image, or, much later, for the last editions of the *Boîte-en-valise* when he had roughly one hundred extra copies run off of his *Réseaux des stoppages-étalon* (Network of Stoppages, 1914) when that work was being reproduced in the catalog to his first retrospective at the Pasadena Art Museum, or even his use of the color images of his three "erotic objects" from the 1950s when Arturo Schwarz had them reproduced in 1964 for *The Complete Works of Marcel Duchamp* (New York: Harry Abrams, 1969). See Bonk, *The Box in a Valise*, 197–256.

88. My understanding of the details of Duchamp's monographic project is highly indebted to Ecke Bonk's exacting and invaluable study *The Box in a Valise*.

89. As Bonk explains in relation to these oddly authenticated copies: "All legal transactions in France—attestations, deeds of sale, contracts of all sorts—require a revenue stamp and the signature of a notary to give them validity." Ibid., 214. See also Naumann, *Marcel Duchamp: The Art of Making Art*.

90. See Sarat Maharaj's brilliant reading of the tension between original and reproduction in "'A Monster of Veracity, a Crystalline Transubstantiation': Typotranslating the Green Box," in Buskirk and Nixon, *The Duchamp Effect*, 65–66.

91. See Cabanne, *Dialogues with Marcel Duchamp*, 79.

92. Ecke Bonk details the full list of the various specialists involved, suggesting the "magnitude of the logistics" invoked for the project. See Bonk, "Marcel Duchamp," in Kynaston McShine, ed., *The Museum as Muse: Artists Reflect* (New York: Museum of Modern Art, 1999), 52–54, and "delay included," in *Joseph Cornell/Marcel Duchamp, in Resonance* (Houston: Menil Foundation, 1998), 102–105.

93. As Duchamp recounted: "I thought of a scheme. I had a friend, Gustave Candel, who was a wholesale cheese merchant in Les Halles, and I asked him if he could commission me to go to buy cheese for him in the unoccupied sector. He gave me a letter, which I took to the German authorities, and with that letter and a bribe of twelve hundred Francs I got from a secretary that famous little red card, called an *Ausweis*, which allowed me to travel by train from Paris to Marseilles. I thought I had to be very careful and buy cheese, and probably give an account of my expenses when I crossed the border between the two zones, but the Germans never asked me any questions." Conversation with Calvin Tomkins, in Tomkins, *Duchamp, a Biography* (New York: Henry Holt, 1996), 323–324.

94. In a curious twist, the various miniature reproduced works that would be presented in a case like a salesman's wares—thus parodying art's (and the museum's) relationship to the commodity—found their way to safety disguised as France's most banal consumer good, cheese. The irony would repeat when, in order to be transported across the Atlantic, Duchamp shipped the hundreds of loose "items" with the help of Peggy Guggenheim, who declared them her "household effects." Again in 1955, when Duchamp tried to ship the loose reproductions for the *Boîte-en-valise* back to France, he encountered difficulties over the question of their status and thus the appropriate duty fees. The artist had to call on the services of an administrator from the Bibliothèque Nationale to aid in the release of the items, which were finally labeled "samples"—neither works of art nor salable (and thus taxable) merchandise. See Bonk, *The Box in a Valise*, 178.

95. Marcel Duchamp, "Bulletin de souscription" of the *Boîte-en-valise* (January 2, 1941). In fact, although he had wanted to feature sixty-nine items and actually made the necessary reproductions, one of the items, the upright standing celluloid reproduction of *Glisière* (Water Glider, 1920), proved particularly fragile and had to be removed from nearly all the boxes on offer, reducing the total number of items to sixty-eight.

96. Letter mentioned in Pierre Mazars, "Fautrier fait une petite révolution," *Le Figaro littéraire*, November 25, 1950, 8, cited in Rachel E. Perry, "The originaux multiples," in Curtis Carter and Karen Butler, eds., *Jean Fautrier* (New Haven: Yale University Press, 2002), 72.

97. Jean Fautrier, exh. cat., Billiet-Caputo, 1950; cited in Perry, "The originaux multiples," 72.

98. On the museum's preoccupation with originality, see Krauss, "The Originality of the Avant-Garde," 162.

99. "A Conversation with Marcel Duchamp," filmed interview with James Johnson Sweeney, cited in Dawn Ades, *Marcel Duchamp's Travelling Box* (London: Arts Council of Great Britain, 1982), 3.

100. See Buchloh, "The Museum Fictions of Marcel Broodthaers," 48.

101. Calling it a "veritable house of opticality," Donald Preziosi discusses the optical impulse of the museum in "Brain of the Earth's Body," in Paul Duro, ed., *Rhetoric of the Frame: Essays on the Boundaries of the Artwork* (Cambridge: Cambridge University Press, 1996), 107.

102. Krauss, "The Im/pulse to See," 60. In a number of important articles, Krauss has read Duchamp's experimentation with libidinal optics as emblematic of an undoing of modernist visuality. See also Rosalind E. Krauss, *The Optical Unconscious* (Cambridge, MA: MIT Press, 1993), 95–146.

103. It should hardly come as a surprise that these particular deluxe incarnations of the *Boîte-en-valise* were made during the period in which Duchamp had just secretly begun to work on *Étant donnés*, an installation that would extend and crystallize so many of his concerns with the museum, looking, and the body.

104. Christian Zervos published the Matisse catalog in 1931 and two Picasso catalogs in 1932 and 1936. Although entirely in black and white, their unrivaled sumptuousness and the high-quality reproductions used throughout were remarkable, so much so that André Malraux described Picasso as a painter of his own *oeuvre complète*, noting: "His goal was not his paintings, but the albums of reproductions by Zervos in which the breathless succession of works is far more significant than the best single one among them can be by itself." Malraux, *Le Musée imaginaire* (Geneva: Skira, 1947), 53. The Matisse catalog ended with installation shots of several exhibitions of Matisse's work, effectively reinforcing the publication's role as a comprehensive presentation—a virtual museum retrospective—of the artist's work.

105. When in 1959 Robert Lebel wrote to French museum officials proposing an exhibition of Duchamp's work, all of his letters went unanswered. Duchamp's first major retrospective only came in 1963, and at the least likely of places, Pasadena, California (hardly an art world capital).

106. Julien Levy, *Surrealisme* (New York: Black Sun Press, 1936), 36.

107. Walter Arensberg, letter to Marcel Duchamp, May 21, 1943, marked "not sent" (Arensberg Archives, Philadelphia Museum of Art).

108. Cabanne, *Dialogues with Marcel Duchamp*.

109. When art historical literature before the 1980s treats the *Boîte-en-valise* at all, it seems to assume that Duchamp's retrospective project was little more than an easy repetition of previous work, or a repetition that was only important insofar as it led to something else. Only with Ecke Bonk's 1989 *The Box in a Valise* did a major monographic study argue for its significance, notably at a time when scholarly interest in Institutional Critique was burgeoning. Both Francis Naumann and Martha Buskirk take the *Boîte-en-valise* as a central subject in their subsequent studies, but still it is to them that we owe the two

ambiguous citations: Naumann's recent publication titles the chapter that deals with the *Boîte-en-valise* "Vacationing in Past Time: Seven Years to Pack a Valise, 1935–1941," and Buskirk argues for the piece as an "interim step" toward the arrangement of Duchamp's works in a real museum. Naumann, *Marcel Duchamp: The Art of Making Art*, 124; and Buskirk, "Thoroughly Modern Marcel," 198.

110. Buskirk, "Thoroughly Modern Marcel," 198, 202 (emphasis mine).

111. Bonk, *The Box in a Valise*, 21.

112. Buchloh, "The Museum Fictions of Marcel Broodthaers," 49.

113. This is the gist not only of Buchloh's essay "The Museum Fictions of Marcel Broodthaers" but also of a number of his other essays on Broodthaers and the artists who are now known under the moniker "Institutional Critique." Duchamp's relationship to the gestures of those artists is discussed in more detail in chapter 3, with a more thorough list of references.

114. Marcel Duchamp, "A Complete Reversal of Art Opinions by Marcel Duchamp, Iconoclast," *Arts and Decoration* 5, no. 11 (September 1915), 428.

115. In January 1940, at a moment when the reproductions for the *Boîte-en-valise* were nearly complete but the container for the works was still under construction, Duchamp sent several items destined for inclusion in it to represent him at a collective Surrealist exhibition in Mexico City. Making the nature of his contribution explicit, Duchamp asked that the catalog and exhibition checklist specifically label each work a "reproduction." If the force of Alexander Dorner's 1929 exhibition lay in positioning the original next to the copy, resulting in a difficulty in telling the two apart, one notes that Duchamp didn't offer an original against which to judge his copies. He did everything he could to underline the fact that *in an exhibition* he was showing nothing more than *reproductions.*

116. Man Ray was called upon to rephotograph and manipulate an advertisement for the Société Anonyme, Inc., printed in *Art News* (May 14, 1927), which displayed a frontal installation view of the *Large Glass* as it had appeared in the 1926 show of modern art at the Brooklyn Museum organized by the Société Anonyme. See *Joseph Cornell/Marcel Duchamp*, 100–101.

117. In order to represent *Bottlerack,* first conceived and signed in 1914 but subsequently lost, Duchamp had Man Ray photograph a second newly purchased version in 1936; they added a thin, almost colorless lacquer to the image during the intricate printing process so as to suggest a new second shadow. As for the representation of *Why Not Sneeze, Rrose Sélavy?*, Bonk notes: "The plinth turned a photographic viewpoint into a pseudo-spatial impression. Even the cuttlefish bone was given a spatial equivalent in or on the plinth ... [the work] is undoubtedly one of the most complex 'items' in the *Boîte*, and at the end of 1940 it added a new variant, somewhere between the 2nd and 3rd dimension, to the range of facsimile technologies developed by Duchamp." For a detailed description of the production of these and other reproductions, see Bonk, *The Box in a Valise*, 209, 238–240.

118. One cannot help seeing in this miniature industrial drawing an anticipation of the blueprints of the readymades that Duchamp and Arturo Schwarz would have made by professional draftsmen in the 1960s for the industrial originals to be replicated. It was the playful manifestation of all those French elementary school drawing lessons in which industrial drawings were made to be uninventively and repeatedly *copied.* See Molly Nesbit, "Readymade Originals," *October* 37 (Summer 1986), 53–64, and Nesbit, *Their Common Sense* (London: Black Dog, 2000).

119. Roland Barthes, *Camera Lucida* (New York: Hill and Wang, 1981), 87.

120. Walter Benjamin, "Malerei und Photographie," in *Gesammelte Schriften*, ed. Rolf Tiedemann and Hermann Schweppenhäuser (Frankfurt: Suhrkamp, 1980), III, 495–507, translated as "Peinture et photographie: Deuxième lettre de Paris, 1936," in Walter Benjamin, *Sur l'art et la photographie*, ed. Christophe Jouanlanne (Paris: Carré, 1997).

121. Bois, "Exposition: Esthétique de la distraction, espace de démonstration," 62 (translation mine).

122. Robert Lebel, "Marcel Duchamp: Whiskers and Kicks of All Kinds," in Lebel, *Sur Marcel Duchamp*, 97. Dalia Judovitz's astute understanding of Duchamp's relationship to such exchange is relevant here: "Rather than viewing Duchamp's commercial activity as a betrayal of both his artistic detachment and putative disinterest in financial value, his fascination for the speculative value of art can be better understood in intellectual terms. It is a fascination with how artistic and monetary value is generated arbitrarily through social exchange. Duchamp's interest in the speculative character of money does not translate itself into the subservience of his own artistic work to monetary considerations. Instead, it expresses the recognition that value, be it artistic or financial, is embedded in a circuit of symbolic exchange." Judovitz, *Unpacking Duchamp*, 167.

123. The near simultaneity of Malraux's and Duchamp's projects is discussed in the pages of a special issue on Duchamp of *October*, where Malraux's writing on the *musée imaginaire* is suggested as the likely "context" to which Duchamp was responding at the time. This idea is taken up by T. J. Demos, who notes that the primary difference between the two projects is Duchamp's use of a monographic form, which "props up the institution of authorship." Other differences between them and their approaches seem more fundamental and noteworthy, but Demos's conclusion is strategic since, as he posits, authorship "takes on special significance ... in the context of exile," and the construction of an image of Duchamp as anxiously responding to nationalism and exile is the author's central, if specious, thematic. See Benjamin H. D. Buchloh, Rosalind E. Krauss, Yve-Alain Bois, et al., "Conceptual Art and the Reception of Duchamp," *October* 70 (Fall 1994), reprinted in Buskirk and Nixon, *The Duchamp Effect*, 216; and Demos, *The Exiles of Marcel Duchamp*, 33.

124. André Malraux, *The Voices of Silence*, trans. Stuart Gilbert (Princeton: Princeton University Press, 1978), 44, 46. *Le Musée imaginaire* (translated into English as *The Museum without Walls*) was the first volume of a three-part work, *La Psychologie de l'art*, which Malraux published between 1947 and 1949 and which he subsequently expanded and republished in a single volume as *Les Voix du silence* in 1951. The kernel of his argument, however, had appeared already as "La Psychologie de l'art" in the pages of the first issue of *Verve* magazine in 1937.

125. *Art since 1900* discusses Benjamin, Malraux, and Duchamp together, citing the year 1935 as the moment each of them starts their respective project. See Hal Foster, Rosalind E. Krauss, et al., *Art since 1900: Modernism, Antimodernism, Postmodernism* (London: Thames and Hudson, 2004), 271–275.

126. Walter Benjamin excitedly reported to Max Horkheimer that Malraux spoke of his "Work of Art" text in his presentation "Sur l'héritage culturel," delivered in London in 1936 to the Association of Writers for the Defense of Culture, and that the Frenchman held out the prospect of even more serious attention to it. See Benjamin, letter to Max Horkheimer, August 10, 1936, in *The Correspondence of Walter Benjamin, 1910–1940*, ed. Gershom Scholem and Theodor Adorno, trans. Manfred and Evelyn Jacobson (Chicago: University of Chicago Press, 1994), letter 280. Malraux's "theoretical book" would be *Les Voix du silence*, and the section most apparently influenced by Benjamin's reflections on reproduction and photography would be "Le Musée imaginaire."

127. André Malraux, *The Psychology of Art: The Museum without Walls*, trans. S. Gilbert (London: A. Zwemmer, 1949), 32.

128. Foster, Krauss, et al., *Art since 1900*, 273.

129. Such is Hal Foster's characterization of Benjamin in contradistinction to Malraux. I have extrapolated here to suggest that it represents shared ground for Duchamp and Benjamin. See Foster, "Archives of Modern Art," in *Design and Crime: And Other Diatribes* (London: Verso, 2002), 81.

130. See the discussion of Benjamin's relationship to and understanding of Duchamp's work in chapter 1.

131. Dorothea von Hantelmann, "The Curatorial Paradigm," *Exhibitionist*, no. 4 (June 2011), 11–12.

132. Ibid.

133. Ibid.

134. Marcel Duchamp, "I Propose to Strain the Laws of Physics," interview with Francis Roberts, *Art News* 67 (December 1968), 47.

135. For a discussion of the history of artists' roles in exhibition making, see my "When Exhibitions Become Form: On the History of the Artist as Curator," in Elena Filipovic, ed., *The Artist as Curator: An Anthology* (Milan and Cologne: Mousse and Walther König Verlag, 2016).

CHAPTER 3

1. Duchamp in Belle Krasne, "A Profile of Marcel Duchamp," *Art Digest* 26, no. 8 (January 15, 1952), 24; cited in Alice Goldfarb Marquis, *Marcel Duchamp: The Bachelor Stripped Bare* (Boston: MFA Publications, 2002), 275.

2. Marcel Duchamp in Pierre Cabanne, *Dialogues with Marcel Duchamp* (London: Thames and Hudson, 1971), 67, 71.

3. Even when scholarly or curatorial gazes attempt to focus specifically on artists who have been preoccupied with the museum in their practice, *Étant donnés* goes unmentioned. Symptomatic of this were such exhibitions as "The Desire of the Museum" at the Whitney Museum of American Art, New York, in 1989, or "The Museum as Muse" at the Museum of Modern Art, New York, in 1999, both of which offered Duchamp's *Boîte-en-valise* as a kind of avant-garde progenitor to more contemporary questioning of the museum while failing to acknowledge both his exhibition installations and his final work, *Étant donnés*, as part of a sustained and polyvalent preoccupation with the museum and the functions of the display of art. See Catsou Roberts, Timothy Landers, et al., *The Desire of the Museum* (New York: Whitney Museum of American Art, 1989), and Kynaston McShine, ed., *The Museum as Muse* (New York: Museum of Modern Art, 1999).

4. Jean-François Lyotard, *Les TRANSformateurs Duchamp* (Paris: Galilée, 1977), translated into English only in 1990 as *Duchamp's TRANS/formers* (Venice: Lapis Press, 1990). Lyotard's book was the first, and for more than three decades the only, monographic publication on *Étant donnés* to emerge since its unveiling.

5. Of course, the work has, over the years, figured in a number of essays and book chapters in publications devoted to Duchamp (it would be impossible for any such major work to escape those histories) or, simply, collections of diverse scholarly essays, but in much of this literature *Étant donnés* is overshadowed by the readymades and the *Large Glass*. Michael Taylor's exhaustive exhibition catalog *Marcel Duchamp: Étant donnés* (Philadelphia: Philadelphia Museum of Art, 2009) goes a long way toward rectifying the lacunae. My dis-

cussion of this problematic reception concerns the widespread elision of the work (and the pages and footnotes that follow trace this) from broad art historical surveys that contextualize art practices contemporaneous with *Étant donnés*. For an exception to this rule, see Hal Foster, Rosalind E. Krauss, et al., *Art since 1900* (London: Thames and Hudson, 2004), 496–499.

6. This distinction is significant because although Jean-François Lyotard and Rosalind Krauss have written pioneering (and as yet still unsurpassed) studies on *Étant donnés*, which both take the public space of the museum into account and understand its mechanisms as integral to Duchamp's final work, neither devotes any attention to the measures Duchamp took to insert his work there, neither considers the *Manual of Instructions* as part of the artwork itself, neither considers it in light of Duchamp's lifelong preoccupation with institutions (or the gestures that made possible the readymade, the *Boîte-en-valise*, and Duchamp's avid exhibition curation), and, finally, neither reads the work as a progenitor to the kinds of critique of the institution that would be prevalent in the 1960s and '70s. See Lyotard, *Duchamp's TRANS/formers*, and Krauss, *The Optical Unconscious* (Cambridge, MA: MIT Press, 1993), 95–146.

7. Duchamp in *Salt Seller: The Writings of Marcel Duchamp*, ed. Michel Sanouillet and Elmer Peterson (New York: Oxford University Press, 1973), 138.
8. Arturo Schwarz, *The Complete Works of Marcel Duchamp* (New York: Harry Abrams, 1969), 557. Also, "no photograph can communicate the unique visual experience of seeing firsthand ... ," in Michael Taylor, introduction to the new edition of Marcel Duchamp, *Manual of Instructions* (Philadelphia: Philadelphia Museum of Art, 2009), vii.
9. Helen Molesworth, "My Funny Valentine," *Artforum* 48, no. 5 (January 2010), 165.
10. Joseph Masheck, ed., *Marcel Duchamp in Perspective* (Englewood Cliffs, NJ: Prentice-Hall, 1974), 23. See also Clement Greenberg's dismissals of the unnamed "Philadelphia Museum peepshow" in "Convention and Innovation," a revised version of one of his Bennington College seminars from 1971, reprinted in *Homemade Esthetics: Observations on Art and Taste* (Oxford: Oxford University Press, 1999), 56–58. Still more than a decade after *Étant donnés* was revealed, the disparagements continued, as when Roger Shattuck called it "the ultimate bluff against art and its whole superstructure, an obscene diorama pawned off on a reputable museum because of the reputation of the 'artist' and the brilliant literary apparatus lending it prestige." Shattuck, *The Innocent Eye: On Modern Literature and the Arts* (New York: Farrar Straus Giroux, 1984), 291.
11. Paul Wood, Francis Frascina, Jonathan Harris, and Charles Harrison, eds., *Modernism in Dispute: Art since the Forties* (New Haven: Yale University Press, 1993); Amelia Jones, ed., *A Companion to Contemporary Art since 1945* (London: Wiley-Blackwell, 2006); Anne Rorimer, *New Art in the 60s and 70s: Redefining Reality* (London: Thames and Hudson, 2004); Thomas Crow, *The Rise of the Sixties: American and European Art in the Era of Dissent 1955–1969* (London: Calmann and King, 1996); and numerous others could be cited. See as well this chapter's later discussion of the work's absence from histories of installation art and Institutional Critique. Three notable exceptions are Martin Jay's sweeping examination of vision as seen through literary, philosophic, and artistic sources, *Downcast Eyes: The Denigration of Vision in the Twentieth Century* (Berkeley: University of California Press, 1993), 163–170; the exhibition catalog *Premises: Invested Spaces in Visual Arts, Architecture, and Design from France, 1958–1998* (New York: Guggenheim Museum, 1998), 254–259; and Foster, Krauss, et al., *Art since 1900*, 496–499, that last being particularly important given its conception as a basic primer for students. These are among the rare publications to inscribe the work in a broad historical overview and argue for its relationship to the art making and thinking of its time and the era that followed.

12. John Tancock, "The Influence of Marcel Duchamp," in Anne d'Harnoncourt and Kynaston McShine, eds., *Marcel Duchamp* (New York: Museum of Modern Art, 1973), 160–178; and Robert Pincus-Witten, "'Quality Material ...': Duchamp Disseminated in the Sixties and Seventies," in Bonnie Clearwater, ed., *West Coast Duchamp* (Miami Beach: Grassfield Press, 1991), 87–101.
13. As previously mentioned, *Art since 1900* is a notable exception to this rule. The statement "*Étant donnés* constituted a newly wrought paradigm, one that would profoundly affect work from 1968 onward" (497) heralds a call for new consideration of it in light of what came after its unveiling.
14. See Michael Fried, "Art and Objecthood," first published in *Artforum* in June 1967 and reprinted in his *Art and Objecthood: Essays and Reviews* (Chicago: University of Chicago Press, 1998), as well as the debate that ensued around Fried's accusations of Minimalism's theatricality and literalism. Cf. Rosalind E. Krauss, "Sculpture in the Expanded Field," in *The Originality of the Avant-Garde and Other Modernist Myths* (Cambridge, MA: MIT Press, 1985), and Hal Foster, "The Crux of Minimalism," in *The Return of the Real: The Avant-Garde at the End of the Century* (Cambridge, MA: MIT Press, 1996).
15. See Lucy Lippard, *Six Years: The Dematerialization of the Art Object from 1966 to 1972* (1973; reprint, Berkeley: University of California Press, 1997).
16. If one speaks of a specific technical strategy for conveying embodiment, one could further mention the coincidence of *Étant donnés*'s completion with the use of body casting in the work of artists such as Jasper Johns, Robert Morris, Bruce Nauman, and Paul Thek. Although the sculptural complexity and casting techniques of *Étant donnés*, surprisingly, are not addressed in the exhibition "Part Object, Part Sculpture" and its catalog, the impact on the art of the period (by way of the cast and handmade) of Duchamp's so-called erotic objects that emerged in the 1950s from the then still-secret project is brilliantly traced in Helen Molesworth et al., *Part Object, Part Sculpture* (Columbus, OH: Wexner Center for the Arts, 2005).
17. John Baldessari's "*possibly ... impossible*" and, in fact, unrealized installation for the "Information" exhibition suggests that artists close to Conceptual art understood *Étant donnés* beyond its apparent return to realism and indeed beyond its appearance as an erotic tableau. Accordingly, the "subject" of Baldessari's piece, as the artist argued, "is not the cadaver. The subject is rather the issue of breaking and mending aesthetic distance" in a museal context. See Kynaston McShine, ed., *Information* (New York: Museum of Modern Art, 1970), 16.
18. See critic Robert Pincus-Witten's review of Acconci's *Seedbed* in which Duchamp's erotic objects are even discussed as an influence on the work, one that Acconci himself acknowledged when asked about it, but *Étant donnés*, astonishingly, is not mentioned at all. Pincus-Witten, "Vito Acconci and the Conceptual Performance," *Artforum* 10, no. 8 (April 1972), 47–49.
19. Here I have specifically avoided comparison with the work of Edward Kienholz and George Segal, among the few contemporaries who *were* mentioned in relation to *Étant donnés* at the time. Those connections, like some others that were made, were seen literally and formally (and seen from the perspective of Duchamp coming, simply, "too late" in relation to them), rather than conceptually or procedurally. One significant drawback to Michael Taylor's otherwise fascinating publication on *Étant donnés* is that while it similarly only sketches out the direct and literal impact of the work on projects by artists such as Hannah Wilke or Marcel Dzama, it does not adequately draw connections to so much work of its time with which it resonates on deeper levels. See, however, the notable essay with references to Vito Acconci's and Bruce Nauman's performance-based works of the early 1970s

by Michael Lüthy, "*Étant donnés* as a Form of Experience," in Stefan Banz, ed., *Marcel Duchamp and the Forestay Waterfall* (Zurich: JRP Ringier, 2010), 132–145; taken up as well in Julian Jason Haladyn, *Marcel Duchamp: Étant donnés* (London: Afterall, 2010), 21–22, 50.

20. Here I might point to two seminal articles that focused on the legacy of Duchamp for a younger generation, specifically on two central aspects of Duchampian practice—his use of the logic of the index and his critique of institutions—neither of which, strangely, even mention *Étant donnés*. Rosalind Krauss's otherwise prescient discussion of Duchamp in "Notes on the Index" curiously fails to grapple with the tangled ways in which *Étant donnés*—as much as if not even more than any of the Duchampian examples she cites—should be seen in relation to the index and as a precursor to the art of the 1970s about which her article speaks. Krauss, "Notes on the Index: Seventies Art in America," *October* 3 (Spring 1977), 68–81; continued in "Notes on the Index: Seventies Art in America, Part 2," *October* 4 (Autumn 1977), 58–67. And Benjamin H. D. Buchloh's "The Museum Fictions of Marcel Broodthaers," treating Duchamp's interest in and imbrication in the museum (seen primarily through a discussion of his *Boîte-en-valise*), claims Broodthaers as the radical inheritor of Duchamp's critical project but exalts the former's position as administrator and "conservateur" of his own museum while completely failing to mention either *Étant donnés* or the ways in which Duchamp enacted quite similar, parallel operations in a real museum at about the same time. Buchloh, "The Museum Fictions of Marcel Broodthaers," in A. A. Bronson and Peggy Gale, eds., *Museums by Artists* (Toronto: Art Metropole, 1983). I will return to a discussion of both of these texts later in this chapter.

21. Cf. Claire Bishop, *Installation Art: A Critical History* (London: Tate Publishing, 2004); Julie H. Reiss, *From Margin to Center: The Space of Installation Art* (Cambridge, MA: MIT Press, 2000); and Nicolas de Oliveira, Nicola Oxley, and Michael Petry, *Installation Art* (London: Thames and Hudson, 1994). These publications mention 1960s and '70s installation art's foundations in the historical avant-garde, often citing Kurt Schwitters's *Merzbau*, Futurist theories, and Duchamp's coal sacks for the 1938 "Exposition internationale du surréalisme," or the *Sixteen Miles of String* at the "First Papers of Surrealism" exhibition of 1942, but *Étant donnés* goes completely unmentioned. Similarly, accounts of participatory paradigms in art fail to mention Duchamp's perhaps most participatory work of all; cf. Rudolf Frieling, ed., *The Art of Participation: 1950 to Now* (San Francisco: San Francisco Museum of Modern Art; New York: Thames and Hudson, 2008). See also publications as diverse as Douglas Crimp, *On the Museum's Ruins* (Cambridge, MA: MIT Press, 1993), and Martha Buskirk, *The Contingent Object of Contemporary Art* (Cambridge, MA: MIT Press, 2003), where site specificity, Institutional Critique, and the museum are central thematics and where Duchamp is confirmed as a primary and pioneering figure, but *Étant donnés* goes entirely unmentioned.

22. Brian O'Doherty's essays have been collected under the title *Inside the White Cube: Ideology of the Exhibition Space* (Berkeley: University of California Press, 2000). O'Doherty, it should be remembered, was in contact with Duchamp just a year prior to the artist's death, having solicited him to include a reading of his notes in O'Doherty's publication-as-exhibition *Aspen* magazine 5–6 (1967), and was an avid reader of Duchamp's works and texts. It is inconceivable that he, like so many artists and critics interested in Duchamp in the period, did not go to Philadelphia to see the artist's posthumous work when news about it broke.

23. In the period July 1969 to December 1972, covering a span of more than twenty-five issues and hundreds of articles, more than fifty of which make explicit reference to Duchamp, not a single text was commissioned by *Artforum* to speak about the rather newsworthy revelation of the artist's last major work. Aside from a lone letter to the editor, only one article

in this period even mentions *Étant donnés* by name, and in both cases only in passing. See Gary Glenn, "Letters," *Artforum* (November 1972), 6–7, and Jack Burnham, "Unveiling the Consort, Part I," *Artforum* 9, no. 7 (March 1971), 56. Burnham, one of the period's most influential historians among young artists, went on to write a second part of the article as well as a three-part article on Duchamp's *Large Glass* that appeared in *Arts Magazine*, none of which discussed *Étant donnés*. See Burnham, "Duchamp's Bride Stripped Bare: The Meaning of the Large Glass," *Arts Magazine* (March 1972), 28–32, with parts 2 and 3 appearing in the April and May 1972 issues (pp. 41–45 and 58–61, respectively). Other contemporary art journals, *Arts Magazine* in particular, did discuss Duchamp's final work, although hardly as visibly or vigorously as one might easily expect and certainly not comparably with discussions of the readymades. Given *Artforum*'s cultural relevance at the time, it is an important indication of how widespread was the reluctance among artists and critics who admired the "early" Duchamp to speak much about his last work.

24. See Hal Foster's discussion of the early history of *Artforum* in "Art Critics in Extremis," in *Design and Crime: And Other Diatribes* (London: Verso, 2002), 104–122. See also Robert Smithson's last published interview, conducted just before his untimely death and published in the pages of *Artforum* in October 1973, focused specifically on Duchamp and, even, on his overwhelming influence that Smithson called "Duchampitis." Here the younger artist doesn't once mention *Etant donnés*, nor (I might add) does the interviewer press him to speak of it. This is the case even when Smithson is characterizing Duchamp as an artist who created a "complete denial of the work process," a fact that the recently unveiled *Etant donnés* would have contradicted. See Moira Roth, "Smithson on Duchamp," reprinted in Robert Smithson, *The Collected Writings*, ed. Jack D. Flam (Berkeley: University of California Press, 1996), 310–312.

25. T. J. Demos, "Duchamp Homeless? The Avant-Garde and Post-Nationalism" (PhD diss., Columbia University, 2000), 281.

26. Benjamin H. D. Buchloh, "Editorial Introduction," *October* 70 (Fall 1994), 4. Buchloh's lament holds another paradox in this context, as the "Three Conversations in 1985: Claes Oldenburg, Andy Warhol, Robert Morris" that he conducted and that were included in the issue never once mention *Étant donnés*. Interviewer Martha Buskirk (and her respondents) in "Interviews with Sherrie Levine, Louise Lawler, and Fred Wilson," also included in the volume, similarly fail to speak to Duchamp's final work. And finally in the roundtable discussion on "Conceptual Art and the Reception of Duchamp" that closes the issue, Duchamp's last work is mentioned in passing and barely discussed. It is remarkable that in an issue devoted to the "Duchamp effect," not a single essay is included about, and so little mention is made of, the one work that Duchamp left as a deliberately final statement. A similar elision is present in David Hopkins's essay "Rethinking the 'Duchamp Effect,'" in Jones, *A Companion to Contemporary Art since 1945*, 215–245, which was published years after the *October* special issue yet does nothing to rectify this state of affairs.

27. It must be stated that Michael Taylor's 2009 exhibition and catalog on the work are milestones, tremendously important and long awaited. Still, they cannot be said to have entirely solved the problem of the work's lack of inscription in wider histories. See Taylor, *Marcel Duchamp: Étant donnés*. The same can be said of Haladyn's slender volume of the same name.

28. The trajectory of Duchamp's various work spaces is meticulously sketched out in André Gervais, "Détails d'*Étant donnés* … ," *Cahiers du Musée National d'Art Moderne* 75 (Spring 2001), 83–97.

29. For details about the last studio of Duchamp, see Paul Matisse, "The Opening Doors of Étant donnés," *Sites* 19 (1987), 4–6; Dennis L. Dollens, "Interview: Denise Browne Hare on Marcel Duchamp's New York Studio," *Sites* 19 (1987), 7–16; and Melissa Dunn, "New York's St. Denis Hotel—At the Threshold of Secret Affinities," *Convolution* 1 (Fall 2011), 96–113.

30. Michael Taylor mentions this possible genesis: Taylor, *Marcel Duchamp: Étant donnés*, 32.

31. See, among others, and among the earliest of these accounts that largely set the framework of the literature to come, Jean-François Lyotard, "Étant donnés: Inventaire du dernier nu," in Jean Clair, ed., *Marcel Duchamp: Abécédaire* (Paris: Centre National d'Art et de Culture Georges Pompidou, 1977), 86–110; René Micha, "Étant donnés *Étant donnés*," in Jean Clair, ed., *Marcel Duchamp: tradition de la rupture ou rupture de la tradition?* (Paris: Union Général d'Editions, 1979), 157–175; Octavio Paz, "Water Always Writes in Plural," in *Marcel Duchamp: Appearance Stripped Bare*, trans. Richard Philips and David Gardner (New York: Seaver Books, 1981), 91–178.

32. In *Marcel Duchamp: Étant donnés*, Taylor traces the iconographic connections between the exhibitions and Duchamp's final work, as does Sheldon Nodelman, in a more abbreviated way, in his essay "Disguise and Display," *Art in America* 3 (March 2003), 57–62.

33. The Gotham Book Mart window display was meant to announce and celebrate the publication of Breton's *Arcane 17*, while the Brentano's shop window display was meant to do the same for Breton's *Le Surréalisme et la peinture*. Both displays are discussed at length in Thomas Girst, "These Objects of Obscure Desires: Marcel Duchamp and His Shop Windows," in Christoph Grunenberg and Max Hollein, eds., *Shopping: A Century of Art and Consumer Culture* (Ostfildern-Ruit, Germany: Hatje Cantz, 2002), 143–146.

34. Thomas Girst, "Duchamp's Window Display for André Breton's *Le Surréalisme et la Peinture* (1945)," *Tout-Fait* 2, no. 4 (January 2002), 5, http://www.toutfait.com/issues/volume2/issue_4/articles/girst/girst5.html (accessed January 2, 2012).

35. Duchamp, letter to Maria Martins, July 17, 1947, in Taylor, *Marcel Duchamp: Étant donnés*, 404–405.

36. See Kiesler's elaborate sketches currently housed at the Frederick and Lillian Kiesler Private Foundation Archive in Vienna, and Breton's sketches and descriptions housed among the Breton papers at the Bibliothèque Kandinsky of the Centre Georges Pompidou in Paris. I thank both archives for so generously making their holdings available to me.

37. See Frederick Kiesler, *Selected Writings*, ed. Siegfried Gohr and Gunda Luyken (Ostfildern: Hatje Canz, 1997).

38. Eva Kraus, "Breton Duchamp Kiesler: Exhibition Politics 1947," in *Breton Duchamp Kiesler: Surreal Space 1947* (Vienna: Austrian Frederick and Lillian Kiesler Private Foundation, 2013), 6.

39. Kiesler cited in ibid. Jean Arp, "L'Oeuf de Kiesler et la Salle des Superstitions," *Cahiers du Musée National d'Art Moderne* 22 (August 1947), 281.

40. The billiard table was what Marcel Jean, Surrealism's earliest and most indefatigable historian, described as "one of those rare notes of deliberate humor in the exhibition." Jean, *The History of Surrealist Painting* (New York: Grove Press, 1967), 342.

41. From the photographs by Denise Bellon and Willy Maywald, among the only known traces of the now-lost project, we can observe that Duchamp had directed Matta to evoke *Le Soigneur de gravité* cryptically via a tilted table and ball, three stiff pieces of string (as if "fallen" from Duchamp's meditation on measurement, *3 stoppages étalon* [3 Standard Stoppages, 1913]), outsize reproductions from notes in the *Box of 1914* (about the making

of *3 stoppages étalon*), a drawing of bread loaves and a breast-shaped dessert (the "food" offering of the altar), and an element of typically Duchampian wordplay (an iron, *fer à passer*, painted with the words "à refaire le passé" [to redo the past]). See Herbert Molderings's discussion of the ephemeral installation in "The Objects of Modern Skepticism," in Thierry de Duve, ed., *The Definitively Unfinished Marcel Duchamp* (Cambridge, MA: MIT Press, 1994), 259–262.

42. Frederick Kiesler, "L'Architecture magique de la salle des superstitions," in *Le Surréalisme en 1947* (Paris: Maeght Editeur, 1947), 131. On the 1947 (and later 1959) Surrealist exhibition and its various contents, see Alyce Mahon, *Surrealism and the Politics of Eros, 1938–1968* (London: Thames and Hudson, 2005), 118–138. See also the exhibition and booklet by Eva Kraus, *Breton Duchamp Kiesler*.

43. See *Le Surréalisme en 1947*.

44. Letters and sketches suggest that Duchamp originally wanted the photograph, light, and layers of colored filters to be built into the outer casing of a leather suitcase (like those used for the deluxe edition of his *Boîte-en-valise*) and then placed behind its hole in the wall, thereby connecting Duchamp's portable museum and this otherwise temporary project embedded into the wall of an ephemeral exhibition. The suitcase idea went unrealized (even as he was proposing it, Duchamp worried that the lightbulb might get too hot in a closed suitcase), but all other plans for Duchamp's obscure little installation seem to have gone ahead. See Herbert Molderings, "*The Green Ray*: Marcel Duchamp's Lost Work of Art," in Banz, *Marcel Duchamp and the Forestay Waterfall*, 240–257.

45. Conversation with author, December 2000. See also Donati's account of the making of the cover in Taylor, *Marcel Duchamp: Étant donnés*, 70.

46. See *Le Surréalisme en 1947*, cover to the regular edition.

47. Inside the deluxe-edition boxes was a single loose photograph by Rémy Duval taken from a different angle so as to consciously and titillatingly announce that it is not the "false" breast of the cover but instead a real one. Complicating even further the relay of original, reproduction, and photography in this story (which it is hard to imagine Duchamp didn't himself fully orchestrate): that same year Man Ray consciously imitated (*copied*, you could say) the same cropping and frontal view of Duval's photograph on the standard cover to make his own photograph, entitled *Prière de toucher* (1947), which was of the foam breast on Duchamp's cover, nevertheless taken with such care as to look just as "real" as Duval's version (if not more so). And unlike Duval's version, Man Ray's image actually *was* a "photographic reproduction of the original cover by Marcel Duchamp."

48. In the postscript of a letter of March 15, 1947, by Duchamp to gallery owner Aimé Maeght regarding the production of the catalog for the 1947 exposition, the artist instructed, "For the inscription: *prière de toucher*—I would like to use the official font used for such signs in the museums (*Prière de ne pas toucher*)." Duchamp, unpublished letter to Maeght, in the collection of Jacques Kober, Paris.

49. In her work on Duchamp's optic games, Rosalind Krauss has underlined the ways in which his vision experiments and optical illusions "corporealize the visual," offering themselves as counterpoints to those very notions of good form and pure opticality central to aesthetic modernism. See in particular Krauss, "The Im/pulse to See," in Hal Foster, ed., *Vision and Visuality* (Seattle: Bay Press, 1988), 51–75; "The Blink of the Eye," in David Carroll, ed., *The States of "Theory": History, Art, and Critical Discourse* (New York: Columbia University Press, 1990), 175–199; and finally "Where's Poppa?," in de Duve, *The Definitively Unfinished Marcel Duchamp*, 437. If the erotic implications of Duchamp's optical experiments were in any doubt, it is noteworthy that at some point following the 1959 "Exposition inteRnatiOnale du Surréalisme" the owner of Paris's famous Crazy Horse cabaret club approached

Duchamp to contribute to the stage show, and the artist proposed projecting images of his spinning *Rotoreliefs* on the bare breasts of the dancers. In exchange, Duchamp and his guests were granted free access to any of the nightly performances, which the artist attended with glee. Story recounted to author by Jacqueline Matisse, Duchamp's step-daughter, who visited the Crazy Horse with Duchamp and her mother, Teeny.

50. André Breton, "Aux exposants," typescript letter sent to the invited artists on August 1, 1959, published in the catalog of the exhibition, *Exposition inteRnatiOnale du Surréalisme* (Paris: Galerie Daniel Cordier, 1959), 5–8. Cécile Bargues discusses the exhibition and its connections to Duchamp's last piece in her "Traverser l'E.R.O.S.: Marcel Duchamp et le VIII Exposition inteRnatiOnale du Surréalisme," in Marc Décimo, ed., *Marcel Duchamp et l'érotisme* (Paris: Les Presses du Réel, 2008), 255–283.
51. Robert Benayoun, *Érotique du surréalisme* (Paris: Jean-Jacques Pauvert, 1965), 163 (translation mine).
52. This is one of the "Suggestions of Marcel" listed in Breton's notes for the exhibition, housed among the Breton papers at the Bibliothèque Kandinsky of the Centre Georges Pompidou in Paris; reproduced in Marie Bonnet, "Anti-Reality! Marcel Duchamp, André Breton et la VIIIe Exposition international du Surréalisme, Paris Galerie Daniel Cordier, 1959," *Cahiers du Musée National d'Art Moderne* 87 (Spring 2004), 101.
53. Including, for instance, Man Ray's *Virgin* (1955), an oil-on-canvas spread-legged nude tacked to the ceiling; Robert Rauschenberg's *Bed* (1955), its paint-splattered quilt and bedsheets hung upright in a passageway (its first showing in Europe was made possible through Duchamp's encouragement); Joan Miró's *Sleeping Object* (1936), part tree trunk, part machine, placed ominously in a corridor; and Hans Bellmer's giant *Poupée* (1936), its doubled legs akimbo and strung from the ceiling above mirrors.
54. Taylor, *Marcel Duchamp: Étant donnés*, 102, 125.
55. These "Suggestions of Marcel" can be found in Breton's notes for the exhibition, reproduced in Bonnet, "Anti-Reality!," 101.
56. Duchamp, letter to André Breton, December 1, 1960, published in *Affectionately, Marcel: The Selected Correspondence of Marcel Duchamp*, ed. Francis Naumann and Hector Obalk (Ghent: Ludion, 2000), 370–371.
57. See John Canaday, "Art: Surrealism with the Trimmings," *New York Times*, November 28, 1960, 36, and "Nostalgia and the Forward Look," *New York Times*, December 4, 1960, 21; Schwarz, *The Complete Works of Marcel Duchamp*, 824, no. 577; Jennifer Gough-Cooper and Jacques Caumont, "Ephemerides on and around Marcel Duchamp or Rrose Sélavy," in Pontus Hulten, ed., *Marcel Duchamp* (Venice: Bompiani, 1993), unpaginated, November 28, 1960.
58. Michael Taylor's catalog of some of those iconographic links is persuasive. See Taylor, *Marcel Duchamp: Étant donnés*, 32–54, 69–75, 100–106.
59. On the Arensbergs' protracted museum discussions with, it is said, no less than thirty institutions over a ten-year period, see Marquis, *Marcel Duchamp: The Bachelor Stripped Bare*, 261–264.
60. Duchamp mentions the other offers in his interview with Pierre Cabanne: "The Chicago Art Institute offered, I think, to display it on its walls for ten years; after this period, no guarantee: the attic or the basement! Oh yes! Museums are like that. The Metropolitan Museum of Art in New York offered five years. Arensberg refused again. He also refused ten years. Finally, the Philadelphia Museum of Art offered him twenty-five years. He accepted." Cabanne, *Dialogues with Marcel Duchamp*, 87.

61. See Duchamp's lengthy and detailed letters to the Arensbergs from May 8, 1949 (concerning the Philadelphia Museum of Art, hereafter PMA, and including two architectural sketches); October 21, 1949 (concerning the Art Institute of Chicago); July 8, 1949 (concerning PMA); and September 7, 1950 (concerning PMA, and including an annotated tracing made from architectural blueprints); reprinted in *Affectionately, Marcel*, 269–272, 277–278, 288–290, 291–292.

62. Duchamp, letter to the Arensbergs, May 8, 1949, in ibid., 272.

63. Duchamp imagined the space divided into two parts: a portion for his installation, which would be closed off by a massive Spanish door, and a small, empty antechamber. Upon entering this antechamber just adjacent to the main Duchamp gallery where the artist installed his *Large Glass* in 1954, viewers could not pretend that they were there for any other reason or looking at anything other than Duchamp's ultimate work: the nature of the spaces' constellation is such that there is nothing else to be seen. See Michael Lüthy's discussion of this room in "*Étant donnés* as a Form of Experience," 132.

64. The task was not as simple or evident as it might seem today. From our vantage point, it may seem hard to imagine that it could have taken such considerable effort to convince museums to promise the long-term presentation of what have proved to be two of the most significant collections of Duchamp's work in the United States, if not of Modern art writ large. But it is important to remember how late the appreciation of Duchamp's work began, not to mention that of some of the other modern artists, collected on Duchamp's advice, in the Arensberg and Dreier collections. See for example Duchamp's words to Walter Arensberg: "Of course I understand that [the] Phila[delphia Museum of Art] does not want everything in her [Katherine Dreier's] collection but I suspect that F.K. [Fiske Kimball, PMA director] and the Trustees hardly like anything she has, including the glass as well. This is strictly confidential: I have a hunch that the broken glass is hard to swallow for a 'museum.'" Duchamp, letter to Walter Arensberg, April 19, 1951, housed in the Philadelphia Museum of Art, Walter and Louise Arensberg Archives. Perhaps as a result of the Philadelphia Museum being less than enthusiastic about Dreier's collection, almost all of the rest of her vast modernist holdings, which included many works by Duchamp, were instead donated to the Yale University Art Gallery.

65. Conversation with Michael Taylor, 2001.

66. See Michael Taylor, *Marcel Duchamp: Étant donnés*, 89.

67. Henri-Pierre Roché, "Souvenirs sur Marcel Duchamp," in Robert Lebel, ed., *Marcel Duchamp* (New York: Fawcus, 1959), 83.

68. When the Arensbergs, the original sponsors of the *Large Glass*, announced they would move to the West Coast, Duchamp convinced Dreier to buy the piece from them so that the delicate glass would not be at risk due to the long travel. He thus shepherded the work between the two most important collections of his oeuvre. On Duchamp's relationship to the Arensbergs, see Naomi Sawelson-Gorse, "Hollywood Conversations: Duchamp and the Arensbergs," in Clearwater, *West Coast Duchamp*, 25–45. On Duchamp's negotiations with Dreier regarding the final resting place of her collection, see Michelle Anne Lee, "'The Puppeteer of Your Own Past': Marcel Duchamp and the Manipulation of Posterity" (PhD diss., University of Edinburgh, 2010).

69. Several such lists in Duchamp's hand are archived at the Philadelphia Museum of Art. See Mark Pohlad, "The Art of History: Marcel Duchamp and Posterity" (PhD diss., University of Delaware, 1994), 23.

70. See Katherine Kuh, "Walter Arensberg and Marcel Duchamp," *Saturday Review* 53 (September 5, 1970), 36–37.

71. Exceptional here have been Rosalind Krauss's various discussions of the work specifically in relation to the Cartesian, rationalist impulse of its institutional context. See her contribution to Foster, Krauss, et al., *Art since 1900*, 496–499; her response in a round-table discussion in de Duve, *The Definitively Unfinished Marcel Duchamp*, 474; and "Where's Poppa?" in the same volume, 437.

72. A figure from Greek mythology, Cassandra was taught by Apollo to prophesy in exchange for her virginity. But when Cassandra refused his advances after he had carried out his part of the bargain, Apollo cursed her by spitting into her mouth, which ensured that no one would believe her prophecies. See James Metcalf, "The Gift of Cassandra," *Tout-Fait* 1, no. 2 (May 2000), http://www.toutfait.com/issues/issue_2/Notes/metcalf.html (accessed January 2, 2012).

73. For the details of these visits, see Taylor, *Marcel Duchamp: Étant donnés*, 132–133. If Duchamp believed (as he had once said of the museum) that it was "controlled by dealers," his orchestration of *Étant donnés*'s entry into the museum may be seen as a defiantly critical act, showing that he could, acting as if his own dealer, affect the permanent collection of a venerable institution.

74. See contract, reproduced in Taylor, *Marcel Duchamp: Étant donnés*, 427–429.

75. On site specificity, see Miwon Kwon, "One Place after Another: Notes on Site Specificity," *October* 80 (Spring 1997), 85–110.

76. Ibid., 85.

77. Ibid., 86.

78. O'Doherty, *Inside the White Cube*. Numerous are the essays that speak to the museum's role in upholding the supposed autonomy of the artwork; Michael Newman even refers to the museum as the "sanctum of autonomy" in his "After Conceptual Art: Joe Scanlan's Nesting Bookcases, Duchamp, Design and the Impossibility of Disappearing," in Newman and Jon Bird, eds., *Rewriting Conceptual Art* (London: Reaktion, 1999), 216.

79. Crimp, *On the Museum's Ruins*, 17.

80. John Canaday, "Philadelphia Museum Shows Final Duchamp Work," *New York Times*, July 7, 1969, 30.

81. Craig Adcock once said of *Étant donnés* that it "has no exterior. It has only an interior, from which you look at another interior." Adcock in de Duve, *The Definitively Unfinished Marcel Duchamp*, 342.

82. Paz, *Marcel Duchamp: Appearance Stripped Bare*, 117.

83. Note included in the *Box of 1914*.

84. For a further discussion of the visual premises of the museum, see chapter 2 of this book, especially the section "This Is a Curator, Exhibition, Museum."

85. His essay "L'Oeil et l'esprit" (1961), translated as "Eye and Mind," raises the compelling issue of how the artwork (painting, in this case) functions as a form of visibility. We do not, Merleau-Ponty argues, so much look *at* the work of art as we see *with it* or "according to it." See Maurice Merleau-Ponty, "Eye and Mind," trans. Carlton Dallery, in James Edie, ed., *The Primacy of Perception* (Evanston, IL: Northwestern University Press, 1964).

86. Cf. Lawrence D. Steefel Jr., "The Art of Marcel Duchamp: Dimension and Development in 'Le Passage de la vierge à la mariée,'" *Art Journal* 22, no. 2 (Winter 1962/63), 72–80; Jean Clair, "Duchamp and the Classical Perspectivists," *Artforum* 16 (March 1978), 40–49; Craig Adcock, *Marcel Duchamp's Notes from the "Large Glass": An N-Dimensional Analysis* (Ann Arbor, MI: UMI Research Press, 1983) and "Geometrical Complications in the Art of Marcel Duchamp," *Arts Magazine* 58 (January 1984), 105–109; Linda Dalrymple Henderson,

The Fourth Dimension and Non-Euclidian Geometry in Modern Art (Princeton, NJ: Princeton University Press, 1983) and *Duchamp in Context: Science and Technology in the Large Glass and Related Works* (Princeton, NJ: Princeton University Press, 2005).

87. See Clair, "Duchamp and the Classical Perspectivists," 40–49. On perspective and stereoscopy more generally, see Jonathan Crary, *Techniques of the Observer: On Vision and Modernity in the Nineteenth Century* (Cambridge, MA: MIT Press, 1990).

88. Rosalind E. Krauss, "Photography's Discursive Spaces," in *The Originality of the Avant-Garde and Other Modernist Myths*, 290.

89. Ibid., 291.

90. "The vanishing point of the 'cube' (in the perspectivist sense) of *Given* would be given by the vulva." Lyotard then adds an important addendum: "But the position of the vanishing point would be verifiable only by photo (which the *Approximation* freely invites us to do)." Lyotard, *Duchamp's TRANS/formers*, 172.

91. Among the instructions that are part of the seventh operation: "la spot doit tomber vertical[t], exact[t], sur le con." Duchamp, *Manual of Instructions*, 20.

92. Lyotard, *Duchamp's TRANS/formers*, 175.

93. Ibid. Here I have opted for the original French of the now-legendary aphorism, and for the English translation of it that has more widely circulated than the slightly different "A cunt is he who sees" provided by the first English edition of the publication. But there is a play of words in Lyotard's original (a double sense to *con* in colloquial French), such that the viewer as "cunt" (following the shared etymology of the words) could also be the viewer as "idiot."

94. See Tony Bennett, *The Birth of the Museum: History, Theory, Politics* (London: Routledge, 1995).

95. Mason Klein, "The Phenomenology of the Self: Marcel Duchamp's *Étant donnés*" (PhD diss., City University of New York, 1994), 22–24.

96. Krauss, "Where's Poppa?," 438.

97. Krauss, roundtable discussion in de Duve, *The Definitively Unfinished Marcel Duchamp*, 474.

98. Krauss, *The Optical Unconscious*, 112.

99. Ibid., 113.

100. Duchamp, note for the fifth operation ("The Door"), in *Manual of Instructions*, vi.

101. Cf. Clair, "Duchamp and the Classical Perspectivists," 40–49; Henderson, *The Fourth Dimension and Non-Euclidian Geometry in Modern Art* and *Duchamp in Context*; Lyotard, *Duchamp's TRANS/formers*; Krauss, *The Optical Unconscious*, 95–146.

102. Duchamp, *Manual of Instructions*, vii.

103. Jonathan Crary, "Modernizing Vision," in Foster, *Vision and Visuality*, 31.

104. Klein, "The Phenomenology of the Self," 20.

105. Lyotard, *Duchamp's TRANS/formers*.

106. Foster, Krauss, et al., *Art since 1900*, 499. Drawing from Laura Mulvey's groundbreaking 1975 essay "Visual Pleasure and Narrative Cinema," *Screen* 16, no. 3 (Autumn 1975), discussions of *Étant donnés* have been the site of much feminist reading, including Rachel Blau DuPlessis, "Sub Rrosa: Marcel Duchamp and the Female Spectator," in *The Pink Guitar* (London: Routledge, 1990); Amelia Jones, "Re-placing Duchamp's Eroticism: 'Seeing' *Étant donnés* from a Feminist Perspective," in *Postmodernism and the En-gendering of Marcel Duchamp* (Cambridge: Cambridge University Press, 1994); and Susan Best,

"Just Looking? The Body, the Gaze, and Syncope," in *Body* (Melbourne: Bookman Schwartz, 1997). While these important studies on Duchamp's final work have focused on the gender implications of viewership and helped forge my thinking here, I have attempted to suggest that rather than merely unreflexively perpetuating a scopic regime (as much art historical as museological) that puts the female body on display for (heterosexual, male) visual consumption, Duchamp is precisely and consciously using the clichés of that regime—all the better to unmask it.

107. Lyotard, *Duchamp's TRANS/formers*, 157.

108. It is noteworthy that even Michael Taylor's extensive study of the piece devotes little time to questioning the nature of the manual and instead takes it to be an almost transparently useful instruction guidebook. Taylor, *Marcel Duchamp: Étant donnés*.

109. Duchamp, *Manual of Instructions*, second, seventh, and eleventh operations.

110. "Structural" is how Krauss has astutely described it. It thus seems remarkable that Duchamp's complex relationship to photography rarely registers in the histories of photography proper, and this despite Krauss's prescient theory that Duchamp's indexical paradigm profoundly affected the work of artists working in the 1970s. See Krauss, "Notes on the Index," 68–81, and "Notes on the Index, Part 2," 58–67.

111. Benjamin H. D. Buchloh, "Conceptual Art 1962–1969: From the Aesthetics of Administration to the Critique of Institutions," *October* 53 (Winter 1991), 105–143. It is curious that for all their outspoken interest in Duchamp, historians of Conceptual art never once looked to these two specific projects of his—the *Box of 1914* and the *Manual of Instructions*—to seriously question their connections to the practices of artists in the 1960s and '70s. See also John Roberts, "Photography, Iconophobia, and the Ruins of Conceptual Art," in *The Impossible Document: Conceptual Art in Britain 1966–1976* (London: Cameraworks, 1997); David Campany, "Conceptual Art History or a Home for *Homes for America*," in Newman and Bird, *Rewriting Conceptual Art*, 132–133; and Newman, "After Conceptual Art," 214.

112. Dollens, "Interview: Denise Browne Hare on Marcel Duchamp's New York Studio."

113. See Olivier Asselin, "Le mystère de la chambre jaune: Quelques notes sur la dernière oeuvre de Marcel Duchamp," *Le Fait divers: La Recherche photographique* 16 (Spring 1994), 44.

114. Holland Cotter, "Landscape of Eros, through the Peephole," *New York Times*, August 27, 2009, C21.

115. Duchamp, *Manual of Instructions*, 34.

116. The photographic analogy did not escape Lyotard, who wrote of the (male) voyeur: "He sees suddenly, in the snapshot of the opening of the diaphragm. Because of this he sees no more than is seen by a sensitive film, he is impressed, like the film." Its image imprinted upon us in the instant of our gaze, we become as if a photograph of the scene. Lyotard, *Duchamp's TRANS/formers*, 174.

117. The agreement between the Cassandra Foundation and the museum stipulates that "within or adjoining [the] Museum's collections of works by Marcel Duchamp, in a setting especially designed for the purpose of housing the same ... [f]or a period of fifteen years from this date, [the] Museum will not permit any copy of or reproduction of *Étant donnés* to be made, by photography or otherwise, excepting only pictures of the door behind which said object of art is being installed." See "Agreement between the Cassandra Foundation and the Philadelphia Museum of Art," housed at the Philadelphia Museum and reproduced in Taylor, *Marcel Duchamp: Étant donnés*, 427–429.

118. It is hard to know for certain whether Duchamp would have been happy about the ban. He was famously not a man of interdictions, but, according to at least one source, it was important to him that the work *not* be reproduced, if it were possible to keep it from being so. William Copley's adamant statements to Anne d'Harnoncourt (and copied to then Philadelphia Museum director Evan Turner and Teeny Duchamp) about his conversations with Duchamp detailing that the work should not ever be moved or reproduced suggest that Duchamp wanted *Étant donnés* to be viewed in person and in its specific (museal) context. The museum's fifteen-year ban on photographic reproduction of the work was inscribed in the agreement for the acceptance of the work from the Cassandra Foundation but was later revisited, allowing for the exceptional release of images. See the Copley letter housed with the Anne d'Harnoncourt Papers, Philadelphia Museum of Art, and the "Agreement between the Cassandra Foundation and the Philadelphia Museum of Art," in Taylor, *Marcel Duchamp: Étant donnés*, 427–429.

119. Duchamp, additional note for the fifth operation, "The Door (continued)," in *Manual of Instructions*, 15.

120. Ibid., 48.

121. Duchamp, opening words of the *Manual of Instructions*, iii.

122. *Merriam-Webster's Dictionary*.

123. *Inframince* appears for the first time in a note dated 1937, later included in his final box of replicated notes, *A l'infinitif*, published in 1966, just as he was completing *Étant donnés*.

124. Duchamp, *Notes*, trans. and arranged by Paul Matisse (Boston: G. K. Hall, 1983), unpaginated, n. 33.

125. Ibid.

126. Duchamp, *Notes*, unpaginated, n. 35.

127. See Georges Didi-Huberman's discussion of the *inframince* in his *La Ressemblance par contact: archéologie, anachronisme et modernité de l'empreinte* (Paris: Éditions de Minuit, 2008), 279–282. Didi-Huberman takes the term to be another name for "aura" for Duchamp: an approximation manifesting (physical) contact that nevertheless bears visual distantiation (from its model/original).

128. Emblematic of this tendency is DuPlessis, "Sub Rrosa," where she observes: "So it is a pattern book of nudes, an excess of intertextual alliances is part of the shock of the work: one looks at its excrescent self and knows the whole museum is falling on one's head" (75).

129. Asselin, "Le mystère de la chambre jaune," 38. Similar mentions of *Étant donnés* as a replication of art historical references abound; see also Juan Antonio Ramirez, *Marcel Duchamp: Love and Death, Even* (London: Reaktion Books, 1998), 216–224.

130. Rosalind Krauss makes this precise argument concerning Sherman in her "Cindy Sherman: Untitled," in *Cindy Sherman 1975–1993* (New York: Rizzoli, 1993).

131. Krauss, speaking of Sherman, calls her a "concatenation of stereotypes"; see Krauss, "Notes on Photography and the Simulacral," *October* 31 (Winter 1984), 59.

132. Duchamp speaks of the importance of the figure being a "unique and *direct* sculpture" (italics mine), suggesting that he was thinking of the one-to-one indexical quality of a life impression. Duchamp, letter to Maria Martins, March 19, [1950], in Taylor, *Marcel Duchamp: Étant donnés*, 417.

133. See Duchamp, letters to Martins, in Taylor, *Marcel Duchamp: Étant donnés*, 404–425.

134. Ettie Stettheimer [Henrie Waste, pseudonym], *Love Days* (New York: Knopf, 1923), 106; cited in Marquis, *Marcel Duchamp: The Bachelor Stripped Bare*, 120.

135. Molesworth, "My Funny Valentine," 165.

136. Martins was the rumored former mistress of Nelson Rockefeller and sexy socialite artist-wife of a Brazilian ambassador who conveniently kept a duplex on Park Avenue for part of the week in the city while her Washington-based husband tended to diplomacy. She sculpted there, building up the Surrealist-inspired figurative forms for which she had begun to have some renown in the 1940s. She also often met up with Duchamp there, before her husband was transferred to a diplomatic post in Paris. The move posed little obstacle to the affair given how much Duchamp traveled between the two cities anyway and, while apart, they often wrote to each other (or at least we can assume so from Duchamp's letters to her, which she kept; all correspondence from her is presumed lost).

137. Melissa S. Meighan's detailed and exacting chronology and description of Duchamp's working process in the construction of *Étant donnés* is an incalculably useful source. Meighan, "A Technical Discussion of the Figure in Marcel Duchamp's *Étant donnés*," in Taylor, *Marcel Duchamp: Étant donnés*, 241–261.

138. Duchamp, letter to Maria Martins, June 29, [1949], in Taylor, *Marcel Duchamp: Étant donnés*, 413.

139. Molesworth et al., *Part Object, Part Sculpture*, 211.

140. As Sue Malvern has argued: "Modernist art's rejection of the plaster cast could be termed a symptom of a crisis in representation, or a flight from photography or any form of reproduction that, like the photograph, has an indexical relationship to the referent." Malvern, "Outside In: The Afterlife of the Plaster Cast in Contemporary Culture," in Rune Frederiksen and Eckart Marchand, eds., *Plaster Casts: Making, Collecting and Displaying from Classical Antiquity to the Present* (Berlin: De Gruyter, 2010), 351–358.

141. Duchamp, letters to Martins, in Taylor, *Marcel Duchamp: Étant donnés*, 404–425.

142. See Charles Sanders Peirce, "Logic as Semiotic: The Theory of Signs," in *Philosophical Writings of Peirce* (New York: Dover, 1955). Rosalind Krauss's seminal essay "Notes on the Index" was one of the first attempts at theorizing the semiotician's notion of the index in relation to the visual arts.

143. Georges Didi-Huberman has written extensively about what he calls "resemblance by contact," the direct physical transference of a form from one surface or material to another in such diverse objects as archaeological remains, death masks, and a number of Duchamp's works; see in particular Didi-Huberman, *L'Empreinte* (Paris: Centre Georges Pompidou, 1997). Although he never directly treats the reproductive implications of *Étant donnés*, he has given the erotic objects that stemmed from it, and particularly *Feuille de vigne femelle*, a central place in his reading of Duchamp. Both Krauss's theorization of the index and Didi-Huberman's theorization of the resemblance by contact have been vital to my own thinking here and I therefore refer extensively to them, while focusing on an object (*Étant donnés*) that each almost wholly overlooks in relation to their respective readings of Duchamp and the index/imprint.

144. *White Box (In the Infinitive)*, reprinted in *Salt Seller*, 85.

145. Roland Barthes, *Camera Lucida* (New York: Hill and Wang, 1981), 87. See also Susan Sontag, *On Photography* (New York: Farrar, Straus and Giroux, 1977), as well as André Bazin, who wrote: "The objective nature of photography confers on it a credibility absent from all other picture making. In spite of any objections our critical spirit may offer, we are forced to accept as real the existence of the object reproduced, actually *re*-presented, set before us, that is to say, in time and space." Bazin, "Ontologie de la photographie" (1958),

published in English as "The Ontology of the Photograph," *Film Quarterly* 13, no. 4 (Summer 1960), 7–8.

146. Barthes, *Camera Lucida*, 15.

147. Duchamp, letter to Maria Martins, November 9, [1951], in Taylor, *Marcel Duchamp: Étant donnés*, 423 (italics mine).

148. The full citation is as follows, previously discussed in chapter 1: "No matter how fuzzy, distorted, or discolored, no matter how lacking in documentary value the image may be, it shares, by virtue of the very process of its becoming, the being of the model of which it is the reproduction; it *is* the model." Bazin, "The Ontology of the Photograph," 7–8.

149. Duchamp, letter to Maria Martins, June 30, [1949], in Taylor, *Marcel Duchamp: Étant donnés*, 415.

150. To read the list of the "numerous irregular brace elements and connective devices that criss-cross the underside of the supporting substructure" of the nude is to get a sense of the complexity of the project. See Meighan, "A Technical Discussion of the Figure in Marcel Duchamp's *Étant donnés*," 247.

151. Duchamp, letter to Maria Martins, April 7, [1949], in Taylor, *Marcel Duchamp: Étant donnés*, 409. Among the vast scholarship that speculates about the unshapely orifice, see Jones, *Postmodernism and the En-gendering of Marcel Duchamp*, 201; DuPlessis, "Sub Rrosa"; Dalia Judovitz, *Unpacking Duchamp: Art in Transit* (Berkeley: University of California Press, 1995), 201; Francis Naumann, "Étant donnés: 1. Maria Martins, 2. Marcel Duchamp," in *The Recurrent, Haunting Ghost: Essays on the Art, Life and Legacy of Marcel Duchamp* (New York: Readymade Press, 2012).

152. One indication of this is suggested by the fact that none of the smaller drawings, studies, or early fragments used to design the piece has the figure's vulva figured as it is in the final version. Its appearance of being mutilated, then, was seemingly *not* part of the artist's initial conception for the piece.

153. Taylor, *Marcel Duchamp: Étant donnés*, 94.

154. George Baker, *The Artwork Caught by the Tail* (Cambridge, MA: MIT Press, 2007), 69. Georges Didi-Huberman similarly makes a point of insisting on the "strange particularity—erotic and technical—of reproduction" in Duchamp's work. See Didi-Huberman, *La Ressemblance par contact*, 270.

155. Baker, *The Artwork Caught by the Tail*, 149.

156. Stuart Preston, "Diverse Facets: Moderns in Wide Variety," *New York Times*, December 20, 1953, sect. 10, p. 11; cited in Francis Naumann, *Marcel Duchamp: The Art of Making Art in the Age of Mechanical Reproduction* (Ghent: Ludion Press, 1999), 181.

157. Helen Molesworth, "Duchamp: By Hand, Even," in Molesworth et al., *Part Object, Part Sculpture*, 178–200.

158. For precise descriptions of the technical aspects of all of the so-called erotic objects, see Meighan, "A Technical Discussion of the Figure in Marcel Duchamp's *Étant donnés*," 254–255.

159. Duchamp, moreover, seems to have thought that they made ideal gifts for those closest to him. The original version of *Coin de chasteté* became the artist's wedding gift to Teeny in 1954, for instance. Another way of releasing them into the world was to include them in his ongoing project, the *Boîte-en-valise*. Duchamp frequently updated and added to the contents of his portable museum, and in 1955 he added twelve more items to it, including a selection of his erotic objects.

160. From Man Ray's gifted cast, Duchamp had the Paris gallery Rive Droit make a bronze edition in 1961 of the *Feuille de vigne femelle*, which he insisted on signing personally and individually since he wanted the artist's typical mark of authenticity to appear "in a more 'original' way than a 'printed' form on the cast." Cited in Naumann, *Marcel Duchamp: The Art of Making Art*, 219.

161. Molesworth, "Duchamp: By Hand, Even," 178–200. Although the originals were blatantly industrial objects, mass-produced, the 1964 reproductions were the opposite: Schwarz hired professional draftsmen who prepared precise technical drawings of the "original" readymade objects based on the only traces that were left—photographs—and had artisans follow these to construct shiny new urinals, bottleracks, snow shovels, et cetera.

162. Jasper Johns, quoted in Calvin Tomkins, *Off the Wall: Robert Rauschenberg and the Art World of Our Time* (Garden City, NY: Doubleday, 1980), 276; cited in Taylor, *Marcel Duchamp: Étant donnés*, 23.

163. One cannot help thinking here of Jacques Derrida's characterization of the conditions for the critique of authority: "The movements of deconstruction do not destroy the structures from the outside. They are not possible and effective, nor can they take accurate aim, except by inhabiting those structures." Derrida, *Of Grammatology*, trans. Gayatri Chakravorty Spivak (Baltimore: Johns Hopkins University Press, 1976), 24.

164. Foster, Krauss, et al., *Art since 1900*, 497.

165. Duchamp, "The Creative Act," lecture given at the meeting of the American Federation of Art, Houston, April 1957; transcription published in *Salt Seller*, 138. Cited in Thierry de Duve, *Kant after Duchamp* (Cambridge, MA: MIT Press, 1996), 401.

166. Duchamp, interview by Georges Charbonnier, radio interview for the RTF (1961); cited in de Duve, *Kant after Duchamp*, 401.

167. Michel Sanouillet, ed., *Duchamp du signe* (Paris: Flammarion, 1975), 247; cited in de Duve, *Kant after Duchamp*, 401.

168. Krauss, "Notes on the Index," 68–81, and "Notes on the Index, Part 2," 58–67.

169. Foster, Krauss, et al., "1966," in *Art since 1900*, 497.

170. *New York Times* critic John Canaday minced no words: "very interesting, but nothing new," just "an entertaining invention that has arrived a bit late to make a sensation. ... For the first time, this cleverest of twentieth-century masters looks a bit retardataire. Edward Kienholz, as the major specific example, has gone so far beyond the spent and sterile slickness of this final Duchamp work that he makes Duchamp look like Bouguereau." Canaday, "Philadelphia Museum Shows Final Duchamp Work," 30.

171. This reception was not exclusive either to those critical of Duchamp or to the period just after the work was unveiled; it clung to the work even among studies that purported to celebrate Duchamp generally, and even until rather recently. Note the comment by T. J. Demos: "Unlike the fragmented disorder, homeless mobility, and labyrinthine spaces that Duchamp's earlier installations produced, *Étant donnés* presents itself, then, as a *retour à l'ordre* of sorts." Demos qualifies this statement, but the conclusion of his reading amounts to a positioning of *Étant donnés* as the regressive counterpoint to the rest of a practice that is considered radical in its alleged "homeless" articulation of a postnationalistic cause. See Demos, "Duchamp Homeless?," 279.

172. Daniel Buren, "Critical Limits," in *Five Texts* (1970; reprint, New York: John Weber Gallery, 1974), 38; cited in Craig Owens, "From Work to Frame, or, Is There Life after 'Death of the Author'?," in *Beyond Recognition: Representation, Power, Culture* (Berkeley: University of California Press, 1994), 130.

173. Robert Smithson and Bruce Kurtz, "Conversation with Robert Smithson on April 22, 1972," in *The Writings of Robert Smithson*, ed. Nancy Holt (New York: New York University Press, 1979), 200; cited in Owens, "From Work to Frame," 130.

174. Owens, "From Work to Frame," 122–123.

175. Just some examples include: Alexander Alberro, "Institutions, Critique, and Institutional Critique," in Alberro and Blake Stimson, eds., *Institutional Critique: An Anthology of Artists' Writings* (Cambridge, MA: MIT Press, 2009), 2–19; Benjamin H. D. Buchloh, "Formalism and Historicity—Changing Concepts in American and European Art since 1945," in *Europe in the Seventies: Aspects of Recent Art* (Chicago: Art Institute of Chicago, 1977), 83–111, and "Ready Made, Objet trouvé, Idée reçue," in *Dissent: The Issue of Modern Art in Boston* (Boston: Institute of Contemporary Art, 1985), 107–122; Owens, "From Work to Frame," 122–142; and Frazer Ward, "The Haunted Museum: Institutional Critique and Publicity," *October* 73 (Summer 1995), 82. The two major recent publications on Institutional Critique do not contain a single mention of *Étant donnés*; see Alberro and Stimson, *Institutional Critique*, and John C. Welchman, ed., *Institutional Critique and After* (Zurich: JRP Ringier, 2006). It must be said as well that artists as much as critics seem to have avoided the subject. In addition to Brian O'Doherty's flagrant silence, mentioned earlier, one notes the same of other artists such as Daniel Buren and Michael Asher writing at the time specifically about the implications of the gallery-institution nexus. See Buren, "The Function of the Museum" (1970) and "The Function of the Studio" (1971), both reprinted in Alberro and Stimson, *Institutional Critique*, 102–109, 110–119; Buren, "The Function of the Exhibition," *Studio International* 186, no. 961 (December 1973), 216; and Asher, "September 21–October 12, 1974, Claire Copley Gallery, Inc., Los Angeles California," reprinted in Alberro and Stimson, *Institutional Critique*, 150–155.

176. Owens, "From Work to Frame," 127.

177. Mignon Nixon, in "Posing the Phallus," touches on a similar question vis-à-vis how to historicize Duchamp's erotic objects in relation to the neo-avant-garde. There, her rhetorical use of the term "survival" instead of "return" in order to refer to the persistence of the part-object is related to an explicit attempt, as explained in a footnote, to "disrupt a convention of periodization that would distinguish practices of the 1950s and early '60s from those of the late 1960s through the 1990s as belonging respectively to modernism and postmodernism." See Nixon, "Posing the Phallus," *October* 92 (Spring 2000), 98–127.

178. See Benjamin H. D. Buchloh, "Marcel Broodthaers: Allegories of the Avant-Garde," *Artforum* 18, no. 9 (May 1980), 52–59, and "The Museum Fictions of Marcel Broodthaers," in A. A. Bronson and Peggy Gale, eds., *Museums by Artists* (Toronto: Art Metropole, 1983), 45–56.

179. Rosalind E. Krauss, "Post-structuralism and Deconstruction," in Foster, Krauss, et al., *Art since 1900*, 42.

180. In addition to Buchloh's sustained readings, see also George Baker, "This Is Not an Advertisement: Marcel Broodthaers' *Section Publicité*," *Artforum* 34, no. 9 (May 1996), 86–89, 124; *October* 42, special issue on Marcel Broodthaers, ed. Benjamin H. D. Buchloh (Autumn 1987); Douglas Crimp, "This Is Not a Museum of Art," in *On the Museum's Ruins*; Rachel Haidu, *The Absence of Work: Marcel Broodthaers 1964–1976* (Cambridge, MA: MIT Press, 2010); and Rosalind E. Krauss, *"A Voyage on the North Sea": Art in the Age of the Post-Medium Condition* (London: Thames and Hudson, 1999). The one recent exception is Haladyn, *Marcel Duchamp: Étant donnés*, 22.

181. The total eclipse of *Étant donnés* in favor of the readymades in discussions of Broodthaers's *Musée d'Art Moderne*, without consideration of how Duchamp's simultaneously released

last work might connect to and trouble its understanding, continues indelibly to this day, even among artists. See Seth Price, *Dispersion* (2002–), downloadable from http://www.distributedhistory.com, n.p.

182. Buchloh, for example, laments in his seminal reading of Conceptual art that its artists focused almost to exclusion on the readymade and even only on one narrow aspect of the readymade—its status as "speech-act" (leaving out "its structural logic, its features as an industrially produced object of use and consumption, its seriality, and the dependence of meaning on context")—in addition to their avoiding, among other "eminently crucial" works, *Étant donnés* and the *Boîte-en-valise*. But if Buchloh and perhaps even other critics at the time noticed this, why, one might rightly ask, did they not in their readings insist on teasing out the implications of this broader context for the work of the time? Why limit readings to the intention or self-proclaimed references of artists? Buchloh, "Conceptual Art 1962–1969," 126.

183. The quoted terms in this sentence and those that follow are all Andrea Fraser's, defining the specific means and methodologies of Institutional Critique in her article "What Is Institutional Critique?," in Welchman, *Institutional Critique and After*, 306–307.

184. Hal Foster, "Subversive Signs," in *Recodings: Art, Spectacle, Cultural Politics* (Seattle: Bay Press, 1985), 99.

185. A perfect example of this is the comment of artist, critic, and Duchamp admirer Anthony Hill: "A critical issue is that of *Étant donnés*: I do not take this work seriously. ... For me, and perhaps many others, the Second World War is the 'break' after which I sense a complete change and a great deterioration ... a genuine tiredness. *Étant donnés* is the kind of thing Duchamp can be excused for choosing as a means of passing time. I admire a number of contingent features of the work, the 'legislative' aspects (the restriction against reproduction), the idea of keeping it a secret, and best of all—if it is fair to mention it—the judicious timing of his retirement from *life* in connection with its premiere. But it remains in conception a banal affair, a peep-hole tableau." Hill, "The Spectacle of Duchamp," in Hill, ed., *Duchamp: Passim, a Marcel Duchamp Anthology* (London: G+B Arts International, 1994), 158.

186. Peter Bürger, *Theory of the Avant-Garde* (Minneapolis: University of Minnesota Press, 1984).

187. Hal Foster, "What's Neo about the Neo-Avant-garde?," in Martha Buskirk and Mignon Nixon, eds., *The Duchamp Effect* (Cambridge, MA: MIT Press, 1996), 20. In another essay, Foster alludes to at least one of the stakes of his critique: "First published in 1974, [Bürger's] important essay takes no account of the artists mentioned here [including Daniel Buren, Michael Asher, Dan Graham, Hans Haacke, Marcel Broodthaers, Lawrence Weiner, John Baldessari, and Joseph Kosuth as well as Martha Rosler, Sherrie Levine, Barbara Kruger, Louise Lawler, Allan McCollum] who are involved in institutional critique." Foster, "Subversive Signs," 100, fn. 3. See also Benjamin H. D. Buchloh, "The Primary Colors for the Second Time: A Paradigm Repetition of the Neo-Avant-Garde," *October* 37 (Summer 1986), 40–52.

188. One way Foster did so was to claim that "Duchamp, in the guise of R. Mutt, 'chooses.' [The] work [does not] purport to be an analysis, let alone a deconstruction ... the museum-gallery is left intact by the readymade," while, on the other hand, "Marcel Broodthaers, Daniel Buren, Michael Asher, and Hans Haacke were concerned to elaborate these same paradigms in order to investigate this exhibition status and that institutional nexus more systematically." Foster, "What's Neo about the Neo-Avant-garde?," 19, 20. The sustained influence of this reading remains in place even today. An incisive recent article by Buchloh argues (with no indication to suggest that he considers Duchamp among the artists of

the 1960s to which he refers): "And what the artists of the 1960s and 70s finally formulated more clearly than anybody before was the fact that the museum had to be recognized as the site where, and the social institution wherein, these forms of acceptance through affirmation, of control though cultural canonization, of tolerance through quarantine, of inversion of meaning through the process of acculturation, had been most successfully implemented." Benjamin H. D. Buchloh, "Farewell to an Identity," *Artforum* 51, no. 4 (December 2012), 254.

189. Bürger, who declared, "Once a signed bottle drier has been accepted as an object that deserves a place in the museum, the provocation no longer provokes; it turns to its opposite," was far from alone. See Bürger, *Theory of the Avant-Garde*, 52.

190. Foster, "What's Neo about the Neo-Avant-garde?," 20.

191. Frazer Ward, in a footnote to an essay focused on the generation of artists after Duchamp who were involved in Institutional Critique, provocatively wonders: "Here the question might be raised whether, in staging the 'scandal' of the urinal, Duchamp didn't in fact stage the limits of what the institution would sustain, which is to suggest that perhaps he did [already then] begin to explore the discursive parameters of the institution. ... I would suggest that Benjamin Buchloh's account of the *Boîte-en-valise* (1936–41) as Duchamp's own attempt to deal with problems of acculturation and institutionalization might give 1936 as the moment in which the readymade touched on institutional critique, and might also give Duchamp as his own neo avant-garde." Ward, "The Haunted Museum," 82, fn. 31.

192. Clement Greenberg, "Counter Avant-Garde," *Art International* 15, no. 5 (May 20, 1971), 16–19; reprinted in Masheck, *Marcel Duchamp in Perspective*.

CONCLUSION

1. Duchamp himself designed the magazine's cover. Several articles on him appeared in its pages, and Kiesler, for his part, accompanied his six-page centerfold homage with the essay "Les Larves d'Imagie d'Henri Robert Marcel Duchamp: M.D. emeritus for the chronic diseases of the Arts," *View: The Modern Magazine* 5, no. 1 (March 1945), 24–30.

2. As one can tell from the photographs and other documents that Kiesler kept concerning the preparation of his *View* triptych, the smoke was not present in the original photograph but was added later, and the lid of the toilet was removed from the photograph, perhaps so that the "ready made" pipe, as Kiesler called it, with its conventional lidded toilet form would more closely resemble a urinal. I thank Gerd Zillner and Jill Meissner of the Austrian Frederick and Lillian Kiesler Foundation Archives in Vienna for their help in accessing these materials. With typical sly aplomb, Duchamp made sure that the smoke that appears to waft up from his pipe found its way elsewhere in the *View* issue: the cover he designed for the magazine featured an old wine bottle with a doctored label floating in cosmic ether with gas/smoke inexplicably coming from inside the bottle (a bit of trickery created through an invisible DIY smoke system he rigged up and held behind the bottle for that purpose), and the back cover of the magazine bore a cryptic quote by the artist connecting smoke to the *inframince*.

3. In this same issue appeared Harriet and Sidney Janis's article "Marcel Duchamp: Anti-Artist," the first published discussion of Duchamp's readymades. *View: The Modern Magazine* 5, no. 1 (March 1945), 23.

4. Although Seth Price misses the later steps that extend Duchamp's "media manipulations" to what could be called "curatorial interventions," he nevertheless brilliantly captures the essence of the operations of *Fountain*, which as a "gesture does not simply raise epistemological questions about the nature of art, but enacts the dispersion of objects into discourse.

The power of the readymade is that no one needs to make the pilgrimage to see *Fountain*. As with [Dan] Graham's magazine pieces, few people saw the original *Fountain* in 1917. Never exhibited, and lost or destroyed almost immediately, it was actually created through Duchamp's media manipulations—the Stieglitz photograph (a guarantee, a shortcut to history), the *Blind Man* magazine article—rather than through the creation myth of his finger selecting it in the showroom, the status-conferring gesture to which the readymades are often reduced. In *Fountain*'s elegant model, the artwork does not occupy a single position in space and time; rather, it is a palimpsest of gestures, presentations, and positions. Distribution is a circuit of reading, and ... Duchamp distributed the notion of the *Fountain* in such a way that it became one of art's primal scenes." Seth Price, *Dispersion* (2002–), downloadable from http://www.distributedhistory.com, n.p.

5. This is a quote from Craig Owens about Sherrie Levine but could easily describe any number of other artists of the period, certainly including those associated with Institutional Critique. Craig Owens, "Sherrie Levine at A&M Artworks," *Art in America* 70, no. 6 (June 1982), 148.
6. The prevailing opinion that Duchamp's readymades should be held apart from or seen as distinct from his exhibition making, rather than as part and parcel of a related gesture, is exemplified in Benjamin H. D. Buchloh's recent assessment that Duchamp's design of the 1938 Surrealist exhibition, for instance, "distanced itself dramatically from the readymade, that most consequential episteme of radical opposition in 1917." See Buchloh, "The Dialectics of Design: The *Degenerate Art* Exhibition (1937) and the *Exhibition internationale du Surréalisme* (1938)," *October* 150 (Fall 2014), 62.
7. In 1927 the artist had made a practical but unusual modification to his Parisian apartment-studio space to have a single door swing between two adjacent doorframes, so that the opening of one space (in this case, the work studio) meant the closing off of the other (the bathroom) and vice versa. In 1963, at about the moment when Duchamp was likely working on the threshold and the door for *Étant donnés*, he returned to his rigged studio door; although he no longer rented the Paris apartment (at that point a friend and fellow artist, Isabelle Walberg, did), he had it removed from the rue Larrey space and installed a replica of the door made by a carpenter in the apartment. He presented the 1927 "original" door and doubled doorframe as a work of art in its own right, entitled *Door, 11 rue Larrey* (1927/1963). This domestic modification-cum-artwork is arguably one of the many clues he released to his then-current but secret labor on *Étant donnés*.
8. "[Duchamp] had two studios in New York, the one people knew about and the one next door to it, where he did his work, which no one knew about. That's why people were able to visit his studio and see nothing going on. As he expressed later, it was a way of going underground." Moira Roth and William Roth, "John Cage on Marcel Duchamp: An Interview," *Art in America* 61, no. 6 (November–December 1973), 72–79; reprinted in Joseph Masheck, ed., *Marcel Duchamp in Perspective* (Englewood Cliffs, NJ: Prentice Hall, 1974), 151–161.
9. Brian O'Doherty, *Studio and Cube: On the Relationship between Where Art Is Made and Where Art Is Displayed* (New York: Forum Project Publications, 2007), 23.
10. The story goes that when Schwarz learned of the posthumous piece, just as his monograph (declaring itself *The Complete Works...*) was going to print, he literally stopped the press and asked the printer to add four pages to the end of the book so he could slip in a descriptive mention and photograph of the outer door of *Étant donnés*. See Arturo Schwarz, *The Complete Works of Marcel Duchamp* (New York: Harry Abrams, 1969).

INDEX

Publisher contact:
The MIT Press
Massachusetts Institute of Technology
77 Massachusetts Avenue, Cambridge, MA 02139
mitpress.mit.edu

EU Authorised Representative:
Easy Access System Europe, Mustamäe tee 50,
10621 Tallinn, Estonia
gpsr.requests@easproject.com

Printed by Integrated Books International,
United States of America